Working Mothers in Europe

Working Mothers in Europe

A Comparison of Policies and Practices

Edited by

Ute Gerhard,
Professor Emerita of Sociology,
Johann Wolfgang Goethe University,
Frankfurt, Germany

Trudie Knijn,
Professor of Social Science, Utrecht University,
The Netherlands

Anja Weckwert,
Research Fellow, Johann Wolfgang Goethe University,
Frankfurt, Germany

Edward Elgar
Cheltenham, UK• Northampton MA, USA

Published by
Edward Elgar Publishing Limited
Glensanda House
Montpellier Parade
Cheltenham
Glos GL50 1UA
UK

Edward Elgar Publishing, Inc.
136 West Street
Suite 202
Northampton
Massachusetts 01060
USA

A catalogue record for this book
is available from the British Library

ISBN 1 84542 244 9

Printed and bound in Great Britain by MPG Books Ltd, Bodmin, Cornwall

Contents

v

Tables

The Authors

Mary Daly is Professor of Sociology at the School of Sociology and Social Policy at Queen's University Belfast. Among the fields on which she has published are poverty, welfare state, gender, family and the labour market. Much of her work is comparative.

Ute Gerhard is Professor emerita of Sociology with a special appointment in Gender Studies, Department of Social and Political Science, Johann Wolfgang Goethe-Universität Frankfurt, Germany. Main areas of research and publications are gender in the history, theory and sociology of law; women's movements in international comparison; citizenship, welfare states and social policies.

Ingrid Jönsson is Associate Professor in Sociology, Senior Lecturer at the Department of Sociology, Lund University, Sweden. Her research interests are welfare and family policies from a gender perspective and the sociology of education.

Ute Klammer is Professor of Social Policy at the University of Applied Sciences Niederrhein, Mönchengladbach, Germany. Fields of research are: social policy (pension systems, health care systems, family policy), labour market research, flexicurity, European and comparative social policy research, feminist and gender research.

Trudie Knijn is Professor of Social Science at the Department of Interdisciplinary Social Science, University of Utrecht, the Netherlands. Main areas of work are comparative welfare state studies and social policy. In this context she is particularly interested in transformations in care systems and professionalism, in family policy and family relations and in gender and the family.

Arnlaug Leira is Professor of Sociology at the University of Oslo, with welfare state and social policy studies as a main field. In this context she is particularly interested in family and social policies, the reconciliation of work and family, gender, caring and citizenship.

Marie-Thérèse Letablier is geographer and sociologist and a researcher at the CNRS and the Centre d'Études de l'Emploi in Paris, where she is conducting comparative studies on gender and labour market, gender and social and employment policies, public policies and the family-employment relationship.

Constanza Tobío is vice-dean of Sociology at Universidad Carlos III, Madrid. Her main areas of research are urban sociology, social structure and the family-employment relationship. More specifically she has worked on social segregation and exclusion in Spanish cities (particularly in Madrid), space and gender, dual earner families, lone parent families and women's strategies to combine employment and motherhood in Spain.

Rossana Trifiletti is Associate Professor in Social Policy and Sociology of the Family at Florence University's Faculty of Political Sciences 'Cesare Alfieri' and a member of *Dipartimento di Scienza della Politica e Sociologia* (DISPO). Her research interests are in qualitative sociology of the family, social policies and social care, gender issues, work-life balance, qualitative methods and theory.

Anja Weckwert is a research fellow at the Department of Social and Political Science, Johann Wolfgang Goethe-Universität Frankfurt, Germany with gender studies as a main field. Main areas of work are feminist theories, social policies and welfare states, gender and IT.

1. Introduction: Social Practices and Social Policies

Ute Gerhard, Trudie Knijn and Anja Weckwert

All over Europe, increasing numbers of women are keeping their jobs when having children. Whether this is due to financial reasons, women's higher educational levels or changed occupational goals, or whether this trend is connected to the expansion of the services sector that offers women more job opportunities, the phenomenon of the working mother has become part of our everyday life.

There are striking differences in the labour market participation of women, both between and within European countries. In Denmark, Sweden and Finland, women of all ages are far more integrated into the labour market than in Ireland, Italy, the Netherlands or Germany (see Klammer and Daly in this volume). Within the individual countries, considerable differences can be noted between women with higher and lower levels of education (see Rubery, et al., 1999).

Social-policy theorists tend to explain these differences by the particular welfare systems and their policies, which are seen as a means to facilitate or hinder the reconciliation of professional and family life depending on the availability and generosity of care-related provisions. Sufficient supply of child care services, generous parental leave regulations and individualised tax systems are regarded as measures that stimulate mothers to keep their jobs, whereas a low level of support and a high taxation of the second family income are considered to impede mothers' labour market participation. At first sight, these conclusions appear to be correct. Despite remaining differences among them, the Scandinavian countries are an example of how highly-supportive policies for children and parents result in high female employment rates. However, such a coherence of policy measures and employment rates cannot be found all over Europe. Recent research therefore points to the importance of cultural differences in order to explain women's employment rates (see Duncan and Edwards, 1999; Duncan and Pfau-Effinger, 2000; Pfau-Effinger, 2000). Women do not base their decisions regarding paid work solely on the availability of childcare or other benefits, nor are financial calculations about income, taxes and childcare costs necessarily the decisive factor. Rather, women's attitudes towards paid work are also influenced by cultural patterns and norms. Women with children have culturally shaped beliefs about the needs of a young child, gender roles, how to run a household and motherhood. They also have to cope with the expectations of their partners or the value systems of their relatives and colleagues, and in this context will have to look for a satisfying way to balance paid work and motherhood. And yet, reference to dominant value systems cannot explain convincingly why women's labour market participation has increased significantly, or why labour market behaviour varies so much between different groups of women. European value studies show that there is no unidimensional relationship between attitudes and women's labour market behaviour (see Sociaal en Cultureel Planbureau, 2000).

Recent research on lone mothers in Great Britain and the Netherlands illustrates how difficult it is to identify the main factors and to interrelate them. In these countries, new policies were introduced to motivate or even force lone mothers to take up a job instead of – as used to be tolerated in practice – living on welfare. These measures were not very successful though. They were based on the assumption that every family should have at least one breadwinner in order to get out of poverty and social isolation. But many lone mothers in Great Britain and The Netherlands decided to continue relying on welfare because they were acting according to a different maxim, namely that a mother first of all has to take care of her child. Faced with the contradictory expectations of meeting the new obligation to engage in paid work on the one hand, and to comply with the gendered norms on the other (Duncan and Edwards, 1999, 2001), a majority of mothers with low educational levels refuse to enter the labour market, while lone mothers with higher educational levels make use of the few available public childcare provisions and enter the labour market (Van Drenth, et al., 1999; Knijn and Van Wel, 2001a; Millar and Rowlingson, 2001). These and other qualitative case studies show that women's decisions point to a whole range of conditions and motives, which summed up can explain why one woman works and another does not. The present book aims at shedding light on this relationship between individual motives and the socio-political framework by taking both social policies and the social practices of working mothers into account.

WELFARE REGIMES AND GENDER ARRANGEMENTS

Reflections on the relationship between social policies and social practices touch upon a core question of sociology, namely that of the relationship between structure and agency that continues to divide social sciences into different schools of thought. To put it differently, at stake is the old question of whether the conditions – structures and institutions – determine the behaviour of people, or whether and to what extent there is scope for individual agency in social practices and strategies, and for shaping one's own life. Though we do not pretend to solve this debate, we do not want to avoid it either, because time and again our topic gives rise to questions that directly relate to this discussion. To translate some of these questions into socio-political matters: Why do East German women have an ongoing orientation towards full-time work, despite high rates of unemployment and despite the fact that they have been living for more than fifteen years under the same legal and socio-political conditions as West German women? Why do lone mothers in Italy and France work more often and in more full-time jobs than their counterparts in England and the Netherlands? Why did women in several countries enter the labour market in great numbers in periods which saw a lack of public support for working mothers?

Looking at structure and action, social theorists have pointed to the deep interrelation between both (Giddens, 1984; Bourdieu, 1990). Giddens, for example, suggests that structure – in his definition rules and resources – is not external to individual action, but as a matter of fact only attains reality status in social practices. Structure is not limited to constraints either, it is rather both constraining and enabling as it provides an orientation frame for the actors. At the same time, the term structure indicates the durability of social systems. According to Giddens, structural principles are embedded in social institutions, which encompass not only the legal framework but, for instance, also, the family system and gender relations, and which are produced and reproduced through social practices. Thus, without negating the persistence of institutions, a core attribute of which is longevity, this concept still acknowledges the possibility of social change. Following Giddens, social policies and social practices, just like family models and gender roles, have to be seen as part of an interrelating complex which also includes cultural aspects.

By introducing the term 'welfare regime', which has become a key concept for comparative work on social policies, welfare state research has already highlighted cultural aspects in order to characterise different welfare policies. Here the works by Esping-Andersen (1990, 1996) in particular offer a conceptual frame that allows for a comparison of different regimes, of different national models of social policies and their path dependencies. Apart from the relationship between state and economy as a central characteristic of the respective welfare state and its conceptualisation of social policies in relation to economic and labour market policies, 'regime' here means a whole complex of legal, institutional and socio-cultural aspects that has to be taken into account and that determines the typology. As Esping-Andersen puts the specific relationship of state, market and the family into the centre of his analysis in order to explain the various welfare regimes, his approach seems to be open to discussing gender issues. However, extensive feminist research on welfare states and social policies has drawn attention to the blind spots of this approach, pointing out that the role of the family remains theoretically unclear and is only accounted for in the conservative-corporate welfare state but not in the two other regimes, the liberal and social-democratic welfare states. To designate the different types of welfare states, Esping-Andersen introduces the term 'decommodification', which describes the relation of the individual to the labour market and which measures the degree of development that a welfare state has achieved by the extent to which the individual is forced to sell his or her work on the labour market. As women with children or family often have other reasons than men for not engaging in paid work, as their 'independence' from the labour market usually means being dependent on a breadwinner in the family, the systematic impact of the gender category is again ignored.

Still, this theoretical frame also offers starting points for feminist analysis, which has pointed out the different conditions of women's work on the market and in the family, thus showing the particular importance of care for the production and reproduction of life and for the common good (see Sainsbury, 1994; Knijn and Kremer, 1997; Lewis, 1998a; Daly and Lewis, 2000). This also introduces a change of perspective, which allows the formulation of a whole new set of criteria for comparative research on welfare states and welfare regimes. For example, whether care for children or for other relatives is primarily considered as a private or a public task is of crucial relevance for the welfare state arrangements between state and family. From a gender perspective, the question arises of whether, for example, care work is accounted for in social security systems, for instance by guaranteeing paid parental leave or by taking parenting times into account when old-age pensions are calculated. Yet, the individual countries not only differ in regard to specific provisions, but also in the way they acknowledge care. The recognition of care might be oriented mainly towards principles of equality; alternatively, it might rather adhere to gender differences and thus possibly tend to support the gender division of work in some cases, while in other cases care- and work-related policies create incentives for men and women to share paid and care work more equally.

Adopting the regime concept for feminist analysis, Sainsbury (1999a, 1999b) speaks of gender regimes in order to grasp the various dimensions that provide information about the gendered order of welfare regimes. For her, the term regime is attractive because it embraces a set of rules and norms which shape expectations in a society and thus also influences social practices. There remains, however, the question about the precise nature of the relationship between rules, norms and behaviour. In order to describe this relationship, Pfau-Effinger (2000) has recently proposed to distinguish between the gender culture, that is the cultural concepts and reference systems shaping gender relations, and the gender order. Though the gender order is embedded in the cultural context, it still forms an independent structural level which is characterised especially by the division of work and power relations as the main structures that are preserved in social institutions. For the author, the differentiation between gender culture and gender order is a way of describing the diachronicities of social change, which might occur if certain changes in the gender culture – as evidenced for instance in an increased labour market participation of women – precede changes in the gender order.

The outlined approaches have developed new perspectives on the nature of welfare states; the relation of state, market and family; and the functioning and the historical and cultural embeddedness of these institutions. The chapters in this volume take up these discussions with a particular interest in the relation between social policies, normative concepts and the social reality of working mothers. Whereas most of the literature on welfare states and women's labour market participation is based on a macro-level analysis, this volume attempts to add to the comparative analysis of welfare state regulation and statistical data by focussing on the micro-level of everyday practices. It focuses on the strategies and everyday practices of working mothers; based on qualitative case studies, the chapters explicitly introduce an actor's perspective for opening up new prospects of the connections outlined above and for considering social practices not only conceptually or in terms of statistics but as an autonomous field of research. The respective chapters start from the question of how mothers combine paid work and childcare in their daily life. This approach entails an alternative view on welfare production because working mothers do not merely rely on the provisions of the welfare state in order to keep their jobs, they coordinate various resources to be able to combine professional and family life. This includes the help of partners, relatives and friends, the use of private forms of childcare, and various types of working-time arrangements.

To date there is the need for further qualitative research in order to understand the relationship between social policies and social practices from a comparative perspective. In the last decade, cross-national comparisons have already proved to be indispensable in order to provide a corrective, in particular with respect to family and work issues. Sociological and social policy research as well as policymakers too often tend to take their own assumptions on the family, motherhood, women's employment and the like for granted. In particular the presupposition of a family model in which women's duty to provide household work and care for free is an essential condition for the material and conceptual welfare-state arrangement (Kaufmann, 1997: 44) has served to exclude this quasi 'natural' basis of all welfare production from the social-political debate. Particularly in those countries where the provisions of private households, especially care work within the family, is assigned a political area of its own and institutionalised as family politics the compatibility of professional life and care responsibilities can still be treated as a problem that only concerns women and families. The contributions in this volume, which also introduce a comparative perspective on values and everyday practices of working mothers, allow a critical scrutiny of these basic beliefs. Such a perspective corrects some premature statements about what mothers want and parents do.

And so there are a number of reasons why looking across the borders is beneficial, and in view of the current changes indispensable: not only because the goals and needs of women all over Europe have changed rapidly, but also because of the process of European integration, in which the supranational politics of the European Union (EU) gain significance and binding regulations on the labour market and social policies of the member states are developed. The issue of equal rights for women and men is part of various treaties, recommendations and programmes of the EU. As EU gender-equality policies establish a common background for the national contexts considered in this book, we want to outline briefly the most important phases of development in work and care-related policies.

THE LABOUR MARKET PARTICIPATION OF WOMEN AND MOTHERS WITHIN THE LEGAL FRAMEWORK OF THE EU

The history of European gender-related policies goes back to article 119 of the EEC Treaty of 1957, which explicitly inscribed the principle of 'equal pay for equal work' into the founding treaty of the European Economic Community (EEC). At first, the codification of equal pay did not primarily pursue the goal of promoting equal rights for women and men, but economic interests. The fact that women's wages were particularly low in some countries and industries caused concern about competitive distortions. France in particular was afraid of competitive disadvantages, because French law already guaranteed equal pay for men and women; despite some resistance (first of all from the FRG), France eventually pushed the inclusion of article 119.[1]

In the next twenty years, article 119 was hardly noticed. Only when Belgian female workers went on strike in 1966 and referred to article 119 to add force to their demands for better wages, and when two years later the Belgian stewardess Gabrielle Defrenne sued SABENA for equal treatment (see Hörburger, 1991), did the article prove to have some impact.[2] The Defrenne case attracted a lot of attention because it reached beyond the particular lawsuit: at a time in which a strong women's movement and a changed awareness of sex discrimination led to an inclusion of women's and gender issues into the political agenda, European law offered a tool to fight against the unequal treatment of women (Gerhard, 2000). At the same time, the groundwork was laid to carry on gender-related policies at a European level. In 1976, the Directive on the 'application of the principle of equal pay for men and women' came into force, defining among other things that this principle should not only apply to equal work but also to work of equal value (75/117/EEC). Moreover, in the Defrenne case the European Court of Justice (ECJ) ruled for the first time that article 119 of the EEC Treaty is of direct legal application,[3] thus enabling every man and woman to refer to this EEC law in the courts of their own country.

During the 1970s and 1980s, the European Commission took several initiatives to advance equal treatment of men and women at work, which led to further legislation such as the Directive regarding 'access to employment, vocational training and promotion, and working conditions' (76/207/EEC) and the Directives on equal treatment in statutory or occupational social security systems (Directives 79/7/EEC, 86/378/EEC, 86/613/EEC). For the first time, these Directives also contained an explicit interdiction of indirect discrimination, while the ECJ proceeded to a wider interpretation of article 119 and punished indirect discrimination in these cases as well. Indirect discrimination is the case if a rule is de facto mainly to the disadvantage of one sex and if this disadvantage cannot be justified by the needs of company. For example, the Court condemned the practice of companies who employed women mainly part-time while excluding all part-time workers from certain social benefits (for example sick pay or occupational old-age provision).[4] In these and other cases, the ECJ played an outstanding role in enforcing the Directives on the equal treatment of men and women. On the one hand, the ECJ has increasingly guaranteed the right to take action in the courts and has established far-reaching standards for the interpretation and application of the principle of equal treatment. On the other hand, its task is to exert joint control with the European Commission: other than recommendations, Directives have a binding character and have to be incorporated into domestic law within a certain period of time. The Commission must repeatedly take legal action or at least threaten such a step because the member states miss the deadlines for adjusting domestic law or because they implemented insufficient laws.

Despite the fact that not all rulings of the Court were undisputed,[5] and although some legal proposals by the European Commission remained unsuccessful while others could only pass the Council after years of struggle, one has to acknowledge some progress towards achieving equal pay and treatment in professional life – the latter being reinforced in 2002 by a new Directive against indirect discrimination, which now explicitly encompasses harassment and sexual harassment as forms of discrimination (2002/73/EC). However, all these achievements remain focused on paid work and thus follow the logic of the common market. As far as the reconciliation of family and professional life is concerned, progress is much slower. Meanwhile, the Directives on 'the protection of pregnant workers and workers who have recently given birth or are breastfeeding' (92/85/EEC), on parental leave (96/34/EC) and on part-time employment (97/81/EC) establish a minimum legal standard. Whereas the first of these Directives is considered as part of occupational safety and health regulations, the Directive on parental leave explicitly formulates the goal of making family and work compatible, and the Directive on part-time work also states this intention, among other things. The Directives on parental leave and part-time work resulted from particularly long discussions, and go back to proposals by the Commission from the early 1980s (Com 83/686 and Com 82/830 final) which could only be realised in a modified form in the second half of the 1990s. Still, these Directives too only address the working population, and thus also adhere to the focus on paid work that characterises the social policies of the EU and has prevented a more comprehensive consideration of care work.

Meanwhile, the EC Treaty of October 2, 1997 (in the version of the Treaty of Amsterdam, which replaced the Treaty of Maastricht) has created a new legal base for European gender-equality policies. The Treaty confirms the principle of equal pay and treatment in working life (Art. 137 and 141), and explicitly allows for 'measures providing for specific advantages' in order to support the 'underrepresented sex' (Art. 141 Par. 4). Moreover, Art. 2 and Art. 3 Par. 2 provide that promoting gender equality is the binding task of all activities of the Community, thus introducing the concept of Gender Mainstreaming into the EC Treaty – that is the consideration of 'gender issues in the process of design, implementation and evaluation of all policies' (Rubery, 2002). In view of this, the question arises of whether and to what degree EU and member states will in time consider care work and the gendered division of work in the family as issues to be tackled by social and labour market policies.

Whereas childcare has so far only been object to 'soft law' in the form of recommendations and council decisions, one must nevertheless acknowledge a new concern about the reconciliation of work and family life in recent employment policies. The Treaty of Amsterdam was designed vis-à-vis economic recession and a high level of unemployment, and one of its basic ideas was to raise the level of employment (see Art. 2 and the newly introduced Title VIII 'Employment' of the EC Treaty). In this context, and in view of high female unemployment rates, the employment of women is increasingly seen as a factor to be considered in employment policies. The European employment strategy, launched at the Luxembourg summit in 1997 and laid down in annual employment guidelines, country-specific recommendations and national action plans, sets up the strengthening of equal opportunity as one of its four pillars, alongside the objectives of raising employability, adaptability and entrepreneurship. More specifically, the employment guidelines introduced in 1999, demand that gender mainstreaming across pillars be combined with specific actions to enhance equal opportunities for women and men, and in the latter regard issues of childcare and the gender division in professional and family life be acknowledged as crucial (see Rubery, 2002 for details). Following on the Council of Ministers in Lisbon (2000), Stockholm (2001) and Barcelona (2002), by now the guidelines include quantitative targets both for the female EU employment rate (60 per cent by 2010) and for the provision of childcare. Member states are requested 'to provide childcare by 2010 to at least 90 per cent of children between three years old and the mandatory school age and at least 33 per cent of children under three years of age'

(2003/578/EC). Though the envisaged improvement of childcare provision can still be argued to be insufficient, the targets for childcare services could relieve the situation in many European countries considerably if compared to the status quo, particularly in southern Europe and in much of the continent, and as long as provisions offer affordable quality care (for the status quo see Daly and Klammer in this volume, Table 7.2). Moreover, EU employment policies generally problematise the gender division of work within the family as an obstacle to women's equal opportunities on the labour market. At the same time, all forms of employment are currently supported in the name of adaptability, including part-time occupation, temporary jobs and subcontracting work, in which women are overrepresented not in the least because of the gendered division of work (Ostner, 2000). Mary Daly and Ute Klammer (in this volume) point out that non-standard work is partly a strategy of mothers to combine work and family. The increase of non-standard work however goes hand in hand with a number of social problems because it mostly leads to a low income, fosters discontinuous working biographies, and has negative consequences for social security. The Directives on part-time and on fixed-term work (97/81/EC and 99/70/EC) meanwhile agree on a basic framework to avoid discrimination, though they can hardly meet the extent of social risks of labour market flexibilisation.

When taking stock of European gender-related policies, Ilona Ostner and Jane Lewis (1995) speak of 'two needles' eyes'. The first 'needle's eye' is the EU's focus on paid labour that limits social and gender equality policies, and that is given even more emphasis by the current orientation towards employability. Against this background, Ostner (2000) diagnoses a 'recommodification' of the social policies of the EU and its member states, because benefits are increasingly linked to paid work. This is not to say that the focus on paid work undermines the possibility to modify the margin of policymaking and to consider gender equality and care in a more substantial way. Current employment policies indeed pick up on these issues and it is not beyond probability that related targets will be set higher, but the political attention towards gender equality and care is nevertheless a matter of secondary importance which is subordinate to other concerns – presently about labour market and demographic development – and not pursued in its own right (Duncan, 2002). At risk is firstly that the confusion of objects leads to contradicting targets – to the disadvantage of equal opportunities. Secondly, to date recognition for care work remains very low and little effort has been undertaken to tackle the gendered division of work in the family, which continues to establish a backbone of gender inequalities effecting several spheres of life. Though for example the

Directive on parental leave guarantees the return to one's job, it leaves out any regulation regarding payment during leave and in this sense does not value care. Against the background of existing gender cultures, and in view of the income gap between men and women, unpaid leave does not create incentives for fathers to take it up (Moss and Deven, 1999).

The second 'needle's eye' is the implementation of the European policies by the member states. Although EU policies have led to a rapprochement of goals, common objectives and Directives, which by the way only formulate minimum standards, meet various national contexts, divergent traditions, interpretations and implementation strategies (see Letablier and Jönsson in this volume). The European Directive on parental leave may serve as an example again. In some countries it has led to the introduction of new legislation, other countries have had to change the pertinent regulations, but in a number of cases existing provisions went far beyond the content of the Directive (see Falkner et al., 2002; Haas, 2003). Accordingly, payment, length and other components of parental leave schemes still vary considerably among the European member states. Moreover, although the Directive defines the objective of supporting the compatibility of job and family and of advancing equal opportunities for women and men, the implementation of parental leave regulations might in fact be oriented towards very different concerns (Plantenga, 2000). In (West) Germany, for example, parental leave regulation is traditionally linked to concerns of family politics rather than to the question of equity. Together with a blatant lack of childcare places for children under three years of age, generous leave schemes tend to foster the care supply by mothers instead of supporting mothers' employment. In view of these difficulties, both at the EU and implementation levels, observers call for a more holistic approach towards gender equality that would require greater coherence of EU policymaking across measures, policies and areas of direct and indirect concern (for example Rubery, 2002; Lombardo, 2003; Pascall and Lewis, 2004).

Such an approach seems to be even more important in view of current challenges arising from the enlargement of the EU, which contributes to the heterogeneity of gender orders and gender cultures in the member states. Other than for example in Malta, where the breadwinner model has been traditionally strong, the new member states in Central and Eastern Europe (CEE) have mostly retained a commitment from the Soviet era to the dual-earner model and to public policies facilitating women's paid employment (Kotowska, 2004; Pascall and Lewis, 2004). However, the UNICEF report 'Women in Transition' (1999) points to a widening gap between rights and practice. Gender inequalities also existed under communism, as evidenced in labour market segregation and income gaps, and were especially marked in family life. The Soviet legacy of a strong gender division of care and household work might have started to undergo some changes, but women still shoulder a double workload in CEE countries (Paoli and Parent-Thirion, 2003). At the same time, losses in GDP, declining public revenue and changing ideologies about the state have led to cutbacks on public provisions in the fields of childcare, education, health, pensions and family benefits, and to a restructuring of welfare systems. As a result, more responsibilities previously defined as public are left to the family (Pascall and Manning, 2000). More women than men have lost their jobs under transition and female employment rates have fallen below the EU average in Hungary, Poland, Slovakia, and in the CEE candidate countries Bulgaria and Romania (Eurostat, 2004b). Against this background, Pascall and Lewis (2004) see threats to the dual-earner model in several regards, although they do not suggest it will actually dissolve. While a more thorough consideration of these developments is beyond the scope of this introduction, ongoing transition processes in economic and welfare state developments as well as regarding gender arrangements pose new questions and tasks to the equal-opportunity agenda of the EU.

CONTEXT AND THEMES OF THE BOOK

The present book results from the work of the European network 'Working and Mothering. Social Practices and Social Policies', in which social scientists from nine European countries have participated, and which was part of the research program 'Targeted Socio-Economic Research' (TSER) of the European Commission between 1998 and 2001. During this time the authors coordinated their joint work in a series of seminars, which provided for discussing a variety of related issues and methodological questions together with international guests. A core question of the network concerned the continued gender-coding of child-raising and waged labour, which has certainly been modified by women's mass entrance into the labour market but has by no means been eliminated. Against this background, the participants of the network opted for a twofold approach that included a comparison of European welfare systems and an analysis of the everyday practices of working mothers on the basis of national case studies. This approach also characterises the present publication. It would undoubtedly be interesting to take everyday practices of men into account as well, but as women still shoulder most of the responsibility when care and paid work have to be combined, they are the focus of this publication.

The articles about everyday practices and strategies of working mothers are mainly based on qualitative studies the authors have conducted in recent years. These were conceptualised as country-based case studies which nonetheless share a common frame that allows for subsequent comparison in a number of regards. For example, all empirical works contain a focus on working mothers who live together with a partner and have children attending kindergarten or school. In this way, these studies also allow an insight into ways in which today's couples organise professional and family life. Due to the scope and timing of the EU network, research has not yet considered the new member states.

The structure of the book tries to tackle the relationship between social policies and social practices from various perspectives. A number of welfare states now subscribe to the assumption that work is the best form of welfare, and accordingly their goal is to integrate all adults – men and women – who are capable of working into the labour market. This approach no longer seems to take the gender division of work in the family and the labour market as a norm. Lewis (2002, 2003), for instance, talks about a transformation towards the adult worker model that replaces the traditional breadwinner model on which the European welfare states of the twentieth century had based their social security systems. Gender does remain an issue under the new model though: even though women today increasingly take up paid work, they still shoulder most of the responsibility of caring for relatives. Consequently, they are integrated into the labour market to a lesser extent, and thus at a disadvantage when paid work is considered as the guiding norm. The new norms are not uncontested either; rather, the adult worker model presupposes to a high degree the process of individualisation that is widely debated and an object of controversial interpretations in social sciences and politics.

Chapter 2 by Ute Gerhard connects to these controversies on the thesis of an ongoing individualisation, according to which the individual frees himself or herself from traditional ties, but as a consequence enters other, depersonalised dependencies – from the labour market, the welfare state, and so on. Many commentators consider decreasing birth rates and the declining significance of marriage and family as core characteristics of the process of individualisation. In this context the 'delayed individualisation' of women, and in particular their increasing orientation towards paid work, is considered as a problematic development that threatens social cohesion. Against this background, Ute Gerhard tackles the normative assumptions and cultural concepts as expressed in sociological theories and socio-political debates about individualisation, marriage, family and motherhood. Referring to feminist research, the author inquires into the social and socio-political implications of a diagnosis which in its orientation towards individualised market subjects considers female employment merely an adaptation of the male process of individualisation, but which at the same time fails to approach the socially necessary activity of care work in any comprehensive way. Ute Gerhard contrasts present diagnosis with an historical perspective, to show how the bourgeois institution of marriage mapped out a certain gender order that has shaped the welfare state arrangements until today. The author relates the term individualisation to its counterpart, the institutions that are part of the frame of action in which individualisation and social change take place. The differences between processes of individualisation of mothers in East and West Germany serve as an example of how different social policies and regimes influence cultural ideals and gender relations.

Marie-Thérèse Letablier and Ingrid Jönsson in chapter 3 also discuss guiding principles of social policies. Focussing on childcare-related policies, the authors start from the question of what actually motivated states to politically intervene in an area that is often regarded as a private sphere. Looking at these motives, the authors analyse the objectives, principles and cultural ideals which have informed political measures related to childcare in different countries. Relating to the regime approach, they identify five 'childcare regimes' in Europe, which differ not only in the availability and generosity of provisions but also with regard to path dependencies and cultural concepts – for instance of motherhood, childhood and citizenship – that shape social policies. The childcare regimes are marked by particular policy logics which at present do shift in various countries due to social, economic and political change. In part, these changes lead to a convergence of objectives across Europe as they react to common problems and to the increased importance of EU politics. Taking France and Sweden as examples, the authors scrutinise how the policy logics in the field of childcare change, and what consequences this has. While new guidelines and principles still see a specific implementation shaped by the particular national context, the example of France shows that a political re-orientation can also lead to inconsistencies and conflicts.

Chapter 4 by Constanza Tobío and Rossana Trifiletti shifts the perspective and turns to everyday strategies of working mothers. This chapter first attempts to conceptualise the term 'strategy', which in social research literature is often used to refer to the intentional and rational character of social interaction. By contrast, feminist critics have objected that the behaviour of women could not be adequately described within these categories because it is less goal- and purpose-oriented, and rather geared towards processes and meaning. Discussing various concepts of strategy, the authors develop a definition of their own which shall serve as a tool to analyse the social practices of working mothers. The authors generally preserve the rational and intentional connotation of the term 'strategy', but suggest that this term is rather unsuited for describing all kinds of everyday practices and that the strategic moment of social action is particularly important in times of social change. They understand strategies as practices that are characteristic for situations in which new problems arise, for which no institutionalised solutions exist yet. With a view towards the everyday practices of working mothers, their thesis is that strategies are of particular importance for working mothers in those countries that lack sufficient provisions for childcare – for instance because increasing female employment rates are a recent phenomenon and society has not yet reacted to the new situation. On the basis of qualitative case studies about working mothers in Spain and Italy, the authors elaborate on various types of strategies which mothers develop to combine professional and family life.

After conceptual considerations about the term 'strategy', chapter 5 by Arnlaug Leira, Constanza Tobío and Rossana Trifilietti scrutinises how the first generation of working mothers in Norway, Spain and Italy managed to cope with the double responsibility of job and family. Precisely because the social-political framework was still lacking when these women entered the labour market, a look at their everyday practices reveals how working mothers developed their very own strategies in a context of social change to combine paid and care work. In referring to Norway, Italy and Spain, the chapter not only concentrates on very different welfare systems, but on three countries in which mothers entered the labour market at different periods. Accordingly, these mothers faced divergent economic, political and social circumstances that defined the specific context in which they had to develop their strategies. Despite all differences, what these countries have in common is that the first generation of working mothers was first of all dependent on informal resources to be able to combine paid and care work. While traditional family ties and obligations in southern Europe are often seen as a factor that hinders the labour market participation of mothers, the authors clearly point out that intergenerational help by family members – mainly by grandmothers – is essential for working mothers. In Norway too, first-generation working mothers could only cope with their everyday life by using the help of informal resources. The example of Norway also demonstrates that social policies adapted only with great delay to the new requirements.

Looking at everyday practices shows that the labour market behaviour of mothers is not merely based on weighing costs and benefits, and neither is it due to cultural factors only. As Trudie Knijn, Ingrid Jönsson and Ute

Klammer point out, it also depends on the available private and public resources, and on the capacity of mothers to combine and coordinate them. Their chapter takes a look at how working mothers in the Netherlands, Germany and Sweden manage to combine care and work today. At the centre of their analysis are the 'care packages' of working mothers. The term 'care packages' refers to the activity of mothers bundling various resources offered by the state, the market, the family and the voluntary sector in varying combinations. The authors emphasise that not all resources are based on legal rights but that some result from claims: mothers have to claim assistance – from their partners, relatives and friends, as well as from their employers – in order to be able to combine professional and family life. The chapter shows which private and public forms of childcare and work-related arrangements mothers in the three countries, package and, based on qualitative case studies, also provides an insight into the motives and wishes of working mothers. Referring to the difference between claims and rights, the authors emphasise that working mothers suffer from grave disadvantages when rights are rare, and when they have to base their care packages mainly on claims.

The final contribution by Mary Daly and Ute Klammer once again changes the perspective, and based on statistical data gives a comparative overview of the development and patterns of female labour market participation in Europe. In view of the great differences that exist from a cross-national perspective between women's participation rates, the authors scrutinise various supply and demand factors, and in this context also concentrate on the social-political framework. The authors note that the provision of childcare has the most significant influence on the extent to which women join the labour market, whereas the correlation is not as clear regarding other policies such as parental leave regulations or tax policies. Rather, it is the precise mix of policies and the coherence of the particular measures that seem to have a greater impact on the decision of mothers to engage in paid work. Mary Daly and Ute Klammer also address current changes in the labour market as evidenced in the increase of non-standard work as well as in a greater diversity of job situations for men and women alike. According to the authors, the fact that men are increasingly affected by the growing flexibility of the labour market could turn out to be a chance for women, because their patterns of labour market behaviour and discontinuous working biographies can no longer be considered as a deviation from the male norm in the future. In view of the social risks that accompany the changes, the authors refer to the necessity to rethink the system of social security, without abandoning the 'regulating idea' behind the 'standard full-time job' – essential elements of which are a sufficient income and access to social security.

The chapters in this volume show that a restructuring of the social security systems would also have to take the relation of state, market and the family into account. The chapters bring the invisible welfare production of mothers and of their supporting networks – of relatives, friends and neighbours – to light. They show that the first generation of working mothers was only able to combine paid and family work through the help of other women, and that mothers in many European countries today are still dependent on informal resources if they want to engage in paid work. Taking an actor's perspective at the same time documents the difficulties, constraints and disadvantages working mothers have to face when care work is considered a private affair, and that means by and large a private responsibility of women. While current sociological analyses as well as policy models tend to turn their attention one-sidedly towards individualised market subjects and the field of employment, the chapters in this volume are a reminder to distribute the chances for individualisation more equally according to the social rights of citizenship, and to make the concern about care work a pillar of the welfare state. At the same time, it is important that not only paid work but care work too is seen as a responsibility of both men and women.

NOTES

[1] For the development of the EU policies for gender equality, see for example Hörburger, 1991; Ostner and Lewis, 1995; Hoskyns, 1996; Gerhard, 2000; Rossilli, 2000.

[2] The Defrenne case was about internal regulations of Sabena, according to which stewardesses older than age 40 – in contrast to their male colleagues – were only employed as ground personnel and had to accept lower wages. Gabrielle Defrenne achieved a recovery of income damages but lost her trial for raised pensions because at that time the European Court of Justice still interpreted the principle of equal pay in a restrictive way(Hörburger, 1991).

[3] See judgment of 8 April 1976. Case 43/75, ECR 547 (1976), quoted in Ostner and Lewis, 1995: 168; see also Langer, 1999: 183.

[4] For example in the cases of Gisela Rummler v. Dato-Druck GmbH, Case 273/85, ECR 1201 (1986) and Bilka Kaufhaus GmbH vs. Karin Weber von Hartz, Case 170/84, ECR 1607 (1986) quoted in Ostner and Lewis, 1995: 170f.; see also Langer, 1999: 183.

[5] Particularly controversial was the Kalanke case (Case 450/93, ECR I-3051), because the European Court of Justice considered a quota regulation to be a practice that discriminates against men. Meanwhile, Art. 141 (ex. Art. 119 EEC) Par. 4 of the Treaty of Amsterdam explicitly acknowledges the possibility 'to keep or to decide on specific benefits to prevent or to compensate for disadvantages in the professional career or to ease employment of the underrepresented sex'. In the Marschall case (Case 409/95, ECR I-6363), in anticipation of this new regulation the European Court of Justice also ruled that preferring women in case of equal qualifications has to be possible; cp. Langer, 1999.

2. Mothers between Individualisation and Institutions: Cultural Images of Welfare Policy

Ute Gerhard

Should mothers participate fully and equally in the labour market? This question continues to generate controversy in Europe – even though the European Union's 1997 contract of Amsterdam instituted a new equal-opportunity policy promoting the integration of women *and* mothers as waged workers. Already in 1908, the German feminist Helene Lange characterised the conflict between work and family as a battlefield with two fronts (Lange, 1908: 11) – a martial yet clear-sighted metaphor taking the subsequent struggle to harmonise work, wages and equality into account. And so a century-long debate has accompanied the process of industrialisation, modernisation and welfare state formation like a basso continuo. Depending on the historical context, these academic and socio-political controversies, either implied or explicit, find expression in the positive discursive form of the 'protective legislation for female workers' (Scott, 1993), in 'the crisis and dissolution of marriage and family' (Nave-Herz, 1998), in the 'male breadwinner model' (Lewis, 1992) and, recently, in discussions on 'individualisation' (Beck and Beck-Gernsheim, 1994, 2002).

Comparative welfare state research that highlights the relation between state, market and family (Esping-Andersen, 1990, 1997) does not only distinguish welfare regimes but also welfare cultures. Especially recent work on women's labour market participation and different gender arrangements has elaborated cultural aspects as a new strand in welfare state research (see Duncan and Edwards, 1999; Duncan and Pfau-Effinger, 2000; Pfau-Effinger, 2000). According to this approach, the cultural dimension cannot be explained merely by looking at socio-economic determinants, statistical data or normative prescriptions, but must be considered in its own right. Thirty years have passed since women's and gender studies emerged from the new

18

women's movement and began questioning female labour market participation, the incompatibility of care and paid work, and contradictions in women's lives and experience. In those early days, feminist scholars were already declaring the need to modify the evaluation of women's motives and orientations, as women's labour market decisions do not merely follow economic rationality or the logic of the market – and can much less be explained by them. Since then, an almost immeasurable body of work has dealt with the phenomenon of women's double socialisation (Becker-Schmidt and Knapp, 2000) and the contradictory demands women face in the family and at work. At the same time, contradiction and ambivalence in women's lives were seen as elements that could also contain seeds of change and resistance despite being impediments (Prokop, 1976: 10). Time and again, qualitative empirical research has confirmed the inappropriateness of political economy and labour market theory as well as statistical analyses in explaining the differences and convergences characterising women's labour market participation. Nor does a change in the institutional, legal framework guarantee politics are adjusted to the needs and desires of women. Rather, we should be asking how social policies affect social practices, and how they facilitate social change. What drives the social practices of people addressed by social policies, and how can freedom of choice, promised over and over, really lead to freedom and equality, or, as we say nowadays, to more gender democracy?

Interpreting social behaviour is a genuinely sociological task that requires accounting for historical context and developments. From a critical, inter-disciplinary perspective, the cultural turn in welfare research must be a welcome development. But if cultural aspects are to be little more than a joker used for everything otherwise inexplicable (see Kulawik, 1999: 21), we must agree on what we mean – particularly in an international arena. Culture as the quintessence of all signs, customs and rules the human species creates, as an 'objectification of the spirit' in cultural-sociologist Georg Simmel's words (Simmel, 1992: 16), is certainly too broad a definition, too vague to serve as a point of reference in socio-political analyses.

At any rate, cultural variables are particularly treacherous because cultural context not only shapes individual and collective behaviour – just as it is reproduced by it – but is also inscribed in institutions and welfare arrange-ments among state, market and family. Therefore, this chapter discusses the relationship between social practices and social policies by focussing on problematic cultural concepts that have repeatedly played a crucial role in scholarly and socio-political debates about working mothers in various countries. I will concentrate on three discourses related to maternal labour market participation, but which as a counterpart to the theme of the adult worker model (Lewis, 2002) focus on the sphere of reproduction and can be evoked by the keywords 'individualisation', 'family and changed life styles' and 'motherhood'. Even though a German perspective informs this inquiry, the comparison aims primarily to question this very bias and its taken-for-granted cultural assumptions.

One of modernity's key concepts is individualisation. Current social change – largely effected by the increasing individualisation of women – is viewed by sociological theory as based on action resulting from (seemingly) autonomous decisions. In other words, a multiplication of choices and plurality of lifestyles promote individualisation, while traditional ties to social institutions and groups gradually decline. The first part of this chapter, focusing on theories of individualisation from a gender perspective, asks whether the theory of women's delayed individualisation, identified mainly with their increasing labour market participation, can adequately describe major social alterations in women's orientation.

Theorists of individualisation argue that marriage and the family have lost significance as basic social institutions. This thesis is also the starting point for problematising modernised gender relations in sociological diagnoses of our time. The chapter's second part therefore focuses on changes in family structure and lifestyle, and the effects of transformation on welfare state arrangements. Next, an overview of family changes across Europe prefaces an historical discussion of the dilution of marriage, revealing how marriage and family as institutions of nineteenth century bourgeois society not only secured reproduction and social stability, but also gendered the social order. Following the approach of path dependencies, I turn to the processes of institutionalisation and de-institutionalisation of marriage in four legal cultures – British Common Law, the French *Code Civil*, the Prussian General Code (ALR) and the Nordic legal context – to show that this 'gendered programme' was not merely a social practice but also a coercive legal institution based on family law. Without assuming a linear connection between historical legal contexts and current welfare state regimes, legal traditions clearly play a significant role in the relation between welfare state and family. The Swedish experience shows, for instance, that the institutional framework does not necessarily constrain but can also promote autonomous social relations and thus individualisation.

Focusing on culture in relations between welfare states and gender arrangements entails scrutinising the term 'motherhood' because norms and expectations of the 'good mother' are very much culturally influenced and historically shaped. Thus the third part of this chapter outlines the social construction of motherhood in socio-political discourse since the end of the nineteenth century. A comparison of mothers' attitudes in East and West

Germany serves as a concluding example, illustrating how different developments and regimes meld cultural gender arrangements and the self-image of female actors.

THE THESIS OF INDIVIDUALISATION FROM A GENDER PERSPECTIVE

While new initiatives and labour market policies aim to draw more women into employment, experts predict a concomitant increase in social problems. Central to this assumption is the concept of women's delayed individualisation, conceived as an adaptation to the biography of the male worker. Reflected in this interpretation are theories of individualisation that not only claim a better framing of family and labour market research but also offer a diagnosis of the development of Western industrialised countries at the end of the twentieth century and beyond.

Theorising about today's increase in individualisation is by no means new, given that the discussion is as old as sociology itself. This explains innovative relations between the individual and society in modernity as derived from a growing division of labour, increasing differentiation and liberation from traditional forms of community. In addition, the field's classical literature has always described this form of individualisation as ambivalent because it is fraught with risks, disorganisation and loss (see Tönnies, 1963; Simmel, 1970). 'Why does the individual,' asks Emile Durkheim in *About the Social Division of Labour*, 'while becoming more autonomous, depend more upon society? How can he be at once more individual and more solidary?' (Durkheim, 1964: 37) For Durkheim, individualisation was linked to the increasing division of labour as a chore characteristic of modern societies, which, at the same time, rely on solidarity. He was concerned with how social solidarity can be maintained or continuously re-established. He emphasises: 'But if the division of labour produces solidarity, it is not only because it makes each individual an exchangist, as the economists say; it is because it creates among men an entire system of rights and duties which link them together in a durable way' (ibid.: 248). This process of individualisation, advancing together with modernity, is also stressed by more recent theorists (see Beck and Beck-Gernsheim, 1994, 2002; particularly Elias, 2001). What is new, however, are the signs of 'the radicalising of modernity' (Giddens, 1994: 57), embodied since the 1960s and 1970s in the qualitative leap towards a 'new modernity', or 'reflexive modernisation' compared to the previously 'simple' industrial society form. Since the publication of *Risk*

Society, Ulrich Beck (1992) has inspired theories of individualisation, provoking strong criticism as well as agreement.[1] Here I question his contribution to an analysis of gender relations.

Individualisation is not to be confused here with individuation, which is an increase of opportunities for individuals to make significant life decisions on their own, free from traditional and societal constraints. Rather, Beck distinguishes three analytical dimensions of individualisation. First, it means release from traditional social structures and relationships (dimension of liberation); second, a loss of traditional certainties (dimension of disenchantment); and third, new forms of social integration, which reverse the liberating and disenchanting dimensions of individualisation (dimension of reintegration) (Beck, 1992, see also Beck and Beck-Gernsheim, 2002). Reintegration, also known as 'institutionalised individualisation', means that 'the liberated individuals become dependent on the labor market *and because of that*, dependent on education, consumption, welfare state regulations and support, traffic planning, consumer supplies, and on possibilities and fashions in medical, psychological, pedagogical counselling and care' (Beck, 1992: 130-131). In this inevitability, we can perceive a one-sided market logic privileging determinism and the economy which – in contrast to Durkheim (1964) – gives neither social solidarity nor mutual rights and duties a chance. It remains unclear how anyone can shape a life when faced with such overwhelming dependencies. The emancipation of individuals has less and less to do with free choice. People are doomed to individualisation (Beck and Beck-Gernsheim, 1994), because one characteristic of reflexive modernity is its involuntary dynamic unfolding as a risky, yet unnoticed or hidden consequence for everyone involved (Beck, 1992). At the same time, individuals constantly have to make decisions in everyday life, and the standard biography turns into a do-it-yourself-biography, into a patchwork biography (Beck, 1993: 152).

According to Ulrich Beck and Elisabeth Beck-Gernsheim, a model for our time's new risks and liabilities is the 'battle of the sexes' (Beck, 1992) with new liberties and restrictions created in dramatic fashion through female individualisation. It is not merely gender relations, that is 'male versus female', that are under the microscope here, but a range of issues, the 'normal chaos of love' that is nothing less than family, marriage, parenthood, sexuality, the erotic and love (Beck and Beck-Gernsheim, 1995). Marriage and family, institutions under state protection in which the inequality and subordination of women had been sealed and justified, are indeed paradigmatic of an internal contradiction imminent in a gendered 'divided modernity'. According to this traditional gender order, work at the home or in the job market, living for others in contrast to a life of one's own (Beck and

Beck-Gernsheim, 2002: 54-84), represents two different paths through life whose gendered connotation has been problematic from the start. Though exemption from waged labour was never possible for large segments of the population, the ideology of incompatibility had far-reaching political and practical consequences. If it is taken for granted – as Beck (1992) does – that industrial society is a driving force for gender conflict within the private, indeed intimate sphere setting off far-reaching social processes (see also Ribbens McCarthy et al., 2002: 207), then accountability is again turned upside-down. Beck does problematise the individual's difficulties to combine care with paid work, yet does not consider that these constraints are modelled vis-à-vis the male norm of 'the system of standardised full employment' releasing the worker not only from property but also from family responsibilities. In contrast, we might object that it is not the individualisation of women, their liberation from dependencies and institutionalised tutelage, which endangered breadwinner wages guaranteeing provision for spouse and family, or triggered off the erosion of gender relations and the asserted dissolution of family morale (Beck, 1992). The culprit is rather lack of responsibility for and participation in childcare by market subjects living a traditional masculine biography.[2]

After all, the vision of a 'fully mobile society of singles' in which 'the market subject ... is ... "unhindered" by a relationship, marriage or family' (Beck, 1992: 116) contrasts with everything we know about the concepts, values and social practices of women – and working mothers in particular – which this volume discusses by focussing on mothers in various European countries. It is true that to associate the responsibilities for reconciling care and paid work solely with women is problematic, but the well-known Janus face of individualisation does show in these findings. It becomes evident that 'according to gender, individualisation means something different' (Rerrich, 1994: 202, see also Gilligan, 1982; Benhabib, 1987 and Lewis, 2001), so any theory of the female's delayed individualisation geared towards the male professional biography is too one-dimensional to capture the complexity of women's individualisation processes. In her empirical study of female youth, Angelika Diezinger found that female individualisation, in contrast to the dominant form of labour market individualisation, necessarily includes individualisation within bonds, not only from bonds. But keeping within bonds does not mean delayed development, nor does it prevent the individual from shaping her life (Diezinger, 1991: 25-28). Individualisation based on the male model 'is a negative ideal of freedom: freedom as release from bondage, individuality stripped bare of its relationship with and need for others' (Benjamin, 1988: 187-88).[3]

Since the 1970s, gender studies in various countries have tackled women's work at home and in the labour market as a key for analysing the gender order in contemporary societies.[4] Feminist research highlighted the ambivalence inherent to the double orientation and 'daily double conduct' (Jurczyk and Rerrich, 1993), which turns women not into latecomers but rather into pioneers of a new, modern way of life. Elisabeth Beck-Gernsheim has also contributed importantly to women's and gender studies (Beck-Gernsheim, 1980, 1983, 1999), and introduces a gender perspective into the individual-isation debate by describing with sympathy the dilemma in women's role and their everyday balancing acts (Beck and Beck-Gernsheim, 1994, 2002). However, she sees this as a result and against a background of loss of security, intimacy and closeness, thus reinforcing the culturally pessimistic thesis of dissolution (ibid.).

If we ask what another prominent author in the individualisation debate, Anthony Giddens, has to say about the gender question, it is striking that his analysis is much more restrained, although the question of gender *relations* does become an issue in some parts of his work (for example Giddens, 1991, 1994, 1999). Social movements play an important role in the context of potential democratisation (Giddens, 1994: 193), and feminism in particular deserves credit for innovating a politics of identity, life and body, thus re-inscribing moral and existential problems of modernity and the modernisation process on the political agenda (Giddens, 1991: 209-226). Giddens emphasises that the 'me generation is a misleading description of the new individualism, which does not signal a process of moral decay. Rather the contrary …' (Giddens, 1999: 35-36). Though predicting crucial changes in the democratic family towards increasing gender equality, greater female labour market participation and changed sexual behaviour, Giddens' politically programmatic work *The Third Way* remains vague and non-committal, as he is primarily concerned about family change, lone parenthood and fatherlessness (ibid: 89-99). If, as he argues, educating children should be joint parental work one can only agree, but once again missing is any explanation of what care means, in political or practical terms.

This is important because the debate on care has received great attention in Great Britain as well as internationally thanks to feminist research, which perceives care both as a socio-political concept and as a daily social practice of women at home and at work.[5] In her study of working mothers in the welfare state, Arnlaug Leira carefully explains her preference for 'care' as it being more fitting and adequate to analyse care work than applying terms such as reproductive work or distinguishing between housework and paid work – concepts used in the early days of women's studies. Care also includes paid care work, and the analysis of relations between caregiver and care receiver resolves the distinction between public and private responsibilities

(Leira, 1992: 29-30). The Scandinavian context has introduced the concept of a 'rationality of care' into the social scientific and socio-political discourse, arguing for a new moral economy to replace a rationality geared only towards efficiency and profitability as guiding principles of care practice both at home and in the public sphere (see Waerness, 2000). Finally, these considerations are supported by a care ethic developed within feminist theory (Gilligan, 1982) which, even though it takes a concept of autonomy as its point of departure, does not regard the individual as an isolated being in pursuit of his/her own interests but as someone who remains in nurturing relationships and responsible for others. Joan Tronto (2000) refers to this idea and develops a new concept of 'democracy as caring practice' (see also Sevenhuijsen, 1998).

In view of this broad feminist discussion that is particularly significant for welfare research (Leira and Saraceno, 2002), Selma Sevenhuijsen criticises Giddens' familial-political notions of a 'third way' as contradictory and inadequate mostly because they completely ignore the political consequences of feminist findings about care and work. A society that posits paid work as the unique foundation of social welfare and understands access to remunerated employment alone as a means of inclusion and social integration should not be dominated by a work ethic, as Giddens agrees (1999: 110). But what Giddens implies by the slogan 'positive welfare' – non-governmental institutions for public benefit, plus family and friends as the main sources of social solidarity – appears in social democracy as a fissure catering to criticism from the right (ibid.: 111-112) which demands state withdrawal, increased individual responsibility, citizen participation and counselling, and finally results in empty phrases such as the 'active development of civil society' (ibid.: 118). The gap, according to Sevenhuijsen (2002: 140), could be filled by recognising an 'ethics of care': 'Instead of talking about individuals as the basic units of social policy, we could take notions like "selves in networks of care and responsibility", and "working and caring citizens" as indices of moral subjectivity for social policy' (Sevenhuijsen, 2002: 140).

However, a social politics of caring should not abandon the protection and enforcement of individual freedom and rights (see Leira and Saraceno, 2002: 78), because these were and are the necessary foundation of all social and democratic practices. Therefore, following Thomas H. Marshall – who, in addition to defending individual political and civil rights, considers 'the right to a modicum of economic welfare and security' as well as 'the right to share to the full in the social heritage and to live the life of a civilized being' absolutely essential (Marshall, 1950: 10-11) – the concept of social rights for citizens can be adopted, even extended, by feminist theory and social policy

(Hobson, 1996; Knijn and Kremer, 1997; Lister, 1997; Siim, 2000; Hobson and Lister, 2002). From a gender perspective, however, these rights must be further developed towards realising new standards of justice. At any rate, the individualisation debate shows that differing experience and lifestyles – not in the least due to persistent structures of gender inequality – obviously legitimise different values and paths towards a self-defined, civilised life. Therefore women's various ways of combining work and family, their everyday strategies to organise childcare by packaging different resources (Knijn, Jönsson and Klammer, in this volume) within a social context of solidarity networks, which provide a crucial source of aid, could and should apply new standards for democratic politics. As a 'third way' for innovative welfare policy to be sufficiently sustainable to meet global challenges, it is not enough to demand the revival of civic culture by encouraging, for instance, state supported non-profit work (Giddens, 1999: 127). Instead, men must take responsibility for private labour, thereby modifying the concept of the adult worker – until now always presented only as a market subject within the model of the standard male biography (see Eckart, 2000; for fatherhood in Europe, see Hobson, 2002).

THE OTHER SIDE OF INDIVIDUALISATION: FAMILY CHANGE AND MARRIAGE'S DECLINING SIGNIFICANCE

Gloomy predictions of the dissolution of the family, raised in theories of individualisation, also have a long tradition in the social sciences. 'Discourse on the family', writes Rosemarie Nave-Herz (1998: 286), 'equates discourse on the crisis or disintegration of the family'. Whether it be the threatened authority of the father, the functional loss of the family or increasing childlessness since the foundation of family sociology through Ferdinand LePlay in France or Wilhelm H. Riehl in Germany, the stumbling block has been either the 'notorious emancipation of women' (Riehl, 1855) or, more to the point, the work outside the home of mothers with small children. The argument has always concerned not only the family as the basic institution of the state or as the venue of private partnership conflicts, but has always been associated with a deterioration of values that threatens society and the state as a whole.

Demography and family sociology serve as points of departure for individualisation theory, which considers lower birth rates, the dissolution of traditional ties and institutions such as marriage and family, and a plurality of lifestyles and family structures (a decrease in weddings together with an increase in divorce, non-married couples and single households) as the main indicators of current transformations. Family researchers, however, have often differentiated among and interpreted these developments in divergent ways.

Many of their findings on which individualisation theories rest – negotiated as pluralisation, de-institutionalisation and polarisation – have meanwhile been heavily criticised, qualified or differentiated. Thus the pluralisation of lifestyles is by no means an historically new phenomenon, but has appeared in the history of the family in various phases of social transformation as a sign or motor of social change (Rosenbaum, 1978). Historical family research has described the variety of family forms in European modern times as a distinctive European background for the development of the family. In the same vein, what is known as the law of contraction (see Durkheim, 1964), the widespread cliché of a development from the extended to the nuclear family has repeatedly been revealed as myth (Laslett, 1972; Mitterauer and Sieder, 1982, see also König, 1969). After all, one can at best talk about a pluralisation of family forms when comparing our times with the era between World War II and the mid 1960s, the phase in Western industrial countries generally characterised as the 'Golden Age of Marriage', 'because never before in the history of our cultural area ... have there been so many married people, so few divorces, and such a relatively high number of children per family, [with] non-married couples ... as good as unknown' (Nave-Herz, 1998: 294).

Indeed, family research in Europe notes a convergence in family and lifestyle changes since the 1970s – a convergence towards diversity, an increasing differentiation of family forms. Anton Kuijsten condenses the major trends into a time scale: the 1960s are marked by alterations in family size due to decreased births; the 1970s by an increased number of couples living together before getting married, an increased number of divorces and a deferral of children; the 1980s by marriages after a child is born; and the late 1980s and 1990s by fewer and fewer people marrying, regardless of whether they have children (Kuijsten, 2002: 21). Of course, behind these major trends hide nation-specific variants and developments, such as divergent rates of out-of-wedlock births, the highest number of which can be seen in Scandinavia, the former GDR, France and Great Britain – all of them in contrast to Ireland, which in many aspects is a wild card (ibid.: 37 and 65). It is interesting that the increased number of divorces in almost all countries began in the 1970s (albeit at differing levels), independently of reforms in divorce legislation sometimes implemented only later (ibid.: 30). Applied to these developments are always moral standards operating mainly with pejorative terms such as loss, decay, disintegration, erosion, and so on. In periods of social change, family orientation or familialism, a firmly established cultural norm, must compete with newly formulated values such as self-realisation, equality and autonomy. The decline of marriage both in numbers and in cultural significance indicates most clearly a convergence of various family traditions in Europe. Therefore, in what follows I consider the relation of family to welfare state in terms of de-institutionalisation as the other side of individualisation.

Liberal political theory considers marriage or family to be a basic institution, a fundamental part of communal relations, and at the same time a pillar of the state. As a legally binding contract, the marital institution means here more than the sociological concept of long-standing social practices might suggest (see Giddens, 1984: 69). As an institution, marriage exemplifies the state's control and legitimisation of a gender order in which the man as head of the matrimony was granted all juridical power, controlled all marital property, and was obligated to provide, whereas the woman was obliged to fulfil her marital duties, be subservient and obedient, and according to a gendered division of labour – an 'invention of tradition' (Hobsbawm, 2000) – was constrained to offering personal services of any kind to the family and to any business enterprise the man might run. This bourgeois family model, which sacrificed women's individual rights to a higher moral community and a political purpose, proves to be the common point of reference both for classical liberal theory and for the followers of political restoration in their reaction against emancipation and equal rights for women, which in the nineteenth century already had become conceivable as a consequence of enlightenment. Both liberal and restoration theorists maintained that the family was 'the foundation of the state' and of 'all nobler human and civil happiness' (Brockhaus, 1834 and von Rotteck, 1837, both quoted in Schwab, 1979: 289; see also Vogel, 2000). The point is therefore that marriage, more than a contract, exceeds a mere legal relationship, and as a moral relationship can by no means be subjected to the free will of the parties involved. In practice, this meant no divorce (Blasius, 1987; Gerhard, 1978: 167).

To evaluate European welfare cultures and their developmental trajectories, it is interesting to trace how this liberal and restorative understanding of marriage continues to influence legislation today, for indeed it plays no insignificant role in accounting for various gender arrangements in specific relations of market, state and family, and may still be present in various national family policies (see Kaufmann, 1993, 2002).

Great Britain's *Common Law* held jurisdiction over the largest leap from the total disenfranchisement of married women to the insignificance of marriage for the legal status of women. Until the nineteenth century, a wife lost her status as a legal subject and acquiesced in 'civil death' – according to the often-quoted formula by William Blackstone, whose commentary to

English Common Law was considered an authoritative source: 'In law husband and wife are one person, and the husband is that person' (quoted in Vogel, 1990: 219). The legal situation of wives not only contradicted the legal position of unmarried women, but was also a blatant defiance of early constitutional institutions in England – its parliamentary traditions, its separation of powers and constitutional guarantee of property – and came under increasing pressure with growing industrialisation and commercialisation. Starting in about 1870, the first suffrage campaigns of the English Women's Movement and John Stuart Mill's famous intervention led to a number of laws – the Married Women's Property Acts. Although the family property of married women was protected, they had not yet attained equal status. This legislation however linked the idea of individual freedom to the right to hold property, in accord with the theory of the individual right to property (see Vogel, 1988: 425-426). In England too, inspired by the principle of equity, a number of legal steps had been necessary before family law reached a degree of individualisation with the major reform of the divorce law in 1969 (Lewis, 2001: 25). Now permitting divorce by mutual consent and abandoning the principle of guilt, the state basically abdicated all responsibility for regulating marriage and family because, in contrast to continental marriage laws, the marriage contract in Common Law is a purely private affair. It resembles a labour contract by presupposing the autonomy and equality of the contracting partners, thereby essentially excluding intervention of the state (see Steinmetz, 2000: 20-21; for the work contract see Simitis, 2000). In this sense, changes in the mode of socialisation from status to contract predicted by Sir Henry Maine were realised in British marriage law, although with some institutional delays. As Kathleen Kiernan et al. note, in the course of the twentieth century marriage has been considered 'less an institution, in terms of both law and popular opinion, and more a relationship' (Kiernan, et al., 1998: 62). This leads Jane Lewis, supported by her analysis of family discourse and a wealth of empirical findings from Great Britain, to raise the fundamental question of the 'end of marriage' (Lewis, 2001). Obviously, the relation between social change and law, or behaviour and legal reform, is much vaguer, more liberal in countries with Common Law – including the US – than in jurisdictions where explicit family policy regulates marital relations through legal provisions concerning marriage contract contents. Moreover, the British welfare state does not link benefits to families but instead to individuals; children's allowance, for instance, is for the children themselves, not for their parents. A considerable part of welfare provision is exclusively tied to special programmes for families particularly in need. The main motive is to alleviate destitution, in accord with the general orientation of social policy on the problem of poverty. Unlike Germany, British welfare thinking is not linked to worker's status, nor is it, as in Sweden, derived from a principle of equality (Kaufmann, 1993 and 2002: 472).

Whether successful family policy in France, and in particular the strong socio-political commitment to childcare, is still owing to cultural traditions stemming from the 1804 *Code Civil* is very much in doubt. This bold assumption seems even more absurd considering that the French *Code Civil*, in contrast to other codifications of Enlightenment thought such as the Prussian General Code, gave fathers unrestricted, even despotic, power over their children while neither offspring born out of wedlock nor their mothers enjoyed any rights or protection whatsoever – even inquiring into paternity was forbidden (Art. 340 Code Civil, see Gerhard, 1990; see also Weber, 1971: 318). At any rate, the rigidity of paternal authority and at the same time the attention that has been paid to this issue is noteworthy. Can we therefore interpret the paternalistic character of the French welfare state (see Letablier and Jönsson, in this volume), which has made a special effort to support and protect mothers and children since the end of nineteenth century, as a compensating policy that was considered necessary vis-à-vis demographic problems? After all, the particularly misogynistic provisions of the French *Code Civil*, giving unrestricted authority to the husband, were valid until 1938, with French women given the right to vote as late as 1944 even though they had already formulated and claimed women's rights during the French Revolution. In any case, French legal development with respect to women's status testifies to strong reactions and cultural changes. The enormous increase in out-of-wedlock births – 40 per cent of all infants at the end of the twentieth century – has meant more variety of family forms, a fact finally confirmed by the Supreme Court in 1989 which granted marriages and non-marital partnerships equal status (see Kaufmann, 2002: 462). It would be interesting to also discuss the legislative differences in countries whose civil law has been influenced by the French Code, such as the Netherlands. It becomes apparent that in treating marriage and family as a private affair, the Dutch liken their welfare policy to the Anglo-Saxon liberal approach. By contrast, Mediterranean welfare cultures, which take for granted subsidies provided by an extended family and supportive networks, meet other conditions in the process of modernisation, which at first led to postponing claims for individual subjective rights (see Leira, Tobio and Triffiletti, in this volume). These deviations warn us not to give too much mono-causal significance to legal traditions.

The family appears most clearly as an anchored institution and 'foundation of German social policy' (Riehl, 1855) in German-speaking countries. Considering the particularism of private law and the heterogeneity and complexity of legal facts in pre-imperial Germany (before 1871), the institutional doctrine on marriage was a product of jurisprudence in reaction to the relatively liberal divorce regulation of the Prussian General Code and some woman-friendly provisions for non-married mothers and their children. This reactionary turn in family law made divorce more difficult, and restricted both the property rights of women and the legal rights of 'illegitimate' children. These regulations found their way into the family-law provisions of the Civil Code that came into force in 1900, and in fact still underlie the particular protection guaranteed to marriage and family in Art. 6 of the West German Basic Law of 1949. The elevation and idealisation of marriage as an institution are based on a notion of the union which – following Johann G. Fichte's ideas about natural law – justified women's 'voluntary' submission to the prerogative of men, given their 'natural impulse' and in the spirit of romanticism 'making herself means to satisfy man from love for a particular one' (Fichte, 1970: 398, 401). 'Through this, her nature, [marriage] obtains an independent mode of being, a right to recognition that is independent of individual will and opinion' (Savigny, quoted in Gerhard, 1978: 171). Juxtaposed to the transition from status to contract as a general characteristic of legal development, family law had remained an enclave of unequal law (Grimm, 1987: 33). Still, we perceive a certain tension between Art. 3 of the constitution guaranteeing equal rights to women and Art. 6 ensuring special protection to marriage and family, all the more so before 1977 when the housewife marriage as legal norm had not yet been erased from the Civil Code. And there remained a long road to be travelled from the rather formal 1957 finding of the Federal Constitutional Court that a wife's labour market participation cannot in principle be seen as destructive of marriage (BVerfGE 6, 55) towards the 1998 ruling that established the basis for new political initiatives regarding child subsidies and the expansion of childcare services. The Court ruled that 'the state ... must create adequate conditions to ensure that fulfilling educational tasks within the family does not lead to disadvantages at work' (BverfGE, 99, 234). In particular, it obliged the state to take measures which improve the provision of institutional childcare and which allow for both parents to return to work, to combine care and paid work, and to pursue a professional career while and after raising a child.

Considered from a family-political perspective, the Swedish example – a model of successful social policy in which family and work are compatible – confirms the relevance of law as an instrument of politics. This, however, is not in the name of the family but as an instrument of individualisation and the institutionalisation of citizenship rights. Comparative legal studies and the history of law treat the Scandinavian countries as a jurisdiction all of its own that, though closer to continental legal traditions than Great Britain or North America, is characterised by rather pragmatic interpretations and practical reforms. This development has to do with the lower influence or non-acknowledgment of Roman law and a lack of codification. Since the end of the nineteenth century, there has been an increase in 'northern legislative cooperation' unifying contract and trade law that initially leaves family law aside due to national particularities (Tamm, 1987). It is remarkable how early, that is to say in 1845, Swedish legislation proclaimed the equality of men and women, at least with regard to marital property and inheritance (Regner and Hirschfeldt, 1987). Explaining this particular development would exceed the parameters of this chapter, since besides the legal environment, political context, protagonists and structural opportunities all come into play (see Hobson, 1996; Kulawik, 1999). We must nonetheless emphasise that the crucial advance of a social policy treating men and women justly has been actualised in Sweden for the past thirty years by means of a distinct and radical policy of equality since the late 1960s. Next to the collectivisation of childcare through the increased availability of public childcare and the introduction of separate taxation for married couples in the early 1970s, the Swedish welfare state has consistently individualised social and family law, and gradually abolished women-specific protective legislation. Once health insurance for spouses and widows' pensions were eliminated in the late 1980s, marriage as a maintenance institution vanished from political discourse for good. It remains to be seen whether or not the family will overcome the remaining gendered divisions of work within it and in the labour market through the 1995 reform of parental leave regulation, which introduced a 'daddy quota', thus creating some – albeit limited – enforcement for fathers to participate in raising small children (see Kolbe, 2002: 212 and 406).

Legal traditions and legislative cultures thus play a significant role in the relation between welfare state and family, yet how the development of family law is embedded into different welfare regimes becomes apparent when various nations are juxtaposed. The German welfare state exemplifies the marginalisation and subordination of family policies to social policies despite an autonomous and institutionalised political focus on the family, and despite an ideologically charged family rhetoric. This is due to the fact that social policy as social insurance still focuses on paid work, its risks and rights, whereas private services and work at home constitute an invisible dimension of welfare production that is taken for granted (Wilson, 1977; Gerhard et al., 1988; Gordon, 1990). The male breadwinner model has been and still is supported by various policies, not least through the joint taxation and splitting system. By contrast, family and demographic policies in France are at the core of welfare state development (Kaufmann, 1993: 157). In Great Britain there is no explicit family policy as the state follows the principle of non-intervention into the private sphere and shows no interest in family law and marriage status. This is because the welfare state awards its benefits primarily to single parents and children according to the principle of need. In Sweden, the family is not the recipient of welfare state benefits either; these are paid instead to the individual as a citizen with equal rights, regardless of his or her family status.

Since marriage as an institution has lost significance, feminists have repeatedly asked about the extent to which the welfare state itself as an institution has reinstated women's tutelage. Indeed, women have been liberated from dependence on marriage, but hasn't the state welfare system followed in the footsteps of the husband? Women – in particular single mothers – who receive social benefits find themselves dependent once again, this time on the state. 'The old kind of bourgeois patriarchy', says Ursula Beer, 'provides every married man with a woman ready to serve him ... Today, patriarchy appears in an entirely different guise. Labour power and the non-paid work of married women are no longer "planned" by the husband but by bureaucracy; they become part of the scheme of consciously calculating socio-politicians' (Beer, 1983: 145). Helga Hernes counters this legal scepticism with reference to the Scandinavian 'women-friendly' system, noting that 'the modern state is potentially one of the most important arenas for political action and ... coalitions ...'. Indeed, it 'might [even] become a base of empowerment for women' (Hernes, 1986: 167).

MOTHERHOOD AS A SOCIAL CONSTRUCTION

Turning now to the protagonists in this individualisation process, we will ask whether social policy has in fact influenced women's concepts and values. This is really a cultural issue, one which, since the nineteenth century when female individualisation first evolved, has repeatedly played a dominant role in the discourse on mothers' labour market participation. In debating gender-specific protective labour legislation, for instance, or restricting women's work in factories, as social democratic and union terminology puts it, a remarkable consensus emerged: it was not the working conditions of women that were considered problematic, but rather them working at all (Hausen, 1997). In her essay *The Female Worker*, Joan Scott points to the inordinate attention focused on female workers' problems in the nineteenth century, which cannot be explained only with reference to the historical process of the separation of household and factory. Instead, the 'female worker in need of protection' was constructed by the political, national-economic, medical and social reformatory discourse of the times (Scott, 1993), and thus was restricted not for her own sake or out of concern for her health, but primarily because she was expected to bear healthy children. No matter how the fears were specifically justified – be it through reference to health risks, decline of birth rates, threats to morality or the well-being of the family – the overall discourses and politics revolving around women's labour market participation resulted in social policies that were anchored in wage inequality, gendered division of labour and female responsibility for home and family as foundational elements of the welfare system. Even though in many European countries at the end of the nineteenth century the first protective legislation benefiting women in childbed signalled the start of governmental social policy, it served as a pretence for patronisation and discrimination and thus established a gendered welfare state design, leaving the 'women question' marginal to matters of paid work in insurance-based welfare systems.

A virtual flood of advice books then appeared, dictating what mothers should believe, how they should behave, and even how much they should bear. In the 1920s and certainly after World War II, these books – at first educating and moralising, then medicalising, disciplining and supervising mothers educating children (see Donzelot, 1980) – made the mother-child relationship a popular subject of psychology (Schütze, 1986), disseminated in a deluge of counselling literature.

Family sociology again played a significant role after the war in restoring the normative model of devoted motherliness to compensate for the loss of paternal authority and re-establish safety and normality in the post-war family (Baumert, 1954; see also König, 1974: 214). The universality of the core family, a thesis expanded in Talcott Parsons' structural-functional theory with its traditional gender role model (his pattern variables), was designed, as René König critically noted, to mistake a whole number of theoretical prejudices for the reality of family (König, 1969: 53). After World War II, conservative family sociology in Western Europe and the United States was part of a so-called normalisation process, and the defence of the traditional family was linked to a re-masculinisation of state and politics (Moeller, 1993, 1998; see also Leira, 1992). As late as 1962, a UNESCO study of various countries uncovered the following norms: 'Single women *must* work; married women without [any children] or [with] grown-up children *may* work; married women with small children *must not* work' (quoted in Sommerkorn, 1988: 132, see also the overview there).

Twentieth-century women's movements have reacted in various ways to protective legislation. On the one hand they have explicitly supported a policy of organised motherhood, and as social reformers have pioneered entirely new fields of socio-political practice and professional social work. Calling their politics 'the maternal applied to the world', they opposed restrictions on traditional femininity and argued for gender differences as a female counter-concept to the 'rationalism of the modern capitalistic world, which is alien and hostile to nature' (Bäumer, 1931: 16-17). This concept, also described as 'spiritual maternity', is aimed at the participation of women 'not only in day nurseries, kindergarten and schools, but also in ministries and parliaments' (von Zahn-Harnack, 1928: 77; see also Stoehr, 1994: 222). On the other hand, reference to motherhood and maternal protection inspired gender-specific legal demands and socio-political measures specifically directed at women and mothers, based on a right to difference as against a policy of equality. In the 1920s this maternalism or welfare feminism (Banks, 1981; see also Bock, 1994) was influential in many European countries and in the United States, as it offered an intellectual framework easily combined with cultural patterns of femininity. Its success is very much debated though – even in retrospect (Kessler-Harris, et al., 1995; Kulawik, 1999; Lewis, 2001). In the 1920s the question of women-specific protective labour regulations, on which the otherwise sparring factions of the German women's movement (the social democrats and the liberals) actually agreed, led internationally to bitter struggles and divisions between the supporters of a maternalistic policy or welfare feminism and the followers of individualistic positions in the Anglo-Saxon and Scandinavian women's movements (the Open Door Movement) (Banks, 1981; Bock and Thane, 1994).

The social practices of working mothers do not follow a uniform pattern either. Nonetheless, it is striking that small children have not prevented their mothers from hurling themselves onto the labour market despite welfare state delay in creating conditions to ease the dilemmas they face (see Leira, Tobio and Triffiletti, in this volume). Nor do the working patterns of women allow planning for their use as a labour reserve, a concept market researchers have often tried to apply. When female participation rates started increasing slowly but gradually in the late 1970s despite labour market bottlenecks and dire economic predictions, experts could only explain it as a 'resisting behaviour which shows an inclination toward paid work' (ANBA, 3/1986:203). Another example reveals erroneous expectations after reunification of the two Germanys in 1989. Experts predicted a 'normalisation' in labour market participation of East German women, meaning a decline to align with the West German level. It is true that East German women's participation rates, which had amounted to 80-90 per cent in the former GDR, have declined dramatically (Winkler, 1990). Yet, they remain higher than women's participation rates in the West – although the latter have seen an increase during the last years. In 2000, 72.2 per cent of women were in the labour market in East Germany compared to 62.1 per cent in the West (Statistisches Bundesamt, *Mikrozensus*, 2001). The unwillingness of single mothers in the Netherlands and in Great Britain to adapt to new social policies urging them to take up paid work shows a concept of motherhood as a social relationship focused on children's needs (Duncan and Edwards, 2001: 36-37; Knijn and Van Wel, 2002). One might interpret this behaviour in terms of a 'moral rationality' (Barlow et al., 2002: 118) that turns away from economic means-end motivations.

One example from the divided history of the two German states makes us think hard about the effect of various social policies on behaviour. It concerns the different attitudes and everyday practices of working mothers in West and East Germany, which have been examined by a qualitative study on the strategies of working mothers in Frankfurt am Main and Leipzig (Ludwig, et al., 2002; see also Knijn, et al. in this volume). This comparison is particularly telling because here – as in a sociological experiment – after forty years of separate history the social policies of two very different political systems and their effects on behaviour can be observed against the background of a formerly shared cultural tradition and political history. Part of this shared history involves vestiges of pronatalist – and racist – national socialist women's policy, state pressure on women to give birth, and sanctioned annihilation of unwanted population groups (see Bock, 1986). The effects of the ideology of motherhood, which was supported in many different ways, are undoubtedly still detectable long after the fall of the Nazi regime. These remnants should not be underestimated, particularly with regard to the legal system (see Niehuss, 1997; Schubert, 1997; Schwab, 1997). To be sure, not all socially and politically relevant factors can be identified, nor can all socio-political measures be compared since the two systems had such different approaches to rights, particularly civil rights (Dilcher, 1994). A principal difference between the systems, however, was the distinction in policies designed to ease or hinder women's participation in the labour market. As a result, to question the effects of policy on behaviour, tentative comparison seems justified.

Essential distinctions are here simply etched in keywords (see Gerhard, 1994): equal rights for women was considered one of the greatest achievements of the GDR (Dokumente, 1975: 235), its realisation the propagated trademark of socialist politics used by all concerned as proof of the superiority of socialism to capitalism (Kuhrig and Speigner, 1979: 22). Apart from the fact that the GDR equal rights paragraph, Art. 7, was enforced immediately, its wider implementation in the early 1950s assured material and social assistance for mothers and children, and particularly an increase in childcare facilities. In the 1970s various socio-political laws easing compatibility of family and work strengthened the desire for a child while also recruiting women into the workforce; they were later characterised as 'mummy policies' for one-sidedly privileging mothers, but not all women. In 1970 the participation rates of East German women were already 20 per cent higher than those of their West German counterparts, and in 1989 the ratio of East German women in the workforce reached almost 90 per cent (including students and apprentices), in contrast to 55 per cent in the West. But this elevated rate appeared in tandem with another astonishing statistic: the fact that more than 90 per cent of working.women had at least one child (Winkler, 1990). Consider this in comparison to the 35 per cent of married women between ages 25 and 55 in West Germany who worked but had no children (Bundesministerium für Frauen und Jugend, 1993: 83).

The sample of working mothers[6] we interviewed is by no means representative, but the homogeneity of their statements regarding the difference between East German and West German mothers is striking. Asked how they judge themselves as mothers, the West Germans unanimously betrayed insecurity, confusion, and sometimes also resignation. Many were plagued by feelings of guilt. The 'guilty conscience' was a constant formula. Many vindicated themselves when charged with being 'egotistical' or 'bad mothers', alleging any number of good arguments in their defence. They realise that their feelings of culpability have been artificially instigated, yet ambivalence in light of the irresolvable contradiction in their situation remains: 'I say to myself, if you have children, you somehow have to decide whether you want to have money or stay at home. I want both, but I don't really manage.'

By contrast, East German working mothers have never faced this problem. To work and mother at the same time was normal: 'the children don't know it any differently.' 'For us in the GDR, this has never been an issue. Women who stayed at home or worked only part-time were the great exception. Thus it was obvious to us that we had to learn some profession, which we actually practiced, and of course we also have a family.' Neither pangs of conscience nor feelings of guilt were even mentioned: 'we don't have that sort of culture', an interviewee said, laughing and slightly defiant. Still, the practical problems of 'combining the two' are mentioned time and again, their management seeming to increase East German women's self-confidence. 'I realise that I am only happy if able to do both to a certain degree.' Or: 'I handle all that quite well and get by.' Although the daily juggling of family and work has tended to burden almost exclusively mothers, and hardly ever fathers, in East Germany too these mothers appeared rather content with existing gender arrangements and less disappointed in their partners' lack of support.

Another international study comparing the attitudes towards the role of women in family and work shows that East Germans – in this case men and women – do not fear damage to relations between mother and child when mothers work, whereas 70 per cent of West German interviewees still assume that pre-school age children suffer (Schäfgen and Spellerberg, 1998: 82-83; see also Spellerberg, 1996). Now, do these differing findings result from specific socio-political and institutional regulations? Without a doubt, any number of conditions, measures and social conventions that take the working mother as a norm facilitate openness and a pragmatic approach. However, such a politically and economically derived norm also puts pressure on women who might have preferred to stay longer with their children. Furthermore, the fact that so many mothers worked does not necessarily correlate with a higher degree of emancipation: another analysis reveals that attitudes in East Germany and West Germany towards women's social role, that is the cultural understanding of gender roles, are not significantly different, and thus cannot be seen as the cause of differing concepts of motherhood. Rather, the opportunity costs of the family are crucial, being determined by the socio-political framework as well as measures taken to ease combining motherhood and work (Klein, 1993: 288). In sum, and as confirmed by the Scandinavian welfare regimes, governmental social policy is a productive act that can help overcome traditional gender roles and thus lead to increased justice in gender relations.

CONCLUSION

At the beginning of the twenty-first century, the conflict between waged labour and care work remains, just as women continue to cope with it. For a theory of individualisation this can only mean that the individualisation of women does not and should not follow a male pattern. Women's experience in dealing with contradictory expectations when combining work and care makes them experts in social practices that are indispensable for society's survival. After all, this is not a matter of catching up or of women's adaptation to market requirements, but concerns the social practice of sympathy or, to phrase it differently, civilisation of the male ego. The concept of civilisation is found in the work of Norbert Elias, who, more profoundly than other theoreticians of individualisation, resolves the conflict between the individual and society by proposing a dynamic relationship among individuals as distinct units. In *The Society of Individuals* he writes: '... the whole relationship of individual and society can never be understood as long as "society" is imagined, as is so often the case, essentially as a society of individuals who were never children and who never die. One can only gain a clear understanding of the relation of individual and society if one includes in it the perpetual growing up of individuals within a society, if one includes the process of individualization in the theory of society. The historicity of each individual, the phenomenon of growing up to adulthood, is the key to an understanding of what "society" is' (Elias, 2001: 25).

This approach, taking children's needs into account, comes very close to an ethics of care, and rules out a view of work as limited to isolated, self-centred market subjects. Even the strongest individualisation does not alter the fact that human beings depend on each other, the essential human characteristic being our sociability. Although I do not want to claim Elias as a theorist of gender, nor can I detail his broad theory of civilisation here, of relevance is his citing the increasing social influence of women 'as a crucial ... driving force behind socio-historical advances' (Klein and Liebsch, 1997: 20-21) giving two supporting historical examples, ancient Rome and the feudal court society. Institutions themselves play only a marginal albeit possibly underestimated role in Elias's process theory of individualisation, but they too can facilitate emancipation and open space for agency – as evidenced in the history of struggle for legal rights, equality and recognition of women's needs. After all, the constitutional welfare state played a crucial role in responding to the demands of the women's movement by supplementing social citizenship rights. If traditional institutions based on gender hierarchy and present lifestyles are no longer adequate, this 'crisis' and the ubiquitous calls for welfare-state remodelling should be seen as a chance to create new forms of solidarity between the sexes and elevate children to citizenship status. This would mean redefining social policy priorities – not least as a gesture towards achieving European standards – according to principles of gender equality.

NOTES

[1] As regards Beck's and Beck-Gernsheim's work, in recent publications the authors have become more cautious and more defensive against misunderstandings of the concept of individualisation. In the introduction of their English publication on 'Individualization' (2002), which has a sample of former German articles, the authors argue: 'It is necessary to keep in view the distinction between the neoliberal idea of the free-market individual (inseparable from the concept of 'individualisation' as used in the English-speaking countries) and the concept of *institutionalized individualism,* as it will be developed in this book' (XXI). However, as U. Beck himself in an interview in the end of this new publication talks about 'zombie categories' as explanations for 'epochal changes' the terminology remains in many respects confusing.

[2] See Ribbens McCarthy, et al. (2002: 202), who fittingly talk about 'the differential gendered

involvement of parents in caring for children'.

[3] After all, in Beck and Beck-Gernsheim (2002) there is some clarification to this point: 'The ideological notion of the self-sufficient individual ultimately implies the disappearance of any sense of mutual obligation – which is why neoliberalism inevitably threatens the welfare state. A sociological understanding of individualization is thus intimately bound up with the question of how individuals can demystify this false image of autarky.' (XXI).

[4] From a wealth of literature: Dalla Costa, 1973; Oakley, 1974;Becker-Schmidt et al., 1984.

[5] See Finch and Groves, 1983; Waerness, 1984; Lewis and Meredith, 1988; Ungerson, 1990; Lewis, 1998a, 2000c; Feministische Studien, 2000; Leira and Saraceno, 2002.

[6] This is an empirical study supported by the Hans-Böckler-Stiftung, which analysed and compared the strategies and social practices of working mothers in the two Germanys. The sample was made up of 53 mothers in Leipzig and Frankfurt who lived in partnerships (married or not married), had to take care of at least one child between the ages of three and ten, and worked full-time or almost full-time. See Ludwig et al. 2002. See also Knijn, Jönsson and Klammer in this volume, reference 1.

3. Caring for Children: The Logics of Public Action

Marie-Thérèse Letablier and Ingrid Jönsson

State commitment to childcare varies between European countries. The variations are not only in generosity, but also in quality and in the form of support, in cash or in kind. In some countries, the main responsibility for provisions as well as for funding lies with the state, in others it lies with the market or the family, or with the civil society, and more often with a mixture of different institutions. However, the general trend all over Europe is that of a transfer of childcare responsibilities from the family towards the collective. The 'de-familialisation' of childcare responsibilities is related to policies implemented in order to increase the work commitment of mothers and to improve economic gender equality, as recommended by European institutions (EC, 1999). The increased interest in childcare issues can also be related to a future expected population crisis and to demands for autonomy and gender equality promoted by the women's movement (Hantrais, 1999).

These general trends contribute to a convergence in justifications of public action in all European countries. Recommendations regarding employability in order to increase the number of persons employed, equal access to jobs for men and women, and equal treatment in the workplace will have an impact on policy actions. Moreover, reconciliation between work and family life is a prioritised area, specifically the need for improved access to childcare and child services (EC, 1999). The principles of action are inspired by similar objectives but their implementation encounters different national contexts. Different ideas, values and norms about mothering, education of children and gender conventions or gender culture have an impact on social policy. This chapter focuses on the logics driving public action in the area of childcare in some European countries, and on the reasons that have led certain states to provide childcare. What principles legitimise state intervention in an area some consider as a private affair? The argument centres on the logics determining public action concerning childcare and early childhood education rather than on the generosity of states, as numerous studies have already done. It attempts to identify the historical background of policies related to childcare so as to understand the path dependency that drives policy responses to the EU recommendations and to the changes in family structures and practices. If there is undoubtedly a convergence in socio-demographic trends all over Europe, as well as in policy principles of acting, there is also a dependency on the historical background of each country and each welfare state, which underlies the interpretation of the recommendations and the implementation of policies. Thus childcare policies are deeply imbedded in the trade-offs within families between working and mothering. They are also imbedded in the trade-offs between families and the states concerning work and care. These trade-offs are associated with values of motherhood and fatherhood, and with the conceptualisation of state action.

To begin with, different childcare regimes in European countries are identified, with regard to the different forms of regulation and share of responsibilities between the state, the family, the market or the company, and civil society. Childcare arrangements will be examined in relation to family obligations, labour market and working-time policies, and values on motherhood and the socialisation of children. Childcare regimes also refer to different welfare regimes and the gender convention on which they are based.

Next, the focus shifts to the logic behind public action and the justification given to childcare policies in relation to principles of solidarity, gender equality and family values. The emphasis is on France and Sweden, where childcare policies have been implemented for a long time and where state responsibility towards children is still highly legitimised by public opinion. However, comparison between the two countries points to similarities as well as differences in the principles of public action.

Finally, recent trends of change are examined to outline new principles and new forms of regulations occurring at the turn of the century. In referring to France and Sweden, a hypothesis can be formulated according to which children tend to become the central figure targeted by family or social policies rather than the family itself. This process occurs under the double pressure of individualisation of social relations and the affirmation of a broader notion of citizenship. Justifications for public action that invoke the interests of the child, the rights of children or equal opportunities appear to lead to the promotion of the child-citizen. Since the 1990s, childcare in both countries is not just regarded as a measure for reconciling work with family life but is included in a broader childhood policy.

CHILDCARE REGIMES IN EUROPE

Variations in public childcare provision are related to how family obligations are interpreted in different countries, that is to what extent the state, the market, the family or civil society is expected to carry the main responsibility for childcare. Family obligations are linked to labour markets, and especially to the forms of mobilisation of female labour. They are particularised for working life and family life, not only in how families organise their time and everyday life but also in working time and labour market policies as well as in family policies. The social construction of gender equality, childhood and motherhood is interrelated with family obligations. In general, such norms and values are related to historical and cultural developments among which women's struggle for public support to childcare cannot be ignored, as well as the struggle of other social actors such as trade unions and family organisations (Daly and Lewis, 1998).

When relating the provision of public childcare in European countries to cultural factors, five childcare regimes can be identified. Each can be illustrated by a country of the European Union.

The Nordic Childcare Regime: Gender Equality and Childcare as State Responsibilities

This childcare regime can be illustrated by the case of Sweden. Long before its integration into the European Union, Sweden and the other Nordic countries implemented policies leading to a transition from a male-breadwinner family model to a model consisting of two equal parents responsible for their own support. The transition to the dual-earner family model implied individualisation of social rights. Individual social benefits and social services were prioritised to tax reductions and family allowances. Gender equality became integrated into family policy, social policy and labour market policy.

The Nordic model is characterised by a high level of economic integration of women into the labour market, a high level of women in political bodies at the national as well as local levels, and a high rate of shared parental responsibilities, at least compared with other Western European countries. Women are encouraged to enter the labour market and to remain economically active also after having children. Reconciliation of work with family life was facilitated by a range of measures such as public childcare, parental leave with the ambition of including fathers in the care of children, and flexible working time for parents. In 1974 parental leave replaced maternal leave with the aim of changing gender roles in the family as well as in working life. By making some part of parental leave non-transferable between the parents in 1995, a further step was taken towards influencing the division of labour within the family.

At the same time as the childcare system was established for the benefit of the child, women and the labour market, a new family norm emerged based on shared parenthood. This meant a more equal division of labour in the household as well as shared legal responsibilities of both parents for the child after a separation or a divorce, even if the parents entered new family relationships. The relative political consensus around the 'new' family policy implemented in the 1970s was followed in the 1990s by more diverse opinions. The introduction of childcare benefits (abolished after six months by the return to power of the Social Democrats in 1995) pointed in the direction of a traditional male-breadwinner family model (Bergqvist, 2001). At the same time, the male parental role and the low male take-up rate of parental leave appeared on the political agenda. The division of labour within the household was brought into the discussion. Men's roles as parents became visible, and gender equality and reconciliation of work with family life was approached as an issue that also concerns men.

The Nordic model has advocated gender equality long before it became an issue at the European level. However, the increase of employed mothers preceded the expansion of public childcare (Leira, 1993; Nyberg, 2000; see also Leira, Tobio and Trifiletti, Chapter 5). In the early industrialisation era the women's movement had already formulated the demand for childcare, but the main political decisions that led to its expansion in Sweden were not taken until the 1960s and 1970s. A contributing factor was the large number of women involved in the political decision processes, especially that concerning social and family policy (Bergqvist, 2001).

An emphasis was put on the social and psychological development of the child, and public childcare integrated pedagogical, social and supervisory elements to provide in the best way for all children. The pre-schools established in the 1970s merged the inheritance of developmental aspects of the kindergarten and social care aspects with their roots in the *crèche* (Persson, 1994). For most of the period since the 1970s, the demand for public childcare exceeded the supply (Skolverket, 2001a and b). By the turn of the twentieth century, further expansion made childcare available for all parents, not only working or studying parents but also those unemployed or on parental leave (Ds, 1999).

Childcare as a Family Policy Issue: Collective Socialisation of Children and Demography

This childcare regime can be illustrated by the case of France where, as in the Nordic countries, the state has a great legitimacy for intervening in childcare issues. Here the social and political consensus is constructed historically upon a certain idea of childhood and early socialisation of children. Over time, childcare support has become a large part of family policy, which used to be an autonomous branch of the social security system. In France, this idea is rooted in the republican and secular tradition and culture. *L'école maternelle* is the most comprehensive component, and is viewed as a preparation for school rather than as childcare. Even though it is not compulsory, almost all children aged 3 – 6 attend it on a regular basis, and the demand for a place is steadily increasing among two-year-olds: 37 per cent of them currently attend pre-school on a regular basis (Leprince, 2003). The *crèches* are used to respond to similar needs of children below the age of three. They are seen as a public service for dual-earner parents as well as for lone parent families. Although only 10 per cent of young children are cared for in a *crèche*, this service is highly valued by parents, who apply in large numbers for a place.

The history of public childcare in France is tied to a conception of the state, *l'Etat paternaliste* with its obligation of protecting children and mothers, a conception that arose at the end of the nineteenth century under the Third Republic (Rollet-Echallier, 1990). The French state protects the mother and motherhood, irrespective of whether mothers are working or not. Motherhood is linked to citizenship (Knibiehler, 1997). And despite policies that might discourage women from entering the labour market (particularly for demographic reasons), employment of women, especially mothers of young children, has remained politically important, especially since the 1960s (Martin, 1998). It was the 1970s, a period of changing social and cultural norms, that saw the rise of the notion of the *neutrality* of the state with regard to forms of private life and to the freedom of women to work or not outside the home. However, if mothers decide to pursue their professional activity, it is widely admitted that the state should help them with facilities for childcare, be it through allowances, services or paid leave. The consensus about the double commitment of women in working and in mothering remains strong in France. The issue is also a source of tensions between politicians, family organisations and feminist groups. Most of the feminist organisations have supported equal employment opportunities for working mothers. This explains why most of them, as well as trade unions, are opposed to part-time work as well as to parental leave, two highly gendered measures considered as being a source of inequalities in the labour market and an obstacle to women's careers.

The second objective behind state intervention is linked to a conception of the state as a protector of childhood and a guarantor of equal opportunities for children. Therefore, the question of childcare was debated long before the idea arose of reconciliation between motherhood and working outside the home (Lanquetin, et al., 1999). Children are acknowledged as 'common beings' and the wealth of the nation that has in return some obligations to them. The introduction of *école maternelle* at the end of the nineteenth century implies that early and collective socialisation aimed at giving all children equal opportunity to participate in society, regardless of their economic or social origins. French public opinion continues to strongly support the notion of public services as a state responsibility in the education, health and well-being of children (Letablier, et al., 2002). Early collective childhood education and care is still highly valued in France.

The third objective of state action is concerned with the relationship between public policy and demography. Demographic reasoning has played an important role in the political tradition of France. This explains why the French state is relatively generous with childcare provision, not only through childcare facilities but also in the form of cash transfers, tax reductions, and paid and unpaid parental leave. Demographic objectives are no longer explicit in French family policy though.

The rise of the Left in the 1980s led to a new programme for the family and children, and even if all the projected parts were not entirely realised, the changes in policy have led to a break with certain major orientations of the Right (Jenson and Sineau, 1998). In the late 1990s, the Socialist government attempted to build a new consensus on family support. The focus of the 'new family policy' is on solidarity between social groups and equality between men and women. Several allowances became means-tested in order to focus state support on those families most in need. To improve gender equality, a focus was put on measures to facilitate everyday life for working mothers, especially increasing available childcare facilities and improving the work-family balance. Two major options were introduced: the reduction of working time and the creation of paternity leave (Letablier, 2003). These two measures aimed at encouraging fathers to take a larger role in domestic work and parental responsibility. In addition, parents got the right to take parental leave for at least one year (can be extended twice until the child is three years old). Parental leave is linked to employment rights. The leave period is unpaid but family policy offers a flat-rate parental leave allowance from the second child onwards (Fagnani, 2001).

Since the late 1980s, the supply of childcare increased at the same time as diversification of publicly financed childcare was supported. A tax credit was introduced in 1989 for all parents to meet childcare costs, either in the form of domestic employees at home, registered childminders or institutional childcare (Martin, et al., 1998).

Childcare as a Private Responsibility

This childcare regime is illustrated by the UK, where publicly subsidised childcare for young children has always been minimal except during World War II (Randall 1999; Marchbank, 2000), as can be expected in a Liberal welfare regime and according to a traditionally strong male-breadwinner model (Lewis, 1992). Historically, the family, the voluntary sector and the private sector have been the main providers of care for both children and adults in the UK. The role of the state is limited and the decision to offer public childcare is taken at the local level. Local authorities only provide childcare for handicapped or sick children, or to children of handicapped parents, and more recently also to children 'at risk'. For other groups of children, there are no obligations to provide childcare (Rostgaard and Fridberg, 1998). In the 1980s, during the Thatcher era, the aim was to replace the state by the independent sector in the field of care (Land and Lewis, 1998). Studies from the late 1980s indicated the lack of affordable childcare as an obstacle to labour market participation among mothers, especially lone mothers (Bertram and Pascall, 1999). But it was only in the 1990s when policies started to address this problem more explicitly. In 1996 the introduction of the Working Families Tax Credits scheme, which permitted tax deduction of childcare costs, aimed particularly at encouraging lone mothers to enter the labour market. In 1997, all parents of four-year-olds became entitled to vouchers covering the cost for half-day care in an educational setting; other than care, education is considered to be a right of children.

The voucher scheme was abandoned by the new Labour government in 1998 and replaced for the first time in the UK by a childcare policy formulated in the initiative paper 'Meeting the Childcare Challenge', which introduced the National Childcare Strategy. The National Childcare Strategy explicitly linked childcare provision to the labour market restructuring. The welfare initiatives of Labour aimed to encourage employment, combat social exclusion, decrease poverty (every third child was living in poverty in 1998) and ensure that young children were prepared to take their place in the workforce of tomorrow (OECD, 2000). Another aim was to enable women to balance family and working life. The idea of privatisation of childcare was not really reconsidered, and parents are supposed to buy childcare on the market by means of a childcare tax credit. Local private agencies are seen as the main source for implementing childcare policy with parents as consumers. State provision remains very poor and the role of the state remains limited (Lewis, 2000b). At the same time, the question of welfare dependency is still a main issue in government thought.

Childcare remains a family issue, to be carried out mainly by mothers. As a consequence, women are seen as secondary earners taking up part-time work, jobs on fixed-term contracts and with flexible working hours. The rate of women who are employed part-time is the highest in Europe after the Netherlands. However, new trends in labour market participation indicate increasing differences among groups of women. The socialisation of children takes place in the family, which contributes to a strict division of labour between men and women. Both the UK and Ireland opposed European directives on Maternity Leave (1992) and Parental Leave (1996), and it was not until 1999 that the UK fell into line with the minimum standards set by the European directives. Parental leave is unpaid and usually only covers 13 weeks. Apart from a skeleton regulation, the state left the concrete terms of use mainly to the workforce or collective agreements, or to individual agreements with the employer.

Public childcare has not become a political issue in the UK in the same way as in the Scandinavian countries, for example, and to a lesser extent in France. The 'opportunity structure' has been less favourable in the UK due to social conservatism among political parties and trade unions, and due to the English kind of state tradition (Randall, 1996). As Bergqvist (2001) argues for the case of Sweden, the role of women in local and national politics should not be neglected for the provision of public childcare. For the UK, Randall (1996) and others claim that the feminist movement 'missed the boat' by not being present at the same time in mainstream political institutions and in grass-roots movements. But there is also the fact that state intervention in public life is not well accepted. And thus it is from businesses that family-friendly policies are expected, through career breaks for women or through the implementation of new ways to work.

In the UK, the appearance of New Labour meant that social policies emphasised social integration achieved through paid employment rather than the fight against poverty (Lister, 1998; Lewis, 1999). This is the touchstone of the concept of equal opportunity, and an essential element for the creation of individual responsibility. The role of the state is to develop opportunities to work, and to aid citizens in seizing them. To accompany the employment programme, the government set into motion a policy in 1998 (for the first time in Great Britain) to develop after-school care inside the schools. Even though the sums spent on this effort remains well below those spent in most other European countries, it reveals a new recognition of the intervention of the state in an area hitherto viewed as the responsibility of the family. The new childcare provision policy was explicitly geared towards enabling parents, especially women, to reconcile work with family life.

Childcare as a Mother's Responsibility

An illustration of this childcare regime is found in the former West Germany. The German childcare regime is linked to the conservative welfare state regime, and to a strong institutionalised division of labour between men and women. The social protection system is to some extent related to the gender division of labour and care by recognising female care work as an entitlement to social rights, for example up to three 'baby years' give credits in the pension system under the condition that the parent does not pay her/his contribution (Scheiwe, 1995). So a first step to recognise care has been done, but only to a very limited extent both with regard to the pension schemes and to parental leave payments.

The socialisation of children primarily takes place in the family, and the relation between mother and child has a prime place in the perception of good education. Mothers are encouraged to take parental leave and to work part-time as a way of reconciling work and family and hence to assume childcare. Parents are entitled to parental leave for three years and to a child-raising benefit (*Erziehungsgeld*) for a maximum of two years depending on the income of the partner. Other than in Sweden, where parents receive a wage replacement (of 80 per cent during the first year of parental leave) instead of a child-raising flat rate, in Germany the benefit is independent of former employment status. Parental leave is 'family-oriented' rather than aimed at keeping mothers employed. In fact, public action in childcare for the very young remains weak because childcare is considered a private matter, a mother's responsibility (see Knijn, Jönsson and Klammer, Chapter 6). But whereas mothering is valued in this society, the tension between working and mothering is strong, as reflected in the low fertility rate, especially for well-educated women (Fagnani, 2001). And although dual-earner families are growing in numbers, they are not dual-career families.

Labour market policy for women functions in line with this idea of motherhood. In West Germany, women make a temporary market exit when the children are born, followed by a return to the labour market on a part-time basis after a long break. Their long withdrawal from the labour market often means that they lose connection with their former job. In East Germany the idea of the working mother is still prevalent, and here women usually only take part of the leave and more often return to a full-time job (see Knijn, Jönsson and Klammer, Chapter 6). Yet, in both parts of Germany it is almost exclusively mothers who make adjustments to labour market conditions. Being a mother with small children is not considered compatible with a professional life unless she works on a part-time basis. Such an idea of motherhood explains the limited public investments in childcare for young children. The childcare reform of the mid-1990s offering a part-time place in a kindergarten for all 3-year-olds does not interfere with the principle of subsidiarity. The reform, however, announces a shift in balance from unpaid care to a new mix of paid and unpaid, formal and informal care (Ostner, 1998). Voluntary organisations are the main providers of childcare while the state plays a role in funding and supervision.

Over time, the relationship between work and family is becoming less rigid and the sharp division between paid work and child rearing is weakening. Present labour market policies aim at promoting a flexible integration of women into the workforce on a part-time basis. Diminishing employment and earnings influence the need for a second income in families. The increased political emphasis on the dual responsibility of the state and the families for children's well-being is justified by both the family and children being endangered as Germany moves towards increasing poverty and polarisation after re-unification (Ostner, 1998). The concept of the family is being changed through a broader range of accepted forms of private life on the one hand, and by making the well-being of children a cardinal principle of public intervention on the other (Richter, 2000).

The Mediterranean Childcare Regime:
Childcare as a Family and Kin Issue

This childcare regime will be illustrated by the case of Spain. In southern Europe, with the exception of Italy, the issue of reconciliation has only recently appeared on the political agenda. Traditionally, the family consisting of several generations and constituting a resort for parenting has taken care of the socialisation of children. The family is built on mutual obligations, which are inscribed in the Constitution. The state only intervenes when the family is unable to cope with its duties. According to existing norms and values, the responsibility for children and young adults rests on the family, that is on women – mothers and grandmothers (Tobío, 2001; see also Leira, Tobío, Trifiletti, Chapter 5). Solidarity within the family means solidarity between generations and between women. It is not a male concern, and it remains so in spite of increased rates of women in the labour market. Men and women are nowadays able to participate in the labour market on 'equal terms'. The traditional housewife is disappearing and women are earning an income at the same time they care for family members. Neither the male population nor the public sector of the economy are working actively for a more equal distribution of domestic and care tasks (Carrasco and Rodríguez, 2000). The help for the new mothers – by grandmothers and sisters – make it possible for mothers with young children to enter the labour market, while those with sufficient incomes hire babysitters (Wall, 1995; Tobío, 1998). Only a minor part of the childcare for 0 – 3-year-olds is publicly funded. As in many other

European countries, the expansion of childcare services for older children mainly aims at improving education rather than enabling parents (mostly mothers) to combine work and family life (Valiente, 1996). School hours are often not scheduled to match parents' working hours. The policy logic is thus based on close relationships, and consequently many local variations are found in these countries. Parental leave has only recently been implemented in Southern Europe, and is mostly unpaid. The entitlement is often based on having a contract for permanent employment, while many women hold jobs on fixed-term contracts. Without help from informal networks, current care- and work-related policies would lead to an even more serious decline of birth rates.

JUSTIFICATIONS OF PUBLIC POLICIES – THE LOGICS OF STATE INTERVENTION

Childcare regimes indicate differences not only in the role of the state in childcare management but also in the conceptualisation of the role of the state and the family. The relationship between the state, the market and the family or civil society implies different conceptualisations of solidarity and equality between social groups and between men and women. In this section, similarities and differences in principles behind public childcare policies are identified in France and Sweden by looking into how different forms of solidarity and social and gender equality are referred to over the years.

In France, child and family support are rooted in a double tradition: *nataliste*, supporting a rising birth rate, and *familialiste*, supporting the redistribution of wealth between families with children and families without children. These two justifications have been the basis for family policies since the beginning of the twentieth century, but their appeal has faded progressively over the course of the last few decades.

The natalist demographic policy remains enshrined in regulations and programmes but has weakened as a reference for public action and as an object of national consensus. The idea of increasing births is rooted in a conception according to which children represent the wealth and future of the nation. At the beginning of the twentieth century, children were primarily seen as a resource for the future military and economic power of the nation. The call for increased births was intended to supply plenty of soldiers for the defence of the French colonial empire. Later, in the 1930s, those in favour of increasing births saw the economic crisis as being rooted in decreasing birth rates, and the loss of moral and family values (Deprez, 1999). In the 1970s, incentives for the birth of a third child (at a time when the national average was consistently two) went along with measures intended to encourage mothers to leave the workforce. This demographic reasoning is present in France even today, and its supporters in family associations and in the conservative political arena point to a dwindling and ageing population as well as the necessity for society to respond to this situation. One of the current demands of the 'natalist stream' is to increase the parental leave allowance in order to make it the equivalent of a salary. This is intended both to free up jobs, thereby lowering unemployment, and to reassert the value of motherhood by paying for it (Deprez, 1999; Büttner, et al., 2002).

In the same way, the *familialiste*, or pro-family reasoning, at the basis of the French redistribution system has weakened under the effect of means testing. The necessity to reduce public spending on the one hand, and social inequality in a context of high unemployment rates on the other, has led successive governments to target several family allowances for those families most in need. Proponents of *familialisme* in the family movement claim that French family policy has lost its consistency, and denounce the re-orientation of public action towards more social objectives. It has to be reminded that in France families are organised interest groups. The family movement has always been strong and powerful, given that it has been institutionalised as a partner for the making of family policies since the 1940s, when the French welfare state was put together. Family actors participate in the decision process in all issues related to state support to families (Chauvière et al., 1999).

Compensation for the costs of child rearing constitutes the primary mechanism of the child and family support policies in France. These policies are affected by the financial calculation of the costs of raising children. Yet they cannot be examined solely from the point of view of the generosity of public bodies, as measured by the percentage of the budget they put into these programmes. They reveal different conceptions of social equity, one in which redistribution is horizontal between families with children and those without children, or vertical, between social categories. In general, the forms of compensation are not neutral as regards who is benefited by the granting of financial allocations or tax reductions. France combines the two methods of redistribution, whereas other countries forefront one or the other. Horizontal redistribution is coherent with a conception of the family as the fundamental social institution that the state is bound to protect, while vertical redistribution emphasises the social dimension of family policies. The principle of horizontal equity is controversial since it tends to favour the richest families in the name of the protection due to the family. It is also controversial because tax relief primarily benefits married mothers who are not in paid employment or who are working part-time. This tax advantage encourages these mothers to leave their jobs, especially if their partners have high salaries. This means that the forms of redistribution are not neutral in relation to women's labour market participation (Hantrais and Letablier, 1996, 1997). The measures taken by the Jospin government in 1998, which questioned the principle of horizontal redistribution, were strongly contested, not only by family associations but also by a large part of public opinion attached to the idea of the state protecting the family. The debate was sharpened by the current demographic situation, with the idea that the children of today will pay tomorrow's retirement pensions according to the 'social contract between generations'. For advocates of 'horizontal solidarity', the support that families provide to society as a whole ought to be taken into consideration and compensated (Büttner, et al., 2002). The return of the Right to government brought new changes in childcare policies. The provision system was reorganised and a unique childcare benefit, *Prestation d'accueil du jeune enfant*, replaced five former allowances. The restructuring does maintain the public/private mix, but with an emphasis on the quality of care provided by private subsidised child- minders. This is clearly the option being encouraged, much more than public collective day care centres.

Swedish welfare policy with regard to the family has changed focus from maternity policy in the early twentieth century to population policy in the 1930s and to a modern family policy from the 1970s onwards (Ohlander, 1989). Many of the present family policy ideas can be traced to the family policy proposed by the Myrdal couple in the 1930s, which emphasised the well-being of the child as well as women's emancipation. To curb decreasing birth rates in the 1930s, general social reforms with the aim of improving living conditions were generally prioritised over a specific 'natalist' policy. Universal social benefits, such as maternity benefits and child allowances, were introduced in the 1930s and 1940s. Moreover, the benefits were paid to the mother in order to increase women's independence and to ensure that the benefits were largely used for the child. Benefits introduced in the post-war period have become work-related or means-tested to an increasing extent. In the 1990s, the consequences of the economic recession became especially noticeable for families with children and lone parents (SOU, 2000:3). Concomitantly, a decline in birth rates was experienced. Once again, the focus is on living conditions among families with children and on how to improve these conditions for new generations of parents. Children are seen as necessary for future welfare. Family policy reforms are given high priority and benefits are being restored to previous levels or extended. Continued expansion of public childcare and a ceiling on childcare costs are expected to lead to an inclusion of all children, to make more parents available for employment and to mitigate the marginal effects of increased labour market participation.

In Sweden, tax reductions and tax relief for families and children are not included in the Social Democratic family policy, while the non-socialist parties advocate such measures. Instead, post-war family policy supported universal allowances for children and means-tested benefits for families with children at the same time that tax-paid services, such as public childcare, were expanded. Historically, fees charged for public childcare were income-related. The introduction of a maximum fee for a childcare cost is less re-distributive, as medium- and high-income parents will gain more than low-income parents.

RESTRUCTURING CHILDCARE POLICIES AND FAMILY SUPPORT: NEW PRINCIPLES AND REGULATIONS

The economic restructuring of the European welfare states, the necessity to increase the number of persons employed, and the idea that men and women should enjoy equal opportunities constitute part of the new framework for national policies. Certain countries have not waited for EU recommendations to begin improving access to childcare, even if their actions respond to other principles. For the rest, these recommendations have led to a revision of certain aspects of social policy, particularly the relation between welfare and work, and consequently have raised questions about the motives of public action and the implications of current changes. When returning to work becomes a cornerstone of public policy, a rigid division of labour between men and women, particularly within the family, is questioned. Thus the old debate about the socialisation of children, whether in the family or in society, takes on another form. The idea of the rights of children (to childcare, for example, as is recognised in most of the Scandinavian countries) acquires a new meaning, although such rights are not yet realised in a number of countries.

Most EU countries underwent political changes in the 1990s. The rise to power of leftist political parties in several EU countries modified the political perception of the family. While the majority of conservative governments focused on the family as a value and a norm to be defended, this was not the case by the late 1990s, when most countries recognised the multiplicity of private life forms and changed the definition given to the family. These political changes led to new goals and new emphases. However, the political situation rolled back in many EU member states at the turn of the century, with possible implications for the perception of the family.

Changes in family structures and labour market conditions have also altered basic policy models. To the extent that employability gets at the centre of welfare policies, the male-breadwinner model is being replaced by the 'adult worker model' (Lewis, 2000a), which aims at integrating all adults into the labour market as work is considered the best form of welfare. However, this model is not developing in the same way across Europe even though on a rhetorical level most countries support measures to increase labour market participation and limit welfare dependency. In countries such as France and Sweden, where the reconciliation of care and work has been a political issue for a long time, the policies have been reinforced. At the same time, the logic of political action changed slightly and the French family policy gives an impression of incoherence or lack of consistency (Fagnani, 1998a). Despite certain convergences of values driving public action, new policy options do not develop in a vacuum; they must reckon with former values and policies, and give rise to various compromises across countries. Such situations obviously create tensions.

In France, new justifications behind public action are tied to the necessity for successive governments to demonstrate their capacity to reduce unemployment. Since the 1980s, creating jobs has become a priority for successive governments. Childcare and eldercare were viewed as sectors with employment potential, and programmes were launched in order to develop jobs opportunities in the care sector. These programmes contributed to the development of individualised services to the detriment of public social services and at the expense of collective care such as *crèches*. The re-establishment of childcare allowances for young children is part of this trend (Fagnani, 1998b) leading towards the individualisation and privatisation of childcare, even if the jobs created are subsidised by the state and families are given financial help. All these changes nonetheless respond to parents' growing demands for an extension of childcare options and flexibility. Besides, this evolution in childcare is occurring not only conceptually but also structurally. Childcare and child services are becoming not only more commercial but also more under local control.

These changes also alter the conception of childcare as a public issue. They represent the dissolution of a national consensus regarding an ideal of childhood and equal opportunity. In France, the *crèche* was a symbol of a certain form of equal opportunity for children, the necessary prelude to educational principles that prevailed beginning with the *écoles maternelles*. Rather than simple childcare, the *crèche* represented a certain conception of the upbringing of children, of their early socialisation and preparation to participate in society. In sum, the *crèche* represented service to the public as well as subjection to the common good.

Consequently, in permitting parents' greater choice, rules of the marketplace have entered the interaction between family and working. Indeed, they contribute to a stratification of services: home help, financial subsidies and tax advantages for the wealthier households, *crèches* for the middle classes and mothers with stable employment, and finally, local networks and intra-family help for those households with the lowest income. This situation breaks with the Republican ideal of social justice and equal access to public services. It also creates a situation in which certain women become the employers of other women, sometimes using public resources for the benefit of their own children. It follows that the official rhetoric on the necessity to 'diversify forms of childcare' in order to facilitate 'the free choice of families' creates, in reality, social inequalities in access to childcare (Fagnani, 1998b). In the name of combating unemployment and in response to the demand for new jobs, the public sphere has responded with individualised childcare that is accessible only to the wealthy and middle classes. However, these policies have had the advantage of making visible and legal work which was formerly hidden in the 'informal economy'. Childcare is thus gaining new political and economic recognition while getting incorporated into larger programmes: increasingly, childcare and family policies are linked to employment policies and gender equality.

In contrast to the development in France, Sweden continues to support collective childcare by expanding the number of *crèches*, pre-school education for all 4 – 5–year–olds and leisure-time centres for school children. The rate of children cared for by registered childminders at home has decreased since the mid 1980s. The variety of provisions increased in the 1990s as a consequence of decentralisation of funding and decision-making from central to local governments. Increased 'freedom of choice' was offered to parents. Childcare is still publicly financed but family and personnel cooperatives, voluntary organisations and employers emerged as organisers in addition to publicly organised childcare. In one sense, this leads to a 'de-marketisation' of childcare as the need for privately arranged and privately funded childcare decreases (Szebehely, 1998).

In Sweden, the link between family policy, employment policy and gender equality has existed for a long time; the recent expansion of childcare and the introduction of a maximum level of fees strengthen this trend. The removal of economic marginal effects is seen as a measure to further increase labour market participation among women with young children. High levels of female labour market participation constitute an important aspect of gender equality policy. Another aim of the expansion is to counteract social exclusion by including children of unemployed parents, many of whom are immigrants.

In addition to the above differences between France and Sweden, recent developments in the two countries point in the same direction. Both countries include childcare in a wider childhood policy. The aim is to give a general coherence to different policy areas following the ratification of the UN

Convention on Children's Rights in 1989. All social reforms have to include the perspective of children. Childhood policies become part of family policies.

Finally, the state in both countries takes initiatives to increase childcare services and to reconsider the work and family balance in a more egalitarian way. In comparison to Sweden, childcare is publicly provided in France to a lesser degree, but both countries extend publicly *funded* childcare. Simultaneously, time policies and the role of fathers receive growing attention. Although French laws reducing working time in 1997 and 2000 had a major objective of combating unemployment, they also aimed at increasing the amount of time dedicated to parental activities and leisure. Similar arguments appear in the Swedish debate about working hours, which also reveals a demand for increased flexibility, as some would prefer an extension of the vacation period to a weekly working-time reduction. The right for parents to shorten their weekly working hours was established a long time ago, but at their own expense unless the use of parental leave benefits are stretched over the years. Time policies can be seen as one of the instruments to encourage fathers to take greater responsibility for family tasks.

Undoubtedly, Sweden takes a leading role in addressing fathers. As early as in the 1970s, parental leave regulations included the idea of shared parenthood, which was enforced in the 1990s by reserving a part of the leave exclusively to each parent. Besides, fathers are entitled to paternity leave after the birth of a child. In France too, fathers are increasingly encouraged to take greater responsibility for their children. However, the amount of parental leave allowances does not encourage fathers to take up parental leave: to achieve that, it should be a replacement wage like in Sweden. In 2002, paternity leave was extended to two weeks after childbirth. The regulation is included in the Labour Act as a right for fathers to care. Such measures entail a new perception of fathers as carers and, to some extent, reflect that work and care arrangements within the family cannot be detached from matters of employment and gender equality. Overall, childcare policies are increasingly linked to a variety of policies (such as those relating to family, employment, time and gender equality), and thus owe to several and sometimes even divergent principles and objectives.

4. Strategies, Everyday Practices and Social Change

Constanza Tobío and Rossana Trifiletti

The relationship between working and mothering can be examined from a social policy perspective, which basically corresponds to a macro-level approach, or through social practices developed by individuals in their everyday life to make their responsibilities in both worlds fit. This chapter follows the second approach and concentrates mainly on care because work and family life are not symmetrical. Employment is clearly defined in terms of number of working hours, schedules or work content, whereas care and domestic work are often imprecise and flexible; it is thus mostly for the latter to adapt to the former. Once the traditional family based in a gendered division of labour ceases to be the norm, compatibility between the spheres of family and employment becomes an issue, especially for working mothers who most clearly represent the contradiction between these two worlds. Should both be expected to change, it is the household rather than the workplace that adapts to the new situation, mainly through women's strategies, even when the adult worker norm, that is the assumption that all adults will engage in paid work, is socially accepted (Lewis, 2000a).

The concept of strategy has to do with purposive social practices. It is a concept that has become popular among sociologists even though it is not a traditional sociological term like structure, action or social class. It is commonly used in different fields (international relations, industrial relations, social policy, sociology of the family, gender, people's everyday lives), levels of analysis (nations, governments, social groups, individuals) and theoretical approaches (rational choice theory and game theory, theory of structuration, theory of *habitus,* organization theory). Such widespread use of the term strategy has been a question of debate (Del Boca, 1982; De Sandre, 1984; Saraceno, 1986; Sgritta, 1986; Crow, 1989; Morgan, 1989) focusing on the types of individual or collective action that can be considered as strategies, that is actions which are rational and purposive and in which there is some degree of choice and calculation.[1] To what extent there is an agreement on the concept of strategy underlying the term is a matter open for discussion. For example, several authors (Hammersley, 1987; Morgan, 1989; Edwards and Ribbens, 1991) have pointed out that the term strategy articulates agency and structural constraints, but it is not really clear whether this aspect is included in the concept of strategy as it is understood in the rational choice approach, where it clearly focuses on agency (Elster, 1986). The emphasis on strategies as an element that makes the link between agency and structural constraintsis, by contrast, characteristic of Giddens' (1984) theory of structuration as well as Bourdieu's (1980) theory of *habitus*.

This chapter explores the concept of strategy as a theoretical tool to understand women's everyday practices. The first part of the chapter reviews the concept as it is understood in different theoretical backgrounds and national contexts. In French sociology, strategies are often assimilated to social practices that reproduce social order. Bourdieu, for example, uses the concept of strategy to study how *habitus* is reproduced in practices, and speaks of partially unconscious strategies, that is actions without a conscious strategic intention. In Italy and the UK, historians and economists working on the family, usually focusing on how resources are combined for survival, have developed the use of the concept in quite a different way.

In the second part of the chapter, the use of the concept of strategy to study working and mothering is discussed, focusing on women's practices in a context of social change of which they are the main subjects. One of the questions to be asked is to what extent women's everyday lives can be understood with a concept that stresses aspects like goals, purpose and calculation. Some authors (Edwards and Ribbens, 1991) have pointed out that women's lives are based on processes rather than goals, on activities and ways of being which are valued in themselves rather than as means to ends. We will argue that social change is a key variable that explains the purposive and quasi-rational elements in social practices. In this sense, strategies can be considered as practices characteristic of periods of social change when most individuals face new problems for which no given solutions are yet established and experienced. Where social policy is less developed, the strategic component of women's practices is stressed, and private and informal resources to combine family and employment become more important. This is often coincident with times and places where modernisation demands have to be met rapidly, typically when women's involvement in paid work increases over a short period of time and the acknowledgement of the new situation by the social organisation (state, employers, trade unions, men) still stands at a very low level.

The third part of the chapter presents different types of strategies developed by working mothers to make working and mothering compatible. These can in fact be organised along a continuum that runs from *rational strategies* on the one end, those clearly and consciously seeking an objective and deploying the means to reach it, and *indirect* or *unconscious strategies* on the other, which include strategies related to reducing or delaying the number of children that are not usually recognised explicitly as a way to make women's double presence in family and employment more easily manageable. In-between these extreme types of strategies there are *packaging strategies*, based on the combination of very different kinds of available resources (collective services, organisation of time, kinship support, and so on), *coping strategies*, when solutions are urgently required and there is little choice left.

CONCEPTS OF STRATEGY

Strategies in Bourdieu's theory are closely related to *habitus*. The link between agency and structural constraint, objective and subjective, active and passive is made by the concept of *habitus*, which is the way through which structures are reproduced, but this happens in a rather unpredictable way. The *habitus* is a predisposition to act in a certain way acquired in the process of socialisation, even if the actor shares a sense of freedom of choice. Structural constraints are incorporated into agents as a part of themselves and forgotten as constraints. Héran (1987) has pointed out how in Bourdieu's approach the rather deterministic concept of *habitus* has to be balanced with the concept of strategy, which widens agents' scope of action. At the same time, the concept of strategy in Bourdieu is quite open – or light – in the degree of purpose required. In fact, strategies are ways or means through which the *habitus* is put into practice. The *habitus* is unconscious and strategies are normally conscious, though there are cases of unconscious strategies – those that can only be considered as such when looked at from the outside. The *habitus* cannot be empirically observed, it is through the empirical analysis of the strategies developed by social groups that the *habitus* can be analysed.

Bourdieu (1994) focuses on the strategies that reproduce the social order, the *stratégies de reproduction* organised in a system, which includes, among other things, biological, educational, economic, social and symbolic strategies. In all these cases the family appears as the basic unity at which level the different reproduction strategies are integrated and developed. In fact, for him family strategies were in a sense the first example of how individual purposive actions can reproduce the structure (Bourdieu, 1976). Class domination or gender domination (Bourdieu, 1998: 103-115) are thus reproduced.

The concept of strategy requires an agent who is the subject of the aimed practice, which conversely constitutes the subject. Bourdieu's general approach to the concept seems to point to social structures as an abstract subject of strategies rather than families or individuals. There is, though, a rather marginal mention (ibid.: 6) of conscious individual strategies, sometimes collective, inspired by the crisis of the established mode, that do not necessarily contribute to the mode's reproduction. These kinds of strategies appear in Bourdieu's theory as exceptional cases linked to a situation of crisis and are not much elaborated beyond a short mention in a few sentences. In short, there is an ambiguity in Bourdieu's concept of strategy. On the one hand, the same term is used to name the process through which existing social structures are reproduced and (marginally) the actions that challenge the dominant *habitus*, even if he describes a sort of circularity among them. On the other hand, the subject of strategies are at the same time structures, families and individuals. From our point of view, practices that reproduce social order and those that challenge it should be distinguished, even if in both cases rationality and purpose is present. This applies to those with an abstract subject (structures) and those with a concrete one (individual or collective agents).

The wide range of actions that are considered as strategies in Bourdieu's approach means that this concept is often used almost as a synonym of social practices.[2] Undoubtedly, it is not easy to find examples of human actions where purpose or intention is absolutely absent. At the same time, practically all actions are explained one way or another by a certain *habitus*. Giddens' understanding of strategies bears a clear resemblance with Bourdieu, but there is a clearer difference between strategic conduct and institutional analysis, which expresses the 'duality of structure' (Giddens, 1979, 1984). In fact, social institutions are reproduced through the recursiveness of social practices, but the latter can regenerate them as historically-bound, constructed structures. Still, they are two sides that cannot be separated. The analysis of strategies focuses on practical and discursive consciousness of actors, but structures are always there and are thus reproduced (Crow, 1989: 16).

A different concept of strategy has been developed from an economic perspective focusing on the combination of resources in the family. Looking at the specific characteristics of the Italian labour market, especially in the peculiar case of the networks of small firms in the *Terza Italia* (Third Italy), Paci (1980) found that the traditional form of family solidarity in its renewed form was the main variable towards understanding the success of the industrial districts. Survival is based on a combination of paid and unpaid work, full-time and part-time jobs, participation in the formal and informal sector, agriculture for subsistence and work in the industry or in services.

Solidarity and combination of resources within the family explain the existence of small firms that would otherwise be difficult to understand. The organisation and coordination of such resources to assure survival is conceptualised in terms of strategies.

The packaging of resources has proven very important for family economies under subsistence level, in poor minorities (Stack, 1975) or in developing countries. Especially in Latin America, people near the poverty line have to develop complex strategies in order to deal with the consequences of the new emerging form of dependent capitalism. Their strategies consist of putting together a salary, other public benefits, revenues from the informal sector, and forms of aid from solidarity networks (Lomnitz, 1977; Schmink, 1984). All this points again to the link between informal economy and strategic agency.

Historians of the family have also put an emphasis on strategies to show how the combination of different resources by the members of the family was necessary to survive or in migration processes (Hareven, 1982). For example, Corner (1993) has studied how in spite of the banishment of women from the labour market during the fascist period in Italy, in certain agricultural areas – where traditionally survival was based on an intertwining of agricultural work and rural manufacturing (silk spinning and reeling mills) – their participation in employment increased, as men left for the war and the extension of pluri-activity to more members of the family permitted the survival of the multiple family unit. In the United Kingdom, Pahl's (1984) exploration of survival strategies focuses on the combination of resources by the different members of a family in a way that very much resembles the Italian approach to family strategies. Yet, these concepts owe much to the pathbreaking work of Tilly (1979), Anderson (1980) and Tilly and Scott (1989), who have developed a notion of strategy that reaches beyond that of conscious calculations.

These two perspectives coming from two other social sciences (economics and history) have heavily influenced the sociology of the family, especially in Italy and in Spain, where the role of kinship support is of considerable importance. 'Family strategies' is a commonly used concept in sociology of the family even among sociologists with quite different theoretical and ideological backgrounds (Del Boca, 1982; Ingrosso, 1984; Saraceno, 1989; Garrido Medina and Gil Calvo, 1993). Whether it is correct to describe such coordinate patterns of behaviour without distinguishing among the actions of different individual members of the family is a matter of discussion (Saraceno, 1989). Authors like Commaille (1993) or Brannen and Moss (1988) have focused on individual strategies within the family and more specifically on women's strategies. Women's individual strategies are sometimes coincident with family strategies and sometimes in conflict with them. There is not a symmetrical relationship between individual women's strategies and individual men's strategies towards family and employment. In fact, family strategies are to a considerable extent men's strategies, as Nicole-Drancourt (1989) shows in her research on men's and women's professional careers: when a man develops a professional career, the entire family is mobilised around this objective; when it is the woman who follows this path, she has to provide by herself, individually, the means to make it compatible with family responsibilities. Men's career is a family strategy; women's career is an individual strategy. To what extent this makes it more difficult for women is an interesting subject of research.

The literature on the individual's (especially women's) everyday lives in terms of strategies (Finch, 1983; Graham, 1987; Brannen and Moss 1988; Anderson et al., 1994; Condon, 1998) conceives these lives in a rather broad or 'light' way, both in the rational and in the choice component. The strength of the term 'strategy' and the emphasis on rationality it implies is often balanced by adjectives like coping, compromise, evasion, and so on. Jacques Commaille (1993) tries to integrate into the concept of strategy will and constraint as the two main elements of a complex process which at the same time expresses and reproduces women's autonomy. In this perspective, rational and identity-oriented behaviour, goals and processes do not appear as opposed but rather as intertwined components of new and complex forms of action which have to be tuned into and given meaning by women's practices in a context of social change.

From our point of view, it is not necessary to suppose that the family group acts as if it were an individual, exactly because of this mixed nature of the conscious/unconscious patterns of behaviour Bourdieu or Giddens underlined in strategies. As Louise Tilly puts it, 'strategies are *principles* that inform bargained interdependent decisions' (1987: 124). In other words, some negotiation process among members is part of the concept, which implies that each member will start negotiating from a different degree of authority as well as build on past patterns already stabilised in time. Consequently, we will address family strategies as described by the voice of women, and in this context especially consider those strategies which reflect and try to adjust interdependent behaviours, even if they may assume different meanings for different members.

WOMEN'S STRATEGIES AND SOCIAL CHANGE

The concept has been criticised as an inadequate analytical tool for certain topics like people's everyday lives. For example, Stephanie Condon (1998) argues that people's plans for the future are rather made up of 'successive or parallel short-term plans, decisions or adjustments, including a number of contingency plans to allow for changing or unforeseen circumstances'. The concept of such rational thinking by individuals, she goes on, should be refuted, as the view people have of themselves, their attitudes and desires is much more vague and unstable. A similar argument is developed by Rosalind Edwards and Jane Ribbens in an article that looks at the concept of strategy from a gender perspective. They argue that the meanings of the concept of strategy are based on 'masculinist "world"[3] understandings' (1991: 484) because these meanings include connotations of hierarchy, view people as resources and imply competitive activities. The needs of individuals are disregarded and subordinated to an overall goal, and activities assumed to be means-ends are motivated within rational frameworks. Women's family lives, on the contrary, are based on processes rather than goals, on activities and ways of being which are valued in themselves rather than as means to ends.

Strategies are certain types of social practices that involve some degree of rational calculation and purpose; this can vary in some approaches. Crozier and Friedberg (1977) have rightly pointed to the fact that the rationality of strategies is often a limited one, going through conflicts and negotiations: it is the outcome and not the starting point of social interaction. It has to be deduced discursively, with reference to the frame of constraints and chances each actor faces. The limited rationality of strategies is also evidenced by the fact that different strategies at the same moment may be equally ational.[4]

Periods of social change can be expected to be moments when the purposive and rational component of human action is stressed. Individuals face new problems for which there are not yet any given solutions already experienced by others, for example the preceding generations. Individuals do not simply reproduce in a more or less original way the past behaviour, but act differently in a new context, which poses new problems and requires new solutions. They necessarily have to innovate and seek answers to respond to situations not faced before. Tilly and Scott (1989: 7-8) define the notion of strategy as.'how people make decisions in the face of changing economic circumstances'. In this sense, strategies have to do with action to change the position of the actor and to respond to the new problems this arouses. Bourdieu's theory of *habitus* is useful to make the link between structure and agency but does not leave much space for social change nor for the change of individual trajectories. Dubar (1991) has criticised in Bourdieu's approach the reduction of 'objectivity' to differential positions in the social structure and 'subjectivity' to the trend toward its perpetuation, the result being the reproduction of the established system of positions. Instead, Dubar conceptualises the system of positions as a strategic opportunity for individuals' objectives, rejecting the mechanic association of positions and strategies (with regard to individuals' trajectories). The latter can be a resource to challenge the established system. The result cannot be forecasted as its reproduction – subjective strategies can lead to social change.

Following this approach, we might think of a tension between *habitus* and strategy, the former referring to the reproduction of old roles and past behaviour, to the inertia of social practices, the latter referring to new practices in contradiction with old roles and institutions. In this sense, social practices would be composed of varying degrees of *habitus* and strategy according to the relative weight of reproduction and innovation. We will use the term strategies to name practices in which the assessment of purposive and innovative components is especially relevant.

From this perspective, women's strategies would be those practices aiming for a change in their economic and social position and for solutions to the new problems, and the individual or collective answers they demand. Thus our approach to the concept of strategy picks up Dubar's reconceptualisation of the link between structure and agency through active trajectories in an established system of positions with opportunities (and constraints) for women's objectives. We follow Dubar, who re-conceptualises the link between structure and agency by introducing a notion of active trajectories within an established system of positions with opportunities (and constraints) for women's objectives.

In all European countries, working mothers are facing a new situation, that of combining employment and motherhood. In some countries like Spain, Greece and the Netherlands, women's involvement in paid work has increased rapidly and recently. In others, like Sweden, Norway, Denmark, France and Germany, women's participation in the labour market has been the norm for many years now (Rubery et al., 1998, 1999). In some countries, women's economic activity has been strongly supported by the state; in others, few social policies address this issue (Hantrais and Letablier, 1996; Gornick, et al., 1997; Moss and Deven, 1999; Gornick and Meyers, 2003).

In countries where female employment has increased rapidly and recently over a short number of years, and where the state and the social organisation remain quite unaware of the new demands this poses, women have to make decisions to be able to combine their double presence as workers and mothers. They have to develop social practices with a high component of rational calculation and purpose to manage their everyday lives in family and employment (cf. Wallace, 2002). However, these social practices can probably be conceptualised as strategies in a broader sense than they have in the rational choice theory. Rationality is often mixed with feelings or with social pressure. Choice is sometimes very limited, it happens rather in the form of gradual steps, whereas, as Bourdieu poses it, [the strategy] 'will retrospectively appear as the only thing to be done or told' (Bourdieu and Wacquant, 1992: 142).

In some cases, strategies are indirect or maybe even unconscious, as it happens with those related to reducing and delaying the number of children. The combination of very different resources (public and private, paid and unpaid, permanent or temporary, formal and informal) plays an important role in the effort to make work and family life compatible. In the southern countries, and to a lesser extent also in Germany, working mothers' social practices often mean coping between a small number of options, most of them hardly desirable. In the Northern European countries, working and mothering include to a lower extent a strategic component, as this is no longer a new behaviour. Being worker and mother is what the state and the social organisation expect most women to be. In spite of that, the high proportion of women working part-time, the low participation of women in the private sector and the still low level of involvement of men in care (even if it is the highest in Europe), among other issues, configure a situation in which women's action to change it could also be conceptualised in terms of strategies.

TYPES OF STRATEGIES

Rational Strategies[5]

Money is often a clear indicator of rational strategies. Hiring somebody to take care of the children and the home can be a normal way of organisation among upper class households or a carefully planned strategy in other cases. For example, mothers who want to develop a professional career know that this means long working hours and an attitude of 'being available' whenever they might be needed. In short, they have to adopt a 'masculine' working model, meaning that their commitment to their job comes in the first place. The problem is that they often have to deploy the means to do that before they are 'successful' in their careers, before it is clear the effort was worthwhile. Full-time household help is a considerable expense for most families, and there is often the idea that it is a kind of expense that can be easily cut down as one (usually the woman) can manage one way or another. There is a contradiction between a family strategy (cutting down expenses on something that is not perceived as absolutely necessary for the family) and the individual strategy of women who know that if they do not travel or attend business dinners because they have to stay with their children they will not progress in their professional activity.

'*I used to stay with the children* [when they were ill she did not go to work] *until I decided I would not, that I preferred to cut down on other expenses. I decided I would not accept cutting down the maid. You always tend to think that you can reduce that expense but I have kept cool and said "I prefer to eat potatoes" .... I have always had a very atypical job for a woman, under a lot of pressure, with a lot of stress, not a typical job for a woman. Circumstances have been that way, I have never desired a certain post, but I have never said no to the challenges I have been confronted with.*'
(Married mother, Madrid, Spain, DG of a state-owned company, age 44)

Another example of a rational strategy might be the case of lower-class mothers who begin to work before the school or *crèche* opens. If they cannot count on a relative or friend, they have to hire somebody just for one or two hours to fill in the gap. The same happens in the summer during school vacation. The amount of domestic help is in this case carefully calculated and weighed, limited to what is strictly indispensable.

'*When our schedules change in the summer I have to look for domestic help for a longer number of hours. Normally it is just three hours a week for the heavy tasks. In the summer I need somebody in the morning to take care of the children until I get back from work. This costs a lot of money, half of my earnings, but there is nothing else I can do.*'
(Lone mother, Madrid, Spain, receptionist, age 35)

For upper-class families, hiring domestic help is not really a strategy but just a social practice coherent with the *habitus* of the social class they belong to. For other women who want to make a career without that same background, or simply for women who need or want to work, domestic help seems to be a strategy in the strong sense of the word.

Packaging Strategies[6]

In Mediterranean countries, the continued employment of both partners in a couple, or even of a lone parent, is hardly assured by the exclusive use of services. They mostly use *crèches* or other childcare services only with the support of assistance from their kinship networks. This means that they regularly have to face changing sets of resources and constraints in their working and family lives. The constellation of adjustments and new strategies they deploy to meet their changing demands is always the result of a mix of public and private solutions; unpredictability becomes the worst risk and many people are constrained to create highly individualised and at times completely original strategies to balance their work and family dilemmas. The range of practices runs from management-style organisation of family life, with clearly defined and routinised assignments of tasks for each partner and relative involved; to the co-involvement of many other people at many different levels; to difficult-to-predict care-giving shifts that vary with each carer's involvement in paid work or other circumstances. In any case, a very complex texture of daily life has to be kept under control.

> *'I was the manager of my daughter with a number of other people. I could count on my mother only in part because she worked, on my mother-in-law only in part because she had a lot of things of her own to do, and on the great-grandma only when she could. When the baby was at the crèche, a common cold was an organisational tragedy .... For me, not managing during the crèche years meant having to do everything myself, my husband was never there, he wasn't there to help organise.'*
> (Lone mother, Bologna, Italy, physiotherapist, age 33)

> *'Materially, then, I had drawn up a timetable for each day of the week, who was free in those hours, who was available, so I could rely on them when I wasn't there .... To completely organise all the work to be done, well, we're always short of time, always on the go, and there's never enough time for ourselves and our children.'*
> (Lone father, Florence, Italy, freelance theatre technician, age 39)

> *'Managing a child, it's something like managing a business.'*
> (Lone mother, Vicchio, Italy, dealer in a store, age 30)

Some families (more evidently one-parent families) depend on a varying combination of assistance from services (both public and private) and relatives to whom they have to appeal for support. They also depend for a really substantive part of friendship and community networks.

> *'I made an exchange with one of these moms, she was working afternoons and I was working mornings, when my children woke up they phoned this mom and she came and picked them up, they stayed at her house, there were four or five children there, she had them do their homework, they played and then she usually left them a half-hour or so in front of the TV, then I came and took them to the park. We did this for a week, then I did it with this lady's girl, she phoned me in the morning and I went to pick her up, we're very creative, we're a little group of*

parents who invent lots of things, there's no problem about adding another child
at the last minute, we all know one another pretty well.'
(Lone mother with two children, Bologna, Italy, childcare worker, age 40)

'The baby wakes up and he's there [the grandfather], she has breakfast and all,
then she goes downstairs to the neighbour's.'
(Lone mother, Vicchio, Italy, store clerk, age 30)

In all types of families, the idea is very clear that childcare services can only solve a (little but important) part of the problem, to be 'packed' together with the crucial support of the elder generation, a resource clearly available to them in an unprecedented way:

'I think the task of the services is one of giving the most possible space and the
most possible elasticity, but also space with respect to the solidarity networks,
however attentive it may be a service cannot go into the details of a situation ....
It's clear that everything helps because the assistance needed is just so vast, so
particular, so specific, the work shifts are so different that only private help can
guarantee, can give people the chance of meeting, getting together to structure
spaces and times.'
(Married mother, Florence, Italy, public administration manager, age 42)

Packaging strategies show a more extreme form in recent years, now that the general flexibilisation of the labour market has opened many chances for atypical jobs, often covering unsocial hours (Rubery et al., 1999). Mothers of young children, especially those with low qualifications, often prefer working weekends or evenings, when their partner is at home or when different combinations of informal care resources may be put together (Emerek, 1999; Ellingsaeter and Rønsen, 1996; Trifiletti, 2003). Another available strategy seems to be to combine two shift jobs for the couple or a short vertical part-time job with the partner's shifts, a strategy which of course compresses even rest time for both. High personal costs, however, do not discourage a creative use of disadvantages or constraints.

Coping Strategies

A coping strategy may often be a good way of avoiding a choice between alternative practices that do not leave much space for real choice, as they are all hardly acceptable. When women have no choice or face undesirable alternatives, they can sometimes reframe the choice in different terms, often not legitimised in current practices but grounded in a different, often more traditional culture.

A classic coping strategy of young working mothers with no care resources when they need a quick solution is to take the child to the workplace with them. In terms of the dominant culture this is of course a sub-optimal choice both for the relationship with the employer and as an experience for the child itself, as well as in relation to the self-image as a 'serious' worker. On the other hand, such a decision may avoid an even worse coping strategy, which of course other working mothers sometimes have to accept – for example, leaving the child at home alone. This clearly illustrates how many strategies are grounded on limited rationality and many choices are only sub-optimal ones (Crozier and Friedberg, 1977).

Perhaps the most extreme case of a coping strategy on the part of working mothers has to be recognised in the practice many immigrant women in Western countries have to accept sooner or later, especially if they work in domestic or care services: sending their children back home at a thousand kilometres distance.

> *'My daughter ... was going to the crèche ... then, for a lot of reasons, for what we were just talking about, this year I left her with my mother in Morocco. Because here, here you can see it, you can really see how hard it is for "foreigners" with children .... She didn't get to see me very often, she didn't want to stay with anyone else, she kept getting sick, she even had allergies; in the winter she was always sick ... So I decided to try it for a year, to leave her with my mother .... On the other hand I was scared to death to leave her down there. I thought "it's for her own good", I said, "it's better if I leave her with my mamma". It's been 4 months now, it feels like 4 years. But she's doing really well.'*
> (Mother, lives with a partner, Bassano, Italy, clerk in a butcher's store, age 32)

Indirect and Unconscious Strategies

The decision about the number of children and when to have them is often an indirect strategy to make family and employment compatible, but it is not always recognised as such. Spain and Italy are the European countries with the lowest fertility levels.[7] Paradoxically, these are also countries with a low female activity rate, in contrast to the Northern European countries where fertility is higher than the European average and female activity is the highest. This difference between Northern and Southern Europe – both regarding the productive and the reproductive sphere – might be more easily understood if we take into account the recent and rapid development of the labour market participation, especially of Spanish women.[8] Spain as well as Italy seems to be living a process of transition towards a new dual-earner family model, but the social organisation has not yet adapted to the new situation.

There is no direct link in working mothers' discourse between number of children (or their timing) and employment (Tobío et al., 1996). What is explicitly said is that the household economy is the main factor to explain fertility. Children 'need' a lot of things that are nowadays perceived to be necessary, and parents want them to have these things.

> 'The number of children? It is not about having a job or not having a job. It has more to do with the economy, with money, you give them more and more, you want them to have them, maybe some of those things are not so necessary really, but you think they are...'
> (Married mother, Valencia, Spain, factory worker, age 35)

> 'Only, I feel really well now, this way [with an only child], but I would like to have another child... this of course would upset everything; on the other hand, I am not for an only child. In my mind an only child will suffer in life, I do not want him to suffer. But this is a question mark, now our situation is the right one, the child is quiet and for the moment it's all right like this.'
> (Married mother, Florence, Italy, clerk in a family store, age 37)

If the family economy is the main variable that determines the number of children (or having any children at all), employment is not an obstacle for fertility but rather what makes it possible, though limited to just one or two children. This was most clearly put by one interviewee:

> 'We thought (she and her husband) that the best would be two children and I think it will be two. If I was not employed we might have had three children, but you cannot afford three children with only one income.'
> (Married mother, Valencia, Spain, civil servant, age 34)

The best choice, according to this argument, seems to be one or two children in a dual-earner family. More than two children for working parents is too much domestic work, which would require a full-time housewife, but for most people just one income is not enough for a family with three children. Discourse on children and fertility develops around economic need, which blurs the idea of women's involvement in paid work as a cause of low fertility. The considerations and arguments of women could also be interpreted as an indirect or maybe even unconscious strategy to protect their involvement in paid work, which is not just an obligation but a desired activity that helps build a new identity as citizens and autonomous individuals (Tobío, 2001). The repeated argument, not always explicitly said, is that mothers' employment is nowadays a condition for higher fertility rates. What is implicit is that going back to old family models of the past is no longer possible. The example of France and the Scandinavian countries supports this perception.

CONCLUSION

The concept of strategy has often been used in a somewhat critical way to describe women's practices related to the reconciliation of work and family life, sometimes preceded by an adjective (like coping or compromise) that counterbalances the association with rationality. This chapter has explored different ways in which strategies are understood in different theoretical contexts, and has discussed to what extent it can be a useful tool to understand how working mothers make decisions and act to make these two still contradictory worlds compatible. Following Tilly and Scott (1989), our main conclusion has to do with the conceptualisation of strategies as social practices characteristic of periods of social change, such as working mothers are experiencing nowadays. This applies especially to the southern European countries, where the involvement of women in employment is increasing rapidly and with scarce state support. In this sense, we conceive strategies as a concept opposite to *habitus*. If the latter explains the reproduction of social structures through the action of individual agents, the former would be applied to cases in which social structures cannot be reproduced anymore and actors are forced to innovate.

Still, there are very different kinds of strategies according to the degree and type of rational calculation, freedom of choice and consciousness. Four main strategies have been found through empirical research of working mothers (rational, packaging, coping, and indirect or unconscious). For example, intergenerational help of close relatives (cf. Chapter 5 'Kinship and informal support for the first generation of working mothers') seems to be a common and recurring element in the strategies of working mothers. The issue of kinship support also points to the relevance of the social context of strategies: kinship support may assume profoundly diverse aspects, depending not only on available alternatives but also on the quality of interpersonal pacts of reciprocity and on the constellation of meanings in which women's strategies are embedded. Freedom of choice is often a *result* of interpersonal negotiations about concrete alternatives in which the cultural means to read them and the way the family story is told afterwards play an important role. From this point of view, the dimension of viable reflexivity between structure, action and meaning is crucial, and quite different from a simple presupposition of rationality. In fact, the strategies that involve the highest emotive costs for women clearly seem to be the unconscious and indirect ones, maybe because purpose cannot be clearly acknowledged as such.

NOTES

[1] Crow (1989: 2) considers that 'strategic analysis applies to only certain types of action, ones which must amongst other things be in at least some senses rational, and take place within broadly predictable social situations'. Wood and Kelly (1982: 84) describe the concept of strategy with 'connotations of comprehensiveness, coherence, long term perspectives and consciousness'. Palomba and Sabbadini (1997: 143) describe the three main elements that are necessary to define an action as a strategy: there must be 1) a subject with a purpose capable of making a choice, 2) different alternatives to choose. and 3) a period of time along which the strategy is developed.

[2] Examples of this use of the concept of strategy can be found in Nicole-Drancourt (1989) and Commaille (1993).

[3] Emphasis on 'world' by the authors.

[4] In fact, Bourdieu himself has often underlined that a same *habitus* may originate different practices.

[5] Data for this section and for 'Indirect and unconscious strategies' from Tobío, et al. (1996), a qualitative research project subsidised by the Women's Institute of the Ministry of Social Affairs. The investigation was based on twenty-five in-depth interviews and six discussion groups with working women between the ages of 20 and 49, with a partner and at least one child under 18. The field work was carried out from February to June 1995 in Madrid, Barcelona, Valencia and Bilbao.

[6] Data from the Soccare Project, a TSER funded comparative project (cf. http://www.uta. fi/laitokset/sospol/soccare). Quotations are taken from the Italian reports by Trifiletti, et al., 2001.

[7] The 2001 total fertility rate for Italy is 1.24 and for Spain 1.25, while it was 1.47 in the EU as a whole and the higher values of the indicator within Europe were 1.98 (Ireland), 1.90 (France), 1.74 (Denmark) and 1.73 (Finland) (Eurostat, 2002).

[8] In 1981, less than 30 per cent of women in their thirties, a very significant group as a majority are mothers of small children, were in the labour market; the figure for 1999 is more than two-thirds (64 per cent) (Fernández Cordón, 1999: 60).

5. Kinship and Informal Support: Care Resources for the First Generation of Working Mothers in Norway, Italy and Spain

Arnlaug Leira, Constanza Tobío and Rossana Trifiletti

Strong kinship support tends to be interpreted as characteristic of traditional societies, whereas the nuclear family, standing on its own, is often presented as one of the main elements of the modernisation process. While the involvement of women in paid work and state provision of childcare services are both low, there is a rationale behind why the family is important as provider of the care and welfare of its dependent members. By contrast, where female activity rates are high, high levels of state support are generally regarded as being a necessary condition for the employment of mothers. This is the underlying hypothesis in the approach of Gornick et al. (1997), who focus on policy variation and mothers' employment in different countries, or of Barrère-Maurisson (1995), who establishes a typology of historical phases in the combination of economic sectors, family types, work and state regulation. According to this typology, dual-earner families correspond with the last phase, where the tertiary sector is dominant and domestic care work is replaced by collective services provided by the state. The three ideal types of welfare state regimes developed by Esping-Andersen (1990, 1999) also problematise the link between policies and female employment. Only the social democratic model is presented as clearly promoting the presence of women in the labour market; the liberal or conservative models tend to maintain families based on a male-breadwinner model. Social policies are therefore interpreted by some scholars as contributing to the reproduction of a traditional, gendered division of work, and by others as challenging it.

In this chapter we approach welfare state and kinship support for mothers' employment from a different perspective. Starting from an examination of how the first generation of working mothers managed to combine paid employment and the care for children, we argue that support provided by the welfare state may be overrated, and the use of kinship and other forms of informal support underrated. There is a relevant gender dimension to all of this because intergenerational support in childcare, like extra-parental childcare in general, is usually a women's affair.

The importance of welfare state policies in promoting motherhood change is disputed (see for example Leira, 1992, 2002; Duncan and Edwards, 1999; Pfau-Effinger, 1999). Even in Scandinavia, where social reproduction is commonly seen as 'going public', the mass entry of mothers into the labour market preceded generous public support for childcare (Leira, 1992). In the 1990s, comparative data from Western Europe indicated that the rising labour market participation of mothers was not triggered by the extensive provision of childcare services but rather by market demand for labour (EC Childcare Network, 1996; Moss and Deven, 1999). An overview of childcare arrangements in the European Union suggests that informal resources are often used, but since these are not registered their relative importance is difficult to assess (Karlsson, 1995). When the labour market participation of mothers of children under three years of age is compared to the level of public childcare, the gap between demand and supply indicates that in most EU member states there are other forms of childcare in use – for example, childcare provided by family and kin, friends, neighbours, private childminders, even commercial services.[1]

Comparative data show considerable differences among EU countries in the role kinship support plays in families with small children (Eurostat, 1997b). In Italy or Greece, more than 20 per cent of women over 50 years of age provide free childcare on a daily basis, normally to their grandchildren. In Spain the proportion is lower, but the childminders do it for more hours than the average. In Denmark,[2] less than 5 per cent of women over 50 carry out this kind of function. There seems to be a relationship between high levels of kinship support and lower female activity (Portugal being one of the obvious exceptions). Traditional values or ways of life apparently run parallel with a dominantly gendered division of work.

We argue, however, that kinship ties and intergenerational support are among the resources that working mothers can mobilise in managing their care arrangements for small children when state support is not forthcoming, when it is insufficient, or when they prefer not to rely on it exclusively.[3] Thus, contradicting much of the welfare state literature of the 1990s (Esping-Andersen, 1990, 1999), we contend that kinship support can play a role in changing the traditional division of work between men and women. In several countries, kinship support has been and still is a resource used in particular by first-generation working mothers, who have often had no other available resource to turn to for childcare. Our main hypothesis is that intense intergenerational support is a provisional solution in a period of transition from the male-breadwinner/single-income family model to a viable dual-earner model. In some countries, strong traditional family ties are often necessary for women to enter the labour market – a new situation that changes the family. Whether this is a cultural specificity of southern countries is open to question.

The particular point of view we have chosen entails comparing a process of social change (the mass entry of women into the labour market) that takes place at different moments in different countries. We look in some detail at the arrangements working parents make for accommodating the obligations of job and childcare. Focussing on Norway, Italy and Spain, we concentrate mainly on kinship and informal support as resources that have facilitated social change. Thus we investigate the importance of these resources for those first-generation mothers whose labour market participation rose to become a 'critical mass' – understood here as making up 30-40 per cent of mothers of children under three. Accordingly, we explore the arrangements working mothers have made for childcare at different times in different welfare states. For Italy and Spain, the discussion centres on the surge of mothers going into employment and on the use of kinship support in the 1990s; for Norway the focus is on the early 1970s. In other words, in order to obtain more detailed information about how mothers managed the modernisation process witnessed in the transition into employment, we look at similar processes occurring at different historical moments in the three countries. Our examination is based on scrutiny of national data sets and on individual case studies of the authors, which have been conducted at different times in different countries.

We first present the three national cases. Special attention is paid to the changing labour market opportunities of mothers and the relative importance of formally and informally provided childcare services in the early stages of mothers entering employment. We follow with a comparison of the 'coping strategies' (see Tobío and Trifiletti in this volume) used among mothers in the three countries to balance work and childcare commitments, and highlight important elements in the social and political construction of motherhood. Cultural and ideological conflicts over which motherhood models and family values should be supported are noted only in passing. In conclusion, we return to the questions raised concerning the importance of kinship and informal support for mothers pioneering entry into formal employment.

THE NORWEGIAN STORY: HOW WORKING MOTHERS MANAGED BEFORE PUBLIC POLICIES WERE IMPLEMENTED

The 10-15 year period following World War II has come to be identified as the 'housewife era' in Norway. For women, the common pattern was to leave the labour market upon marriage or when the first child was born; this for a prolonged period, sometimes even for good. The male-breadwinner family represented the norm and was not contested. In a literal sense, a married mother's place was in the home, while unmarried mothers were largely expected to be the main providers for themselves and their children. The impact of marital status is captured in the 1960 census, which shows that only 5 per cent of married mothers with children aged under seven were gainfully employed, while 42 per cent of previously married mothers and 55 per cent of the unmarried ones had paid work (Selid, 1968: 15).

Ideological barriers against women's employment were pronounced at the time. Married mothers who did go out to work often met with social disapproval as well as practical difficulties. Part-time work was not widely available and public day-care services were almost non-existent anyway. How these working mothers managed to combine work and family responsibilities is not systematically recorded. Well-educated, well-off women were likely to hire domestic help to do the housework and look after their children, while lower-income working mothers might get the assistance of family and kin, grandmothers, aunts, or the older siblings of younger children.

The Modernisation of Motherhood

Norwegian society started to go through a profound transformation in the late 1960s, as evidenced in labour-market restructuring, welfare state reforms and in changes in families and the labour force, processes in which women took an active part. The numbers of married women entering the labour market started increasing. According to a nationwide survey conducted in 1968, four out of ten married women aged 15-59 were in some form of gainful employment working full-time or part-time, or taking on occasional or seasonal work. Among married working women, one in three was the mother of children under 11. Lacking the support of formal childcare services, how did mothers reconcile job and family? Half of the children were cared for by their parents, mainly by the working mothers themselves. Childminders, domestic helps and neighbours functioned as carers for one in four of the children, and one in ten was cared for by grandparents (Statistisk Sentralbyrå

1969, Table 41: 60). In extraordinary situations, such as when a child was ill or during school vacations, mothers reported that kin were the most important extra-familial childcare assets.

By the late 1970s, half of the mothers of pre-schoolers were gainfully employed, the majority on a part-time basis, but with weekly working hours on the increase. What actually caused these new trends in women's employment has been much debated in Scandinavia. Important in Norway was a restructuring of the demand for labour, a tightening labour market (although with regional variations), and from the late 1960s/early 1970s an expansion of the welfare state as a service provider state. The public sector labour market in health and welfare, social and educational services, and in middle- and lower-level administration often meant jobs in local labour markets and in fields traditionally regarded as 'typically' women's work. Labour supply also changed; women in the 1970s commanded much greater control over their labour and reproductive capacities than women of earlier generations. Fertility rates declined from 2.88 in 1960 to 1.7 in 1980. Smaller families and improved educational attainments facilitated women's employment. Furthermore, a shift in motherhood and family ideology was on its way, highlighted for example in the revival of the feminist movement. Gender equality entered the political agenda and legislation was passed that made women's access to paid work a main target. The reconciliation of working and parenting was re-conceptualised as a political issue, and from the late 1970s included fathers as well as mothers. As the gender balance in employment shifted, the dual-earner family became predominant even among families with very young children. In normative terms, support for the gender-differentiated family remained strong, but was contested as mothers took on more of the economic provider functions of the family. The rapid increase in mothers' employment contributed to a rising demand for state-sponsored childcare services, thus challenging the traditional boundaries between public and parental responsibilities.

Political support for investment in public day-care for children developed slowly compared to the activity rates of mothers. In the 1970s, the welfare state did not intervene in any large-scale way to facilitate the reconciliation of work and childcare. Mothers' balancing of work and family was managed by two largely informal strategies: one is seen in the growth of part-time jobs, termed by one analyst as an 'informal labour market reform' (Strømsheim, 1983); the other is evidenced in the flourishing of private and/or informal arrangements for childcare (Leira, 1992, 2002). We will now focus on the arrangements for childcare.

Two Trends in Childcare Provision: Collectivisation and Privatisation

Almost thirty years of deliberation preceded national legislation concerning public childcare. Politically, there was pronounced ambivalence and opposition to public intervention in the private sphere of the family, as well as concern over the costs to the public purse. Introduced by a Labour minority government, the 1975 Act governing day care for children gained parliamentary support.

In 1975, a nationwide survey recorded the forms of care in use for children aged 0-6 (Statistisk Sentralbyrå, 1975). For families in which the mother was employed, two findings were striking: first, half of these families reported that they managed without any extra-familial support; second, private agreements – used by almost 40 per cent – were far more common than use of the publicly funded childcare facilities, reported by only 11 per cent (Leira, 1992: 136). In some of the families who managed childcare with no help from others, mothers would look after the children while at work. For everyday, regular childcare, 'parent shifts' were also used, that is, the parents went to work at different hours of the day and took turns looking after the children. This is highly interesting, since it shows an involvement of fathers with their children not often reported. Private agreements included domestic help, nannies or a private childminder; alternatively, the families deployed close friends or kin. No doubt grandmothers were important in some of these arrangements. However, since a considerable proportion of the grandmother generation was likely to be in the labour market, there might not be a pool of grandmothers to mobilise for full-time childcare. If we are to take survey information from the 1970s at face value, friends and neighbours – perhaps also relatives – did get paid in cash for childcare services. In this perspective, social networks shade into informal labour markets.

Some of the private informal arrangements for childcare were based on close relationships between mothers and childminders, mobilised for example via kinship, friendship or between neighbours or colleagues. Social networks too were important in mediating between mothers and minders, and women reported in interviews that childminders were 'passed on' between mothers. In other cases the relationship was more distant, or market-based, for example when an au pair or a nanny was employed to look after the child, or when childminding was organised via job announcements and employment agencies. When added up, private childminding agreements (including support from kin and social networks) represented informal labour markets in childcare, in which the informal labour of some women supported the formal employment of mothers of young children. From a labour market perspective, informal childminding was one of the important job categories for women (Leira, 1992).

In 1985, more than half of the mothers of children under three were in the labour force, as were 70 per cent of the mothers whose youngest child was between the ages of three and six. State-supported childcare services were increased, but demand still exceeded supply. A 1985 survey of childcare arrangements among families with pre-school children (Bogen, 1987) shows that the use of family-based childcare was in decline, used by only one in eight families, while the use of de-familialised childcare increased in two different ways: almost half of the families used private arrangements for childcare, usually a childminder or paid domestic help, while approximately one in three made use of state-sponsored childcare facilities. Other studies show that family and kinship provided important childcare resources in special circumstances, for example when a child or parent was ill, or when a babysitter was needed outside the hours of the childcare services (Gautun, 1990).

From the 1960s and well into the 1980s, when Norwegian mothers of pre-schoolers entered employment, publicly funded childcare was not well developed. To a considerable extent, the employment of mothers depended on other women's labour being available for informal childcare arrange-ments. However, as public services expanded, the combination of job and childcare was facilitated. An important shift in childcare arrangements was recorded from the late 1980s onwards. For the families of employed mothers, the use of publicly funded childcare surpassed private arrangements. The shortage of high-quality, publicly funded childcare remained a problem though, and by 2002 supply was still not sufficient to meet demand in some regions.

Policy Reforms of the 1990s

Family policy reforms of the 1990s again showed different processes at work in the reconciliation of work and family. On the one hand, state support for de-familialised childcare increased, that is for the provision of childcare services. On the other hand, important policy reforms targeted the '(re)familialisation' of childcare, witnessed for example in the prolongation of paid parental leave and legislating of a cash benefit for childcare schemes:

- During the 1990s, governments of different political leanings promised to make state-supported childcare facilities universally available; the latest message is to achieve this by 2005.
- Paid parental leave has been prolonged to 52 weeks at 80 per cent wage compensation (or 43 weeks at 100 per cent). The rights of fathers to be the familialised carer for children have been strengthened. In addition to two weeks of leave for fathers at the time of birth of their child, and the

right to share the greater part of the paid parental leave period with the mother, four weeks of the parental leave period is earmarked for the fathers on a 'use or lose' basis.
– A cash benefit for childcare schemes makes a cash grant available to parents for all children aged 12 to 36 months on the condition that the child does not make use of a place in state-sponsored childcare.

Apparently, the reforms promote different family values and forms. Since the cash benefit does not represent a living wage, the reform presumes a traditional family form in which the cash-benefit recipient depends on someone else for economic provision. State sponsoring of childcare services supports the employment of mothers and the dual-earner family, while parental leave and the father's quota aim to promote the dual-earner, care-sharing family. Although not much is known about the combined effects of the policy reforms, some studies indicate a polarisation among the families of young children with respect to how employment and childcare are combined by mothers and fathers (see Leira, 2002): at one end are those families who opt for a conventional gender division of work and care, at the other the families in which fathers and mothers share both childcare and economic provision more equally between them.

KINSHIP SUPPORT FOR CHILDCARE: A NECESSARY RESOURCE IN ITALY FOR WORKING MOTHERS

The female activity rate in Italy is still very low, but the traditional model of participation, in which many young women entered the labour market and gave it up at the time of the first or second childbirth, has already changed. Usually they knew there would be no chance of returning to work, except to unregistered jobs in the informal labour market, where they could often find the part-time jobs lacking in the official market. Today, many young women remain out of the market longer, investing in their cultural capital, but a growing proportion of married women tend to hold on longer in full-time jobs by delaying and compressing fertility. Family support is indispensable for these working mothers. They are able to maintain employment only thanks to important family support (substituting the support of their husband) and at the price of a deep feeling of hardship and fatigue. No wonder they also tend to have shorter working lives afterwards.

Italian women in general have wanted to work since the late 1970s as the normal way to realise their autonomy and be entitled to citizenship rights: they usually accept working long hours *on male conditions* in order to gain a worker identity for themselves. In fact, the mere existence of an important informal labour market has long induced a serious mistrust on the part of women, as well as trade unions, towards part-time arrangements. The proportion of female activity explained by part-time jobs remained around 11-12 per cent until very recently, when it increased along with temporary or semi-autonomous jobs to 16 per cent after the last Act (2000) favouring part-time arrangements. Rather than offering an opportunity for re-entry into the labour market after a break (Solera, 2001), longitudinal studies on status transitions in Italy show clearly that a part-time contract puts the woman at greater risk of exiting the labour market than a full-time contract (Bernardi, 1999), that is it grants mostly a precarious first entry for young women or a soft exit at pre-retirement (Addabbo, 1997). Paradoxically, this may explain why part-time arrangements are often described as desirable by women in opinion polls, but the proportion of involuntary part-timers already working part-time is higher in Italy than elsewhere, with the sole exception of Portugal. It can therefore be understood why the former generation of women, who participated in the labour marker for only a short while (usually ended by the first childbirth) and at a young age, now as mothers (and grandmothers) are so willing to support their daughters in maintaining a good job and prevent them by any means from falling into the informal labour market. They are two generations very close to each other in the Mannheim sense (cf. Arber and Attias-Donfut, 2000).

All this is a consequence of the strong rigidity of a dual labour market, much more so than it is an outcome of a prevalent model of the family. We could try to synthesise that since Italy never reached a fully developed Fordist economy, ideologically it never supported a strong male-breadwinner family – at least not in the post-war years, when most other countries did. This happened of course because the fascist regime had pushed women out of the labour market with some very explicit laws, and it was no longer possible for the democratic regime to risk similar measures. Family obligations endorsed by welfare measures never encouraged housewifery. Even the fiscal system did not explicitly discourage women's work; it rather encouraged a second revenue in the family only if it was high enough (Gambale, 1994), something clearly very different from the classic 'a job and a half' solution.

The mere fact that, unlike in many other countries, the activity rate is not growing steadily but is deeply affected by recessions, seems proof of the enduring precariousness of women with a lower education. If the 'spirit' of the double presence (Balbo, 1978) is shared by all women, they appear really polarised between two groups: of course not between women who invest in family *or* in career (Hakim, 1995), but between women who can afford to and are supported to invest in both, and others who cannot and have to sacrifice one of the two against their will. The second group have less well-paid and more insecure jobs, no help from social policies, even less help from relatives, and have a much greater likelihood – if for some reason they interrupt working – of falling out of the labour market after the first spell.[4] As is clear in Portugal (Wall et al., 2001: 229), there is some evidence in Italy that women with a lower education receive less informal help when working, particularly in the south of the country: 52 per cent of working mothers' children are cared for by grandparents in the south against 56 per cent in the north. Only 6 per cent of working mothers have access to day-care as against 15 per cent when their child is 18-20 months old (and 63.2 per cent of these mothers do work in the centre-north, only 34.5 per cent in the south. Also southern working mothers re-enter work much earlier, before the child is six months old, almost double the northern women (ISTAT, 2003).

And still, on a national level the percentages of families with children under the age of 14 in which both parents work were 30.9 in 1983, 36.8 in 1988-89 and 40.4 in 1998. This is a growth of 10 percentage points in 15 years (faster than the activity rate) – a rapid change of the model, at least in the first years of maternity.

Intergenerational Help for Working Mothers

Unlike mothers in other European countries, Italian women with very young children tend to hold on to a job more than women with children of school age and not to take advantage of parental leave entirely. Paradoxically, the highest women's activity rates tend to coincide with the phases or circumstances of life in which care work is in most demand: mothers of young children as well as lone mothers of all ages.

A crucial element of this paradoxical situation is the intergenerational help young mothers receive from elder-generation kinswomen. They share a strong sense of complicity with their daughters (or nieces or daughters-in-law) in changing a society of men. In other countries, students have underlined the vicarious realisation of the grandmother through the professional success of her daughter as a possible source of conflict (Bloch and Buisson, 1998). Reality is of course more complex, but it has to be borne in mind that these forms of help are embedded in Italy in a more general pattern, one that mobilises the entire family network in favour of the young couple. This supports the social mobility of the new family (cf. Arber and Attias-Donfut, 2000) and prevents its impoverishment.

Nuclear families with some aggregated member or extended families produce a higher activity rate than nuclear families made up of parents and children alone; lone mothers do work more than mothers in nuclear families, but the percentage is often higher if they have another cohabiting relative (usually the grandmother). It is peculiar that in recent years this type of support seems to have facilitated the work of mothers, even though lone parents or extended families form a minority. It is possible to see in these 'traditional' family structures the same mechanism of 'modernisation', as visible for example in the prolongation of the working life of women just like in nuclear families after the mid-century compromise in other countries. The direction of the facilitation effect revealed by cohabitation with relatives is so clear that we can observe similar forms of support for many constellations of non-cohabitation with relatives in which the generations live in residential proximity. This guarantees a similar type of help flows from the elder generations of women to the youngest ones living in residential proximity.

The availability of grandparents – especially the child's maternal grand-parents – is a precondition for mothers going to work. Grandparents are really important and constitute the mainstay of the entire organisation of daily life, even when some other form of childcare is employed at the same time. This happens of course in greater proportion in middle-class families, where women gain enough to pay for childcare; women in poor jobs find in grandparents the most inexpensive care resource, the only one rendering a low salary worth the effort. It is easy to suppose that cohabitation is often a solution for this last condition: in fact, whereas 9.5 per cent of grandparents live in the same house with at least one grandchild, 11.2 per cent of grandmothers do (18.6 per cent if aged 75 or more) (ISTAT, 1999a).

More generally, grandparents 'ferry' their grandchildren across the gap in childcare services for the under-three's until nursery-school age, when coverage becomes more generous. However, they remain of prime importance afterwards, filling all possible gaps in all emergency situations – such as school's or educational services' holidays or strikes, childhood illnesses, longer parental absences.

The special quality of grandparents' aid, their unconditional availability for every unpredicted event and crisis, grants something no child service of good educational quality could ever offer. This, of course, is only possible if they live close to their grandchildren: of all couples married in the period between 1987 and 1997, 11.7 per cent cohabited in the first period after marriage with a grandparent, 34.5 per cent chose to live less than one kilometre away from *her* parents, 36.6 per cent from *his* parents, 20 per cent from both and 51.1 per cent settled less than one kilometre from *at least one* grandparent. In subsequent years, cohabitation diminishes but residential proximity increases (ISTAT, 1999b).

Kinship Support as a Complement

Such grandparent-based arrangements also make use of the available childcare services. Only in the case of very large kin networks living in close proximity can the parents of a working mother cover the entire daily needs of their grandchildren with the aid of other relatives or of paid domestic aids. This could explain the extreme position of Italy in a recent European report on care (Bettio and Préchal, 1998: 13): with the highest percentage of grandmothers taking care of their grandchildren on a daily basis. In a local survey on children in public childcare conducted in the Emilia-Romagna region, which is the richest in Italy in terms of childcare places for the under-three's (and with women's activity rates among the highest), more than 40 per cent of grandmothers took care of their grandchildren several days a week *even if they themselves worked* (Musaṭti and D'Amico, 1996).[5] This indicates that the aid that grandparents provide is probably not one of long hours daily (as seems to be the case in Spain and Portugal), but rather one of strategic hours or periods. Many grandparents also help financially (more than 20 per cent in the same survey), but a small proportion receive economic support (3.3 per cent) usually when they take care of the grandchild all day long; about 15 per cent of all grandmothers receive help from their daughters for housecleaning or shopping.

Such strategic availability shows that behind the paramount figure of the maternal grandmother there is growing space for the grandfather in an important complementary role – perhaps for no other reason than that he has retired earlier than the grandmother. It is noteworthy, however, that he probably belongs to the first cohort of retirees enjoying generous pensions on a mass basis and with long life expectancy. Enjoying grandfatherhood is a widespread social aspiration now, together with the precise – and proud – consciousness of being a modern and 'innovative' young grandfather just like grandmothers were (Attias-Donfut and Segalen, 1998). In any event, their role is of *growing* importance in their being available at strategic periods of the day.

In a sense, care is always a matter of a patchwork of resources (see also Knijn, Jönsson and Klammer, Chapter 6). The very availability of the grand-parents, for example, is often a condition for the use of the educational services whose hours practically never coincide with normal working hours plus transport timetables. This describes the habit of mothers (and fathers) not giving up the function of *managerial* supervision of the overall care arrangement. Working mothers never delegate entirely the quality of care to grandmothers, who have to come to terms with the educational requests or standards of their daughters or daughters-in-law.[6] In principle, they are careful not to play the mother-substitute role – a situation of closeness not without creeping conflicts and perhaps of an entirely new form of reciprocity to be explored by both parts. Full-time working mothers who are away from their children for many hours daily grant some appointments in time to their children that are charged with great symbolic importance. They make a conscious choice in favour of the 'quality' of the parental relationship over the 'quantity' of time it is possible to spend together with their children.

The relationship between the generations can be characterised by a gift ethics, which is however less viable in the case of the lower classes or lone mothers who do not have a choice – when care by grandparents covers the entire day and constitutes an economic good. This probably contributes to a further polarisation between the two groups of women workers, underlining that the arrangement is probably an unstable one and will need to be sustained by the state in the near future. In fact, it has been calculated that in the total 'gift' economy of help exchanges, families of all types receiving aid dropped from 23.3 per cent to 14.8 per cent, even though caregivers increased from 1983 to 1998 (from 20.8 per cent to 22.5 per cent of persons). However, families with minors and a working mother still show a countertrend: in 1998, 31.2 per cent of these families received help from non-cohabiting persons compared to 30.9 per cent in 1983. The figures and their development describe a condition of sufficient care resources for the time being, albeit one that shows an intensifying demand for a larger number of helpers (Freguja and Sabbadini, 2000).

On the other hand, a more radical shift in the responsibility of partners is yet to be realised. Even the largely symbolic law on parental leave (passed on 8 March 2000) introducing the right of both parents to take leave until the children have reached eight years of age and favouring both parents' use of it – even jointly – has no universal coverage and still depends on the contribution of employers. In other words, to be implemented the law requires an unlikely change of mentality in the workplace. Women's work histories are normalising and the extraordinary availability of grandmothers in substituting for the fathers' share of caring has been possible because of their shorter, interrupted work lives. If fathers do not grant a more important presence at home and in the lives of their children, only atypical flexible work arrangements will be open for women in the future. Term contracts, semi-autonomous jobs and temporary agencies are already growing fast.

KINSHIP SUPPORT: A NECESSARY RESOURCE FOR WORKING MOTHERS IN SPAIN TODAY[7]

Contrary to how things have taken shape in central and northern European countries, the generalisation of women doing paid work in Spain is taking place during a period of economic recession and high unemployment rates. The explanation for this paradox is that the economic crisis of the late 1970s and 1980s affected an industrial sector based on male employment in particular, whereas the services and public sector created moderate employment. These were the years when the transition from dictatorship to democracy took place, as well as the acceptance of Spain as a member of the European Union. A social democratic majority governed during the 1982-96 period, and in spite of the unfavourable economic context established some of the basic elements of a modern welfare state in terms of education, health, unemployment benefits and old-age pensions. All this meant job creation, to a considerable extent for women. For example, between 1975 and 1991 the active male population increased only from 9.4 to 9.7 million, while the female active population increased from 3.8 to 5.4 million (Navarro, 1993).

Women's involvement in paid work is low in Spain compared to other developed countries. While the female activity rate for the European Union in 1997 was 45.6 per cent, the figure for Spain was only 36.7 per cent (Eurostat, 1998a). However, female activity rates have increased rapidly in the past 20 years, especially for women below 40 years. The younger generations are introducing a new pattern of activity based on most women entering the labour market and, even more important, remaining in paid work during the period of higher fertility. Only 20 years ago, most middle-aged women, the majority mothers of small children, were housewives; now two-thirds of these women are in the labour market. In 1990, most mothers aged 25 – 44 were inactive; in 2000 a majority were active (Labour Force Surveys, special tabulation).

Social perceptions of women's paid work have changed rapidly. Twenty years ago the ideology of the traditional family based on distinct gender roles was still dominant. Surveys carried out in 1980 and 1981 show that a clear majority of the population (61 per cent) was against the employment of mothers with small children, and even 40 per cent opposed married women's paid work (Martínez and Violante, 1992: 18-20). By 1994, social attitudes towards women's employment and family models had changed. Half of the population (51 per cent) believed that the ideal family was one in which both men and women worked, shared domestic labour and took care of the children (Cruz Cantero, 1995: 56). In a survey carried out in 1997 on young Spaniards aged 15-29, a clear majority (75 per cent) supported a family model based on equal gender roles, with higher percentages among women (82 per cent) and among those with more educational skills (86 per cent) (C.I.S. 1999).

Few Policies for New Mothers

Today, mothers in Spain represent the first generation of women with a majority in the labour market; grandmothers represent the last generation of housewives. Mothers today perceive themselves as a generation in transition, very different from their own mothers but very different too from their daughters, who they believe will continue along the path they themselves have initiated. Grandmothers represent those past times when women depended on the family, or, more precisely, on the men of the family. Now the rules have changed. For mothers today, paid work is the main factor behind personal autonomy as well as a new desired identity. There are many obstacles and difficulties to be overcome if family and employment are to be made compatible though, because the social organisation has not yet adapted to the new reality of working mothers as the norm.

Part-time employment is less important in Spain than in most European countries. Since 1980, there have been different legal reforms clarifying its content and making it more attractive in a context of concern about high levels of unemployment. Recent data show that part-time workers represent 8.1 per cent, with the figure for women more than double at 17.2 per cent (Instituto Nacional de Estadística, 1999). Part-time jobs are increasing slowly, especially among young women with low skills, but seem to be related more to employers' strategies than to women's choices.

In 1999, a law was passed by the Spanish Parliament to help reconcile family and employment. It adapts the legal situation in Spain to the European Directive 96/34CE, 1996 on parental leave and introduces the right of parents to take leave to take care of children below eight years of age for a maximum period of three years and of other relatives who need care for a maximum period of one year. The new law is a first recognition of the problems that the increasing involvement of women in paid work poses, but probably only a minority of mothers and fathers will be able to benefit from it, as these leaves are unpaid.

Crèches and schools would be one main resource making work and family responsibilities compatible. The latest available data for the academic year 2000-01 show that 100 per cent of children aged four and older attend an educational institution – school or pre-school – and that 87 per cent of those aged three attend *crèches* or pre-school centres (Ministerio de Educación, Cultura y Deporte, 2000). The real problem is the first three years (0-2), all the indicators showing that demand clearly exceeds supply. According to the law, the Public Administration has to guarantee places for these ages, but this objective has not been achieved. The diversity of childcare centres for the older age groups, according to their institutional dependence, is wide (local councils, regions, central administration, NGOs), and the private sector is more important than at any other educational level. Up until 1999, parents could set off 15 per cent of the cost of the *crèche* against tax. The new system is based on fiscal deductions, that is in accordance with the age of the child and the number of children.

Grandmothers and the Family Network

Grandmothers play a fundamental role in the rapid extension of women's economic activity. The contradiction between new roles in the labour market and old roles in the family is partly solved by the help of the preceding generation of women who take care of their grandchildren while their daughters are at work. According to a quantitative survey[8] carried out in 1998 (ECFE survey), most Spanish working mothers (77 per cent) have a close relative living in the same town, in 56 per cent of cases their own mother. Their help is one of the main strategies used by working mothers to make their double responsibility compatible.

Most of the help provided by grandparents has to do with taking care of grandchildren. In half of all cases (52 per cent), the maternal grandmother takes care of pre-school children (when they live in the same town and when working mothers have at least one child below age four). In another 44.5 per cent of cases, maternal grandmothers take care of the children when they come home after school, either at their own home or at their daughter's. Often (23 per cent) they prepare meals for their children and grandchildren or take the children to school and collect them in the afternoon (22 per cent).

The help of the older generation seems to follow a double logic of consanguinity and gender. On the one hand, consanguineous relatives help more, thus explaining why mothers help more than mothers-in-law. On the other hand, women help more than men, which explains why mothers help more than fathers and mothers-in-law more than fathers-in-law. The help of grandfathers can be important, but is highly dependent on grandmothers (their spouses) organising, coordinating tasks and often telling them what to do. When grandfathers are alone, their help decreases considerably. The help of grandparents becomes even more important in circumstances such as when the grandchildren are ill or on holiday from school. Two-thirds of working mothers count on their mothers to look after their children in the evenings or on weekends if they live in the same town.

Help from grandmothers is clearly related to space. Half of working mothers with their mother living in the same town live in the same neighbourhood, though seldom in the same home (11 per cent). Lone mothers, who often live with their own mothers[9] (29 per cent), are the exception, especially if they are single. The rate then rises to 60 per cent. As a general trend, the nearer the family network, the bigger the support the family provides. Sometimes living near grandparents is a complementary strategy developed by working mothers to make this help easier.

Mother Substitutes

Paid domestic help is another private and informal strategy used by one in four Spanish working mothers (27 per cent), according to data from the ECFE survey. In most cases (21 per cent) this resource is limited to a few hours per week. It is usually well-off families who can afford to hire a domestic worker to take care of the children, but in cases of non-existing kinship support this is the only available option if mothers want to keep their jobs, even if it means allocating an important part of their income for this purpose.

Paid domestic help and kinship support have in common that another woman substitutes for the real mother during her absence. The contradiction between family and employment therefore remains a woman's problem, a private affair to be solved between women. There are other links between these two strategies. Domestic help can be an alternative for kinship support or a complement if this is not enough to respond to all the different needs of the children and the family. At the same time, kinship support often appears as the strategy used by domestic workers to solve their own problems in making family and employment compatible. Immigrants working as carers often leave their own children in their country of origin with grandmothers or other female relatives in a 'global care chain' (Hochschild, 2000) underlying the increasing marketisation of care. But there is one clear distinction in Spain between these two strategies: kinship support is seldom paid.

Grandmothers play the role of the mother. They are vicar mothers or substitute mothers whose help is usually transmitted through feminine lineage, as happens in other countries (Bloch and Buisson, 1998; Dench and Ogg, 2001). They are often willing to help their daughters, partly because through them they can fulfil a desire for independence which they cannot attain directly by themselves. Grandmothers are available because most of them have been housewives all their lives. According to what their daughters say, many seem to be quite happy taking care of their grandchildren, as it is a continuation of what they have been doing all their lives. The traditional ideology on women and 'sacrifice' might also be related to their commitment to taking care of their grandchildren while their daughters are at work.

The first generation of Spanish working mothers is therefore receiving intensive and necessary help from the older generation. The strong family ties between mothers and daughters, which are a characteristic of the traditional family, are playing a decisive role in the involvement of the younger generations of women in the labour market. The extension of women in paid work is already changing the family and will probably continue to do so. Thus the traditional family is actively collaborating towards its change through the help today's mothers are receiving from the older generation of women.

THE SOCIAL AND POLITICAL CONSTRUCTION OF WORKING MOTHERS IN NORWAY, ITALY AND SPAIN

In all three countries, the traditional housewife model was based not just on being a mother but on being one within marriage. In fact, lone mothers' involvement in paid work was high long before this became the norm for mothers living in partnership. Timing is important where the entry of mothers into the labour market is concerned because of the different economic, political and ideological contexts in which it takes place. In Norway, married mothers joined the labour force at a favourable moment. They were needed as workers in an expanding economy and the feminist movement successfully included its demands in the political agenda. However, there is an inertia of the gendered family model that might explain the long delay before large-scale child-care policies are implemented. In Norway, Italy and Spain, as in many other countries, the tertiarisation of the economy is playing a key role in the increasing participation of women in the labour market (Fine, 1992; Jacobs, 1995). Many service jobs are better suited for women in terms of skills and working conditions, even if not explicitly defined as such. In Spain, the development of the service sector explains why women joined the labour force in such a big way during the 1980s and 1990s despite the unfavourable economic context of industrial decline, decreasing jobs and increasing unemployment. The enormous rise in female occupation partly compensates for the loss in men's jobs. However, women's unemployment rates are higher than men's, which might be the reason why the economic importance of women as workers is not acknowledged even if negative attitudes towards it have largely disappeared. The second income they provide is welcome, in fact it has become necessary, but the social organisation in general and the state in particular do not feel that this new reality requires changes that concern them.

Italy is a different case altogether because the transition towards a dual-earner model is taking place much more slowly than in Norway or Spain, and also because the role of women as helpers in family businesses has a long tradition, as has their presence in the grey economy. At the same time, the increase during the 1980s and 1990s has been small and current female activity rates are the lowest in Europe. In the Italian case it is not so easy to define the first generation of working mothers owing to the existence of a large sector of informal jobs that are to a considerable extent occupied by women. What is clearly a new trend is the increasing participation of women, more specifically married mothers, in good jobs in the formal sector *on male terms*.

In Norway, part-time jobs for women increased substantially during the 1970s. This could be interpreted as a compromise between the acknowledgement of women's work as necessary for the economy and a resistance to changing the traditional ideology of motherhood. Part-time jobs for mothers were modelled according to the combination of the role of mother and worker. Increasingly, mothers worked full-time and had to develop different strategies to be able to remain in the labour market when full-time childcare was not available. There were unsolved care gaps, especially for pre-school children who required private and informal strategies such as kinship support, the help of friends and neighbours or the use of childminders. In Italy and Spain, part-time work has always represented a minor part of women's jobs. There is no social definition of 'adequate' jobs for women, because women are not perceived to be 'necessary' in the labour market (even though they are). There is an inertia of the masculine work model and women have to adapt to it as best they can. The main resource they can count on is help from the older generation of women.

The help of the family network is an important resource for first-generation working mothers in the three countries studied, but there are considerable differences in its meaning and the way it is used. The available data allow the conclusion that childcare done by relatives is a strategy used more often in Italy and Spain than in Norway, where the variety of options is wider, including part-time work or parental shifts that often make resources beyond the nuclear family unnecessary. Even for first-generation Norwegian working mothers, the autonomy of the nuclear family was greater than in the southern countries. In Norway as well as in Italy, the distinction between the younger generations of women (first-generation working mothers) and the older ones (the last generation of housewives) is not as clear-cut as in Spain during the 1980s and 1990s; many grandmothers were in the labour market themselves during the 1970s and thus less available for childcare. There is not much information for Norway about the extent to which kinship support for care was provided on a daily basis, but generally informal childcare was important until the late 1980s. We do have evidence about Italy and Spain reflecting some interesting differences in the use of kinship support. In Italy, the proportion of grandparents providing daily care for their grandchildren is higher but less intense. Grandparents complement nursery schools (which most children attend), filling in the gaps between the children's schedules and the working hours of parents. In one out of three cases in Spain (when the mother works), grandparents take care of small children during the parents' absence, a commonly used resource in periods of transition or crisis that has been reported in countries such as the former East Germany (Herlyn, 2001) and Russia (Gessat-Anstett, 2001). In addition, Spanish grandparents fill in the gaps when the children go to a *crèche* or are old enough to go to school.

A common trend in all three countries is the importance of kinship support in extraordinary situations, which are in fact quite widespread, such as children's illnesses, school holidays, parental outings or absences, or any other unexpected event. Relatives and most especially grandparents are a last resource that dual-earner families can count on when the normal organisation cannot respond to the children's need for care. There is similar evidence even from countries with generous state support, such as France, where the help of grandparents on special occasions related to the children is important and has increased in the past thirty years (Attias-Donfut and Segalen, 1998: 74-79). The prevalence of the feminine lineage in kinship support is another common trend, but it has not been possible to find much empirical evidence for the Norwegian case.

It might be said that in Norway kinship support is mainly conceived as help received from outside the nuclear family, where the childcare responsibility lies, whereas in Spain and Italy the family network, especially grandmothers, often feels responsible both for helping daughters remain in their jobs and for taking care of the grandchildren. Giving or not giving money in exchange for services might also express a different conception of the family in terms of boundaries beyond the nuclear family and what is expected of its members. For example, in the Norwegian case, payment for regular childcare services provided by kin is not excluded. Paying for kinship support is rarely reported in Italy, and out of the question in Spain, but at the same time help provided by relatives for childcare is no longer taken for granted, especially when the future is considered.

Whereas the boundaries between the nuclear and the extended family are defined more clearly in Norway, those between kin support and help from other carers are not as clear as in Spain or Italy. Private childminders were an often-used childcare strategy by first-generation Norwegian working mothers, as well as nannies and domestic help. They were often recruited via informal networks of kin, friends or neighbours, and thus based on confidence and a close relationship between the mothers and the carers.

CONCLUSION

Despite the differences in the national economic and cultural settings of first-generation working mothers in the three countries, certain common aspects of the mothers' situation are noteworthy: for this generation, the welfare state has not made any impressive contribution towards facilitating the combination of work and childcare. Generally, motherhood change has preceded social policy reform. Market demands for women's skills and mothers' demands for paid work have not only increased female employment, but have also changed family models, that is generated lone-parent single-earner and dual-earner families. These families are in need of extra parental resources for childcare. Furthermore, in all three countries – in welfare states of different persuasions – working mothers (and their partners) have managed to balance job and childcare commitments via the mobilisation of family and kin, social networks and other informal childcare services. The significance of the resources represented by the informal childcare arrangements as support for the employment of mothers tends to be underestimated in the literature. Whereas the intervention of the welfare state is often taken as a precondition for the employment of mothers in Scandinavia, and family obligations are interpreted as hindering it in southern Europe, our case studies present another story. For the three cases under discussion, informal support for childcare in the early stages of changing the gender balance of employment has been more important than the services provided by the welfare state.

In addition, the gender dimension is significant everywhere. The everyday arrangements of the mothers who first entered formal employment have largely depended upon other women being available for childcare, be they grandmothers, kinswomen, friends, neighbours, domestic help or childminders. There is an interesting difference in the relative importance of types of informal childcare. While in Italy and Spain the use of kin, especially grandparents, for childcare is more common, in Norway the pioneer generation of mothers in formal employment has depended more on paid domestic help and private childminders.

The Norwegian case shows that welfare state intervention does facilitate the employment of latter generations of mothers. As state-sponsored childcare has expanded in Norway, the use of all types of informal childcare has declined since the late 1980s. Still, such services do not always meet the demand and some informal services are still used, especially for the under-three's.

The higher relevance of kinship support in Spain and Italy could be due either to formal family obligations being more comprehensive, more strongly pronounced and culturally accepted in Southern Europe (Millar and Warman, 1996), or to 'familialism' – the subsidiarity of the state to the family – being more influential as a policy guideline (Saraceno, 1994). Not to be neglected is the labour market situation of grandparents and kin, and their availability for other commitments such as daily, time-consuming childcare.

Working from the assumption of 'path dependence' (Esping-Andersen, 1999) in the formulation of welfare-state response to working mothers, it appears unlikely that Italy and Spain will follow in the tracks of Norway and other Nordic countries where social reproduction has 'gone public'. However, if the labour market participation of mothers of young children remains at present levels or increases, as it probably will, the availability of kin for childcare cannot be taken for granted when the second and third generations of mothers enter the labour market. The childcare arrangements of Italian and Spanish mothers may come to depend upon a varied repertoire of services, including more domestic help (with state support as in France, or without), an expansion of services provided by 'third sector' organisations and a general increasing marketisation of childcare. Recently, domestic help (childminders who take care of children in the childminder's home are practically non-existent) seems to have increased, replacing the less available kinship support. This is clearly related to the supply of an immigrant workforce, increasing participation of mothers in the labour market and persistently scarce social policies. But lack of state support should not just be assumed as a fact. A state of limited social policies has to do with collective priorities and options that might change, especially in a future horizon of ageing demographics where women are increasingly needed as workers and mothers. At the time of writing, something seems to be moving in Spain, where public support for working mothers is a subject of debate between the two main political parties. At the same time, the European Commission is proposing more ambitious national policies for childcare; the aim by 2010 is to accommodate a minimum of 1 in 3 children under the age of three, and 9 in 10 of older children (report presented in Barcelona in mid-March 2002). If the proposals are transformed into binding recommendations for national policies, the provision of childcare services might converge across Western Europe to meet the gradual convergence reported in mothers' labour market participation.

NOTES

[1] National figures may mask considerable differences with respect to kinship support for childcare, for example by class, regions, ethnicity.

[2] Denmark was the only Nordic country represented.

[3] The role played in different contexts by kinship support to make women's transition from the household to the workplace possible is not the only example of the importance of help and solidarity between generations in current modern societies. In fact, recent research shows the increasing importance of intergenerational relationships in Europe beyond the nuclear family both in transfers of wealth and in services, and not just in the Mediterranean countries (Attias-Donfut, 1995; Smith, 1995; Attias-Donfut and Segalen, 1998; Hagestad, 2000; Trnka, 2000; Bengston, 2001).

[4] By contrast, women who are able to re-enter the first time and find another job can manage a much more mobile career afterwards, in which the fact of having children acts as a *lesser* risk of exiting the labour market (Bison et al., 1996).

[5] In another EC-funded comparative research conducted in 1999/2002 (the Soccare project), we even found cases of grandmothers working only in those days the grandchild could be cared for by someone else; these cases were of course few and of self-employed women, but the sample was small too. (cf. http://www.uta.fi/laitokset/sospol/soccare/).

[6] This last condition was again different in Portugal in the Soccare project, where several mothers complained about vicarious mothering of the children by the maternal grandmothers.

[7] This part of the chapter is based on findings from three different research projects: 'Estrategias de compatibilización familia-empleo. España años noventa' supported by the Instituto de la Mujer, Ministerio de Asuntos Sociales (convocatoria 28-3-94), 'Las Familias Monoparentales en España' financed by the Ministerio de Asuntos Sociales (Convenio con la Universidad Carlos III de Madrid 1996-1998) and 'Análisis Cuantitativo de las Estrategias de Compatibilización Familia-Empleo en España' financed by the III National Plan for R+D, Programme for Research on Women and Gender (1996).

[8] Based on 1200 interviews representative of Spanish working mothers (Tobío et al., 1996). This project was financed by the III National Plan for R+D, 1996.

[9] Data from lone motherhood are based on a special analysis of the Spanish Census of Population of 1991 (Fernández Cordón, Juan and Tobío, 1999).

6. Care Packages: The Organisation of Work and Care by Working Mothers

Trudie Knijn, Ingrid Jönsson and Ute Klammer

Today women's labour market participation is increasing at a much more rapid pace than public care services for children in many European countries, and we cannot be sure of reaching any equilibrium between women's employment and public care services in the near future. By contrast, the tendency of welfare states to withdraw public investments, the neo-liberal credo of self-responsibility and the revival of stressing the responsibilities of 'civic society' reaches toward a welfare pluralism in which the role of the state is diminishing. Non-state pillars of the 'welfare mix', in particular markets, local governments and families, are gaining importance in the delivery of social services. In the meantime, mothers in all European countries are rapidly entering the labour market. In combination with the ambiguity of welfare states to take full responsibility for childcare while mothers work in paid jobs, this leads to the question Kristin Smith (2000) raises in her US Census article on childcare, 'Who is minding the kids?'

In the present chapter we will answer this question by integrating the macro-level of social policies and statistical data and micro-level interviews with employed mothers in three countries – Sweden, Germany and the Netherlands.[1] We introduce the concept of 'care packages', indicating the combination of resources packaged by mothers in order to become or remain employed; the concept includes all kinds of support for childcare (private, market or public) and work-related resources (part-time work, leaves, irregular working hours and shifts). Care packaging refers to the activity of personally mixing available resources provided by the institutional pillars of the welfare mix; the state, voluntary organisations, the market and the family (see for other strategies Leira, Tobío and Trifiletti in this book). Care packaging is derived from the analogous concept of 'income packaging' introduced by Martin Rein and Lee Rainwater (Rein and Rainwater, 1980; Rainwater, et al., 1986), who use it to analyse, from an actor's perspective, the assembling of various income sources by low-income families. This concept points at the way people use and substitute financial resources from the institutional pillars of the welfare mix, and has proven its empirical value by comparing the way different categories of the population combine and/or substitute financial resources over the life course (Hobson, 1994). It is also valuable in cross-national comparisons because resources differ per country, as Lewis (1997) showed in a study on lone mothers.

People not only package income. Laura Balbo, inspired by Rein and Rainwater, analysed in her famous article *Crazy Quilts* (1987) that women's work mainly exists in 'packaging services'. By doing quilting or patchwork, women pool and package resources in a way that serves not only their families and neighbourhoods, but also society at large.

'In today's society resources are channelled to individuals, or rather families, from a variety of external social institutions. They must choose from existing alternatives; "combine" available resources from various agencies and institutions, whether public or private; 'adjust' them to the specific requirements of each family member, and provide services that are not available enough through other institutions.'
(Balbo, 1987: 48)

We can assume that the same goes for childcare. Employed mothers do not simply withdraw from caring, they claim alternative care for their families from the state or their employers in order to assemble enough resources to continue employment and feel comfortable with the way their children are cared for. Rainwater, et al. (1986) also state that, because of the particular character of the institutional pillars of the welfare state, not all parts of the income package will come as 'rights'. Some care resources will have to be claimed, on the basis of moral rules, reciprocity or solidarity. Also some care resources come as rights, while others will result from pleas and bids and from a process of convincing alternative care providers that a mothers needs support to keep her job. Concepts like 'claim' and 'claiming' therefore point at informal care resources. What mothers will claim depends on social conventions and their ideas about good care, and is embedded in systems of legal and customary entitlements and collective institutions that may or may not take into account the need of employed mothers for alternative care. 'Claiming' points at what mothers want, hope for and sometimes get.

We realise that it would be more politically correct to start from the position of employed parents instead of that of the employed mother. The father cannot be neglected in this analysis. However, mothers do the bulk of care work and their jobs are evidentially the ones that are more elastic. Although fathers increasingly do their share of caring in some European countries, in particular the Scandinavian countries and the Netherlands, their jobs are seldom contested if parents cannot find a way to solve childcare in a satisfying way. That is why we, at present, see the father as one of the potential resources of care needed if the mother has a job.

Claiming Alternative/Additional Care

The *nature of care claims* (Rainwater, et al.,1986) presupposes that childcare is stable, secure and affordable. Employed mothers will demand childcare to be continuous, stable and of good quality; only then are their jobs guaranteed. Mothers will not keep their jobs if the well-being or the development of their children is harmed. In addition, access to childcare depends on its costs. Childcare costs in relation to employed mothers' income, the quality of care and even the objectives of childcare differ from country to country.

Paradoxically, while in countries like Sweden or Denmark the formal objective is defined in terms of providing stimulating and developmental activities for young children that combine education and care, such a definition might contribute more to mothers' employment than when purely defined in terms of stimulating mothers' employment, as it is formally defined in the Netherlands. The educational objective probably contributes to the trustworthiness of the childcare centres, while the employment objective might give mothers the impression that childcare centres are the only places you can leave your children when working.

Such claims however do not say at whom these claims are directed. In line with the idea of the welfare mix we identify the state, voluntary organisations, the market and the family as the institutions that can be held responsible for delivering care for young children. Each institution has its own logic and related vocabulary concerning care claims (Knijn, 1998, 2000). The welfare mix of childcare is currently shifting. Two overall trends are marketisation and decentralisation. Marketisation is very prominent in the Netherlands, where public childcare only started to develop in the early 1990s. Right from the beginning, the Dutch government stated that childcare should be a 'tripartite responsibility', implying that the government, the employers and the family should share the costs. Decentralisation to the local level was realised, and local councils became responsible for developing childcare. The funds, no longer earmarked for childcare, became part of municipalities' general social services budgets. Municipalities now had the task of getting 'childcare contracts' with local companies for places at the local childcare centres. This quickly resulted in an increase of the number of childcare facilities (from 4 per cent of all children below school age in 1990 to 17.5 per cent in 1999) as well as a higher contribution of employers and parents towards the costs of childcare (Portegijs, et al., 2002). The Basic Childcare Provision Act (*Wet Basisvoorziening Kinderopvang*, 2004), which will come into force on 1 January 2005, states that local authorities will only direct the quality of childcare and its providers, but that private companies will be the only providers of childcare. There will be no guaranteed childcare places. However, if parents succeed in getting access to childcare, they themselves and their employers are supposed to share the costs while getting a tax deduction.

In Germany and Sweden companies hardly contribute to the costs of childcare; the main purchaser is still the government, but the provision is organised at the regional and local levels. In Germany, the 1996 Childcare Act grants each child over three a place in kindergarten; this however has not yet been realised in all regions due to limited state subsidies. In East Germany most childcare centres are run by municipalities, but in West Germany 40 per cent of all childcare centres are run by voluntary organisations, such as churches. Municipalities pay most of their budget (more than 90 per cent of the budget in addition to parents' fees) (Kreyenfeld, et al., 2001). In Sweden the expansion of public childcare, either in municipal or other publicly paid settings, has even led to a de-marketisation. During the 1990s, local governments were liberated from strict central regulations in order to promote a welfare mix at the local level (Kröger, 1997). Since the early 1990s there has been a substantial growth in childcare arrangements that are publicly financed and privately operated, mainly by parent cooperatives and other non-profit organisations. By 2003 these arrangements accounted for about 12 per cent of Swedish childcare placements (SCB, 2004). The introduction of fixed rates for public childcare in 2001, and the offer of a special state grant to municipalities when providing childcare at a fixed rate – which has not been refused by any Swedish municipality – have led to further uniformity and de-marketisation of childcare.

Patterns and Conventions of Care and Care Packaging in Sweden, Germany and the Netherlands

The various institutional pillars of the welfare mix and their particular logics make up the context in which employed mothers can formulate their claims for childcare. In packaging childcare they make a selection from a range of alternative care sources. Which care package they use will partly depend on the care system and its options in their country, and partly on conventions and personal preferences. We will therefore look at the care systems in our three welfare states to see what kinds of options are available. Also important is how these options change when children grow older. We cannot restrict this investigation to the social-policy side of childcare, firstly because there is no consistency and purpose in governmental issues concerning childcare,[2] and secondly because mothers will use other sources of care than public facilities only. Therefore we will start with outcomes and then trace government activities that have contributed to creating the situation as it is.[3]

Dutch, German and Swedish women who have children have to deal differently with working and mothering. What are the most common patterns of childcare in these three countries the moment a woman has a baby, during the early childhood years and during school age? The analysis focuses on the use of parental leave schemes and career interruptions, on reductions and adjustment of working time, on the use of public childcare and other forms of paid childcare, and on unpaid childcare by fathers, relatives and friends. The final paragraphs focus on how these resources are packaged and how rights and claims come together in the actual care packages.

Taking a break

Interrupting paid work after a child is born is an important component in the care package of Dutch and German mothers. Half of the Dutch mothers of young children (0 – 5) were not employed in 1998, although the per centage of Dutch mothers that interrupted paid work went down significantly from 46 per cent in 1980 to 24 per cent in 1998. Interruptions for caring for a child increase the employment gap between mothers with higher and lower educational levels, about 33 per cent of mothers with lower educational levels withdrew from the labour market, compared to only 12 per cent of those with a higher education (Portegijs, et al., 2002). In the Netherlands, most mothers who take a break from paid work do this without any financial compensation. Seventy-five per cent of all working mothers have a right to take parental leave, but only 27 per cent take the leave because for most of them it is unpaid (OECD, 2001b).[4]

West German mothers come closest to the Netherlands in their employment behaviour. Withdrawing from the labour market is the most common way of managing care of the newborn child. In Germany, the parental leave act (*Bundeserziehungsgeldgesetz*) allows parents to leave the labour market for a maximum of three years after the child's birth. They have the guarantee that they can return to their jobs thereafter. Payments are modest and do not replace a full wage: depending on income thresholds, up to EUR 300 a month is provided by the state for up to two years, whereas the third year is always unpaid. Since 2001, after a revision of the parental leave scheme, parents who only take one year of parental leave can receive a higher payment (up to EUR 450 per month). Parental leave has become highly popular among German mothers. In the last decade, more than two-thirds of all employed West German mothers extended maternity leave for a period of parental leave, interrupting paid work for the entire three-year duration. In East Germany the per centage of mothers taking parental leave is even slightly higher than in West Germany, but East German women on average take leave for a shorter time (Beckmann and Kurtz, 2001; Engelbrech and Jungkunst, 2001b). One-third of all East German mothers who recently returned to the labour market after parental leave had not taken more than one year of leave. This seems to be influenced by economic reasons, but also by the still-surviving former GDR concept of parental leave consisting of one baby year only. Due to the different income thresholds for the first six months and afterwards, 92 per cent of all parents received parental leave cash benefits during the first six months of 2000, but only 51 per cent afterwards. Between 1987 and 2001 there was a continuous decline of the share of parents who had the right to claim payments after six months because the income threshold was not dynamised (Engstler and Menning, 2003: 115).

Hardly any Swedish mothers leave their jobs for a long time; only 15 per cent of the mothers of 1-5-year-olds are not employed. However, almost every Swedish mother takes parental leave for an average of eleven months when the child is young. On average, 12 per cent of the mothers of 1-5-year-olds are actually on parental leave (Haas and Hwang, 1999). Swedish parental care insurance is the best of all three countries; it is paid to either parent with 80 per cent income replacement (90 per cent for civil servants) for 390 days of which the other parent has to use 60 days. A flat-rate benefit is paid for an additional 90 days. This parental leave can be used on a part-time or full-time basis, and holds until the child is eight years old. Mothers used 93 per cent and fathers used 7 per cent of the leave days during the first year of children born in 2001; it is more common among fathers to take parental leave when the child becomes older (22 per cent of fathers of children aged two, born in 2001). In addition to parental leave, fathers have the right to a 10-day paternity leave around the birth date of the child. Almost all fathers use this right (SCB, 2004).

In all three countries, taking a break from employment means that the mother will be the main caretaker for her children and will probably need additional care only incidentally. Opting out in Sweden therefore means that mothers get a relatively generous benefit and continue to be part of the labour market. By contrast, opting out in the Netherlands often means disconnecting oneself from the labour market without any income compensation. In Germany it means remaining part of the labour market for the duration of the parental leave (up to three years), but getting only moderate payments for six months in most cases. Employed mothers in the Netherlands, Germany and Sweden give various arguments for interrupting paid work when becoming a mother. Half of the interviewed Dutch mothers with lower educational levels withdrew completely from the labour market after having had their first baby. Most said that it had always been their intention to become a full-time housewife during the first years of their children's life:

'Yes, I have always said that I will stay at home when I have children. And when they go to school I will feel free to decide what I will do then, maybe still stay at home, maybe find a job.'
(Dutch mother of two children, works now 20 hours a week)

The same argument can be heard from West German mothers, but in Sweden and East Germany housewives are scarce. Those women who are at home full-time are either on parental leave or, as is the case in East Germany, unemployed (in some East German regions more than 20 per cent of women are unemployed). This is not to say that all mothers are satisfied with the length and compensation of parental leaves. Some would like to stay at home for several additional years, but said they could not afford it. Most Dutch mothers did not take up parental leave because it was not financially compensated. Indeed, the take-up rate is much higher among employees who can claim paid parental leave than among those who only can claim unpaid parental leave. Moreover, among those employees who have a right to parental leave, many more women (42 per cent) than men (12 per cent) actually took up that leave (Keuzenkamp and Oudhof, 2000; Portegijs, et al., 2002). A reason for not taking parental leave is the option to switch to a part-time job:

> '*When my employer agreed that I could return to my job for three days a week, it was not necessary to take parental leave. But if I had not been allowed to reduce my working hours, I would had taken the leave.*'
> (Dutch mother of one child, works now 24 hours a week)

Men take a break from employment less often when becoming fathers. In Sweden[5] a certain portion of parental leave is non-transferable between the parents, and is based upon the principle of 'use it or lose it' (OECD, 2001b). In the Netherlands and in Germany both parents can claim parental leave on the same conditions. The take-up rate of parental leave by fathers is 40 per cent (2002) in Sweden and 12 per cent (1996-1998) in the Netherlands. In Germany, less than 2 per cent of all parents taking parental leave since 1992 were fathers (Engstler and Menning, 2003), and only very recently did the share of fathers taking up parental leave start to rise slightly. In addition to low take-up rates, fathers in all three countries only take a small part of the available days (for example 13.8 per cent of 480 days in Sweden) (Riksförsäkringsverket, 2002). In the Netherlands and Germany it seldom happens that both parents share the leave (Keuzenkamp and Oudhof, 2000). In Sweden, by contrast, mothers take for granted staying at home with the newborn baby, but all partners of the interviewed Swedish mothers took the 'daddy month', not least because the benefit would have otherwise been lost.

Reasons for fathers not taking more parental leave are related to their higher income. To lose the best income in the family simply has a negative effect on the family budget:

'If you have one smaller and one larger income, and if the one with the higher income is going to stay at home, then you will lose money.'
(Swedish mother of three children now working 30 hours a week)[6]

For that reason most women take this gender division for granted. The corporate culture in the father's job will also influence his readiness to take the leave; it is easier for men working in the public sector to make use of their right; fathers working in sectors with high unemployment rates might fear losing their jobs, and others fear for their career:

'My husband has also considered taking parental leave and reducing his workweek to four days, but this will probably be an obstacle to his career. We have decided that he should not take the leave, one does not throw away a career because of such a leave!'
(Dutch mother of one child, works 24 hours)

Whereas in all three countries a majority of the employed mothers would have liked to extend the period of parental leave, some mothers wanted to return to their jobs within a few months of childbirth. Not all mothers enjoy staying at home:

'I went back to work for one night a week when my son was about four months old. I did it for my own sake. I enjoyed being back at work.'
(Swedish mother of two children, works 34 hours a week)

'I only took maternity leave. I liked to go back to work. I felt no need to take parental leave. You are just at home, no car is available and it is like being locked up in the house.'
(Dutch mother of three children, works 24 hours a week)

'When I was staying at home at the time my child was very small, I nearly went mad …. It means "only being at home", always on call. You can't do anything and finish it, and this goes on for years. I simply can't bear that.'
(West German mother of two children, works full-time)

In all three countries a majority of mothers want to interrupt their careers to care for their children for a while, but a variety of attitudes exists in each country. Statistically, there are clear differences between these countries. About half of the Dutch mothers, in particular those with lower educational levels, stay at home until their children reach school age. Most West German mothers take a break of three years, and the majority of Swedish and East German mothers return to work within one to two years of childbirth. Differing parental leave schemes offer some explanation for the various leave periods, for example the differences between the behaviour of Dutch and

Swedish mothers. However, the difference in employment behaviour between West and East German mothers shows that mothers from both parts of Germany behave differently under the same parental leave scheme: both groups use it, but the average time of parental leave (still) differs considerably, being much longer in the West. Social conventions about care and the family's economic situation structure mothers' behaviour as well as social policy.

Part-time work and the reduction of working hours

After returning to the labour market or as a source of care packaging, many mothers reduce work hours. The three countries differ enormously in mothers' choice of part-time jobs and in what is *understood* to be a part-time job. In Sweden most mothers return to a part-time job, but part-time work in Sweden means working for so many hours a week that these jobs are not even considered as part-time jobs by the European Commission (Blossfeld and Hakim, 1997). The number of working hours increases by educational level; 70 per cent of all mothers of children aged 0-18 works full-time compared to about half of mothers with the lowest educational level (SCB, 2000). In the Netherlands, by contrast, almost no employed mother works more than 32 hours a week (Knijn and Van Wel, 2001b). Of the mothers with the lower educational levels, about a third withdraw from their jobs and an additional 22 per cent reduce their working hours, while among those mothers with higher educational levels only 12 per cent withdraw and an additional 50 per cent reduce their working hours (Portegijs, et al., 2002).

In West Germany, most mothers return to a part-time job after parental leave, whereas in East Germany the majority of mothers return to a full-time job. West German women, especially those with children below 10, work part-time after a period of parental leave. At the turn of the twenty-first century, 52 per cent of all West German working mothers with a child below 10 works less than 20 hours a week, another 17 per cent works 'long' part-time jobs (between 21 and 36 hours). Less than one-third (31 per cent) works full-time. In East Germany, on the contrary, about two thirds (65 per cent) of all working mothers with a child below 10 works in a full-time job, 23 per cent between 21 and 36 hours, and only 12 per cent less than 20 hours a week (Federal Office for Statistics, Microcensus 2000). Hence if East German women work part-time, their working patterns are more similar to the Swedish patterns with long part-time jobs than to the West German patterns.

Reducing working hours is an important strategy for employed Dutch mothers with lower educational levels. They all say that if they were not allowed to reduce their working hours they would not have kept their jobs. These mothers claim time to care by reducing their working hours, the implication is, however, that they do so at the cost of income; they pay for 'caring time' themselves, not only during the time they work less, but also for future pensions.

Also, some West German and Dutch mothers working full-time feel stressed and wish to reduce working hours, or even want to stop working. Earlier studies in the 1990s showed that East German mothers, by contrast, regarded their full-time employment as something very normal even if they had small children. One very remarkable result of the interviews in the current research project was that many East German mothers have obviously begun to think about shorter working hours to reconcile work and care. Almost two-thirds of the interviewed East German mothers mentioned part-time work (mostly for themselves, in some cases for both partners) as the ideal solution to their shortage of time, like the mother who said her big wish was:

> '*to get the chance to work part-time one day. That would be good when the children start to go to school. But I don't have that option, we simply don't have part-time jobs.* '
> (East German mother of two children, works full-time)

There were surprising similarities in the East German mothers' personal visions: in most cases, 30 hours of paid work per week was regarded to be the ideal way of reconciling work and care. This ideal of 'long part-time' is again more similar to the Swedish case. A decade after reunification, mothers' ideas about working and mothering have obviously started to change in East Germany, although almost none of the interviewed women actually did have *concrete* plans to reduce their working hours, due to either financial reasons or the impossibility to find an appropriate part-time job.

In all three countries, part-time work is now rather well regulated. Part-time workers in the Netherlands have the same work protection as full-time workers; minimum wages, working conditions, health insurance, and so on are all similar. Moving from full-time to part-time work is facilitated even more since the introduction of the Working Hours (Adjustment) Act in 2000. This law gives employees the right to reduce or extend their working hours, and employers can only refuse when they can prove that the company's interest is threatened. In Germany a similar law was passed under the red-green government in 2001. In Sweden, parents are entitled to reduce their working hours by 25 per cent until the child is eight years old, and in 2002 the rights of parents to decide about when to take time off was strengthened.

Adjusted and/or flexible working time
Mothers working full-time as well as part-time often try to claim flexible working time arrangements. Such arrangements exist for working only during

school hours, starting early in the morning, shortening lunch breaks, working night and weekend shifts, and working (partly) at home. Mothers with higher educational levels, the majority working in the public sector, often have better options than those with lower educational levels. Working as a teacher implies that the working hours fit in with the children's schooldays, and working as a civil servant can offer the opportunity to work at home now and then.

> *'Being a teacher is the only job you can do without having all these problems [with care during school holidays] all the time. I am happy that I could realise this.'*
> (West German mother of one child, works full-time)

Mothers with lower educational levels often work in care/healthcare jobs or lower-rank administrative jobs in which working times are less easy to change. In all three countries, interviewed mothers say that working non-standard working hours is a prerequisite for being able to work, or for working as many hours as they do. The meaning of adjusted working hours, however, is all but the same in these countries. Although they work part-time, many Dutch mothers claim working times that fit in with their children's school hours, their partners' working hours, and sometimes even with their children's holidays. In particular, working mothers with lower educational levels regard their job as an option that may not harm their family life. These mothers stress that they would not have taken these jobs if the working times contradicted their family time, they claim adjusted working times take 'the best of both worlds', not putting much value on the loss of economic independence. This behaviour could only be successful, however, under the booming Dutch economy of the 1990s, when employers were more than happy to get any employees at all.

For mothers working full-time, adjusting working hours often means working outside office hours. This may help fulfil other 'motherly' responsibilities, albeit at the expense of tiredness and feelings of guilt that easily result from not being available at all times when the children are at home:

> *'You feel guilty. It was hard but it had to go. And you have to think like this; the children have never been used to anything else. So they don't know anything else. But I would like to stay at home. But then we had bought this house and the interest rates went up. We simply had to pay.'*
> (Swedish mother of two children, works 40 hours a week)

For many Swedish, some German and a very small minority of Dutch working mothers, adjusting working hours is one way of arranging care for children when having a full-time job. In Sweden, the government has rejected a claim for a general reduction of working hours (to 35 hours a week). Instead, an extension of vacation time is discussed along with an increased flexibilisation in the use of working time over the day and over the year. Most West German interviewees found that combining a full-time job with childcare was a very tiring strategy; however they were quite content with *how they had adjusted* their working time. What they regarded as tiring was more the *combination* of work with a range of household and care tasks. Dutch mothers, in particular the ones with lower educational levels, regard flexible working hours as a claim to reconcile part-time work and care, under the domination of family time.

Public childcare and other forms of paid childcare
Formal and paid childcare provisions differ considerably in the three countries. In Germany there was a ratio of 90 available places in kindergarten per 100 children aged 3-6 in 2000 (with a ratio of 88/100 in West Germany and even more than 100/100 in East Germany). The high coverage in East Germany is the result of the decreasing number of children despite the fact that some kindergartens have closed down. In West Germany the coverage increased steadily after the 1996 law that guaranteed every child aged three and older a place in a kindergarten. Available places for children below the age of three are still very scarce; the overall ratio in 2002 was 8.5 places per 100 children (2.7 in West Germany and 37 in East Germany) (Statistisches Bundesamt, 2003; Bäcker et al., 2004). In Sweden 48 per cent, 77 per cent and 82 per cent of respectively all one-, two- and three-year-olds attended pre-schools in 2002. Almost no children below the age of one attended pre-school (65 per cent of all 1-5-year-olds attend for more than 28 hours per week) (Skolverket, 2004), while in the Netherlands 17.5 per cent of children below school age attended a kindergarten, albeit almost none on a full-time basis (Portegijs, et al., 2002). Going to formal childcare for a part of the week (usually half-days) is much more common for West (51 per cent) than for East (31 per cent) German children, and is the dominant pattern in the Netherlands. Spending the afternoons in formal childcare (*Hort*) is quite widespread (22 per cent) among schoolchildren in East Germany, but this habit does not exist at all in West Germany (6 per cent) (Bäcker et al., 2004). Many mothers have to make the decision to take their children to a childcare centre at a young age if they do not want to lose a substantial part of their income; only Swedish mothers have the option of caring for their children for one year while getting relatively high benefits. Swedish mothers who are employed or studying are also privileged because municipalities are obliged to offer childcare for children aged 1-12, and because childcare is highly subsidised. All the interviewed Swedish mothers expect to get a public

childcare place, and few had to wait for a place.

Most East German mothers did not meet difficulties in finding municipal childcare centres for their children (Lindon, 2000). In West Germany and the Netherlands the situation is very different. Although the 1996 German law that guarantees every child aged three and older a place in a public childcare institution has led to a considerable increase of the coverage of public childcare in West Germany, West German mothers still have problems getting a place in a kindergarten if they want a specific childcare facility, if they are looking for a full-time place (which is not guaranteed by law), or if they live in certain regions. Although parents with low incomes and parents with several children in the same childcare institution often get reduced fees, childcare costs undoubtedly influence mothers' labour supply (especially those with lower educational levels). In the interviews with women who currently did not work at all or only in a small job, the combination of high marginal tax rates for the second income and additional care costs was repeatedly mentioned as the main reason for not working or not extending one's working hours. Several other mothers who had recently taken up a full-time job complained that hardly any extra money was left after taxes and additional childcare costs. Given this institutional setting, many partnered women with lower educational levels prefer to do the care themselves for a number of years:

> '*In my tax group one doesn't earn that much, it is not worth working full-time, I have figured that out. I would have to pay more for after-school care, for childcare, so there is not much left, no, part-time is enough.*'
> (West German mother, two children, works 24 hours)

On the other hand, there is evidence that West German mothers would be willing to pay more for care; for the majority of parents, *costs* of care are a minor problem compared to the deficits in *availability* of care (Engelbrech and Jungkunst, 2001a).Very few of the interviewed Dutch employed mothers with lower educational levels use paid childcare, although many had considered taking their children to a childcare centre. Many Dutch people reject the importance of public childcare as a suitable form of care for young children (about 60 per cent disagrees with bringing babies and one-third disagrees with bringing toddlers to childcare) (Portegijs, et al., 2002). For the rest, the main complaints of the mothers concern the costs of childcare and the long waiting lists.

> '*[Because of the costs of childcare] only EUR 50 of my monthly salary were left. In retrospect I could have better stopped working, then my husband also would have had a higher net income.*'
> (Dutch mother of two children, works 18 hours a week)

In contrast to the majority of Dutch and West German mothers, Swedish and East German mothers regard public childcare as a 'social benefit' for their children. Only a few Swedish mothers think that their children would like them to stay at home, also because it could be difficult to find playmates during daytime.

In all three countries the use of public childcare is the dominant form of paid childcare, but not all employed mothers use it to the same extent. In the Netherlands, employed mothers with higher educational levels make use of public and subsidised childcare much more than mothers with lower educational levels. In Sweden, mothers with higher and lower educational backgrounds use municipal day-care centres to about the same extent. However, mothers with a higher education use privately run (but publicly financed) day-care centres more often than less well-educated mothers (18 per cent compared to 3 per cent) (Skolverket, 2001a and b). When childcare centres, like the Swedish, are known for their good professional care, this becomes an important reason for taking children to public childcare. Availability, affordability and in particular continuity are other important motives. Despite the fact that day-care mothers/guest parents are part of the public childcare system in Sweden, childcare centres are more stable resources than private childminders or day-care mothers; parents can count on centres much more than they can count on day-care mothers. Day-care mothers therefore only provide a marginal portion of the care for young children, for about 6 per cent of all German families (Ludwig et al., 2002), about 7 per cent of all Swedish families (SCB, 2004) and about 3 per cent of Dutch children (Portegijs, et al., 2002).

Although mothers in Germany, Sweden and the Netherlands tend to prefer public childcare, there may be reasons to opt for private childcare facilities, such as having no choice because of working schedules, preferring the intimate relationship between the family and the day-care mother, the small number of children attending, and fewer risks of infections and diseases. Swedish and German day-care mothers only take care of young children temporarily; if a place in a childcare centre becomes vacant, children will go there. In Germany, day-care mothers are also employed for small children under three because of a lack of public childcare facilities and the wish to get more personal care for one's child.

A final privately paid option for childcare is workplace childcare. This option is not well developed in Sweden, where childcare is public and most of it is publicly financed. Only 1 per cent of Swedish children is enrolled in childcare facilities provided by employers (Skolverket, 2001a; OECD, 2001b). In the Netherlands, 25 per cent of all childcare places in 1999 were publicly subsidised, while 45 per cent of all childcare places were paid for by employers. The percentage of childcare places that is paid by the parents' company increased steadily from a third in 1996 to almost half of all places in 1999 (Portegijs, et al., 2002). In Germany, kindergartens at the workplace are mainly restricted to big firms. Among the interviewed German mothers, hardly anyone made use of company-financed childcare, while among the Dutch mothers several made use of childcare that received a financial contribution from their company:

> *'The childcare centre is in our building and is in particular available for our employees. It is very expensive if your company does not pay for it but now we only pay EUR 130 per month and the boss (= company TK) pays the rest. That is reasonable, for that money we could never get a private childminder.'*
> (Dutch mother of one child, works 16 hours a week)

In both Germany and the Netherlands, most firms that invest money in childcare have contracts with private childcare agencies that help mothers find the right day-care mother or childcare centre. Such work-related childcare makes parents rather dependent on their jobs and can hamper their job mobility; childcare facilities or fees bind them to their companies.

Unpaid childcare by fathers, relatives and others
Equal sharing of work and care with fathers is still an objective of many mothers, but in practice this is not so easy. Promoting fathers' involvement is also an official goal of some European countries, for instance through parental leave schemes. After this period of caring for a new-born baby, fathers seldom reduce their working hours or adjust their working times. In the Netherlands and Sweden, only 10 per cent and 4 per cent respectively of all fathers of children below the age of five work part-time (Knijn and van Wel, 2001; SCB, 2002). In Germany, 8 per cent of all fathers with minor children in the household work part-time (Engstler and Menning, 2003). Fathers are nonetheless of some help to employed mothers as informal carers. Dutch mothers say that their partner is the most important informal care resource for an average of one day a week. Some fathers working full-time have adjusted their working times a bit in order to be at home when the mothers work, or they care for the children when mothers work odd shifts:

> *'I start to work between 7 and 8 in the morning to be able to come home at a reasonable time around four o'clock .... As my partner takes the youngest child to the childcare centre in the morning, he will not be at his work until 9 o'clock and then will not be home until 6:30 when we are having our evening meal.'*
> (Swedish mother of two children, works 30 hours a week)

Overall, in the 1990s fathers were more engaged in caring for children and housework than they were in the past.[7] In Sweden and the Netherlands, their share even doubled. In Germany there was a considerable increase in paternal engagement in childcare, but only a modest increase in the engagement in housework. The most recent time budget data (from 2000) reveals that the burden of housekeeping and childcare is more evenly distributed among East German couples than among West German couples. The reason, however, is not that East German fathers spend more time on housekeeping and childcare than their Western counterparts, but that East German mothers spend less time on it than West German mothers (Künzler et al., 2001; Klammer and Klenner, 2004). In all three countries we found mothers who are satisfied as well as dissatisfied with their partners' help in care work, irrespective of the mother's workload and the amount of help she gets from other resources. In Germany, employed mothers are generally more content with their life than housewives (Ludwig et al., 2002). Interestingly, the overall satisfaction was highest among the relatively few partnered mothers working full-time in West Germany and their part-time counterparts in East Germany, precisely the groups that do *not* follow the most common working pattern in their part of the country.

Other women apologise for their partners' lack of help by referring to the husband's inability to care:

'No, it wouldn't be of any help if he got up in the morning with us. Like us he is also in a bad mood in the morning. It would just be another one standing around not knowing what to do.'
(West German mother of two children, works full-time)

Some women were very discontent with their partner's unwillingness to share care work:

'I said stop and demanded a more fair division of labour. I ended up taking care of his aquarium. So I have taken my hands off his aquarium, to the fright of the fish. Many times they have been hanging on the surface. Then I could hardly hold back. That is what's wrong, you usually just do it. But I am NOT doing it again, so they will die.'
(Swedish mother of three children, works 40 hours a week)

Many Dutch mothers with lower educational levels argue that they do not want to take any risk concerning their husbands' income and career; they are the breadwinners and consequently they just want them to be happy in their jobs. In addition, some mothers say that they do not want their partners to interfere in their domain:

'It would be nice if he worked less, but it should absolutely not be the opposite. I can do my things at home rather easily ..., it is a bit my domain. Neither of us would like it if it was the other way around.'
(Dutch mother of two children, works seven hours a week)

In Sweden, better-educated parents of children below the age of seven ideally see both parents working part-time and sharing care work. However, a third of the parents with lower educational levels with children younger than seven prefers a family with a working father and a homemaking mother. Few parents, irrespective of educational background, see two full-time working parents as the ideal family type (SCB, 1994). In addition, fathers with higher educational levels and relatively higher incomes as well as fathers whose wives have higher educational levels take parental leave to a higher extent than fathers with lower incomes and educational levels (Riksförsa-kringsverket, 2002). In the Netherlands, the dominant trend among parents of young children is the one-and-a-half earner family, with mothers doing the part-time job and most of the care work. Both parents working part-time, both parents working full-time and the single-earner family are exceptions to this pattern. Of these 'deviant' family types, couples in which both father and mother work part-time and share the care work with their partner have the least wishes of changing their life patterns. Housewives and couples in which both parents work full-time have the most wishes for change. Mothers working full-time wish more time for care for themselves as well as their partners, while about half of the housewives wishes to find a large part-time job (Knijn and Van Wel, 2001b).

Despite its importance, only some figures are available about informal paid and unpaid childcare. Grandparents – especially grandmothers – play by far the most important role as additional informal carers:

'Grandma and grandpa close by, that would of course be the best, for grandma and grandpa and also for us. Because it keeps them young and we have the feeling that we wouldn't give the child to just anybody. People I don't know well ..., that is not what I would like.'
(German mother, one child, works full-time)

In the late 1990s, the grandmother was one of the three most important private carers in 18 per cent of all German families with children aged 3-10. In 25 per cent of the families with both partners working full-time, grandmothers even care on a regular basis, with some differences between West (28 per cent) and East Germany (22 per cent), where fewer grandmothers have time to care for their grandchildren because many of them work full-time themselves (Ludwig et al., 2002). Probably the role of grandmothers as a stable resource in families' care packages will also

diminish within the next generation, when labour market participation of
West German women increases (Klammer, 2001b). Compared to mothers,
fathers and grandmothers, other relatives only play minor roles as *regular*
carers.

In the Netherlands, working mothers rely on the grandparents to a great
extent. The use of informal childcare is at least as high as the use of formal
childcare (Keuzenkamp and Oudhof, 2000; Knijn and Van Wel, 2001b).
About half (49 per cent) of the employed mothers of young children (0-12)
make use of informal childcare. Informal and unpaid childcare by
grandparents is by far the most important among the informal childminders in
these families (35 per cent, for 1.6 days a week on average). Other relatives
take care for children in 9 per cent of all families with children (0-12 years
old) for one day a week on average, and 10 per cent of those families share
care with other parents and friends for 0.7 days a week on average (Knijn and
Van Wel, 2001b).

In Sweden, help from grandparents is welcome occasionally, but not on a
regular basis. Swedish parents rely very little on grandparents, friends and
relatives for structural care, but they are helpful in filling the gaps in-between
public and parental care. Only 1 per cent of Swedish 1-5-year-olds was cared
for by a private childminder or by relatives in 2002, but the proportion has
risen to 5 per cent for children aged one (SCB, 2004).

Care by fathers and relatives sometimes constitutes an important part of
the care package of employed mothers. Although it is still low, fathers' share
in childcare seems to be increasing in all three countries, but many mothers
still wish that fathers did a greater share. Care support by grandmothers (and
other relatives) obviously is negatively related to the availability of public
childcare and to the employment patterns of the older generation of women.
It hardly exists in Sweden, but is of major importance in the Netherlands and
West Germany. In the latter countries, grandparents cover the gaps in care
that result from a lack of public childcare, irregular school times and long
school vacations. Grandparents are often available to fill the gaps or to care
in cases of emergency.

School attendance and after-school care
School attendance relieves mothers from arranging care during the school
day. In Sweden, 98 per cent of 6-year-olds attend one year of pre-school or
regular school before starting compulsory school at the age of seven. Care is
offered for most schoolchildren before and after the school day (66 per cent
of 6-9 year-olds). A hot lunch is served during the day and a light meal in the
afternoon. The contrast is sharp with the Netherlands and Germany,
especially the West. In the Netherlands, compulsory school starts at the age
of five and almost all children attend pre-school classes at the age of four.

Many children, especially in the countryside, still come home at lunchtime, schools end no later than 3 o'clock, and after-school care is only available for 2 per cent of all school-aged children and is not always of good quality (Portegijs, et al., 2002). In Germany, school starts at the age of six and usually covers half a day only; in West Germany, primary school (ages 6-10) usually ends between noon and 1 o'clock. Only about 6 per cent of all German schoolchildren aged 6-14 go to public care in the afternoons (*Hort*). The average of 6 per cent disguises big differences between both parts of the country: whereas coverage of afternoon care (by *Horts*) was still about 22 per cent in East Germany in 2002, in West Germany it was only 3 per cent (Statistisches Bundesamt, 2003; Bäcker et al., 2004).

In Sweden, municipalities are obliged to organise care for schoolchildren before and after schooldays. Out-of-school care, also open during vacation time, is offered at leisure-time centres, by day-care mothers or by clubs organising leisure-time activities. These services are often offered in school buildings and there are no sharp boundaries between pre-school arrangements, regular school hours and leisure-time centres. Consequently, parents are relieved from arranging transport of the children from one activity to another. The children of the interviewed Swedish mothers continued attending those public services even during the first years at school. Almost all visited a leisure-time centre during schooldays, although mothers often try to minimise that daily stay for schoolchildren. Sometimes they continue to pay for a place in the centres while the children come home directly after school to manage a few hours a day themselves. A mother explains this double strategy:

'*they know that when they don't get along and don't manage, then they have to go back to the leisure time centre.*'
(Swedish mother of two children, works 40 hours a week)

In the Netherlands, only a few children (2 per cent) go to after-school care. Mothers with lower educational levels in particular want to be at home when the children's school day is over, and most of them do not think about after-school care at all:

'*There are those parents with high incomes and fast careers. The children of these parents are in childcare from the time they are only six months old. When they are 4 they go to after-school care, being brought at 8 in the morning and picked up at 6 in the evening. I think these children are emotionally neglected, even if it is good childcare. I feel sorry for these children.*'
(Dutch mother, two children, works 24 hours a week)

Those (few) Dutch mothers whose children go to after-school care are usually satisfied with these care facilities.

Breaks in the children's regular school schedules, such as long vacations and other school breaks, demand additional care arrangements supplementing the regular ones. In the Netherlands as well as in West Germany, this problem has even increased during the last decade due to a reduction of teachers' working hours, a lack of teachers and continuous reorganisation in schools. A consequence is that many children do not have full regular school weeks, and often get unexpected days or hours off from schools. Such interruptions of children's school weeks are hard to plan and demand flexibility from parents; again, mothers often solve this. Twelve-week long school vacations take more than double the free days of employed parents. In Germany, some schools and regions have recently started projects to guarantee reliable half-day schooling, sometimes combined with lunch facilities, while in the Netherlands some schools have started to offer good quality after-school care.

Care Packaging

As has become obvious, typical care packages mothers use for children of different age groups vary considerably in the three countries. The central pillar of the package system is the state in Sweden and the family in the Netherlands. Germany is an interesting case because mothers in West and East Germany have different historical traditions and still different public provisions and private resources. Varying ideas of motherhood, fatherhood, and of socialising and educating children influence the care package in the four social contexts.

Childcare is above all a mixed economy of welfare. In none of the countries we studied, and probably in no other country, is it provided by one institutional domain only. All four domains of the welfare regime – the state, the market, voluntary organisations and the family – are involved, but to a different extent in each country. By comparing three countries cross-nationally, considerable variation shows in the way institutional domains take responsibility for childcare. The state is the main provider and purchaser of childcare and after-school care in Sweden and East Germany, it is extending in West Germany, but (still) plays a minor role in the Netherlands. In West Germany, voluntary organisations are the main providers of pre-school and after-school care, while the market plays a prominent role as purchaser and provider of childcare in the Netherlands.

In all three countries the national welfare state has decentralised childcare responsibilities to the lower local and regional levels. In Sweden and Germany (except for Bavaria) this decentralisation is accompanied by a legal obligation for municipalities to offer childcare, but in Germany this right is limited to children that are already three years old and only covers half-day childcare. In the Netherlands such rights do not exist, parents depend much more on what municipalities and private companies will provide.

The same goes for parental leave. The Swedish welfare state really contributes to this form of facilitating care too; mothers, and in a more limited way fathers, are supported in taking care themselves of their very young children without losing much of their financial resources. In Germany the state also facilitates care by parents themselves by providing a long period of parental leave; payments are limited though. In the Netherlands, the state only supports its own employees, that is civil servants, with paid parental leave, while other employees only have the legal right to unpaid parental leave and have to negotiate the payments in collective labour agreements. The Dutch state behaves more as an employer than as a representative of the 'common interest' with respect to care for young children. State control of childcare facilities exists in Sweden and is limited in the Netherlands, not only with respect to publicly provided childcare but also for privately provided day-care such as day-care mothers, guest parents or work-related childcare centres. This is an expression of the state's responsibility for public childcare; financial control is needed because parents are subsidised for using formally recognised private day-care.

The market acquires increasing importance as a purchaser of childcare in the Netherlands, but is still of minor importance in the other countries. Again, the Dutch interpretation of 'who is responsible for childcare' stresses the domination of economic logic above welfare-state logic and leads to parental dependency on family-friendly attitudes of employers. Sweden and Germany do not have a strong tendency towards marketisation of childcare; companies provide only very small per centages of childcare and do not contribute its costs directly. The voluntary sector provides most childcare in West Germany, where churches and voluntary organisations run publicly financed and controlled kindergartens.

The family, and in particular the mother, is the main source of childcare in all countries and also the one who is ultimately responsible for packaging care when she is employed. We have seen that many West German and Dutch mothers do not package care when their children are still very young; they just stay at home to care for the children themselves. Especially mothers with lower educational levels in both countries are full-time carers, resulting in an increasing income gap between mothers with higher and lower educational levels, although to a lesser extent in West Germany, where these mothers get at least some money during parental leave. Dutch mothers who want to stay in the labour market work part-time. The same goes for West German mothers after the (sometimes extended) period of parental leave. In both countries, employed mothers claim and get support from their partners and/or other kin. Fathers increasingly care for children in all three countries by taking some parental leave as a substitute for the mother when both parents work in shifts, some even by combining part-time work and a 'care day' (in the Netherlands) and by bringing the children to childcare. However, in none of the three countries do fathers take a substantial role in caring for the children. Grandparents, finally, are approached less often in Sweden and East Germany than they are in the Netherlands and West Germany.

Most Swedish and East German mothers make use of their right to paid leave, then try to use public childcare, and only sometimes claim additional informal care to bridge changes in care or work. Swedish and East German mothers package care by jigsawing informal care and flexible working hours, but the main piece of the puzzle getting is stable public childcare for school and pre-school children offering continuity, security and quality. The state is the main provider and the state logic dominates; family and market systems (and logics) are supplementary.

Dutch and West German mothers, by contrast, use either none or all kinds of resources in their care package. There is a sharp division between women who stay at home (often those with lower educational levels) to care and those who stay in the labour market, mostly working part-time (often those with higher educational levels). If care is 'packaged' during the child's first years, it is usually family members (fathers and grandmothers) stepping in. The traditional predominance of care by mothers during the first years is deeply rooted in cultural values in West Germany and in the Netherlands, and has been reinforced by the laws on parental leave since the early 1990s. However, many mothers do not acknowledge these values anymore. In both countries, more mothers would prefer to take their children to a *crèche* or a similar childcare institution, a tendency that is only partly supported by the growth of childcare places.

The shortage of public childcare for children under three and the limited access to kindergartens for over-three's are problematic for West German women. Long parental leaves followed by part-time work and help from informal carers are part of West German women's care package. Lack of childcare facilities for school and pre-school children and interrupted school times lead to employment insecurity among Dutch and West German parents, and those mothers with lower educational backgrounds also struggle with childcare costs. Reducing and adjusting workweeks as well as the support of grandparents and fathers are therefore substantial elements of the care package in both the Netherlands and (West) Germany.

Claims and Rights

Rainwater, et al. (1986) introduced the 'claim perspective' in analysing income packaging by low-income families because not all parts of income come as rights. If one applies the approach of 'rights' and 'claims' on childcare, it becomes obvious that some rights referring to childcare are guaranteed in the analysed countries:

- Parental leave is guaranteed in all three countries, although by Dutch law it is minimal and still unpaid.
- Public childcare is a guaranteed right at the national and municipality levels in Sweden for all children aged 1-12. It also is a guaranteed right for half-days for German children from age three to the beginning of school, although this right has not yet been realised everywhere.
- Part-time work is a guaranteed right for all employees in the Netherlands, it is a right restricted to parents in Sweden and has recently become a right – albeit limited – for all employees in Germany.[8] In addition, German and Dutch parents have the right to combine part-time work with parental leave.

However, East German mothers fear that the coverage and quality of public childcare (in particular the care for under-three's and after-school care, for which there is no right) might remain insufficient and an obstacle for their employment. They also fear that the bad situation in the labour market might hinder them from claiming flexible, adjusted working time arrangements. At present, however, public childcare facilities in Sweden and East Germany offer a stable basis and are much more precarious in West Germany and the Netherlands. In these latter countries, putting together a care package really means 'quilt work', demanding a lot of mothers' creativity and flexibility.

When rights are guaranteed, claims diminish, and vice versa. Claims, not rights, concern informal care (directed towards the partners and kin) and flexible working hours (directed towards employers); it also includes access to childcare facilities and (part of) the costs for childcare in the Netherlands. In particular the claim aspects of care can lead to problems, such as insecurity about one's future work perspectives. Many Dutch and West German mothers face work insecurity because of unpaid or minimally paid parental leave, and because childcare is not guaranteed. In these countries the whole care package needs to be reconsidered at children's school age and because of long school vacations, short school days and unreliable school schedules. The conclusion that the future work perspectives of mothers depend highly on the claims they have to make on their informal network of friends and relatives, on informally paid childminders and on their employers has important social and political implications. It means that women are still envisioned as mother-citizens who depend on private relationships to become a worker. A claims-based care package is all but a guarantee for developing a stable relationship with the labour market, current and future income security, and full citizenship. Inclusive citizenship presupposes that the right to care is included in the state-guaranteed employment conditions (Knijn and Kremer, 1997). This chapter shows how urgent such a right is and how vulnerable women are when they have to base their care package on claims.

This chapter has also revealed that the concepts and ideals of working mothers in the countries under study slowly converge. East German and Swedish mothers have started to think about part-time work; about half of all Swedish mothers actually do so when they have children under five. Dutch and West German mothers are claiming good public childcare and uninterrupted school times. It remains to be seen whether new legislation, for example the recent laws on part-time work that give employees the right to reduce their working hours, will accelerate this convergence.

NOTES

[1] The German study contains 53 in-depth interviews with partnered mothers with at least one child aged 3-10. About half of these families are from West Germany, about half from East Germany. The focus is on households in which both partners work full-time or at least 30 hours a week. Additional data is added from German data sources such as the Microcensus, the German Socio-Economic Panel (GSOEP) and various surveys. The Dutch study contains a survey among 1285 partnered mothers with children aged 0-12 and 31 in-depth interviews with less educated, employed mothers living with a male partner and at least one child aged 1-12 (Knijn and van Wel, 2001b). The Swedish study contains in-depth interviews with 40 employed partnered mothers with children aged 2-18. Half of these Swedish mothers have higher educational levels, half have lower educational levels. Although the samples of the three studies differ, we could detect patterns and preferences by comparing our samples with the results of national surveys. The qualitative studies are used here to elaborate the conventions underlying the claims and packages of the employed mothers.

[2] For similar scepticism towards income guarantees, see Rainwater, et al., 1986.

[3] Although our findings are based on our national studies for Germany, the Netherlands and Sweden, we can assume that care packaging is not restricted to these countries.

[4] Parental leave is financially compensated only for civil servants and for specific employees through collective labour agreements. Until 1999, only employees who worked more than 20 hours per week could take parental leave, so many part-time employed mothers were excluded.

[5] And also in Austria, Denmark, Norway and Finland.

[6] In a recent German survey, both fathers and mothers claimed the insufficient, flat-rate level of *Erziehungsgeld* (child-reading allowance) as the main reason for men's abstinence from parental leave (Beckmann, 2001).

[7] In Sweden, women reduced their time spent on unpaid work by 40 minutes, and men spent 20 minutes less on paid work in the period between 1990 and 2000. Among fathers of young children, the decrease in paid work amounts to 40 minutes per week. The largest difference is found among parents of young children: women do 60 per cent of the work and men 40 per cent (SCB, 2004). In the Netherlands, the share of fathers (children 0-5) doing housework decreased from 8.9 hours in 1985 to 8.3 hours in 2000. In 1985 they spent 6.4 hours on childcare, in 2000 it was 8.4 hours (Nermo, 1994; Portegijs, et al., 2002).

[8] All in all, it is East German mothers of small children who have the highest workload (Klammer and Klenner, 2004).

[9] Provided there are no serious objections as far as the company is concerned. The right does not exist in small firm.

7. Women's Participation in European Labour Markets

Mary Daly and Ute Klammer

Women's decision to participate in paid work is governed by a complex series of factors that extend beyond individual choice to embrace key sets of societal arrangements. In effect, the balance between female and male levels of labour market participation is embedded in a much larger balance – between the state, market, and family in terms of the distribution of resources and services in general and particularly in relation to the provision of care. This chapter explores the sets of relationships that are involved in the demand for and supply of female labour across countries. It is especially interested in identifying factors that make a difference to women's propensity to be employed across countries. The main purpose of the chapter therefore is to identify variations in female employment patterns and investigate how a range of factors affect these variations. We also wish to place this analysis in a broader context and especially to consider how recent trends in the labour market might impact on women's employment. Women's own views are also briefly considered here. The trend towards greater flexibility is considered especially important from the point of view of women's well-being and their access to employment.

WOMEN'S LABOUR MARKET PARTICIPATION ACROSS THE EU

Female Labour Force Participation Rates

Women's employment levels vary hugely. In 2003, for example, almost 30 percentage points separated the member states of the European Union (EU) in regard to the proportion of women at work (see Table 7.1 and OECD, 2004). The female labour force participation rate ranged from a 'high' of 76.9 per cent in Sweden to a 'low' of 48.3 per cent in Italy. The Scandinavian countries cluster together to form a block at the top, with over 70 per cent of women employed. The Mediterranean countries, apart from Portugal, form the opposite pole with approximately half of all women of working age being economically active. Ireland, Belgium and Luxembourg, being low female employment countries, tend towards the Mediterranean pattern. Apart from these countries, the cross-national patterning is less definite. The continental European nations of Austria, France, Germany and the Netherlands appear to form a middle way between the Scandinavian route of a highly feminised labour force and the Mediterranean pattern of half home, half market work for women. Around 65 per cent of women in these 'middle way' countries are economically active.

Male participation patterns present a stark contrast, in terms of both absolute level and the range of variation (Table 7.1). Between 73 and 84 per cent of men are in the labour force. It is interesting to note that men's employment rates vary much less from country to country as compared with those of women. When one compares gender differences in terms of the female/male ratio, the Scandinavian countries have the least differential and are unchallenged in this regard. In comparison, the continental European nations have achieved much less gender equality in labour force participation with a gap of between 11 (France) and 17 (Belgium) percentage points separating women's and men's employment rates. Once again, the Mediterranean nations of Greece, Spain and Italy, together with Ireland and Luxembourg, are in a class apart with relatively high male and low female levels of labour market participation.

It is important to note that participation rates, in recording both the numbers at work and those seeking work, cannot reveal the success of the economy in providing employment opportunities for the working age population. When examined, this too is gendered in character within and across countries – even though the gender difference in unemployment rates has declined over the last years (see Table 7.1 and for a comparison Eurostat, 1999). Women in the EU are still more likely to be hit by unemployment than men. The countries most marked by a gender gap in unemployment are Greece and Spain, and to a lesser extent Italy. Women's risk of being unemployed in these countries is about double that of men. In France, Luxembourg and the Netherlands the gaps between female and male rates of unemployment are still noticeable, whereas in half of the EU countries the figures for men and women have converged considerably.

Looking at women's labour market participation patterns over time indicates further important differences within and across countries. In contrast to the downward direction of labour market participation generally, the female trend has been determinedly upwards. The 1970s and 1980s were the high points of this trend, all countries except Ireland having seen a steady upward movement in female labour force participation in one if not both decades (OECD, 1997). Patterns in the 1990s appear to have followed a different course – it was a decade characterised by cross-national diversity. In the northernmost part of Europe, the trend in female labour force participation rates was of decline. Sweden and Denmark led this trend.[1] In some contrast to the Scandinavian pattern, the trend in countries of a liberal provenance during the 1990s was for stability. The continental European and Mediterranean nations present evidence of a further trend: women's labour force participation continued to rise in these countries although at a slower pace than in the 1980s. The Netherlands is an exception to all of these trends by virtue of the scale and rapidity of the growth it has seen in women's economic activity. In the last 25 years the participation rate of Dutch women more than doubled, with the last 15 years having seen the most growth. Only Ireland can rival this pace during the 1990s, the period of the so-called 'Celtic Tiger'. Between 1993 and 1997, the number of Irish women in regular employment grew by 26 per cent and between 1997 and 1998 alone the proportion of women in the labour force grew by 7 per cent (Ruane and Sutherland, 1999).

Women's decisions and behaviour play a central role in the change that is taking place in employment in developed economies. Indeed, calculations carried out by Eurostat suggest that the behaviour of women rivals the demographic effect (that is, changes in the size of the population of working age) as the main factor explaining the overall change in the economically active population in the member states of the EU in the last decades (Eurostat, 1996: 72). Rubery, et al. (1996: 12) demonstrate that when growth in the employment rate occurred in the EU in the 1980s and early 90s, it was growth in women's rates that accounted for the bulk of it and that without the impact of women's rising participation rates the overall change in EU employment rates over the period would have been negative rather than weakly positive.

The Amount and Continuity of Women's Labour Force Participation

Participation rates *per se* are a relatively poor guide to the extent of women's involvement in and the nature of their relationship to the labour market. The amount of women's involvement in the labour force is worthy of attention because reduced working time and the increasing availability of paid and unpaid leave for childcare and other purposes, among other factors, mask the real nature of women's attachment to the labour market (Gornick, 1999). To uncover this, the degree of participation has to be taken into account. Part-time and other forms of less than full-time work must therefore be distinguished and counted in.

Table 7.1 Labour force participation, unemployment and part-time employment rates in the EU, 2003

Country	Labour market participation rates in the European Union¹ 2003 (in %)			Unemployment rates in the European Union² 2003 (in %)			Part-time rates in the European Union³ 2003 (in %)		
	women in %	men in %	gender difference (women – men) in %-points	women in %	men in %	gender difference (women – men) in %-points	women in %	men in %	gender difference (women – men) in %-points
Austria	63.9	79.4	-15.5	4.3	5.1	-0.8	26.1	3.2	22.9
Belgium	55.8	72.6	-16.8	8.0	7.5	0.5	33.4	5.9	27.5
Denmark	74.8	84.0	-9.2	5.8	5.2	0.6	21.9	10.5	11.4
Finland	72.1	76.1	-4.0	8.9	9.3	-0.4	15.0	8.0	7.0
Finland	62.5	73.8	-11.3	10.4	8.3	2.1	22.8	4.7	18.1
France	64.5	78.0	-13.5	8.9	9.7	-0.8	36.3	5.9	30.4
Germany	51.0	77.0	-26.0	13.8	5.9	7.9	9.9	2.9	7.0
Greece	57.6	78.3	-20.7	3.9	4.9	-1.0	34.7	8.1	26.6
Ireland	48.3	74.8	-26.5	11.7	6.8	4.9	23.6	4.9	18.7
Italy	53.5	77.0	-23.5	3.6	1.9	1.7	28.1	2.3	25.8
Luxembourg⁴	68.4	84.2	-15.8	3.8	3.5	0.3	59.6	14.8	44.8
Netherlands	65.6	78.5	-12.9	7.7	5.9	1.8	14.9	5.9	9.0
Portugal	55.7	81.1	-25.4	16.0	8.2	7.8	16.5	2.5	14.0
Spain	76.9	80.8	-3.9	5.3	6.4	-1.1	20.6	7.9	12.7
Sweden	69.2	83.9	-14.7	4.1	5.5	-1.4	40.1	9.6	30.5
United Kingdom	61.3	79.2	-17.9	8.6	7.2	1.4	30.1	6.3	23.8
EU-countries. Total average⁵									

Notes: 1) Labour force in % of population age 15-64. 2) Unemployed persons in % of the labour force. 3) Part-timers in % of all employed persons. - 4) Data from 2002. - 5) Without Luxembourg.
Source: OECD: Employment Outlook 2004. Own calculations.

As Table 7.1 confirms, part-time work is a very important form and component of female employment. Thirty per cent of employed women across the EU (compared with about 6 per cent of men) works on a part-time basis. The Netherlands is a clear outlier in terms of the significance of part-time work – about 60 per cent of all employed Dutch women works part-time. The Mediterranean countries – except for Italy – make up the opposing pattern with between 10 per cent and 17 per cent of women working on a part-time basis. The trends over time indicate diversity (OECD, 1998, 2004). In the Scandinavian countries, in particular in Denmark and Sweden, part-time employment as a proportion of women's employment has been on a clear decline for quite a while now. In most of the continental countries (for example Austria, Belgium, France, the Netherlands) newer data also reveals a standstill or even decline in female part-time quotas. In some other countries, for example the Mediterranean countries of Greece and Italy or the liberal country of Ireland, there is still an upward trend in female part-time employment. This has recently led to a (slight) convergence between female part-time rates throughout Europe.

It is important, if perhaps unnecessary, to point out that part-time work is highly gendered. As the last column of Table 7.1 shows, the predominance of women over men in this type of employment is especially marked in Germany, the Netherlands and the UK. Other countries where the gap between the numbers of women and men engaged in part-time work is on the high side include Austria, Belgium, Ireland and Luxembourg.

Part-time work is not the only factor complicating women's labour supply. There is also the matter of continuity of employment. Unlike that of men, women's employment tends to be peppered by short and sometimes long interruptions. Differences in employment rates between women and men across countries are thus not only due to differences in labour supply and labour force attachment but also reflect differences in employment stability and labour market flexibility over time. According to European Community Household Panel data, about 53 per cent of all male EU citizens of working age were continuously employed over the five-year period from 1995 to 1999, compared to only 30 per cent of all female citizens (European Commission, 2003: 136). Shares of the latter ranged from about 16 per cent in Spain to almost 43 per cent in Denmark and Finland. Although there is insufficient longitudinal data on this issue, Zighera's data (1996) and other data (for example Eurostat, 1997a; Klammer and Tillmann, 2002: 172-189) indicate that there are 'dips' in the years associated with early family formation. European countries are far from uniform, however, since they manifest three general patterns of age-specific female labour force activity. First, there is the pattern, found especially in the Scandinavian countries, of relatively continuous participation rates across age groups. Second, the opposite of this, is a more or less permanent exit from the labour force during the years of child-bearing. This, although decreasing, is still widespread in Ireland, Italy, Luxembourg and Spain. The third pattern is of high participation for women generally but lower participation rates among women when they are older. France and Portugal show this picture as do Austria, Germany and the UK.

The information presented thus far on female labour force participation rates shows that, even if there are certain common experiences, one must pay due attention to the considerable diversity that characterises the situation and developments in the EU countries. Taking status and trends together, a number of country clusters are identifiable which are characterised by particular female labour profiles. The Scandinavian nations tend to be high female activity countries in respect of both the amount and continuity of women's employment. They are also countries in which women's economic activity rates tend to be relatively stable. They are joined by France and Portugal which could also be characterised as 'high female employment' countries. A second female labour market profile is represented by the UK which tends to have high female participation rates as well – yet in combination with a high share of both part-time work and interruptions for child-bearing. In a third pattern, true especially of continental European states like Austria, Germany and the Netherlands, the trend in female labour force participation is on a steadily upward course. However, participation rates are especially deceptive in these countries. With relatively high levels of part-time work (especially in the Netherlands) and an established pattern of women interrupting employment for both child-bearing and child-raising, the actual involvement of women in the labour market is lower than it might seem in some of these countries. A further cluster of countries are the three Mediterranean nations of Greece, Italy and Spain. In absolute participation terms, these countries have remained at the bottom of the female labour force participation league over the course of the last decades. It should be noted, however, that when women in these countries are employed, they tend to work continuously and on a full-time basis. Only Italy has started to become somewhat of an exception to this trend with part-time rates increasing among women over the last five years (see Table 7.1 and for comparison Eurostat, 1999). This kind of clustering is helpful in indicating some factors that are associated with variation in women's employment. The matter of cause and effect is a subject to which we now turn.

THE EFFECTS OF DEMAND AND SUPPLY FACTORS

Women's employment behaviour is undoubtedly a result of a range of factors. The context is broad, involving, along with the structure and organization of the labour market, the arrangement of home and private life as well as norms and values prevailing in society. While we cannot examine them all, our strategy in this section is to focus on those factors which appear to be most likely to be associated with women's participation in employment.

Demand-oriented Explanations

Economic and structural characteristics and the processes that they engender in the labour market are the main factors theorized to affect the demand for labour. Among them, the temporal structure of jobs and their sectoral distribution as well as the availability of particular kinds of work are to be emphasized.

Part-time employment

As has been shown, part-time work accounts for an average of almost a third of female employment across the EU. To what extent does the availability of part-time employment covary with the female employment ratio?

In the past there used to be a covariation between female labour market participation and the volume of part-time employment: high female labour force participation tended to go along with high part-time rates and vice versa. Whereas the Scandinavian nations (except Finland) and the UK manifested a high part-time/high female employment relation, the Mediterranean nations (apart from Portugal) displayed its obverse form. This covariation can still be seen at the 'lower end', in particular in Greece and Spain. In the 'upper end' countries, however, it has become less clear, since female part-time rates in the Scandinavian countries (Denmark, Sweden) have decreased. Today the Netherlands can be regarded as the most outstanding example of the high part-time/high female employment relation, since female employment participation in the Netherlands has gone up remarkably during the last couple of years. But there are some countries, in particular Portugal and Finland, that indicate that high female labour market participation does not always go along with a high volume of part-time work. Given the existence of such exceptional cases, there is no automatic or necessary relationship between the volume of part-time employment and the female employment rate. It is certainly not the case that a large availability of part-time work is a necessary condition of high female employment. If one looks at developments over time, however, rising part-time work usually went along with rising female labour market participation. Part-time work therefore seems to serve as an entry gate to the labour market in (transitional) phases when women start to enter the labour market.

Service sector employment
Women's employment also tends to be closely identified with the service sector. Indeed, it would not be far-fetched to predict that, given its tendency to increase the demand for female labour, a large service sector is crucial for female employment levels. Do countries with high rates of service sector employment have higher female employment levels than those with low service sector employment?

Although a gap of some 23 percentage points exists in the proportion of employment located in the service sector (data not shown but see Eurostat, 2003), most countries cluster around the average, wherein the service sector accounts for about two-thirds of total employment. When the size of the service sector and female employment are examined together, there is in fact a close relation. Indeed, the size of the service sector appears to correspond even more closely with the female employment ratio than does the volume of part-time employment. Overall though, the continental European nations are quite dispersed in this regard and give the lie to a straightforward relationship between the size of the service sector and female employment. There is a large group of countries that are high in both, comprising the Scandinavian nations (except Finland), the UK and the Netherlands with a share of service sector employment of between 73 per cent and 76 per cent. At the other end, one sees a correspondence for Greece, Italy and Spain in terms of the co-existence of relatively low service sector employment (below 64 per cent) and low female employment. There are exceptions too, however, especially Portugal and Finland which have relatively small service sectors but high female employment rates. This information overall suggests that while a large service sector is not necessary for high female employment, it does facilitate female employment in most European countries.

Public sector employment
The Scandinavian model leads to the expectation that a large public sector is critical for increasing the demand for female employment. If so, countries with high rates of public sector employment should have higher female employment rates than those with low public sector employment.

If one analyses government employment (data not shown but see OECD, 1997) as a proxy for public employment,[2] the size of the public sector has the weakest relationship with the female employment ratio of any of the demand factors considered thus far. The Scandinavian block, apart from Finland, is the only real cluster. Apart from the Scandinavian grouping, the country cases are more exceptional than confirmatory. Among the notable exceptions is the UK which has relatively high levels of female employment co-existing with a rather small public sector. Once again, the continental European nations are quite dispersed. The analysis suggests that the Scandinavian high public sector employment route to high female employment is quite exceptional in a European context.

Overall, the demand factors considered correspond moderately well with female employment ratios. There appears to be a systematic relation between the prevalence of part-time as well as service sector employment and women's propensity to be employed. This relationship is particularly robust in the Scandinavian and Mediterranean nations where high or low female employment is associated consistently with high or low part-time employment and high or low service sector employment. In general though, the analysis speaks against a singular understanding of the factors that shape the demand for female labour. In the liberal nations, it is the private services sector rather than the public sector that exerts the greater influence on female employment rates. In addition, there is no continental European block in terms of the relationship between the number of women in paid work and the availability of either part-time, service sector or public sector jobs. In sum, the relationship between labour demand and women's employment is very complex within and across countries.

Supply-oriented Explanations
In conventional labour market analysis, supply-side factors tend to be conceived of relatively narrowly, appearing often as human capital stock. Hence, the resources at people's disposal, such as education and training level, career experience and so forth, are taken as accounting for who is employed and who not. We believe that narrow conceptualizations of individual attributes are inappropriate for understanding women's labour market presence given that this is a phenomenon embedded in and shaped by, *inter alia*, family considerations and prevalent norms and beliefs about appropriate gender roles as they are expressed in policy. A broader analysis is therefore necessary.

Of primary significance for the labour supply of women are policies relating to the family. Over time one can see a greater differentiation in family-related policies in developed welfare states and a growth in the extent to which states are introducing or changing their policies on the care of children and the elderly (Gornick, et al., 1997; Knijn and Kremer, 1997; Rostgaard and Fridberg, 1998; Daly and Clavero, 2002). This means that the range of factors to be considered for their effects on labour supply should be broadened. As well as policies for families with children, the following analyses will also consider tax provisions as potential influences of female labour supply.

Policies on care of children
Welfare states have at their disposal a variety of instruments through which

they can provide support for child-rearing and childcare-related activities. These include cash allowances, different types of paid and unpaid leave, social security credits, and services. But the dimensions of policy that must be considered as crucial for women's labour market participation are the existence and coverage of childcare services and the existence of and conditions attaching to maternal and parental leave and benefits. Table 7.2 summarizes selected key features of childcare-related social programmes across Europe.[3]

The cross-national variation in provisions is striking. There appear to be three general work-family policy models in operation in Europe (Bettio and Préchal, 1998). The first is found in the Scandinavian countries and is a strategy of variety. Cash benefits are relatively generous in these countries but so also are leave and childcare services. The second model, found mainly in the continental European countries, tends to privilege and promote maternal caring for children. These countries – especially Austria and Germany – offer generous provisions with regard to parental leave. Child care services exist but operate mainly on a part-time basis. The orientation of this policy model seems to be to assist the family with, but not substitute for, family or maternal care. In the third pattern, care is also privatised to the family but this occurs because the state provides little or no alternative. This is a pattern typifying both the Mediterranean countries and also Ireland. Here women are given limited choice by public policy: little if any paid parental leave exists and the public authorities provide only limited childcare facilities – especially regarding children under the age of three. Women are left to their own devices in deciding whether to organise care in the marketplace or with the help of relatives and friends.

When one compares the patterns of family policy with the employment rate of mothers, it becomes clear that there is a relation (Table 7.2). It appears that when the policy package offers women a choice most of them elect to be in the labour market. This is well known from Scandinavia (although Table 7.2 does not contain information about mothers' employment rates in Denmark and Sweden).

Medium levels of policy support for maternal employment also appear to have the intended effect, as the cases of Germany and the Netherlands demonstrate. While these countries are not always consistent in their approach to maternal employment, they tend to opt for a set of policies that enable (or entice) mothers to be out of employment or in it only on a part-time basis. Low levels of choice are also associated with the expected pattern of maternal employment. However, at least part of the constraint on mothers' employment in Greece, Ireland, Italy, Luxembourg and Spain is the low availability of part-time employment.

Table 7.2 Childcare provision and maternity and parental leave policies

Country	Proportion of young children using formal childcare, late 1990s[1] (2000/2001)		Maternity/parental leave indicators (2003/2004)				Employment rate of mothers with child under 6 (1999)
	Children under 3 years	children aged 3 to mandatory	Duration of maternity leave (in weeks)	Maternity benefits (% of earnings)	Parental leave	Parental leave benefits	
Austria	3	80	16	100	24 months (including maternity leave) until child is 2	Flat-rate: € 13,50 for 18 months for mother, 24 months for father	66.5
Belgium	30	97	15	82% for first month, 75% thereafter	3 months each parent until child is 4	Flat-rate +/- € 495	69.5
Denmark	60 [2]	85	18	On the basis of the hourly pay for employees and of the income from the business activities for self-employed, ceiling	32 weeks	A maternity leave	n.a.
Finland	48 [2]	73	17.5	43%-82% of earnings, average: 66% € 406 per week (2002)	26 weeks + 10 for multiple births; further period until child is 3	A maternity leave. Flat-rate: € 250/month + supplement for other children	58.8 [4]
France	29	99	16-26	84%	36 months (including maternity leave) up to child's 3rd birthday	Flat-rate if 2 or more children: € 460/month	56.2
Germany	10	85	14	100%	36 months (including maternity leave) up to child's 3rd birthday, max. 12 months of it may be taken until child is 8	Up to € 300 for 24 months or 460 for 12 months, means-tested	51.1
Greece	3	70	14	100%	3 months each parent until child is 3.5	Unpaid	48.6
Ireland	n.a.	55	14	70%	14 weeks each parent until child is 5	Unpaid	44.4 [5]

Italy	6	95	5 months	80%	10 months until child is 8; 11 months if at least 3 taken by father	30% of earnings	45.7
Luxembourg	n.a.	n.a.	16	100%	6 months each parent until child is 5	Flat-rate of €412/month for 22 months with no re-employment guarantee (not tied to childcare) or €1490 for 6 months with employment guarantee (tied to childcare)	47.4
Netherlands	8	95	16	100% with ceiling	3 months each parent until child is 8	Unpaid	60.7
Portugal	12	65	120 days	100%	6 months each parent until child is 3	Unpaid	70.6
Spain	5	84	16	100% with ceiling	36 months (including maternity leave) until child is 3. If child below 6, reduced	Unpaid	41.8
Sweden	48[2]	79	12	80%	18 months each parent until child is 8	80% of earnings for 360 days and €6,50/day for 90 days with ceiling	n.a.
United Kingdom	34[3,4]	60[3,4]	18 (40 if employed for over 12 months with same employer)	90% for 6 weeks and flat-rate for 12 weeks (rates depending on earnings)	13 weeks each parent until child is 5	Unpaid	55.8

Notes:
1) The data include both public and private provision. 2) 1-3 years. 3) England only. 4) Mostly private provision, much lower if only public provision is regarded.

Sources: For child care provision: Kamermann (2000); OECD (2001a, b); Hofäcker (2004); for leave schemes: Eurostat (2004).

133

The picture looked similar in Italy and Luxembourg some years ago, but in these two countries participation rates of women have recently increased along with levels of part-time employment. The UK is something of an exceptional case in that mothers' labour force participation is relatively high despite a relatively low degree of support from public policies. The reason is most likely the existence of low-cost private childcare facilities in combination with a lack of 'decommodifying' social security benefits for non-working persons and a taxation system that strongly encourages labour market participation. This makes it necessary, but also feasible, for most British mothers to return to the labour market quite soon after a child is born. Overall, these analyses show that mothers' employment is quite complex and cannot be read off in any simplistic way as a function of public policies' treatment of families with children.

Taxation policy and the treatment of spousal earnings
Taxation has long been used as a measure to affect labour supply. For women's employment, the most important element of taxation arrangements is the treatment of spousal incomes. Where the male breadwinner model is supported, the second income is burdened by high marginal taxes. Privileging the one-earner household has become less common nowadays in Europe as countries attempt to increase female labour supply. However, the situation still differs from country to country, although one can identify a general trend in the direction of individualised taxation for spouses or partners.

Table 7.3 displays some of the relevant features of countries' tax structures. In general, national taxation systems tend to be either neutral in respect of earnings on the part of the second partners or to penalise them. Neutrality in this case means that the income taxes to be paid on the second income in the household are more or less the same as the taxes a single person would have to pay on the same gross income. Neutrality towards the household situation can of course go along with different absolute levels of taxation. As the table reveals, the countries where a second income in the household more or less leads to the same net income as a similar gross income on the part of a single person belong to quite different welfare state regimes.

If one considers an (additional) income of two-thirds of an average production worker – a typical female low-paid full-time job or long part-time job – the marginal tax burden of the second earner equals the tax burden of a single person in Finland, Greece, Luxembourg and Sweden. Ireland, Italy, Spain and Germany, on the contrary, are the countries where the marginal tax rates of a second earner are highest compared to a single person.[4]

Table 7.3 Comparison of tax rates of single persons and second earners, 2000/2001

Country	Type of taxation system. (1999)[1]	Person earning 67% of APW. 2001			Person earning 100% of APW. 2000			Family Tax Ratio[3]. 2000	Labour market participation rate of mothers in couple families, 1999
		Second earner[2]	Single	Ratio second earner/single	Second earner[2]	Single	Ratio second earner/single		
Austria	Separate	25.0	22.0	1.4	29.0	28.0	1.1	94	65.7
Belgium	Separate	51.0	34.0	1.5	53.0	42.0	1.3	74	71.8
Denmark	Separate	50.0	41.0	1.2	51.0	44.0	1.2	85	n.a.
Finland	Separate	26.0	26.0	1.0	34.0	34.0	1.0	100	57.7
France	Joint	26.0	21.0	1.2	26.0	27.0	1.0	78	56.8
Germany	Joint	50.0	34.0	1.5	53.0	42.0	1.3	47	51.4
Greece	Separate	16.0	16.0	1.0	18.0	18.0	1.0	100	48.4
Ireland	Optional/joint	24.0	10.0	2.3	31.0	20.0	1.5	50	45.5
Italy	Separate	38.0	24.0	1.6	39.0	29.0	1.4	84	44.9
Luxembourg	Joint	20.0	19.0	1.0	28.0	27.0	1.1	53	46.1
Netherlands	Separate	33.0	27.0	1.2	41.0	36.0	1.1	86	62.3
Portugal	Joint	17.0	13.0	1.3	20.0	18.0	1.1	77	70.2
Spain	Separate (Joint)	21.0	13.0	1.6	23.0	18.0	1.3	50	41.5
Sweden	Separate	30.0	30.0	1.0	28.0	33.0	0.9	100	n.a.
United Kingdom	Separate	24.0	19.0	1.3	26.0	24.0	1.1	90	61.3

Notes:
1) It has to be noted that while Austria, Greece, Italy and the Netherlands have separated taxation systems, they have a number of family-based tax measures. Some other countries with separate taxation also give small amounts of tax relief in respect of a partner who does not work or only working very little. 2) Assumption: First earner earns 100% of Average Production Worker. 3) Income taxes plus employee contributions of an average earner with family (wife and two children) in percentage of income taxes plus employee contributions of a single person.
Sources: OECD (2001b), Tables 4.1, 4.6; Jaumotte (2003: 30); Koopmans and Schippers (2003: 20);

The taxation system is more or less similar for a second full-time income of 100 per cent of the Average Production Worker as the respective income of a single person in Greece and Finland and Greece as well as in France, and is quite similar in Austria, Luxembourg or Portugal. In Belgium, Germany, Italy and Spain, however, second earners with full-time jobs have to pay much higher taxes than singles (data for 2001, see Table 7.3). One would assume that in the latter countries married women are discouraged from taking up of employment.

Some countries penalise a full-time job on the part of the second earner more than a part-time job, thereby giving incentives for a one-and-a-half-earner model. Some of the continental welfare states – Germany but also Belgium and France – 'punish' married women when they take up employment, or at least in the case of Germany when they take up employment that exceeds a marginal job. In Germany for example, an additional 40 per cent of gross income (a typical part-time job with a low female wage) increased the net family budget by less than 30 per cent in 1997. An additional 100 per cent of gross income (equivalent to a full-time job) increased the net family income in Germany only by 63 per cent, whereas it led to a gain of about 90 per cent in Portugal, Spain and the UK (Dingeldey, 2000; OECD, 2001b). In comparison to a single earner, tax and contribution 'savings' for a breadwinner-family household are highest in Germany and Ireland: in Germany, an average production worker with a non-employed wife and two children only pays 47 per cent, in Ireland 50 per cent, of the income taxes and compulsory social security contributions of an equivalent single person (see Table 7.3; Koopmans and Schippers, 2003). This illustrates that public subsidies for the breadwinner model still exist in some countries in Europe.

One possible hypothesis of the relationship between taxation and women's employment could be the following: if the taxation system in general, and the treatment of spousal incomes in particular, are factors affecting women's labour supply, it will be manifested in the labour force participation rates of married women. This turns out not to be the case. Actually both the relationship between the orientation of the tax system to the income of married couples as well as the relationship between the tax systems and married women's labour force participation rates is quite weak (see Table 7.3). For example, Germany, although most strongly supporting the single earner model, has a middle rate of labour market participation of married women. In contrast in Denmark a high percentage of married women engage in paid work although taxes on the second income are high. It is variations between the continental and Mediterranean countries which most undermine the strength of the relationship between the treatment of couples' earned income and married women's employment rate. While there is congruence for some of the countries where tax systems encourage participation, especially Finland, Portugal and the UK, and to a certain extent also Sweden, in general the extent of married women's participation in the labour force does not covary clearly with taxation arrangements. Nevertheless, some recent studies on the determinants of female labour force participation have again stressed the (negative) impact of high marginal tax rates for the second household income. Smith et al. (2003) show for Britain, Denmark, Ireland and East and West Germany that the tax system – joint, split or separate taxation – as well as the level and progressivity of tax rates have considerable effects on the labour supply of married women. Jaumotte in her econometric analysis of factors influencing female labour force participation in OECD countries also stresses the 'positive impact on female participation of a more neutral tax treatment of second earners (relative to single individuals)' and of 'stronger tax incentives to share market work between spouses' (2003: 2, 25).

Overall, both congruence and exceptionalism can be found in the relationship between the labour force participation of different groups of women and public policies on caring for children and the nature of taxation arrangements. Of the two factors considered, childcare policies appear to have the more consistent relation to female labour supply. However, it is important to point out that all policies operate in an environment in which they interact with other policies. Hence it is *policy packages* that count rather than individual policies. While it is difficult to demonstrate this in practice, the results of the analyses undertaken here shed two main insights into the significance of policy in relation to women's employment. The first point is that a variety of policies affect women's employment and that policies do not have to be specifically targeted at the female employment rate for them to have an effect on it. Secondly, consistency across different policy spheres matters. One of the most interesting aspects of the Scandinavian countries, for example, is how consistent policies are. In most other European countries, public policy is neither clear nor consistent in regard to women's employment. Either individual policies have opposing objectives or the overall package of policies is inconsistent. When this is the case women are receiving mixed messages about what is considered appropriate for them.

EMERGING TRENDS

Thus far the chapter has focused on some of the driving factors behind the overall level of female participation in employment and its patterning in different European countries. We turn now in the final pages of the chapter to some emerging trends and to how women feel about them. The process of growing flexibility is among the most crucial of developments from the perspective of gender, having already led to greater differentiation between women and men in regard to employment and also among women (Klammer, 2001a; Klammer and Tillmann, 2002). What is the nature of flexibility and diversity in today's labour market and how do they affect women's situation in the labour market?

Flexibility and diversity are closely connected to the growth of the non-standard workforce (external flexibility). Not only have the number and share of part-time jobs grown in the last years in Europe but so also have temporary jobs and subcontracting work. In addition, the nature and organisation of work within a company has also changed (internal flexibility). This growth of flexibility is highly gendered.

It is known that employers develop different strategies within their firms in trying to adapt to the changing requirements of the market. The flexibility adopted to support the continually shifting production of specialised goods that requires a skilled, committed workforce can vary significantly from the flexibility that allows a firm, when producing only a few products at the lowest cost possible, to take on and cast off a low-skilled workforce. Therefore enabling strategies (when firms upgrade labour processes and cultivate long-term relations with a core workforce) as well as restrictive strategies (when firms downgrade the employment relationship and de-skill work processes) are to be found (Smith and Gottfried, 1998: 96). Some groups of employees profit from these processes whereas others lose ground and have to bear unstable employment, low wages and new risks. Although gender is only one aspect, analyses have shown that a high proportion of women belong to the relative 'loser' group (Holst and Maier, 1998; Smith and Gottfried, 1998; Granqvist and Persson, 1999; Nickel, 1999).

Flexible, non-standard work is today much more common among working women than among working men in all member countries of the EU (Klammer, 2001, for more recent data see Europäische Kommission, 2003; OECD, 2004). It is not only in part-time work that the share of women is much higher than that of men; many women work on temporary contracts or their jobs combine part-time work and temporary work. While about one-third of all working women work on a part-time basis (Eurostat, 2003 and Table 7.1), among women who take up employment after a period of unemployment or household work the part-time quota is much higher. Throughout the last decade, Europe also saw a steady rise of both fixed-term contracts and subcontracting work. In 2002, 12 per cent of all male employees and 14 per cent of all female workers, throughout the then EU 15 worked on a temporary contract. In Spain – the EU country with the highest share of fixed-term contracts – as many as 31 per cent of all work contracts are fixed-term, and women are more affected than men (34 per cent compared to 29 per cent respectively) (Europäische Kommission, 2003: 118-119). One reason for employers' preference for fixed-term contracts might be the strict rules for dismissals. However, uncertain future expectations are generally regarded as the driving force in this development (Europäische Kommission, 1997: 51, 53). Fixed-term contracts also seem to be one of the entry routes after unemployment. As the European Commission has already pointed out several years ago (Europäische Kommission, 1997), more than half of the employees who had taken up employment after a period of unemployment during the previous year had a fixed-term contract.

This hints at a twofold significance of the move toward labour market flexibility for working women. On the one hand flexible forms of employment offer a chance for women to enter the labour market, for example, after a period of childcare or unemployment. International comparisons have shown that there is a (slightly) negative correlation between strict employment protection legislation and the level of female employment (OECD, 1999: 72-73; OECD, 2004: 61-125). Strict employment protection legislation (for example high barriers on dismissals, limited possibilities for fixed-term contracts) obviously protect the 'core' labour force (prime-aged men) whereas outsiders (primarily young people and women) are kept away from the labour market, at least in countries with strong breadwinner models where female employment has been low in the past. Denmark presents a counter case, however, in this regard. Where employment protection legislation is low and the labour market flexible female labour market participation tends to be high, as is the Danish case. The relaxation of employment protection legislation in many countries during the 1990s and the gradual removal of employee protection via labour law in some respects eased women's access to the labour market .

On the other hand, many of the new jobs are precarious and contain new risks because they involve low wages as well as a low level of social protection or no protection at all. More than one-fifth of employed mothers in the EU work in part-time jobs of less than 20 hours per week (Europäische Kommission, 1999: 24). Non-standard work is the preference of some employed women, being a constituent part of their family-work reconciliation strategy. At a broader level, the entry of women into the labour market alters the male breadwinner model while at the same time still supporting it and thereby keeping it alive. This is because in many cases women's occupational involvement is meant to add a second income to the family's earnings whereas it leaves the gendered responsibilities for care and work untouched. Women's labour force experiences therefore have been called an 'integration/resegregation process' (Smith and Gottfried, 1998: 104). The extent to which this is the case, however, varies from country to country.

Part-time work offers one example of the very heterogeneous situation of working women. Part-time work can mean very different things in different countries, even within a single country, in terms of quality of work, career chances, working time, income and social rights. In some countries, in particular in the liberal countries of Ireland and the UK, women's part-time work frequently means 'short part-time'. On average, female part-time employees work 18.6 hours in the UK and 18.5 hours in Ireland and more than 20 per cent of the part-timers work less than 10 hours per week (Europäische Kommission, 2003: 156-157). Germany also has a high percentage of marginal part-time jobs ('minijobs'). Short part-time jobs are in many cases precarious jobs in terms of income and social protection – mostly jobs that allow women to earn an additional, supplementary income. They can in no way be compared with long part-time jobs (those above 30 hours), which account for a considerable share of all part-time jobs in some of the Scandinavian countries – in particular Sweden – but also in France and the Netherlands, as well as Italy. The average weekly duration of female part-time work currently varies between 17.6 hours in Spain and 23.2 hours in France and Sweden (Europäische Kommission, 2003: 156-157). In addition to the number of hours that part-timers work, it is important when they work and whether they have influence over this. While flexibilisation and pluralisation have in some cases improved employees' influence over their working times, research on German developments has revealed that flexibilisation of working hours is usually determined by the employer's needs.[5]

Non-standard work contracts such as part-time and fixed-term contracts do not always reflect employees' preferences (that is, the labour supply side). This becomes clear when people, especially women, are asked about their reasons for working part-time or on a fixed-term contract. Barely 10 per cent of female part-time workers in Belgium and Spain and no more than 20 per cent in Austria, Germany and the UK say that they 'did not want full-time work'. On the contrary, more than a quarter of female part-timers in Finland, France, Greece, Italy and Sweden say that they 'could not find full-time work' (Table 7.4). Especially in Austria, Germany and the UK the main reason to work part-time was to care for children or adults.

Among women with a temporary contract, an overwhelming majority in many countries and nearly half of all women with temporary contracts in the EU could not find a permanent job (Table 7.4). In other words, their temporary contract is involuntary. Hence, the way that women participate in the labour market is influenced not only by the existing welfare system and cultural values but also, to a high degree, by the structure of labour demand and companies' employment strategies.

Table 7.4 Women's reasons for working part-time or on a temporary contract, 2002/2003

Country	Part-time[1]		Temporary contract[2]		
	'Don't want full-time work'	'Couldn't find full-time work'	'Have to care for children or adults'	'Don't want to have a permanent job'	'Couldn't find a permanent job'
Austria	19.9	8.7	46.4	n.a.	n.a.
Belgium	9.9	15.2	27.8	7.6	88.3
Denmark	48.6	18.2	n.a.	28.5	51.5
Germany	16.7	11.1	62.5	2.6	12.4
Greece	33.3	42.8	n.a.	4.8	73.6
Finland	23.0	33.8	9.2	23.3	69.6
France	66.4	22.3	n.a.	20.5	67.8
Ireland	74.1	9.5	n.a.	44.7	26.3
Italy	28.0	27.5	n.a.	4.4	40.4
Luxembourg	61.2	6.9	9.7	n.a.	n.a.
Netherlands	73.9	1.9	7.1	11.9	21.2
Portugal	21.9	20.4	14.0	n.a.	69.9
Spain	9.5	18.8	12.9	1.2	67.6
Sweden	49.0	23.2	n.a.	21.5	18.3
United Kingdom	16.1	6.3	45.2	31.4	23.3
EU 15	**32.2**	**12.8**	**31.5**	**10.5**	**44.6**

Notes:

1) Other options were: Education. illness/invalidity. other reasons. no answer.

2) Other options were: Apprenticeship. probation. no answer.

n.a.   = not available.

Source: Eurostat (2003): Labour Force Survey (part-time employment; data for 2002); Eurostat (2004b): New Cronos Database (temporary employment; data for 2nd quarter 2003).

CONCLUSION

The discussion in this chapter shows that the border line between 'women in the labour force' and 'women outside the labour force' is no longer as decisive as it was. The majority of women of working age have now entered the labour force and all projections are that in most European countries the labour market participation rate of prime-aged women will continue to rise.

Indeed, this group is seen to comprise the main potential for the future extension of the European workforce (Europäische Kommission, 1999: 22-23). Along with their rising involvement in paid work, the diversity in women's situation has grown. Actual work patterns as well as preferences concerning paid work differ to a much greater degree among women than among men. Non-standard employment of women goes along with non-standard life forms. These and other changes become even more obvious when one adopts a longitudinal perspective. Women's interruptions of their employment career have become shorter, but they now switch more often than formerly between household, unpaid work outside the household and different positions in the labour market.

In this chapter a series of factors typically assumed to be predictive of female labour demand and supply were investigated. Some factors stand out as being more important for women's employment participation than others. On the demand side, the structure of the labour market, especially the extent of part-time and service sector employment, has an influence on the form of the female labour profile. In addition, while the state's support of caring appears to have some effect on the extent to which and how continuously women are economically active, the impact of particular aspects of the taxation system on women's employment is less clear. Overall, it is important to point out that women's employment in Europe is not determined by any one factor. The variation within and across countries is strong. At best we can say that a complex of factors affect whether women are in paid work or not. A gender analysis makes it clear that women's employment is embedded in a wider social process, involving not only the content of family and other domain of policy but also the structure of the labour market itself.

The chapter also looked at recent and possible future developments. The trend to create jobs that are more flexible and often low-paid has led to a differentiation between 'losers' and 'winners' even if it has favoured a growth in overall female employment. One point of note in the emerging patterns is an increase in the average number of transitions made by women, between employment and unemployment, different kinds of employment, different amounts of hours of paid work and so forth. Another significant change is the growth in diversity in the situation of women in general and in that of women in the labour market in particular.

This is related to factors like education, employment sector and motherhood. Future analyses of women's attachment to the labour market will have to focus on these differentiations within countries. However, the fact that men, too, are increasingly hit by discontinuous work biographies and resulting problems of social protection seems to have led to a rising interest in the question of how social security can be adapted to the needs of growing diversity and flexibility and discontinuity in the labour market and in private life. This might turn out to be a chance for many women since their labour market behaviour can no longer be regarded as a deviation from the (male) norm. The problematic point is, however, that much of this new work is contingent or precarious in so far as it is connected with low income and a lack of social protection. To change this, it will be necessary to think about the *regulating idea* that underlies the 'standard full-time job'. Part of the original idea was a sufficient income and complete access to social protection. In the age of flexibility where a diminishing share of the workforce has such employment, this set of idea(l)s still has to be kept in mind. A key task will be to transpose the highest standards to other forms of work and to adapt them to the new requirements of discontinuous biographies and frequent transitions between one status and the other.

NOTES

[1] However, falling female economic activity is not a Scandinavia-wide phenomenon: Finnish rates are relatively stable and the Norwegian pattern is for continued growth.

[2] Information on the former is available on a more detailed and comparable basis than that on the latter.

[3] It has to be emphasized that these rather general indicators miss some important aspects of variation within and across programmes such as the duration of childcare per day and up to what age the child is eligible to attend as well as the costs associated with it.

[4] In absolute terms, however, the tax burden is highest in Belgium, Denmark and Germany and lowest in Greece and Portugal.

[5] Internal evaluation of data from the WSI-Archive for Collective Agreements, Düsseldorf.

References

Achinger, Hans (1979), *Sozialpolitik als Gesellschaftspolitik*, Hamburg: Rowohlt.

Addabbo, Tindara (1997), 'Part-time work in Italy', in Hans Peter Bloßfeld and Catherine Hakim (eds), *Between Equalization and Marginalization*, New York: Oxford University Press, pp. 113-132.

Anderson, Michael (1980), *Approaches to the History of the Western Family 1500-1914*, London: MacMillan.

Anderson, Michael, Frank Bechofer and Jonathan Gershuny (1994), *The Social and Political Economy of the Household*, Oxford: Oxford University Press.

Arber, Sara and Claudine Attias-Donfut (2000), 'Equity and solidarity across generations', in Sara Arber and Claudine Attias-Donfut (eds), *The Myth of Generational Conflict. The Family and State in Aging Societes*, London /New York: Routledge/ESA, pp. 1-21.

Attias-Donfut, Claudine (1995), *Les Solidarités entre Générations. Vieillesse, Familles*, État, Paris: Nathan.

Attias-Donfut, Claudine and Martine Segalen (1998), *Grand-parents. La famille à travers les Générations*, Paris: Odile Jacobs.

Bäcker, G., R. Bispinck, K. Hofemann and G. Naegele (2004), *Sozialpolitik und soziale Lage in Deutschland*, internet update, www.sozialpolitik-aktuell.de, download 14/10/2004.

Balbo, Laura (1978), 'La doppia presenza', *Inchiesta*, **32**, 3-6.

Balbo, Laura (1987), 'Crazy quilts: Rethinking the welfare state debate from a woman's point of view', in Anne Showstack Sassoon (ed.), *Women and the State*, London: Hutchinson, pp. 45-71.

Banks, Olive (1981), *Faces of Feminism. A Study of Feminism as a Social Movement*, Oxford: Martin Robertson.

Barlow, Anne, Simon Duncan and Grace James (2002), 'New labour, the rationality mistake and family policy in Britain', in Alan Carling, Simon Duncan and Rosalind Edwards (eds), *Analysing Families. Morality and Rationality in Policy and Practice*. London, NewYork: Routledge, pp. 110-129.

Barrère-Maurisson, Agnès Marie (1995), 'Regulation familiale, march- ande ou politique: les variations de la relation famille-emploi', *Socio- logie et Societés*, **2** (XVII), 69-85.

Bäumer, Gertrud (1931), *Die Frau im neuen Lebensraum*, Berlin: Herbig.

Baumert, Gerhard (1954), *Deutsche Familien nach dem Kriege*, Darmstadt: Roether.

Beck, Ulrich (1992), *Risk Society: Towards a New Modernity*, London: Sage.

Beck, Ulrich (1993), *Die Erfindung des Politischen. Zu einer Theorie reflexiver Modernisierung*, Frankfurt am Main: Suhrkamp.

Beck, Ulrich and Elisabeth Beck-Gernsheim (1994), *Riskante Freiheiten. Individualisierung in Modernen Gesellschaften*, Frankfurt am Main: Suhrkamp.

Beck, Ulrich and Elisabeth Beck-Gernsheim (1995), *The Normal Chaos of Love*, Cambridge: Polity.

Beck, Ulrich and Elisabeth Beck-Gernsheim (2002), *Individualization. Institutionalized Individualism and its Social and Political Consequences*, London: SAGE.

Beck-Gernsheim, Elisabeth (1980), *Das halbierte Leben. Männerwelt Beruf, Frauenwelt Familie*, Frankfurt am Main: Fischer.

Beck-Gernsheim, Elisabeth (1983), 'Vom Dasein für andere zum Anspruch auf ein Stück eigenes Leben: Individualisierungsprozesse im weiblichen Lebenszusammenhang', *Soziale Welt*, **34** (3), 307-340.

Beck-Gernsheim, Elisabeth (1999), 'On the way to a post-familial family. From a community of need to elective affinities', *Theory, Culture and Society*, **15** (3-4), 53-70.

Becker-Schmidt, Regina and Gudrun-Axeli Knapp (2000), *Feministische Theorien zur Einführung*, Hamburg: Junius.

Becker-Schmidt, Regina, Gudrun-Axeli Knapp and Beate Schmidt (1984), *Eines ist zu wenig, beides ist zuviel*, Bonn: Verlag neue Gesellschaft.

Beckmann, Petra (2001), 'Neue Väter braucht das Land! Wie stehen die Chancen für eine stärkere Beteiligung der Männer am Erziehungsurlaub?', *IAB-Werkstattbericht*, **6**, Nürnberg.

Beckmann, Petra and Beste Kurtz (2001), 'Erwerbstätigkeit von Frauen. Die Betreuung der Kinder ist der Schlüssel', *IAB-Werkstattbericht*, **10**, Nürnberg.

Beer, Ursula (1983), 'Marxismus in Theorien der Frauenarbeit. Plädoyer für eine Erweiterung der Reproduktionsanalyse', *Feministische Studien*, **2**, 136-147.

Bengston, Vern Luis (2001), 'Beyond the nuclear family: The increasing importance of multigenerational bonds', *Journal of Marriage and Family*, **63**, 1-6.

Benhabib, Seyla (1987), 'The generalized and the concrete other: The Kohlberg-Gilligan controversy and feminist theory', in Seyla Benhabib and Drucilla Cornell (eds), *Feminism as Critique*, Minneapolis: University of Minnesota Press, pp. 77-95.

Benjamin, Jessica (1988), *The Bonds of Love: Psychoanalysis, Feminism, and the Problem of Domination*, New York: Pantheon.

Bergqvist, Christina (2001), 'Jämställdhetspolitiska idéer och strategier', *Arbetsmarknad & Arbetsliv*, 7 (1), 15-29.

Bernardi, Fabrizio (1999), *Donne fra famiglia e carriera*, Milan: Angeli.

Bertram, Tony and Christine Pascall (1999), *The OECD Thematic Review of Early Childhood Education and Care*, Background Report for the United Kingdom, University College Worcester: Centre for Research in Early Childhood.

Bettio, Francesca and Sacha Préchal (1998), *Care in Europe*, Brussels: European Commission, Joint Report of the Gender and Employment and the Gender and Law Groups of Experts.

Bison, Iganzio, Maurizio Pisati and Antonio Schizzerotto (1996), 'Disuguaglianze di genere e storie lavorative', in Simonetta Piccone Stella and Chiara Saraceno (eds), *Genere. La construzione sociale del femminile e del maschile*, Bologna: Il Mulino, pp. 253-279.

Blasius, Dirk (1987), *Ehescheidung in Deutschland 1794-1945*, Göttingen: Vandenhoeck & Ruprecht.

Bloch, Françoise and Monique Buisson (1998), *La garde des enfants, une histoire de femmes*, Paris: L'Harmattan.

Blossfeld, Hans-Peter and Catherine Hakim (1997), 'Introduction: a comparative perspective on part-time work', in Hans-Peter Bloßfeld and Catherine Hakim (eds), *Between Equalization and Marginalization. Women Working Part-Time in Europe and the United States of America*, Oxford: Oxford University Press, pp. 1-21.

Bock, Gisela (1986), *Zwangssterilisation im Nationalsozialismus: Studien zur Rassenpolitik und Frauenpolitik*, Opladen: Westdeutscher Verlag.

Bock, Gisela (1994), 'Poverty and mothers' rights in the emerging welfare states', in Georges Duby and Michelle Perrot (eds), *A History of Women in the West, vol. V: Toward a Cultural Identity in the Twentieth Century*, vol. ed. by Françoise Thébaud, Cambridge, Mass. and London: Belknap Press of Harvard University Press.

Bock, Gisela and Pat Thane (eds) (1994), *Maternity and Gender Policies. Women and the Rise of European Welfare States 1880s-1950s*, London/New York: Routledge.

Bogen, Hanne (1987), *Barnepass – drøm og virkelighet*, Oslo: FAFO-rapport 87 (4).

Bourdieu, Pierre (1976), 'Marriage strategies as strategies of social reproduction', in Robert Forster and Orest Ranum (eds), *Family and Society: Selection from the Annales E.S.C.*, Baltimore: John Hopkins University Press, pp. 117-144.

Bourdieu, Pierre (1980), *Le Sens Pratique*, Paris: Editions de Minuit.

Bourdieu, Pierre (1990), *The Logic of Practice,* Cambridge: Polity.

Bourdieu, Pierre (1994), 'Stratégies de reproduction et modes de domination', *Actes de la recherche en sciences sociales,* **105**, 3-12.

Bourdieu, Pierre (1998), *La domination masculine,* Paris: Seuil [Engl: (2001), *Masculine Domination,* Cambridge: Polity.

Bourdieu, Pierre and Lois Wacquant (1992), *Réponses. Pour une anthropologie réflexive,* Paris: Seuil.

Brannen, Julia and Peter Moss (1988), *New Mothers at Work: Employment and Childcare,* London: Unwin Hyman.

Bundesministerium für Frauen und Jugend (1993), *Frauen im mittleren Alter. Lebenslagen der Geburtskohorten von 1935 bis 1950 in den alten und neuen Bundesländern,* Stuttgart/Berlin/Köln: Kohlhammer.

Büttner, Olivier, Marie-Thérèse Letablier and Sophie Pennec (2002), 'L'action publique face aux transformations de la famille de France', *Rapport de recheche,* No. **2**, Paris: Centre d'Études de l'Emploi.

C.I.S. (1999), 'Los jóvenos dehoy', *Boletín Datos de Opiniòn,* **19**.

Carrasco, Cristina and Arantxa Rodríguez (2000), 'Women, family and work in Spain: Structural changes and new demands', *Feminist Economics,* **6** (1), 45-57.

Chauvière, Michel, Monique Sassier, Bernard Bouquet, Roger Allard and Bruno Ribes (eds) (1999), *Les implicates de la politique familiale. Approaches historiques, juridiques et politiques,* Paris: Duno/unaf/Cedias.

Commaille, Jacques (1993), *Les stratégies des femmes. Travail, famille et politique,* Paris: La Découverte.

Condon, Stephanie (1998), 'Compromise and coping strategies: Gender issues and Caribbean migration in France', in Michael Chamberlain (ed.), *Caribbean Migration. Globalised Identities,* London/New York: Routledge.

Corner, Paul (1993), 'Women in fascist Italy. Changing family roles in the transition from an agricultural to an industrial society', *European History Quarterly,* **23**, 51-68.

Crow, Graham (1989), 'The use of "concept" in recent sociological literature', *Sociology,* **23** (1), 1-24.

Crozier, Michel and Erhard Friedberg (1977), *L'acteur et le système. Les contraintes de l'action collective,* Paris: Seuil.

Cruz Cantero, Pepa (1995), *Percepción Social de la Familia en España,* Madrid: Centro de Investigaciones Sociológicas.

Dalla Costa, Mariarosa (1973), *The Power of Women and the Subversion of the Community,* Bristol: Falling Wall Press.

Daly, Mary and Sara Clavero (2002), *Contemporary Family Policy,* Dublin: IPA.

Daly, Mary and Jane Lewis (1998), 'Introduction: Conceptualising social care in the context of welfare state restructuring', in Jane Lewis (ed.), *Gender, Social Care and Welfare State Restructuring in Europe*, Aldershot: Ashgate Publishing Company, pp. 1-24.

Daly, Mary and Jane Lewis (2000), 'The concept of social care and the analysis of contemporary welfare states', *British Journal of Sociology*, **51** (2), 281-299.

De Sandre, Italo (1984), 'Famiglie, strategie et politiche sociale', *Inchiesta*, **65**, 3-10.

Del Boca, Daniela (1982), 'Strategie familiari e interessi individuali', in Guido Martinotti (ed.), *La città difficile*, Milan: Angeli.

Dench, Geoff and Jim Ogg (2001), 'Grand-parents par la fille, grand-parents par le fils', in Claudine Attias-Donfut and Martine Segalen (eds), *Le Siécle des grand-parents. Une génération phare, ici et ailleurs*, Paris: Autrement, pp. 187-199.

Deprez, Anne (1999), 'Femme et famille dans le natalisme français (1985-1995)', in Anne Devillé and Olivier Paye (eds), *Les femmes et le droit: Constructions idéologiques et pratiques sociales*, Bruxelles: Publications des Facultés universitaires Saint-Louis, pp. 197-220.

Diezinger, Angelika (1991), *Frauen: Arbeit und Individualisierung: Chancen und Risiken. Eine empirische Untersuchung anhand von Fallgeschichten*, Opladen: Leske+Budrich.

Dilcher, Gerhard (1994), 'Politische Ideologie und Rechtstheorie, Rechtspolitik und Rechtswissenschaft', in Hartmut Kaelble, Jürgen Kocka and Hartmut Zwahr (eds), *Sozialgeschichte der DDR*, Stuttgart: Klett Cotta, pp. 469-482.

Dingeldey, Irene (2000), 'Einkommensteuersysteme und familiale Erwerbsmuster im europäischen Vergleich', in Irene Dingeldey (ed.), *Erwerbstätigkeit und Familie in Steuer- und Sozialversicherungssystemen. Begünstigungen und Belastungen verschiedener familialer Erwerbsmuster im Ländervergleich*, Opladen: Leske+Budrich, pp. 11-47.

Dokumente (1975), *Forschungsgemeinschaf, Geschichte des Kampfes der deutschen Arbeiterklasse um die Befreiung der Frau*, Dokumente der revolutionären deutschen Arbeiterbewegung zur Frauenfrage 1848-1974, Leipzig: Verlag für die Frau.

Donzelot, Jacques (1980), *Die Ordnung der Familie*, Frankfurt am Main: Suhrkamp.

Ds (1999), *Maxtaxa och Allmän Förskola*, Stockholm: Socialdepartementet.

Ds (2001), *Barnafödande i fokus: Från befolkningspolitik till ett barnvänligt samhälle*, Stockholm: Socialdepartementet.

Dubar, Claude (1991), *La socialisation. Construction des identités sociales et professionnelles*, Paris: Armand Colin.

Duncan, Simon (2002), 'Policy discourses on "reconciling work and life" in the EU', *Social Policy & Society*, 1 (4), 305-314.

Duncan, Simon and Rosalind Edwards (1999), *Lone Mothers: Paid Work and Gendered Moral Rationalities*, Houndmills/Basingstoke: Macmillan.

Duncan, Simon and Rosalind Edwards (2001), 'Alleinerziehende Mütter, moralische Rationalität und der Rationalitätsfehler von New Labour', *Feministische Studien*, 19 (1), 34-47.

Duncan, Simon and Birgit Pfau-Effinger (2000), *Gender, Economy and Culture in the European Union*, London/NewYork: Routledge.

Durkheim, Emile (1964), *The Division of Labour in Society [1893]*, New York: Free Press.

Eckart, Christel (2000), 'Zeit zum Sorgen. Fürsorgliche Praxis als regulative Idee der Zeitpolitik', *Feministische Studien extra*, 18, 9-25.

Edwards, Rosalind and Jane Ribbens (1991), 'Meanderings around strategy: A research note on strategic discourse in the lives of women', *Sociology*, 25 (3), 477-489.

Elias, Norbert (2001), *The Society of Individuals*, edited by Michael Schröter, translated by Edmund Jephcott, New York: Continuum.

Elster, Jon (1986), 'Further thoughts on Marxism, functionalism and game theory', in John Roemer (ed.), *Analytical Marxism*, Cambridge: Cambridge University Press, pp. 202-220.

Engelbrech, Gerhard and Maria Jungkunst (2001a), 'Erwerbsbeteiligung von Frauen. Wie bringt man Beruf und Kinder unter einen Hut?', *IAB-Kurzbericht* 7, Nürnberg.

Engelbrech, Gerhard and Maria Jungkunst (2001b), 'Erziehungsurlaub. Hilfe zur Wiedereingliederung oder Karrierehemmnis?', *IAB-Kurzbericht* 11, Nürnberg.

Engstler, H. and S. Menning (2003), *Die Familie im Spiegel der amtlichen Statistik, Erweiterte Neuauflage*, Berlin: Bundesministerium für Familie, Senioren, Frauen und Jugend.

Esping-Andersen, Gøsta (1990), *The Three Worlds of Welfare Capitalism*, Cambridge: Polity.

Esping-Andersen, Gøsta (1996), 'Welfare states without work: The impasse of labour shedding and familialism in continental European social policy', in Gøsta Esping-Andersen, *Welfare States in Transition, National Adaptions in Global Economies*, London/Thousand Oaks/New Dehli: Sage, pp. 66-87.

Esping-Andersen, Gøsta (1997), 'Toward a post-industrial welfare state', *Internationale Politik und Gesellschaft*, 3, 237-245.

Esping-Andersen, Gøsta (1999), *Social Foundations of Postindustrial Economies*, Oxford: Oxford University Press.

Europäische Kommission (1997), *Beschäftigung in Europa 1997*, Luxembourg: Eurostat.

Europäische Kommission (1999), *Das europäische Arbeitskräfteangebot der Zukunft*, Luxembourg: Eurostat.

Europäische Kommission (2003), *Europäische Sozialstatistik. Erhebung über Arbeitskräfte. Ergebnisse 2002*, Luxemburg: Amt für amtliche Veröffentlichungen der Europäischen Gemeinschaften.

European Commission (1999), *The European Employment Strategy and the ESF in 1998*, Luxembourg: European Commission.

European Commission (2003), *Employment in Europe 2003. Recent Trends and Prospects*, Luxembourg: Office for Official Publications of the European Communities 2003.

European Commission (2003), *European Social Statistics. Labour Force Results 2002*, Luxembourg: Office for Official Publications of the European Communities.

European Commission Childcare Network (1996), *A Review of Services for Young Children in the European Union 1990-1995*, Brussels: Abteilung für Gleichstellung von Frauen und Männern.

Eurostat (1996), *Social Portrait of Europe*, Luxembourg: Eurostat.

Eurostat (1997a), *Labour Force Results 1996*, Luxembourg: Eurostat.

Eurostat (1997b), 'Les responsabilités familiales – comment sont-elles partagées dans les ménages européens', *Statistiques en bref. Populations et conditons sociales*, 5.

Eurostat (1998a), *Labour Force Survey Results 1997*, Luxembourg: Eurostat.

Eurostat (1999), 'Labour force survey – principal results 1998', *Statistics in Focus, Population and Social Conditions*, **11**.

Eurostat (2002), 'First results of the demographic data collection for 2001 in Europe', *Statistics in Focus, Population and Social Conditions*, **17**.

Eurostat (2003), 'Labour force survey – principal results 2002', *Statistics in Focus, Population and Social Conditions*, **15**.

Eurostat (2004a), *Development of a Methodology for the Collection of Harmonised Statistics on Childcare*, Luxembourg: Office for Official Publications of the European Communities

Eurostat (2004b), 'European labour force survey – principal results 2003', *Statistics in Focus, Population and Social Conditions*, **14**.

Eurostat: New Cronos Database.

Fagnani, Jeanne (1998a), 'Lacunes, contradictions et incohérences des mesures de conciliation famille/travail. Bref bilan critique', *Droit social*, **6**, 596-602.

Fagnani, Jeanne (1998b), 'Recent changes in family policy in France: Political trade-offs and economic constraints', in Eileen Drew, Ruth Emerek and Evelyn Mahon (eds), *Women, Work and the Family in Europe*, London/New York: Routledge, pp. 58-65.

Fagnani, Jeanne (2001), 'Les françaises font toujours plus d'enfants que les allemandes de l'Ouest: Une esquisse d'interprétation', *Recherches et Prévisions*, **64**, 49-64.

Falkner, Gerda, Miriam Harltapp, Simone Leiber and Oliver Treib (2002), 'Transforming social policy in Europe? The EC's parental leave directive and misfit in 15 member states'. *MPIfG Working Paper* **02** (11).

Feministische Studien (2000), *Fürsorge – Anerkennung – Arbeit*, spezial issue 2000.

Fernández Cordón, Antonio Juan and Constanza Tobío (1999), *Las Familias Monoparentales en España*, Madrid: Ministerio de Asuntos Sociales.

Fernandéz Cordón and Juan Antonio (1999), *La situación sociolaboral de las mujeres, informe de investigación*, Madrid: Fundación Alternativas.

Fichte, Johann Gottlieb (1970), *The Science of Rights [1796]*, translated from the German by A.E. Kroeger, New York: Harper.

Finch, Janet (1983), *Married to the Job*, London: Allen and Unwin.

Finch, Janet and Dulcie Groves (eds) (1983), *A Labour of Love: Women, Work and Caring*, London: Routledge and Kegan Paul.

Fine, Susan B (1992), *Women's Employment and the Capitalist Family. Towards a Political Economy of Gender and Labour Markets*, London/New York: Routledge.

Freguja, Christina and Linda Laura Sabbadini (2000), *Women as Crucial Pivots of the Normal Support Networks: Evidence from Italian Multi-Purpose Surveys*, Working paper no. 19 to the Conference of European Statisticians, Orvieto, October 11 to 13.

Gambale, Sergio (1994), *Il trattamento fiscale della famiglia, Presidenza del Consiglio dei Ministri: Per una politica della famiglia in Italia*, Rome: Dipartimento affari sociali.

Garrido Medina, Luis and Enrique Gil Calvo (eds) (1993), *Estrategias Familiares*, Madrid: Alianza Editorial.

Gautun, Hanna (1990), *Eldre kvinner som ressurspersoner fo vosken barn med foreldreforpliktelser. Hovedroppgae*, Institutt for sosiologi og samfunnsgeografi, Oslo: Universitetet i Oslo.

Gerhard, Ute (1978), *Verhältnisse und Verhinderungen: Frauenarbeit, Familie und Rechte der Frauen im 19. Jahrhundert*, Frankfurt am Main: Suhrkamp.

Gerhard, Ute (1990), *Gleichheit ohne Angleichung. Frauen im Recht*, Munich: C.H. Beck.

Gerhard, Ute (2000), 'Die Europäische Union als Rechtsgemeinschaft und politische Gelegenheitsstruktur – Feministische Anfragen und Visionen', *L'Homme. Zeitschrift für feministische Geschichtswissenschaft*, **11** (2), 234-249.

Gerhard, Ute, Alice Schwarzer and Vera Slupik (1988), *Auf Kosten der Frauen: Frauenrechte im Sozialstaat*, Weinheim: Beltz.

Gessat-Anstett, Elisabeth (2001), 'Du collectif au communautaire: A propos des réseaux familiaux dans la Russie post-soviétique', *L'Homme, Revue fançaise d'anthropologie*, **157**, 115-136.

Giddens, Anthony (1979), *Central Problems in Social Theory*, Basingstoke: Macmillan.

Giddens, Anthony (1984), *The Constitution of Society*, Cambridge: Polity.

Giddens, Anthony (1991), *Modernity and Self-Identity*, Standford: University Press.

Giddens, Anthony (1994), 'Risk, trust, reflexivity', in Ulrich Beck, Anthony Giddens and Scott Lash (eds), *Reflexive Modernization: Politics, Tradition and Aesthetics in the Modern Social Order*. Cambridge: Polity, pp. 184-197.

Giddens, Anthony (1999), *The Third Way: The Renewal of Social Democracy*, Cambridge: Polity.

Gilligan, Carol (1982), *In a Different Voice: Psychological Theory and Women's Development*, Cambridge, Mass.: Harvard University Press.

Gordon, Linda (ed.) (1990), *Women, the State, and Welfare*, Madison, London: University of Wisconsin Press.

Gornick, Janet C. (1999), 'Gender equality in the labour market: Women's employment and earnings', in Diane Sainsbury (ed.), *Gender and Welfare State Regimes*, Oxford: Oxford University Press, pp. 210-242.

Gornick, Janet and Marcia K. Meyers (2003), *Families that Work. Policies for Reconciling Parenthood and Employment*, New York: Russell Sage Foundation.

Gornick, Janet C. Marcia K. Meyers and Katherine E. Ross (1997), 'Supporting the employment of mothers: Policy variation across fourteen welfare states', *Journal of European Social Policy*, **7** (1), 45-70.

Graham, Hillary (1987), 'Being poor: Perceptions and coping strategies of lone mothers', in Julia Brannen and Gayl Wilson (eds), *Give and Take in Families: Studies in Resource Distribution*, London: Allen and Unwin.

Granqvist, Lena and Helena Persson (1999), 'Career mobility in the private service sector – are women trapped in "bad" jobs?', in *European Commission, EC/DG V – OECD/DEELSA seminar: Wages and Employment*, Luxembourg, 71- 91.

Grimm, Dieter (1987), *Recht und Staat der bürgerlichen Gesellschaft*, Frankfurt am Main: Suhrkamp.

Haas, Linda (2003), 'Parental leave and gender equality: Lessons from the European Union', *Review of Policy Research*, **20** (1), 89-114.

Haas, Linda and Philip Hwang (1999), 'Parental leave in Sweden', in Peter Moss and Fred Deven (eds), *Parental Leave: Progress or Pitfall?* Brussels: CBGS, pp. 45-68.

Hagestad, Gunnar (2000), 'Adults' intergenerational relationships, in United Nations generations and gender programme', *Exploring Future Research and Data Collection Options*, New York/Geneva.

Hakim, Catherine (1995), 'Five feminist myths about women's employment', *British Journal of Sociology*, **46** (3), 429-455.

Hammersley, Martin (1987), 'Ethnographic and accumulative development of theory: A discussion of Wood's proposal for "phase two research"', *British Educational Research Journal*, **13**, 283-296.

Hantrais, Linda (ed.) (1999), *Gendered Policies in Europe: Reconciling Employment and Family Life*, London: Macmillan.

Hantrais, Linda and Marie-Thérèse Letablier (1996), *Families and Family Policies in Europe*, London: Longman.

Hantrais, Linda and Marie-Thérèse Letablier (1997), *Familles, travail et politiques familiales en Europe*, Paris: CEE/PUF.

Hareven, Tamara (1982), *Family Time and Industrial Time. The Relationship between Family and Work in a New England Industrial Community*, Oxford/New York: Oxford University Press.

Hausen, Karin (1997), 'Arbeiterinnenschutz, Mutterschutz und gesetzliche Krankenversicherung im Deutschen Kaiserreich und in der Weimarer Republik. Zur Funktion von Arbeits- und Sozialrecht für die Normierung und Stabilisierung der Geschlechterverhältnisse', in Ute Gerhard (ed.), *Frauen in der Geschichte des Rechts. Von der frühen Neuzeit bis zur Gegenwart*, Munich: C.H. Beck, pp. 713-743.

Héran, François (1987), 'La seconde nature de l'habitus. Tradition sociologique et sens commun dans le language sociologique', *Revue Française de sociologie*, **28** (3), 385-416.

Herlyn, Isabelle (2001), 'D'Est en Ouest, les styles des grand-méres allemandes', in Claudine Attias-Donfut and Martine Segalen, *Le siécle des grand-parents. Une génération phare, ici et ailleurs*, Paris: Autrement, pp. 116-126.

Hernes, Helga Maria (1986), 'Die zweigeteilte Sozialpolitik: Eine Polemik', in Karin Hausen and Helga Nowotny (eds), *Wie männlich ist die Wissenschaft?*, Frankfurt am Main: Suhrkamp, pp. 163-176.

Hobsbawm, Eric John (2000), 'Introduction', in Eric Hobsbawm and Terence John Ranger, (eds), *The Invention of Tradition*, Cambridge: Cambridge University Press. pp.1-14.

Hobson, Barbara (1994), 'Solo mothers, social policy regimes, and the logics of gender', in Diane Sainsbury (ed.), *Gendering Welfare States*, London/Thousand Oaks/New Dehli: Sage, pp. 170-187.

Hobson, Barbara (1996), 'Frauenbewegung für Staatsbürgerrechte – Das Beispiel Schweden', *Feministische Studien*, **14** (2), 18-34.

Hobson, Barbara (ed.) (2002), *Making Men into Fathers. Men, Masculinities and the Social Politics of Fatherhood*, Cambridge: Cambridge University Press.

Hobson, Barbara and Ruth Lister (2002), 'Citizenship', in Barbara Hobson, Jane Lewis and Birte Siim (eds), *Contested Concepts in Gender and Social Politics*, Cheltenham: Edward Elgar, pp. 23-54.

Hochschild, Arlie Russell (2000), 'The nanny chain', *American Prospect*, **11** (4), 32-36.

Hofäcker, Dirk (2004), 'Typen europäischer Familienpolitik – Vehikel oder Hemmnis für das "adult worker model"?', in Sigrid Leitner, Ilona Ostner and Margit Schratzenstaller (eds), *Wohlfahrtsstaat und Geschlechterverhältnis im Umbruch. Was kommt nach dem Ernährermodell?* Wiesbaden: VS Verlag für Sozialwissenschaften, pp. 257-284.

Holst, Elke and Friederike Maier (1998), 'Normalarbeitsverhältnis und Geschlechterordnung', *MittAB*, **3**, 506-518.

Hörburger, Hortense (1991), *Europas Frauen fordern mehr. Die soziale Dimension des EG-Binnenmarktes am Beispiel der spezifischen Auswirkungen auf Frauen*, Marburg: Schüren Presseverlag.

Hoskyns, Catherine (1996), *Integrating Gender. Women, Law and Politics in the European Union*, London/New York: Verso

Ingrosso, Marco (1984), *Strategie familiari e servizi sociali*, Milan: Angeli.

Instituto Nacional de Estadística (1999), *Encuesta de Población Activa*, 2° Trimestre 1998.

ISTAT (1999), *Vita di coppia e figli*, Rome: Istat.

Jacobs, Jerry (ed.) (1995), *Gender Inequality at Work*, London: Sage.

Jaumotte, Florence (2003), 'Female Labour Force Participation: Past Trends and Main Determinants in OECD Countries, OECD Economics Department', *Working Papers* **376**, ECO/WKP 30, Paris.

Jenson, Jane and Mariette Sineau (eds) (1998), *Qui doit garder le jeune enfant? Modes d'accueil et travail des mères dans l'Europe en crise*, Paris: LGDJ.

Jurczyk, Karin and Maria S. Rerrich (1993), *Die Arbeit des Alltags. Beiträge zu einer Soziologie der alltäglichen Lebensführung*, Freiburg: Lambertus.

Kamermann, Sheila B. (2000), 'Early childhood education and care: an overview of developments in the OECD countries', *International Journal of Educational Research*, 33, 7–29.

Karlsson, Malene (1995), *Family Day Care in Europe*, Brussels: DG V (V/5187/95).

Kaufmann, Franz-Xaver (1993), 'Familienpolitik in Europa', in Bundesministerium für Familie und Senioren (ed.), *40 Jahre Familienpolitik in der Bundesrepublik Deutschland: Rückblick/Ausblick*, Festschrift. Neuwied: Luchterhand, 141-167.

Kaufmann, Franz-Xaver (1997), *Herausforderungen des Sozialstaates*, Frankfurt am Main: Suhrkamp.

Kaufmann, Franz-Xaver (2002), 'Politics and policies towards the familiy in Europe. A framework and an inquiry into their differences and convergences', in Franz-Xaver Kaufmann, Anton Kuijsten, Hans-Joachim Schulze and Klaus-Peter Strohmeier (eds), *Family Life and Family Policies in Europe*, vol. 2: *Problems and Issues in Comparative Perspective*, Oxford/New York: Oxford University Press, pp. 419-490.

Kessler-Harris, Alice, Jane Lewis and Ulla Wikander (1995), 'Introduction', in Ulla Wikander, Alice Kessler-Harris and Jane Lewis (eds), *Protecting Women. Labour Legislation in Europe, the United States, and Australia, 1880-1920*, Illinois: University of Illinois Press.

Keuzenkamp, Saskia and Ko Oudhof (2000), *Emancipatiemonitor 2000*, The Hague: Sociaal en Cultureel Planbureau.

Kiernan, Kathleen, Hilary Land and Jane Lewis (1998), *Lone Motherhood in Twentieth-Century Britain*, Oxford: Oxford University Press.

Klammer, Ute (2001a), '"Flexicurity" als zukünftige Leitidee sozialer Sicherung in Europa. Eine Antwort (nicht nur) auf die neue Vielfalt weiblicher Erwerbs- und Lebenszusammenhänge', in Katrin Andruschow (ed.), *Ganze Arbeit: feministische Spurensuche in der Non-Profit-Ökonomie*, Berlin: edition sigma, pp. 241-274.

Klammer, Ute (2001b), 'Managerin gesucht. Erwerbstätige Mütter in Europa zwischen Sozialpolitik und sozialer Praxis', *WSI-Mitteilungen*, 5, 329-336.

Klammer, Ute and Katje Tillmann (2002), *Flexicurity – Soziale Sicherung und Flexibilisierung der Arbeits- und Lebensverhältnisse*, Düsseldorf: Ministerium für Arbeit und Soziales, Qualifikation und Technologie des Landes Nordrhein-Westfalen.

Klammer, U. and C. Klenner (2004), 'Geteilte Erwerbstätigkeit – Gemeinsame Fürsorge. Strategien und Perspektiven der Kombination von Erwerbs- und Familienleben in Deutschland', in Sigrid Leitner, Ilona Ostner and Margit Schratzenstaller (eds), *Wohlfahrtsstaat und Geschlechter- verhältnis im Umbruch. Was kommt nach dem Ernährermodell?*, Opladen: Verlag für Sozialwissenschaften, pp. 177-207.

Klein, Gabriele and Katharina Liebsch (1997), 'Zivilisierung zur Zweigeschlechtlichkeit. Zum Verhältnis von Zivilisationstheorie und feministischer Theorie', in Gabriele Klein and Katharina Liebsch (eds), *Die Zivilisierung des weiblichen Ich*, Frankfurt am Main: Suhrkamp, pp. 12-38.

Klein, Markus (1993), 'Die Rolle der Frau im geteilten Deutschland. Eine exemplarische Untersuchung über den Einfluß gesellschaftlicher Kontextbedingungen auf die Einstellungen zur Rolle der Frau und die Frauenerwerbstätigkeit', *Politische Vierteljahresschrift*, **34** (2), 272-297.

Knibiehler, Yvonne (1997), *La révolution maternelle depuis 1945: Femmes, maternité, citoyenneté*, Paris: Perrin.

Knijn, Trudie (1998), 'Social care in the Netherlands', in Jane Lewis (ed.), *Gender, Social Care and Welfare State Restructuring in Europe*, Alderhot: Ashgate, pp. 85-110.

Knijn, Trudie (2000), 'Marketization and the struggling logics of (home) care in the Netherlands', in Madonna Harrington Meyer (ed.), *Care Work, Gender, Labor and the Welfare State*, New York/London: Routledge, pp. 232-248.

Knijn, Trudie and Monique Kremer (1997), 'Gender and the caring dimension of welfare states: Towards inclusive citizenship', *Social Politics*, **4** (3), 328-361.

Knijn, Trudie and Frits Van Wel (2001a), 'Does it work? Employment policies for lone mothers in The Netherlands', in Jane Millar and Karen Rowlingson (eds), *Lone Parents, Employment and Social Policy: Cross-National Comparisons*, Bristol: Policy Press, pp. 107-128.

Knijn, Trudie and Frits Van Wel (2001b), *Een wankel evenwicht. Arbeid en Zorg in Gezinnen met jonge Kinderen*, Amsterdam: SWP Uitgeverij.

Knijn, Trudie and Frits Van Wel (2002), 'Careful or lenient: Welfare reform for lone mothers in the Netherlands', *Journal of European Social Policy*, **11** (2), 235-252.

Kolbe, Wiebke (2002), *Elternschaft im Wohlfahrtsstaat. Schweden und die Bundesrepublik im Vergleich 1945-2000*, Frankfurt am Main/NewYork: Campus.

König, René (1969), 'Soziologie der Familie', in René König and Leopold Rosenmayr (eds), *Handbuch zur empirischen Sozialforschung*, vol. 7: *Familie – Alter*, Stuttgart: Enke, pp. 172-305.

König, René (1974), *Materialien zur Soziologie der Familie*, Köln: Kiepenheuer & Witsch.

Koopmans, Ivy and Joop Schippers (2003), 'Female Employment and Family Formation – The Institutional Context', paper prepared for the joint meeting of MoCho, FENICS, DynSoc and AGIR, Brussels, 18-20 February 2003.

Kotowska, Irena E. (2004), 'Fertility and nuptiality in the CEE countries in the context of weakening families and a weakening state', in Trudie Knijn and Aafke Komter (eds), *Solidarity Between the Sexes and the Generations*, Cheltenham: Edward Elgar, pp. 111-132

Kreyenfeld, M., K. Spieß, and G. Wagner (2001), *Finanzierungs- und Organisationsmodelle institutioneller Kinderbetreuung*, Neuwied: Luchterhand.

Kröger, Teppo (1997), 'The dilemma of municipalities: Scandinavian approaches of child care provision', *Journal of Social Policy*, **26** (4), 485-507.

Kuhrig, Herta and Wulfram Speigner (1979), *Wie emanzipiert sind die Frauen in der DDR? Beruf – Bildung – Familie*, Köln: Pahl-Rugenstein.

Kuijsten, Anton (2002), 'Variation and change in the forms of private life in the 1980s', in Franz-Xaver Kaufmann, Anton Kuijsten, Hans-Joachim Schulze and Klaus Peter Strohmeier (eds), *Family Life and Family Policies in Europe*, vol. 2: *Problems and Issues in Comparative Perspective*, Oxford/New York: Oxford University Press, pp. 19-68.

Kulawik, Teresa (1999), *Wohlfahrtsstaat und Mutterschaft – Schweden und Deutschland 1870 – 1912*, Frankfurt am Main/New York: Campus.

Land, Hilary and Jane Lewis (1998), 'Gender, care and the changing role of the state in the UK', in Jane Lewis (ed.), *Gender, Care and Welfare State Restructuring in Europe*, Aldershot: Ashgate, pp. 51-84.

Lange, Helene (1908), *Die Frauenbewegung in ihren modernen Problemen*, Leipzig: Quelle & Meyer.

Langer, Rose (1999), 'Kompetenzen in der Europäischen Union auf dem Gebiet der Gleichbehandlung', *Zeitschrift für ausländisches und internationales Arbeits- und Sozialrecht*, **13**, 178-189.

Lanquetin, Marie-Thérèse, Jaqueline Laufer and Marie-Thérèse Letablier (1999), 'From equality to reconciliation in France?', in Linda Hantrais (ed.), *Gendered Policies in Europe: Reconciling Employment and Family Life*, London: Macmillan, pp. 68-88.

Laslett, Peter (1972), 'Introduction: The history of the family', in Peter Laslett and Richard Wall (eds), *Household and Family in Past Time*, Cambridge: Cambridge University Press, pp. 1-89.

Leira, Arnlaug (1992), *Welfare States and Working Mothers. The Scandinavian Experience*, Cambridge: Cambridge University Press.

Leira, Arnlaug (1993), 'The "women-friendly" welfare state? The case of Norway and Sweden', in Jane Lewis (ed.), *Women and Social Policies in Europe. Work, Family and the State*, London: Edward Elgar, pp. 25-48.

Leira, Arnlaug (2002), *Working Parents and the Welfare State. Family Change and Policy Reform in Scandinavia*, Cambridge: Cambridge University Press.

Leira, Arnlaug and Chiara Saraceno (2002), 'Care: Actors, relationships and contexts', in Barbara Hobson, Jane Lewis and Birte Siim (eds), *Contested Concepts in Gender and Social Politics*, Cheltenham: Edward Elgar, pp. 55-83.

Leprince, Frédérique (2003), *L'accueil des jeunes enfants en France: état des lieux et pistes d'amélioration*. Rapport pour le Haut conseil de la population et de la famille, Paris: La documentation française.

Letablier, Marie-Thérèse (2003), 'Work and Family Balance: a new Challenge for Policies in France', in Janet Z. Giele and Elke Holst (eds), *Changing Life Patterns in Western Industrial Societies*, Oxford: Elsevier Science Publishers, pp. 189-210

Letablier, Marie-Thérèse, Sophie Pennec and Olivier Büttner (2002), 'Opinions, attitudes et aspirations des familles vis à vis de la politique familiale en France', *Rapport de recherche*, no. 6, Paris: Centre d'Etudes de l'Emploi.

Leprince, Frédérique (2003), *L'accueil des jeunes enfants en France: état des lieux et pistes d'amélioration*. Rapport pour le Haut conseil de la population et de la famille, Paris: La documentation française.

Lewis, Jane (1992), 'Gender and the development of welfare regimes', *Journal of European Social Policy*, **2** (3), 159-173.

Lewis, Jane (ed.) (1998a), *Gender, Social Care and Welfare State Restructuring in Europe*, Aldershot: Ashgate.

Lewis, Jane (1998b), 'The problem of lone-mother families in twentieth-century Britain', *Journal of Social Welfare and Family Law*, **20** (3), 251-284.

Lewis, Jane (1999), 'New Labour, nouvelle Grande-Bretagne? Les politiques sociales et la "troisième voie", Lien social et politiques' *RIAC*, **41**, 61-70.

Lewis, Jane (2000a), 'Care and work', *Social Policy Review*, **12**, 48-67.

Lewis, Jane (2000b), 'Les femmes et le workfare de Tony Blair', *Esprit*, no. **273**, März-April, 174-186.

Lewis, Jane (2000c), 'Wohlfahrtsstaat und unbezahlte Betreuungsarbeit', *L'Homme, Zeitschrift für feministische Geschichtswissenschaft*, **11** (2), 251-268.

Lewis, Jane (2001), *The End of Marriage? Individualism and Commitment in Intimate Relationships, Cheltenham*: Edward Elgar.

Lewis, Jane (2003), 'Erwerbstätigkeit versus Betreuungsarbeit', in Ute Gerhard, Trudie Knijn and Anja Weckwert (eds), *Erwerbstätige Mütter. Ein europäischer Vergleich*. Munich: C.H. Beck, pp. 29-52.

Lewis, Jane and Benedict Meredith (eds) (1988), *Daughters Who Care. Daughters Caring for Mothers at Home*, London: Routledge.

Lindon Jennie (2000), *Early Years of Care and Education in Europe*, London: Hodder & Stoughton.

Lister, Ruth (1997), *Citizenship: Feminist Perspectives*, Basingstoke: Macmillan.

Lister, Ruth (1998), 'From equality to social inclusion: New labour and the welfare state', *Critical Social Policy*, **2**, 215-225.

Lombardo, Emanuela (2003), 'EU gender policy: Trapped in the "Wollstencraft Dilemma"?', *The European Journal of Women's Studies*, **10** (2), 159-180.

Lomnitz, Larissa (1977), *Networks and Marginality*, New York: Academic Press.

Ludwig, Isolde, Vanessa Schlevogt, Ute Klammer and Ute Gerhard (2002), *Managerinnen des Alltags. Strategien erwerbstätiger Mütter in Ost- und Westdeutschland*, Berlin: edition sigma.

Marchbank, Jennifer (2000), *Women, Power and Policy: Comparative Studies of Childcare*, London: Routledge.

Marshall, Thomas Humphrey (1950), *Citizenship and Social Class*, Cambridge, Cambridge University Press.

Martin, Claude, Antoine Math and Evelyne Renaudat (1998), 'Caring for very young children and dependent elderly people in France: Towards a commodification of social care?', in Jane Lewis (ed.), *Gender, Social Care and Welfare State Restructuring in Europe*, Aldershot: Ashgate, pp. 139-174.

Martin, Jacqueline (1998), 'Politique familiale et travail des mères de famille: perspective historique 1942–1982', *Population*, **6**, 119-154.

Martínez, Quintana and Maria Violante (1992), *Mujer, trabajo y madernidad. Problemas y alternativas de las madres que trabajan*, Madrid: Instituto de la Mujer, Ministerio de Asuntos Sociales.

Millar, Jane and Karen Rowlingson (2001) (eds), *Lone Parents, Employment and Social Policy: Cross-National Comparisons*, Bristol: Policy Press.

Millar, Jane and Andrea Warman (1996), *Family Obligations in Europe*, London: Family Policy Studies Centre.

Ministerio de Educación, Cultura y Deporte (2000), *Estadisticas de la Educación*, www.mec.es/estadistica.

Mitterauer, Michael and Reinhard Sieder (1982), *Historische Familienforschung*, Frankfurt am Main: Suhrkamp.

Moeller, Robert G. (1993), *Protecting Motherhood. Women and the Family in the Politics of Postwar West Germany*, Berkeley/Los Angeles/Oxford: University of California Press.

Moeller, Robert G. (1998), 'Forum: The "'remasculinization" of Germany in the 1950s', *Signs. Journal of Women in Culture and Society*, **24** (1), 104-127.

Morgan, David H.J. (1989), 'Strategies and sociologists. A comment on crow', *Sociology*, **23** (1), 25-29.

Moss, Peter and Fred Deven (eds) (1999), *Parental Leave: Progress or Pitfall*, Brussels: NIDI/CBGS Publications.

Musatti, Tullia and Roberta D'Amico (1996), 'Nonne e nipotini: lavoro di cura e solidarietà intergenerazionale', *Rassegna italiana di sociologica*, **37** (4), 559-84.

Navarro, Manuel (1993), 'Tipos de empleo', in Salustiano del Campo (ed.), *Tendencias Sociales en España 1960-1990, Fundación BBV*, vol. I, pp. 355-369.

Nave-Herz, Rosemarie (1998), 'Die These über den "Zerfall der Familie"', in Jürgen Friedrichs, Rainer Lepsius and Karl Ulrich Mayer (eds), *Die Diagnosefähigkeit der Soziologie. Sonderheft 38 der Kölner Zeitschrift für Soziologie und Sozialpsychologie*, Opladen: Westdeutscher Verlag, pp. 286-315.

Nermo, Magnus (1994), 'Den ofullbordade jämlikheten', in Johan Fritzell and Olle Lundberg (eds), *Vardagens villkor. Levnadsförhållanden i Sverige under tre decennier*.

Nickel, Hildegard Maria (1999), 'Erosion und Persistenz. Gegen die Ausblendung des gesellschaftlichen Transformationsprozesses in der Frauen- und Geschlechterforschung', in Hildegard Nickel, Susanne Völker and Hasko Hüning (eds), *Transformation – Unternehmensreorganisation – Geschlechterforschung*, Opladen: Leske+Budrich, pp. 9-33.

Nicole-Drancourt, Chantal (1989), 'Stratégies professionnelles et organisation des familles', *Revue Française de Sociologie*, **40** (1), 57-79.

Niehuss, Merith (1997), 'Eheschließung im Nationalsozialismus', in Ute Gerhard (ed.), *Frauen in der Geschichte des Rechts*, Munich: C.H. Beck, pp. 851-870.

Nyberg, Anita (2000), 'From foster mothers to child care centers: A history of working mothers and child care in Sweden', *Feminist Economics*, **6** (1), 5-20.

Oakley, Ann (1974), *The Sociology of Housework*, New York: Pantheon Books.

OECD (1997), *Statistical Compendium*, Paris: OECD.

OECD (1998*)*, *OECD Full-time/Part-time database*, Paris: OECD.

OECD (1999), *Employment Outlook*, Paris: OECD.

OECD (2000), *OECD Country Note: Early Childhood Education and Care Policy in the United Kingdom*, Paris: OECD.

OECD (2001a), *Employment Outlook*, Paris: OECD.

OECD (2001b), *Starting Strong. Early Childhood Education and Care*, Paris: OECD.

OECD (2004), *Employment Outlook 2004*, Paris: OECD.

Ohlander, Ann-Sofie (1989), 'Det osynliga barnet? Kampen om den socialdemokratiska familjepolitiken', in Klaes Misgeld (eds), *Socialdemokratins samhälle: SAP och Sverige under 100 år*, Stockholm: Tiden, pp. 170-190.

Ostner, Ilona (1998), 'The politics of care policies in Germany', in Jane Lewis (ed.), *Gender, Social Care and Welfare State Restructuring in Europe*, Aldershot: Ashgate, pp. 110-138.

Ostner, Ilona (2000), 'From equal pay to equal employability: Four decades of gender politics', in Mariagrazia Rossilli (ed.), *Gender Politics in the European Union*, New York: Peter Lang, pp. 25-42.

Ostner Ilona and Jane Lewis (1995), 'Gender and the Evolution of European Social Policy', in Stephan Leibfried and Paul Pierson: *European Social Policy. Between Fragmentation and Integration*, Washington, DC: The Brookings Institution, pp. 159-193.

Paci, Massimo (ed.) (1980), *Famiglia e mercato del lavoro in un'economia periferica*, Milan: Angeli.

Pahl, Rymond E. (1984), *Divisions of Labour*, Oxford: Blackwell.

Paoli, Pascal and Agnès Parent-Thirion (2003), *Working Conditions in the Acceding and Candidate Contries,* Dublin: European Foundation for the Improvement of Living and Working Conditions.

Pascall, Gillian and Jane Lewis (2004), 'Emerging gender regimes and policies for gender equality in a wider Europe', *Journal of Social Policy*, **33** (3), 373-394.

Pascall, Gillian and Nick Manning (2000), 'Gender and social policy: comparing welfare states in central and Eastern Europe and the former Soviet Union', *Journal of European Social Policy,* **10** (3), 240-266.

Persson, Sven (1994), *Föräldrars föreställningar om barn och barnomsorg*, Stockholm: Almqvist & Wiksell International.

Pfau-Effinger, Birgit (1999), 'Change of family policies in the socio-cultural context of European societies', in Arnlaug Leira (ed.), *Family Change: Practices, Policies, and Values, Comparative Social Research*, **18**, Stanford, Conn.: JAI Press.

Pfau-Effinger, Birgit (2000), *Kultur und Frauenerwerbstätigkeit in Europa. Theorie und Empirie des internationalen Vergleichs*, Opladen: Leske +Budrich.

Plantenga, Janneke (2000), 'Parental leave and equal opportunities – an international comparison, in 4. Bericht des TSER-Netzwerkes', *Working and Mothering: Social Practices and Social Policies: Proceedings of the seminar Available Provisions and Policy Deficits*, March 23 – 25 in Paris, 196-206.

Portegijs, Wil, Annemarie Boelens and Saskia Keuzenkamp (2002), *Emancipatiemonitor 2002*, Den Haag: Sociaal en Cultureel Planbureau.

Prokop, Ulrike (1976), *Weiblicher Lebenszusammenhang: Von der Beschränktheit der Strategien und der Unangemessenheit der Wünsche*, Frankfurt am Main: Suhrkamp.

Rainwater, Lee, Martin Rein and Joseph Schwartz (1986), *Income Packaging in the Welfare State*, Oxford: Clarendon.

Randall, Vicky (1996), 'Feminism and child day-care', *Journal of Social Policy*, **25** (4), 485-505.

Randall, Vicky (1999), 'Childcare Policy in Britain', paper presented for the conference *Labour Market and Social Policy. Gender Relations in Transition*, Brussels, May 31 - June 1.

Rangelova, Rossitsa (2002), 'Gender labour relations and EU enlargement', *South-East Europe Review*, **3**, 105-126.

Regner, Nils and Johan Hirschfeldt (1987), 'Schweden', in Helmut Coing (ed.), *Quellen und Literatur der neueren europäischen Privatrechtsgeschichte. Dritter Band: Das 19. Jahrhundert*, Munich: C.H. Beck, pp. 235-373.

Rein, Martin and Lee Rainwater (1980), *From Welfare State to Welfare Society*, Cambridge, Mass.: Joint Center for Urban Studies.

Rerrich, Maria S. (1994), 'Zusammenfügen, was auseinanderstrebt. Lebensführung von Berufstätigen', in Ulrich Beck and Elisabeth Beck-Gernsheim (eds), *Riskante Freiheiten. Individualisierung in modernen Gesellschaften*, Frankfurt am Main: Suhrkamp, pp. 201-218.

Ribbens McCarthy, Jane and Rosalinds Edwards (2002), 'The individual in public and private: The significance of mothers and children', in Alan Carling, Simon Duncan and Rosalind Edwards (eds), *Analysing Families. Morality and Rationality in Policy and Practice*, London/NewYork: Routledge, pp. 199-218.

Richter, Ingo (2000), 'La politique familiale en Allemagne', paper presented for a conference of the Caisse Nationale des Allocations Familiales (*CNAF*) in January 2000 in Paris.

Riehl, Wilhelm H. (1855), *Die Naturgeschichte des Volkes als Grundlage einer deutschen Social-Politik: Die Familie*, Stuttgart/Augsburg: Cotta.

Riksförsäkringsverket (2002), *Spelade pappamånaden någon roll? – pappors uttag av föräldrapenning*. Rapport 2002:14. Stockholm.

Rollet-Echallier, Catherine (1990), 'La politique à l'égard de la petite enfance sous la Troisième République', *Travaux et documents,* **127**, Paris: PUF/Ined.

Rosenbaum, Heide (1978), *Formen der Familie*, Frankfurt am Main: Suhrkamp.

Rossilli, Mariagrazia (ed.) (2000), *Gender Politics in the European Union,* New York: Peter Lang.

Rostgaard, Tine and Torben Fridberg (1998), *Caring for Children and Older People – A Comparison of European Policies and Practicies. Social Security in Europe 6,* Kopenhagen: The Danish National Institute of Social Research 98: 20.

Ruane, Frances, S. and Julie M. Sutherland (1999*), Women in the Labour Force*, Dublin: Employment Equality Agency.

Rubery, Jill (2002), 'Gender mainstreaming and gender equality in the EU: the impact of the EU employment strategy', *Industrial Relations Journal,* **33** (5), 500-522.

Rubery, Jill, Mark Smith and Colette Fagan (1998), 'National Working-Time Regimes and Equal Opportunities', *Feminist Economics,* **4** (1), 71-101.

Rubery, Jill, Mark Smith and Colette Fagan (1999), *Women's Employment in Europe: Trends and Prospects*, London: Routledge.

Rubery, Jill, Mark Smith, Colette Fagan and Damian Grimshaw (1996), *Women and the European Employment Rate: The Causes and the Consequences of Variations in Female Activity and Employment Patterns in the European Union*, Brussels: European Commission, DG-V.

Sainsbury, Diane (ed.) (1994), *Gendering Welfare States*, London: Sage.

Sainsbury, Diane (1999a), 'Gender and social-democratic welfare states', in Diane Sainsbury (ed.), *Gender and Welfare State Regimes*, Oxford: Oxford University Press, pp. 75-114.

Sainsbury, Diane (1999b), 'Gender, policy regimes, and politics', in Diane Sainsbury (ed.), *Gender and Welfare State Regimes*, Oxford: Oxford University Press, pp. 245-275.

Saraceno, Chiara (1986), 'Stratagie familiari e modelli di lavoro: alcuni problemi concettuali e di metodo', *Inchiesta,* **74**, 1-9.

Saraceno, Chiara (1989), 'The concept of family strategy and its application to the family-work complex: Some theoretical and methodological problems?', Marriage and Family Review, 14, 1-18.

Saraceno, Chiara (1994), 'The ambivalent familism of the italian welfare state', Social Politics, 1 (1), 32-59.

SCB (1994), Att klara av ...arbete-barn-familj. Demografi med barn och familj, Stockholm: SCAB.

SCB (2000), Children and their families 1999.Stockholm: SCB.

SCB (2003), Tid för vardagsliv - Kvinnors och mäns tidsanvändning 1990/91 och 2000/01. Rapport 99, Stockholm: Statistiska Centralbyrån.

SCB (2004), Barnens tid med föräldrarna. Demografiska rapporter 2004:1. Stockholm: Statistiska Centralbyrån.

Schäfgen, Katrin and Annette Spellerberg (1998), 'Kulturelle Leitbilder und institutionelle Regelungen für Frauen in den USA, in West- und Ostdeutschland', Berliner Journal für Soziologie, 1, 73-90.

Scheiwe, Kirsten (1995), 'Family obligations in Germany', in Jane Millar and Andrea Warman (eds), Defining Family Obligations in Europe, University of Bath, Bath Social Policy Papers, 23, 107-128.

Schmink, Marianne (1984), 'Household economic strategies: Review and research agenda', Latin America Research Review, 19, 87-101.

Schubert, Werner (1997), 'Die Stellung der Frau im Familienrecht und in den familienrechtlichen Reformprojekten der NS-Zeit', in Ute Gerhard (ed.), Frauen in der Geschichte des Rechts, Munich: C.H. Beck, pp. 790-827.

Schütze, Yvonne (1986), Die gute Mutter. Zur Geschichte des normativen Musters 'Mutterliebe', Bielefeld: B. Kleine Verlag.

Schwab, Dieter (1979), 'Familie', in Otter Brunner, Werner Conze and Reinhart Koselleck (eds), Geschichtliche Grundbegriffe. Historisches Lexikon zur politisch-sozialen Sprache in Deutschland, Stuttgart: Klett-Cotta, pp. 253-301.

Schwab, Dieter (1997), 'Gleichberechtigung und Familienrecht im 20. Jahrhundert', in Ute Gerhard (ed.), Frauen in der Geschichte des Rechts, Munich: C.H. Beck, pp. 790-827.

Scott, Joan W. (1993), 'The woman worker', in Georges Duby and Michelle Perrot (eds.), A History of Women in the West, vol. IV: Emerging Feminism from Revolution to World War, vol. ed. by Geneviève Fraisse and Michelle Perrot, Cambridge/London: Harvard University Press, pp. 399-426.

Selid, Betty (1968), Kvinner I yrke, hjem og samfunn, Oslo: Fabritius og sønners forlag.

Sevenhuijsen, Selma (1998), Citizenship and the Ethics of Care. Feminist Considerations on Justice, Morality and Politics, London/New York: Routledge.

Sevenhuijsen, Selma (2002), 'A Third Way? Moralities, ethics and families: An approach through the ethic of care', in Alan Carling, Simon Duncan and Rosalind Edwards (eds), *Analysing Families. Morality and Rationality in Policy and Practice*, London/NewYork: Routledge, pp. 129-145.

Sgritta, Giovanbattista (1986), 'Strategie familiari e infanzia', in Franca Bimbi and Vittorio Capecchi (eds), *Strutture e strategie della vita quotidiana*, Milan: Angeli, pp. 223-238.

Siim, Birte (2000), *Gender and Citizenship. Poltitics and Agency in France, Britain and Denmark*, Cambridge: Cambridge University Press.

Simitis, Spiro (2000), 'The case of employment relationship: Elements of a comparison', in Willibald Steinmetz (ed.), *Private Law and Social Inequality in the Industrial Age. Comparing Legal Cultures in Britain, France, Germany, and the United States*, Oxford: Oxford University Press, pp. 181-202.

Simmel, Georg (1970), *Grundfragen der Soziologie [1907]. Individuum und Gesellschaft*, Berlin: de Gruyter.

Simmel, Georg (1992), *Schriften zur Soziologie. Eine Auswahl*, Frankfurt am Main: Suhrkamp.

Skolverket (2001a), *Barnomsorg, skola och vuxenutbildning i siffror. Del 2. Barn, personal och lärare*, Stockholm: Skolverket, rapport 198.

Skolverket (2001b), *Barns omsorg. Tillgång och efterfrågan för barn 1-12 år med olika social bakgrund.* Stockholm: Skolverket.

Skolverket (2004), *Barn, elever och personal – Riksnivå avseende år 2003.* Officiell statistik för förskoleverksamhet, skolbarnsomsorg, skola och vuxenutbildning. Rapport nr 244. Del 2. Stockholm: Skolverket.

Smith, Kristin (2000), 'Who's minding the kids? Childcare arrangements', Fall 1995, *Current Population Reports*, p.70, Washington, DC: U.S. Census Bureau.

Smith, Nina, Shirley Dex, Jan-Dirk Vlasblom and Tim Callan (2003), 'The effects of taxation on married women's labour supply across four countries', *Oxford Economic Papers*, 55 (3), 417-439.

Smith, Peter K. (1995), 'Grandparenthood', in Marc Bornstein, *Handbook of Parenting,* Vol. 3: *Status and Social Conditions of Parenting*, London: Lawrence Erlbaum.

Smith, Vicki and Heidi Gottfried (1998), 'Flexibility in work and employment: The impact on women', in Birgit Geissler, Friederike Maier and Birgit Pfau-Effinger (eds), *FrauenArbeitsMarkt. Der Beitrag der Frauenforschung zur sozio-ökonomischen Theorieentwicklung*, Berlin: edition sigma, pp. 95-125.

Sociaal en Cultureel Planbureau (2000), *Nederland in Europa. Sociaal en Cultureel Rapport 2000*, Den Haag: Sociaal en Cultureel Planbureau.

Solera, Cristina (2001), 'Women's transitions in and out of the labour market in Italy and Great Britain: What changes across cohorts?', paper presented for the conference *European Societies*, Kerkrade, Oktober 6 – 10.

Sommerkorn, Ingrid N. (1988), 'Die erwerbstätige Mutter in der Bundesrepublik: Einstellungs- und Problemveränderungen', in Rosemarie Nave-Herz (ed.), *Wandel und Kontinuität der Familie in der Bundesrepublik Deutschland,* Stuttgart: Enke, pp. 115-144.

SOU (2000:3), *Välfärd vid vägskäl,* Stockhom: Socialdepartementet.

Spellerberg, Annette (1996), 'Frauen zwischen Familie und Beruf', in Wolfgang Zapf and Roland Habich (eds), *Wohlfahrtsentwicklung im vereinten Deutschland. Sozialstruktur, sozialer Wandel und Lebensqualität,* Berlin: edition sigma.

Stack, Carol (1975), *All Our Kin. Strategies for Survival in a Black Community,* New York: Harper.

Statistisches Bundesamt: *Mikrozensus,* Statistisches Jahrbuch (fortlaufend).

Statistisches Bundesamt (2003), *Statistik der Kinder- und Jugendhilfe,* Wiesbaden: Statistisches Bundesamt.

Statistisk Sentralbyrå (1969), *Ønsker om og behov for sysselsetting blant gifte kvinner,* Oslo: Rapport fra en intervjuundesøkelse 1968.

Statistisk Sentralbyrå (Statistics Norway), (1975), *Undersøkelsen om barnetilsyn 1975* (Survey of forms of childcare). Rapport 39, Oslo.

Steinmetz, Willibald (2000), 'Introduction', in Willibald Steinmetz (ed.), *Private Law and Social Inequality in the Industrial Age. Comparing Legal Cultures in Britain, France, Germany and the United States,* Oxford: Oxford University Press, pp. 1-41.

Stoehr, Irene (1994), 'Housework and motherhood: Debates and policies in the women's movement in imperial Germany and the Weimar Republic', in Gisela Bock and Pat Thane (eds), *Maternity and Gender Policies. Women and the Rise of the European Welfare States, 1880s-1950s,* London/NewYork: Routledge, pp. 213-232.

Strømsheim, Gunnar (1983), *Working Hours and Segmentation in the Norwegian Labour market,* Oslo: IRS working paper.

Szebehely, Maria (1998), 'Changing divisions of carework: Caring for children and frail elderly people in Sweden', in Jane Lewis (ed.), *Gender, Social Care and Welfare State Restructuring in Europe,* Aldershot: Ashgate, pp. 257-283.

Tamm, Ditlev (1987), 'Einführung', in Helmut Coing (ed.), *Quellen und Literatur der neueren europäischen Privatrechtsgeschichte.* Vol. 3: *Das 19. Jahrhundert,* Munich: C.H. Beck, pp. 3-13.

Tilly, Louise A. (1979), 'Individual lives and family strategies in the French proletariat', *Journal of Family History,* **4,** 137-152.

Tilly, Louise A. (1987), 'Beyond family strategies, what?', *Historical Methods*, **20** (3), 123-125.

Tilly, Louise A. and Joan W. Scott (1989), *Women, Work and Family*, New York and London: Routledge.

Tobío, Constanza (1998), 'Roles de género y la relación familia-empleo', *Asparkia, Investigació Feminista*, **9**, 21-44.

Tobío, Constanza (2001), 'En Espagne, la abuela au secours des mères actives', in Claudine Attias-Donfut and Martine Segalen (eds), *Le Siècle des Grand-Parents: Une génération phare, ici et ailleurs*, Paris: Editions Autrement – Collection Mutations, **210**, pp. 102-115.

Tobío, Constanza, Enriqueta Arteta, Cordón Fernández and Antonio Juan (1996), *Estrategias de compatibilización familia-empleo. España años noventa*, Madrid: Departamento de Humanidades, Ciencias Politicas y Sociología, Universidad Carlos III de Madrid/Instituto de la Mujer.

Tönnies, Ferdinand (1963), *Gemeinschaft und Gesellschaft. Grundbegriffe der reinen Soziologie*, Darmstadt: Wissenschaftliche Buchgesellschaft.

Trifiletti, Rosanna, Alessandro Pratesi and Simonetta Simoni (2001), Care arrangements in single parent families. National report Italy. SOCCARE Project report 2.3. Http://www.uta.fi/laitokset/sospol/soccare.

Trnka, Silvia (2000), *Family Issues between Gender and Generations*, Luxembourg: European Commission.

Tronto, Joan (2000), 'Demokratie als fürsorgliche Praxis', *Feministische Studien extra*, **18**, 25-42.

Ungerson, Clare (1990) (ed.), *Gender and Caring: Work and Welfare in Britain and Scandinavia*, New York: Harvester Wheatsheaf.

Valiente, Celia (1996), 'Women in segmented labour markets and continental welfare states: the case of Spain', in Linda Hantrais and Marie-Thérèse Letablier (eds), *Comparing Families and Family Policies in Europe*, Cross National Research Papers, European Research Centre: Loughborough University, pp. 86-93.

Van Drenth, Annemieke, Trudie Knijn and Jane Lewis (1999), 'Sources of income for lone-mother families: Policy changes in Britain and the Netherlands and the experiences of divorced women', *Journal of Social Policy*, **28** (4), 619-642.

Vogel, Ursula (1988), 'Patriarchale Herrschaft, bürgerliches Recht, bürgerliche Utopie. Eigentumsrechte der Frauen in Deutschland und England', in Jürgen Kocka (ed.), *Bürgertum und bürgerliche Gesellschaft*, Stuttgart: Klett-Cotta, pp. 406-438.

Vogel, Ursula (1990), 'Zwischen Privileg und Gewalt: Die Geschlechterdifferenz im englischen Common Law', in Ute Gerhard et al. (eds), *Differenz und Gleichheit. Menschenrechte haben (k)ein Geschlecht*, Frankfurt am Main: Ulrike Helmer, pp. 217-223.

Vogel, Ursula (2000), 'Private contract or public institution? The peculiar case of marriage', in Maurizio Passarin d'Entreves and Ursula Vogel (eds), *Public and Private: Philosophical, Political and Legal Perspectives*, London: Routledge, pp. 172-199.

Waerness, Kari (1984), 'Caring as women's work in the welfare state', in H. Holter (ed.) *Patriarchy in a Welfare Society*, Oslo: Universitetsforlaget, pp. 67-87.

Waerness, Kari (2000), 'Fürsorgerationalität', *Feministische Studien extra*, 18, 54-67.

Wall, Karin, Sofia Aboim, Vanessa Cunha and Pedro Vasconcelos (2001), 'Families and informal support in Portugal: the reproduction of inequality', *Journal of European Social Policy*, 11 (3), 213-33.

Wallace, Claire (2002), 'Household strategies: Their conceptual relevance and analytical scope in social research', *Sociology*, 36 (2), 275-92.

Weber, Marianne (1971), *Ehefrau und Mutter in der Rechtsentwicklung [1907]*, Aalen: Scientia.

Wilson, Elizabeth (1977), *Women and the Welfare State*, London, Tavistock.

Winkler, Gunnar (ed.) (1990), *Frauenreport '90*, Berlin: Verlag Die Wirtschaft.

Wood, Stephan and John Kelly (1982), 'Taylorism, responsible autonomy and management strategy', in Stephan Wood (ed.), *The Degradation of Work?*, London: Hutchinson, pp. 74-89.

Zahn-Harnack, Agnes von (1928), *Die Frauenbewegung. Geschichte, Probleme, Ziele*, Berlin: Deutsche Buch-Gemeinschaft.

Zighera, Jacques A. (1996), 'How to measure and compare female activity in the European Union', in Petra Beckmann (ed.), *Gender Specific Occupational Segregation*, Nürnberg: Institut für Arbeitsmarkt und Berufsforschung der Bundesanstalt für Arbeit, pp. 89-105.

Index

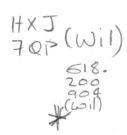

WOMEN & CHILDBIRTH

IN THE TWENTIETH CENTURY

A History of the National Birthday
Trust Fund 1928–93

A. Susan Williams

SUTTON PUBLISHING

First published in 1997 by
Sutton Publishing Limited · Phoenix Mill
Thrupp · Stroud · Gloucestershire · GL5 2BU

British Library Cataloguing in Publication Data
A catalogue record for this book is available from the British Library

ISBN 0 7509 1209 X

TM
ALAN SUTTON™ and SUTTON™ are the trade marks of Sutton Publishing Limited

Typeset in Baskerville 10/13 pt.
Typesetting and origination by
Sutton Publishing Limited.
Printed in Great Britain by
Hartnolls, Bodmin, Cornwall.

Contents

Foreword

This book will prove to be an important contribution to social and medical history in the twentieth century. The National Birthday Trust Fund was not among the most famous or the best known of charities, but it deserves its place for the achievements recounted here. It was started in 1928, one year before the Royal College of Obstetricians and Gynaecologists, at a time of serious concern about the health of women and the high death rate of mothers. Death of a mother in pregnancy or childbirth is a tragedy which may include the death of her baby and which will involve a whole family.

The beginning of the Trust by a group of noble and affluent women – soon to include Mrs Stanley Baldwin, wife of the Prime Minister – who worked and raised money for the 'Extension of Maternity Services', is in itself remarkable.

The history of the 1930s is a sorry tale of depression, unemployment and poverty. In parts of the country, the situation was unbelievably awful. In areas such as South Wales, where women were literally dying of starvation, food supplements were provided by the Trust. The status of midwives as independent and professional trained workers was improved by a new Midwives Act. Abortion among the poor was an appalling problem. Women in childbirth received little or no pain relief. The Fund encouraged and supported new developments to assist women, including the provision of gas and air machines.

Recommendations were made for an adequate maternity service in advance of the coming of the National Health Service in 1948. Important surveys of maternity services, such as the 1958 Perinatal Mortality Survey, were supported and organized. These have to be recognized as classic and historic studies.

This work could not have been done without the efforts and enthusiasm of many. Of these, two stand out: Dame Juliet Rhys Williams was the driving force; and the Secretary, Miss Doreen Riddick, served the Trust from its earliest years until her retirement. Her meticulous record-keeping provided the material on which this history could be based.

Since 1993 the work of the Fund has continued with the charity WellBeing. Many of its objects have already been realized, but there is still much to do and learn. Mothers and their babies still need the best that medicine, midwifery and advances in medical science can offer.

This remarkable and unique record of events since 1928 demands study and gives a vista for an even better future.

Josephine Barnes, June 1996

Dame Josephine joined the Trust in 1945. She was involved in the major national surveys of 1946, 1958 and 1970, and was Chairman of the Steering Committee for the 1958 and 1970 surveys; she has also been Chairman of the Trust's Scientific Committee. She was President of the Birthday Trust between 1981 and 1993.

Acknowledgements

The story of the National Birthday Trust Fund would never have been written if it had not been for two people. The first of these is Miss Doreen Riddick, who devoted her working life to the Trust. She was secretary to the Trust's Joint Council of Midwifery from 1934 to 1939 and then to the Trust itself from 1939 to 1972, and kept detailed records of its activities for the whole of this period. The second person is Mrs Margaret Wynn, who as a young woman witnessed the Hunger Marches of the 1930s and has campaigned against poverty for most of the century. She recognised in Miss Riddick's collection of papers an important story of women and childbirth, particularly women who were poor, and set about making sure that the story was written. Mrs Margaret Matthews, Miss Riddick's successor, organised the removal of the Trust documents to the Contemporary Medical Archives Centre (CMAC) at the Wellcome Institute for the History of Medicine, where they were catalogued and stored for consultation by scholars. Mrs Wynn has kept me company throughout my research: my sternest critic, but always encouraging and always unselfishly offering suggestions and sharing her insights and memories.

The Birthday Trust funded the work for this book, with a level of generosity that is a joy to historians who need the time and resources to carry out detailed archival research. I have been assisted also by WellBeing, with whom the Birthday Trust joined forces in 1993. I am grateful to Mrs Rosie Barnes, Director of WellBeing, and Mr Paul Barnett, Secretary of the Royal College of Obstetricians and Gynaecologists.

I have been privileged to have the help of a distinguished Steering Committee, which included Dame Josephine Barnes, who was active in the Trust from 1945 and knew many of the people whose work is the subject of the postwar chapters of this book; Professor Eva Alberman, who was co-editor of *Perinatal Problems* with Professor Neville Butler; and Professor Geoffrey Chamberlain and Mr Elliot Philipp, co-authors of the 1970 survey report. The Hon. Mrs Susan Baring, Chairman of the Trust, Professor Jane Lewis of the LSE, Professor Ann Oakley of the Institute of Education, University of London, Dr Charles Webster of All Souls College, Oxford, and Mrs Margaret Wynn, were also members of the Steering Committee, which met regularly to review my work. I am extremely grateful to the committee all of whom read and commented on drafts of every chapter.

I had interviews with Professor Neville Butler, co-author of *Perinatal Mortality* and co-editor of *Perinatal Problems*; Professor Albert Claireaux, who was responsible for the pathology component of the 1958 Perinatal Mortality Survey; and Professor Harvey Goldstein, who contributed to *Perinatal Problems*. As an historian relying so heavily on archival evidence, I was uniquely fortunate to have the willing help of those who had contributed to the Trust's work for more than half a century.

Professor Ann Oakley has been involved in the work of the book from the very beginning. She introduced me to the world of maternity research and made suggestions about people to contact and clues to follow up; she also furnished me with some key documents, especially those relating to Richard Titmuss. I have a happy memory of our visit together to a freezing stable in the middle of Leicestershire to look through trunks and boxes of old papers.

I owe Dr Charles Webster a special debt. About a third of the way through writing the book, I realised that my point of view had shifted in a subtle but important way and I was unhappy about my historical perspective. In dismay I turned to Charles, who helped me to sort out my problem. I emerged with a clearer and, I think, better grasp of how to approach the story of the Trust. I am also grateful to Charles for suggesting the title of this book and for some important historical leads.

I thank Alison Macfarlane at the NPEU for the use of her statistical data on maternity and for permission to duplicate some of her graphs. I was very fortunate to have the assistance of James Thomas, who carried out research in various sets of archives and produced a systematic account of the Birthday Trust's financial data over the century. He produced most of the graphs and figures in the book.

I am indebted to the families of former Birthday Trust members for their assistance with my research. The daughters of Lady Juliet Rhys Williams – Susan, Lady Glyn, and Elspeth, Mrs Chowdharay-Best – gave me access to many family records and shared their memories of their mother with me. The family of Mr Richard Cahn, son of Sir Julien Cahn, gave me great help with my research into the life and work of Sir Julien. Lady Baldwin's niece, Mrs Molly Anderson, and her grandson, Mr Miles Huntington-Whitely, gave me invaluable information about Lady Baldwin. Lady Mairi Bury shared with me her memories of her mother, Edith, Marchioness of Londonderry.

I interviewed many mothers who were pregnant and gave birth in the 1930s; some of these had received the Birthday Trust's special nutrition for pregnancy. I also interviewed a number of midwives who had worked in the interwar and early postwar years. I shall not forget their welcome and the hours I spent listening in their homes. Their unique contribution is acknowledged in the endnotes to the chapters.

Other people who have helped me with information, comments on my work, and in other ways, include: Lord Archer, Miss Ruth Ashton, Charlotte Bellman,

Tony Benn, Dennis Bonham, Virginia Bottomley, Jo Bowyer, Philippa Burrell, Professor John Bynner, Iain Chalmers, Andy Croft, David Crook, Ann Dally, Kevin Dodwell, Lady Ebbisham, Frank Field, Enid Fox, Jenifer Gilbey, Walter Gilbey, Sir George Godber, Christine Gowdridge, Dr J.A. Heady, Frank Honigsbaum, Simon Israel, Mrs Toby Israel, Lord Jenkins, Lara Marks, the staff of *Midwives Chronicle and Nursing Notes*, Wendy Moore, Ornella Moscucci, Dr Mary Paterson, Lady Palmer, Sarah Perry and the Queen's Nursing Institute, Sue Richards, Peter Shepherd, David Smith, Marjorie Tew, Betty Vernon, Professor Michael Wadsworth, Dr Elsie Widdowson, and Ann Wraight.

For a study like this, I was dependent on the cooperation and goodwill of librarians and archivists. I should like to thank the staff of CMAC at the Wellcome Institute for their efficient help over the years of the research, in particular the archivists Lesley Hall and Julia Sheppard; P.A. Baker catalogued the Birthday Trust collection and the Wellcome Institute Photographic Library, notably Michele Minto, supplied me with photographs. The friendly assistance of the staff at the Public Record Office made my work there even more enjoyable; and the Department of Health opened some closed files for me. Sir Stanley Simmons, then President of the Royal College of Obstetricians and Gynaecologists, gave me permission to consult the College archives, whereI had the help of archivists Gervaise Hood and Clare Cowling. I was assisted at the Library of the Royal College of Midwives by Mrs Jan Ayres, Judith Ions and Lesley Moss. I must also thank David Webb at the Bishopsgate Institute, Angela Raspin at the LSE, and the librarians of the Bodleian Library, the Institute of Historical Research and the British Library. Dame Rosalinde Hurley kindly gave me permission to consult the documents of the Human Milk Bureau at Queen Charlotte's Hospital, Hammersmith Hospitals NHS Trust, and Gillian Weaver, Coordinator of the Milk Bank, gave me invaluable help; I am grateful to Georgina Going, the Librarian of Queen Charlotte's, for supplying photographs of the Human Milk Bureau. Angela Clarke, the Marmite Librarian, unearthed important material for me, as did Molly Robinson at the Cambridgeshire Libraries & Information Service and the Librarian of the Information Department of The BOC Group.

My work was done at the Institute of Education in the Social Science Research Unit, of which Ann Oakley is Director, and where I have enjoyed all kinds of support. Sandra Stone and Jackie Lee provided continual administrative and secretarial help.

Sutton Publishing has taken a very real interest in the content of the book and I am grateful for this to Roger Thorp, Head of Academic Publishing, Jane Crompton, Commissioning Editor, and Sarah Fowle, Project Editor, who has shown meticulous attention to the text and unfailing patience. Susanne Atkin compiled the index.

Acknowledgements

My husband Gerald Bloom was at all times my support and helped me with the most difficult part of all – accepting that the book was finished. Finally, I thank my daughter, Tendayi, who energetically joined in the hunt for old records and documents and came with me to many interviews in different parts of Britain. I treasure the memory of our adventures on these trips we took together.

ASW
December 1996

Chronology

1928 **National Birthday Trust Fund**
The National Birthday Fund for Maternity Services is founded by Lady George Cholmondeley and Lady Londonderry.
12 November: Inaugural meeting of Birthday Fund.

Great Britain
Maternal mortality rate is 442 per 100,000 births in England and Wales.
Conservative government, with Stanley Baldwin as Prime Minister (PM) and Neville Chamberlain as Minister of Health.
Voting age of women lowered from thirty to twenty-one.
Departmental Committee on Maternal Mortality and Morbidity established.

1929 Mrs Baldwin offers to run her anaesthetics campaign with the Birthday Fund.
Wireless fundraising appeal from Chequers by Mrs Baldwin.

General election. Labour forms minority government, with Ramsay MacDonald as PM and Philip Snowden as Chancellor of the Exchequer.
Local Government Act.
October: Crash of New York Stock Exchange.
British College of Obstetricians and Gynaecologists (BCOG) founded.

1930 Trust Deed drawn up reconstituting the Birthday Fund as National Birthday *Trust* Fund.
Sir Julien Cahn becomes Chairman and Lady Juliet Williams is invited to join the Trust.
National 'Mother's Day' started by Mrs Baldwin.

2½ million unemployed.
Interim Report of Departmental Committee on Maternal Mortality and Morbidity.

1931 *August:* Formation of National government.
October: General election. National government with Conservative majority.
November: Second National Cabinet: Baldwin as Lord President, Neville Chamberlain as Chancellor, and Snowden as Lord Privy Seal.
'Means Test' introduced.

1932   Snowden resigns from government.
        Final Report of Departmental Committee on Maternal Mortality and Morbidity.
        Depression deepens: hunger march to London.

1933   Opening of Birthday Trust headquarters for midwifery at 57 Lower
        Belgrave Street in London, housing the Midwives' Institute and the
        Queen's Institute for District Nursing.
        Start of Birthday Trust work in Rhondda Valley.

        Unemployment rises to three million.
        Hitler becomes Chancellor of Germany.
        Dr R.J. Minnitt designs gas and air apparatus.

1934   Joint Council of Midwifery (JCM) created by Trust.
        Miss Riddick appointed as Secretary to JCM.

        Maternal mortality peaks at a rate of 460 for every 100,000 births.
        Hunger march to London. Start of demonstrations against new
        Unemployment Assistance Board (UAB). Disturbances in South Wales.
        Special Areas (Development and Improvement) Act.

1935   Broadcast Appeal for the Birthday Trust by Mrs Baldwin.
        Report by JCM on the *Desirability of Establishing a Salaried Service of Midwives*
        BCOG report approves Minnitt machine.

        Maternal mortality starts to decline, at 410 deaths for every 100,000
        births.
        June. Baldwin becomes PM.
        November. General election. National government, mostly Conservative,
        has large majority.
        Discovery of sulphonamides.

1936   JCM Committee of Enquiry into Non-Therapeutic Abortion set up.
        Grant from Commission for Special Areas for nutrition scheme.
        Final allocation to Cooperating Hospitals.

        Midwives Act passed.
        George V dies.
        Beginning of Spanish Civil War.
        December. Edward VIII abdicates, succeeded by George VI.
        'Jarrow March' of unemployed to London.

1937 *Interim Report* of JCM enquiry into abortion.
      Research Committee set up by JCM.

      Inter-Departmental (Birkett) Committee on Abortion appointed.
      Baldwin resigns as PM and is replaced by Chamberlain.

1938 JCM report on abortion submitted to Birkett Committee.
      Invasion of Austria; Munich crisis.

1939 Human Milk Bureau opened at Queen Charlotte's Hospital.
      28 March: Birthday Trust Reception at the Guildhall in London.
      JCM report identifies risk of midwife shortage.

      Publication of Margery Spring Rice's *Working-Class Wives*.
      3 September: War declared on Germany.
      Women and children evacuated from London.
      Maternal mortality rate drops to 313 for every 100,000 births.
      Emergency Medical Services created.

1940 JCM dissolved.

      Coalition government formed under Winston Churchill as PM and
      Minister of Defence.
      Battle of Britain and London Blitz.
      Ministry of Food set up.

1941 Germans invade Russia.
      Japanese attack US fleet at Pearl Harbor.
      Rushcliffe Committee set up, which considers conditions of midwives.
      Midwives' Institute becomes College of Midwives.

1942 Beveridge Report published.

1943 Maternal mortality rate is half the 1935 rate.

1944 Julien Cahn dies. Louis Nicholas becomes Chairman of Birthday Trust.

      Butler Education Act.
      Willink's White Paper on a National Health Service.

1945 *May*: Germany surrenders.
      Wartime Coalition disbanded. Caretaker government.
      General election: Labour government formed under Attlee as PM.

Aneurin Bevan is Minister of Health.

Atomic bombs dropped on Hiroshima and Nagasaki.

End of Second World War.

Blackout ends; street lights lit.

Statement by Royal Commission on Population on fall in birth rate. Start of baby boom.

Perinatal mortality is 45.2 for every 1,000 births.

1946 *3–9 March*: All women giving birth this week interviewed eight weeks later for survey, *Maternity in Great Britain*.

A.J. Espley becomes Chairman of Birthday Trust.

National Health Service Act, England and Wales.

Rationing tightened in UK, including bread.

54 per cent of confinements take place in institutions.

6 August: Family Allowance Day.

1947 Coal industry nationalized.

Independence granted to India and Pakistan.

Working party set up by government to enquire into shortage of midwives.

College of Midwives becomes Royal College.

British College of Obstetricians and Gynaecologists becomes Royal College.

1948 *Maternity in Great Britain* published.

Public meeting run by Married Women's Association on Safer Motherhood.

Lady Baldwin dies.

Technical Advisory Sub-Committee set up by Birthday Trust.

Maternal mortality drops to 102 per 100,000 in England and Wales.

5 July: Appointed Day: NHS inaugurated.

Soviet coup in Czechoslovakia.

1949 William Penman becomes Acting Chairman of Trust.

Report of the Working Party on Midwives.

Introduction and defeat of Thorneycroft's Analgesia in Childbirth Bill.

1950 Lady Rhys Williams becomes Deputy Chairman of Trust.

General election: slim Labour majority.

1951 Festival of Britain.

Bevan resigns.

General election: Conservative majority. Churchill becomes PM.

1952 Contraceptive pill developed.
Elizabeth II becomes Queen.

1954 Lady Juliet Rhys Williams becomes Acting Chairman of Birthday Trust.

Food rationing ends.
RCOG publishes *Report on the Obstetric Service under the National Health Service*, advocating 100 per cent hospital births.

1955 *May*: General election, Conservative majority.
Anthony Eden becomes PM.

1956 *Report of the Committee of Enquiry into the Cost of the NHS* (Guillebaud; presented November 1955).
Maternity Services Committee set up (Cranbrook).
Natural Childbirth Association (later Trust) set up.
Suez crisis.

1957 Lady Juliet Rhys Williams becomes Chairman of Birthday Trust.

Harold Macmillan is PM.
Perinatal mortality rate is 36.2 for every 1,000 live births.

1958 *3–9 March*: Perinatal Mortality Survey, investigating all babies born in this week in England, Wales and Scotland.

1959 *October*: General election, Conservative majority.
Report of the Maternity Services Committee (Cranbrook Report) recommends 70 per cent hospital delivery.
1960 Association for the Improvement of the Maternity Services (AIMS) founded.

1961 Natural Childbirth Trust becomes National Childbirth Trust (NCT).

1962 Publication of *A Hospital Plan for England and Wales*.

1963 Publication of *Perinatal Mortality*, first report of the Perinatal Mortality Survey.
Report of the Trust's Maternity Services Emergency Informal Committee.

Sir Alec Douglas-Home is PM.
National Fund for Childbirth Research set up as research arm of RCOG; its name soon changes to Birthright (and then in 1993 to WellBeing).

1964 Technical Advisory Sub-Committee renamed Scientific Advisory Committee. Inaugural meeting of National Child Development Study, follow-up of Perinatal Mortality Survey.
Death of Lady Rhys Williams.

General election: Labour Party elected. Harold Wilson is PM.
70 per cent of deliveries take place in hospital.

1965 Child Poverty Action Group set up; poverty 'rediscovered'.
NHS prescription charges abolished.

1966 HRH Princess Alexandra becomes Patron of Birthday Trust.
Sir George Haynes is first President of the Trust; Walter Gilbey is Chairman.
Jeffrey Archer employed briefly as fundraiser for the Trust.

General election: Labour returned.

1967 Abortion Act provides for legal termination of pregnancy.
Family Planning Act.
Standing Maternity and Midwifery Advisory (Peel) Committee set up.

1968 Prescription charges reintroduced.

1969 Publication of *Perinatal Problems*, second report of the 1958 Perinatal Mortality Survey.

Voting age reduced to eighteen.
Perinatal mortality rate is 23.4 for every 1,000 births.

1970 *5–11 April*: British Births Survey, investigating all babies born in Great Britain this week.

Election: Conservatives win. Edward Heath is PM.
Equal Pay Act.
Peel *Report* recommends 100 per cent hospital delivery of babies.
12 per cent of deliveries take place at home.

1971 Reorganization of Trust: General Committee merged with Executive Committee to form much smaller General Committee.

Decimalization of currency.
Abolition of free school milk.

1972   Miss Riddick retires.
Dame Josephine Barnes becomes Vice-President of the RCOG until 1975.

1973   NHS Reorganization Act.
UK joins EEC.
Queen's Institute for District Nursing becomes Queen's Nursing Institute.

1974   Two general elections, both producing a minority Labour government under Wilson as PM.
NHS reorganization.

1975   Volume 1 of *British Births 1970* published.

Sex Discrimination Act.

1977   Sir Brandon Rhys Williams becomes Chairman of Birthday Trust.

1978   Volume 2 of *British Births 1970* published.
National Perinatal Epidemiology Unit set up in Oxford.

1979   General Election: Conservative government. Margaret Thatcher becomes first woman PM in Britain.
DHSS decides against fourth national perinatal mortality survey.
Maternal death rate is 11 per 100,000.

1980   *Report of the House of Commons Social Services Committee on Perinatal and Neonatal Mortality* (Short Report).

1981   Dame Josephine Barnes takes over Presidency of Birthday Trust.
The Maternity Alliance founded.
Perinatal mortality rate is 11.8 for every 1,000 births.

1982   Unemployment passes three million.

1983   General election: Conservatives returned.

1984   *First day of August, September, October, November.* Birthplace survey.

1987   Publication of *Birthplace. The Report of a Confidential Enquiry into the Facilities Available at the Place of Birth.*

General election: Conservatives returned.

1989   57 Lower Belgrave Street sold.

1990   *25 June–1 July*: Pain relief survey of all births in this week.

       98 per cent of deliveries take place in hospital.

1992   Report of the House of Commons Select Committee on Health enquiry
       into *Maternity Services* (Winterton Report).

1993   *4 November*: Birthday Trust joins forces with WellBeing (formerly
       Birthright), the research arm of the RCOG.
       Geoffrey Chamberlain becomes President of the RCOG.
       Pain and its Relief in Childbirth published.

       Publication of *Changing Childbirth* (Cumberlege Report).

1994   Home Births Survey.

List of Abbreviations

AIMS	Association for the Improvement of the Maternity Services
ALRA	Abortion Law Reform Association
BBS	British Births Survey
BCOG	British College of Gynaecology and Obstetricians
BCS70	British Cohort Study 1970
BMA	British Medical Association
BMJ	British Medical Journal
BOC	British Oxygen Company
CAB	Citizen's Advice Bureau
CMAC	Contemporary Medical Archives Centre
CMB	Central Midwives Board
CMO	Chief Medical Officer
CNA	County Nursing Association
COS	Charity Organization Society
CPAG	Child Poverty Action Group
CPHC	Central Public Health Committee
CRD	Conservative Research Department
DH	Department of Health
DHSS	Department of Health and Social Security
DNA	District Nursing Association
EBM	Expressed Breast Milk
EUG	Eugenics Society
GLC	Greater London Council
GLRO	Greater London Record Office
GP	General Practitioner
GPU	General Practitioner Unit
GRO	General Register Office
HMB	Human Milk Bureau
HO	Home Office
ICCS	International Centre for Child Studies
JCM	Joint Council of Midwifery
LA	Local Authority
LAB	Ministry of Labour
LCC	London County Council
LHA	Local Health Authority
MH	Ministry of Health
MI	Midwives' Institute

MMC	Maternal Mortality Committee
MMR	Maternal Mortality Rate
MOH	Medical Officer of Health
MP	Member of Parliament
MRC	Medical Research Council
MSEIC	Maternity Services Emergency Informal Committee
MWA	Married Women's Association
NBTF	National Birthday Trust Fund
NCDS	National Child Development Study
NCT	National Childbirth Trust
NCW	National Council of Women
NFWI	National Federation of Women's Institutes
NHS	National Health Service
NPEU	National Perinatal Epidemiology Unit
NSHD	National Survey of Health and Development
ONS	Office of National Statistics
OPCS	Office of Population Censuses and Surveys
PAC	Public Assistance Committee
PEP	Political and Economic Planning
PIC	Population Investigation Committee
PLH	People's League of Health
PMS	Perinatal Mortality Survey
PNMR	Perinatal Mortality Rate
PRO	Public Record Office
PRS	Pain Relief Survey
QCH	Queen Charlotte's Hospital
QIDN	Queen's Institute for District Nursing
QNI	Queen's Nursing Institute
RCM	Royal College of Midwives
RCOG	Royal College of Obstetricians and Gynaecology
RCT	Randomised Controlled Trial
RSM	Royal Society of Medicine
RUDC	Rhondda Urban District Council
SAC	Scientific Advisory Committee
SCF	Save the Children Fund
TASC	Technical and Advisory Sub-Committee
TUC	Trade Union Congress
UAB	Unemployment Assistance Board
UCH	University College Hospital
WAAF	Women's Auxiliary Air Force
WCG	Women's Cooperative Guild
WHO	World Health Organization

CHAPTER ONE

Introduction

"The Queen views with grave concern the continued high rate of maternal mortality. Her Majesty feels that a very real endeavour should be made to remove this reproach from our national life." This declaration of royal concern was made by Queen Mary in 1928, when nearly one in 200 women in Britain lost their lives in childbirth every year.[1] Every pregnant woman was faced with the knowledge that she might not survive to care for her baby, and just about everyone had suffered the loss of a friend or a loved one in childbirth. Even more chilling was the fact that this risk to mothers was increasing: the rate of maternal death had been rising steadily since 1911, as shown in figure 1.1. The time had come, said the Queen, "for concerted action to be taken in dealing with so pressing an evil."[2]

Less than six months after this urgent message from Queen Mary, the constitution of a new charity was drawn up on 2 July 1928 with the express aim of reducing death in childbirth. It was called the National Birthday Fund for Maternity Services and was to be a "real crusade to solve the problem of maternal mortality".[3] Its initial aims were simply philanthropic, but they soon developed into an ambitious and determined campaign to influence government policy on maternity care. The name of the Fund (which became a trust in 1930, when its name was changed to reflect this) was derived from a plan to collect at least one shilling from every member of the British public on their birthday, or the birthday of their mother or one of their children.[4] In 1928 this would have amounted to 42 million shillings, or £2,100,000, a sum that was comparable in value to about £714,000,000 in the mid-1990s.[5]

THE GREAT AND THE GOOD

The Birthday Fund was the idea of Ina, Lady George Cholmondeley,[6] who founded it with the help of her friend Edith, the Marchioness of Londonderry, the foremost social and political hostess of her day.[7] They recruited to their new organization Lucy Baldwin, wife of the Conservative Prime Minister,[8] who was preoccupied with the demands of the coming general election but was unable to resist a cause she cared about so passionately.[9] At a fundraising dinner in 1929, she announced that women in labour were as much at risk from death as soldiers in the trenches had been in the 1914–18 war. "Do you realise," she asked her audience, "that our women daily, hourly, are 'going over the top'?"

FIGURE 1.1: MATERNAL DEATH RATE PER 1,000 LIVE BIRTHS

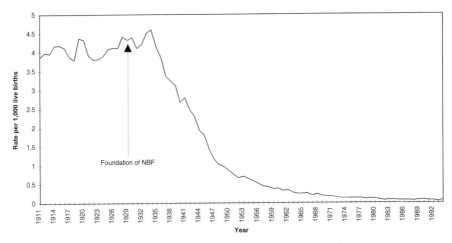

Source: A. Macfarlane and M. Mugford, *Birth Counts: Statistics of Pregnancy and Childbirth*, 2 vols (HMSO, 1984) p. 271. This graph includes the most recent data to be included in the next edition, provided by Alison Macfarlane. It does not show revisions in classification over the century.

When a mother gave birth, she said, it was just like "going into battle – she never knows, and the doctor never knows, whether she will come out of it alive or not".[10]

Other members of British High Society soon joined the Fund, most of them women. They were free of many of the restrictions placed on the female sex at this time because of their social class, wealth and connections: albeit indirectly, they were able to exert power and influence through their husbands and other male members of their families, through whom they were linked to both Houses of Parliament. They belonged to a small circle that was closely connected, through blood, friendship, business or politics, especially those of the Conservative Party. Lady Baldwin's grandson has pointed out, for example, that Lord Strathcona was Lucy Baldwin's son-in-law's brother, Lady Congleton was Lord Strathcona's sister, and Agatha Lady Hindlip, the Countess of Plymouth and Lady Vansittart were neighbours to the Baldwins in Worcestershire.[11] The privileges afforded by social class were clearly understood by Lady Londonderry. Although she had joined in demands for the female vote, she took the view that women like herself did not really need it: "It is not 'for the noblest women in England' as such," she said, "that the vote is really desired, except for the recognition of the principle."[12]

These 'noblest women' were nearly all titled, which caused a headache for the Fund's secretary. Lady Dawson of Penn complained, "Will you be kind and see I am rptd [sic] *Viscountess* Dawson of Penn and *not* Lady Dawson of Penn. I do not personally mind but it is incorrect. I had to mention this before! Another lapse."

'*Lady George Cholmondeley's chief interest just now is the National [Birthday] Fund for Maternity Services, of which she is chairman and founder. All the London maternity hospitals have amalgamated under this trust.*' Vogue, *6 March 1929. (Reproduced courtesy of The Condé Nast Publications Ltd)*

Edith, Marchioness of Londonderry, Vogue, *late June 1918. Lady Londonderry was at this time head of the Women's Service Legion, supplying army cooks and motor drivers to the War Office. (Reproduced courtesy of The Condé Nast Publications Ltd)*

She was also concerned that due title be given to others and wrote, "I see that the new Lady Melchett is down as the Hon. Mrs Henry Mond. It may have been overlooked, but I mention it as a reminder for the new paper." No wonder the secretary was relieved at the arrival on her desk of the latest edition of *Who's Who*.[13]

Although Lady George was the first Chairman of the Fund, this position was taken over in 1930 by Sir Julien Cahn, an eccentric millionaire businessman.[14] He had a particular bond with Lady Baldwin, whose niece recalls their shared passion for cricket: Sir Julien had his own private cricket team, which he took to Jamaica in 1929 and to the Argentine in 1930; while Mrs Baldwin belonged to the only women's cricket team in Britain.[15] Sir Julien, who was President of the City of Nottingham Conservative Association, was extremely generous and built an up-to-date maternity hospital in Stourport in Mrs Baldwin's honour, which was called the Lucy Baldwin Hospital. One of the few men on the charity's central committee, he was content to leave the decision-making to the women leading 'this very feminine charity', as it was described in 1939 by the magazine *Sketch*.[16] However,

THE LADY GEORGE CHOLMONDELEY, O.B.E.
(Founder and Vice-Chairman, National Birthday Trust Fund).

SIR JULIEN CAHN, Bart.
(Chairman, National Birthday Trust Fund).

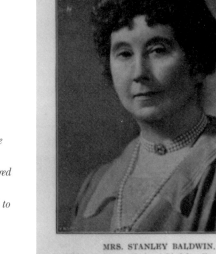

MRS. STANLEY BALDWIN.
(Vice-Chairman, National Birthday Trust Fund).

Key members of the Birthday Trust in the 1930s: (clockwise from top left) Lady George Cholmondeley, Sir Julien Cahn and Mrs Stanley Baldwin. These photographs appeared in the programme for Elijah, *which was performed at the Royal Albert Hall in 1935 to raise funds for the Trust.*
([NBTF/uncatalogued box] Reproduced courtesy of the Wellcome Institute Library, London)

he was at times perplexed by the women's behaviour and after a meeting in 1931 he wrote irritably, "I do not pretend to understand the psychology of women."[17]

The driving force behind most Trust projects throughout the century was Lady Juliet Williams (becoming Lady Juliet Rhys Williams in 1938)[18], who joined in early 1930 after writing a letter of enquiry about the new charity.[19] Lady Bearsted made enquiries about Lady Williams, reporting to Lady George that she was very keen on helping with maternity work and "seems a really energetic worker".[20] This proved to be an understatement: the Trust relied more and more heavily on Lady Rhys Williams, especially after the deaths of Sir Julien and Lady Baldwin in the 1940s, and never really recovered from her death in 1964. According to the novelist and Conservative politician Jeffrey Archer, who was employed by the Trust as a fundraiser in 1966, "they talked of her as if she was some sort of matriarch and you know, if she'd said they must do something, then they all did it."[21] Her son, Sir Brandon Rhys Williams,[22] became Chairman of the Birthday Trust in 1971, but was unable to devote as much time and energy to the Trust as his mother because of his commitment to parliamentary duties. The baton of leadership was not picked up for over a decade after Lady Rhys Williams's death, when Geoffrey Chamberlain,[23] an obstetrician, emerged from the 1970 survey work as a new leader of the Trust.

THE EARLY YEARS

In the autumn of 1928, Lady George and Lady Londonderry sent out invitations for an Inaugural Meeting of the Fund on 12 November at Wimborne House in London,

Lady Rhys Williams, who in the early 1930s persuaded the Birthday Trust to start an energetic campaign to improve the status and conditions of midwives. (Reproduced courtesy of the National Birthday Trust Fund)

The Marchioness of Londonderry

and

Lady George Cholmondeley

request the pleasure of your Company

at the Inaugural Meeting of the

National Birthday Fund for Maternity Services

at Wimborne House, 22, Arlington Street, W.1.

(by kind permission of the Viscountess Wimborne)

on Monday, 12th November, 1928, at 3 p.m

Speakers:

    Mrs. Stanley Baldwin.

    Mr. Neville Chamberlain

Chairman: The Lord Ebbisham, C.B.E.

R.S.V.P. The Secretary,

Room 72, Carlton House,

Regent Street, S.W.1

Tea 4.15 p.m.

Invitation to the Inaugural Meeting of the National Birthday Fund for Maternity Services on 12 November 1928. ([NBTF/C1] Reproduced courtesy of the Wellcome Institute Library, London)

the home of the very rich Wimborne family. The meeting was chaired by Lord Ebbisham and the speakers were Lucy Baldwin and Neville Chamberlain, Minister of Health. Philip Snowden, who had been Chancellor of the Exchequer in the former Labour government, was unable to come but sent a warm letter of support. The occasion was covered by the national newspapers, but mostly as a fashion event. Lady Londonderry looked "extremely well in black velvet, with a helmet hat," reported the *Daily Express*, adding, "Another was Lady Islington, who also wore black. So did Lady Carlisle. Black is being rapidly restored to the favour of the *chic* – if, indeed, it ever lost it. Mrs Baldwin wore brown."[24]

Not only fashionable ladies joined the Fund's General Committee, but also representatives of the voluntary maternity hospitals cooperating with the Fund; these hospitals are listed in table 1.1. Initially, it was planned to have three classes of Cooperating Hospitals, depending on the level of work and money provided by their principal ladies,[25] but these categories were soon disregarded. Each hospital received a small donation every year, usually between £10 and £30 (comparable in value to £340 and £1,020 in the mid-1990s).[26] The hospital representatives are easily recognizable in a list of Trust members, because they were not titled (lists of various Trust committees over the century are given in Appendix B). The representatives included Seymour Leslie, the Appeal Secretary of Queen Charlotte's Hospital, Mrs Model of the Jewish Maternity

---

TABLE 1.1: HOSPITALS COOPERATING WITH THE BIRTHDAY FUND

In London
British Hospital for Mothers and Babies
City of London Maternity Hospital
Clapham Maternity Hospital
East End Maternity Hospital
General Lying-in Hospital
Jewish Maternity District Nursing and Sick Room Help Society
Mothers' Hospital of the Salvation Army
Queen Charlotte's Maternity Hospital

In the provinces
Leeds Maternity Hospital
Plaistow Maternity Hospital

In Kenya
Kikuyu Alliance Women's Industrial Home
Pumwani African Maternity and Child Welfare Hospital and Training Centre

---

District Nursing and Sick Room Help Society, Dr Annie McCall of the Clapham Maternity Hospital, and Commissioner Catherine Booth of the Salvation Army Mothers' Hospital. They had very little influence on the decision-making of the organization.

On 2 April 1930, a Trust Deed was drawn up, reconstituting the charity as the National Birthday Trust Fund. In early 1929, Lady George had presented to the General Committee her plan for this new approach. Instead of banking all donations and subscriptions on deposit, she said, "all sums should be invested, the interest only distributed according to the constitution of the Fund, any surplus to be re-invested."[27] The chosen Trustees were all experts at high finance. They were the Earl of Cromer, the Lord Chamberlain, who was the director of several large banks and of an insurance company; Lord Melchett, who transformed his highly successful chemical organization into Imperial Chemical Industries (ICI); Viscount Philip Snowden, who was Chancellor of the Exchequer in the current Labour government; and J.W. Beaumont Pease (who became Lord Wardington six years later), the chairman of several banks, including Lloyds, and director of an insurance company. The Trust's Finance Committee, who were husbands of Birthday Trust members and familiar with the ways of business, took charge of investments. They were Lord George Cholmondeley, Lord Annaly, the Earl of Bessborough, and Lord Ebbisham.

Lady Williams soon discovered that the new name, 'Trust Fund', "was very useful in the country, it gave prestige".[28] The *Daily Sketch* observed that: "The Birthday Trust is something to talk about because it is the first time that a charity has been put on a really sound business footing. . . . Now that is infinitely sounder than the average charity, which relies on continual donations.[29] The *Evening News* agreed, pointing out that Lady George was "the first person to have worked out a plan by which all the money collected in an appeal is invested."[30] Certainly this plan put the Birthday Trust on a different footing from other women's organizations concerned with women's health, such as the Women's Cooperative Guild, which relied for its survival on a subscription membership. But it was not an original idea, since many voluntary organizations had a tradition of investing their funds, like the King's Fund and voluntary hospitals.

THE CAMPAIGN AGAINST MATERNAL DEATH

The Trust Deed gave Lady George the opportunity to set down in a legal framework the objects of the charity. However, these were fairly vague, involving a general commitment to the support of voluntary maternity hospitals, midwifery, and "any other purposes connected with maternity" (see Appendix A for a list of aims). At first, they produced little more than the donation of modest sums to the Cooperating Hospitals. It was unanimously agreed and minuted that "the Fund should have imperial scope" and that its work should extend throughout the Empire,[31] but this imperial scope was limited to an affiliation in 1931 with two institutions in Kenya. These were the Kikuyu Alliance Women's Industrial Home, which had opened in 1923 for the "Rescue and Preventive Work among African women of all tribes",[32] and the Lady Grigg African Maternity Welfare Hospital and Training Centre in Pumwani, Nairobi (the Pumwani Hospital today), which had been founded by Lady Grigg, a member of the Birthday Fund. Like the British voluntary maternity hospitals, these Kenyan institutions were sent small donations every year. They were sent other forms of assistance, too, such as a parcel of the chloroform capsules that were developed by the Trust in the course of its efforts to diminish the pain of childbirth. In October 1933, the Matron of the hospital in Pumwani reported on her patients' reaction to these capsules: "I have tried them on many cases, in the first stage, in the second stage, and Episitomy [sic] and stitching," she said, "but the native women flatly refuse to inhale."[33] In 1936, as shown in chapter 6, the judgement of these mothers was confirmed by the British College of Obstetricians and Gynaecologists (BCOG), which ruled that the capsules were too dangerous for use.

Shortly after these modest beginnings, the Trust started more earnest efforts to tackle maternal mortality. This was largely due to the influence of Lady Williams. Her joining of the Trust in early 1930 coincided with Lady George's resignation from the position of chairman (because she felt that someone with more time was needed) and a growing disinterest on the part of Lady Londonderry. This meant that an opening appeared for Lady Williams's energy and drive: at her suggestion, an Executive Committee of core members was created in September 1930. This would meet monthly, while the General Committee would meet only once or twice a year.[34] Since the representatives of the Cooperating Hospitals were not brought on to the Executive Committee, their influence in the organization became even weaker than it already was.

At about the same time that these administration changes were being put into effect, the Trust turned its attention to the needs of the poor. By 1930, the Depression had made two and a half million people unemployed, which made the lives of working-class mothers even more of a struggle than they already were. A Report produced for the Pilgrim Trust in 1936 on the effects of unemployment stated that the wives of unemployed men suffered more than anyone else and showed "obvious signs of malnutrition". According to the Report, their lack of nourishment and the strain of caring for a family in adverse conditions had produced a general lowering of vitality and "a marked increase in the number of women suffering from anaemia, neurasthenia, and . . . in the occurrence of septic hands, boils and skin troubles."[35]

Before the National Health Service, working-class women had less access to health care than anyone else in Britain. Under the National Insurance Act of 1911, most workers were entitled to care when they were ill, but wives received nothing for illness and only 30s maternity benefit. Margery Spring Rice, chairman of the North Kensington Women's Welfare Centre, observed in *Working-Class Wives*, an account of poor women's lives in the 1930s, that, "Owing to the fact that the National Health Insurance system makes no provision for the wife of an insured man, she has still to call in a private doctor when she feels ill" or, more likely, postpones this step for as long as possible.[36] The Maternal and Child Welfare Act of 1918 empowered Local Authorities to care for mothers, but "the question of turning the present maternity and welfare powers into duties was much more difficult."[37]

The Trust decided to do all that it possibly could to help pregnant mothers who were poor – to "secure for the poorer mother the same relief from suffering as is invariably offered to her well-to-do sister."[38] This priority underpinned most of its work in the 1930s: a request for a gas and air machine for middle-class patients was specifically rejected because the Trust's funds were reserved for "the working class women who cannot afford analgesics".[39]

THE STATUS OF MIDWIVES

Lady Williams believed that simply assisting maternity hospitals with small amounts of money would do little to reduce the maternal death rate. "The Fund gets no kudos," she told the Trust, "and in fact it gets ridicule rather than gratitude for what it is doing now."[40] For ideas about how the Trust could really make a difference, she turned for advice to Dame Janet Campbell,[41] the Senior

Medical Officer in the Department of Maternal and Child Welfare at the Ministry of Health. Lady Williams had already established contact with Dame Janet in the course of her work for the Queen Charlotte's Anaesthetics Fund, which she had founded in 1927.[42] Dame Janet, who regarded an improvement in midwifery as a priority in the struggle to reduce maternal death, welcomed this opportunity to influence the direction of the Trust. She suggested that the Trust devote its energies and resources to the assistance and support of midwives – that "the best contribution possible to the cause of maternal welfare at the moment would be the establishment of a proper headquarters where midwives can take postgraduate courses and [with] club rooms and other facilities."[43] Lady Williams reported this advice to the Trust, explaining that there was no question of altering the Fund's original policy, "but merely of allocating a larger proportion of its income than hitherto to the second of its objects, namely, the assistance of midwives, rather than to the first of them, namely assistance of hospitals." She persuaded her colleagues that this was "work which no other organization is engaged upon, and by doing which the N.B.T.F. would be meeting a real need, and possibly contributing materially to the reduction of the maternal mortality rate."[44] It would be of particular benefit to mothers who were poor, since it was they – and not better-off mothers, who invariably were attended by doctors – who relied on midwives for care in childbirth.

From this point in the history of the Trust, it is possible to detect a shift in its direction. In 1933, it established a national midwifery headquarters at 57 Lower Belgrave Street in London's genteel Belgravia, where many of the Trust members had their London homes (both Mrs Baldwin and Lady Williams, for example, lived on Eaton Square, which adjoins Lower Belgrave Street). Sir Julien bought the lease for the building and paid for it to be equipped and decorated. Not only did the Trust, which had first been at Empire House in Piccadilly and then at Carlton House on Regent Street, move in, but it also offered free accommodation to the Midwives' Institute and the Queen's Institute for District Nurses, which together were responsible for 60 per cent of all births in 1933. The Midwives' Institute had been founded in 1881 and produced *Midwives Chronicle and Nursing Notes*; it became the College of Midwives in 1941 and was granted a Royal Charter to become a Royal College in 1947.[45] The Queen's Institute had been founded as Queen Victoria's Jubilee Institute for Nurses in 1887 and in 1889 was issued a Royal Charter to provide "the training support and maintenance of women to act as nurses for the sick and poor";[46] it provided Queen's Nurses with midwifery training for rural areas. In 1973 it was renamed the Queen's Nursing Institute.[47]

The Midwives' Institute and the Queen's Institute were delighted to move out of their cramped accommodation into this "beautiful house".[48] Their new physical proximity was described as a key measure in the advancement of midwifery in a 1934 study of the relations between the statutory and voluntary social services by Elizabeth Macadam, a leading social worker; her book refers approvingly to "the unexpected acquisition of stately headquarters in a London West End square".[49] The midwifery organizations had the benefit not only of office accommodation, council and lecture rooms, but also of hostel accommodation for midwives attending refresher courses, and a canteen.

The headquarters were officially opened on 25 October 1933 by the Parliamentary Secretary to the Minister of Health, Sir Hilton Young, who had hoped to come himself but had been detained by a Cabinet meeting. Lady Hilton Young attended the ceremony, at which Miss Rosalind Paget, the first Inspector General of the Queen's Nurses and a senior member of the Midwives' Institute, gave flowers to Lady Cahn. A month later, on 23 November, Queen Mary paid an informal visit to the headquarters,

57 Lower Belgrave Street, London SW1, the home of the midwifery headquarters in the 1930s. The NBTF and the Queen's Nursing Institute stayed here until 1989, when the building was sold. (Reproduced courtesy of the Queen's Nursing Institute)

and the day after sent a gift of an electric clock for the midwives' sitting room. Although unable to give her patronage to a new appeal fund, the Queen had indicated her support for the charity from the very start and Lady Cynthia Colville, her Lady-in-Waiting, became a keen member. In 1933, the Queen attended a fundraising premiere of the film *The Great Barrier* at the New Capitol Theatre in Haymarket (with special chocolates for the occasion supplied by the Army and Navy Stores). In 1939, Queen Elizabeth continued the support of the Royal Family by attending a lavish reception at the Guildhall.

In early 1934, the Trust stepped up its campaign to assist midwives by setting up the Joint Committee on Midwifery, which was shortly afterwards renamed the Joint Council of Midwifery (JCM). The task of this Council was the evaluation of national policy on the employment of midwives and the development of recommendations to improve this. It was chaired by the Earl of Athlone, Queen Mary's brother, who was Personal ADC to King George V and also President and Chairman of the Queen's Institute of District Nursing. The Council comprised members of the Houses of Commons and Lords and of all those organizations and individuals most concerned with midwifery, including distinguished representatives of the British College of Obstetricians and

Gynaecologists, which had been founded in 1929, and of the British Medical Association (BMA). The secretariat of the JCM was located in the new midwifery headquarters at 57 Lower Belgrave Street. Lady Williams became Honorary Secretary and Miss Doreen Riddick,[50] who was later to become a key member of the Trust, was appointed administrative secretary. A big step had been taken towards raising the midwife's status , which was now "one of the main objects of the Fund".[51]

This campaign to professionalize the midwife was consistent with the growing importance of professional groups in the 1930s. In 1933, the same year that saw the opening of the midwifery headquarters, *The Professions* by A.M. Carr-Saunders and P.A. Wilson was published, which was the first proper study of the professions.[52] For the rest of the 1930s, well over half of the Trust's expenditure was allocated to the JCM and the midwifery headquarters, as shown in figure 1.2; in 1936, the Trust's donations to the Cooperating Hospitals were stopped (with the exception of Queen Charlotte's Hospital in London, with which the Trust enjoyed an increasingly close relationship over the 1930s, and the Pumwani Hospital in Kenya).[53]

RAISING FUNDS

Most of the charity's funds came from a few major benefactors, of whom Sir Julien was the most important.[54] Lord Strathcona's backing helped the Fund get started: he gave £1,000 in 1929, then £2,000 to be spread over seven years, and a further £1,000 in 1936; he entreated Lady George to let "the gift . . . remain

FIGURE 1.2 NBTF EXPENDITURE IN 1937 (EXCLUDING FUNDS FROM COMMISSION FOR SPECIAL AREAS)

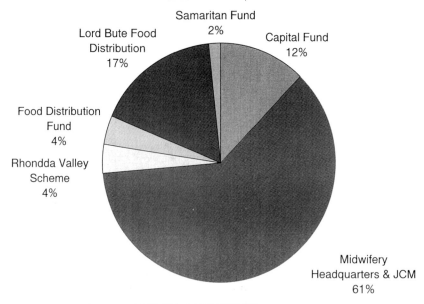

Source: NBTF Annual Report 1937 [SA/NBT/C17/7]

anonymous as far as the General Public is concerned although – it is obvious that your finance committee – and others, must know".[55] The flour magnate Robert McDougall donated 1,042 shares in his company, McDougall Trust Ltd, in response to a Wireless Appeal by Mrs Baldwin in 1935. "My special interest," he told Lady Londonderry, "is in the Anaesthetic Appeal Fund section of the work of your Fund," and he asked her to create an 'Elizabeth McDougall Trust', in memory of his mother.[56] The value of these shares in 1936 was about £1,875.[57]

Efforts at raising funds from the public were not successful. The idea of the Birthday Shilling never really captured the public's imagination and a complaint was made that the birthday reminder card was in "very bad taste".[58] Another problem was the name of the Trust, according to Jeffrey Archer. "If you said to a person in the street, I'm supporting the National Birthday Trust," he remembers, "they would say, 'Happy Birthday!' They had no idea it had anything to do with the birth of children."[59] Sir Julien thought it was an "asinine title" and complained that, "a quick glance at the heading gives me the idea that the Trust is founded to give us presents on our birthdays!"[60] In 1943, he made a request to the Charity Commissioners to change the name to the 'National Maternity Services Trust', but this was not approved. When the Natural Childbirth Trust became the National Childbirth Trust in the

Skilful draping gives softening lines to these new MATERNITY FASHIONS

A Splendid selection of Maternity Gowns is always to be seen on the Second Floor at Dickins & Jones, revealing the latest styles in charming variety.

GOWN AND COATEE for Maternity wear of Black Lace, lined throughout crêpe-de-chine. Cut on slender lines with easy adjustments.

MATERNITY GOWN AND COATEE of daintily patterned Chiffon on Black ground. Lined throughout crêpe-de-chine. Simple adjustments.

7½ Gns.   7½ Gns.

Maternity Salon—Second Floor

DICKINS & JONES LTD

REGENT STREET   LONDON, W.1

This 1930 advertisement for maternity wear reflects the fashion of disguising pregnancy. Illustrated London News, *2 April 1930. (Reproduced courtesy of the* Illustrated London News *Picture Library)*

1960s, the similarity between the names generated endless problems.[61]

Fundraising in the 1930s was hampered by the Depression, which led several events to be postponed or cancelled, and by the general discomfort attached to the idea of talking about childbirth and pregnancy in public. In any case, the Birthday Trust was competing with so many other charities: when the department store Barkers opened a letter from the Fund in 1929, it had already seen sixty-seven demands in the post that morning.[62] Violet Astor, who was Chairman of the Trust's Safer Motherhood Appeal, sent out "no less than 1,875 letters and . . . got in only £28 10s 0d."[63] The Fur Coat Competition in 1930 was equally unsuccessful, because "guessing the number of skins does not appeal to people very much".[64] Lady Howard de Walden's secretary protested that she was "really too busy to have time to eliminate the names of the people she knows from the letter 'M' onwards in the Telephone Directory".[65]

Charity balls were more popular: large-scale private dances had been supplanted by charity affairs since the 1914–18 war, according to the *Brighton Standard* in 1930.[66] These dances lasted through the night, like the British Porcelain Ball at Claridge's on 24 November 1931, which started at 10.00 p.m.; supper was at 11.30, and a grand 'Porcelain Ballet' followed at 12.30. There was a 'running' buffet and carriages were arranged for 3.00 a.m. In 1930, there was a Strauss Ball, which was conducted by Johann Strauss, the nephew of the composer of the Blue Danube, and at which Lady George, Lady Londonderry and two of her daughters wore dresses from 1873. In 1931 there was a Lace Ball and in 1933, a Midnight Gala performance of a play called Ballerina. The organization was keen to exploit its connections: a notice about Mrs Baldwin's Bridge Ball advertised the sale of tickets from "Mrs Stanley Baldwin, OBE, 10 Downing Street, S.W.". At such an address, At Homes were bound to be successful, with the exception of a Poetry Recital and Madrigals at 10 Downing Street on 27 October 1936, which was organized by Lady Buckmaster, Vice-President of the

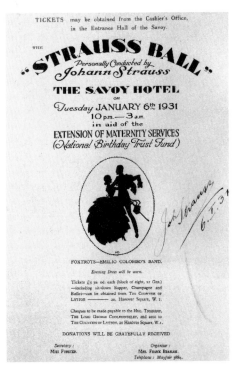

The programme for the Strauss Ball, 6 January 1931. It was signed by Johann Strauss, nephew of the composer of the famous Viennese waltzes, who conducted the ball. ([NBTF/G15(1)] Reproduced courtesy of the Wellcome Institute Library, London)

WITH THE DOWAGER LADY SWAYTHLING : MRS. S. BALDWIN.

CHATTING TO MRS. CLEAVER : MR. STANLEY BALDWIN.

A FAMOUS AIRWOMAN : THE DUCHESS OF BEDFORD, WITH MRS. BENTLEY.

A WELL-KNOWN SPORTING PEER : THE MARQUESS OF CHOLMONDELEY WITH HIS WIFE.

A KNIGHT OF THE AIR : SIR ALAN COBHAM, WITH LADY COBHAM AND CAPTAIN WARD.

MEMBERS OF THE COMMITTEE : THE COUNTESS OF BESSBOROUGH AND LADY GEORGE CHOLMONDELEY.

WITH THE COMTE DE SEGONZAC : MISS SONIA CONVERSE.

OFFICIALS OF THE AIR RACE TOTALISATOR : (L. TO R.) MISS DOROTHY DUNKELLS, MISS ELMA REID, AN ASSISTANT, PRINCESS MELIKOFF, AND CAPTAIN ANDREWS.

A Flying Rally was held at Hanworth airfield on 19 July 1930 to raise funds for the NBTF. It "was not only a most successful gathering from the flying point of view, but was attended by many notable people, both of airy and earthly distinction". Sketch, 30 July 1930. (Reproduced courtesy of the Illustrated London News *Picture Library)*

Poetry Society. It made only £67: Sir Julien adamantly refused to attend, even though the Trust's secretary wrote to his assistant, "Am I right in assuming that Sir Julien definitely does not require any tickets at all for Lady Buckmaster's P. R.? Surely he cannot be so hard. Please ask him to have pity on me, and take even half a dozen little ten shilling tickets – after all tea is thrown in, and several other things probably thrown out."[67]

In 1930, an Aerial Meet and Rally was held at Hanworth Airfield and was attended by the official ambassadors in Great Britain of nations all over the world. Aviation was still being developed at this time and was less a means of getting from place to place, than a leisure pursuit that was popular with the very rich. The Birthday Trust was always interested in new technology and used the cinema, which was still novel and exciting, for propaganda purposes. They arranged for trailers to be displayed on the screen in cinemas in London and provincial towns, with the message: "When is your birthday: Do send 1s or more to Lady George Cholmondeley's National Birthday Trust Fund, which has been started because 69,892 mothers have died in the last 16 years."[68] Mrs Baldwin used the wireless to make two appeals: the Empire Appeal in 1929, and a Safer Motherhood Appeal in 1935. These produced many gifts of money and warm wishes of support. A contribution of 10 guineas was accompanied by a letter of admiration for "your work to see that poor women were also given anaesthetics."[69] 'A Small Giver' wrote to Lady Baldwin, "You speak, dear Lady, very kindly of the suffering. . . . We heartily hope and pray that God will support you all in this effort, that the people through the mighty Press will be touched to the heart, and the result will be a great and glorious victory over pain and suffering." A 'Working Man' said he was sure that "if the appeal meets the eye of men and women who have the slightest idea of a woman's suffering in childbirth it will meet with a good response."[70]

Mrs Baldwin's appeals to the British public invariably won their hearts. When she started 'Mother's Day' as a flag day for maternal welfare on 29 March 1930, the day before Mothering Sunday, stamps and flags were sold on behalf of the Trust in many parts of Britain. "A new movement," enthused the *Nottingham Guardian*, "has been inaugurated by Mrs Stanley Baldwin – 'Mother's Day'."[71] It was "growing rapidly in public favour," according to the *Express & Star*. "Towns extending from Peebles to Camarthen, from Worcester to Burnham-on-Sea in Somerset, and from Newcastle-under-Lyme . . . are already busy preparing for the sale of emblems printed in what has come to be known as 'Mother's Blue'."[72]

THE START OF RESEARCH

The pursuit of research, which became the Trust's primary concern in the postwar period, developed out of earlier negotiations with the government to pay for a food relief programme for pregnant women. The Trust applied in 1935 to the Special Areas Commission, which had been set up the year before, for funds to extend its nutrition work into the so-called Special Areas, which had been badly affected by the Depression. This was initially rejected by the Commission, on the grounds that it was supposed to promote the economic and social development of the Special Areas, not to assist with "what is in fact relief of the poor".[73] But because the Prime Minister's wife was backing the proposal and was also (mistakenly) thought to be a president of the Trust, pressure from the highest levels was put on the Commissioner to reconsider the request. It was also thought that something should be done to appease Lady Williams, because she "had the ear of Cabinet Ministers . . . and was going up and down the country stating that maternal mortality was frequently attributable to malnutrition."[74]

The Commissioner decided to dress up the Trust's nutrition work as a research experiment to investigate the value to mothers of the extra food. While he could not assist with a "poor law function", he explained, he was nevertheless empowered "to conduct experiments in the realm of social improvement in the Special Areas."[75] He asked the Trust to create a committee of experts to supervise the research, which he hoped would reassure colleagues who were doubtful about the Trust's capacity to conduct scientific work.[76] The Trust referred this task to the Joint Council of Midwifery, which on 28 April 1937 set up a Research Committee of scientific experts.

In this way, through the agency of an outside influence rather than an internal development, the Trust began its long career in research. In 1938, Dr Haden Guest, who worked for the Medical Research Council (MRC), wrote to Ebbisham to suggest that "a definite percentage of the funds should be earmarked for the purpose of research, just as a percentage is earmarked for investment."[77] The outbreak of war in 1939 interrupted these plans, but they were vigorously implemented after the war.

ADAPTING TO POSTWAR BRITAIN

The Trust's growing interest in research helped it to redefine its mission after the Second World War. This was essential for its survival: maternal mortality, the original reason for its foundation, fell so steeply between 1935 and 1950 that the later rate was only a fifth of the earlier rate. On top of this, the creation of the welfare state was supposed to remove the need for philanthropy and this brought into question the role of the voluntary sector in the provision of health care. The Trust reacted by channelling all its energies and funds into "the field of research, in which it is felt that there will be for some time continued scope for voluntary effort".[78] As well, its earlier narrow focus on mothers expanded into a broader approach to reproduction that included babies; in particular, it turned its attention to perinatal mortality, the rates for which had been falling much more slowly than for maternal mortality.

In 1948 Lady Rhys Williams consolidated the research base of the Trust by creating a committee of professional experts, the Technical Advisory Sub-Committee (TASC); its name was changed in 1965 to the Scientific Advisory Committee (SAC). It usually had about four members and relied for expert advice on a larger group of distinguished Consultative Members, who were mostly men and were obstetricians, paediatricians, sociologists, epidemiologists and statisticians; by 1965, there were ten members of this group, all men. As the influence of the TASC and its Consultative Members grew, the larger committees, which were dominated by laywomen, became relatively unimportant. Gradually, passionate pleas like 'Save Our Mothers', which had characterized the Trust work of the 1930s, were replaced by a more prosaic language: "The Trust is dedicated to research into abnormalities in childbirth", announced the 1967 Christmas cards in a matter-of-fact way.[79] The Trust still referred in 1956 to "the unique position it holds of speaking for the mother herself",[80] but without much conviction. In any case, women were now starting to campaign on their own behalf for better maternity services, just as the women in the Trust had done in the 1930s. In 1960, for example, the Association for the Improvement of the Maternity Services (AIMS) was founded by women to put pressure on the government to provide more hospital beds for pregnancy and childbirth.

The chief postwar achievement of the Trust was its role in nationwide surveys in 1946, 1958, 1970, 1984, 1990 and 1994. The first three investigated every birth that took place in one week in England, Wales and Scotland, while the last three looked at special subjects related to childbirth. The Trust has also supported follow-up studies of the cohorts of children generated from the first three surveys.

END OF AN ERA

The generation that created the Birthday Trust had mostly disappeared by the end of the war. Many of those who took over were upper class, but they did not wield the same kind of power after the postwar victory of the Labour Party. The only important link with political power and influence was provided by Lady Rhys Williams, who was a close friend of Harold Macmillan, the Conservative MP who was Prime Minister between 1957 and 1963. Other new members of the Trust belonged to the rising postwar elite of doctors and other professionals. These included Josephine Barnes[81] and Elliot Philipp,[82] consultant obstetricians and gynaecologists who were to become key members of the Trust over the rest of the century. In 1945, Miss Barnes joined at the invitation of Lady Rhys Williams, following her move to a house in Belgravia that was very near the London home of the Rhys Williams family; she already had an indirect link with the Trust, since she had been a consultant at Clapham Maternity Hospital when it was one of the Trust's Cooperating Hospitals. Mr Philipp was invited by Lady Rhys Williams to join the Trust in 1952, following an introduction by another Trust member; this was Sydney Walton, who had interested him in the work of the Trust as early as 1939, when he was Governor of the hospital where Mr Philipp worked.

The Trust nurtured a close relationship with the Royal College of Obstetricians and Gynaecologists, which replaced its earlier link with midwives and midwifery. Even though the College (which became a Royal College when it was granted a Royal Charter in 1947) was founded just one year after the Trust, there had been no alliance between the two organizations before the war. The College, for its part, regarded the Trust as a set of amateur dilettantes. The obstetrician William Fletcher Shaw complained in 1930 to Blair-Bell, then President of the College, that the Trust was meddling in affairs it did not understand. "I object," he said, "to being rushed by a pack of London Titles through a letter in the press [which had been sent by the Fund to *The Times*]. If they want us to do anything they should circulate each hospital and ask for the considered opinion of the staff."[83] In a conversation with Mrs Baldwin about the Trust, Blair-Bell "made it plain that she had got hold of the wrong end of the stick and that there was much more in the subject that she had realized;

Miss Doreen Riddick, secretary of the Birthday Trust (left), and Sir George Haynes, who became the Trust's first President in 1966. The Trust relied heavily on Miss Riddick, who started work for the organization in 1934 and retired in 1972. ([NBTF/B5/10(4)] Reproduced courtesy of the Wellcome Institute Library, London)

that lay folk should not rush into such questions."[84]

The style of the Trust was not affected by its change in alliances after the war, but retained its Interwar air of refinement. The minutes of committee meetings over the century show that differences of opinion were always tackled in a spirit of respectful delicacy, while money was hardly ever mentioned (and then, only discreetly). Miss Riddick had grown up in British India and had old-fashioned notions of behaviour. Right up to her retirement in 1972, recalls Geoffrey Chamberlain, who had joined the Trust four years before, she "used to tick us all off if we turned up without bowler hats on – she used to say to me, 'appearing in town on a weekday in brown shoes, Mr Chamberlain?'"[85] Discussions about work were sometimes held at the Belgravia home of Lady Rhys Williams over breakfast, while she sat up in bed, holding court.[86] A statistician who provided expertise with computer analysis in the 1960s has described Trust meetings as "rather quaint. . . . It was a very unworldly sort of situation. Like a sort of garden party."[87]

The world of Britain, however, had changed dramatically. The fundraising schemes of the 1930s were no longer feasible: balls through the night were now rare events, since most people had to get up before lunchtime the next day in order to earn a living. The Trust arranged some small events, like a Radio Appeal by the actor Richard Attenborough in 1963, and in 1964 it made a more determined effort to raise money by setting up an Appeals Committee, under the chairmanship of Lady Helen Nutting. In 1966, Lady Helen persuaded Princess Alexandra to become the Trust's official patron, which greatly boosted the morale of the organization. The Princess attended various Trust events, including a premiere in 1971 of the film *Nicholas and Alexandra*, which raised £2,000.

But the Trust needed a major injection of funds in order to meet the vast expenses of survey work. It therefore arranged to use some of its capital to employ a Director-General, with the express task of raising funds. Jeffrey Archer was selected for the job and started in 1966, the same year in which he was elected as a councillor on the Greater London Council (GLC). He tried to resurrect the idea of the Birthday Shilling, asking mothers to send a pound and join Britain's 'Million Mothers', but he had even less success than Lady George. Then, when he arranged for cards of congratulation to be sent to mothers in hospital, asking for a donation to the Trust, the Ministry of Health refused to allow them to be sent to NHS hospitals.[88] Equally unsuccessful was the collection of Shell 'Make Money Notes', which were dispensed in halves as an inducement to buy Shell petrol (when matched up, they could be exchanged for real money). Archer organized the collection of over 310,000 of these half notes, but was not able to match any of them.[89] An account of his work for the Trust is given in a biography of Lord Archer, in a chapter called 'Birthday Boy'.[90] It argues that Archer's manner of working was entirely at odds with the style of the Birthday Trust.[91]

REORGANIZATION OF THE TRUST

Towards the end of the 1960s, the Trust was faced with serious difficulties: a lack of leadership following the death of Lady Rhys Williams in 1964, a shortage of funds, and the imminent retirement of Miss Riddick. Several strategies were developed in an effort to solve these problems. First, the position of President was created in 1968, as a figurehead for the Trust to fill some of the gap left by the death of Lady Rhys Williams. The first President was Sir George Haynes, who had been the UK delegate to the UN Social Commission between 1962 and 1966 and to the UN Commission for Social Development in 1967. The second and last President, between 1981 and 1993, was Dame Josephine Barnes.

Plans were also developed by Sir Brandon Rhys Williams and Mr Walter Gilbey,[92] who was Chairman at the time, for a merger with the RCOG. Other members of the Trust were generally in favour of the plan, although a few shared Lady Hutchison's fear that "if we have too many *medical* people on the committee, we might find that some of them might press their own pet schemes, rather than keep the essential original ideas of the Trust to carry out our primary duty of making childbirth safer for mother and babies."[93]

Sir Brandon wrote in a personal capacity to John Peel, President of the College, to propose the idea, which was taken up with enthusiasm. "The Trust is anxious for this College to take over the future administration of the Trust," Peel told the College's solicitors in 1968, adding, "and we ourselves are anxious to do this."[94] A sense of mutual interest enhanced preliminary negotiations: HRH Princess Alexandra, patron of the Trust, was awarded an Honorary Fellowship by the College in July 1969, while the Birthday Trust offered the College a Pathology Exhibit on the 1958 survey.[95] When Peel wrote to a friend to solicit financial support for the 1970 survey, he explained 'in confidence' that negotiations were in progress for the Birthday Trust to come "under the aegis of this College". He added, "if you decide to support this particular appeal you will indirectly be supporting this College."[96] But by 1973, negotiations for the merger had petered out.

In the early 1970s, Mr Gilbey streamlined the Birthday Trust. The massive committees, which had been so successful in the 1930s, were no longer properly attended and in 1971, the General Committee was merged with the Executive Committee to form a new General Committee; four members of this Committee were asked to act as an executive core. The former Finance Committee and the Scientific Advisory Committee were dissolved: four members of the new General Committee formed a new financial committee, while five members of the new committee formed a medical advisory panel, which was later called the Medical Committee and then the Scientific Committee. All those Trust members who had not been brought into the new General Committee were asked to become 'Friends of the National Birthday Trust Fund', with the role of raising funds and attending annual meetings. This new arrangement ensured better attendance at meetings and ended the duplication of secretarial work; this was an advantage to Mrs Margaret Matthews, who took over from Miss Riddick as secretary and played an important role in keeping the Trust together over the next two decades, even though she was employed for only one day a week.

This administrative change eased the Trust's difficulties, but it also confirmed that it was growing into a small research organization with a narrow base and limited ambitions. This trend can be seen in the graph showing the Trust's expenditure over the century (see figure 1.3): it reached a short-lived peak between the wars, fell and then rose during the analysis of the 1958 survey data and preparations for the 1970 survey, and then started a final overall drop in 1970. An irreversible point in the life of the Birthday Trust was reached in 1989, when 57 Lower Belgrave Street was sold and the Trust no longer had a home. The life of the midwifery headquarters was over: Trust meetings were henceforth held at the RCOG in Regent's Park, and the Queen's Nursing Institute (which had paid rent for their accommodation after the war) had to find new premises. The Royal College of Midwives was not affected, since it had moved into its own building on Mansfield Street in 1957.

THE TRUST OVER THE TWENTIETH CENTURY

This book tells the story of the National Birthday Trust Fund from its foundation in 1928 until it joined forces in 1993 with WellBeing, the

FIGURE 1.3 NBTF EXPENDITURE 1931–1985, ALLOWING FOR INFLATION

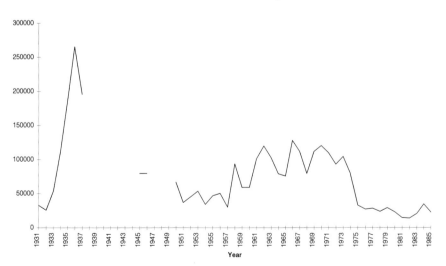

Source: NBTF Annual reports, balance sheets. Long-term Prices Index CSO.
[SA/NBT/C17/1-C19/22, D1/3/10-D1/4/12]

fundraising body of the RCOG. Chapter 2 analyses the Trust's relationship with the social and political reality of the interwar period, with particular attention to Conservative and feminist politics. This is followed by a chapter on the background to the Midwives Act of 1936. The next chapter covers the nutrition programme of 1934–9, and chapter 5 gives an account of the abortion enquiry of 1936–9. Then follows a chapter on the development of pain relief for childbirth, which has been a priority for the Trust throughout its life. The Human Milk Bureau is the subject of chapter 7.

Chapter 8 gives an account of the Trust's adaptation to the reality of postwar Britain and of its efforts to influence the new National Health Service; this is followed by a short chapter on the maternity survey of 1946. The Perinatal Mortality Survey of 1958 is the subject of chapter 10, which assesses the role of the Trust in the postwar shift from home to hospital birth. Next follows a discussion of the 1970 perinatal survey, *British Births*, and of three single-subject national surveys; this chapter also traces the development of the maternity consumer movement. The conclusion to the book covers the winding down of the Trust's affairs in the 1990s and the work for maternity that has yet to be done.

CHAPTER TWO

The Trust in the 1930s

The National Birthday Fund emerged in the late 1920s from a network of political developments that were transforming the shape of British society. Chief among these were landmark events in the women's and the labour movement. In 1928, the year in which the Birthday Fund was created, a law extending the vote to all women over twenty-one meant that women now formed over 50 per cent of the total electorate. As well, the working classes had moved into the political arena: the General Strike of 1926, which briefly brought Britain to a standstill, and the election in 1924 of the first Labour government, were unprecedented events in British history. One woman who was interviewed for this book recalls that when the first Labour government came to power in 1924, "I carried the photos of the Cabinet around with me as others might of their favourite film stars."[1] At the same time, reforms like the Local Government Act of 1929 were strengthening the role of the state sector in the provision of welfare and health services.

Although the Birthday Trust aimed to help poor women, not one single working-class woman sat on its committee. There were not many middle-class members, either: although some joined as representatives of the Co-operating Hospitals, their influence was marginal. Rather, the organization was run entirely

WOMEN VOTERS
IF YOU WANT
Healthy Homes in place of Slums
Medical Care for Mothers & Babies
Food Prices Reduced
Better Factory Conditions
An Open Door to College & University Education for your Children

SUPPORT THE PARTY THAT KEEPS ITS PROMISES!

VOTE CONSERVATIVE

An election poster for the Conservative Party, 1929. Political parties worked hard to win women to their cause following the extension of female suffrage in 1928. (Reproduced courtesy of the Bodleian Library, Oxford)

by members of the social and political elite of Britain.[2] At the centre of this circle was Lucy Baldwin, Vice-Chairman between 1932 and 1945. Her influence derived from her marriage to Stanley Baldwin, leader of the Conservative Party and the dominant figure in British politics when the Birthday Fund was created: he was Chancellor of the Exchequer in 1922–3; Prime Minister in 1923, 1924–9, and 1935–7; Lord President of Council in 1931–5; and Lord Privy Seal in 1932–4.

Edith, Marchioness of Londonderry, who was Honorary Treasurer of the Trust in its first seven years, was "a dazzling symbol of wealth, power, glamour and influence".[3] She was powerful in her own right and if anything, her husband Charles was dependent on *her*: he might not have managed to manoeuvre his way into the Cabinet without her social cachet and political cunning. Such was the lavishness of Londonderry House entertaining that Birkenhead accused the Marquess, who was Secretary of State for Air between 1931 and 1935 in MacDonald's second National Cabinet, and briefly Lord Privy Seal in Baldwin's National Cabinet, of "catering his way into the cabinet". The Marchioness enlarged her influence through her close relationship with Ramsay MacDonald, which was characterized by affection on her side and besotted love on his. "With MacDonald under her spell", observes a biographer, "she could be more effective than ever."[4] Many socialists blamed Lady Londonderry for MacDonald's acceptance of the leadership of the National government, which led to his expulsion from the Labour Party. The National government, observed Beatrice Webb, was "acclaimed by the whole of the Conservative Party and newspapers as the one and only bulwark against the spread of Socialism, and against the coming into power of the Trade Union and Co-Operative Movements. . . . Within the new Ministry are the most prominent enemies of the Labour Movement, such as Mr Baldwin and Mr Neville Chamberlain."[5] Baldwin was a key player in MacDonald's National Cabinet, living at 11 Downing Street as Lord President; Chamberlain was Chancellor. Londonderry House became a social centre for the National Government.[6]

The Marchioness gave regular receptions at Londonderry House for the State Opening of Parliament. At the reception in 1928, the year in which the Birthday Fund was created, Stanley Baldwin stood beside her at the top of the stairs; the guest list took up a whole page of *The Times*. Other regular functions at Londonderry House included the gatherings of the Ark, a group of friends who met for dinner, conversation, and fun. Anyone invited to join had to take the name of a real or mythological beast: Lady Londonderry was 'Circe', while Ramsay MacDonald was 'Ram' and John Buchan was 'Buck'.[7] Two other Prime Ministers – Stanley Baldwin and Neville Chamberlain – belonged to the Ark, as well as their wives. Lady George, the founder of the Trust, was evidently a member, since a letter to her from Lady Londonderry is signed 'Circe'. Social occasions like the meetings of the Ark created useful obligations that extended into politics, business and charitable work: when Lady Londonderry asked

Chamberlain, then Minister of Health, to speak at the Inaugural Meeting of the Fund, he readily agreed.[8]

There was occasional friction between these powerful individuals. In 1929, Lady Londonderry threatened to resign from her role as Treasurer of the Trust because she objected, she told Lady George, to a letter that had been sent by the Birthday Fund to *The Times*: "I do dislike these long wordy – badly written, lengthily expressed letters in the Press, which perforce I have to sign – and I have not the time to write them myself but ty [sic] really are bad – Can't you shorten them or the lady down!!"[9] The 'lady' was Lucy Baldwin, a source of irritation to Lady Londonderry at this time. Tension between the two families became high when Baldwin moved to bypass Londonderry at the Air Ministry by installing his own nominee. "With one stroke," Londonderry accused Baldwin in 1938, "you wiped me off the political map."[10] Londonderry and Baldwin had disagreed over foreign policy. But also, the Marquess had become a liability to the party through his and Edith's efforts to befriend Hitler, Goering and Ribbentrop. "Now I admire Londonderry in a way," commented Harold Nicolson in 1936, "since it is fine to remain 1760 in 1936; besides, he is a real gent. But I do deeply disapprove of ex-cabinet Ministers trotting across to Germany at this moment. It gives the impression of secret negotiations and upsets the French."[11] The Londonderrys' friendship with the fascists may explain why Queen Victoria Eugenie of Spain was invited as Guest of Honour to a Birthday Trust fund-raising tea on 9 May 1938, after two years of Civil War in Spain. It may also explain why the German Ambassador and his wife were invited to the Trust's Guildhall Reception in March 1939, thirteen days after Hitler entered Prague.

Lady Londonderry at the Strauss Ball, wearing a dress from 1873 "trimmed with old lace and caught up with roses and a period wig with hanging curls". Sketch, 14 January 1931. (Reproduced courtesy of the Illustrated London News *Picture Library)*

Other members of the Birthday Trust were less celebrated than Lucy Baldwin and the Marchioness of Londonderry, but were also key members of British 'society'. They included its founder Lady George Cholmondeley; the Marchioness of Cholmondeley; Viscountess Bearsted; the Countess of Bessborough, whose involvement with the Fund was interrupted between 1931 and 1935, when her husband was Governor-General of Canada; Lady Ebbisham and her husband, who was President of the Federation of British Industries (1928–9) and Treasurer of the Conservative Party Organization (1931–3); and Lord Melchett, who was a Trustee, and his wife. Lord Melchett was both a successful businessman in the chemical industry, notably in the creation of ICI, and also a prominent politician (in spite of much anti-Semitic abuse[12]): he was a Liberal MP and briefly Minister of Health in the 1918–22 coalition government, then joined the Conservative Party in 1926. Lord Strathcona and Mount Royal, who was briefly a Vice-Chairman, was a member of the Indian Statutory Commission between 1928 and 1930, Captain of the King's Bodyguard between 1931 and 1934, then served as Parliamentary Under-Secretary of State for War until 1939. Sir Julien Cahn, who was Chairman of the Birthday Trust between 1930 and 1944, was "the leading Conservative in Nottingham".[13] While not himself at the centre of political and social events, he mixed with those who were: the Visitors' Book kept at Stanford Hall, his luxurious stately home, is sprinkled with the names of important connections through the Trust, like Lady Melchett, the Dalrymple-Champneys and Lord Ebbisham; Neville Chamberlain visited in October 1934, a year before Lucy Baldwin.[14] It has been argued that Cahn's baronetcy was given by MacDonald in 1934, on Stanley Baldwin's advice, as a reward for paying £30,000 to spirit abroad an honours tout who had operated a network of agents for all three parties and was now under investigation (officially, it was given for services to agriculture in the form of a generous gift to the University of Wales).[15]

The Trust ladies and gentlemen had little contact outside their circle apart from the master/servant relationship. Typical of this relationship was Lady Bessborough's offer to lend her servants for a day to sell flags for the Trust: "My Maid, my Cook, and 1 of the Kitchen maids, and 1 Hse [sic] maid would love to sell flags for you . . . I'm sorry I can't help myself, but I shall have a hectic day with my boy, who doesn't go back to Eton till the evening."[16] The only representatives of the working class at the Birthday Trust headquarters were Mr Chudley the hall porter and Mrs Chudley and Ethel, who helped him. Ethel made the mistake of asking for a raise in her wages, which were 15s a week. Following lengthy discussion at an executive meeting, it was agreed that although Ethel was entirely satisfactory, "her duties were more those for a younger girl and did not warrant higher wages". Ethel was therefore told to find another job, though she was promised an extra 2s 6d until her departure.[17] When the page-boy was given notice because of ill health, Mrs Baldwin advised that "we should apply to Dr Barnardo's Home for such a boy, provided it was possible to arrange for him to sleep in the building".[18]

As part of a deliberate policy to appear 'apolitical', there were representatives on the Birthday Trust of all three major political parties of the period (Conservative, Liberal and Labour). Lady Williams, for example, stood for election as a Liberal, while Lady Buckmaster was married to a Liberal MP. Ethel Snowden, one of four women elected to the Labour Party's National Executive in 1919, sat on the committee, while her husband, Philip Snowden, became a Trustee in 1930. Snowden had been Chancellor of the Exchequer in the first Labour government in 1924 and was prominent in the National Cabinets between 1929 and 1932, as Chancellor of the Exchequer and Lord Privy Seal. Dr Haden Guest, a physician at St George's Dispensary in Southwark who was a member of the Trust's Finance Committee, was a Labour MP (he resigned from the Labour Party in 1927 but returned to it in 1930).

Like the National Governments of the period, however, the National Birthday Trust Fund in the 1930s was Conservative in all but name. The dominant members of the committee were either directly involved in, or supporters of, the Conservative Party. Lucy Baldwin advertised this connection when she made her 1929 Broadcast Appeal for the Birthday Fund from Chequers, her country retreat as wife of the Conservative Prime Minister. The Trust's firm place within the establishment was further guaranteed by the support of the royal family, through the trusteeship of the Earl of Cromer, Lord Chamberlain of His Majesty's household, and the membership of Lady Cynthia Colville, Lady-in-Waiting to the Queen. Philip Snowden had been brought into the Fund as a representative of the Labour Party, but he gradually moved to the right of the Labour Party, remaining with Ramsay MacDonald in the National government despite the vigorous objections of the Party, until he eventually resigned over the government's protectionist policies.

OTHER WOMEN'S ORGANIZATIONS

The Birthday Trust was not the only organization run by women that took an interest in the high rate of maternal death and morbidity. Other groups, as shown in table 2.1, included the Maternal Mortality Committee (MMC), the Women's Cooperative Guild, the Labour Party Women's Organization, the National Council of Women, the Fabian Women's Group and the National Union of Societies for Equal Citizenship. At a meeting in May 1930 of the National Federation of Women's Institutes (which had started in 1915 and had 5,000 institutes by 1934), 8–10,000 women expressed their unanimous concern about the inadequate provision by Local Authorities of antenatal care.[19]

The Maternal Mortality Committee was set up in 1927, a year before the creation of the Birthday Trust, "when we realised that so little public attention was being given to the high maternal death rate, though it had then not declined for thirty years."[20] The chief organizers were May Tennant, an infant welfare campaigner, and Gertrude Tuckwell, a trade unionist and activist in the Labour movement (who was described by Sir Arthur Robinson at the Ministry of Health as "the wild woman"[21]). The MMC was "representative of all shades of opinion"[22] and Conservative Party delegates on the MMC included Lady Iveagh, Chairman of the Party, and Lady Maureen Stanley, the eldest daughter of Lady

Table 2.1: KEY WOMEN'S ORGANIZATIONS TACKLING MATERNAL MORTALITY IN THE
1930S

Fabian Society Women's Group
Family Endowment Society
Labour Party Women's Organization
Maternal Mortality Committee
National Birthday Trust Fund
National Council for Maternity and Child Welfare
National Council of Women
National Federation of Women's Institutes
National Union of Societies for Equal Citizenship (NUSEC)
National Women's Citizens' Association
Standing Joint Committee of Industrial Women's Organizations
Women Public Health Officers' Association
Women's Cooperative Guild
Women's Health Enquiry Committee

Londonderry. It advocated a national maternity service and was active at a local level, putting pressure on laggard Local Authorities to deliver a better service.[23] Their deputations to the Minister of Health demanding better maternity care provoked severe irritation at the Ministry with "these good ladies".[24] Sir Kingsley Wood, Minister of Health, was told that, "They have not shown great discretion in the past, and a good deal of harm might easily result from the dissemination of such ill-considered criticisms as are submitted in their Memorandum."[25] However, Dame Janet Campbell, who attended several meetings, approved of the committee's efforts.

Given their shared agenda, it might have been expected that the Birthday Trust and the MMC would collaborate, especially since there was some cross-membership (for example, through Lady Cynthia Colville, Alice Gregory, Mrs Crozier, Viscountess Fitzalan and Miss Haldane). There was a promising start to the relationship: in the early days of the Birthday Fund, May Tennant was invited to join the committee and although she refused on the grounds of overwork, she offered to attend a meeting and sent a small donation;[26] and Gertrude Tuckwell visited Lady George before going on holiday.[27] But the Trust were not really interested in the MMC and did not bother to find out about their activities: when asked by Lady Londonderry to speak at a meeting, Neville Chamberlain told Lady George that he had already promised to speak on that day "at a similar meeting organized by Mrs Tennant and Miss Tuckwell", which Lady George did not know about.[28] By 1935, the relationship between the two organizations had deteriorated into mistrust and rivalry, at least on the side of the Trust: Lady Williams complained to Miss Meyer in 1935 that it was

FIGURE 2.1: IMPORTANT RELATIONSHIPS OF THE NATIONAL BIRTHDAY TRUST FUND,
MATERNAL MORTALITY COMMITTEE AND WOMEN'S COOPERATIVE GUILD IN THE 1930S

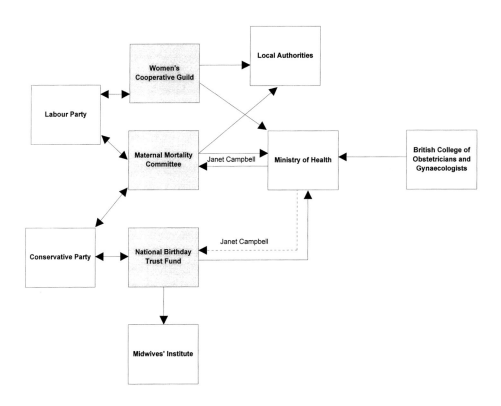

"preposterous of Miss Tuckwell not to invite the Trust, as such, to be present at the Maternal Mortality Committee Meeting. They are about a year late in everything they are doing, and they must be taught not to try and leave us out!"[29] The differences between the functioning of the MMC and the Birthday Trust (and also the Women's Cooperative Guild, which is discussed below) are shown in figure 2.1.

On the controversial issues of the day, the MMC took a more radical position than the Trust. Like many women's groups in the 1920s and 30s, it advocated birth control as an integral part of maternal policy, and the committee invited to its meetings women like Mrs Margaret Pyke of the National Birth Control Association (which later became the Family Planning Association); also, some members openly sought the legalization of abortion. Matters were quite different at the Birthday Fund. When Lady George reported in early 1929 that Dr Marie Stopes, who in 1921 had opened the first birth clinic and was a prominent champion of contraception, had offered to speak at a private meeting of the committee, Lady Bearsted quickly killed the plan. She was afraid, she said, that "it might re-act against the Fund to have Dr Stopes' name actively associated with it, and Lady Jekyll agreed that the Fund could not have

FIGURE 2.2: BIRTH RATE, ENGLAND AND WALES (PER 1,000)

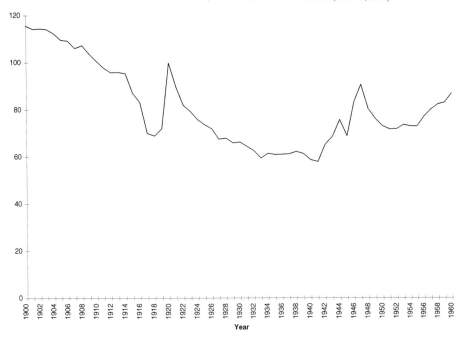

Source: A. Macfarlane and M. Mugford, *Birth Counts: Statistics of Pregnancy and Childbirth,* 2 vols (HMSO, 1984) pp. 2–4

this lady officially connected with it."[30] Lady Williams wrote to Miss Meyer in 1935, "Thank you for the details of the Birth Control controversy. I think it is better for the N.B.T.F. to keep out of this."[31]

The Trust did not really keep out of the birth control controversy, though, as chapter 5 of this book will show. Some dominant members of the Trust, notably Lady Williams, publicly opposed making birth control available because they were afraid that the British population was dying out. "National suicide is being committed," she warned, "by the failure of the majority to maintain the population."[32] The fall in the birth rate, which is shown in figure 2.2, was a cause for widespread concern. David Glass, a social scientist who was investigating the population question at the London School of Economics, predicted in his book, *The Struggle for Population* (1936), that "if 1931 conditions of fertility and mortality persist, the total population will soon begin to fall. Eventually it will reach a stable age composition, and after that stage there will be a decrease of almost 20 per cent in each successive generation."[33] A woman who accompanied a friend on a visit to the doctor to ask for birth control in the 1930s, recalls that her friend was asked, "Are you certain you want birth control? After all, you've only two children now, that's only replacing you and your husband, that's not doing anything for the population."[34]

When the Chancellor of the Exchequer introduced the Budget in 1935, he linked a decline in population (in particular, of "the right breed") to the possibility of diminished control over British colonies.[35] In 1936, the Eugenics Society set up the Population Investigation Committee (PIC) to "examine the factors influencing contemporary population trends in England and Wales with special reference to the fall of the birth-rate."[36] David Glass and Lady Williams were both members of the PIC; financial supporters included Lord Melchett, who gave the PIC a "substantial grant".[37] Anxiety about the birth rate reached fever pitch towards the end of the 1930s, as a result of the expansionist behaviour and rising populations of Germany and Italy.

Birth control did receive support from some quarters, however, especially from eugenists. Some of these were prominent individuals linked to the Trust through their wives, such as Lord Dawson and Lord Buckmaster, who maintained that "the birth-rate should be judged by quality rather than quantity"[38] and that the availability of contraception would contain the population of the poor and 'unfit'. In Germany, eugenist sentiment centred on the language of race but in Britain, the birthplace of the eugenics movement, it centred on the language of class. Lady Williams was passionately opposed to this kind of social Darwinism, believing that "unhealthy and subnormal children" were the product of inadequate nutrition and deprived surroundings, not of genetic deficiency.[39]

Birth control was also advocated on the grounds of women's health and quality of life, by some doctors, feminists and women's organizations. In 1923, the Women's Cooperative Guild (WCG) was the first women's organization to come out openly in support of birth control. "Probably no organized body has done more to further the national protection of motherhood" than the Guild, maintained Elizabeth Macadam.[40] All its members were working-class women, who were married and belonged to the Cooperative Movement. It was founded in 1883 and was a vigorous campaigning organization by the First World War, with an active membership of 32,000. In 1915, it published *Maternity*, a volume of letters by working-class women that described pregnancy and childbirth in the homes of the poor. It sold out almost immediately. In 1931, the Guild produced *Life As We Have Known It*, in which women recounted their experiences and aspirations, going back as far as the 1850s. The Women's Cooperative Guild "naturally leans to the left"[41] and was treated with suspicion by Conservative-controlled local government. Following an application to the County Council in Surrey for home helps for necessitous mothers, the Medical Officer of Health for that area was "of opinion that this request was made mainly through the Women's Cooperative Guild, that is to say, that it was an "engineered request", and the County Council was not convinced that there was genuine need."[42]

In 1933, a Women's Health Committee Enquiry was set up by the WCG, the National Union of Societies for Equal Citizenship, the Standing Joint Committee of Industrial Women's Organizations, and the North Kensington

Women's Welfare Centre; the chairman of the committee was Gertrude Tuckwell of the MMC. It investigated the health of some 1,250 married working-class women, and the results were used by Margery Spring Rice of the North Kensington Women's Welfare Centre to produce *Working-Class Wives*. This book concluded that the chief difficulties of married working-class women were poverty, ill-health and ignorance, and it advocated the provision of family allowances, health insurance for all women, and a reduction in pregnancies through birth control.

Cross-membership was common among organizations that campaigned to improve the health of women and children. Eleanor Rathbone, Eva Hubback and Marjorie Green, for example, were leading figures in both the Family Endowment Society, which was created in 1924, and also the Children's Minimum Council, which was set up ten years later. These organizations supported each other: the notepaper of the Children's Minimum Council listed 30 affiliated organizations, including the Nursery School Association of Great Britain, the Workers' Educational Association, the Maternal Mortality Committee, the WCG, the National Union of Societies for Equal Citizenship, the National Women's Citizens' Association, and the Women's Group of the Fabian Society.[43] Significantly, there was no cross-membership between groups like these and the Birthday Trust.

The ladies of the Trust differed also from those women philanthropists who did 'frontline' work among the poor. These women were usually middle class and worked under the auspices of the Charity Organization Society (COS), which was the most influential charitable association of the day. Their house-to-house visiting was often unpleasant, because of the filth and bad smells in many homes of the poor.[44] Neville Chamberlain evidently expected the Trust to do this sort of work. At the Inaugural Meeting of the National Birthday Fund in 1929, he said it would enjoy "actual contact with the people" and have a role that was not open to the Ministry of Health. A government department, he explained, "is not really equipped for that sort of work, a Voluntary Association will beat a Government Department at that job every single time."[45] But Trust members had no intention of enjoying contact with the people. When an opportunity for this arose, in the operation of the Samaritan Fund, they employed someone else to do it. Working in a charity shop was also beneath them. Having agreed as an organization to participate with other charities[46] in the sale of unwanted clothing and other articles at an Opportunity Shop on Buckingham Palace Road, the Trust "was not doing its share, and in one week had not even paid [its] share of expenses – £2 7s 6d".[47] Sir Julien smoothed matters over by writing a very large cheque for the purchase of new articles to be sold at the shop as 'secondhand' goods.[48]

The women providing local social welfare were mostly excluded from the decision-making committees of their organizations,[49] which were controlled by men. But the Birthday Trust committees were different, because they were dominated and managed by women. Number-work was done by men, as Trustees and as members of the Finance Committee, but this was because the women did not want to. When the Marchioness of Londonderry was Honorary Treasurer, she refused to do anything but sign cheques. The Viscountess Buckmaster only agreed to take over the position on condition that "the post does not mean my undertaking any sort of technical mathematical work as the mathematical side of my brain is quite useless, and I cannot undertake any responsibility that demands a clear grasp of figures!";[50] this must have been an affectation, since the Birthday Trust archive collection contains evidence that Lady Buckmaster could add and subtract perfectly well.

THE TWO NATIONS

In 1929, less than a year after the Inaugural Meeting of the Birthday Fund, the crash of the New York Stock Exchange heralded a severe economic depression, which aggravated the already harsh living conditions of the poor. In 1934 the government acknowledged the difference in the quality of life between the areas of unemployment and the rest of Britain, by passing the Special Areas Act – "to facilitate the economic development and social improvement of certain areas which have been specially affected by industrial depression."[51] In many of these Special Areas, almost the whole population was unemployed and dependent on insurance benefit and help from the Unemployment Assistance Board. A Special Area, bleakly observed the social critic, James Hanley, "is a new kind of social hell, with nothing special about it except the demoralization of a whole people".[52] When a plan to investigate conditions in these designated areas was announced in the House of Commons, Macmillan remarked with bitter irony, "I am glad that there has been on this occasion a visit from Whitehall to the Passchendaele of Durham and South Wales."[53]

Applying for relief was a miserable experience. According to one woman living in a village in the Rhondda Valley:

> Parish relief was very degrading. You had to be desperate. The people who gave parish relief, we didn't like them . . . The Means Test was to see how much money you had in the house. If there was any over that, you got no more. That had to keep you, whether you were ten or less. And then the other, if you were sick, you went on the parish. The Means Test was with the dole. I'd be old enough to go on the parish.[54]

Another woman living in a town in the Rhymney Valley, South Wales, remembers her mother suffering the indignity of the Means Test: "They wanted the eldest son to keep the children. It was a cruel thing. Like the poll tax today, very mean. The struggle my mother must have had . . . and then there was the strikes. That's why I could never go away and leave my mother."[55]

In her memories of the interwar period in Birmingham, one woman recalls that the impossibility of surviving on parish relief forced her to give up her children to Dr Barnardo's homes; it was eight years before she could offer them a home again.[56] Most of the girls in the Rhondda, reported Lady Williams in 1936, "are trained by the local Council and fitted out with uniforms to go away into domestic service. The rest go as low paid shop girls in the poorer types of shops."[57] One woman in South Wales recalls going away to service in 1927: "I went to service when I was 14. There was nothing else. Times were very hard. . . . I survived. You went home once, got two weeks holiday and one half day and every other Sunday. Everyone was in the same boat. There was no work about. I used to send so much home. I had to pay for uniform. You saw yourself about 10s a week."[58] A woman living in the Midlands remembers starting work in 1924 at the age of fourteen in a hosiery factory, earning 7s 11d for tying knots on a long winding machine all day long, 8 till 6, and 6 till 12 on Saturdays. Her family were all on the Means Test. Her sister, proud of her home and her little girls, "had to suffer the visits of the Means Test man and his probing questions, even looking into the pan on the stove because something smelt particularly appetizing".[59]

Questionnaires completed at municipal hospitals for an enquiry into abortion by the Joint Council of Midwifery reveal some details about the lives of working-class women. A family typical of those consulted in the enquiry lived on £4 per week income and in two rooms at a rent of 8s 7d per week. One woman living in Greenwich in two rooms at a cost of 9s per week, "occupies top rooms of a house and has to carry pails of water up about 34 steps, there being no water supply at the top of the house. She considers this heavy lifting caused her abortion." A Liverpool family with four children had a father who was an unemployed labourer; they lived in four rooms at a rent of 10s per week and received 35s from the Public Assistance Committee. Another family with thirteen children lived off 17s 6d per week in three rooms that were rented at 7s 4d per week. Many of the women living in Dublin endured even more gruelling conditions. For example, in one family with eleven children, the father earned £2 a week as a part-time cattle-drover and they all lived in one room, at a weekly rent of 7s.[60]

The life of Birthday Trust members was entirely different from that of the women they aimed to help. The Depression did not seriously threaten the standard of living of the very rich, so failure to attend meetings was often the result of World Cruises; notes of apology were sent from Belgravia and the exclusive (and Conservative) Carlton Club and Ladies Carlton Club. Sir Julien's grand trips abroad continued unabated and in the early 1930s he was photographed next to the pyramids with an extensive entourage, all atop camels.[61] At the Strauss Ball in January 1931, tickets were three guineas for a sit-down supper, champagne and a buffet. The women for whom this money was raised would have spent even less than three guineas for a month's supply of meals for four people: for example, a family of two adults and two children, who received 26s a week from the Unemployment Assistance Board, "paid ten shillings a week rent and had 15s 9d left for clothing for four persons and for food for four persons – flour, potatoes, two tins of condensed milk, a pint of fresh milk on Sundays, minced meat, and one penny-worth of bones once a week for soup."[62]

The operation of the JCM investigation into abortion illustrates the Two Nations aspect of the Birthday Trust's work. The women consulted for the questionnaires were in-patients at municipal hospitals, in conditions that were very often spartan; many of them had risked injury, death and life imprisonment, in order to obtain an abortion. No effort was made to collect information on the abortions of better-off women, who were able to pay for an operation by a qualified doctor in a private nursing home, and questions about working-class women's wishes regarding birth control or abortion were absent from the abortion questionnaire. Unlike the WCG and the Women's Health Enquiry Committee, the Trust did not actually ask working-class women about their lives, or consult them on their opinions. They believed they already knew what they wanted and what was best for them: Mrs Baldwin said that the Fund was like the British Provident Association (which later became BUPA), which is "helping the middle-class mother to provide for herself what we are trying to provide for the poor mother."[63] Even in the Trust's strenuous efforts to improve midwifery services for the poor, working-class women were not invited to express their own wishes. If they had been, they might have opposed the JCM's plan for the 1936 Midwives Act, which disqualified from practice handywomen and monthly nurses, who were invaluable to many mothers because they helped out in the home as well as at the birth.

On a unique occasion in the 1930s, the Birthday Trust brought rich and poor together. This was the Guildhall Reception on 28 March 1939, which was attended by Queen Elizabeth and the elite of many countries. Two hundred recipients of Birthday Trust supplementary nutrition were also invited to attend, all from families that had been hit hard by the Depression and unemployment. "Working class mothers, debutantes and peeresses presented the purses, just to indicate that all women are pulling together," reported *Sketch*.[64] One of the working women, who was from New Tredegar in South Wales, had seven children between the ages of 16 years and five months; her husband "wasn't working. He couldn't get a job. . . . He collapsed in the pit. He had dust. But they wouldn't certify him." Her daughter recalls:

> I don't know how [my mother] was chosen, but they thought she was the best one to send, I suppose. She was a perfect mother. They used to say, it was like Dr Barnardo's homes, our house. . . . What my mother used to do, you see, my mother used to take in washing, and she used to have 3s a week for taking

The Guildhall Reception on 28 March 1939, a lavish fundraising event organized by the NBTF. ([NBTF/G7/9/4] Reproduced courtesy of the Wellcome Institute Library, London)

in this washing. She used to save that and that was our outings. Because this came up, we used to have little meetings, with our aunts, and we all decided that mam should have the money to buy the clothes to go. I can remember the hat![65]

The Sister Superior of the Nursing Sisters of St John the Divine in Deptford, which had sent twenty mothers, pointed out that, "it is not often that working women have the chance to see the Queen at close quarters in evening dress."[66] A daughter of one of the invited women recalls, "She was pleased. Oh she was. And I was in school and the teacher came to me, do you know who this is, the picture of my mother in the paper. When she came home, everyone welcomed her back . . . we all had a party because she went."[67]

Since the aim of the Guildhall Reception was to raise money, the tickets were expensive: two guineas for supper and 10s 6d for a buffet in the 'red and yellow refreshment room'. Inevitably, only the wealthy could afford them: that is, the class that produced Lady Londonderry's Guard of Honour, a group of debutantes between the ages of seventeen and twenty-three, who wore white and carried a bouquet and a cushion with a pattern in pale blue, holding a dainty collecting tin of the same colour.[68] Orders were given to the Guard of Honour to "Please stitch label with owners' name and address to cushion. Guard will be on duty with Her Majesty until 10.30 approximately, after which they are free to dance."[69]

Rich women and poor women meet together at the NBTF Guildhall Reception, 1939. Lady Rhys Williams is second from the right, next to the Queen. Her DBE is pinned to her dress. ([NBTF/G7/9/4] Reproduced courtesy of the Wellcome Institute Library, London)

These women certainly looked different from their poorer sisters, to judge by photographs that were taken of the event and by the following report in the *Daily Mail*:

> Debutantes in fluffy white frocks, carrying fresh-flower posies and silk cushions, were shoo-ed away at the Guildhall . . . to make way for working-class mothers to form a guard of honour for the Queen. . . . Two hundred mothers gave their Sunday best an extra ironing, had a dry shampoo overnight, and polished their least-worn shoes.[70]

They were also treated differently. Whereas the ladies with tickets enjoyed a hot supper or a buffet, the working mothers had to make do with a cold snack. It was found "impossible to give the 200 mothers a meal in the Guildhall after the Reception, so it has been decided to give them a nice packet of food each."[71] This 'nice packet' of food was the cheapest 'Standard Picnic Luncheon Box' available from J. Lyons and Co., which cost 9*d* and contained "1 Beef Sandwich; 1 Small Pork Pie; 1 Junior Swiss Roll; 1 Dessert

Fruit; 1 1*d* Bar Chocolate."[72] The 'Working Women' were given typewritten instructions on how to behave:

> All the women must eat before they arrive: no parcel of sandwiches etc. must be taken into the Guildhall. Chocolate may be taken in hand-bags, but no paper must be thrown on the floor or the corridors. Each consignment [this word is changed by hand to 'party'] of women must be in the charge of *two* responsible people (male or female).[73]

The attitudes of the Birthday Trust towards the poor reflected an assumption that 'our' needs were different from 'theirs'. The Birthday Trust's initial plan to collect at least one shilling from every member of the British public on their birthday, reveals a high degree of ignorance or indifference (or both) about the life of the working class. It was most unlikely that *everybody* would be able to contribute a shilling, which was more than a fifth of the weekly income, net of housing costs, of many British people. According to a report by the British Medical Association in 1936, "The average income per head, exclusive of rent and rates, is shown to range from 4*s* 9*d* for the unemployed, to 10*s* 6*d* for the employed. This weekly sum has to cover not only food but clothes, heating and lighting."[74] B. Seebohm Rowntree observed in *The Human Needs of Labour* that, "to-day millions of working-class people in this country are inadequately provided with the necessaries of life, simply and solely because the fathers of families are not in receipt of incomes large enough."[75]

These attitudes underpinned reactions to the General Strike of 1926, which took place two years before the foundation of the Birthday Fund and "displayed all the overtones", claims one of Baldwin's biographers, "of a class war as between 'We' and 'They'."[76] It was sparked off by the miners' dispute with the coal owners, which was described in 1927 by Sir Alfred Mond of the Birthday Trust as "the longest and most devastating industrial dispute in the history of the country."[77] The General Strike lasted only nine days and the miners were eventually forced back to work by cold and starvation, having to accept both longer hours and lower wages; Baldwin then introduced the Eight Hours Act to lengthen the seven hour day. It was followed by the 1927 Trades Disputes Act, which made any repetition of a general strike illegal.

Members of the Birthday Trust would have identified themselves as 'We' – that is, those who opposed the strike. Even if their consciences were pricked by the conditions endured by miners, they would have agreed with Stanley Baldwin that, "Constitutional Government is being attacked. . . . The General Strike is a challenge to Parliament, and is the road to anarchy and ruin."[78] Mrs Baldwin supported the efforts of troops, police and volunteers to maintain essential services, by organizing a special convoy of motor cars to assist business women and girls living in the suburbs of London to reach their places of work, and to convey them back to their homes. Car owners were asked to communicate immediately with Mrs Baldwin in writing or by telephone to 10 Downing Street. The response "was considerable, owner-drivers willingly putting their vehicles at Mrs Baldwin's disposal as a patriotic duty".[79]

Working-class women, on the other hand, mostly backed the General Strike. They ran soup kitchens, raised £300,000 for boots and clothing for miners' families, adopted miners' children during the period of absolute deprivation, and organized meetings of up to 10,000 miners' wives.[80] One woman has recalled how hopeful she was then that the strike "signified complete change for this unequal society"; she wanted to strike herself, but was not called out.[81] Another woman who was fifteen in 1926 remembers how "men used to go and steal coal off the colliery for the fire. Some of their wives were pregnant. Someone would give a whistle if a policeman was coming. Looking back, never ever, would I want to see [such difficult times] come back."[82] Strikes, national hunger marches, and campaigns against the Means Test and the operation of the Unemployment Assistance Board were commonplace in the 1930s. Several hundred women from the Merthyr area in South Wales, for example, marched upon the UAB offices in 1935, wrecking them and burning the records.[83] In an essay in *Civil Journey*, Storm Jameson asked, "And how long will this country bear the burden of its ruined areas?"[84]

Not only the Baldwins, but other Birthday Trust families too, were directly affected by this social disaffection. Lord Plender, who served on the finance committee and became a Trustee when Snowden died, was the first independent Chairman of the National Board for the Coal Industry, 1921–5, and independent Chairman of the Durham Coal Industry in 1927. Sir Rhys Williams, who owned coalfields in the Special Area of the Rhondda Valley, was "V. heavily hit by Coal Trouble,"[85] in the words of Lady Bearsted. Lord Londonderry, whose vast fortune was supplemented by extensive coal-owning interests in the Durham area, wrote angrily to Baldwin in 1924, "We have a desperate struggle before us in the next few years and I am proposing to devote a great deal of my time to defeating the Socialist menace in one of the reddest portions of the kingdom [he meant Co. Durham]."[86] There was criticism of the Marquess's position on the dispute even within his own family: "Before the last war," stated his son Robin in the *Spectator* in 1946, "over half of all industrial disputes were to do with coalmining. The average owner is rarely seen by his men; in fact, the only times they see him are when there are differences of opinion which call for strikes. The miner can hardly be blamed for regarding his employer as a man who is more interested in profits than welfare."[87]

Behind the strikes and marches, the classes of wealth saw the threat of revolution, which had transformed Russia and given impetus to communist teachings throughout Europe. This threat was met with a variety of approaches. One was suppression and force. A typical casualty of this was Lewis Jones, a miner and political activist in South Wales between the wars, who was imprisoned for sedition during the General Strike.[88] Another strategy was negotiation, which was advocated by the Trust's Alfred Mond. In the wake of the General Strike, he invited a group of influential industrialists to meet the General Council of the TUC; these meetings between 1928 and 1929, which became known as the Mond-Turner talks, were a first effort at cooperation between unions and business. Mond believed that profit-sharing would eliminate the threat of working class anger; "The best answer to socialism," he remarked in 1927, "is to make every man a capitalist."[89] Yet another approach to the threat of social disorder was the dispensing of charity: providing relief to the destitute in order to diminish anger and despair. This has been described by David Cantor, an historian of the interwar period, as "the benevolent means by which elites tried to maintain social order."[90] As the Depression deepened and agitation for work and improved poor relief became more and more familiar, the Birthday Trust regarded its own charitable work in this light. Lord Strathcona remarked to Lady Baldwin,

> Personally, I think that the work which you are doing, combined with the fresh efforts being made in the direction of providing suitable nutrition for the poorer classes, are among the most praiseworthy undertakings that can be adopted now with a view to benefiting the conditions *of all classes.*[91]

At times, the attitude of the Fund recalled that of the 1834 New Poor Law, which had drawn a distinction between the 'deserving' and the 'non-deserving' poor. In this respect, it was no different from many other charitable organizations, which chose to help 'decent' families and to leave the state to help those that were not.[92] When considering a request from the Zachary Merton Convalescent Home, the Trust decided that it "might perhaps, pay the expense of eight *deserving* mothers and babies at 30s per week for two weeks."[93] This discretionary method of allocating assistance was a particular feature of the Samaritan Fund, which was set up by the Trust to assist pregnant women with blankets, baby clothes, and other essentials. The Fund started at Christmas in 1934 with the distribution of food to poor families in South Wales, and continued to operate until 1942. Mrs Janet Pugh, a local nurse, was hired at a salary of 10s a week to investigate the conditions of applicants; when funds became limited, she worked on a voluntary basis for an honorarium of £1 per month and expenses. Most of the work of the Samaritan Fund took place in the Rhondda Valley, but it also brought assistance to other Depressed Areas; at the end of 1938, the Medical Officer of Health for Sunderland, A. Stuart Hebblethwaite, sent thanks for a bale of sixty-six blankets for expectant mothers.[94]

Mrs Pugh went to great efforts to distinguish which mothers deserved Samaritan assistance. "I shall call on Mrs [P].," she wrote to Miss Riddick, "and if she is *deserving* shall give her all the help I can."[95] She was quite ready to dismiss a woman as being unworthy of help: of one woman, she concluded,

"I do not really think she is so *deserving* as she would have us believe";[96] of another, she remarked, "She has a boy with one leg, and she appears very poor, but I am sure there are lots of women in the Rhondda far more *deserving* of help than Mrs [G]." She added, however, "I felt sorry for Mrs [P]. I feel sure they are a very respectable family."[97] Respectability, coupled with acute deprivation, qualified a woman for help. A sixteen-year-old who was evidently undernourished and was "practically without clothes . . . she need never have lost her baby if we had known of her care in time, poor little soul"[98], was an ideal candidate. Mrs Pugh approved of mothers who were "clean and deserving",[99] but objected to those who took some initiative to obtain help, such as a woman who sent a detailed account of her income and expenditure.[100] Despite taking such great care to identify the 'right' women, the sums involved were very small (see table 2.2), relative to the level of established need and the vast wealth of Trust members.

The Trust's Cooperating Hospitals were "in competition for a seemingly declining slice of the philanthropic cake," according to Queen Mary's Hospital for the East End.[101] The maternity hospitals always begged for more:[102] Alice Gregory, the Honorary Secretary of the British Hospital for Mothers and Babies, complained in 1934 that, "We are in the most urgent need of a Second Ward (Isolation) Block – all our beds are already blocked up till June. (We have this week refused 35 women for May, and they have mostly gone away in tears) . . . If only we could find some generous donor. . . . It has occurred to me that possibly Lady Williams might be willing to lay our case before Sir Julien Cahn . . . ?"[103] Annie McCall of Clapham Maternity Hospital asked Lady Williams in 1937 for £50 for an antenatal department.[104]

	£	s	d
TABLE 2.2: SAMARITAN FUND			
Year ending 31 October 1936			
Cost of blankets, clothing, etc.	21	13	6
Balance carried forward	31	7	3
	53	0	9
Year ending 31 October 1937			
Cost of blankets, clothing, etc.	45	15	10
Balance carried forward	16	8	10
	62	4	8
Year ending 31 October 1944			
Balance carried forward	60	11	10
Interest on deposit		5	10
	60	17	8

Another charity like the Trust, created by very rich ladies to help the poor, was the Personal Service League. It aimed to make or give, and then distribute, clothing to the unemployed. A doctor consulted by the League reported a meeting with Lady Londonderry, who was busy in the League, where she "talked at me about starving and dying children, ordered cocktails, phoned to a servant to take the dogs out for their exercise. . . ."[105] This "disgusting patronage of the plutocracy"[106] was frequently resented by the recipients of charity. In her book about *Growing up in Lambeth*, Mary Chamberlain records that one woman's father

> became a Salvation Army man and he said that it was the only way he could get anything to wear. He got a uniform. And then me and my three sisters became Sunbeams and we had a little grey uniform with red piping. *I've never worn that colour since.*[107]

In contrast with this kind of charitable relief, working-class organizations like the Women's Cooperative Guild simply collected and sent money, clothing and other goods to the poor in distressed areas, to be distributed as they saw fit.[108]

FEMINISM IN THE 1930s

Before 1928, however much poor and rich women were divided by social class, there was a degree to which suffragists of all classes and political affiliations were united in the single cause of the franchise. This unity was reflected at the parliamentary level: after Lady Astor's election as a Conservative MP, Ethel Snowden and Edith Picton-Turberville refused to stand against her as a Labour candidate. "I am a Labour woman," said Ethel Snowden, "but the work which Lady Astor is doing for women and children both in parliament and the country makes her services invaluable."[109] Astor and Mrs Wintringham, a Liberal and the second woman to become an MP, exchanged telegrams of mutual support at elections. Vera Brittain recorded this solidarity in her novel *Honourable Estate*, where she quoted Stanley Baldwin's words at a meeting of the United Franchise Demonstration in March 1928: "This wonderful meeting," he said, "represents the greatest common measure of agreement on one great political issue amongst women who, on every other subject, probably hold diverse views."[110]

Many members of the Birthday Trust had campaigned in the suffrage movement, including Ethel Snowden, author of *The Feminist Movement*, who represented Socialism in the National Union of Societies for Equal Citizenship with Mary Stocks and Edith Picton-Turberville, and also her husband Philip. Lady Londonderry, despite strong disapproval from her father and mother-in-law,[111] was an active suffragist. In a letter to *The Times*, she displayed a sense of solidarity with working-class women, insisting that the vote

43

is chiefly wanted for *her poorer sister* . . . it is almost beside the mark to tell her that the vote is intended to hang a murderer or shut a public house, when she knows she could use it for all the factory laws and housing laws – in fact in a hundred ways in which legislation deals directly now with women. . . . In the last 50 years [women have] been forced into the open labour market, as all the home industries, which she did at home, have gradually been absorbed by the factories, and for this very reason, she requires the extra protection of the vote.[112]

The Marchioness of Londonderry was the founder and president of the Women's Legion during the First World War. The success of women's efforts to keep Britain functioning while the men were away fighting, highlighted the absurdity of withholding the franchise from them. This led in 1918 to the granting of the suffrage to women aged thirty and over. Other reforms soon followed, which opened the professions to women, granted divorce to women on equal grounds with men, gave women equal guardianship of children, introduced widows' pensions, and established the right to legitimize a child by marriage to the father.

Women were more frequently the target of advertisements after obtaining electoral power. Sketch, *17 October 1928. (Reproduced courtesy of the* Illustrated London News *Picture Library)*

Once the full vote had been won in 1928, the struggle for equal rights for women generally lost its impetus, though it was maintained by Lady Rhondda and some others. For the most part, energy was now directed towards the welfare of women in the home, which was called 'New Feminism' by Eleanor Rathbone, a feminist and social reformer who was an Independent MP.[113] The choice for suffragists between class and gender loyalties became sharper. Nearly all working-class, and a handful of middle-class, activists committed themselves to the Labour Party. Those who were better off mostly turned to the Liberal and Conservative Parties, while some feminists were attracted by the British fascist movement.[114] New Feminism took many forms, such as the Birthday Trust's work to improve conditions around childbirth. Other organizations tried to improve and make more interesting the task of running a home. This development was reflected in the changing activities of the National Union of Societies for Equal Citizenship, which up to 1927 had been chiefly concerned with the issue of the franchise. From 1932, however, it turned its attention to the development of the National Union of Townswomen's Guilds, which focused on handicrafts and gardening. These activities were less an extension of the tradition of the National Union of Societies for Equal Citizenship, than a departure from it.

A major strand of New Feminism was the campaign for family allowances, which was led by Eleanor Rathbone. Believing that women needed an independent income, she had already argued in *The Disinherited Family* (1924) that "nothing can justify the subordination of one group of producers – the mothers – to the rest, and the deprivation of all share of their own in the wealth of a community which depends on them for its very existence."[115] Lady Williams shared Rathbone's vision and drew up plans for "a straight-forward insurance scheme, to provide family allowances in the same way as National Health Insurance benefits."[116] She had great hopes for the improvement of mothers' lives and would have shared the optimism of a character in one of her novels: "We're in the twentieth century now, don't forget, and women are going to come into their own!"[117]

The attention to marriage and childbearing was seen to provide women with an opportunity of uniting over causes that – like the franchise movement before 1928 – were separate from issues of class. In this spirit, Mrs Baldwin prefaced her wireless appeal for the Fund in 1935 by saying to her listeners, "I want to speak to you just as a woman and as a mother, and as one who has for many years been pleading on behalf of mothers."[118] The threat of maternal death and the pain of childbirth were links between rich and poor women that could not be shared by men. Supposing that there were as many rich women as rich men, argued Virginia Woolf in *Three Guineas*, "What could you not do?" As well as financing a woman's party in the House of Commons, she said, you could "bring down the maternal death-rate from four in every thousand to none at all, perhaps."[119] Mrs Baldwin identified male prejudice against women as a key enemy in the campaign to make childbirth safer. "Prejudice dies hard," she said, "and I must say that when a man shewing prejudice talks to me . . . I have very great difficulty in preventing myself from telling him what I think. And it is rather a tremendous thing if a man once hears what a woman thinks of him, because he so rarely does."[120] When Sir Hilton Young, Minister of Health, referred in 1932 at a meeting of the Maternal Mortality Committee to a need to "grow . . . enlightened mothers", he provoked "Murmurs of 'And fathers'".[121] Many women maintained that they were more capable than men of talking sensibly about childbirth. This was the spirit of a campaign for women to serve on the committee of management of Queen Charlotte's Hospital.[122] In 1933, Mrs Baldwin wrote to Hilton Young:

where the Maternity Services are in Question it is more important to have a woman than a man. You know and all men ought to know that their knowledge on this subject is merely second hand and for so long the question of maternal welfare has been shelved by them and put in the background. Do I beseech you on behalf of us poor women, do give us a couple of representatives [on the Departmental Committee investigating maternal mortality]. I apologise profusely but I do feel it personally.[123]

The Minister promised to arrange for two women to join the committee;[124] he could hardly refuse, given that her husband's position in the Cabinet as Lord President of Council was superior to his own.

The Birthday Trust displayed limited interest in the welfare of children, relative to their concern with mothers. When Lady Cynthia Colville invited the Fund to participate in a day called 'Child Welfare Day', Lady George and Mrs Baldwin were asked by Trust members to insist that unless 'Maternity' were added to 'Child Welfare' in the name of the day, the Fund would not participate.[125] When the question arose of selling flags on Children's Day, Mrs Baldwin said that she "did not wish to see 'Mother's Day' sunk in 'Children's Day'" and that the Fund ought to concentrate on mothers.[126] This was not the product of disinterest in children, but the conviction – which was the cornerstone of New Feminism – that mothers themselves deserved attention.

A 'NON-PARTY' ORGANIZATION

The Birthday Trust was one of several middle and upper-class women's organizations of the period that described themselves as 'non-party', in the spirit of cooperation that had characterized the suffrage movement.[127] When the Birthday Fund's secretary in 1929 asked members to suggest speakers for the Inaugural Meeting, many replied that all the main political parties and religions should be represented. Mr Seymour Leslie suggested Mrs Snowden as the third speaker, adding, "It is a common mistake to forget the Liberal and Labour Parties. The Meeting must be non-political and really representative. It must also have representatives of different religions. Lady Bearsted could help you about the Chief Rabbi. The Bishop of London we have always found impossible, but perhaps he would come for a General Meeting like this."[128] Dr Annie McCall proposed Miss Ishbel MacDonald, the eldest daughter of Ramsay MacDonald. There was a consensus that, as a temporary paid organizer insisted, "We must keep all politics out."[129] To indicate to the public the apolitical nature of the Fund, an appeal letter to *The Times* was signed by: Lucy Baldwin; Margaret Lloyd George, the wife of the former Liberal Prime Minister; M.E. Clynes, the wife of J.R. Clynes, a Labour politician who had been Lord Privy Seal in the 1924 Labour Cabinet and was Home Secretary between 1929 and 1931; Ethel Snowden; Cynthia Colville, Lady-in-Waiting to the Queen; Beatrix Lyall of the Mothers' Union; Lady George; and Lady Londonderry.

Mrs Baldwin insisted that her work for the Fund should not be construed as partisan. Her secretary asked Mrs Constance Lloyd Baxendale if a meeting could be held at her house because she was

. . . so afraid that a meeting in Newbury [at Chequers] itself might easily be misconstrued into a party meeting. Mrs Baldwin is most anxious that her appeal should be strictly non-political, she has been very careful to always stress its 'national' importance; she does not want to give anybody the chance to say it is under political auspicies [sic].130

However, an organization that was so dominated by one political party could not seriously expect to avoid politics – Mrs Henry Lewis, a

MRS. BALDWIN'S MESSAGE.

Every thinking man and woman deplores unnecessary suffering. We have our societies for the protection of children and animals, but the unnecessary suffering of mothers in child-birth is apt to be ignored. We ask you to help to make this a thing of the past, both by propaganda and by supporting the work of this fund.

Lucy Baldwin

VISCOUNTESS SNOWDEN'S MESSAGE.

Is there a man who would not have sacrificed everything to have saved his Mother unnecessary suffering at his birth? With that in his heart, he simply cannot say "No" to this appeal for the Mothers of our country.

Ethel Snowden

DAME MARGARET LLOYD GEORGE'S MESSAGE.

Not only of Motherhood do I ask you to think. I would that you remember your own Mother, her love, her cease-less care and concern. With that lovely memory prompting you, how can you fail to make your gift that Motherhood may be as safe as it is noble?

Margaret Lloyd George

YOUR DONATION

There are 44,000,000 people in Great Britain, and 44,000,000 shillings when invested, would enable the National Birthday Trust Fund to attain its object.

We ask for Birthday Donations to help the Birthdays of others, either 1/-, or the number of shillings (or pounds) according to the number of birthdays you have celebrated.

Please send 1/- now, and 1/- on each birthday, if you cannot send more.

An appeal from the Birthday Trust in the early 1930s which is deliberately 'apolitical' – it is signed by Lady Baldwin, wife of the Conservative Party leader, Viscountess Snowden, wife of a prominent member of the Labour Party, and Dame Margaret Lloyd George, wife of the former Liberal Prime Minister.

member of the Birthday Trust, said that she preferred Lady Snowden to Mrs Baldwin as a drawing room speaker, because "she would rather not have Mrs Baldwin to speak in her house, although she realises the Fund is non-political, as she is a Liberal!"131 In any case, however much Mrs Baldwin protested that she did not want the Birthday Trust to be associated in the public mind with the Conservative Party, she appears (by broadcasting from Chequers, for example) to have sought such a link. So did the Prime Minister: when the Gramophone Company issued three double-sided records of his broadcast speech on the death of King George V, he instructed it to make the royalties on these records payable to the National Birthday Trust Fund.132 All this was welcome publicity for the Conservatives, since the welfare of mothers was a key electoral issue.

Once women got the vote, they became important for the first time in the eyes of the political parties. As Lady Londonderry had observed in the years of the suffrage campaign, "It is only human nature, that a Parliamentary candidate attends to the wants and wishes of a voter in preference to a non-voter."133 In

1918, only four out of ten voters had been women; but in 1929, women comprised 53 per cent of the total electorate. The Ministry of Health acknowledged women's new power when it opposed research into the extent of mothers' morbidity; such an investigation, it feared, "would inevitably arouse public opinion and create a demand, which in present political emancipation and the special interest in this question among labour women would have to be met."[134] After 1928, the Conservative Party conducted a 'special survey' of new voters and appointed a large number of full-time women as organizing secretaries.[135] Personal connections with women quickly became an established feature of election literature – candidates published photographs of themselves with wives and children, and messages from their wives.[136] Now, politics had to reflect "the viewpoint of the homemaker as well as that of the breadwinner."[137] The commitment of government to the reform of women's conditions was a response to their developing political power. Between 1918–19 and 1927–28, there was a rise in Ministry of Health grants to Local Authorities for child and maternal welfare, from £218,000 annually to £983,000.[138]

A file at the Public Record Office, labelled 'Brief to Counter Labour Party's Campaign',[139] contains documents by Conservatives reporting on the efforts of the Labour Party to address women-related issues. One memo complains, "It

FIGURE 2.3: INSTITUTIONAL RELATIONSHIPS OF THE NBTF IN THE 1930S

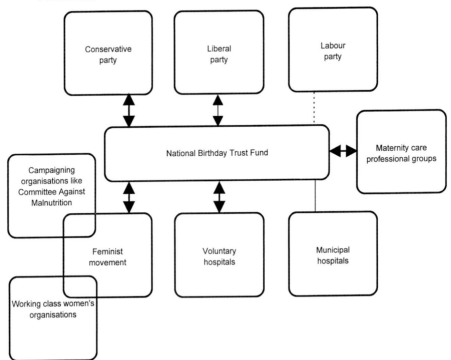

appears that the Labour Party are beginning an intensive campaign against the Government on the subject of maternal mortality. The Minister would be grateful if a full brief could be prepared setting out all that has been done and is being done in this matter. I understand that the Central Office will prepare counter propaganda . . ." There is also a draft statement, evidently rushed, protesting that, "The National Government, and the Conservative Government prior to 1929, have been no less active than the Labour Party in their measures to deal with the problem of maternal mortality."[140] In fact, though, the Conservative record on women's health was not impressive. Although the Labour Party had not yet been in a position to be properly tested on this issue, it had at least put social reform high on its political agenda and had supported women's struggles in this area – which could not be said of the Conservatives.

The association between the Birthday Trust and prominent Conservatives was therefore a happy development for the Conservative Party, because it demonstrated to the nation that the Party was concerned about women's welfare. But this did not mean that the Birthday Trust was simply a political tool. Determined to help reduce the rate of maternal death, the Trust exploited its political and social connections (as shown in figure 2.3) in order to achieve this goal. At the top of its ambitious agenda, as the next chapter will show, was the reorganization of the midwifery services.

CHAPTER THREE

The 1936 Midwives Act

The high maternal death rate of the late 1920s was the reason for the foundation of the National Birthday Fund. An additional cause for concern was the prevalence of maternal morbidity: even if a woman survived childbirth, her life might be ruined by consequent ill health. Indeed, one authority estimated that twenty times the number of mothers who died were disabled annually.[1] Little had changed since the publication of mothers' letters in *Maternity* more than a decade before, which described some of the long-term effects of injuries sustained in childbirth. One mother reported, "I am suffering from the ill-effects today. This is 31 years ago", while another said, "I know I shall have to suffer while I live through being neglected at childbirth."[2] In his novel *Once in Every Lifetime*, Tom Hanlin depicted the misery of a woman who became "a semi-invalid till the day she died", following a difficult childbirth. "From our one room," comments her husband, "we looked down on a backyard of clothes poles and cats raking buckets. In this back room she lived her life and died."[3]

District nursing in the 1930s. The Birthday Trust was determined to help mothers like this, whose pregnancy and labour was made harder by poverty. (Reproduced courtesy of the Queen's Nursing Institute)

The Birthday Trust was determined to make motherhood safer. Guided by Dame Janet Campbell, it decided to improve the status and working conditions of midwives, who attended approximately 60 per cent of all confinements in England and Wales in the mid-1930s.[4] Its first step in this strategy was to create a national headquarters for midwifery in 1933, as described in chapter 1. Then, the following year, it set up the Joint Council of Midwifery as an unofficial body "to discover a practical solution to the growing problem of the underpayment of midwives".[5] In

TABLE 3.1: CONSTITUTION OF THE JOINT COUNCIL OF MIDWIFERY

Chairman

Major-General the Rt. Hon. the Earl of Athlone (President, Queen's Institute of District Nursing)

Vice-Chairmen

The Lord Aberdare
Sir Francis Fremantle

Council

T. Watts Eden	British College of Obstetricians and Gynaecologists
J.S. Fairbairn	as above
L.C. Rivett	as above
R.D. Smedley	Association of County Medical Officers of Health
Dame Louise McIlroy	British Medical Association
E.W.G. Masterman	as above
W.H.F. Oxley	as above
Miss L.H. Wooldridge	Association of Inspectors of Midwives
Miss M. Coleman	as above
Miss E.M. Pye	Midwives' Institute
Miss M. Burnside	as above
Miss G.B. Carter	as above
Sir William Hale-White	Queen's Institute of District Nursing
Mrs Bruce Richmond	as above
Miss M. Wilmshurst	as above
Miss E.M. Doubleday	College of Nursing
Sir Julien Cahn	National Birthday Trust Fund
Mrs Stanley Baldwin	as above
Lady Williams	as above (Hon. Secretary of Council and Committee)
R.H.P. Orde	British Hospitals Association
Rhys Davies, MP	Independent
Miss Megan Lloyd George, MP	Independent
Major E. Longmore	County Councils Association
J.M. Newnham	Association of Municipal Corporations
The Lord Strathcona	

other words, it organized a method to evaluate and change national policy on the employment of midwives.

This was work that the Trust was best placed to do, because of its powerful connections. It had no difficulty in persuading distinguished and influential members of the establishment to join the JCM (see table 3.1), which was chaired by the Earl of Athlone, Queen Mary's brother and President and Chairman of the Queen's Institute; the Vice-Chairmen were the Lord Aberdare and Sir Francis Fremantle. The independent members included Rhys Davies, a Labour MP, Miss Megan Lloyd George, a Liberal MP, and the Lord Strathcona. The majority of its members were formally nominated by the various bodies which they represented: for example, John Fairbairn,[6] Thomas Watts Eden[7] and Louis Carnac Rivett[8] were asked to serve by the BCOG; the Society of Medical Officers of Health sent Dr Buchan; the College of Nursing sent Miss Doubleday; the Midwives' Institute sent Miss Edith Pye, who was its President between 1929 and 1949, Miss Burnside and Miss Carter; and the Queen's Institute of District Nursing sent Sir William Hale-White, Mrs Bruce Richmond and Miss Mercy Wilmshurst, its General Secretary. The Birthday Trust was represented by Sir Julien Cahn, Lady Williams and Mrs Baldwin. In late 1934, Gertrude Tuckwell observed, "of course, if there was a married woman who had had a difficult labour at the head of affairs or at the Ministry of Health, our work would practically be done."[9] The Birthday Trust provided the next best thing – the wife of the leader of the Conservative Party, who became Prime Minister just as the real work of the JCM was starting.

At its second meeting on 30 May 1934, the JCM appointed a Midwifery Services Committee, with two members of the BCOG acting as Chairman and Vice-Chairman: Eden and Fairbairn, respectively.[10] The first meeting was held on 25 October 1934, which drew up terms of reference involving the preparation of "a detailed scheme" for the "enlistment of Midwives throughout the country in an organised service, suited to the needs of each district, and having due regard to the retention of the mother's freedom of choice of attendant."[11] An Administrative Sub-Committee and a Training and Distribution Sub-Committee were established to support this work.

Dame Janet was an invisible presence, using the JCM to achieve her own ambitions for midwifery. As early as 1917, she had advocated an improvement in the "status and position" of the midwife;[12] and in *The Protection of Motherhood* (1927), she presented her vision of a midwife-based national maternity service, in which many normal deliveries and all maternity nursing would be performed by midwives, with the support of the patient's own doctor.[13] It was this kind of national scheme that she described at a 'confidential' meeting on 5 June 1934, less than one week after the JCM had been set up, to Miss Pye, Miss Burnside, Miss Carter, and Lady Williams.[14] Dame Janet kept firmly in the background, though. On 31 May 1934, reporting to Dame Janet on the first meeting of the JCM, the day before, Lady Williams acknowledged her preference "not to be associated with the committee's work officially"; she assured her, "I will of course keep quiet as to the origins of the suggestions if you would prefer it, but, as you know, we are not likely to reach any very useful conclusions without your help."[15] Even Eden, Chairman of the committee, was not told of the degree of her involvement: Lady Williams simply told him that she had "ascertained privately from the Ministry of Health that a detailed scheme worked out on these lines would be acceptable."[16] With the use of the word 'privately', she avoided identifying her source.

A NATIONAL MATERNITY SERVICE

In 1928 the Ministry of Health appointed a Departmental Committee on Maternal Mortality and Morbidity, which was chaired by Sir George Newman and included F.J. Browne, an obstetrician, Janet Campbell, Walter M. Fletcher, and W.H.F. Oxley,[17] a general practitioner in London's East End who was highly respected for his obstetric skills. It produced an *Interim Report* in 1930 and a *Final Report* in 1932, which called for a reform of the maternity services. Anxiety about the rising rate of maternal death had already led to a number of suggestions for a national maternity service. Arthur Greenwood, Labour Minister of Health, reflected wryly on these schemes at a meeting of the Maternal Mortality Committee in 1930. "I have read with the very greatest interest every proposal that has been made within recent years for what is called a National Maternity Service," he observed, adding, "I am not sure yet that I have met the person who quite understood what it meant. It is the easiest thing to invent phrases." In any case, as Henry Brackenbury, Chairman of the Council of the BMA, pointed out, there were "all sorts of interests to consider when we get down to the practical work of establishing a service."[18]

In 1929, a government committee had recommended the creation of a national maternity service in which the midwife, the doctor and the specialist would each play their part. Services would be provided free of charge at the time, but linked to the National Insurance Scheme. This scheme was not pursued, chiefly because of the financial crisis generated by the Depression. Also, according to a memorandum written for internal use at the Ministry of Health, there were "doubts as to whether it would deliver the goods".[19] A consultant-based maternity service was proposed by the President of the British College of Obstetricians and Gynaecologists, Blair-Bell, who outlined a scheme run by a central independent administrative body with representatives of every interested group except midwives.[20]

The BMA, for its part, published plans for a national maternity service that centred on GPs, which "should always be the bedrock on which the medical services of the country, including midwifery, must be built up."[21] Brackenbury maintained that "every woman who is about to become a mother should have at her service a general medical practitioner of her own choice"; he mistrusted

TABLE 3.2: CHAIRMEN AND DEPUTY CHAIRMEN OF THE CENTRAL MIDWIVES BOARD
1902–1983 (WHEN CMB DISSOLVED)

Chairmen		Deputy Chairmen	
1902–30	Sir Francis Champneys	1944–6	Sir Arnold L. Walker
1930–6	John S. Fairbairn	1946–52	J. Prescott Hedley
1936–46	Sir Comyns Berkeley	1953–67	Sir Alan Moncrieff
1946–67	Sir Arnold L. Walker	1967–73	Miss Margaret I. Farrer
1967–8	Sir Alan Moncrieff	1973–8	J.S. Tomkinson
1973–9	Miss Margaret I. Farrer	1978–83	F.J.W. Miller
1979–83	Miss N. Hickey		

Local Authorities, suspecting they would try to squeeze out GPs.[22] His glorification of the role of the doctor led to some incredulity. "But does Sir Henry Brackenbury really suggest," asked one newspaper, reporting on a meeting of the BMA, "that no woman can have a child without the attendance of a doctor?"[23]

The Women's Cooperative Guild called in 1929 for a National Maternity Service that was paid for by the state and centred on midwives: a "municipal service of qualified midwives" that covered Britain, so that every village with a population of 4,000 had "a certified midwife supplied by the State".[24] John Fairbairn, who was Chairman of the Central Midwives Board (CMB) at this time (a list of the Chairmen of the CMB is given in table 3.2), advocated the same kind of service; in so doing, he departed from the proposal of the BCOG, of which he was soon to become President (a list of Presidents is given in table 3.3). In 1927, in an article

TABLE 3.3: PRESIDENTS OF THE ROYAL COLLEGE OF OBSTETRICIANS AND GYNAECOLOGISTS

1929–32	William Blair-Bell	1969–72	Thomas Norman Arthur Jeffcoate
1932–5	John Shields Fairbairn		
1935–8	Ewen John MacLean	1972–5	Stanley George Clayton
1938–43	William Fletcher Shaw	1975–8	Christopher John Dewhurst
1943–6	Eardley Holland		
1946–9	William Gilliatt	1978–81	Edward Anthony John Alment
1949–52	Hilda Nora Lloyd		
1952–5	Arthur Alexander Gemmell	1981–4	Rustam Moolan Feroze
		1984–7	Malcolm Campbell MacNaughton
1955–7	Charles David Read		
1957–60	Andrew Moynihan Claye	1987–90	George Douglas Pinker
1960–3	Arthur Capel Herbert Bell	1990–3	Stanley Clifford Simmons
		1993–4	Geoffrey Victor Price Chamberlain
1963–6	Hector Ross MacLennan		
1966–9	John Harold Peel	1995–	Naren Babubhai Patel

praising the midwifery service of the Queen's Institute, which had a death rate of 2.1, about half the rate for England and Wales, Fairbairn proposed copying this model nationwide – a maternity service built on the foundation of a salaried service of midwives, with medical help in difficult cases.[25] He justified this by referring not only to the results of the Queen's Institute midwives, but also to those of the midwives of voluntary hospitals and Nursing Associations, who also worked within a salaried service and whose rate of maternal mortality was below the national average.[26]

This kind of salaried service was proposed by the JCM's Midwifery Services Committee: "We have definitely decided to try to hammer out some kind of scheme on the lines of Dr Fairbairn's Resolution," wrote Lady Williams to an approving Dame Janet.[27] It took a little time, however, for a consensus to be reached on the plan for a salaried service. "The mother's freedom of choice," argued Miss Burnside, "was the first consideration, and in her opinion this could best be assured by the formation of a panel of independent midwives" on the same lines as the National Health Insurance panel system. This suggestion, which was also supported by Dr Oxley,[28] had been part of an earlier plan for a national maternity service that had been abandoned by the Ministry of Health.

THE STATUS OF MIDWIVES

There were 52,872 midwives on the Roll of the Central Midwives Board in 1934, though only 15,442 were in practice; of these, only about 10 per cent were paid-up members of the Midwives' Institute. Of the midwives in actual practice, 6,255 were salaried, working in a hospital or district practice, and 9,187 were in independent practice.[29] The livelihood of these midwives was being gradually eroded. Women received 30s maternity benefit under the National Insurance Act of 1911, if their husband was employed, but this sum barely covered the cost of a midwife's services. "In the East End of London," reported the Medical Officer of Health for the London County Council, "the average midwife's fee is, for primiparae, between 25s and 30s and for multiparae between 16s and 21s. The corresponding fees in West London are between 42s and 50s and between 30s and 35s."[30] It was not uncommon for a midwife to receive only a part of her fee, or nothing at all.

This situation had been aggravated by the Depression, which put so many people in insurable employment out of work, thus causing the maternity benefit to lapse. The 1935 Report of the Medical Officer of Health for the Rhondda Urban District Council observed that "the midwives practising in the district were not able to recover any fees or any adequate payments for attendance on the confinements of a large number of mothers in the district." A retired midwife who worked in South Wales recalls that before the 1936 Act, "There was so much poverty. The midwives were working for nothing half the time."[31] In *Love on the Dole* (1933), the midwife Mrs Bull pitied the "Poor soul wi' a tribe o' kids as lives in next street's bin confined agen . . . Couldn't even afford t'pay me for tendin' her i' childbed, an' him workin', too!"[32]

On top of these difficulties, midwives were also faced with a loss of work. The birth rate was falling, which reduced the number of possible deliveries, and the provision by some Local Authorities of free clinics took cases away from many single-handed independent midwives. A 1936 report by the Midwives' Institute into the state of 'The Midwife in Independent Practice Today' quoted a midwife as saying that following the opening of a new maternity home four years before, new cases were going to the hospital and she had only one case a month, with "nothing coming in except what a relation allows me. Some days I have nothing to eat". Another midwife complained about a hospital which "immediately on settling in this borough commenced a swift campaign of undercutting the midwives, charging about one-half our fees and offering other benefits besides."[33]

When midwives did have work, it was hard and, sometimes, unpleasant. A midwife who worked in Birmingham in the 1930s recalls that in one district, "bugs came out of the wall at night when I was staying there all night with the mother. They were all back to back, houses joined to other houses. They were big insects." These houses had no running water and she had to rely on carbolic lotion in order to maintain hygiene, which ruined the skin of her hands. Research carried out by the JCM showed that the average yearly earnings of a midwife dependent upon her profession were £80, and in certain areas as low as £50.[34] Out of this, midwives had to buy their own equipment, drugs and disinfectants, and in some cases even dressings. They had no time off, no holidays and no security.

Midwifery had become a closed occupation to any woman who had pretensions to gentility, because it was so poorly paid and arduous. Miss Eleanor Rathbone recalled that in the course of debate in the House of Commons over the Midwives Bill of 1902, which she had watched from the Ladies' Gallery (and seen her father fighting for the Bill), "It required courage in those years to work for a Midwives Bill, when even the mention of midwifery was the cause of ribald jokes in the House."[35] Midwifery had none of the respectability created for nursing by Florence Nightingale in the Crimea and by the courage of the women who became VADs (as members of the Volunteer Aid Detachment were known) during the First World War. A letter written in the 1930s to the Editor of *Time and Tide* remarked that, "A new midwife is still considered by upper class and (male intelligentsia) as something that, if mentioned at all, is meant to be funny (like Wigan) or vulgar (like tripe)."[36] This was not the case among the poor, however, who relied on midwives for their maternity care. In working-class communities, a midwife was usually safe and respected, her uniform letting her pass safely where many other women would not venture. One retired midwife who trained in the late 1930s chose her profession because she had been so impressed, as a child growing up in her Yorkshire village, by the high esteem in which the local midwife was held. "When we were at school," she explains, "I thought it was wonderful to be so respected."[37]

Midwives were keenly aware of their low status and wanted new entrants to the profession to come from a 'respectable' background. Mrs Richmond of the Queen's Institute "emphasised the importance of preventing the uneducated type of candidate from taking the C.M.B course".[38] They were annoyed that health visitors, who worked shorter hours, were given greater respect and higher pay. One midwife wrote to *Nursing Times* in 1935, "We midwives do feel that something ought to be done with regard to our position as compared to that of the health visitor . . . to raise the status of midwives."[39]

In her 1917 *Report on the Physical Welfare of Mothers and Children,* Janet Campbell had argued that it was difficult to raise the status of midwives when some of them were incompetent.[40] This was evidently true of some midwives. Hannah Mitchell, a leader in the suffragist and labour movements in the north of England, recalled in her autobiography, *The Hard Way Up*, that when she gave birth at the turn of the century, her baby was born after twenty-four hours "of intense suffering which an ignorant attendant did little to alleviate, assuring me at intervals that I should be much worse yet".[41] In a public address in 1935, the Minister of Health, Sir Kingsley Wood, implicitly criticized the work of midwives. Their low level of pay, he said, "is not such as to attract to the profession those we would desire to see in this important service."[42] His remarks generated much indignation in *Nursing Notes* and the Midwives' Institute complained that, "it is both unjust and false to lay the blame for the alleged high rate of maternal mortality at the door of the independent midwife."[43] In any case, as *Nursing Notes* reasonably pointed out, "we have no proof that the still high maternal death rate can be laid to the account of insufficient training of the practising midwife."[44]

Handywomen were blamed for maternal mortality even more than qualified midwives, although there was no direct evidence that they were an important cause of the problem.[45] They had been protected by the first Midwives Act of 1902, which had recognized midwifery as a profession separate from that of doctors or consultants and had created the Central Midwives Board; any woman of good character who could produce evidence that she had been in practice as a midwife for at least one year when the Act was passed, was admitted to the Roll of the CMB. They often assisted at deliveries, sometimes taking full responsibility. A midwife who started work in 1937 recalls,

> I worked with an old bona fide midwife until she retired. And I learnt such a lot from her. She couldn't tell you why she did things, but she was right. If a mother was nearly due, she'd have a tape and she'd measure from the umbilicus up, you see, and I remember a doctor said, now why do you do that? And she couldn't say. She knew that if the tape dropped a bit, if it was six inches one week and came down to five the next, the baby was due, but she couldn't explain why.[46]

Another midwife has recalled that when she was working in the 1930s, handywomen "were respected all round".[47] Handywomen were especially appreciated by poor mothers, who relied on their help with child care, making fires, and washing and cooking for the family, the kind of work that was not provided by a qualified midwife.

But some doctors complained vigorously about these handywomen: a Dr Finer, whose patients in Essex in the 1930s arranged their own handywomen, said they were "mainly ignorant, their duties being to cover the bed with old newspapers and to keep water boiling . . . they knew virtually nothing about parturition."[48] The chief gain of a national service, believed the Honorary Secretary of the Association of County Medical Officers of Health, would be the "gradual elimination of the handy woman."[49]

CAUSES OF MATERNAL DEATH

It made sense to focus on midwifery in raising the standard of the maternity services, since midwives attended the majority of confinements. Also, it was they who cared for the poor, and there was a widespread assumption that poverty was the crucial factor in maternal mortality. In his research in 1936 for the Pilgrim Trust enquiry into the effects of unemployment in the most depressed areas of Britain, Hans Singer reported a "clear connection" between unemployment and maternal mortality. If the figures for the county boroughs could be taken as representative of the country as a whole, he said, the number of victims of unemployment among mothers dying of puerperal disease might be estimated at 32,000, because of nervous strain, malnutrition, and economies in the public medical services.[50] In *High Maternal Mortality in Certain Areas* (1932), Dame Janet Campbell, Isabella Cameron and Dilys Jones explored reasons for an excessive maternal death rate in the regions of Yorkshire, Lancashire and Wales, which suffered a high degree of poverty.

But overall, better-off women were more at risk of maternal death than working-class women. This was because those who could afford it were buying the services of doctors, many of whom were inexperienced in obstetrics. Poor women usually escaped this risk because they were attended by midwives. In his study *Death in Childbirth*, the historian Irvine Loudon refers to studies in the 1920s and 1930s that demonstrated this differential in the death rate: in Glasgow in 1929–31, for example, it was 50.4 among women who attended a doctor (mostly the middle classes), but 26.0 among women who attended a midwife (the working classes). "The important conclusion," he comments, "is not that poverty and malnutrition had no effect on the risk of dying in childbirth, but rather that the effect was surprisingly slight compared to the effect of the standard of maternal care and the type of birth-attendant."[51] He suggests that at least one-third of all maternal deaths were due to careless obstetric practice and were avoidable.[52]

The chief problem with the attendance of doctors was inadequate antisepsis and their willingness to intervene in normal labour with forceps and other instruments. "Premature intervention," said Professor F.J. Browne, the Director of the Obstetric Unit at University College Hospital in London (who has been credited with the invention of antenatal care[53]), "is the mother of disaster"; he advised that the GP "should not carry forceps ready sterilized in his bag, for if they are ready the temptation to use them may be too great to resist."[54] A retired midwife recalls, "In those days on the district, the doctors didn't worry. They never waited for the mother to be fully dilated. They would just put on forceps and try and bring out the baby. They would tear the mother to bits."[55] Dr Oxley, who represented the BMA on the JCM, estimated in 1934 that his colleagues used forceps in 60 per cent of their cases.[56]

In fact, though, there was little accurate data about the cause of death in pregnancy and childbirth, with the exception of results from some small enquiries, like the Departmental Committee's 1932 report of an enquiry into 4,655 deaths. When the Director of the Central Bureau of Hospital Information, Mr R.P.H. Orde, sent Lady Williams some particulars of births in voluntary hospitals in 1933, he did so "alas in fear and trembling". He admitted, "They are the best we can do with the material at our disposal." In another letter, which notes that "these great hospitals" make no mention in their reports of the births of babies, he added as an afterthought in pen and ink, "I did, rather flippantly, suggest that no one could check any figures however incorrect and you very properly rebuked me but I did not mean to be flippant: it was rather a cry of despair."[57] There was a suspicion that the real reason for the patchy records on maternal death was their potential to expose doctors as responsible. Miss G.B. Carter, President of the Midwives' Institute, commented, "No one keeps a very careful record of the differential rate of death in domiciliary practice as between Doctors' cases and midwives' cases – *too invidious.*"[58] Blaming the midwife had the advantage for the GP, suggested an article in *The New Statesman* in 1928, of deflecting attention away from his own work. "Uninformed medical commentators," observed the author, "ask us to believe that the continuance of the midwives – a rival to the medical practitioner – is the evil which we must remedy."[59] But for the most part, no one really understood the cause of maternal death or knew what to do about it. It was "in very large degree preventible", said Neville Chamberlain, Minister of Health, at the Inaugural Meeting of the Birthday Fund in 1929, adding that, "we are nowhere near the irreducible minimum".[60] But he was unable to suggest exactly how this minimum should be reached.

THE JCM REPORT

On 13 December 1934, Lady Williams reported to the Midwifery Services Committee that the current Minister of Health, Sir Hilton Young, had asked for the JCM's conclusions to be presented to him as soon as possible. This would enable him to consult the representatives of the Local Authorities at the same time as the Council consulted its Constituent Bodies. It would then be possible to receive all the relative comments in time to introduce legislation next session, should this course be approved.[61]

This level of interest is not surprising. From the point of view of the government, the issue of a national maternity service was intricately bound up with the support of the electorate. Sir Kingsley Wood, who took over as Minister of Health in the new National government of 1935, wrote to a senior Ministry official in August 1935, "I suspect the subject will find a place in any election manifesto of the government". He added, "subject to the Chancellor's consent and to the holding of an election by next spring and the return of this government, the Ministry may be required to embody this scheme in a bill to be passed next year."[62] It was important to the government to be seen to be acting on the issue of maternal death, now that half the voters were women, and there are a number of references in Ministry correspondence to the urgency of pressing ahead with the Midwives Bill.[63]

At every stage the government's interest was carefully nourished by the JCM. Lady Williams was an able politician and she knew that the support of the Ministry and of its high ranking civil servants, such as A.J. Machlachlan, Assistant Secretary, was key to the success of the JCM's strategy. "It is vital to get the sympathetic support of Mr McLachlan [sic]," she wrote to Miss Carter in January 1935, "as it is he who will be drafting the actual Bill, and I don't want to go against him if I can help it. At this stage, of course, he is speaking only as a private individual, and I am not officially allowed to quote him. In practice, the Minister will speak with his voice later on, and he matters immensely!"[64] She made a point of visiting Mr Machlachlan when the opportunity arose and listening to his views with studious attention.

In 1935, the Midwifery Services Committee finished the *Report of the Joint Council of Midwifery on the Desirability of Establishing a Salaried Service of Midwives.* The first part of the Report reviewed the conditions of midwives and considered alternative proposals. It made three key recommendations: it endorsed the patient's "own home" as the ideal place for a normal confinement; it advocated the conduct of every maternity case by a qualified midwife, adding that unqualified persons should not be permitted to nurse maternity cases for gain; and it declared that there was no satisfactory alternative to the establishment of a municipal salaried whole-time midwives' service. It also supported the continuance in practice of independent midwives.

The second part of the Report outlined a scheme for the establishment of such a service. It included the following proposals: that it should be the duty of every Local Authority to provide an adequate domiciliary service; that the Local Supervising Authority should administer the service; that the cost should be met by the fees payable to the Authority or the voluntary organization; that midwives entering the Municipal Service should receive adequate pay and pension rights and be accorded the same rights as a health visitor; that midwives not accepted to the service should be entitled to compensation; and that midwives should be inspected by other, experienced, midwives (previously, inspectors had been medical women or, most often, health visitors). The committee stressed that experience of general nursing, even in the case of State Registered Nurses, was not an adequate substitute for experience of the practice of midwifery.

The Midwifery Services Committee defended the practice of home delivery. The JCM report stated that "although adequate hospital accommodation for antenatal cases and abnormal confinements is essential, normal confinements can be satisfactorily, safely and preferably conducted in the patient's own home, except where this is unsuitable." Louise McIlroy,[65] representing the BMA on the JCM, remarked, "I thoroughly agree that it will be a bad day for British midwifery if domiciliary midwifery is cut out and hospital substitution takes its place."[66] One powerful reason for recommending the continued practice of home delivery was, of course, its cheapness. The External Affairs Committee of the British College of Obstetricians and Gynaecologists concluded in 1935 that even if some of the public were asking for increased hospital provision, in order to obtain relief from pain and for social reasons, "Adequate provision could only be made at great expense, because overcrowding in maternity hospitals is a great peril. It will be safer to keep hospital admissions strictly to the normal accommodation and, meantime, improve domiciliary service until increase of hospital beds adequate to meet the need is secured."[67]

When the JCM Report was sent out to its Constituent Bodies for comment, all but the BMA and the Association of County Medical Officers of Health approved it. *Nursing Notes*, the journal supported by the Midwives' Institute, ran a series of articles on the Report. It urged its readers to become familiar with it and to be mindful of "the jealousy of a certain section of the medical profession". Remember, it advised them, that

> you are in a very different position to-day from the time when the Act of 1902 was passed. You are State Certified Midwives (S.C.M.). Don't remain a solitary unit. There will have to be a new Bill. You all have votes; see that when the time comes your member understands how to vote. Show that you are a power in the land and remember one thing, viz., the power for good you possess. The mothers of England trust you and cannot do without their midwives.[68]

The Midwives' Institute was in favour of the scheme but insisted on the need to uphold the rights of the independent midwife. Like the author of a letter sent to the Minister of Health, it was afraid that "new arrangements may fall rather heavily on the Independent Midwives."[69] *Nursing Notes* complained about the absence on the Midwifery Services Committee of any member who had had experience of independent practice.[70] "The midwife in independent practice is rather a voiceless person and few hear her views or ask for them," it pointed out, adding that "NURSING NOTES does ask for them. We seem to be the only opportunity they have of voicing their needs and views." But in fact, Sir Comyns Berkeley, an obstetrician who was a member of the JCM and became Chairman of the CMB in 1936,[71] had fully expressed his concern about their future[72] and the JCM Report sought to protect their position. "There is no intention expressed in the report of the Joint Council," noted Miss Carter, "to prevent the practice of independent midwives. Those midwives who do not wish to be employed by the Authority may continue their practice as before."[73]

The College of Nursing put forward the view that a midwifery service should be composed of midwives who were also registered nurses. Only such a training, it argued, could form the basis of an efficient midwifery service.[74] However, this idea was rejected in the JCM Report. In the eventual Act, it was expressly stated that the experienced independent midwife who was not a State Registered Nurse should have equal opportunity of inclusion in the salaried service with those who were trained nurses.[75]

Consultants were anxious to protect their own position, too. In an article in the *British Medical Journal*, Sir Ewen MacLean stressed that calling in the specialist when problems arose was "the proper thing to do".[76] The External Affairs Committee of the BCOG reported in April 1935 to the Council that it approved of the recommendations of the JCM Report.[77] Eden explained, though, that this was because "they believe there is no alternative".[78] Lady Williams appreciated Fairbairn's efforts to persuade the British College officially to approve the JCM Report, since she had understood "from Dr Eden that this was not altogether easy".[79]

The BMA refused to approve the Report. In a defensive argument, it stated (quoting from a resolution passed at an Annual Representative Meeting in 1935) that: "Maternal mortality is a scientific and administrative problem which deserves careful and scientific study, but, in the experience of practising doctors, the publicity which it is receiving to-day is tending to terrify child-bearing women, and is, in itself, a cause of increased mortality."[80] Lady Williams caustically remarked, "I do not think they [the BMA] have done themselves any good by the resolution condemning publicity, and stating that obstetric shock is caused by political propaganda!"[81] She was outraged by the doctors' intransigence. "For one professional organization, so well-known for its activities in keeping up the standard of payment of its members," she marvelled, "to condemn efforts to increase the remunerations of the midwifery profession, which is at present little more than 6*d* per hour, would not I think be considered very sporting by the British Public."[82] She told Eden, "I think the B.M.A. will be more unwise than they realise if they proceed with this rejection of a scheme destined to provide a living wage for what might be described as a rival profession, although it isn't really. Dog shouldn't eat dog, nor one trade's union interfere with the efforts of another to improve the pay and conditions of service of its members."[83]

THE MIDWIVES BILL

Using the JCM Report as its basis, the Ministry moved quickly to draft the Midwives Bill. Throughout this process, the Midwifery Services Committee worked hard to ensure that the eventual Act would reflect its own recommendations to the fullest extent. Lady Williams was concerned about the absence of any reference to pensions for elderly and infirm midwives, and persuaded the committee to send a Resolution declaring that there was "an immense difference in the status of a woman retained upon State Pension as against a recipient of Out-relief".[84] Miss Carter persisted in the midwives' battle against health visitors, suggesting that midwives should be paid more than them.[85] Meetings were held to consider these and other amendments to the Bill but when the committee was given to understand that the Bill might be lost if there were any further Resolutions, it was decided to drop them.[86] In any case, the Bill was generally welcomed by midwives and their organizations. Dame Rosalind Paget wrote to the Minister of Health, "I feel we shall be able to welcome your Bill . . . [and] your insights into the question that we never before had from Ministers of Health." She added, "Pardon the views of an old woman", which rather belied her influence over the midwifery professions.[87]

The Joint Council had invited Megan Lloyd George, a Liberal MP, and Arthur Greenwood, a Labour MP, to join the Midwifery Services Committee, in order to guarantee support in Parliament from all three major parties. When Miss Riddick wrote to Greenwood to express her regret that he had been absent from all the meetings so far, and to ask him to suggest another representative of the Labour Party, she explained, "The Council is of course entirely non-political, but representatives of the House of Commons are naturally included as so many of the aspects of the problems under consideration involve legislation."[88] Rhys Davies, who took over, did not attend meetings either but guaranteed his "interest in the problem when it comes before the House of Commons";[89] he was true to his word and vigorously defended the Bill in debate.

Mr Ritson of the Labour Party brought up the question of the falling birth rate in the House of Commons. "We talk about the birth rate", he commented in reference to the Bill, adding, "I am more anxious for the birth rate than I am about anything else with which we deal in this House."[90] Hopes were expressed that a new Midwives Act would not only increase the rate of births, but also improve the quality of those who were born. Arthur Greenwood relied heavily in his defence of the Bill on the desire for 'quality' babies. "What this nation may in future lack in numbers," he urged, "it ought to be the aim of statesmanship to make up in quality. That has a very distinct bearing upon this problem of maternal well-being."[91] This justification for the Midwives Bill trickled down to the popular press. An article entitled 'Better Britons' in the *Evening News* in May 1936 complained that, "As a nation we are holding out against any sort of compulsory improvement of the national physique." It added, "we can at least do something for it by seeing that future Britons are brought into the world efficiently and that is what Sir Kingsley Wood's Midwives Bill attempts to do. . . . It is but one of many things that the nation must make up its mind to do if C3 Britons are to be the exception and not the rule."[92]

The most powerful link between the government and the JCM was Mrs Stanley Baldwin, whose husband was now Prime Minister. During debate in the House of Commons, Miss Rathbone remarked that the Bill owed a good deal to a number of people, but "to none more than the lady who is the wife of the head of the Government, and whose unfailing and patient interest in the welfare of the mother has done so much to stimulate interest in this question." The Prime Minister himself gave his personal support to the Bill. Maternity and midwives, he stated in the House of Commons in January 1936, was a subject which "had been near his heart for many years". He begged the House to see that "when they came to that Bill . . . if it commended itself to the House they might do their best to get it through this session."[93]

In the House of Lords, too, the JCM exploited its connections. What Lord Aberdare would like, Miss Carter told Lady Williams, was "a message from the Jt Council [sic] which he could make use of in the Lords, would this be possible? There would only just be time to get a message down to the House. He doesn't think it would be safe to come to the Jt himself first – in case the Bill came in earlier."[94] But in fact, all this trouble and effort was not really necessary, since the Bill proved to have a broad basis of support. "For once," remarked the *Nottingham Guardian*, "the Opposition found itself unable to fulfil its duty of opposing. No Socialist could dare to vote against a measure of such obvious social benefit."[95] Indeed, in the area of maternity care at least, the Bill fulfilled Labour's pledge of 1934 to build a health service available to all.

'For Motherhood's Sake Read Every Word of This'
– a leaflet produced by the NBTF in the early
1930s. ([NBTF/G3/3] Reproduced courtesy of
the Wellcome Institute Library, London)

While there was broad agreement on the content of the Midwives Bill, there were differences between the two sides of the House on how to administer it. This is hardly surprising, since the Midwives Bill was promising a nationalized midwifery service – a radical reform that was unprecedented in Britain.

In particular, there was disagreement over whether the Local Authorities should have full responsibility for the service, or should share it with voluntary organizations. Following the Local Government Act of 1929, which had transferred direct supervision of maternal and child welfare from the Ministry of Health to the various Local Authorities, the LAs had developed a suitable apparatus to take full control; however, the voluntary organizations had accumulated plenty of valuable experience in the provision of midwifery services. Views on this matter largely followed political lines: Labour MPs hoped that the role of the voluntary sector would be diminished, and the Socialist Medical Association wanted to see at the very least a clearly defined relationship between Local Authorities and voluntary organizations.[96] Conservatives, on the other hand, were determined to defend the role of the voluntary sector; without this, argued some, the planned state service would be the start of a downward slide into the totalitarian world of the Soviet Union.

Since the National Government was largely made up of Conservatives, the role of the voluntary sector was protected. The Conservative Minister of Health, Kingsley Wood, told representatives of the London County Council that it would be impossible to carry the Midwives Bill through Parliament, unless due regard was paid to the position of voluntary organizations. On the point of principle, he added, it would be necessary for him "to see that no efficient voluntary service was squeezed out."[97] In the end, every effort was made to safeguard "as far as possible the position of all voluntary Organizations, and the established work they are doing on the Midwifery Side."[98]

A number of midwives did not wish the state, in the form of Local Authorities, to take over their profession. While the Bill was under review, Miss Burnside of the Midwives' Institute wrote a letter to *Nursing Notes* saying,

> We are at present recognised by the State as 'practitioners' governed by certain rules, but free and independent to fulfil our duty to the mothers whom we serve. Will it be the same when the midwife becomes the servant of the Local Authority bound by any rules and regulations imposed by the Medical Officer of Health, limiting the scope of the midwife's work? It is for the younger midwives to visualise and think far enough ahead and realise that for good or ill, the future of the profession is in their hands, and to make quite certain that it is going to be worthwhile to sacrifice the birthright of status and freedom so hardly won in 1902.[99]

A 'Rural Midwife' was dismayed by the idea of a state service, on the grounds that the inevitable bureaucracy would remove the 'heart' from the service. She warned, "A State-paid Maternity Service will be a great mistake. The state is too cold and cumbersome a machine for such a purpose. Human feelings are negligible to the State but vital to midwifery."[100] Viscountess Astor agreed. "I have seen people who started off by thinking the state could do everything, but who have found that the soul was missing from its work," she observed in the House of Commons.[101]

Eleanor Rathbone wanted to see the role of the voluntary organizations maintained because they were "naturally very largely women", as compared with the Local Authorities. During debate on the Midwives Bill in the House of Commons, she said that

> an hon. Member who objected to this work being left to voluntary organisations told me a few minutes ago that his particular local authority has only one woman on it among 50 men, and he claimed that she was an expert on this subject. There you have the case of a local authority with one woman among 50 men dealing with a problem which the most ardent anti-feminist must admit to be a woman's problem, and it is suggested that all the expert work of the voluntary organisations should be swept away because of a stupid, old-fashioned, musty prejudice against voluntary organisations.[102]

Mrs Baldwin had used the same sort of argument as Miss Rathbone to oppose state-run maternity care. "Now, we women are temperamental," she told her audience at a fundraising event, "as I think a good many men friends here would agree – (laughter) – some of us more so, some less, but never more so than when a baby is on its way. You are up against that mystic psychology of motherhood. And therefore I venture to think that you cannot run the maternity services the same way as you can the health services."[103]

Miss Rathbone accused the Labour Opposition ("with which I very often find myself in agreement") of doctrinaire prejudice that neglected the needs of women. "Even Mr and Mrs Sidney Webb, and if ever there were people who believed in the bureaucrat, they do", she said, were not taking the Opposition's line regarding voluntary organizations. In any case, she added, the days of voluntary organizations run by "Lady Clara Vere de Vere and the Lady Bountiful" were over (this was not quite accurate. Even leaving aside the Birthday Trust, which was entirely run by Lady Vere de Veres, there were plenty of voluntary organizations concerned with health that were run by the great and the good. The President of the Hampshire Nursing Association, for example, was the Countess of Selborne).

On the one hand, Miss Rathbone and Mrs Baldwin had plenty of evidence to support their argument, since women were by no means proportionately represented in parliamentary politics. It was as recently as 1919 that Viscountess Astor had become the first woman MP to take a seat in Parliament, following which the percentage of women MPs had been as low as 2.3 in 1929 and 1.5 in 1935.[104] But in local government, women were increasingly represented on local elective bodies. From their foothold in the pre-war period, writes Martin Pugh, an historian of the women's movement, "women extended their presence so that they were represented on almost two in every three local authorities by the late 1930s."[105] Significantly, the Women's Cooperative Guild, which was entirely composed of women but which identified with the political left, did not want to see the voluntary sector involved in the administration of the proposed Midwives Act: it recommended that "appointment of midwives shall be made directly by the Local Authorities; and the Public Funds shall not be handed over to the voluntary charitable organisations."[106]

The question of the state's role in the provision of maternity care had been raised in the earliest years of the Birthday Fund. In a letter of support for the Fund that was read aloud at the Inaugural Meeting in 1928 (because he was unable to attend), the Labour MP Philip Snowden had made a case for the provision of maternity services by the state. He insisted that the work of the Birthday Trust was "the primary responsibility of the state" and regarded the Fund's work as a temporary measure; it was only until the state "fully realises and acts up to its duty," he said, that "private help and organization is needed".[107]

THE 1936 MIDWIVES ACT

The Bill became the Midwives Act on 31 July 1936. It was "based largely upon the recommendations made in the important report presented . . . by the Joint Council of Midwifery," stated Sir Kingsley Wood, the Minister of Health, at a public meeting.[108] He was always eager to identify the key role of the JCM, because its membership was so distinguished in the maternity field: he commented in a letter to the President of the Hampshire Nursing Association that the Bill was based "on the scheme drawn up by the JCM which was representative of all the interests concerned."[109] It was generally recognized that creating the Joint Council was the work of the Birthday Trust: *Nursing Notes* gratefully observed that, "The Birthday Trust Fund . . . has worked for many months on the scheme that is now laid before us."[110]

As proposed by the Report, the Act secured the organization throughout England and Wales of a domiciliary service of salaried midwives under the control of Local Supervising Authorities, who were required to provide enough full-time midwives for all their areas' needs by July 1937. They could do this directly or through voluntary organizations. The Minister urged that "as many as possible of the independent midwives at present in practice should be absorbed into the new service."[111] However, there was no coercion: a qualified midwife who did not surrender her certificate could continue in independent practice anywhere she liked, provided she gave notice each year of her intention to practise to the appropriate Local Supervising Authorities.[112] Those midwives who did not want to become employees of the Local Authority, or who were considered unsuitable because of their age or lack of training, were to be paid compensation on surrender of their certificates. The "prohibition of maternity nursing by unqualified persons in any area"[113] effectively abolished the role of the handywoman.

The Act required the periodical attendance at post-certificate courses of all practising midwives. As well, it empowered the CMB to grant a Midwife Teachers Diploma, on the basis of an examination; the first residential courses were established in London and Liverpool in 1937 and 1938 respectively. Qualifications were also prescribed for the post of supervisor of midwives, who was to be taken from the ranks of midwives themselves. In the past, these supervisors had usually been health visitors, few of whom had any experience of attending childbirth.

Provision was made for adequate remuneration, comparable with that applicable to health visitors employed in the same district (which mollified those midwives who had bitterly resented the higher pay of health visitors). This amounted to not less than £200 a year. In addition to a salary, a telephone, travelling expenses, equipment and certain professional costs were allowed. These expenses, together with 3s 6d a week for professional laundry and £10 a year uniform allowance, were worth approximately £50 a year.[114] In addition, midwives were given time off duty, annual leave and a pension.

It had been estimated that the net annual cost to the Local Authorities of a salaried service of midwives would be in the neighbourhood of £500,000.[115] The challenge of providing this money generated much correspondence between the Ministry of Health and the offices of the Chancellor of the Exchequer,[116] resulting in funds for the Local Supervising Authorities from the national exchequer. The Special Areas, promised the Minister of Health to a meeting of the Midwives' Institute, would get a proportionately larger grant.[117] Local Authorities set charges for midwifery and were given the power to recover them. One midwife who started work just after the passing of the Act, recalls that she and her colleagues were encouraged to exert this power:

> When we started in this new midwifery, with off duty and pay, then the mothers had to pay to have their baby and the fee was 30s. When you'd delivered the baby and you were busy bathing the baby, downstairs, we had a meeting about this in the hall, then you'd say to the father, the fee for delivering this baby is 30 shillings. Can you afford it or not? And they were so thrilled at having the baby that they'd pay you there and then. We were told at this meeting, take it for goodness' sake, because they won't pay you again. So if they couldn't afford to pay, we would put on the birth card, cannot afford to pay fee. Someone would investigate and they wouldn't have to pay. If they said they could pay, and they didn't pay at the end, then they were taken to court.[118]

One recommendation of the Act not made in the JCM Report was that married midwives be allowed to practice. The circular sent to the Local Supervising Authorities urged authorities to select midwives for a salaried post solely on the basis of their efficiency and their ability to undertake whole-time employment, adding that a refusal to act on this basis was a "sort of discrimination against married women".[119] Sir Kingsley made the same appeal at public meetings.[120] In the light of the relatively recent (1927) refusal in the House of Commons to remove the prohibition on married women in many of the professions, this recommendation set an important precedent. It appears to have been generated from a letter sent to the Ministry by Charis Frankenburg, a member of the Midwives' Institute Council who wrote for *The Woman Citizen*. "We have just realised," she observed, "that Local Authorities who have a by-law against employing married women, will not employ any of our first-rate full-time married midwives, and this may wreck the scheme!" As Frankenburg pointed out, "Many women most emphatically prefer a married woman for the job."[121] Also, the nation could not afford to lose any skilled midwives.

ASSESSING THE ACT

Midwifery was no longer the Cinderella of the health care services. When the Minister of Health, Sir Kingsley Wood, addressed a meeting of some 1,200 midwives from 107 branches of the Midwives' Institute to discuss the implications of the Act, there was a "storm of applause". Midwives hoped this would convince him "of the gratitude of his hearers".[122] Their working lives had been transformed: "That's the first time midwives had ever had a salary, after the 1936 Act. That was the first time they had off duty. They had a day off a week, from 8 o'clock until 11 o'clock. And one weekend a month, which was 8 on a Friday evening until 11 on a Sunday night."[123] The central importance of midwifery in obstetric care was now confirmed, laying the basis for its role in the NHS after the war. In *Death in Childbirth*, Irvine Loudon comments that the 1936 Act "was a major advance, revolutionizing the prospects for midwives. Some have said that the decades following this Act were the golden age of district midwifery . . . It not only provided much better prospects for midwives; it was symbolically important, for it gave substance to the official view that domiciliary midwifery would remain the backbone of a national maternity service."[124]

The enhanced status of the midwife is reflected in the very structure of a novel called *The Squire* by Enid Bagnold, which was published two years after the passing of the Act and which centres on childbirth. All events and opinions are presented through the point of view of a midwife: behind her, "into the Middle Ages and far behind that . . . stretched the medieval line of priestesses, wise-women, gamps, midwives, threading their way slowly up to the fine instrument which she had become."[125] This is no Sarah Gamp, the maternity nurse created by Charles Dickens in *Martin Chuzzlewit* (1844), whose incompetence endangers life and whose sole function in the novel is to amuse the reader.

The passing of the 1936 Act improved the lives not only of midwives, but also of mothers, because it is likely to have been one of the factors that promoted a dramatic fall in maternal death, starting in 1935. Loudon argues that this decline was not due to any single factor, but "to several which came into operation at different periods", one of which was the raised standard of care provided by midwives, which "probably improved most of all as a consequence of the Midwives Act of 1936".[126] The most important factor in the decline of maternal death, suggests Loudon, was the introduction of Prontosil and its ally sulphonamide. Leonard Colebrook, who had served as the expert bacteriologist on the Interdepartmental Committee on Maternal Mortality, tested these drugs in the 1930s in his laboratory at Queen Charlotte's Hospital, and established their value in the treatment of puerperal infections. This weapon against maternal death was welcomed with much excitement: "I was going to ask you about this wonderful new drug being used at – Its name is Prontosil – Q C – for fever – shd [sic] we not know more details of it, and its prices?", wrote a Birthday Trust member to the Trust headquarters.[127] "The use of . . . slufonamide [sic] preparations and results are extremely satisfactory,"[128]

WAGING WAR ON GERMS

This is an age of research; when men, working in the isolation of the laboratory, with incredible patience and marvellous devotion, wage ceaseless war on the disease germ — studying him, analysing him, coldly and implacably planning his downfall and defeat.

In the van is Wright's Coal Tar Soap — product of research—the matchless emollient and antiseptic, promoting perfect skin-health, giving no reprieve to disease germs.

WRIGHT'S COAL TAR SOAP
GUARDS AGAINST INFECTION
6d. per tablet   BATH SIZE 10d.

The 1930s "war on the disease germ" led to the development of Prontosil, an important weapon in the battle against puerperal sepsis. Illustrated London News, 5 April 1930. (Reproduced courtesy of the Illustrated London News Picture Library)

observed the Medical Officer of Health for Caerphilly in his Annual Report for 1937. A midwife who worked in South Wales during the Depression has said that, "in my day, Prontosil had come in. When I was in hospital, doing my training, we used it . . . in 1937. And it was very interesting, because the first time I saw it, when they had a wee, they weed pink. It was a big tablet. Before that, if there was a fever, the mother died, you see."[129] But there was evidence, in any case, to suggest a decline in the virulence of the infection that was occurring independently of the new drug treatment, because the case-fatality rate was falling among non-Prontosil cases at Queen Charlotte's and elsewhere.[130] Figure 3.1 shows the dramatic fall in maternal death due to puerperal sepsis at this time.

Not everybody was pleased with the 1936 Act. As far as Sylvia Pankhurst was concerned, the Act was "a good little measure" in so far as it ensured

FIGURE 3.1: MATERNAL DEATH RATE DUE TO PUERPERAL SEPSIS (PER 10,000 BIRTHS)

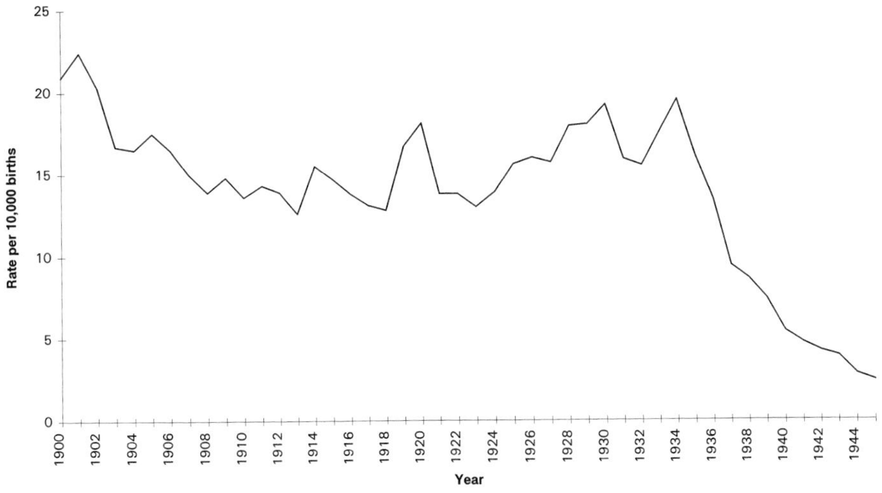

Source: Irvine Loudon, *Death in Childbirth* (Clarendon Press, 1992), pp. 542–4

employment for the midwife, but "it does not get within a mile of a tithe of what the mother needs!" Pankhurst wanted the implementation of "a Specialist Service, equipped with all the latest medical and other knowledge of use to mothers . . . Every mother must have the option of confinement in hospital."[131] Handywomen were particular casualties of the Act, since they were now forbidden by law from assisting at childbirth.

But from the point of view of the development of national policy, the passing of the Midwives Act was a remarkable phenomenon. First, it was the product of an enquiry by an unofficial committee. Second, it was responsible for the creation of a state service of midwives, giving mothers maternity care as a right enshrined in the law; this was the first time that the principles of the state medical service, which had been set down in the 1910 Minority Report of the Poor Law Commission, had been put into effect. "That a Conservative administration adopted the radical remedy of nationalization so quickly, and after a voluntary initiative rather than an official inquiry, is some measure of the crisis in midwifery," comments Enid Fox, an historian.[132] However, the Act was not inevitable, even given the crisis. It would not have been drawn up and passed without the commitment of the Birthday Trust and the quiet advice of Dame Janet Campbell.

The role of the Birthday Trust and the JCM Report have been completely forgotten in the history books. Frank Honigsbaum, an historian of British medicine in the twentieth century, comments that, "Kingsley Wood did more than any other Minister of Health to develop the public health service between the wars. His great achievement was the Midwives Act of 1936 . . . and, when it passed, the public-health world had nothing but praise."[133] But perhaps the absence of credit for the Trust is appropriate, for it had not actually pioneered the idea for a salaried service of midwives. This had been recommended by the Women's Cooperative Guild as early as 1929 and had received support from a number of sources, especially the Labour movement. What was different about the Trust was its power and influence, which enabled it to make this idea a reality.

THE JCM AFTER 1936

After the achievement of the 1936 Act, the JCM still had work to do for midwifery, but this was much less successful. On 14 December 1938, it appointed from its members a Maternity Hospitals Nursing Staff Committee under the chairmanship of Louis Rivett. Its terms of reference were to consider the problems of maternity nursing and staffing of maternity hospitals, and to suggest ways of preventing a serious shortage of midwives.[134] There was plenty of debate and disagreement over this at committee meetings: Sir Julien said that Sir Comyns Berkeley's "scheme has puerperal fever but . . . a dose of Prontosil at the Meeting may bring it back to life!"[135] A report was produced in 1939 which pressed for the formal training of maternity nurses other than midwives, who would provide a lower rank of maternity care.[136] This would establish the midwife as a practitioner within her own sphere of a tier of workers, not simply as an assistant to the GP.

The Report was sent directly to the Ministry of Health on 3 May 1939 by Lady Rhys Williams, on the grounds that Lord Athlone, the Chairman, was absent. "Owing to the urgency of the matter," she explained, "I have been requested to present it for your consideration, without waiting to receive the comments of the Constituent Bodies."[137] She argued that there was a pressing need to create legislation to deal with the matters in the Report. However, the Constituent Bodies of the JCM – especially the BMA and the College of Obstetricians – were furious that the Report was submitted directly to the Ministry of Health, without approval from them first. The Ministry of Health was not pleased, either, since it was not keen on any plan to create yet another class of attendant in the maternity services.

A flurry of internal memos circulated the Ministry. "It is obviously a matter in which Lady Williams and her friends are trying to rush the Ministry and on which we ought not to be rushed," observed one of these. Eden was assured that the Minister would not come to a decision on the matter without informing himself of the views of the bodies on the Joint Council, and a letter was sent to this effect to Lady Rhys Williams and to the BMA. The conflict continued to fester, as Lady Rhys Williams continued her campaign and the medical organizations resisted it. The Ministry wearily wrote one letter after another to calm tempers down;[138] it had to allocate considerable resources during this period to the Birthday Trust, since it was also having to deal with problems created by the Trust's nutrition and abortion projects, which are discussed in the next two chapters of this book. In the end, the JCM Report came to nothing. In 1942, Lady Rhys Williams wrote a letter to *The Times* warning that the recommendations of the 1939 Report were "disregarded, and it was claimed that no shortage would be likely to occur".[139]

The JCM was finally dissolved in 1940. War had begun and Lord Athlone left Britain to become Governor-General of Canada. A Ministry of Health official reported to his colleagues that he and Lady Rhys Williams had decided to disband the JCM, "since its reference is really discharged".[140] He added that there was still the outstanding matter of staffing in maternity hospitals and the "whole question of neo-natal mortality", which called for urgent study and in which "the boundless energy of Lady Williams might be valuable". But the JCM was not needed for this, he added, "and I hope they will cease to exist".[141]

CHAPTER FOUR

Nutrition for Poor Mothers

Between 1935 and 1939, the Birthday Trust distributed extra food to nearly 26,000 impoverished pregnant women in the Special Areas of England and Wales. This project developed out of an earlier scheme that was started in the Rhondda Valley in 1933, but which focused on the need to improve maternity care. The maternal death rate in the Rhondda was almost 7 per 1,000 that year, which was higher than the overall rate for England and Wales of nearly 5.[1] This coalmining area in South Wales had been severely affected by the economic depression and was selected for special economic aid under the Special Areas Act of 1934. Lady Williams, who lived at Miskin Manor just south of the valley, witnessed the difficulties endured by mothers and was determined that the Trust should help reduce the rate of maternal death. She and Mrs Baldwin, who travelled down to the Rhondda for this purpose, had meetings with the Medical Officer of Health (MOH) for the Rhondda Urban District Council to discuss this. When offered some additional maternity services for the mothers of the region, he gratefully accepted.

The Trust arranged for two District Sister-Superintendents, C.E. Bryson and M. Neatly, to come from Queen Charlotte's Hospital in London to work in the valley as Assistant Inspectors of Midwives. They were provided with a motor car to get around this scattered region, on the model of Queen's Institute nurses who were offered this facility when covering a large rural area. Increased antenatal care was provided and local midwives were supplied with refresher courses at the maternity department of Cardiff Royal Infirmary, as well as with disinfectant and rubber gloves. The Trust guaranteed compensation to midwives for any loss incurred when their patients were sent to the nearby hospital at Llwynypia for emergency care, and also paid for the attendance of an obstetric consultant, Mr R.G. Maliphant, in the case of any woman who needed but could not afford specialist care. This extra help from the Trust was similar to the package of increased maternity services organized by Dr Andrew Topping in Rochdale in Lancashire, an industrial town with high unemployment. When Dr Topping took up the post of MOH in 1930, this region had the highest rate of maternal death in Britain, at 9 for every 1,000 deliveries; but when he made major improvements in the quality of maternity care, the rate fell to 1.75 by 1935.[2]

The Trust invited the BCOG to nominate three representatives as advisors to the Rhondda scheme.[3] The College nominated John Fairbairn, Thomas Watts

74

Eden and Louis Rivett and was so impressed by the Rhondda project[4] that it had internal discussions about the possibility of a takeover bid: the Secretary proposed creating a separate College committee, which could "either co-operate with the Birthday Trust Committee, or – what I should prefer – if the local conditions would allow it – would be for our committee to take complete supervision and guidance of the Scheme."[5] In the end, though, the role of the College was minimal.[6]

The Queen's Institute, which in any case was not on good terms with the County Council, was less pleased about the intervention in the Rhondda. It regarded it as an intrusion that undermined the Glamorgan County Nursing Association's attempt to promote District Nursing Associations on the provident basis, whereby a user's regular payments, such as a penny a week, would guarantee the services of a nurse as required[7] (Lady Williams doubted the feasibility of the provident scheme in the Rhondda, on the grounds that it was opposed by doctors). It was also annoyed that it had not been consulted on the provision of extra personnel by the Trust and complained that when referring to Miss Weiss, a former Queen's Nurse Superintendent who had been engaged by the Trust, they gave the impression that she was still a Queen's Nurse. The Queen's Institute Counties Committee "endeavoured to censure Lady Williams in Wales" and then reported the matter to their headquarters.[8] This regional difficulty must have caused some embarrassment in London, given that Lady Rhys Williams had joined the Queen's Institute Council in 1932. Furthermore, the central office of the Queen's Institute was now being housed free of charge by the Birthday Trust at 57 Lower Belgrave Street. The problem was eventually solved at a special meeting of both parties, where the Trust agreed to support the Queen's Institute efforts to develop the Provident Subscription Scheme in the Rhondda.[9] It also released Miss Weiss to work for the Glamorgan County Nursing Association, so long as she carried out some educational duties for the Trust.[10]

By the end of 1934, the MOH for the Rhondda was able to report that the Birthday Trust scheme was in operation. Results were disappointing, however. Not only did the rate of maternal deaths not fall, but it actually rose – to 11.29 per 1,000 births.[11] This figure was especially shocking when compared with the national rate, which had not risen at all.[12] The Birthday Trust was forced back to the drawing board in its mission to save mothers' lives in the Rhondda.

At this point, Sisters Bryson and Neatly brought to the Trust's attention the undernourishment of many women in the Rhondda. The spread of malnutrition, they argued, was "so striking" as to explain the high maternal death rate.[13] The hunger of miners and their families was evident throughout the region. Already weakened by the hardships of more than a decade of coal strikes and the General Strike of 1926, they were now impoverished by widespread unemployment. The Birthday Trust was convinced by the sister midwives and decided to supplement the scheme in the Rhondda with a

An advertisement for Marmite in the 1930s.
([NBTF/G25/2] Reproduced courtesy of the
Wellcome Institute Library, London)

distribution of food. During 1935, 3,776 4 oz jars of Marmite, 3,053 8 oz jars of Brandox Essence of Beef, 2,510 9 oz tins of Ovaltine,[14] 20 1 lb packets of Natyo (made of herbs and minerals[15]) and 121 1 lb packets of Dorsella Milk Foods were distributed to pregnant women at clinics in the Rhondda Urban District.[16] The adjoining district of Llantrisant and Llantwit Fardre was given similar foodstuffs.

A 'sharp fall' in the maternal death rate followed immediately, reported Lady Williams.[17] Whereas the death rate in the previous six years had averaged over 7, rising to over 11 per 1,000 total births in 1934, it then fell in 1935 to nearly 5.[18] Armed with these results, Lady Rhys Williams led the Birthday Trust into a vigorous crusade to improve the nutrition of impoverished pregnant women.

THE HUNGER OF THE POOR

Overall, people were eating better in the 1930s than ever before. Comparing the average of the years 1909–13 with 1934, John Boyd Orr and David Lubbock, two nutrition experts, observed in 1940 that "the consumption of cheese, eggs, butter, vegetables and fruit increased by 43, 46, 57, 64 and 88 per cent respectively and the consumption of fat by 25 per cent."[19] The development of the food industry simplified shopping: the family firm of Sainsbury grew from 123 branches in 1919 to 244 in 1939. An increasing range of foods was available, including prepared foods and a variety of chocolates and sweets wrapped in individual packages.

But despite these developments, 50 per cent of the nation were underfed, according to John Boyd Orr in *Food, Health and Income. Report on a Survey of Adequacy of Diet in Relation to Income* (1936). In his view, this widespread undernourishment was the result of poverty. Women in South Wales who were interviewed for this book have bitter memories of these years of hunger. One woman in the Rhymney Valley recalls that three months after her marriage in 1928, her husband lost his job in the mine. When their baby was born the year after, "it was terrible. I had one pound two and six per week unemployment. . . . My husband's mother used to bring us up a dinner every day. And my parents kept us in vegetables."[20] Not everybody had this kind of help. In an article about the hunger of families in South Wales in the *Evening Standard* in 1936, Lady Williams said that in one home, to which she brought some soup, "Two tin mugs and one plate were the whole equipment of a family of nine. There was no pot in which to warm the soup. Neither could the neighbour provide one. . . . Both households had been unable to cook anything at all for months, and had apparently lived on bread and margarine and tea."[21]

An added difficulty for the wives of unemployed miners was the shortage of fuel for cooking. They were guaranteed a free supply of coal when their husbands were in work; but without it, they had to rely on small scraps from pit tips. Because of the uneven distribution of resources *within* households, the women in poor families ate the least nourishing food of all. *Working-Class Wives*, Margery Spring Rice's account of working women's lives in the 1930s, observed that women were almost always going without food, in order to feed their husband and children. "In an undernourished family," she observed, the mother "is certainly the worst sufferer."[22] This was also found by the Pilgrim Trust Enquiry, which reported that mothers "obviously did without things for the sake of their husbands and children, and it was by no means certain they keep for their own use the 'extra nourishment' provided expressly for them in a large number of cases by the Unemployment Assistance Board."[23]

There was increasing evidence of a link between poverty, undernutrition and poor health. "The main cause of sub-optimal and inadequate nutrition," observed the social researcher Richard Titmuss in *Poverty and Population* (1938), "is poverty, which precludes the purchase of a diet sufficient and properly balanced to promote growth and to maintain health."[24] This view was also held by the biochemists Dr R.A. McCance and Dr E.M. Widdowson, who investigated the diets of pregnant women of different classes. They found "physical differences (almost certainly of a nutritional origin) between the poor and the rich."[25] The Maternity and Child Welfare Authorities were supposed to ensure that expectant nursing mothers and young children received the nourishment they needed, but in 1935, only 235 out of 316 Local Education Authorities were providing food, and many of these gave as little as possible.[26] The Rhondda Urban District Council was one of the few authorities to take its responsibility seriously: it had distributed milk to malnourished mothers since 1919, greatly increasing provision during the 1926 General Strike, and then developed a food programme in the 1930s that aimed to help everyone in need.[27]

The marches of the unemployed were for jobs, not for food, but they were called 'Hunger Marches'. The heavy policing was not needed to keep control of weary and footsore men and women, but indicates the government's anxiety about the level of anger and unrest. The situation in South Wales generated particular concern, since there was a history in that region of repeated social disturbance. In the same month of 1928 in which the National Birthday Fund was inaugurated, the Minister of Labour was warned about the explosive nature of conditions in South Wales. The situation there, he was told, "is becoming dangerous . . . the screw may . . . have been turned too tight."[28]

The political parties were eager to appear concerned about undernutrition. The Conservative Research Department (CRD) was very worried when it discovered in 1935 that Boyd Orr was writing a report that would reveal the inadequate consumption of milk by lower income groups under the Conservative government. The Minister of Agriculture persuaded Boyd Orr to hold back his report until after the imminent general election.[29] "We wish to avoid doing any damage to the party," Boyd Orr reassured the CRD, "and will probably hold back our report until after the Election." He recommended that the Conservative Party include a cheap milk policy as one of the planks of the election, and set up a commission to look into the nation's diet. This would "be an astute political move," he pointed out. "You would have spiked the guns attacking the present Government on what is probably its only weak point."[30] The Conservatives were eager to find opportunities "of countering the very persistent socialist propaganda against us on the subject of Nutrition".[31] To some degree, the nutrition work of the Birthday Trust achieved this end, since the Trust was associated so closely, and so publicly, with the Conservative Party.

THE NUTRITION MOVEMENT

Nutrition was important not only in the world of politics, but also within the scientific community, where it "was just becoming a subject".[32] At the League of Nations in 1935, nutrition was described as "the most important factor influencing the public health" since the sanitation movement of the nineteenth century.[33] In 1932, a British Advisory Committee on Nutrition produced a scale of food values that was supposed to be necessary to maintain health. In 1933, the British Medical Association produced its own Minimum Diet that worked out, on a weekly basis, at 5s 11d for a man and 4s 11d for a woman.[34] While some reformers welcomed the diet as a tool to help defeat malnutrition, others were scornful. "Instead of discussing minimum requirements, about which there has been so much controversy," wrote Boyd Orr in *Food, Health and Income*, his own survey considered "optimum requirements".[35] The Committee Against Malnutrition, which had been set up in 1934 (and was regarded as "rather troublesome" by the Ministry of Health[36]), refused to accept even the principle of a minimum standard of diet.[37]

The Birthday Trust entered this debate by producing a minimum diet for pregnant women. This was a response to a letter it received in 1935 from a Yorkshire woman asking for a diet sheet for expectant mothers. She explained that she was married to a miner earning £2 a week and "am always such a wreck for about two years after my confinements, and that is what I am trying to avoid, so I thought if you could give me any advice I would gladly follow it." The Fund promised to follow up her request[38] and asked the BCOG to produce schedules of diets that would be suitable for pregnant women on an income of 10s, 15s and 20s per week. Sir Julien then decided that the scale of diets was too high, so requested diets for women who could afford only 4s 9d to 5s a week.[39] The College refused to do this, on the grounds that no pregnant woman could be adequately nourished on this sum, so drew up diets for the income levels that were originally asked for.[40] To demonstrate that it was possible to eat nourishing food very cheaply, the diet sheet advised the consumption of sheep's heads, which cost 8d each and would provide four meals:

> The brains are removed, rolled in breadcrumbs, fried and served on toast. This will provide the 'meat' of the meal for one day. The head is then covered with cold water, onions, carrots, pepper and salt added and the whole head cooked. . . . The soup is sufficient for several days. The tongue is removed, skinned and serves as the meat meal for the second day. The meat is scraped from the head, and together with breadcrumbs is placed in a small pie dish and cooked.[41]

Both the Unemployment Assistance Board and the Committee Against Malnutrition asked to see copies of the diet sheet and the Ministry of Health produced comments on the diets, approving of them in principle.[42]

The Birthday Trust was just one organization in a broad movement of individuals and organizations that were concerned about the nutrition of pregnant women. Dame Janet Campbell, for example, suggested in 1932 that nutrition played a more important part in maternal illness than was generally realized.[43] The Children's Minimum Council, which was created by Eleanor Rathbone in 1934 (and of which Dame Janet was one of the Vice-Presidents), argued that from the nutritional point of view, the needs of mothers and children should claim priority.[44] The Committee Against Malnutrition produced a pamphlet on the "very important factor" of the nutrition of the expectant mother in 1936,[45] while the Trades Union Congress General Council passed a resolution stressing the need for a better provision of meals for expectant and nursing mothers and sent a copy of this in 1934 to the Minister of Health.[46] Then, in 1935, the People's League of Health (PLH) set up a special committee to consider the effect of nutrition on maternal and infant mortality and morbidity. In the same year, the Annual Report of the Women's Cooperative Guild referred to the "necessity of adequate feeding . . . if we are to secure healthy motherhood. The Guild has taken up this question."[47]

FROM RELIEF TO RESEARCH

The Birthday Trust applied in November 1935 to the Commission for the Special Areas, which had been created the previous year, for funding to extend the Rhondda scheme to other Special Areas. At first, the Commissioner rejected the request, pointing out that the Commission had been set up not to provide poor relief, but to promote regional development; paying for food, he said, would be the beginning of a "very slippery slope".[48] However, he was put under considerable pressure to reconsider, because the Trust was identified with Lucy Baldwin, who sent a letter from 10 Downing Street to the Minister of Health, pleading with him to support the application.[49] As Lady Williams and Lady Dawson pointed out, turning down this opportunity to feed starving women would not be good propaganda for the government. After careful consideration, the Commissioner thought of a way to fund the Trust without appearing to serve a poor law function. He proposed that instead of simply distributing food, they conduct an "experiment with different type of foods"; in this way, he said, the scheme would qualify as research.[50] He himself was "never . . . enamoured of the scheme",[51] but altogether the Commission gave a total of £15,900 (£626,778 at current prices, allowing for inflation) to the Birthday Trust nutrition programme before it came to an end in 1939. This use of state money to fund charitable work was not unusual at the time: Constance Braithwaite observed in *The Voluntary Citizen* (1938), an enquiry into the role of philanthropy in the community, that a growing feature of charitable finance between the wars was the proportion of funding received from the state or municipality.[52]

In March 1936, the Special Areas Commission funded the Birthday Trust to provide additional nourishment in South Shields, Sunderland, Gateshead, Merthyr Tydfil and the Scheduled Areas of Monmouthshire. A donation from the Marquess of Bute, who owned several collieries in South Wales, paid for food distribution in Aberdare, Caerphilly, Cardiff Rural District, Gellygaer and Pontypridd, and ensured a continued supply of foodstuffs in the Rhondda and Llantrisant districts. The Ministry of Health was invited by the Commissioner to help the Trust plan the experiment. It suggested that Dorsella (dried milk) should replace Brandox Essence of Beef, which was regarded by nutrition experts as deficient in nutritional value.[53] Otherwise, the foods were the same as those distributed before, so each mother received 6 lb of Dorsella, 3 lb of Ovaltine and ½ lb of Marmite during the last three months of her pregnancy.

The results of this phase of the nutrition scheme seemed to be as impressive as those of 1935. Lady Rhys Williams reported in a letter to *Public Health* that between 1 January 1935 and 30 June 1937, the puerperal death rate per thousand births for the 10,384 women who received extra nutrition, was 1.64; among other cases, she said, the death rate was 6.15. Moreover, "among the 3,064 cases assisted [between January and June 1937], the stillbirth and neo-natal death rate has been nearly 50 per cent less than that of the 4,781 other cases in the same areas."[54] It appeared, therefore, that the Trust programme diminished not only the maternal death rate, but stillbirths and infant mortality, too.

DOUBTS ABOUT THE RESEARCH

However, doubts were already developing about the value of the Trust's nutrition research. When Lady Rhys Williams produced a long article on the project for *Public Health* in October 1936, several of the Constituent Bodies of the Joint Council of Midwifery were annoyed that she signed herself as Honorary Secretary of the Joint Council, since this implied an endorsement from the JCM that they felt unable to support.[55] The College of Obstetricians was acutely embarrassed by a letter from the Scottish Board of Health objecting to the article's conclusions.[56] Nor were senior civil servants at the Ministry of Health happy about the research. A.J. Machlachlan, Assistant Secretary, told the Special Areas Commission that "we retain the view that this scheme has no value as scientific investigation."[57]

Certainly there were major problems in the design and implementation of the study. This is not surprising: the 'randomized controlled trial', which would have been an appropriate research method for this kind of enquiry, was not 'invented' until 1946.[58] The control group in the 1936–7 nutrition experiment comprised, quite simply, the women in the selected areas who were not fed. In other words, the 'fed' cases were subtracted from the total figures of the areas involved and the remainder was used to provide some basis of comparison. These two groups were not comparable, however. For one thing, the women receiving supplements all attended antenatal clinics, while the majority of the other group did not. Also, deaths from abortion were automatically excluded from the 'fed' category, owing to the fact that foods were given during the last three months of pregnancy; but these deaths were included in the area figures, which gave no indication of the period of pregnancy at which the death occurred.

Other factors, too, biased the experiment. Many women in the control group are likely to have received extra nourishment from their Local Authority, like the daily milk and fresh butter with bread or biscuits that were given to mothers in Sunderland.[59] The Milk Marketing Board started to distribute milk in the Rhondda and then other Special Areas.[60] In some areas, like Gateshead, Marmite and Ovaltine were supplied by the Birthday Trust both through the nutrition scheme *and* through the Samaritan Fund, but only the food given through the channels of the experiment was reflected in the research data.[61] On top of all this, a quantity of disinfectant and packages of sterilized dressings,[62] both of which are likely to have reduced the risk of puerperal infection, were issued to the women receiving the food. The company Reckitt &

ANTISEPTICS
and
CHILDBIRTH

A test conducted under the auspices of the National Birthday Trust Fund

During the past year an important test in connection with the incidence of sepsis in childbirth has been conducted in the Rhondda Urban District. The figures obtained for 1935 are shown below. It will be noted that for cases where 'Dettol' was the antiseptic used, the incidence was only 10.6 per thousand confinements, as compared with 30.4 per thousand where other disinfectants were employed.

Disinfectants used	No. of Midwives	No. of Confinements attended	Incidence of septic cases per 1000 confinements	Death rate from sepsis per 1000 confinements
'DETTOL'	54	1,598	10.6	2.5
OTHERS	15	395	30.4	5.1

These figures are taken from a report which has been submitted to the Ministry of Health by the National Birthday Trust Fund.

'DETTOL'
TRADE MARK
THE MODERN ANTISEPTIC
RECKITT & SONS LTD., (PHARMACEUTICAL DEPT.) HULL, AND LONDON

An advertisement for Dettol in a programme for the Birthday Trust premiere of the film The Great Barrier Reef, *1937. The Trust did not identify Dettol as having any role in the reduction in maternal death in the Rhondda, attributing this improvement entirely to the supply of extra food. ([NBTF/G25/2] Reproduced courtesy of the Wellcome Institute Library, London)*

Sons were quite annoyed that Lady Williams did not give Dettol "its due share of the credit".[63] Also, maternity services were being improved in many regions: under the Special Areas Act, for example, money was allocated for increased hospital accommodation for maternity problems and for birth control clinics at welfare centres.

HOPES FOR MARMITE

The Special Areas Commissioner disliked the Trust's choice of foods, because "they are largely proprietary articles".[64] Edward Mellanby, too, "severely criticized [Lady Rhys Williams's] handing out proprietary preparations in her well-meant efforts."[65] They objected to Marmite in particular, because they regarded it as a vitamin supplement; milk and other 'natural' foods, they maintained, were a better form of nourishment. Milk was developing an image of cleanliness and health in the 1930s[66] and Boyd Orr argued that the supply of clean milk for working-class mothers and children at a price within their means "should be a corner-stone of Public Health Policy for the country".[67] H.E. Magee at the Ministry of Health advocated 'natural' foods, too. When reviewing the College diets for pregnant women, he reported that the government Advisory Committee on Nutrition was unanimous that nutrients should be supplied in the form of natural foods, rather than as a synthetic preparation; Marmite, he said, was unnecessary in an adequate diet.[68]

The Birthday Trust foods had been recommended to Lady Rhys Williams by Professor F.J. Browne, whom she thanked later for "your advice in the choice of foods (particularly Marmite)".[69] The views of Dame Janet Campbell are also likely to have influenced the selection of foods. In 1932, she argued that a vitamin deficiency was the most obvious defect to remedy in the case of maternal death. It was worth considering, she added, whether some of the money spent by the Local Authorities on dried milk could not be spent to better advantage on giving irradiated ergosterol or some vitamin-containing preparation.[70] Lady Williams referred to this document on several occasions, so she must have read it.

Dame Janet's hopes for the potential of food supplements, which were at odds with the preference for milk of the Advisory Committee on Nutrition and the Special Areas Commissioner, were generated from recent research in nutrition. Various problems of ill health, it was now being discovered, were due to deficiencies of vitamins and of other essential constituents in the diet, though little was known of the nature, occurrence and mode of action of these.[71] If Marmite had been discovered to produce a dramatic reduction in maternal mortality, "midwifery practice would be revolutionised",[72] as Dr Oxley (who was sceptical about the research) remarked with gentle irony to Lady Williams. In fact, modern research has demonstrated the value of yeast extract to the health of pregnant women and their infants.[73] In 1992, the Department of Health issued a pamphlet advising pregnant women to eat folate-rich foods like yeast extract, to reduce the risk of

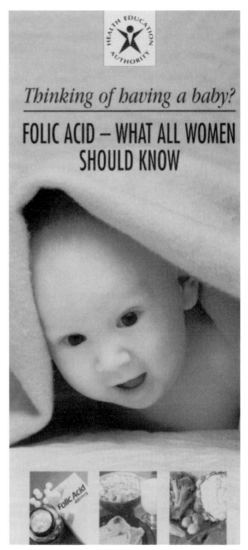

A leaflet (1996) advising pregnant women of the value of folic acid, distributed by the Health Education Authority.

neural tube defects in their babies. In the situation of the 1930s, however, the interest in micronutrient deficiencies led to a reduction in the caloric value of supplementary meals fed to poor and malnourished children, according to Celia Petty. In a study of the relationship between primary research and public health, she argues that a nutrition intervention strategy evolved between the wars that was totally inappropriate for the target population. This remained underfed: "clinical, dietary survey, and anthropomorphic evidence all corroborate the view that underfeeding, rather than qualitative dietary deficiency . . . was the real nutritional problem facing inter-war Britain."[74]

The idea that Marmite was an active principle in the Trust food was vigorously advocated by Lady Williams, who consumed Marmite regularly when pregnant with her second daughter.[75] The perception of Marmite as very beneficial to health was not uncommon: a Labour Women's Committee in Coventry, with representatives from the Women's Labour League and Women's Cooperative Guild, subsidized the sale of Marmite, along with Bemax and Ovaltine.[76] The records of the Special Antenatal Clinics at the Carnegie Welfare Centre in Trealaw, South Wales, show that Marmite was actually prescribed for several difficult pregnancies between 1934 and 1942 (though this may have been simply the influence in the region of the Birthday Trust nutrition scheme).[77]

The Marmite company was more than willing to promote its product as a type of medicine. The pamphlet *Marmite: In Preventive and Curative Medicine* creates this image by providing a 'dosage table' and recommending for several ills a small teaspoonful of Marmite in a cupful of hot water, with a well-beaten egg and one or two teaspoonfuls of sherry.[78] At every stage of the nutrition work, the Marmite company cooperated with the Birthday Trust and offered attractive discounts (as did all the companies whose foods were distributed by the Birthday Trust). At the company's request, Lady Rhys Williams wrote an account of Marmite's role in the Trust's nutrition scheme for the *Daily Herald*. She and Dr Balfour also organized the distribution through Medical Officers of Health of 5,000 leaflets explaining *Why Marmite, the Great Yeast Food, definitely does you good.*[79]

CREATING A RESEARCH COMMITTEE

In 1937, despite his reservations, the Commissioner for Special Areas agreed to make funds available for a further supply of food and sterile dressings. This additional support enabled more of the Special Areas to be involved in the study and would thereby, he hoped, establish the extent to which maternal mortality was affected by the Trust foods.[80] It also meant that the Trust now derived just over a quarter of its funds from the state and that half of its expenditure was allocated to the nutrition programme (see figures 4.1 and 4.2).

To allay the growing doubts of colleagues about the Trust's ability to conduct research, the Commissioner asked it to create a committee of experts to supervise the work. The Trust referred this task to the Joint Council of Midwifery, not all of whose medical members shared Lady Williams's enthusiasm for the project. "After a more or less sleepless night," wrote Eden to Lady Williams, "I have come to the conclusion that it would be wrong of me to continue to oppose the proposal that the Joint Council should set up a Research Committee. My opposition, whether successful or not, may do a good deal of harm: the Joint Council is deeply indebted both to Mrs Baldwin and to

FIGURE 4.1: INCOME 1937

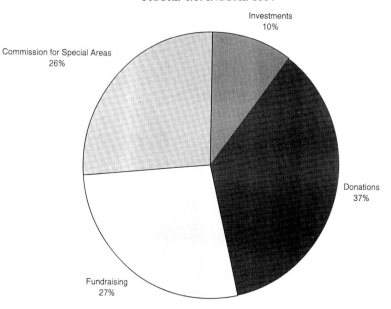

Source: NBTF Annual Report 1937
[NBTF/C17/7]

FIGURE 4.2: NBTF EXPENDITURE 1937

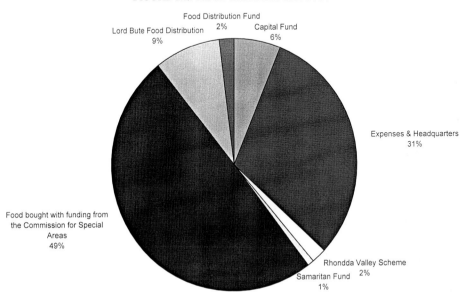

Source: NBTF Annual Report 1937
[NBTF/C17/7]

you; to alienate either of you (I think you used the word 'insect' last night) would be an egregious mistake . . . Now let us bury this unfortunate hatchet and get on with our work!"[81]

The Research Committee was set up on 28 April 1937. It was chaired by Louis Rivett and Lady Williams was Honorary Secretary. Also on the committee were James Young, Professor of Obstetrics and Gynaecology at Hammersmith Hospital,[82] and Dr Margaret Balfour, who had been Chief Medical Officer to the Women's Medical Service in India.[83] Professor Young became involved through writing a letter of enquiry about the nutrition research to Lady Williams, in which he observed that "it does definitely look as if you are making an undoubted impression on the maternal death rate".[84]

On the advice of Edward Mellanby at the Medical Research Council (in order "that the money should not be frittered away"),[85] Dr R.A. McCance, secretary of the MRC Nutrition Committee, and his colleague Dr E.M. Widdowson, both of whom were soon to become distinguished and international figures in nutrition, were invited to join the committee as scientific experts. Dr Widdowson has recalled, "We felt our job was to look at it [that is, the nutrition work of the Trust] objectively, put it to a scientific test. The results were so striking . . . and they'd been published and publicised. So it was only right that we should look into it further."[86] Dr McCance wrote to Mellanby:

When Lady Rhys Williams came to us at your suggestion our reaction to these results of hers were: 1. They ring true. 2. What should now be done? We set out to plan the work with the feeling that – (a) her results should be checked up again this year, (b) if they are true, Marmite is probably the active agent, c) we must not assume Marmite to be the active agent until it has been proved.[87]

Steered by Dr McCance and Dr Widdowson, the Research Committee proposed a massive scheme covering approximately 12,000 cases within a period of twelve months, starting in April 1937. It would test the respective value of the different constituents of the diet so far supplied, paying special attention to the effects of the autolysed yeast extract contained in Marmite.[88] There were four groups: "(1) women having Marmite (or yeast extract specially prepared) alone; (2) those having Marmite (or the same yeast extract) with milky foods; (3) those having Minadex with milky foods; (4) women getting no special foods."[89] The division of women into these four groups was left to health workers at the local level. The food was given during the three months before confinement or for nine weeks before delivery and three weeks after. Every fortnight each woman was given 1 lb of Ostermilk and ½ lb of Ovaltine or Colact, in addition to either a 4 oz carton of Marmite or an 8 oz bottle of Minadex. Sterile dressings and disinfectant were also supplied, as before.

Minadex, a preparation containing vitamins A and D, calcium, phosphorus and iron, was chosen as a control on the yeast because it had no B vitamins in it. However, this did not develop into the useful control that McCance and Widdowson had hoped for; instead, the mothers taking Minadex ended up simply as a component of the overall 'fed' group. The group that was used as a control comprised women who were not receiving special foods, as before, with the difference this time that, like the 'fed' mothers, they attended antenatal clinics. To create this group, the MOHs were asked to give figures for the women who attended antenatal clinics but did not receive Birthday Trust foods. The Research Committee requested that all cases of abortion and miscarriage be excluded from both the 'fed' group and the control group.

Ovaltine was one of the foods used in the NBTF nutrition experiments. This advertisement appeared in the programme for the NBTF's Bridge Ball, December 1935. ([NBTF/G21/3] Reproduced courtesy of the Wellcome Institute Library, London)

This phase of the nutrition scheme, which lasted from April 1937 to June 1939, distributed food to over 15,000 women in ten areas in the North of England and eighteen areas in Wales; these are listed in table 4.1.[90] In all, 16,821 6 oz bottles of Minadex, 111,446 1 lb tins of Ostermilk, 32,737 1 lb tins of Colact, and 254,679 oz of Marmite or a similar yeast extract, in 8 oz and 4 oz bottles, were distributed. The results were measured by neonatal and stillbirth rates, maternal mortality rates (divided into deaths due to sepsis, 'other causes' or 'associated causes') and toxaemia rates. The Medical Officers of Health for each participating area kept a card for each woman, on which the following details were entered: the date when the foods were started, the nature of the foods, the age of the woman, and the number of her confinements. Dr Balfour visited the participating regions, sometimes accompanied by Professor Young, in order to give MOHs advice on procedure.

The foods "were an exceedingly popular gift", noted Drs McCance and Widdowson in the course of an independent study.[91] They have "done a tremendous amount of good work in my area," wrote the MOH for Caerphilly,

TABLE 4.1: AREAS PARTICIPATING IN THE BIRTHDAY TRUST NUTRITION SCHEME BETWEEN APRIL 1937 AND JUNE 1939

England
County Durham
Gateshead
Hartlepool
Jarrow
Newcastle upon Tyne
South Shields
Sunderland
Tynemouth
Wallsend
West Hartlepool

Wales
Aberdare
Bridgend
Caerphilly

Cardiff Rural Area
Cowbridge
Gellygaer
Glynmorryg
Llantrisant
Maesteg
Merthyr Tydfil
Monmouthshire
Mountain Ash
Neath
Ogmore
Penybont
Pontypridd
Pembroke Cock
Port Talbot

RECORD CARD

NON-CLINIC.

JCM/ 1 /39 /N /32

Oldham

JOINT COUNCIL OF MIDWIFERY
NUTRITION EXPERIMENT (EXPECTANT MOTHERS)
1937/38

Place Chins Street   Name of Mother   Age 36

No 13   Occupation Housewife   No. of Confinements 9

DATE OF 1st FOOD DISTRIBUTION	PERIOD OF PREGNANCY	SPECIAL FOODS GIVEN (DETAILS)	TOTAL AMOUNTS SUPPLIED	WERE STERILE DRESSINGS SUPPLIED?	DATE OF BIRTH
6.2.1939	7 Months	MARMITE	Hospital Pack	No	17-3 1939

An example of a record card used in the NBTF nutrition experiment of 1937–9. ([NBTF/T11/1] Reproduced courtesy of the Wellcome Institute Library, London)

Dr Nash. "The women attending my antenatal Centres are in the main so poor," he explained, "that it is necessary to supplement and adjust the diet in almost every case."[92] Dr J.H. Rankin, the Medical Officer of Health for Gellygaer, thanked Lady Rhys Williams "for all you are doing for this district".[93] The MOH for Gateshead, Dr James Grant, remarked that he "personally would not know how to meet the situation were the distribution of foodstuffs to be withdrawn."[94] In his district, he said, "the women call the Birthday Trust children, 'Ovaltine Babies'."[95] Some Medical Officers of Health requested more food. The MOH for Glyncorrwg asked, "I wonder would it be possible for you to allow us a larger supply, as I find that many mothers who would benefit by this extra, have to go without."[96] The popularity of the food parcels indicates the extreme degree of deprivation suffered by mothers, since they did not in fact contain much food – certainly not enough calories to diminish problems of malnutrition. Lady Williams herself pointed out that "the amount given was not sufficient, in all probability, to make the diet of the poorest group more than equal in quantity to that of the better-off group [among the mothers in each area]."[97]

Not only the food, but also the sterile dressings, were welcomed. According to the MOH for South Shields, "The sterile dressings received from the Birthday Trust Fund have proved a great help to the midwives and added to the comfort of their patients."[98] The Medical Officer of Health for Merthyr Tydfil appears to have been more interested in obtaining the dressings than the food.[99] In fact, though, under the Midwives Act of 1936, which became operational in July 1937, the Local Authorities were supposed to supply sterile dressings for use by midwives. For this reason, Dr Severn, MOH for Pontypridd, wrote to explain he would not need any more.[100]

During this period, the Trust was also organizing some smaller food programmes that were not part of the experiment in the Special Areas. These were: an experiment paid for by Sir Rhys Williams, involving a special yeast preparation that was given to 1,000 mothers in Cardiff; the distribution of Marmite in Oldham, paid for by Lord Bute; the provision of Yeast-Vimal to 500 mothers in Deptford, which was funded by Mrs Beddington Behrens; the distribution of Natyo, also in Deptford, paid for by Lord Bute and the makers of Natyo; a supply of Ambrosia dried milk to mothers in Pitsea, which was paid for by the Ambrosia Company; and the provision of dinners for expectant mothers at the antenatal centre at Islington, funded by the Trust itself. Although records were kept on each of these schemes, no conclusions were drawn from any of them.

ANALYSING THE 1937–9 DATA

Dr Balfour directed the analysis of the data that were generated from the research in the Special Areas. This proved difficult, since – despite the strenuous efforts of Drs McCance and Widdowson – many of the problems that had plagued the nutrition scheme in its preliminary stages had still not been sorted out. It was impossible, for example, to know whether or not the women who were given the foods, actually ate them. Some may have given them to their children; one woman whose mother received the extra nourishment recalls that, "my mam didn't use it all for herself, she used it for us three children as my dad was a 1914 wounded soldier and we had very little to live on."[101] In a few cases, the food was given to dogs. According to Miss Riddick, some husbands fed the milk foods in the Birthday Trust parcels to their whippet dogs – and these dogs always won their races![102] Dr Rennie complained in early 1939 that about 50 per cent of his mothers flatly refused to continue eating Marmite once they had taken the first pound. He wondered "if the taste of the Yorkshire women is different from that in the South because it does seem to me rather strange that one section of the community will take the product and another will not."[103] There was evidence, too, that some women were not getting the supplement they were supposed to receive. "I find that a small number of mothers who had previously received Marmite under the original scheme," confessed Dr Campbell Lyons in August 1937, "have recently inadvertently been given Minadex since the supply of Marmite has been exhausted. . . ."[104]

Once again, the experiment did not take into account any other sources of additional nourishment for mothers, such as that generated by the Interim Milk Act of 1938, which increased by £250,000 the government subsidy for schemes to increase the consumption of cheap milk by mothers and children. The transfer of patients from one area to another presented yet another problem. "The reason for the increase in the number of neo-natal deaths and slight reduction in the stillbirths," explained Dr Nash, MOH for Caerphilly, "was due to notifications received stating stillbirths from hospitals outside my area, and then transferred at a later period as having died a short while after birth."[105] The Acting MOH for the Maesteg Urban District Council apologized for the fact that, "having made a re-check of the figures given you . . . it is found that by an oversight, due to a change in staff, the figures are not in all respects correct."[106] Some Medical Officers were doubtful about official figures for puerperal sepsis. In the Rhondda, only one case of sepsis had been notified during a half year, which the Medical Officer of Health thought was too low a figure to be likely.[107]

Several Medical Officers of Health showed little commitment to keeping records for the Trust. Dr J. Jamieson of Northumberland County wrote to say that the task was rather difficult, "as we were some time in getting distribution started and many of the mothers ceased attendance before the distribution was completed."[108] Dr Williamson of Durham, whose terse letters indicate growing impatience with the scheme, concluded that "it is not possible to get the information you require with any degree of accuracy."[109] The submitted records were often confused and unreliable. In the returns from Cymmer, there are cases of duplicated healthy births in the 'fed' group. One Mrs A., who received one tin of Ostermilk and one carton of Marmite, appears to have given birth to three children within seven months.[110] "It is very difficult," admitted Lady Rhys Williams, "to get such an experiment as this carried out as scientifically and accurately as we should like."[111]

In order to enlarge the 'control' group, Medical Officers of Health were asked in May 1939 to produce further cases of women not receiving food but attending antenatal clinics. For this extra work, a payment was offered to the MOHs of 7s 6d per hundred women;[112] up to this point, they had participated on a voluntary basis. Few agreed to cooperate with this additional task; Dr Chalmers Oddie, MOH for Oldham, explained that he was too short staffed.[113] In any case, it was difficult to follow women who did not visit clinics on a regular basis. Some of the figures that were submitted were unreliable: "The number of persons not attending A.N. Clinics and not receiving NBT Foods," warned the Assistant MOH for Jarrow, Robert Good, " . . . cannot be regarded as an exact record."[114] An added problem was the fact that some mothers visited private practitioners to receive the same kind of care that was available at an antenatal centre.[115] Dr T. Islwyn Evans, the Medical Officer of Health for Llantrisant and Llantwit Fardre, who praised the nutrition scheme as relief work, questioned its value as an experiment. He was concerned, he said, that the study did not take into consideration the general health of the mother or the fact that his mothers received foods at the clinic that were similar to the Birthday Trust foods. "I beg to point out these," he wrote to Lady Rhys Williams, "as only a few of the difficulties I find in getting at a true estimate of the value of the experiment.[116]

In July, 1939, Lady Rhys Williams reported in a letter to *Public Health* on 48,881 women who had been part of the experiment between 1 July 1937 and 31 March 1939. Of these, 15,333 women had been fed supplementary foods and 33,548 had not; to create the group of 'fed' women, the Marmite and Minadex data were combined, and no attempt was made to distinguish between the Marmite and the Minadex groups. The maternal death rate of the 'fed' group was 3.72 per 1,000; in the control group of 'unfed' mothers, the rate was 5.42. The stillbirth and the neonatal death rates for the 'fed' group were 34 and 25, respectively; the rates for the control group were 46 and 38. These figures were less impressive than the results of the earlier phases of the nutrition scheme. This was due, said Lady Rhys Williams, to the reduction in the number of deaths from sepsis that had occurred throughout the country during the period under review, "no doubt as a result of the introduction of new methods of chemotherapy".[117]

PLANNING A PROPERLY CONTROLLED TRIAL

Lady Rhys Williams was determined to continue the nutrition programme. She was haunted by the consequences of ending the scheme, believing that "women and babies will die if we do, who could otherwise be safe".[118] Aware of the weakness in the design of the 1937–9 experiment, she turned for advice to A. Bradford Hill, a statistician at the London School of Hygiene and Tropical Medicine who had been a member – with Edward Mellanby and John Boyd Orr – of the government Advisory Committee on Nutrition. He was not encouraging. It would be impossible, he said, to reproduce "exactly your procedure in the fed areas – and an exact reproduction is essential."[119]

Drs McCance and Widdowson suggested ways of ensuring that the groups in a new study would be strictly comparable. "We suggest," wrote McCance, "that the general plan should be to have two groups, one having yeast or Minadex or both, and the other group having a preparation made to look and taste like Minadex but to contain no minerals or vitamins. The Medical Officers should not be told that any group is being used as a control. . . . Further, the results would carry more weight if you yourself did not know which areas were receiving the active and which the inactive preparation."[120] The idea of giving a placebo to malnourished pregnant women was greeted with horror by Lady Rhys Williams. Her eldest daughter, who remembers her mother's growing irritation with Drs McCance and Widdowson, said that her reaction was to shout, "These are women, not rats!"[121] Her opposition to the principle of withholding food to create a control group was not uncommon in this period of widespread hunger. Dr Islwyn Evans, an MOH in South Wales, had stated that, "as things are at present it is quite impossible for me to withhold foodstuffs from a sufficient number of people to form a control."[122] A minute in the Ministry of Labour asked, "Will anybody deliberately select a 'control group' and watch them do without extra nutrition which might save their lives?"[123]

Eventually, Lady Rhys Williams came up with a plan that seemed likely to qualify as a controlled trial without using a placebo. Because the maternal death rate had fallen very steeply, which meant that an extremely large sample of women would be needed to show any statistically significant difference, it dispensed with any investigation into maternal deaths – which had been the primary focus of all previous work. Instead, the focus of this new experiment was limited to the effect of food supplements during pregnancy on the welfare of infants. The new study, explained Lady Rhys Williams to Miss Pye of the Midwives' Institute, would "watch 5,000 cases on a strictly alternative basis, in order to test the stillbirth and neonatal results."[124] In a draft letter intended for the Medical Officers of Health in the Special Areas, she outlined her plan. It would be their task, she explained, to arrange that the names and addresses of all the expectant mothers in their area who desired to receive the foods, regardless of their economic position, be forwarded to the Birthday Trust office. "Fifty per cent of these cases," she explained, "would then be selected upon a strictly alternate basis, and the foods would be sent to them by post in five monthly consignments."[125] Bradford Hill was cautiously optimistic about this plan. It seemed, he said, "to come very much nearer to the desired controlled experiment than the past schemes." Though weakened by such difficulties as the impossibility of knowing whether or not the women ate the food, he said, it ought to give material that could be properly analysed.[126] At last, Lady Rhys Williams seems to have designed a proposal that had the potential to deliver accurate results. However, it was never put into operation.

THE END OF THE NUTRITION SCHEME

Anxious that mothers in need all over Britain should benefit from the Birthday Trust food, Lady Rhys Williams consulted Boyd Orr on a plan to extend the nutrition scheme to Scotland. At first he was fired with enthusiasm. "You can depend upon me doing my best to get the experiment extended to Scotland," he assured her, adding confidently, "I am pretty sure that the Scientific Advisory Committee [to which he belonged] will approve of it." He said he felt "rather strongly about giving everything which we think can help in the supplementary feeding, including, of course, yeast to get out the maximum effect."[127]

But a year later, the department of the Commissioner for the Special Areas of Scotland wrote to say that the Scientific Advisory Committee (SAC) had concluded it would not be advisable to operate a scheme.[128] "With regard to the specific nutrition scheme which you propose in your letter," explained Dr McGregor, the Medical Officer of Health for Glasgow and a member of the SAC, "I find myself involved in serious doubts and difficulties."[129] A letter from Boyd Orr was evasive.[130] The full story finally emerged from R.W. Johnstone of Edinburgh, who also sat on the committee. He wrote in May 1939 to tell Lady Rhys Williams that, "Personally, I was very much disappointed that our Scientific Advisory Committee reached the decision it did, but, *writing confidentially, Dr Mackinlay and Sir John Orr were definitely of the opinion that your results were statistically such that no definite conclusions could be drawn.*"[131] In the government, too, earlier doubts about the value of the Birthday Trust work had developed into a complete loss of faith. A minute in a Ministry of Labour file reported in spring 1939 that

> The statistics with which we have been supplied in justification of the benefits derived from the scheme seem entirely misleading and calculations appear to have been based on such an inadequate selection of cases as to render them practically worthless. I think it was often suspected there might be a 'snag' in the extraordinary results claimed by Lady Williams.

A note was added to this minute on the following day, saying, "We have always suspected Lady Williams' figures".[132] Evidently, there was a consensus among the scientific community and civil servants that the Birthday Trust experiment had failed to produce accurate results.

The Nutrition Committee of the Medical Research Council produced a scathing report on the research, claiming that its results could not be ascribed to any one factor, such as improved nutrition.[133] Realizing that this report would jeopardize future funding, Lady Rhys Williams urged Mellanby to suppress the tone of the report. "It would be very kind," she told him, "if you would send an official letter from the Medical Research Council to the Joint Council of Midwifery, couched perhaps in less derogatory language than the actual report of the Nutrition Committee, which Dr McCance proposed should, on no account, be shown to the Joint Council."[134] Mellanby obliged. He sent a letter that referred only briefly to the number of variables and uncontrollable factors in the previous experiment, adding that the MRC would welcome a new and properly controlled investigation.[135]

Lady Rhys Williams turned this letter to her advantage. Enquiring into the possibility of funds from the Leverhulme Trust, she informed Dr Haden Guest, who was secretary of the Leverhulme Trust (as well as a member of the Birthday Trust Finance Committee), that the JCM had received a formal letter from the MRC stating that it would "welcome an investigation to test the effect of dietetic factors on the pregnant and lactating mother and her offspring".[136] Haden Guest's reply expressed interest – no doubt the implied endorsement of the MRC made a difference. In July 1939, the Leverhulme Trust agreed to supply a grant of nearly £1,000.

However, efforts to obtain more funds from the Special Areas Commission failed.[137] Although the Ministry of Health "reluctantly and grudgingly" supported the Trust's application to the Commission, because it did not wish to seem unwilling to provide extra food to pregnant women, the Treasury was unwilling to approve this allocation of funds.[138] In any case, the Commissioner was determined not to "re-enter a field that we had no reluctance in leaving."[139] Then, when Britain declared war on Germany on 3 September, all negotiations were brought to an end.

WRITING UP AND PUBLISHING THE DATA

While the armed forces went to war, Dr Balfour soldiered on with her analysis of the records of the 1937–9 nutrition experiment in England and Wales; she was assisted by Mrs Ellis, Dr McCance's assistant. Although 15,333 mothers had received supplementary foods,[140] the cards for only 14,181 women had been submitted. Many of these had to be discarded because they were not properly filled in, so that in the end the cards for only 11,618 women were used to evaluate the experiment.[141] This represents a loss of 24 per cent altogether. In July 1942, Dr Balfour produced a draft report. This claimed that, "In the fed group there is a reduction in the neonatal and stillbirth mortality which is statistically significant. The reduction in the maternal mortality rate is very suggestive but not quite statistically significant."[142] To reach this conclusion, she had compared the 'fed' group, which included all those women who had received special foods, including Minadex, with a group of mothers who had not received any extra food.

Drs McCance and Widdowson were not impressed. Having devoted considerable time to reading the report, they said, they were "unhappy about the whole thing". Dr McCance complained in particular that the Marmite and Minadex data had still not been separated and described phrases like 'not quite statistically significant' as examples of special pleading. He was mystified, he said, as to how numbers of deaths in some of the tables "can be fractions of a whole number". He added:

You have written the whole paper on the assumption that the supplementary feeding does produce a real difference in maternal and infant mortality. When the results support your beliefs you make a lot of them, when they do not you tend to gloss them over. You have not convinced us that the supplementary feeding has had the beneficial effect that you attribute to it.

He and Dr Widdowson had consulted Dr Irwin, a statistician working for the Medical Research Council in Cambridge, who had found "a tendency to gloss over any differences which don't support the hypothesis that the supplements are advantageous."[143]

Lady Rhys Williams was outraged. "I was horrified," she wrote to Balfour, "at the childishly worded letter of Dr McCance." She added, "He accuses you of exactly what he seems to me to be practising himself, namely, bias in favour of the results whereas he is against them." She attributed the scientists' criticism not to a difference in opinion over methods, but to personal animosity. "If you think that his opposition is due to your kind remarks about me at the beginning," she told Balfour, "please omit them. I am inclined to think that this may be part of the trouble. . . . Go on keeping your end up."[144] Miss Riddick was equally indignant. "I especially liked his remark that you had written the whole paper on the assumption that the feeding did produce a real difference in maternal mortality and infant mortality . . . one, I should think, usually wrote a paper with some belief as the basis, or why write at all!"[145] Even though Lady Rhys Williams had finally recognized the weakness of the study's design and had gone to considerable trouble in 1939 to develop a plan for a properly controlled trial, she had no reservations about Dr Balfour's conclusions. "You are right," she enthused, adding, "You should go ahead and express yourself freely at every medical meeting you can . . . Don't let anything put you off."[146]

Dr Balfour produced another draft of the report, which met some of the criticisms made by Drs McCance and Widdowson. This time, she made no claims for any effect on maternal mortality, explaining instead how difficult it was to assess this when there were so few maternal deaths in the limited series studied. It gave the stillbirth and neonatal figures with more confidence – "feeding with Marmite, or a similar yeast extract, during pregnancy," it claimed, "results in a statistically significant reduction in the stillbirth rate and neonatal mortality."[147] The Marmite group was not compared with the Minadex group, but with a group of women who had not received any special foods; the number of women taking Minadex was explained as being too small to draw any conclusions. Dr Balfour referred for confirmation of her conclusions to two contemporary studies: one conducted by a group of scientists at the University of Toronto in Canada, and another carried out by the British People's League of Health, in cooperation with ten London hospitals. These were similar to the Birthday Trust experiment in their objectives, but were conducted in a hospital context rather than with women who lived at home. Conducting this sort of experiment in a hospital situation would have been much easier than in a domiciliary one.

The Canadian study was undertaken by J.H. Ebbs, F.F. Tisdall and W.A. Scott in the antenatal clinic of Toronto General Hospital and was written up in 1941 in an article entitled, 'The Influence of Prenatal Diet on the Mother and Child'. Vitamin B1 was supplied to the Supplemented Group by giving wheatgerm, milk, egg, orange and tomato, and by changing from white bread to wholewheat bread. A major difference between this study and that of the Birthday Trust lay in the use of a placebo – "In order to offset any possible psychological factor due to the taking of medicine, patients not receiving supplemental food were given gelatin capsules resembling the viosterol capsules, but containing instead plain corn oil." The Canadian study concluded that the nutrition of the mother during the prenatal period influences to a considerable degree the whole course of pregnancy, and directly affects the health of the child during the first six months of life.[148]

The study of the People's League of Health into the effect of the nutrition of expectant mothers was carried out by a special committee, under the chairmanship of James Young (who was a member of the Research Committee of the JCM). Its main investigation took place between March 1938 and the end of 1939, when it distributed vitamin and mineral elements to pregnant women. An interim report of the study, which was published in both the *Lancet* (4 July 1942) and the *British Medical Journal* (18 July 1942), claimed that this supplementary feeding protected the mothers against the risk of toxaemia and reduced the number of premature births.[149]

Unlike the PLH, Dr Balfour did not manage to publish her results in the *British Medical Journal*, because the editor maintained that her report was "open to criticism on statistical and other grounds".[150] She had more success with the *Lancet*, which agreed to publish the article on the condition that some alterations were made. The editor was puzzled to find under the heading, 'deaths: number', such figures as 127.6 and 243.6. "How did fractions of babies manage to die?" he asked, adding, "It makes me think of the harassed food controller who told the farmer that he mustn't kill a whole pig at once."[151] At last, on 12 February 1944, the results of the experiment were published in the *Lancet*. Once again, Balfour's overall conclusions were based on combining the Marmite and the Minadex data into one single 'fed' group, which was compared with a group of 'unfed' mothers. "In a feeding experiment covering 10 areas in the North of England and 18 in South Wales," reported Balfour,

> 11,618 pregnant women received food supplements consisting mainly of vitamins A, D and B-complex, and calcium, phosphorous and iron. They were compared with 8,095 pregnant women who received no such supplements. Both classes were getting extra milk in some form.
>
> There was a significant reduction in the stillbirth and neonatal mortality rates of the fed group as compared with the controls.[152]

Mrs. ....

A Gift from

THE NATIONAL BIRTHDAY TRUST FUND

(for Extension of Maternity Services)

SPECIAL ANTE-NATAL NUTRITION

With
Best Wishes

from the

National Birthday Trust
Fund

Examples of labels and stickers attached to NBTF parcels of food. ([NBTF/T18] Reproduced courtesy of the Wellcome Institute Library, London)

ASSESSING THE NUTRITION RESEARCH

The Birthday Trust nutrition research was inconclusive and was criticized by the scientific community for its methods and results. There was "no properly designed scientific study," recalls Dr Widdowson, "because they couldn't understand what we were trying to do. I don't think Marmite could have saved women's lives. It might have done, but I think it's very doubtful."[153] Despite this, many social critics and reformers were enthusiastic about the Trust's nutrition work. If they were aware of the experts' criticism, they disregarded it; and they do not appear to have questioned the design and conclusions of the research. Richard Titmuss, for example, referred to "the results of the extraordinarily useful work recently carried out by the National Birthday Trust Fund", while the Committee Against Malnutrition described the "evidence of these results" as "overwhelming".[154] In 1939, S. Mervyn Herbert observed in *Britain's Health* that after the distribution of food to mothers in the Rhondda Valley, the reduction in the rate of maternal death was "remarkable".[155] This tone of approval has continued in discussions of the nutrition scheme by later historians, who do not indicate any knowledge of the negative verdicts of scientists and government officials.[156]

The assumption that Trust foods reduced the rate of maternal death appears to have been less an evaluation of the research, than a statement of support for a programme of relief that reached more than 26,000 impoverished women. Even though not enough food was distributed to make a real difference to undernutrition, the lasting image of the nutrition project reflects the principle that brought it about in the first place – the need to supply food to mothers who were hungry. This underlying principle was seen by some as more compelling than the matter of scientific accuracy. Viscountess Astor asked the Minister of Health in the House of Commons in 1938, "Will the right hon. Gentleman ask expectant mothers what they think about [the Trust nutrition work], and then they need not bother about having any experimental stage?"[157]

The Birthday Trust nutrition project was part of a much larger movement in the 1930s that linked good health to a decent diet. This provided the basis for the establishment of the Ministry of Food in 1939, as a key weapon in the war against Germany. The Ministry organized not only the rationing of food, but also the provision of adequate nutrition for pregnant and nursing women and for children.

CHAPTER FIVE

Investigating Abortion

In 1930s Britain, abortion carried the threat of life imprisonment for mother and abortionist: until the passing of the 1967 Abortion Act, it was punishable by law under the Offences Against the Person Act of 1861. It also carried serious risks to the woman's life and health, especially since antibiotics and blood transfusions were not widely available until after the Second World War. But despite these dangers, many woman risked an illegal abortion. (The word 'abortion' is used in this chapter to refer to an induced termination of pregnancy, although in the 1930s it was used to refer to both spontaneous and induced abortions.)

Poverty was a common reason in the 1930s for ending a pregnancy, as in the case of a woman who "dosed myself with quinine until my ears buzzed and jumped down stairs". One mother complained that her husband refused to use rubber contraceptives but that she "cannot let the children go without shoes. We must look after those we have got and I can't manage to clothe them anymore." She supported two children on a weekly income of just over £1 and paid 11s 6d rent for two rooms. In Nottingham, a married nurse chose to have an abortion out of "fear of losing her employment if the marriage was disclosed". Another woman "Has no parents and must keep her post at Players [cigarette factory]. Says that knowledge of her condition would secure her dismissal. . . . Says she would take any risk – even of death – to keep her post." A 23-year-old in London with three children, whose labourer husband was out of work, "bought three bottles of Dr Rospail's quinine pills and took one bottle".[1] According to the East Midlands Working Women's Association, "In places like Nottingham, Derby, Mansfield, etc., where the bulk of the industries are light, women and juveniles are the wage-earners. The women feel that so long as their wages are necessary for keeping the home going, a pregnancy would be a disaster."[2]

There were other reasons, too, for wanting to terminate a pregnancy. Having an illegitimate child brought shame on mothers and their family: some women in South Wales have recalled that when they were teenagers in the 1930s, they associated unmarried mothers with the workhouse:

If your parents were willing for you to come out of the workhouse and take the child, you could go home. But a lot were in there, they could never come out . . . they couldn't get a job. At the workhouse there were long tables and chairs all around and there was an old lady there we always used to go in and see. Every Sunday we used to take her for a walk around the table. And she never went out. She had a child and she had to work in the laundry. She had to stay there all her life. She could have had it adopted but then there was no place for her.[3]

Some mothers were motivated by fear: a thirty-year-old woman had "a dread of childbirth, as her husband's first wife died through it." Another woman with eight children risked an abortion because she had been made pregnant by a "Husband . . . in prison, convicted of incest with eldest daughter (mentally deficient since fall on head as a baby)." At the end of the 1930s, under the shadow of imminent war, some women preferred "to prevent the birth of a child rather than run the risk of having a son who might be killed."[4]

An illegal abortion was procured through drugs or through physical interference. The drugs were available from chemists or through magazines and had names like 'Widow Welch's Female Pills', 'Dr Patterson's Famous Pills', 'Towle's Pennyroyal and Steel Pills' and 'Triumph Female Pills', and were advertised as ideal "For all irregularities. Safe, sure and speedy. Never been known to fail in even the most obstinate cases. The only infallible remedy."[5] These drugs were considered by most experts to be risky when taken in large doses but unlikely to produce an abortion.

Active interference in pregnancy was far more likely to achieve a termination. This could be done by the pregnant woman herself, through the insertion into

Triumph Pills and Lightning Pills were unlikely to produce an abortion, despite the veiled claims made for them in these advertisements.
([NBTF/S4/10(2)] Reproduced courtesy of the Wellcome Institute Library, London)

the uterus of slippery elm bark, or foreign objects like a button hook, a crochet hook, a darning needle, a knitting needle, a hair or hat pin, a skewer from a mill, a spatula, wax tapers or pieces of wood, such as a pencil; in one reported case, the raw liver of a young rabbit was plugged into the vagina. Sometimes, fluids were injected, such as hot water, potassium permanganate solution, lysol solution, soap solution (one form was known as 'lively Polly'), vinegar, and washing soda solution.[6] The Ministry of Health reported that a "syringe is handed on from one woman to another"; in one district, "the syringe is said to have been circulated 'round the village', or 'round the factory'."[7]

Other methods had to be done by somebody else; if the mother could not afford a doctor who was willing, she turned to an unqualified abortionist. Some of these passed uterine sounds; the 'Italian method' involved passing a uterine sound with carbolic acid for 2½ inches into the uterus. Slippery elm bark was frequently used. Both silver and glass female catheters were used, and water and glycerine was sometimes injected. Many abortionists used a 'Higginson' syringe for the injection of very hot water or soap solution, and turpentine in olive oil was used in one reported case. The stem of a clay-pipe was used by one abortionist, who became known as the 'clay-pipe woman'. The use of an instrument always carried the risk of sepsis. One doctor working at St Giles' Hospital in Camberwell, London, published a report in late 1935 stating that in 88 per cent of abortions following the use of instruments, septic complications were noticeable.[8]

In many working-class neighbourhoods, despite the risk of complications and death, abortionists were valued members of the community. Their fees were usually between two and three guineas[9] but sometimes no charge was made. A member of the Sheffield Women's Welfare Clinic told Mrs Margaret Pyke, the Secretary of the National Birth Control Association, "Did I tell you that one elderly woman who brought a patient confessed that until she heard of the Clinic she used to keep a jar of Slippery Elm and Pennyroyal in the oven for the neighbours? . . . She did not make any charge – did it from kindness of heart."[10] The confidentiality of abortionists was often protected: "There is a death and everyone knows who has done the abortion, but no one will tell."[11] One woman who was terrified of having an illegitimate child and "douched and inserted Slippery Elm Bark on two occasions – managing to retrieve the first piece but not the second", admitted she had been given the bark by someone but "states she inserted it herself". Another woman "Admitted to City Hospital with an incomplete abortion . . . gives the impression that she is shielding someone."[12]

Women of at least moderate means could pay for operations by trained doctors, which were usually safer. A doctor who worked at a family planning clinic in this period recalls that "a great many of the gynaecologists had been doing it privately for a fee, using their own discretion. That's why the nursing homes were used so much.[13] These fees could rise as high as 100 guineas.[14] Lady Rhys Williams obtained evidence that at a nursing home in St John's Wood in

London, six abortions were done a day, which were called 'straightening'. The doctors worked in groups of three, so that different names could be used. The lowest fee for a curettage was £42.[15] "The morbidity resulting from abortions done in private by properly qualified doctors," observed Dr Helena Wright, a pioneer of birth control between the wars, "is very low indeed."[16] Nevertheless, abortions were much more risky in the 1930s than in the postwar period, when antibiotics and blood transfusions became available.

Because of the inevitable secrecy, there was not much accurate information available at this time on criminal abortion. When Lord Dawson of Penn asked the Home Office about the abortion rate, he was told that "there is really little or no positive information available on the topic . . . beyond what may be described as intelligent guesswork."[17] The *Report of an Investigation into Maternal Mortality* revealed that the information "on which conclusions could be based was found to be very limited. The gravity of the problem was admitted, but even its extent was found to be unknown."[18] It was generally assumed, however, that the rate of abortion was increasing. "All the midwives agree," maintained one woman with information about her own district, "that there is an increase in the number of

Slippery elm bark, which was used to produce an abortion: the bark expanded with moisture and so dilated the mouth of the uterus when inserted into the vagina. It was very risky: for example, it caused the death of a cleaner with five children (whose husband was in a mental hospital), through perforation of the uterus and peritonitis (JCM Interim Report, p. 7). The slippery elm bark shown in this photo is held in the NBTF archives. ([NBTF/S4/10(2)] Reproduced courtesy of the Wellcome Institute Library, London)

abortions in the County, but it is extremely difficult to get information."[19] Lady
Rhys Williams referred to an increase in abortion in a letter in September 1936,
stating it was "such a scandle [sic] that everyone knows that something must be
done".[20] However, Dr Oxley did not agree there was an increase. His work in
the East End of London led him to the conclusion that "with the increasing
hospitalisation of such cases in recent years, certification has been more exact,
giving rise to a fictitious increase in the number of deaths."[21] Loudon in *Death
in Childbirth* suggests that the greater part of the increase in puerperal sepsis
between 1910 and 1935 was due to a rise in deaths due to post-abortive sepsis.
However, it is difficult to assess the contribution of abortion to the maternal
death rate, since in England and Wales at this time, deaths for post-abortive
sepsis and post-partum sepsis were placed in the single category of puerperal
sepsis.[22]

There was a fear that the rate of abortion would be increased by the 1936
Midwives Act, which threw out of the profession a number of midwives who
were experienced but did not qualify to practice under the new rules. "If no
tightening up on these lines can be brought about," observed the National
Birthday Trust Fund in a memorandum distributed among its members, "there
is likely to be an increase in the number of abortionists after the coming into
force of the Midwives Act."[23] Midwives were often under suspicion of
performing abortions. In late 1934, *Nursing Notes* offered 'A Warning to
Practising Midwives', who "run a risk of being accused". It described in detail
the case of a midwife who had been indicted for performing an illegal abortion
on a young waitress. In "these difficult times, when any midwife may find herself
the victim of a false accusation", urged the journal, she should seek assistance
from such bodies as the Midwives' Institute.[24]

THE JOINT COUNCIL OF MIDWIFERY STARTS AN ENQUIRY

Whether or not there was an increase in the number of abortions, there was
certainly a growth of interest in the subject. In 1934, the BMA set up a
committee of enquiry into abortion and the Women's Cooperative Guild passed
a resolution calling for more liberal laws. In 1935, the Guild Congress called for
a reform of the abortion laws of 1861, "making abortion a legal operation", and
establishing an amnesty for mothers who were in prison for attempting an
abortion.[25] In 1936, the Abortion Law Reform Association (ALRA) was founded
and at its first conference, a nurse commented that "Working women want
abortion. Why should not the poor have it? Let the poor have what the rich
have already got."[26] The National Council for Equal Citizenship in 1936 urged
the Ministry of Health "to consider measures which will permit abortion to be
performed under proper medical auspices, in order that the present illegal and
dangerous practices may be wiped out",[27] and the National Council of Women,
which had a membership of nearly two million, sent a deputation pressing for

legal abortion to the Minister of Health. Abortion played a role in fiction, too, notably in Virginia Woolf's *Between The Acts* (1941). This novel refers to a rape in 1938 of a fourteen-year-old girl, which led to the test case of Aleck Bourne, a gynaecologist, who openly terminated her pregnancy on the grounds of preserving her life. He was charged with "unlawfully using an instrument with intent to procure miscarriage" but was found not guilty; this "fired the opening shot in his campaign for abortion law reform."[28]

The JCM also took up the issue of abortion. In October 1936, it set up a Committee of Enquiry into Non-Therapeutic Abortion ('non-therapeutic' was used to mean 'not for medical reasons'). The aim of the enquiry was "To enquire into the incidence in different areas of abortion induced for non-medical reasons, and to consider what practical steps can be taken within the framework of the existing law, or by further legislation, to combat this practice."[29] From the very start, the committee identified the prevention of abortion as its chief priority: it was "laid down at the first Meeting that the duty of the committee was to consider means of stopping the practice of self-induced abortion."[30] The committee was high-powered, boasting representatives of all related organizations. It was chaired by Thomas Watts Eden of the BCOG and included Professor James Young, who had chaired the BMA Committee on Medical Aspects of Abortion. The law was represented by W. Bentley Purchase, a coroner, and Sir Leonard Dunning, who had just retired as Chief Inspector of Police. The National Council of Women sent its Vice-President, Lady Ruth Balfour, and the National Birthday Trust Fund was represented by Sir Julien Cahn and Lady Williams. Independent Members included Sir Comyns Berkeley, Chairman of the Central Midwives Board and Mr R.K. Burge, Director of the London Office of the International Labour Office, League of Nations.

Lady Williams, who was Honorary Secretary, believed that the problem of abortion should be solved by "economic and other commonsense measures" that would improve social conditions,[31] and wanted to prevent either the medical establishment or the government from controlling any discussion of the subject. In a letter inviting Mr Burge of the International Labour Office to join the committee, she explained that she did not want it to be dominated by doctors. "I have such a tremendous preponderance of Doctors," she told him, "that I am beginning to feel that it is additional civilians that I need most to help me out 'if the Doctors disagree'." She also wanted to keep the issue out of the hands of the government, in case it was "driven to appoint some kind of an Official Committee later on if we do not forestall them. If they had you may be sure that they would have seen to it that economic factors were left completely out of the terms of reference, and little progress would be made."[32]

Two sub-committees were set up. One was the Legal Sub-Committee, which was given the task of collecting information that was already available on the legal status of abortion, in order to write an interim report. A General Purpose Sub-Committee set about obtaining further information through the distribution of a questionnaire; the decision to gather data in this way was very possibly informed by the recent shift to research in the nutrition project. Some difficulties arose in the organization of these committees. Eden wrote to Lady Williams, "Of course we must welcome Lady Ruth Balfour and Sir Julien Cahn, but I hope they will not want to serve on the Sub-Committees . . ."[33] When Dr Blacker of the Eugenics Society decided against joining a sub-committee, Eden was relieved and remarked, "I can shed no tears."[34]

From its very inception, the overall consensus of the Committee of Enquiry into Non-Therapeutic Abortion was that abortion was an evil. The enquiry was less an investigation into abortion and its role in the lives of women, therefore, than an attempt to 'combat this practice', as the committee's terms of reference put it. In effect, the committee was collecting data in order to establish a conclusion it had already reached. Lady Williams assured a doctor who had provided information about abortion in the USSR, that "we were extremely interested to note your remark that from a physiological point of view abortion is very harmful to the women. This is the opinion of members of the Committee."[35] Similarly, she assured the Town Clerk of Croydon, "It is difficult for me to believe that abortion, even under the most perfect conditions, is anything but harmful to the health and 'morale' of any young woman."[36] Quite simply, said Dame Louise McIlroy, it was "a question of murder". Some members of the committee regarded abortion in a different light, however. When Sir Comyns Berkeley remarked that "no one believed in the legalisation of abortion in any case", Lady Ruth Balfour retorted that "the committee had not properly considered the point." She believed it was necessary to interpret the law "more widely than to save life. There was the question," she pointed out, "of mental condition."[37] Dr Oxley objected strongly that "in the minds of the Committee", abortion was "all criminal".[38] In this respect, the committee differed from most other groups engaged with the issue of abortion, such as the Abortion Law Reform Association.

There was support for liberalization of the abortion law from some quarters of the medical establishment. An investigative committee set up by the British Medical Association in 1934 produced a report in April 1936 advocating reform of the law, "so that doctors should not only be clearly free to do the operation on serious medical grounds, but also on wider medical grounds".[39] Although it was eventually decided by the Representative Body that the report should not be published under the authority of the Association, the fact that it was approved by 91 votes to 80 indicates the high level of support for its conclusions.

There was widespread interest in the enquiry and Eden observed drily to Lady Williams that, "Our Committee is evidently going to be one of the attractions of the Season."[40] The Minister of Health sent a message of interest to the JCM and senior civil servants saw "good reasons for its being undertaken by a responsible body such as the Joint Council". They also thought it would be "convenient to cite this inquiry as a reason for not initiating a difficult and embarrassing inquiry on the part of the Ministry."[41] The National Council of Women, which was a loose federation of charitable and religious organizations concerned with women's issues, was less enthusiastic, even though it was represented on the JCM committee. In 1935 it had pressed for an enquiry into the relation between abortion and maternal death and now told the Ministry that this should be carried out officially, not by a voluntary organization.[42] Miss G.B. Carter, who had recently resigned her post in the Midwives' Institute at the midwifery headquarters, was anxious about what her own role in the investigation might involve. When she mentioned this on a visit to the Ministry, she was advised to "wait and see".[43]

ABORTION AND THE BIRTH RATE

Abortion was widely associated with a negative influence on the birth rate. In the USSR, a law permitting abortion on demand, which had been passed in 1920, was repealed in 1936. In a speech to the Academy of the Red Army, Stalin explained that he wanted all Russians to enjoy parenthood, home and marriage.[44] According to an article in *News Review* in 1937, he had been alarmed by the low rate of births and the high rate of abortions throughout the Soviet Union.[45] In Germany, an increased severity in the application of the abortion law and the granting of marriage loans had led to a marked fall in abortions in 1934 and 1935. Abortion was allowed only for reasons of alleged 'racial hygiene', for example in the case of Jews or of those with inheritable diseases.[46] In Britain, too, abortion was identified as at least partly responsible for the fall in the birth rate. Dame Louise McIlroy, who represented the BMA on the JCM Committee, spoke to the House of Commons in late December 1936 "on abortion in its relationship to the decline of the population". David Glass demonstrated a link between abortion and the birth rate in *The Struggle for Population*.[47] If a system of family allowances were implemented, argued Lady Williams, the problem of abortion would not arise. In her view, most women would welcome their pregnancies if they had adequate means to care for their children. In any case, she believed there were "sound medical reasons for opposing legalised abortion".[48]

However, in December 1931, a judge by the name of Justice McCardie (who in 1933 was found shot in a suspected suicide) stunned the nation when he sentenced an abortionist in Leeds called Lily Scruton, who charged 4s 6d and 5s 6d a time,[49] to only seven months imprisonment, although she had been charged with wilful murder. McCardie believed that abortion should be made available under the law, because "one-tenth of the population of this country was either physically or mentally deficient as a result of the random output of unrestricted breeding. The ending of an unborn child's life . . . should be made compulsory in certain cases."[50] McCardie's verdict encouraged some members of the public to submit requests for state approval of an abortion.[51] This forced the Home Office to state its official policy on abortion. It complained that Justice McCardie's

> frantic excursions into the regions of pseudo-science, half-fledged eugenics and topsy turvy morality are calculated to embarrass the Secretary of State at innumerable points, so that the position must be explored. . . . 'D' Division will have to consider the bearings of all these outpourings on its policy in respect of preventive checks and abortifacients . . . and bye and bye the Secretary of State will almost certainly have to consider pleas, by prisoners whom other judges have sentenced, that they were only trying to do what Justice McCardie told them it was their 'moral duty' to do![52]

In *Maternal Mortality* (1924), Janet Campbell had stated that 3,000 women died each year from childbirth; but at no point in the report did she make any reference to birth control. At this time it was rarely mentioned. One doctor who advised women on the use of birth control recalls that while working in Cambridge between the wars,

> I found it wasn't a good idea to announce that I was doing the Family Planning Clinic. Cambridge is very old-fashioned, or it was at that time. You called on people with gloves on and a hat and all that, and left your card. And I found that it was very unwise to announce that I was starting up a new family planning clinic and so I used to use the euphemism, Women's Clinic.[53]

Birth control in the 1930s was still associated "with the pornographic literature of rubber-shops"[54] and sexual licence. It was also condemned for its negative effect on the birth rate. The Fourth Annual Report of the Sheffield Women's Welfare Clinic for 1936–7 stated on a defensive note, "As a voluntary Clinic we are at liberty to give Birth Control advice to any married woman who seeks it, but I propose, in view of the much discussed question of a falling birth rate, to give a more detailed report of the kind of patient we are dealing with."[55] The JCM questionnaires on abortion indicate a high level of ignorance about birth control. One woman of thirty-nine with eight children said that "Contraception was 'tried' after birth of second baby, but . . . her husband and she 'didn't know much about it and didn't ask anyone'." She was grateful for information about a birth control clinic. Another woman who was advised to avoid pregnancy because she had a "Difficult forceps delivery with first baby . . . followed by puerperal fever", was not given any information about birth control. When she fell pregnant again, "she was so frightened of dying at the confinement" that she injected quinine tablets and water into her uterus. Even when women did manage to obtain some kind of birth control, their husbands might veto its use. "My husband so dislikes the idea of anything in that way," reported one woman, that "even soluble pessaries would repel him." One woman who took pennyroyal, steel and quinine because her "Husband won't be careful", said that, "My mother-in-law told me to break the waters with a knitting needle at four months. She said she had always chosen this and brought it away . . ." Yet another woman of twenty-four in London, whose husband deserted her regularly because "We both 'scrap a bit'", said that, "anything in the shape of birth control would entirely spoil his pleasure and he won't have it", so she took pills every pregnancy.[56] A woman living in the Rhondda Valley between the wars recalls that, "After I had my first child, I was told not to have any more, so I was privileged to go to the clinic, you would call it family planning clinic today . . . But you had to have permission from the doctor to go. They didn't fit you with a cap, but they showed you how to use it. A mucky process."[57]

In some quarters, attitudes towards birth control were growing more liberal. The Women's Cooperative Guild had supported the use of birth control from 1923 and argued at its 1929 Congress that this would reduce the rate of abortion: "for, in the opinion of this Congress, unscientific attempts at contraception are responsible for a great number of maternal deaths."[58] In July 1930, a government memorandum conceded that married women whose health would be injured by further pregnancy, could be given birth control instruction by Local Authorities. At the 1930 Lambeth Conference, the Church of England gave limited approval to the practice of birth control. By that year, there were five birth control societies and over thirty independent birth control clinics in various parts of the country, all organized on a charitable basis. The National Birth Control Association came into being in 1931 and was the forerunner of the Family Planning Association, which was established in 1939.[59]

There was disagreement on the JCM Abortion Committee over the issue of birth control. Lady Williams was opposed to it, especially the eugenist notion that contraception should be made available to the working classes to encourage them to limit their families. Margaret Pyke wrote to her in 1936 to complain that, "I was in South Wales recently and was informed that you had stated that wherever a birth control clinic had been started the Maternal Mortality from sepsis had increased. I should be very glad," she added with some acerbity, "if you would let me know the source of the figures to which you are referring."[60] Lady Williams wrote back to say that yes, she had said such a thing, but had done so informally.

Because methods of contraception were not readily available, abortion served as an essential means of family limitation.[61] It was common knowledge, observed Dr Oxley, that very large numbers of married women were prone, if they missed one or two periods, to take strong aperients or to use a soap and water douche to "bring themselves on". He added, "the women who resort to it have good social reasons for not wanting another child at present."[62] The questionnaires collected by the JCM support the theory that many women attempted abortion on a regular basis. A 26-year-old Londoner, for example, took "Gin and hot salts repeatedly from 4th–8th week of pregnancy"; her "Mother told her there was 'no danger in taking anything up to the third month, but it was very dangerous after that'." Another woman practised douching "fortnightly for 'cleansing' purposes: Douched with soap and water the day before abortion." In some cases, the woman's partner assisted in this practice: "Husband bought a syringe and tried to inject water into uterus but entirely failed. 'It hurt me but I didn't have any bleeding'." A distinction was often drawn between pills and instruments. One mother was "afraid to use any method for attempted abortion other than by large doses of aperient when she thought she was pregnant." Another "had no scruples about taking gin and cascara, but would not attempt vaginal interference – for the sake of her other children."[63]

Eden, Lady Balfour, Oxley and James Fenton, the Medical Officer of Health for Kensington and a representative of the Society of Medical Officers of Health on the JCM Committee, supported birth control as a key measure in the reduction of criminal abortion. "The prevalence of abortion in Kensington two years ago," said Dr Fenton, "prompted me to start a propaganda against the practice. This campaign has resulted in a much larger use of contraceptives, and a consequent decrease in the number of abortions during the last year."[64] Eden complained to Lady Williams: "I do not see how we are to keep the subject of Birth Control out of the enquiry: we shall probably find that married women would prefer to practise prevention than resort to abortion, if they knew how, and if reliable methods were open to them."[65]

THE JCM QUESTIONNAIRE ON ABORTION

The task of the General Purpose Sub-Committee was to collect information about the reasons for abortion and its results, through the distribution of a questionnaire. Several drafts of the questionnaire were drawn up and Mrs Spring Rice was asked for advice based on the work of the Women's Health Enquiry Committee (WEHC) that led to *Working-Class Wives*.[66] The final version of the JCM questionnaire shared the same focus on women's daily lives that informed the WEHC questionnaire, though problems of space meant that a question about whether or not there was running water laid on in a woman's home was eventually removed. The questionnaire was divided into two parts: Part One, which contained questions about social conditions, type of house, district, occupation, and income; and Part Two, which dealt with health and the medical history of the woman involved.[67] There are questions about the economic status and occupation of both mother and father and the reproductive history of the mother (as well as inquiries about the result of her Wasserman Test for syphilis). There are also detailed questions about the housing of the family: whether it is a house, flat, tenement, furnished or unfurnished rooms, the number of rooms, the number of persons per room,

DATE May | 57

COUNTY, CITY, OR COUNTY BOROUGH
L.C.C

CO

JOINT COUNCIL

DISTRICT (LOCAL AUTHORITY)

KINDLY
THE JOINT COUNCIL

DISTRICT CASE NO.

(1) SOCIAL AND ECONOMIC POSITION

INSTRUCTIONS FOR FILLING UP FORM.

A. Please put "Yes" or "No" in square below questions marked with question mark and dash in non-relevant square.

B. Please put first letter (shown in Block Capitals) of relevant word in those squares in which several alternatives are suggested.

C. In remaining squares please supply information asked for, if available.

D. If it is thought undesirable to ask any question please put "N.A." (not asked) in square.

E. If answer is in doubt please put question mark. Blanks and dashes will be treated as negatives.

F. If commenting on an answer given in squares provided, please quote Number of question referred to.

G. Re Question (3) If married more than once please give dates of respective marriages and also dates of widowhoods.

(11) Please do not deduct rent from total income.

(12 & 24) "Dependants" includes all persons supported out of family income, including parents.

(15) An affirmative answer should be given when parents are living together whether married or not.

(25—28) Under "Notes and Comments" please put any information bearing on mentality and physique of children.

(33) Please indicate in "Notes" which pregnancies are attributed to failure of contraceptive methods with particulars of methods if known.

(36) By Rural is meant small villages and outlying cottages.

(37) No. of rooms occupied should exclude Sculleries, Landings, Lobbies, Closets, Bathrooms or any Warehouse, Office, or Shop rooms.

(38) Each person including babies should be counted.

(40—55) Please put "Yes" under more than one heading if this appears correct, and give full details of any additional causes in space provided, e.g., Avoidance of Family Cares, Fear of undesirable future for children, etc.

MEDICAL REPORT.

Re Question (61) Please indicate whether twins, giving sex of both infants.

(69) If Medical cause is known, please put "K" in square and provide details under heading "Medical Report."

(70) All abortions following miscarriage or accident, whether intentional or not, should be placed in Square 70.

(71) Please give reasons for Therapeutic abortion under heading "Medical Report."

(72—76) Please give all available particulars re methods of obtaining abortion and the results under heading "Medical Report." All such information will be treated as confidential.

(77) Please state whether patient was attended by Hospital or at home by Doctor, Midwife, District Nurse or Untrained Help.

PARTICULARS RE MOTHER

CIVIL STATE Single Married Widow	AGE (last Birth-day)	DATE OF MARRIAGE (year)	RELIGION C of E Non-Con. R. C. Jewish No Denom.	MENTALITY Good Average Poor	SOBRIETY Abstainer Moderate Excessive	OCCUPATION OR PROFESSION (a) (Before Marriage)	(b) (After Marriage)	EMPLOYMENT POSITION Is occupation Regular or Casual	Was Mother Employed when Pregnancy began?	Was M. Employed during Pregnancy?	ECONOMIC Ill Single, Employed Separately Total Weekly Income
1	2	3	4	5	6	7		8	9	10	11
M	32	1924	C of E	A	NA	rubutactory hand	house work	nil	—	—	

PARTICULARS RE FATHER

CIVIL STATE Single Married Widower	AGE (last Birth-day)	MARRIAGE Are Father and Mother Living To-gether?	RELIGION C of E Non-Con. R. C. Jewish No Denom.	MENTALITY Good Average Poor	SOBRIETY Abstainer Moderate Excessive	OCCUPATION OR PROFESSION	EMPLOYMENT POSITION Is Employm'nt Regular or Casual	Was F. in Empl. when H. became pregnant?	Is Father now in Employm't?	ECONOMIC Total Weekly Income to Family
13	14	15	16	17	18	19 jute-mill	20	21	22	23
M	32	yes	C of E	NA	NA	store keeper	R	yes	yes	65/

PARTICULARS RE FAMILY

PARTICULARS RE HOU

RE CHILDREN				RE CONTRACEPTION						TYPE OF DWELLING		ACCOMMODATION	
Number born alive	Total Number now alive	No. Under 5 Years of Age	No. Over 5 and under 15	Did Mother Desire to Limit Family?	Did Father Desire to Limit Family?	Has Contraception ever been Practised?	Inter-mittently or Regularly?	Has it been known to Fail?	Has Abortion been tried bec. of Failed Contra'c'p'n?	House. Flat Tenement Rms. Unfd. Rms. Frnd.	Are Sur-roundings Rural or Urban	No. of Rooms Occupied	No. of Persons in Room
2	2	0	2	yes	No	yes	I	yes	No	flat	U	3	2

MOTIVES FOR AVOIDING PREGNANCY.

(A) ECONOMIC								(B) HEALTH					
High Cost of Confinement?	Restricted Accommodation?	Mother in Employment?	Father out of Employment?	Fear of Future Unemploy'm't?	Inability to Maintain Present Social Position?	Actual Poverty?	Desire to Provide for Other Children?	Poor Health of Mother?	Poor Health of Father?	Poor Health of One or More Children?	Fear of Producing Defective Children?	Desire to Space Family?	Dread of Risks of Childbirth?
40	41	42	43	44	45	46	47	48	49	50	51	52	53
no	no	no	no	no	yes	no	yes	No	No	No	No	No
55													

(C) OTHER CAUSES (IF ANY)

NOTES AND COMMENTS

An example of the abortion questionnaire used in the Joint Council of Midwifery's Enquiry into Non-Therapeutic Abortion, which was started in 1936. ([NBTF/S9/4] Reproduced courtesy of the Wellcome Institute Library, London)

the rent, and whether the surroundings are urban or rural. Questions about motives for abortion refer to a possible fear of producing defective children and of the pain of childbirth. Further questions cover the number of children (alive and dead) and the mentality (good, average, or poor) and sobriety (abstainer, moderate, or excessive) of the parents. Questions were asked about methods: drugs or infusions, douches or injections, instruments or bark.

```
─IAL                                          No. J.C.M./_ 1843

                                              NAME OF HOSPITAL
WIFERY  ENQUIRY                                              St Aeges
─PLETED TO
─WER BELGRAVE STREET.
                                              HOSPITAL CASE NO. 94983
                                              (IF PATIENT IN HOSPITAL)
                    (2) MEDICAL REPORT
```

PARTICULARS RE MOTHER

LMP ? end May/37 — GYNAECOLOGICAL CONDITION

vag haem from mid May/37

on exam. Uterus size of 10 wks preg. Os closed . V. little loss p.v.   a-febrile

? Threatened abortion.

Wasserman Test +   Wasserman Test neg

HISTORY OF PREGNANCIES

MATURITY	SEX	RE INFANT					ATTEMPTED but Failed	SPONTANEOUS			THERA-PEUTIC	NON-THERAPEUTIC		RE METHOD USED			ATTENDED After Abortion by whom?	RESULT TO MOTHER		
	Male or Female	Still Birth	Baby Died within 24 Hours?	Baby Died between 1 Day and 4 Weeks!	Baby Died Between 4 weeks and 12 Months!	Baby Lived Over 12 Months		What Month of Preg'cy?	Cause Known Unknown	Attributed to Accident		Procured !	Self-Induc'd	Drugs or Infusions	Douches or Injections	Instruments or Bark		Good or Poor	Sepsis ?	Death ?
T	F						7wo											G		
T	M						7wu											G		
10.½wk									U									G		
12.½wk									U									G		

AL REPORT, INCLUDING HISTORY OF LAST ABORTION AND ANY OTHER PARTICULARS OBTAINABLE RE MEANS OF ABORTION

larly desired to learn whether the grave dangers of abortion to the life and health of the mother are fully appreciated (a) by the mother herself, and (b) by the father or other relatives and friends who
─d her to procure it.

 of Patient is in the habit of giving herself a weekly vaginal douche
using a "spray" and a watery solution of Life buoy soap.
She realises the danger of abortion

─ure of present threatened abortion ? use of vaginal douche .

The questionnaire was specifically designed in order to "discover the proportion of induced to spontaneous abortions".[68] However, parts of it already assumed that the abortion had been induced: Boxes 40 to 54 are set out under the heading, 'Motives for Avoiding Pregnancy', and enquire about these motives. Since muddled questions are likely to generate muddled answers, many mothers who insisted they had not sought an abortion, offered at least

TABLE 5.1: ABORTION QUESTIONNAIRES WERE DISTRIBUTED TO:

London County Council Hospitals
St James's Hospital
Mile End Hospital
St Alfege's Hospital
St Mary Abbott's Hospital
Hackney Hospital

Also the Rotunda Hospital in
Dublin

**Local Authorities in England and
Wales**
County Borough of Blackburn
City of Bradford
City of Cardiff
City of Coventry
Royal Borough of Kensington
City of Leicester

City of Liverpool
County Borough of Merthyr Tydfil
City of Nottingham
City of Portsmouth
Urban District of Rhondda
City of Sheffield
City of Southampton
County Borough of Swansea
County of Essex
County of Hertford
County of Northampton

Also the National Birth Control
Clinic in Sheffield

Local Authorities in Scotland
City of Dundee
City of Glasgow

one motive for doing so. In any case, as the MOH for Edinburgh remarked in a letter to Lady Balfour, "there is probably no group of cases in which it is more difficult to get reliable information than abortion – I mean in respect to whether they were procured or were spontaneous – and unless the information is reliable its value is obviously vitiated."[69]

In early 1937, the questionnaires were distributed to the institutions shown in table 5.1. Most of the institutions participating in the enquiry were municipal hospitals, and none of them were voluntary hospitals. Less than one tenth of the questionnaires were filled in by private health practitioners or at clinics. As a result, the women consulted in the course of the enquiry were chiefly working class. In each case, a health worker filled out the questionnaire on behalf of women who were in-patients at the hospital as a result of abortion, whether procured or spontaneous.

Mrs Pyke was enthusiastic about the questionnaire and Dr Buchan, who sat on the JCM Committee as a representative of the Society of Medical Officers of Health, commented, "I have gone over this, and think it is excellent and we should obtain some quite good information from the enquiry."[70] The Sheffield Women's Welfare Clinic warned, however, that, "so often the information is too casual to warrant the full enquiry that this form entails. Women are so resigned to physical pain and anxiety that the additional discomfort following an abortion is taken for granted as a part and parcel of married life!"[71]

Medical Officers of Health were not very keen on taking part. Several MOHs who initially agreed to help refused once they had seen the size of the questionnaire,[72] while others were apprehensive about investigating such "intimate matters".[73] Dr J.A. Charles, the MOH for Newcastle upon Tyne, refused on the grounds that the questions were of "a very intricate and searching kind", so that it was "doubtful whether any reliance at all could be placed upon the answers."[74] R.V. Veitch Clark, MOH for Manchester, was critical of the section headed 'History of Pregnancies'. In this section, he said, the enquiries relating to abortion involved the criminal aspect of abortion and had little or no medical relevance. He suggested that the JCM "should consider this issue seriously inasmuch as such questions, if put by anyone representing the police, would be preceded by a warning to the effect that such statements might be used in evidence later."[75] H.P. Newsholme, MOH for Birmingham, confessed to Lady Williams that he felt "a little uneasy" about the section on 'Motives for Avoiding Pregnancy'. Pointing out that the character of the heading and of the queries might "lead the investigator unconsciously into a frame of mind which will assume that the abortion has, in fact, arisen from a desire to avoid pregnancy", he wondered if this might result "in some degree of bias towards pre-judgement which will itself damage the value of the data obtained?"[76] Lady Williams was starting to despair and asked the Minister of Health to issue a circular to Local Authorities, with instructions that they should help the JCM; however, he refused, pointing out that the Ministry had no responsibility for the enquiry.[77] In the end, thirteen MOHs agreed to help, but grudgingly in some cases. Three refused (Birmingham, Manchester, and Newcastle upon Tyne), while two (Leeds and Swansea) did not respond to the request at all.

The BCOG shared some of the concerns felt by MOHs and commented that it felt "uncertain" about the whole question of the abortion questionnaire.[78] At around this time, Eden visited the Chief Medical Officer, Sir Arthur MacNalty, at the Ministry of Health and indicated that the committee would be prepared to desist from the enquiry. "My impression, confirmed by Lady Williams's activities," noted MacNalty after the visit, "is that the Committee want to drop the Abortion investigation as they find it too difficult. They want an excuse to say they do so in accordance with the Minister's wishes which, of course, is not the case."[79] Without such instructions from the Minister, the JCM felt obliged to carry on.

In the same year that the JCM Committee distributed its abortion questionnaire, the Population Investigation Committee (PIC) was designing a questionnaire regarding the causes of the decline of the birth rate.[80] Although this questionnaire did not focus directly on the issue of abortion, it contained a number of related questions. This created a conflict of interest and by April 1937, Blacker was complaining to Lady Williams that, "Co-operating between your Committee and mine seems now to be limited to not transgressing on each other's field."[81] In the end, about half of the questions relating to abortion on the PIC questionnaire were made optional.

THE RECOMMENDATIONS OF THE JCM

The Interim Report for the abortion enquiry was released by the JCM for the information of the Constituent Bodies in April 1937. This was over a year before the abortion questionnaires were returned to the JCM in 1938. It was also just a couple of months after some further discussion between the Ministry of Health and the JCM about whether or not the abortion enquiry should go ahead.[82] The Minister again refused to take responsibility for the decision, referring it back to the JCM.[83] Once again, in order to save face, the JCM had to continue with the investigation.

The Report presented an account of the present situation and seven recommendations: that steps be taken to enlighten the public on the dangers of abortion; that the supply of slippery elm bark and essential oils of pennyroyal and parsley be restricted; that the word 'noxious' be omitted from Sections 58 and 59 of the Offences against the Person Act, 1861, in order to assist the prosecution of offenders; that the advertising of abortifacients be prohibited; that a medical practitioner should not be allowed to terminate a pregnancy for therapeutic reasons without the approval of a second practitioner; that a list of consultants for this purpose be compiled by the Minister of Health; and that deaths following abortion be distinguished in the returns from other maternal deaths. The "most important" proposal, though, was "the compulsory notification of all abortions, whether spontaneous or induced, to the Medical Officer of Health of the Area", with the clear understanding to the mother that medical assistance would be available upon notification.[84]

Some of the Constituent Bodies, notably the Queen's Institute and the Midwives' Institute, welcomed this recommendation. So did the College of Nursing, though wanting to "place the onus on the householder",[85] as it would be less easy for a nurse to gain the confidence of her patient if the legal obligation were placed on professional persons only.[86] However, the BCOG,[87] the BMA and the organizations of the Medical Officers of Health vehemently opposed the proposal. They feared that if notification were made compulsory, women would become even more reluctant to visit a doctor after an abortion and would therefore be at greater risk of death. Dr Oxley, who had persisted in making objections to the proposal at committee meetings, said he was "dead against this proposition of notification – women will not see their doctor, more will die."[88]

The idea of notification had been conceived and refined by Sir Comyns Berkeley, who had earlier attempted to have a reference to notification inserted in the government's *Maternity Mortality Report*. He was prevented from this by the Chief Medical Officer, who remarked, "I am not in favour of any reference being made to notification in the report. The investigators are against it."[89] Sir Comyns believed that the obligation to notify an abortion would protect the reputation of midwives which, as Chairman of the CMB, he was eager to defend. He complained to Lady Williams that "it must be known that I for years have been advocating it and first thought of it. The BMA, however, have always been all out for the doctor – and no one else."[90]

CREATION OF A GOVERNMENT INVESTIGATION

Just a month after the release of the Interim Report, while the issue of notification was still a cause of controversy on the Committee of Enquiry, the Ministry of Health and the Home Office set up their own Inter-Departmental Committee to deal with the "urgent national problem"[91] of abortion; it was chaired by W. Norman Birkett, KC. Six out of the sixteen members of this Inter-Departmental Committee were members of the JCM Committee on abortion. These were Lady Ruth Balfour, Sir Comyns Berkeley, Eden, Sir Ewan MacLean, Bentley Purchase and Lady Rhys Williams. Lady Baldwin was also brought on to the committee, although she had not been on the JCM Committee, which further enlarged the influence of the Birthday Trust. The JCM decided to send the Interim Report and the comments of the Constituent Bodies to the Inter-Departmental Committee.[92]

The creation of the government committee, claimed Dr Eden in his capacity as Chairman of the JCM investigation, had come "as a bombshell". But this is unlikely, since Kingsley Wood had sent a letter to Lady Williams in early March stating that he would give "very close consideration to the whole question of the incidence of abortion when the [Maternal Mortality] Report is available".[93] Also, it was known to anyone involved with the subject that the NCW was pushing for an official inquiry and that the Ministry had promised to look into the matter.[94]

The terms of reference of the two committees were strikingly similar. Birthday Trust minutes report Eden remarking that, "It looks almost like a case of plagiarism, although one would never accuse the Government of doing anything of that kind. (Laughter)."[95] There was an important difference, though, between the two sets of aims. Whereas the JCM Committee aimed simply to combat the practice of abortion, the focus of the government investigation was the death and injury it caused: the Inter-Departmental Committee set out "to consider what steps can be taken by more effective enforcement of the law or otherwise to secure the reduction of maternal mortality and morbidity arising from this cause."[96]

It seems likely that the creation of the Inter-Departmental Committee was at least partially an attempt by the government to extinguish the JCM Committee. Lady Forber, who was briefly a member of the Birkett Committee, evidently suspected this. When she resigned, ostensibly because of her husband's illness, it was privately believed that she had been irritated by the ladies of the National Birthday Trust Fund. "I think I ought to say," said Moshinsky at the Ministry of Health, "that something more may lie behind Lady Forber's wish to resign than is stated in her letter to me, or in her note to Mr Birkett." In her personal letter to Mr de Montmorency, he explained, "Lady F. stated that she would never have gone on the Committee if she had known that it was merely intended to be 'a sop to a few ladies', and that she expressed the opinion that the whole problem could have been satisfactorily dealt with by a few experts sitting round a table in a few hours."[97]

The government may have been motivated to set up its enquiry by a wish to diminish the importance of the JCM questionnaire data, which were still being collected. The Ministry of Health was already under attack over its failure to reduce women's ill health, and data like these would draw attention once more to the problem. But most importantly, the Ministry needed to stop the JCM's Interim Report from becoming a Final Report, because of the notification proposal. "If the report is passed in its present form," observed Oxley, "the strong opposition to it is not likely to be silent."[98]

Sir Comyns certainly believed that the doctors on the JCM Committee had put pressure on the government. If so, Eden played a machiavellian part in the affair; after all, he gave the impression of being surprised at the government inquiry. Shortly before it was created, Sir Comyns had warned Lady Williams, "you will have to play your cards very carefully, as it occurs to me that Eden and Co and B.M.A., finding that they are going to be beaten on your Committee [on the matter of notification] will persuade the Minister to set up a Commission or Departmental Committee to report on Abortion." He had gathered, he said, "that the Government would not take such a step as advising Notification unless they had behind them a recommendation made by an authoritative body specially appointed. . . . Quite apart, therefore, from the opposition trying to side track us by encouraging such a new committee (perhaps they are not clever enough to have thought of this), the Minister may be thinking of setting up his own Committee."[99]

As the government committee started work, discussions about notification on the JCM Committee became heated, especially between Lady Williams and Dr Oxley. His earlier remark to her, "I am rather a thorn in your flesh",[100] proved to be accurate. "Dr Oxley has been hostile to the work of the Abortion Committee from its first meeting," she wrote to Eden, adding bitterly, "I am inclined to think that his views tend to coincide with those of the Abortion Law Reform Association, but I did not realise this at the time."[101] Oxley asked that the following words be inserted in the report: "Dr W.H.F. Oxley desires to entirely disassociate himself from the report."[102] He would not like any of his friends, he said, to think that he had been in any way instrumental in drawing up "such a sloppy and illogical" document.[103] The Verbatim

Report of the committee meeting where this was discussed, on 5 October 1937, shows how this matter was handled:

> Oxley: There should be a little note: 'Dr Oxley desires to entirely dissociate himself from the Report'.
> Miss Stephenson: Does Dr Oxley dissociate himself from the whole Report or from certain recommendations?
> Dr Oxley: The whole Report.
> Lady Williams: Could you not change the wording, to avoid the split infinitive?
> The Chairman: 'entirely to dissociate'?
> Lady Williams: Yes.[104]

It was not long before the whole question of the report was dropped. As Lady Williams remarked, any attempt at revision would be controversial and difficult, and "is not called for in view of the appointment of the Government Committee, which makes further consideration of the subject by a voluntary committee redundant."[105] Typically scrupulous, however, Miss Riddick ensured that Dr Oxley's request was somehow met: a copy of the Interim Report has been found in which she penned in blue ink a footnote to the committee list, stating, 'Dr W.H.F. Oxley desires entirely to dissociate himself from the Report.'

The formation of the Inter-Departmental Committee was welcomed in most quarters. "I do not believe that an inquiry of experts alone," the NCW told the Ministry, "would succeed in getting the information and on that account I felt that the Joint Midwives Board [that is, the JCM] or some such body who had started an inquiry, would be very much less successful than an inquiry working with all the resources of the Minister behind it."[106] Lady Ruth Balfour, herself a member of the JCM Committee, had told a number of women's groups that in her view, one important aim of the JCM enquiry was actually to "stimulate the Government to make an official enquiry into abortion".[107]

Because so many members of the JCM Committee on Abortion joined the Birkett Committee, they were able to determine much of the content (though not the outcome) of the meetings, so notification was frequently on the agenda. When experts and representatives of relevant groups gave evidence, they were asked again and again by former members of the JCM Committee to explain their position on notification. Sir Comyns produced a long report showing that notification in Germany, where it had been made compulsory in 1933 and was a key tool in German pronatalism, was successfully lowering the abortion rate.[108] He had long been interested in the German law on notification of abortion and was annoyed when the Ministry of Health held up all his attempts to arrange a translation of German documents on this issue. He complained to Mr Moshinsky, "I had occasion, during your absence on holiday, to get the Foreign Intelligence Dept. to make another German translation. I took the occasion to enquire about the 14 official forms I sent you, dealing with the German Notification of Abortion. No trace could be found of these forms. This makes me anxious, since I could not get another set and you told me at the last meeting that you had given the proper department all my material, so that they could get on with it while you were away. . . ."[109] Either the Ministry was sloppy or it was obstructing Sir Comyns's attempts to arrange the translation.

The advocates of notification continued their campaign. Even at the last and 46th meeting of the Inter-Departmental Committee, on 10 February 1939, which was intended merely to wrap up matters and to organize a dinner, Lady Rhys Williams was still trying to persuade the committee to agree.[110] But if anything, objections to notification had increased by this time. The BMA was "about as nearly unanimous on this as it is possible for a body of 30,000 people to be" in its opposition.[111] Professor Fletcher Shaw of the British College of Obstetricians and Gynaecologists complained curtly, "You are turning us into policemen, which as medical men we do not like."[112]

When the Birkett Report was published in 1939, it contained only two brief references to the work of the JCM Committee of Enquiry into Non-Therapeutic Abortion, even though its conclusions were much the same as those in the JCM Interim Report. It rejected any plan to inform the public about birth control, on the grounds that as a result, "the tendency of the birth-rate to decline might well be accentuated". It added, "it is computed that the size of the population of this country will before long begin to fall. A proposal that public money should be spent on a measure which is likely to aggravate this position by making contraception universally available on request, and thereby to affect adversely the continuity of the State, is one which we feel we cannot endorse." Eden and Lady Balfour added a reservation stating that they themselves were in favour of making birth control available, pointing out that the rich had access to it anyway.

The Birkett Report did not approve of the notification of non-therapeutic abortion, arguing that it would not yield complete statistics and that notification would deter women from seeking medical assistance. It approved only the notification of therapeutic abortion, for statistical, medical and police purposes (and H.A. de Montmorency and Dr M'Gonigle added a reservation on this issue). Lady Baldwin, Lady Balfour, Sir Berkeley, M.P. Pugh, Bentley Purchase and Lady Rhys Williams had been defeated – the idea of compulsory notification was successfully blocked. They added a long reservation to the Report, arguing their case for the notification of all abortions, especially those that were criminal.[113]

Those who opposed notification argued that it would drive abortion further underground and deter women who had had an abortion from seeking medical help. It would also threaten the reputation of doctors and consultants who were performing abortions themselves or knew of colleagues who were doing so. In any case, there was considerable support from the public for the work of abortionists, whose services were in demand from women of every class. As Dr Oxley pointed out in a note to the Secretary of the Inter-Departmental Committee on Abortion: "many convictions fail on account of the jury's sympathy with the woman and even with the abortionist."[114] The level of demand for abortion can be inferred from the fact that after the Abortion Act of 1967, according to Mr Elliot Philipp, who was working as consultant gynaecologist at the Royal Northern Hospital, "we terminated about 700 in the first year, in 1968–9".[115]

THE ABORTION QUESTIONNAIRES

The early determination of the JCM Committee to explore the social causes of abortion disappeared in the almost exclusive focus on notification. This concern, and the creation of the government committee well over a year before the abortion questionnaires were returned, meant that the questionnaires became irrelevant to the investigation. None the less, 3,300 questionnaires had been collected by 31 August 1938, and attempts were made to analyse the data. This proved difficult, since the failure of the overall enquiry hampered efforts to obtain funds for statistical analysis.[116] "At the moment I am struggling to get an adequate statistical opinion without any money," Lady Rhys Williams told Miss Carter, "as Sir Julien Cahn refuses to allow any more money to be used on this 'unnecessary report'."[117] The analysis eventually got started when Miss Winifred Burt, who had done a similar work for the Midwives' Institute, volunteered her services as a statistician.[118] Miss Burt was enthusiastic about the project and turned down the suggestion of an honorarium. "It would, I feel sure, be a most valuable social document," she told Lady Rhys Williams.[119]

The Research Committee, which had been set up in 1937 to supervise the nutrition experiments, was asked for advice. But, as with the nutrition research, the abortion enquiry was riddled with difficulties. The data did not represent women as a whole, but chiefly those who had been admitted to a municipal hospital in an emergency. A.J.M. Macgregor, MOH for Glasgow, warned that since they were "a municipal hospital class" and therefore drawn "from the poorest section of the community", they could not be accepted "as a cross-section of the population".[120] A more problematic bias, however, resulted from the fact that only women who suffered serious complications following abortion were likely to go to hospital. Women who managed to escape such complications, or died, were not represented in the enquiry.

As in the case of the nutrition research, attempts to create a control group were problematic. It had been hoped initially to use the Dublin figures as some kind of control group, on the grounds that most women in Dublin were Roman Catholic and would not attempt an abortion; the low rate of sepsis in Dublin abortions appeared to confirm this view.[121] "As you know," observed Dr Davidson of the Rotunda Hospital in Dublin, where 200 questionnaires were sent, "we have very little septic abortion here but plenty of ordinary abortions."[122] It soon became obvious, however, that the lack of hard facts on the Dublin abortions made it impossible to use them as a control group.

Not all the questionnaires that were returned could be used in the enquiry. Of the 500 forms submitted by Dr Fenton, 400 had to be excluded because they referred to cases in which no abortion or attempted abortion had occurred. In the end, the total number of papers available for the analysis was 2,912. Methods of interpreting and answering the questionnaire varied from one part of the country to another. For example,

> With regard to the sub-division Spontaneous Health, Gynaecological, it was found that a number of papers mention retroversion of uterus in the notes on the gynaecological condition, but insert the cause of abortion as unknown (U) . . . The Glasgow papers invariably give retroversion as a known cause. Rotunda and Sheffield do not do so, except in rare instances . . . The majority of these forms have, on the advice of Mr Rivett, been placed in Spontaneous Unknown.

In the case of those mothers who took extra aperients when their period was delayed for a day, "some of the writers have marked self-induced with a query . . . most of the doctors in these cases seem to be loath to use Box 73, Self-Induced [and] . . . Some have left all boxes entirely blank, except Box 69 Unknown Cause." The "Birth Control enthusiasts" created further problems, insisting that coitus interruptus should not be counted as contraception. Lady Rhys Williams decided that "where the answer is 'No' except for C.I., I would be inclined to classify it as not practised, particularly in view of the Roman Catholic position."[123]

The sheer mass of data produced confusion and error. Miss Burt wrote to Lady Williams: "Probable error was that Threatened was taken off twice in Spontaneous . . . The 'married only' was my error over the telephone to Miss Riddick. I told her 'All Cases'. . . . The rest of this Table [Economic Circumstances] not yet checked and appears to have some error . . . The total number of replies do not check across with the figures under each group and in consequence, none of the percentages across add to 100%."[124] "I sink into deeper despair – but keep up an average of 100 a day,"[125] reported Miss Burt to Miss Riddick, adding "Personal. Today's great thought. What a mercy that I do not know your private address – I am always pining to telephone you on an urgent query about 8 p.m. – Do not, whatever you do, inform me where you roost in peace."[126]

The last section of the questionnaire was entitled, 'Medical Report, including history of last abortion and any other particulars obtainable re means of abortion.' It invited the health worker interviewing the woman who had suffered the abortion, to identify its cause. The reported causes of spontaneous abortion were various: rats, especially in the kitchen; overwork, notably heavy washing and carrying heavy buckets of water; cycling; riding in a motor car; and a blow from a husband. The most frequent medical cause was a 'fibrotic uterus' and the retroversion of the uterus.

It was particularly desired, stated the questionnaire, to learn whether the dangers of abortion "are fully appreciated (a) by the mother herself, and (b) by the father or other relatives and friends who have assisted her to procure it". This suggests a judgemental attitude on the part of the designers of the questionnaire, as the MOH for Birmingham had suggested. In a sense, the woman was put 'on trial' for the crime of inducing an abortion. Some women were pronounced 'innocent': "Patient attributes her abortion to a fall . . . cause of abortion = patient's statement accepted". Sometimes a protestation of innocence was grudgingly accepted: "Abortion said to be due to shock caused by a mouse running up her legs to her knees (in these days of short skirts and sophistication). All interference denied by the patient." But often, the woman was judged guilty, even when "Inducement [was] denied of course." A woman in Nottingham, for example, was described as having

> no idea of weekly income but says they have £100 debt to pay off and that they are not doing well . . . Admitted with spontaneous abortion because said to be due to a fall [down the stairs]. The mother does not look well but there is no evidence of criminal abortion. She does not want another child (has three) because of economic difficulties and says she would be afraid to procure abortion. She is probably not telling the truth.

In yet another case, a woman "[Denied] attempt to procure abortion . . . it is suspicious that this may have been attempted." One woman who was admitted as an incomplete septic in August 1937, "accounts for the sepsis by having taken a bath after passing pieces of placenta, and denied uses of douche or instruments. . . . She says her age is 50, but she looks 40, i.e. her statement's unreliable." Another mother was suspect because she "likes to look nice – money spent on clothes. Bad manager as regards food – typical dinner fish and chips and cake all bought from shop. Husband very attached to her but reverse probably not the case . . . prefers outside amusements to care of family." Inevitably, many women resented the questionnaire and chose not to co-operate. One woman "was not frank, in my opinion, in her replies to these questions . . . gives no helpful information." When it was difficult to tell whether or not an abortion had been induced, Mr Rivett was consulted for the final judgement. In those cases where purgatives or douches were used on a regular basis, he decided that the abortion was "Induced, not premeditated". The categories of 'Doubtful' and 'Unknown' were used for those abortions that could not be classified as either 'Spontaneous' or 'Induced'.[127]

By October 1938, a report on the abortion questionnaires was ready. It contained tables based on the completed questionnaires about Causes of

Abortion, Recovery, Sepsis, Contraception, Age, Marital State, Number of Children, Religion, Type of Surroundings, Economic Condition, Employment, Overcrowding and Housing. However, it had failed in its chief aim: namely, to discover the proportion of induced to spontaneous abortions. It made a limited attempt to do so, by comparing the spontaneous with the induced figures and vice versa. It was recognized, however, that the spontaneous group "is not a true basis of comparison, in view of the fact that the spontaneous group cannot be considered as a fair sample of the average normal pregnancy, since pathological conditions are present in a large proportion of the cases." The report admitted, too, that the data were influenced by unknown variables, such as the development of Prontosil, "which are tending to reduce the incidence of sepsis in all obstetrical and gynaecological conditions, including abortion".[128]

Dr McCance was scathing about the report. "I have been through the Report as far as possible," he said, "and it seems that you have abandoned the idea of treating the data statistically. If so I am sorry, but please forgive me if I am wrong." He advised Lady Rhys Williams to consult Dr Bradford Hill, who had already advised her on the nutrition enquiry.[129] Lady Rhys Williams wrote hopefully to Miss Carter, "I have got in touch with Dr Bradford Hill himself over our Report and have an interview fixed with him this week . . . so I think we shall be all right."[130] Bradford Hill was not reassuring, however. "My personal opinion," he said, "is that the results that might accrue from a further statistical analysis of the data would be not be likely to repay the effort", because they related to in-patients of large hospitals and institutions in a relatively small group of urban areas and were not a representative sample of all cases of abortion. Indeed, he said, they were not likely to be a representative sample even of the hospital patients that were involved: a woman could be brought to hospital, where she would die, for example, in which case a form would not necessarily be returned for her. Again, if a woman developed sepsis, she might be removed to an isolation hospital. He concluded that, "from the statistical aspect, my view is that only very tentative and very carefully considered conclusions can be drawn from this material and that, as matters stand, no elaborate analysis could compensate for its limitations."[131] As a result of this assessment, analysis of the data was abandoned.[132]

The story of the abortion questionnaires ends with the publication in 1941 of an article by Rivett in a medical journal. The article explained, "Obtaining records to act as controls was not found practical . . . No statistical evaluation of the results has been undertaken by the Research Committee, and it is recommended that a statistical analysis of these figures be made before conclusions are drawn." Of course, some analysis had been done, but been judged as worthless by Bradford Hill. One of the few conclusions offered by Rivett in this article was that abortion was not used as an alternative to contraception.[133] Given Bradford Hill's evaluation of the research, however, his conclusions are unreliable.

The Joint Council of Midwifery's enquiry into abortion came to nothing, despite a tremendous amount of work. This was a serious loss in the case of the questionnaire data, given the scarcity of information available about women's ill health. Since women were not entitled to compensation for accidents or insurance during sickness, Eleanor Rathbone had pointed out in *The Disinherited Family* in 1924, "no public record is kept of their lapses from health . . . [and] it is in vain that the records most likely to contain evidence as to the health of working-class mothers have been searched, without furnishing any evidence worth speaking of."[134] Several women's groups sought to fill this gap: the Women's Cooperative Guild published women's letters in *Maternity* and *Life As We Have Known It*, and the Women's Health Enquiry Committee collected data that were published in *Working-Class Wives*. But only the Joint Council of Midwifery systematically set out to collect data on the role of abortion in the lives of over 3,000 working-class women, a subject that was shrouded in secrecy and fear.

CHAPTER SIX

Pain Relief for Childbirth

At the end of the twentieth century, women in Britain generally expect to be offered pain relief for childbirth. But in the late 1920s, when the National Birthday Fund was founded, chloroform and twilight sleep were the only methods available, and only to those women who could afford the care of a doctor. Poor women were offered mild sedatives or nothing at all. A midwife who worked on the district in Lambeth remembers, "We used to give them horrible stuff called chloral hydrate which used to immediately make them sick.

Mrs Stanley Baldwin, who was determined that all women – poor and rich – should be offered pain relief in childbirth. This portrait was painted by de Laszlo and presented to Mrs Baldwin by Sir Julien Cahn. ([NBTF/E8/3/1] Reproduced courtesy of the Wellcome Institute Library, London)

It was no good. That was the only concession we had to pain relief."[1] Even in hospital, women were not offered pain relief unless they developed serious complications. The Central Public Health Committee of the London County Council (LCC) reported that in 1929, eleven out of twenty-two London hospitals with maternity wards gave no relief to normal cases, even in the form of sedatives; and of 7,454 patients delivered during that year, seven out of eight were offered no pain relief.[2]

Mrs Baldwin was one of a small number of people who believed passionately that all women should be offered pain relief in labour as a fundamental right, regardless of their social status or income. Before joining the Birthday Fund, she had already been involved in efforts to provide resident anaesthetists at maternity hospitals. Then, when she joined the Fund, she insisted that the issue of pain relief be established as a priority in the charity's campaign to improve maternity care. This was pioneering work: not simply because it sought to provide a new kind of service to mothers, but also because it had to confront widespread opposition. Over the centuries in Western culture, the agony of childbirth has been regarded as woman's punishment for her natural sinfulness and has been sanctioned by the Bible: "In sorrow," states Genesis, "thou shalt bring forth children."[3] This led to the common view, observed the LCC Public Health Committee, that a woman was doing "something morally wrong" in evading the pain of labour.[4] "How can a woman have that motherly affection for her offspring," wrote Mr G. in 1949 to the Minister of Health, "if she bares [sic] it without any pain?"[5] Hannah Mitchell complained that her husband, "like most men, had the comfortable idea that women do not feel pain as much as men."[6] Mrs Baldwin had only contempt for men with such opinions. "When a man shewing prejudice talks to me on this subject," she said briskly, "I have very great difficulty in preventing myself from telling him what I think. And it is rather a tremendous thing if a man once hears what a woman thinks of him, because he so rarely does."[7]

The problem of public opinion was compounded by ignorance since, as one mother wrote to the Birthday Trust in 1938, "the mothers don't know such a thing exists".[8] This was particularly the case among the poor: the LCC Public Health Committee reported that "Anaesthesia in labour is still outside the experience of the class of women coming into municipal hospitals."[9] Spreading information about the possibility of pain relief, advised Louis Rivett, must be done carefully. "We shall have to go slowly," he warned in 1930, "as in a conservative country like this it must take some time to get everyone used to such an innovation."[10]

It took time in the Birthday Fund, too. When Mrs Baldwin told Lady George and Lady Londonderry that she planned to bring her 'Anaesthetic Fund' with her into the Fund, they were not very happy. Lady George tried to dissuade Mrs Baldwin from calling attention to it in her Wireless Appeal in 1929 to raise money for the Fund's Empire Campaign. Her secretary wrote anxiously to Judith Jackson, Mrs Baldwin's Private Secretary, to explain that "Lady George Cholmondeley most urgently asked me to ask you to persuade Mrs Baldwin not to mention anaesthetics."[11] Even Lady Londonderry, who had cheerfully dealt with all sorts of prejudice and opposition in the cause of women's suffrage and as President of the Women's Legion, wanted Mrs Baldwin to be quiet on the subject. She complained to Lady George that Mrs Baldwin was being "persistent" about mentioning this "controversial point" in her imminent broadcast. This, she added, "would be too shattering!!! Would it be possible for her just to say 'that personally' she hopes anaesthetics will be used in future, without involving the N.B.T.F.?"[12] The tension was defused when Lady Londonderry was reassured that, "There is nothing in the constitution against the use of anaesthetics so we are all right there", and Mrs Baldwin's secretary told Lady George that her proposed remark on the subject "is most

Flags and stamps used to raise funds for the NBTF Anaesthetics Campaign led by Mrs Baldwin. ([NBTF/G6/4] Reproduced courtesy of the Wellcome Institute Library, London)

innocuous".[13] In the end, Mrs Baldwin replaced a specific reference to the pain of labour ("We know the agony we have had to face in giving birth") with a vague reference to the experience of mothers ("Mothers know *what we have had to face*"); her only comment on pain relief was a plea for funds "to provide more beds, but also *eventually* anaesthetics."[14]

Mrs Baldwin may have given in over the Wireless Appeal, but she was determined not to let Lady George and Lady Londonderry interfere with her ambitious plans for the anaesthetics campaign. This is likely to have been the reason why she insisted that it should not merge with the Trust, but be administered independently: "The Anaesthetics Fund which now bears my name," she said, "works *in conjunction* with the NBTF."[15] A poster for the Hanworth Meet and Rally called for support "To help the National Birthday Trust Fund (for the extension of maternity services), *including* Mrs Stanley Baldwin's Appeal for Anaesthetics." Stamps and flags sold on Mother's Day in 1930 urged the public to 'Help our Mothers with Anaesthetics'.[16] The Trust's Finance Committee acted on behalf of the Anaesthetics Fund, but kept the accounts of this Fund separate from the accounts of the Capital Fund: each Fund was dealt with in turn at meetings, and invested and allocated separately. By October 1935, the Anaesthetics Fund amounted to £7,786 3*s* 4*d*, nearly half the sum of the Capital Fund.[17]

Under Mrs Baldwin's leadership, which was vigorously backed by Lady Williams, the Trust announced that it wanted to make analgesia available to all women, "regardless of income".[18] Because childbirth was a shared experience of women that discounted social rank, pain relief was identified by some feminists as linked to the struggle for women's suffrage. "In Finland, that little progressive nation which was the first in Europe to give the franchise to women," commented Mrs Baldwin, "they always give anaesthetics to women in childbirth."[19] A similar connection was made in the USA in 1910–20 by the National Twilight Sleep Association, which put pressure on the medical profession to provide their chosen method. Many leaders were active suffragists, who regarded the availability of analgesia as a fundamental right,[20] as did Mrs Baldwin and other feminists in Britain. Virginia Woolf, for example, argued in *Three Guineas* that if rich women were as common as rich men, "You could provide every mother with chloroform when her child is born."[21] Vera Brittain (who painted a harrowing picture of the pain of birth in her novel, *Honourable Estate*) said in her autobiography that she wanted to batter down the walls of the Ministry of Health and "to take the Minister himself and give him a woman's inside, and compel him to have six babies, all without anaesthetics."[22]

In fact, poor women were likely to suffer more severe pain than their wealthier sisters, as a result of pelvic disorder caused by inadequate nutrition in childhood. "Rachitis of the pelvis, which was not uncommon," explains an historian of childbirth, Jacques Gélis, "was certainly one predisposition towards a long labour, highly risky and painful. In such cases the baby's head, even if of average size, could not pass properly through the pelvic girdle."[23]

However, many working-class women were suspicious of pain relief when first introduced to the idea in the 1930s. In an investigation into the use of anaesthetics by the LCC in 1931–3, involving the administration of chloroform, gas and oxygen, ether and ethyl-chloride, and nembutal in eight of its hospitals, 1,880 women refused the offer of an anaesthetic, while 4,133 accepted.[24] One reason for the refusal, commented the LCC's Public Health Committee, was that anaesthesia in labour was "associated with obstetrical disasters. The suggestion of its use arouses a fear that the doctor anticipates an abnormal labour."[25] In *Working-Class Wives*, a District Nurse reported that, "they all dread chloroform and beg me not to call the doctor in",[26] while a letter to the Birthday Trust sent by an 'Anxious Daughter', insisted that "No doctor should give chloroform without the husband's permission in confinements."[27]

But in any case, the lives of working-class women – short of money and food for their families, and without running water – were so difficult and exhausting in this period, that relief of pain in labour was not likely to be a priority. This is suggested by the JCM abortion questionnaires that were distributed to hospitals in 1937, which asked in a special box whether women who had sought an abortion had been motivated by a 'Dread of the Pain of Childbirth'. In a set of 250 questionnaires that were filled in on behalf of married women who had had an illegally-induced termination, only ten (and another 'partly') described such 'dread' as a motive, and nearly all of these listed other 'Motives for Avoiding Pregnancy', too. The remaining 239 women regarded economic difficulties as a primary, and poor health as a secondary, motive; they ignored the issue of pain.[28]

However, a number of letters sent to the Trust reveal that some poor women were desperate for help. "I have had to have all my children in the horrible pangs of childbirth," complained a 'Mother in York' to the Trust, "because I never have had money, not even to pay for a doctor." Pregnant again, she felt that "after what I have gone through year after year I cannot go through with it. My nerves are terrible." A woman expecting her third baby lay awake at night dreading the delivery: "I can of course only afford a Midwife. She is very good, and very kind and very efficient, but oh for the knowledge that the last hellish pains could be lost in an anaesthetic." Yet another woman begged for £2 to pay a doctor's bill so that she could have some pain relief: "I am a coward and cannot sleep at night," she explained, "for thinking of the time to come."[29] A mother of seven children wrote to Mrs Baldwin: "I am looking forward with dread to another confinement next month. . . . I'm sure God will bless your efforts to bring this merciful thing [of chloroform] nearer to poor creatures. Then childbirth will not be dreaded nearly so much."[30]

Such a dread of labour was considered to be one possible cause of the fall in the birth rate: a letter to the Minister of Health insisted that "the chief cause of the low birth rate is the fear of bearing children, which is a ghastly experience given good conditions".[31] "Surely at a time like the present when one is continually reading articles about the decreasing birth rate," wrote a mother to the Minister, urging him to take action, "surely this is the time to make it possible for every expectant mother to have the benefit of this wonderful discovery[?]."[32] One doctor wondered in a letter to the *BMJ* if the medical profession had contributed to the decrease in the birth rate, by "the unnecessary withholding of anaesthetics during labour."[33]

This connection between the pain of childbirth and the birth rate was drawn right up until the time when the population trend was reversed, shortly after the Second World War. In the 1945 Report by Mass-Observation on *Britain and her Birth-Rate*, a woman is reported as insisting, "Drastic steps must be taken quickly, for I am of the opinion that our falling birth-rate is a kind of strike from the wives of today to show that they will not have children till matters are improved."[34] In 1945, Lady Rhys Williams received a letter claiming that, "Practically the first sentence the average woman says when the ordeal is over is, 'Thank God – Never Again', which is one of the chief reasons for the one child problem."[35]

THE HISTORY OF PAIN RELIEF

The beginning of anaesthesia in midwifery followed the discovery of the anaesthetic properties of ether by an American dentist, Morton, in 1846. In 1847, Simpson abandoned ether for chloroform, which is less safe but easier to administer. Queen Victoria delivered Prince Leopold under light chloroform anaesthesia in 1853. Following her example, it was not uncommon for Victorian middle- and upper-class women to ask for chloroform for the delivery of their babies. In 1902, Twilight Sleep was developed, which required the administration of scopolamine and morphine. It produced a state of semi-consciousness, in which the woman appeared to feel pain but retained no memory of it. Mainly used by middle- and upper-class women, it was more popular in the USA than Britain and became less frequently used in the 1920s because it was difficult to administer safely.

At this time, pain relief for childbirth was generally described as anaesthesia, not analgesia. But as the movement to widen its use developed over the 1930s, efforts were made to distinguish between these two terms. "In the state of *anaesthesia*," explained a letter to *The Times*, "the patient is quite unconscious of what is going on, and does not respond to any stimulus. In the state of *analgesia*, the patient can hear and understand instructions, and can move in response, but does not feel the sensation of pain."[36] This distinction was useful to the Trust's campaign, since analgesia was regarded as safer than anaesthesia (though this argument was misleading, since analgesia can also produce side-effects).

The Ministry of Health did little in the 1930s actually to increase the provision of analgesia, but it did make a commitment to do so in the *Interim* (1930) and *Final* (1932) *Reports of the Departmental Committee on Maternal Mortality and Morbidity*. Provision by local government was patchy, to say the least, even in the LCC hospitals, which had the support of Dr Laetitia Fairfield, the Senior Medical Officer of the LCC Public Health Department, who had articulated a commitment to the availability of pain relief in 1914.[37] Most doctors, though, "won't trouble about it", as one mother complained to the Birthday Trust.[38] One reason for this was the lack of financial advantage. "In the majority of cases," observed an article in the *British Medical Journal* in 1939, "the practice cannot be made economically sound."[39]

Adequate funds were essential for the pain relief campaign. Mrs Baldwin's efforts before joining the Birthday Fund had focused on this, and Lord Buckmaster had raised money in an appeal in 1929 through *The Times* in order briefly to maintain a resident anaesthetist at London's Royal Free Hospital (at this time, there was talk of Lord Buckmaster becoming Chairman of the Fund, but Sir Julien became Chairman instead). In April 1928, Mr Rivett persuaded the Committee of Queen Charlotte's Hospital to allow Lady Williams to raise £200 a year for a resident anaesthetist (and by October 1930, 93 per cent of mothers in this hospital received relief).[40] The Birthday Trust gave small amounts – usually £50, sometimes £10 – to maternity hospitals to support a resident anaesthetist and to pay for drugs. At first only the Cooperating Hospitals were given money,[41] but it was soon decided to give the grant to other hospitals too.[42] Some of these hospitals put anaesthesia for normal labour low down on their list of priorities and tried to spend the money on other things, but this provoked the ire of the Trust.[43] In 1931, it withheld a grant from the East End Hospital, even though it was a Cooperating Hospital, because the Medical Officer there "only approved of giving anaesthetics in difficult and abnormal cases of labour".[44] Soon, six of the leading maternity hospitals were provided with enough funds to appoint extra resident anaesthetists to administer analgesics to normal cases.[45] The Chairman of the House Committee at the City of London Maternity Hospital expressed the hospital's gratitude. When he first joined the hospital in 1929, he said, analgesics for normal delivery were almost unknown, but now "their use is ordinary routine and they are availed of in practically 100 per cent of cases". This was due, he added, to Mrs Stanley Baldwin, whose achievement ranked "as highly as the work of her husband during his premierships."[46]

But since most British women delivered their babies at home under the care of a midwife, promoting the use of analgesia in hospitals made little difference to them. The only way forward, therefore, was to develop a method of relief that was suitable for use by midwives in the home environment. The Birthday Trust quickly understood how important this was and in 1930, its anaesthetics campaign shifted away from hospitals to women's homes – in effect, from anaesthetists to midwives (although hospitals continued to receive grants for anaesthesia until 1936).[47] This change in direction anticipated and was entirely consistent with the imminent shift in the overall policy of the Trust, from hospitals to homes and midwives.

BRISETTES AND ZOMBS

The first phase in this new stage of the campaign was the development of crushable chloroform capsules, which were thought up by Miss Pye, President of the Midwives' Institute.[48] They were intended chiefly for use during the second stage of labour, by a midwife acting alone. Rivett put the plan into action. "In order to overcome the risk of a midwife applying too much chloroform from the drop bottle," he explained, "I have had [20 minims of] chloroform put up into crushable glass capsules."[49] The midwife put the capsules into rolls of gauze, crushed one of them, then tucked the gauze roll container into a mask. The patient was allowed to sniff the mask at the onset of a pain, and the dose was sufficient to produce analgesia for seven to ten minutes.[50] The capsules were made by Messrs J.F. Macfarlan in the East End of London and a box of a dozen was sold for 1*s* (and was made available through the Trust at the cost price of 9*d* per box). It was agreed that each box should contain three small cards bearing the word 'Motheraid' and the message, "These are presented free to all mothers by the National Birthday Trust Fund, founded by Mrs. Stanley Baldwin, Lady George Cholmondeley and Lady Williams. Chairman: Sir Julien Cahn" (this was not quite true, since Mrs Baldwin and Lady Williams were not the founders of the Trust). Miss Judith Jackson, who was Mrs Baldwin's secretary and also involved in the work of the Trust, observed, "These cards will be given to the mothers as a kind of souvenir!"[51] Later on, Macfarlan sold the capsules under the name of 'Brisettes'; Messrs Warwick Brothers also supplied the capsules, under the name of 'Chloroform Zombs'.

The capsules were tried out in various hospitals. In May 1932, at the suggestion of the Trust,[52] Sir Frederick Menzies, MOH for the LCC, arranged for fourteen LCC hospitals to use the capsules on an experimental basis in fifteen of the LCC hospitals for six months.[53] It was recorded that of 1,121 patients, 613 found the capsules of 'great use', 446 'some use', and only 62 reported that they had been 'no use';[54] the number of women who did not want to use the capsules was not reported. Dr Laetitia Fairfield wrote gratefully to Lady Williams, "We still continue to use thousands of capsules without any ill-effects."[55]

Similar good results were found in the same year in a trial of 200 cases at the Middlesex Hospital, which Rivett described in a report to the Royal Society of Medicine in June 1932.[56] On the basis of this report, Sir Julien wrote on behalf of the Trust to a number of hospitals and Local Authorities, offering to supply them with capsules for three months if they would take part in a large study of their use. He drew on the distinction between analgesia and anaesthesia in order to defend the safety of the capsules: "the effect of the small quantity of chloroform contained in the capsules," he assured them, "is purely analgesia and does not produce anaesthesia."[57] A newly qualified anaesthetist, Dr N. Llewellyn Jones, was employed to visit the participating institutions and

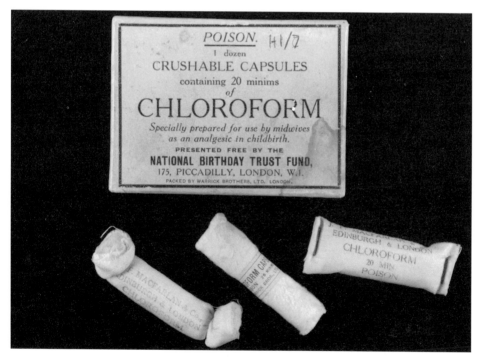

Chloroform capsules, which were developed by the NBTF in the early 1930s to diminish the pain of childbirth. They were no longer used after 1936, when the British College of Obstetricians and Gynaecologists said they were unsafe. ([NBTF/H1/7] Reproduced courtesy of the Wellcome Institute Library, London)

demonstrate the best use of the capsules; in 1934, Dr Hilda Garry took over this position. Sir Julien met all these expenses until October 1933, when they were paid from the income of the Anaesthetic Appeal Fund.[58] At this stage, the CMB sanctioned the use of capsules by midwives, though only under the direction and personal supervision of a doctor; this ruling was reiterated in the 1934 Annual Report of the Board. The Ministry of Health also gave its approval, though unofficially. Lady Williams reported to a meeting of the Birthday Trust Executive Committee that Dame Janet Campbell had personally assured her that the Ministry of Health would take no disciplinary action against midwives who used the ampoules and was prepared to look upon their use, both on the wards and in the hospital districts, as 'legitimate experimental work'.[59]

The hospitals were asked to arrange for health workers to fill out and return a form about the performance of the capsules during normal labour. To supervise the study, a committee was set up, comprising John Fairbairn, Louis Rivett, Mr Herbert Charles, Dr Enid Browne of the British Medical Women's Federation, and Arnold Walker. In 1933, this committee analysed over 1,000 returns from hospitals, doctors and midwives, in which no accidents or deaths were recorded. It found that in the opinion of the patients, the capsules had been of great use in 54 per cent of cases, of some use in 41 per cent, and of no use in 5 per cent.[60] Rivett also tested a series of 342 cases over three months in 1933 at Queen Charlotte's, having already found that the capsules produced "almost perfect analgesia" in at least 95 per cent of over 3,000 cases at this hospital. He obtained equally satisfactory results from the three-month investigation, despite the death of a woman who was given thirty-seven capsules over a period of five and three-quarter hours, and the development of puerperal sepsis in a mother who had been given sixty-six capsules in fourteen hours.[61]

Many of the reports on the capsules were enthusiastic: five of the six patients at Oldswinford who used capsules, "received wonderful relief and can scarcely find words to express gratification".[62] Even "nervous primipara" were grateful.[63] Often, mothers "Did not know the baby was born" and did "not remember birth of child; or the manual removal of placenta and membranes." But not all health workers were happy. The MOH for Greenwich complained they made women wave their arms about and turn over, while a Wolverhampton hospital said that the capsules made women "very hysterical and difficult to manage".[64] The MOH for Wareham and Purbeck Rural District Council said that his midwives flatly refused to use the capsules any more.[65] There were technical problems, too. "The capsules were anything but crushable," observed one doctor,[66] while the Matron at Alexandra Maternity Home reported that some of her capsules had exploded.[67] Another doctor reported "the horrifying experience of entering a house and finding a capsule between a patient's clenched teeth, only a small part showing. She was, of course, semiconscious."[68] A retired midwife interviewed for this book still remembers "one little phase where we had horrible little chloroform capsules. I don't know if anyone's told you about those? They soon stopped it because I think they found it not very successful – and a bit dangerous."[69]

One critic drily observed that they were more likely to satisfy the High Society ladies who were backing them, than the women who were expected to use them. "Whereas I admit these capsules represent an ingenious method of satisfying the sentimental demands of Society," he said, "it will by no means constitute a universal panacea for abolishing the pangs of childbirth."[70] However, the demands of Mrs Baldwin were not satisfied. The Lucy Baldwin Hospital in Stourport, which had been built especially for her by Sir Julien, refused to use the capsules and received an angry letter from her: "it grieves me very much," she told the Director, "to find that my own hospital should be the one to lag behind in this matter. Especially as I have been the pioneer in the work for so long."[71] The Clerk of the Worcestershire County Council explained that nothing could be done, since it was rarely possible to provide supervision by a qualified medical practitioner at the hospital.[72]

As part of its Empire Crusade for mothers, the Birthday Trust distributed capsules to all corners of the Empire: to the Gold Coast, Nigeria and Bombay in 1932, Gibraltar, Canada and Burma in 1933, and Calcutta in 1935.[73] Some British health workers took the capsules with them when they went abroad, such as a nurse working with poor women in India who had watched the use of chloroform capsules in the Rotunda Hospital in Dublin.[74] A British man in Nigeria who had nothing whatever to do with the medical profession, asked for a supply of capsules: "I have a reputation for 'goodness' to maintain," he explained, "and where I CAN help to alleviate suffering I like to do so."[75]

In November 1933, the Birthday Trust asked the BCOG to investigate the safety of chloroform capsules and their administration by midwives in the home.[76] The Trust hoped to discover new information that would persuade the CMB to rescind its requirement that midwives should use capsules only under medical supervision, which seriously limited their use. The Trust promised to meet all the costs of the study, which were over £2,000 by the time it was completed. The College agreed to carry it out, but insisted that it would have to look into other methods of pain relief as well, since chloroform could be dangerous.[77] The following terms of reference were produced: "to investigate the use of analgesics in labour with special reference to the use of chloroform capsules and the employment of any analgesic by midwives."[78] The College set up a Sub-Committee, with John Fairbairn as Honorary Treasurer and Louis Rivett as Honorary Secretary, both of whom had been involved in the earlier investigation into the use of capsules; they were joined by G.F. Gibberd, R. Christie Brown (whose chloroform inhaler was included in the study), Z. Mennell of the Association of Anaesthetics, and Professor Mellanby and Dr Matthew Young of the MRC. Mellanby actively sought membership of the committee: he explained to MacNalty, CMO at the Ministry of Health, "Actually,

I approached the Lord President, then Mr Baldwin, and told him that we would like to help this Committee, as we thought we could improve the value of their results. At a public dinner given by the British College, Mr Baldwin mentioned this in his speech, and the College then acted on the suggestion by co-opting myself and Matthew Young."[79] This account reveals that the BCOG investigation was highly regarded by the scientific community.

Thirty-six hospitals attached to teaching schools and the large maternity hospitals throughout England, Wales, Scotland, Northern Ireland, and the Irish Free State [Eire], cooperated in the study. It was conducted in institutions, rather than domiciliary practice, on the grounds that results would be recorded more accurately there.[80] Consequently, the very reason for initiating the study – to investigate analgesia suitable for use by midwives in a home environment – was neglected, despite the earlier assurance by Fairbairn that "wherever possible the various methods would be tried on the district as well as in the hospitals."[81] This led to bad feeling between the Birthday Trust and the College. When Fletcher Shaw said that a further step would be needed, in order to find out which methods would be "safe and effective in the very different conditions of the patient's home",[82] Sir Julien was quite put out. "My Committee is not quite clear as to the reason for this proviso," he replied sarcastically, "as my Committee originally requested you to investigate this very point."[83]

In all, nearly 10,000 cases were investigated.[84] Almost 4,000 women were given nitrous oxide and air administered with the Minnitt gas and air apparatus, which had been developed in 1933 by Dr R.J. Minnitt, an anaesthetist in the Liverpool hospitals. Five thousand women were given chloroform (2,500 by capsules, 1,500 by the Mennell inhaler, and the rest by the Christie Brown inhaler); and nearly 1,000 women were administered paraldehyde per rectum. There is no record of the basis on which women were allocated the different methods of pain relief. The study was described as a 'controlled trial', but simply in the sense that different methods were investigated at the same time. A form was drawn up for hospitals to fill out and the records were collected each month and then classified and analysed by Group Supervisors, who were given responsibility for a hospital or group of hospitals.

The BCOG's eventual report in 1936 concluded that chloroform should not be used by midwives acting alone, because immediate and delayed dangers had occurred in the investigation. Paraldehyde per rectum was not recommended, either, on the grounds that it did not provide adequate analgesia at the time of the actual birth. The only method that received full approval was the Minnitt Gas and Air apparatus, which was described as a safe and satisfactory method of producing analgesia for use by midwives, so long as they had been specially trained. It was important "to press forward the use of the Minnitt gas and air apparatus," argued the report, "rather than to continue the supply of chloroform capsules."[85] The Midwives' Institute was not at all pleased, especially Miss Pye.[86] The BCOG Report carried such authority, however, that it brought all interest in chloroform capsules to a sudden end. The Trust shifted its allegiance to the Minnitt gas and air machine, which soon became the linchpin of its work to promote pain relief. By 1939, Sir Julien's private secretary in Nottingham wrote to the Birthday Trust, "I would like to descend on you one day, but I am rather nervous lest I meet a midwife in the Hall. If I do, do I murmur 'Minnitt Gas/Air' and hasten by, or have you changed the password?"[87]

GAS AND AIR

Dr Minnitt's machine had developed from a meeting he attended at the Royal Society of Medicine to discuss the use of nitrous oxide and oxygen for obstetric pain relief.[88] The disadvantages of this seemed clear and the suggestion was made of substituting air for oxygen; this had already been tried in America by McKesson, but it had failed, because he had given too high a concentration of the gas. Minnitt resolved to make an attempt himself. He consulted his friend, A. Charles King, a well known medical instrument maker, and within two months they had produced an apparatus that was used for the first time at the Liverpool Maternity Hospital on 16 October 1933. The concentrations of the Minnitt machine were originally 45 per cent nitrous oxide and 55 per cent air,

A Queen Charlotte's gas and air machine, late 1930s. ([NBTF/H3/2/2] Reproduced courtesy of the Wellcome Institute Library, London)

but this was later altered to 50 per cent of each. The apparatus consisted of a reduced pressure regulator attached to a small rubber bag in a metal drum, and an automatic valve shutting off the flow of gas when the patient did not inhale.[89] Dr Minnitt showed his machine to the Association of Anaesthetists in October 1933, after which a similar machine was made for Wellhouse Hospital, Barnet, where an anaesthetist called John Elam embarked on a study of its use. A paper on the two studies was read to the Liverpool Medical Institute on 22 February 1934.

In a small way, the Trust supported this early work of Dr Minnitt, once Dr Elam had drawn its attention to the new machine in December 1933.[90] At first the Trust said it was too preoccupied with chloroform capsules to think about the Minnitt machine, but soon after employed Dr Hilda Garry to test the method at the Liverpool Maternity Hospital (though another part of her job was to demonstrate the use of the capsules).[91] While Elam became very friendly with the Trust, writing passionate letters about the glory of gas and air, Minnitt appears to have kept his distance and Lady Williams described his letters as "cryptic".[92] Following a telephone call in 1934 from the Trust, in which he was urged to consider the suitability of his apparatus for midwives, he said it should not be used in hospitals without trained staff and that it should "*not* [sic] be used by midwives acting alone".[93] Only when he was completely sure of its safety, did he advocate its use by midwives. In 1935 the Trust sent him a cheque for £25 as "a token of appreciation of his splendid efforts".[94]

Immediately after the BCOG report of 1936, the CMB set up a committee under its new Chairman, Sir Comyns Berkeley, to advise midwives on the use of gas and air. It recognized the administration of this analgesia as treatment within the province of the midwife, so long as the conditions recommended by the BCOG were met. These conditions were: that the midwife had been properly trained; that the patient had been examined within the month before confinement by a medical practitioner, who had handed the midwife a certificate stating that the mother was in a fit condition to receive gas and air; and that an additional person – a state registered midwife, State Registered Nurse, senior medical student, or pupil midwife – was present. These conditions were strictly enforced. A midwife who is now retired and started work in 1937 in Wales, says that even though she had studied gas and air on her midwifery course, she had to repeat the training because she did not have a certificate.[95]

The need for the presence of a second trained person seriously limited its use, since in many areas it was difficult enough to find one trained midwife, let alone two. In country districts, observed the *News Chronicle*, "it is the exception for a village to have more than one nurse, and when there are two the poorer homes cannot afford to pay a double fee."[96] In 1938, the CMB asked for the BCOG's opinion on rescinding this regulation, but the earlier recommendation was reaffirmed.[97] In 1945, following sustained pressure from organizations like the National Federation of Women's Institutes and the Trust, as well as medical officers, the regulation was altered to allow members of St John or the Red Cross, or similarly qualified people, to be the second person present.[98]

Despite the CMB's restrictions, the Trust embarked on an energetic campaign to distribute gas and air machines, which were now sent instead of grants to the hospitals that had previously been allocated these.[99] In 1937, an Analgesics Sub-Committee was set up to supervise the distribution, which was chaired by Louis Rivett and included Miss Jackson, Miss Pye, Miss Wilmshurst, Lady Rhys Williams and Sydney Walton. In 1938, Mrs Methuen joined as the representative of the National Federation of Women's Institutes (NFWI) and was replaced by Frances Farrer in 1939; the NFWI had initiated this participation itself, because it was "hoping to push forward the use of Analgesics in country districts".[100]

The models selected for distribution were the Minnitt-Walton apparatus, made by Messrs A. Charles King, and the Queen Charlotte's Model B, made by the British Oxygen Company (BOC); in 1939, the Autogesia Self-Administered apparatus, made by the Dental Manufacturing Co., was also approved by the Trust.[101] Machines bearing the label 'Presented by the National Birthday Trust Fund'[102] were sent to hospitals, District Nursing Associations (DNAs) and County Nursing Associations (CNAs), either free or at a nominal cost of £5. The manufacturers offered discounts to the Trust,[103] and by the mid-1940s, 119 machines had been supplied to hospitals, both voluntary and municipal, and 160 machines had been supplied to 124 DNAs and CNAs.[104]

The machines could not always be used, however. "Having to send two nurses to these cases certainly restricts its usefulness," complained the Hampstead DNA. The Kilburn and West Hampstead DNA reported that, "This year we are facing the difficulty other Associations have in securing the attendance of the second midwife at the time she is needed."[105] Another obstacle was the heavy weight of the machines. Even when cylinders of nitrous oxide were delivered to a mother's home by

A midwife using a bicycle to transport a gas and air machine to a home delivery, late 1930s. ([NBTF/H3/2/2] Reproduced courtesy of the Wellcome Institute Library, London)

BOC, a service provided by BOC throughout the nation for a minimal charge,[106] the midwife still had to transport the actual apparatus; this was easier for midwives who travelled on a bicycle. The Trust did everything it could to help. When the Nursing Sisters of St John the Divine at Deptford said they would welcome gas and air for their district cases, it gave them three machines and £50 a year for three years towards their expenses.[107] In 1939, Queen Charlotte's Hospital was given the first payment of £250 a year for three years, to help provide analgesia on the district.[108] Several machines were sent to the Salvation Army, which cared for working-class mothers (many of them unmarried) in its maternity homes,[109] and the Monmouth NA was given a machine free of charge, because of "the hard times through which Monmouth was passing".[110]

The Trust responded swiftly and generously to requests for machines that referred to economic need, such as one from a nurse working near Nottingham: "We are a very poor colliery district and wide rural areas and it is difficult to get necessary expenses and certainly no margin for such things as this. Is there any means of producing one free of cost?"[111] A midwife in independent practice in North London, working among very poor mothers, pleaded, "Please help me to get one of the bags, as I do not like to see these poor women suffer, knowing as I do, there is something I could give them, if only allowed to."[112] Wallsend Infirmary appealed for a machine on the grounds that it was serving mothers in "a very badly depressed area".[113] The machines were gratefully received, judging by the many letters that were sent to the Trust headquarters. "We are very proud of the Gas and Air apparatus you gave us," wrote two midwives in the Rhondda, "and hope to do good work with it."[114] The West Hampstead DNA said it wanted to "give our patients the benefit of this new boon."[115] Lady Williams herself used gas and air and spoke about it afterwards with rapturous enthusiasm.[116]

Like the short-lived chloroform capsules, gas and air machines were sent all over the world, to Athens,[117] Hong Kong,[118] Calcutta,[119] Mexico,[120] Singapore,[121] Honolulu[122] and Colombo.[123] Whenever Sir Julien went abroad with his cricket team, he took an apparatus with him as a gift for a hospital. Just before Christmas in 1936, his assistant wrote to the Birthday Trust secretary, "Would you be so overwhelmingly kind, my sweets, as to order from the makers of the atrocities four of those what you efficiently call gas/air Minnitt machines, packed in wooden boxes (decorated with a little holly and mistletoe), ready for Sir Julien to take abroad with him?"[124]

The development of the gas and air apparatus coincided with the birth of the modern industrial gases business, which was heralded by the development of a cheap method of producing oxygen by distilling liquid air. Growth was rapid, particularly in the case of the British Oxygen Company (BOC), which led the UK market in the 1930s. In a centenary account of its history, the BOC Group acknowledges the Trust's role in the growth of its success: "Originally involved only in the manufacture of anaesthetic gases," it explains, "the company was asked by the National Birthday Trust to develop a lightweight gas-air machine of simplified construction for use by midwives. The result was the 'Queen Charlotte's Gas-Air Analgesia Apparatus', of which several thousand were sold."[125] BOC used this opportunity to spread its name through the scientific community. Advertisements for the Queen Charlotte's machines referred to the approval of the BCOG (but when Charles King requested permission to do the same in advertisements for the Minnitt machine,[126] the BCOG refused to let either company use its name).[127] The BOC offered machines to the Trust at a "special complimentary discount".[128] During the 1930s, BOC was trying to expand into as many countries as possible. This was difficult before the end of the decade, when it became possible to transport and store gases in liquid form. In the meantime, the distribution of gas and air machines helped to spread BOC's name to foreign parts – "Today, to people in many parts of the world, The BOC Group *is* industrial gases."[129]

The Queen Charlotte's apparatus produced by BOC was based on Louis Rivett's "design of a modification of the Minnitt and Davies Gas and Air machines."[130] Minnitt would "not allow his name to be associated with this model",[131] probably out of loyalty to his friend Charles King, who had used his design to build the first gas and air apparatus in 1933. Eventually, however, his name was given to a gas and air machine by BOC. In September 1939, BOC took over Messrs Coxeter and Son, which had supplied Charles A. King with the Minnitt apparatus.[132] Then, in 1943, the BOC produced a new machine based on the Minnitt principle, but with the advantages of the Queen Charlotte's model – and called it a Minnitt gas/air apparatus.

The training of midwives to administer gas and air was regarded as a priority by the Birthday Trust Analgesics Sub-Committee,[133] but the opportunities for such training were inadequate. British Oxygen reported that it had received "an increasing number of enquiries from bewildered Midwives and Medical Officers of Health on this subject."[134] In 1939, the NFWI reported to the CMB that they had received letters from nurses and midwives in country districts, especially Lancashire and Warwickshire, referring to impossible difficulties in the way of obtaining training.[135] "Very few hospitals," observed the Trust in dismay, "appeared to be holding courses of instruction for outside midwives."[136] John Elam reported to the *Manchester Evening News*, "I have seen gas apparatus provided free of charge by the National Birthday Trust standing in the corner of the labour ward, covered with rust and dust."[137]

In the middle of 1937, the Birthday Trust sought information from hospitals and Nursing Associations about the kind of gas and air training that was available. A few said they did hold courses, which midwives from outside the hospital were invited to attend;[138] some said they could only offer places on their courses to their own midwives;[139] others had not yet been approved by the CMB as a teaching hospital in the administration of gas and air;[140] yet others regretted that the teaching resources in anaesthetics were already taken up by medical students.[141] There were several reasons for this slow progress. One was simple resistance to the idea of midwives providing pain relief, which led the Honorary Secretary of a Berkshire NA to turn down the Trust's offer of a Minnitt machine.[142] Another reason was the CMB's requirement that two trained people be involved in the administration of gas and air – as their nurses were always on their own, said some Nursing Associations, they could not see the point of sending anyone on a course.[143] As a result of all these problems, only 29 out of 188 Local Authorities had provided their domiciliary midwives with training by 1939.[144]

OPPOSITION BY GPS

On the whole, general practitioners opposed the idea of midwives using gas and air, and the BMA passed a Resolution to this effect at its 1939 Annual Meeting. This Resolution had no official bearing on the work of midwives, since the Central Midwives Board, not the BMA, was their statutory body, but it angered many of those who supported the analgesia campaign. Shortly after the BMA meeting, Eleanor Rathbone referred in Parliament to "the selfish attitude of a certain portion of the medical profession who expressed their views the other day",[145] and a letter to the Trust said that it was only because of the "inarticulacy . . . of thousands of working class women" that the strength of the resentment against the "recent decision of the B.M.A. has not been realised."[146] The Department of Health for Scotland anticipated similar opposition from Scottish doctors when it considered giving midwives the authority to use gas and air. When it wrote in 1937 to the Ministry of Health asking for information on the practice in England, it was especially interested in finding out "whether there has been any opposition by the medical profession".[147]

"I quite agree with the BMA. Personally, if I were having a baby, I shouldn't dream of allowing a midwife to give me an analgesic."

This cartoon refers to the BMA's opposition to the idea of midwives administering gas and air analgesia to mothers in childbirth. The BMA passed a Resolution to this effect at its Annual Meeting in 1939. Daily Express, 27 July 1939.

At this time, argues Frank Honigsbaum, the GP was being

squeezed out of midwifery by a pincer movement: pressure from obstetricians trying to consolidate their role as experts and to create a need for women to give birth in hospital; and pressure from midwives, "who, aided by the revolutionary Minnitt machine and the backing they received from public health officers under the 1936 Midwives Act, took over an ever-increasing share of home confinements."[148] During the debate that preceded the passing of the Resolution at the 1939 meeting of the BMA, a number of doctors said they "wanted to stop midwives controlling the midwifery of the country".[149] The GPs' struggle to maintain a central role in childbirth failed. By the end of the Second World War, only about one out of three GPs still practised midwifery.[150] However, their effort to sabotage midwives' use of analgesia was more successful. According to the report of the 1946 survey, *Maternity in Great Britain*, the negative attitude of GPs was "the deciding factor" in the delay to develop and provide analgesia for childbirth.[151] Honigsbaum agrees with this, stating that doctors managed to prevent such use in any extensive way until after the war.[152]

'NATURAL' CHILDBIRTH

In the 1930s, there was growing interest in the nature and cause of labour pains. *The Squire* by Enid Bagnold contains a discussion of whether or not labour pain is really pain at all, since labour is not actually pathological. A woman who has had five deliveries recalls that at the third and fourth times, she started to ask, "Is this really *pain* . . . or is it an extraordinary *sensation*? . . . Pain is but a branch of sensation. Perhaps child-birth turns into pain only when it is fought and resisted?" A woman giving birth, concluded Bagnold, "was not in torture, she was in labour."[153] This was consistent with the ideas of Grantley Dick-Read, a propagandist for 'natural' childbirth who questioned the value of medical intervention in labour, including pain relief. In *Natural Childbirth* (1933) and *Childbirth without Fear* (1942), he argued that the root cause of pain in labour was fear: by the controlled elimination of fear, he said, the need for analgesic drugs could be avoided.

Fear, often generated from ignorance, was certainly a feature of childbirth between the wars, according to midwives and doctors who worked at the time. A doctor specializing in family planning recalls that, "in the 1930s you would find that at least three quarters, if not more, of the women you saw had no idea about the actual facts of life. They had no idea even about coitus before they were married."[154] A district midwife says that when she worked in Birmingham in 1933, "We all had bicycles with the black bag. And the people I've been asking round here, neighbours you see, remember that sort of thing and they all thought the baby came in the black bag, all of them. They weren't told a thing."[155] A woman who gave birth in 1937 at Llwynypia Hospital in the Rhondda remembers, "I didn't know what was happening, where the baby was, what bits of it. I thought it was at the back. I couldn't feel the front."[156] Another woman recalls that, "Right up to the time I was married I thought the babies would come from the tummy, that you split open. I was 13 when I saw my periods and my mother said, now don't you go about playing with boys. If you do, it's to the workhouse you'll go."[157]

Dick-Read's views were regarded as suspect by the medical profession. While many doctors agreed that a better level of information about pregnancy would diminish fear, they were not so convinced that this would reduce the pain of childbirth. In 1945 Professor F.J. Browne made an offer to Dick-Read to lecture to his students of obstetrics at University College Hospital, but Dick-Read's demands were such that it was impossible for these lectures to be given. The Birthday Trust, particularly Rivett, Comyns Berkeley and Dame Juliet, took the view that there was no substance in Dick-Read's claims, and were concerned that his campaign would be "injurious to the publicity for the universal provision of gas and air".[158]

THE END OF THE DECADE

Whereas in 1930, only Queen Charlotte's Hospital had given pain relief on a regular basis to mothers in 'normal' labour, by 1936 there were few voluntary hospitals that did not do so; many municipal hospitals, too, including all those under the control of the LCC, had adopted the policy of providing relief to every mother in labour.[159] By 1939, the administration of analgesics by midwives was included in the Ministry of Health Returns made by each Local Authority.[160] However, the stated objective of the Birthday Trust – to bring pain relief to all women, regardless of income – was still a distant dream by the end of the Second World War. Just 20 per cent of women delivering at home in 1946, and only eight per cent of those attended by midwives, were given any sort of pain relief, reported *Maternity in Great Britain*, which gave the results of a national birth survey that is described in chapter 9 of this book. The commonest analgesic was chloroform, which was used in 14 per cent of domiciliary confinements. By 1946, only one in five practising midwives was qualified to administer gas and air, which was consequently little used: "Gas and Air is used in 5 per cent . . . The use of Gas and Air is practically limited to England, where 7 per cent receive it as compared with only one mother out of 433 women in Wales and none in Scotland."[161] These figures echoed the conclusions of a Birthday Trust report, which was drawn up in 1945 on the basis of answers to a questionnaire that had been sent by the Queen's Institute for District Nursing to affiliated County Nursing Associations. It stated that while 84 CNAs used gas and air analgesia, 1,341 did not. The main reasons for this limited use were listed as: a lack of trained staff, due to inadequate commitment by Local Authorities; the difficulty of meeting the CMB regulations; a lack of funds to purchase apparatus; and opposition from medical practitioners in some cases.

The report also observed that the extension of gas and air analgesia had been further restricted by the outbreak of war in September 1939, which had delayed the supply of apparatus (especially steel and rubber) and created shortages of midwives and lecturers for teaching hospitals.[162]

A substantial shift in attitude had taken place between the late 1920s, when Mrs Baldwin's Wireless Appeal had been considered an embarrassment by Lady George and Lady Londonderry, and the 1940s. In that time, said Lady Baldwin, "one by one I have seen the old arguments against [pain relief] go down."[163] According to *Maternity in Great Britain*, the most commonly stated reason for dissatisfaction with treatment during labour was the lack of analgesia.[164] In 1946, for the first time, the WCG called for pain relief to be made available for normal labour; then, the following year, it demanded that all midwives be trained and equipped to provide this.[165] A building labourer's wife, who delivered her baby at home with the assistance of a midwife, complained that, "Something should be given. I was tired out before I started. People with plenty of money don't have to suffer pain."[166] *Britain and her Birth-Rate*, which was prepared by Mass-Observation in 1945, reported anger among poor women, especially younger working wives, that they did not have the relief afforded to the rich. One woman was quoted as asking, "Rich people don't suffer, why should we?" Another complained, "if you have money you can have the best anaesthetics and everything. That's not right is it?"[167] The disparity between rich and poor in the provision of pain relief had not, after all, been removed. A letter to *The Lady* in 1942 complained that, "this is not democracy. One of the most cruel class divisions yet remaining in this country is that rich mothers need not suffer in childbirth as though we were still in the Stone Age, while poorer ones far too often do."[168]

PAIN RELIEF AFTER THE WAR

This marked disparity between rich and poor came to an end following the Second World War, as a result of the health service established by the National Health Act. It took responsibility for the provision of adequate and safe methods of pain relief to all mothers who required it, although it took some time to develop the resources to deliver a universal service. When the Act came into force, 1,775 Minnitt machines (over one third of those in use) had either been supplied free or through a grant from the Birthday Trust. Now that the Birthday Trust no longer needed to provide these or to take a leading role in this work, it offered its support and financial backing to efforts by obstetricians and by the MRC to improve the safety and efficacy of pain relief methods, especially those that were suitable for use by midwives in a mother's home.

The Trust was instrumental in obtaining permission for midwives to use Pethidine. This is an injectable analgesic method that was developed in 1939 by the German drug industry and used extensively by front-line troops during the war; after the war, the British were granted the patent rights for Pethidine production under the War Claims.[169] Much of the original British research in connection with making Pethidine available for obstetric use was carried out by Dame Josephine Barnes at University College Hospital between 1942 and 1946, with the support of the Trust Fund's Technical Advisory Committee. Dame Josephine, who became a member of the MRC Committee on Analgesia in Midwifery, had a commitment to this work because she was appalled by the unnecessary suffering of women in childbirth.[170] This research led to an article in the *BMJ*, which reported that in 500 cases, 53 per cent of mothers experienced Pethidine as an effective form of analgesia.[171] The drug proved so successful that by 1948, it was used in the first stage of labour in 75 per cent of all hospital cases. It could not be used in a mother's home, however, because it was put under the Dangerous Drugs Act in 1947, which meant that midwives were not permitted to use it on their own responsibility. Because Pethidine was a drug of addiction, there was a fear that giving midwives access would encourage misuse. The CMB asked the Home Office to reconsider the ban on its use by midwives and on 11 November 1948, the Birthday Trust sent a deputation in support, led by Dame Josephine, Arthur Bell, the President of the RCOG, and Mr Espley, the Trust's Chairman. After long discussions an agreement was finally reached in 1951, when midwives were permitted the use of Pethidine in two doses of 100 mg, without the presence of a doctor.

The Trust cooperated with the RCOG in an investigation into Trilene (Trichloroethylene), which is related to chloroform but is less toxic. A machine was developed in 1943 which was suitable for dispensing Trilene and was so small and light that it could be carried in a midwife's bag. The RCOG approved Trilene for use by midwives on condition that an apparatus could be evolved which would deliver the analgesic at a fixed rate, so the Trust contacted a number of manufacturers, urging them to produce such a machine. Finally, several prototypes underwent extensive tests by the MRC in 1951, with the financial backing of the Trust. The MRC Committee on Analgesia in Midwifery produced a report in 1954, which recommended that midwives be allowed to administer Trilene.[172] Two types of machine were finally approved for use by midwives. Trilene is no longer used at the end of the twentieth century, following the CMB's withdrawal in 1983 of its approval for the use of Trilene by midwives working independently.

Minnitt's gas and air machine was used until the early 1960s, when concern developed about its safety: a woman using the apparatus only breathed about 10 per cent of oxygen, which was a problem if the foetus was experiencing difficulties. The first modification of the Minnitt machine involved an exchange of oxygen for air, which led to the Lucy Baldwin machine, named after Mrs Baldwin in recognition of the Birthday Trust's work. With this machine, the mixture of nitrous oxide and oxygen could be varied and preset. These machines were very heavy, however, so could not be carried by midwives to a mother's home.

With the financial backing of the Birthday Trust, Dr Michael Tunstall, an anaesthetist in Aberdeen, worked on the idea of premixing oxygen and nitrous oxide in liquid form under pressure. In 1961, with the cooperation of BOC, Tunstall developed Entonox, a safe mix that could be easily transported in cylinders, including small ones of only six kilos that could be carried by a midwife. This gave the safety of a high concentration of oxygen (50 per cent), with the efficacy of nitrous oxide.[173] A small problem of layering of the liquids in the cylinder occurred if they were left standing for some time, so a gentle rocking was required before use; at very low temperatures, the layering was accelerated. This was unlikely in England and Wales, but meant that the machine was never used in the USA, where approval was not given because of the cold winter temperatures in the Midwest. Entonox, produced by BOC, is used today as a demand analgesic all over the world except the USA.

From 1953 to 1955, the Trust financed a Research Unit devoted to Obstetric Analgesia at Hammersmith Hospital. The work was carried out by Dr Hilda Roberts and the grant allowed postgraduate midwifery students from different countries to study in the department. Dr Roberts made a detailed study of analgesics in childbirth and was able to show the advantages and disadvantages of different methods. She wrote detailed accounts of the use of inhalation analgesia for midwives, which helped them to give maximum relief to their patients. She also made a study of mothers who attended relaxation classes and found that many of them benefited more easily from light types of sedation, than women who did not attend classes. At the same time, she warned that teachers of antenatal relaxation were liable, if they were too enthusiastic, to make mothers feel that any sedation was a confession of failure. This warning was in part a response to the creation on 4 May 1956 of the Natural Childbirth Association, which was set up for the promotion and better understanding of Grantley Dick-Read's system (it became the National Childbirth Trust in 1960).

Discussions in the UK about 'natural childbirth' had thus far been somewhat parochial. Elliot Philipp of the Trust introduced a broader perspective by going to Paris in 1959 to study the Lamaze method of a psycho-prophylactic approach to childbirth. He produced a report on methods in Paris that were based on a combination of the Lamaze method and Dick-Read's theories. These were effective, he suggested, largely because of the supportive role of the monitress who kept the mother company throughout labour.[174]

In its 1958 and 1970 national surveys (see chapters 9 and 10), the Trust ensured that questions were asked about the use of pain relief in labour. Then, in 1990, under the direction of Professor Geoffrey Chamberlain at St George's Hospital in London, it devoted a whole study to the topic. In one week of June 1990, it carried out a national survey to find out the pattern of usage of the various methods of analgesia, and the effectiveness of these methods from the point of view of the woman, her partner, and her professional supporters. The survey team comprised Geoffrey Chamberlain, Ann Wraight, a midwife, who was the coordinator of the study, and Philip Steer, an obstetrician. The study was almost entirely conducted in hospitals, since 99.5 per cent of the women in the survey delivered in a hospital setting; the methodology involved is discussed in chapter 10 of this book.

The results were published in *Pain and its Relief in Childbirth* (1993), edited by the survey team. It showed that Entonox, the apparatus based on the Minnitt machine, was still "amongst the most popular of pain relieving methods in labour and demand for it is likely to go on at least into the next century."[175] It was available in 99 per cent of units, followed closely by Pethidine, which was available in 73.3 per cent of units. Other drugs available in a few units included morphine and heroin. Epidurals were widely available, and non-phamarcological methods were offered by almost all institutions. Discovering what women actually used was complicated by the fact that only 41 per cent of the mothers in the study completed their part of the questionnaire, but of these, 60 per cent chose Entonox, 37 per cent Pethidine, and 18 per cent epidural anaesthesia. While 34 per cent of women considered that they had used relaxation as a method of analgesia, only 3.8 per cent of midwives recorded this as a chosen method. The survey also found that very few women used alternative methods, such as homoeopathy, hypnosis and acupuncture, which comprised less than 1 per cent of the analgesia used.[176]

Fundamental to the survey was the question of choice, which was based on the assumption that all women giving birth in the UK of the 1990s would be offered pain relief for childbirth. A remarkable distance had been travelled since the 1930s, when many working-class women were not even aware of the possibility of relief from pain; and of those who were, few expected to be offered it. Mrs Baldwin and the Birthday Trust had taken a leading role in a revolution that not only transformed the experience of childbirth, but narrowed the gulf between the lives and the expectations of poor women and rich women.

CHAPTER SEVEN

The Human Milk Bureau

The first milk bank in Britain – the Human Milk Bureau – was opened by the Birthday Trust on 1 March 1939 at Queen Charlotte's Hospital. The plan to set it up was developed by Sir Julien Cahn, the Trust's Chairman, who funded Miss Edith Dare, Matron of Queen Charlotte's, to organize and to direct it. The object of the scheme, explained the *Medical Officer* shortly after the opening of the Bureau, "is to make human milk readily available for sick or delicate babies for whom it has been medically prescribed, and whose mothers are not able to provide it themselves."[1] Every morning, nurses went out on their motorcycles to collect breast milk from mothers who had more milk than they needed for their own child. "If you see a nurse on a motorcycle," reported the *Daily Express* in June 1939, "she may be saving a baby's life."[2]

Miss Edith Dare, Matron of Queen Charlotte's Hospital, standing with Princess Marina, Duchess of Kent, in a conversation with the mechanized midwifery squad in 1941. (Reproduced courtesy of Queen Charlotte's and Chelsea Hospital, Hammersmith Hospitals NHS Trust)

147

This milk bank is still operating today, as part of the Paediatric and Neonatal Medicine Department at Hammersmith Hospitals NHS Trust. For over half a century, it has distributed human milk all over the British Isles to newly born babies in need. The current term for this milk is 'expressed breast milk' (EBM), which is a more accurate description since it makes a distinction between human milk that has been expressed and that which is fed to an infant directly from the breast. For this reason, it is used where appropriate in this chapter.

The first milk bank of all was set up in Vienna in 1909; ten years later, another was opened in Boston, USA. By 1931, the Boston Directory for Mothers Milk was collecting 4,400 quarts of milk annually and distributing it to twenty-two hospitals. Other cities followed the Boston example, including Chicago, New York, Los Angeles, Pittsburgh, Detroit and Montreal.[3] In 1939, the Directory published a set of standards describing all aspects of human milk banking and in 1943, the American Academy of Paediatrics issued national standards, based chiefly on those developed in Boston.[4] By this time, there were similar organizations in Germany and in Russia.

Against this background of the growth of milk banks abroad, interest in Britain in the value of EBM was raised by the birth of a set of quadruplets. This was unusual, because multiple births of more than two babies were rare before the development and use of fertility drugs. The babies, who were born at St Neot's in Cambridgeshire on 28 November 1935, were between six and seven weeks premature and very small (one of them was scarcely three pounds in weight), so Miss Dare arranged for a "supply of sterilized human milk" to be sent twice daily for them from Queen Charlotte's Hospital; this milk was diluted with water for the first month's feeds. The chief difficulty was fetching the milk from London twice a day: the local newspaper announced two weeks after the birth that the doctor in charge of the case needed help to bring milk from Queen Charlotte's Hospital, either by car or aeroplane. The milk had to be fetched at 10.00 a.m. and 6.00 p.m. A pilot based at Hanworth, who had earlier written to place himself and his aeroplane at the doctor's disposal, went by road to Queen Charlotte's and back to Hanworth, then flew at 150 miles an hour to St Neot's. On one occasion, just as he started to land, "three women dashed across his path and he had suddenly to climb up again to avoid hitting them. He circled again and landed safely." According to the bulletins provided by the local newspaper, the feeds were given as follows:

Every two hours: Ann, Ernest and Paul fed with tiny bottles of human milk.
Every ½ hour: Michael [the smallest] fed.
Bath time, 11.00 a.m.: Quads bathed in warm olive oil before the fire, then tucked in cotton wool wrappings, flannels and shawls. Ann likes it, the boys, especially Michael, think it a nuisance.

When the special milk did not arrive in time, the babies were given glucose and water.[5]

Thanks to these dramatic efforts to provide the quadruplets with EBM, they survived. Their physician, Donald Paterson, who worked at Westminster Hospital and the Hospital for Sick Children at Great Ormond Street and had written a text book on infant feeding, was so impressed that he wrote to Miss Dare in July 1938 to urge the opening of a centre at Queen Charlotte's – "for supplying breast milk to ailing and premature babies *on a large scale*". The case of the quadruplets, he said, demonstrated the value of such a scheme: "What would I have done in the case of the Quadruplets? They never would have survived had it not been for you supplying day after day, the proper quantity."[6] The importance of this episode in the creation of the HMB was recognized in its early years: the back of a photograph of the Bureau that was taken in 1939 bears the statement, "When the famous St Neot's Quads were born, [Miss Dare] supplied human milk for the Hospital to supplement what their mother was able to give them – *and from this incident, grew the great idea.*"[7]

SETTING UP THE HUMAN MILK BUREAU

While the idea for the Bureau may have derived from the challenge of saving the quads and the enthusiasm of Dr Paterson, it would never have become a reality without the vision of Sir Julien Cahn and the backing of the Birthday Trust. Sir Julien was interested in the idea of a human milk bank as early as 1936, when he was taken to see the Boston milk bank during a visit to America. Since this was less than one year after the birth of the St Neot's quadruplets, it is conceivable that his visit was the result of interest in the story of the quads. As soon as he returned from Boston, he offered to pay all expenses for Miss Dare to go herself to Boston to study the operation of the bank. Before leaving for the USA, Miss Dare visited Stanford Hall, Sir Julien's home, to discuss plans for the trip;[8] once in Boston, she worked for seven

Sir Julien Cahn, Chairman of the Birthday Trust between 1930 and 1944, whose idea it was to start the first human milk bank in Britain. (Reproduced courtesy of the Cahn family)

days "in the Milk Laboratories and completely mastered the technical side of it".[9] After her return, Sir Julien organized setting up the Bureau. He purchased from America "the latest type of pumping machine"[10] and the most modern freezing plant; he also donated £1,000 to start the Bureau and a further £1,000 for the first year's expenses.[11] The long-term responsibility for maintaining the Bureau was assumed by the National Birthday Trust Fund, which fully supported of the project. When the Bureau was set up in 1939, the Trust's supplementary food experiments were coming to an end. Both programmes were concerned to assist families who had been disadvantaged by poverty. The babies who were delivered at Queen Charlotte's came from poorer families: there was a charge for the milk, but special arrangements were made in necessitous cases.[12]

The rate of neonatal mortality (that is, death within twenty-eight days of life) in the 1930s was persistently high: it was just over 31 for every 1,000 live births in 1928, and just over 28 in 1938, as shown in figure 7.1. In contrast, the infant mortality rate overall had fallen, from 65 for every 1,000 live births in 1928 to nearly 53 in 1938.[13] Whereas neonatal mortality had formed about one-third of the total infant mortality twenty-five years before, by 1935 it formed one-half, observed G.F. McCleary, formerly Deputy Senior Medical Officer in the Ministry of Health and Principal Medical Officer on the National Health Insurance Commission. Nearly 34½ per cent of the total neonatal deaths, he added, occurred before the end of the first day, while nearly 37 per cent occurred between the first and seventh days.[14] The increasingly high death rate of neonates fed anxiety about the decline in the birth rate in the years leading up to 1939, when war was declared

FIGURE 7.1: NEONATAL AND POSTNEONATAL MORTALITY RATES, ENGLAND AND WALES, 1905–94

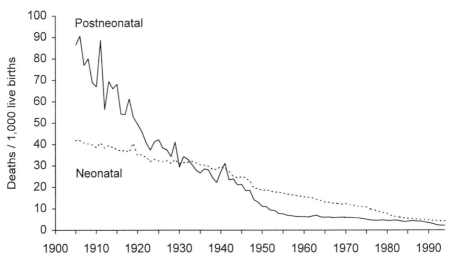

Source: OPCS mortality statistics. Data and graph provided by Alison Macfarlane

(and the Bureau was opened). Donald Paterson remarked in 1938 in a letter to Miss Dare that the need to supply breast milk to "ailing and premature babies on a large scale" was now a matter "of national importance".[15] In December 1939, Lady Rhys Williams expressed a fear that there would be "no gallant twenty-year-olds to stand between England and the horrors of Nazi rule".[16]

Sir Julien had a personal interest in the survival of infants, since he suffered the death of his newly born first child. The woman who became his nurse in the last years of his life recalls that although he later had a daughter and two sons, all of whom thrived, he continued to grieve for his first son.[17] His concern for infant welfare was not limited to the Bureau: he also wanted to meet the needs of delicate babies who were first given EBM but were then fed with ordinary cow's milk. He planned a scheme in which each baby would be kept entirely upon the milk of a single cow during that period. In order to take the scheme a step further, he proposed maintaining a farm to ensure the supply of a particular cow's milk, and hoped to make this a nation-wide scheme once peace had been restored[18] (but he died before the end of the war). Sir Julien was always interested in eccentric projects, comments his former nurse. "To do a milk thing," she explains, "well, that would have interested him because it was unusual. He was on to another person in Manchester about heart disease; you see the Human Milk Bureau wasn't the only scheme."[19]

Lady Rhys Williams assisted Sir Julien in setting up the Bureau, which was splendid, like all Sir Julien's projects. It was housed in palatial quarters in three

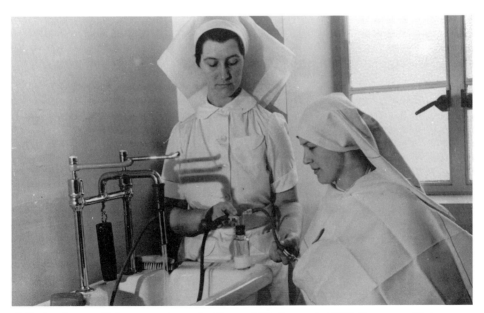

Collecting breast milk from a mother at the Human Milk Bureau in 1939. Strenuous efforts were made to ensure sterile conditions. (Reproduced courtesy of Queen Charlotte's and Chelsea Hospital, Hammersmith Hospitals NHS Trust)

rooms, all floored in blue marble terrazzo with an array of teak and other benching, and the blocks were outlined in gold metal.[20] A tour of inspection of the Bureau was held on 11 July 1939, when Miss Dare showed members of the Birthday Trust around.[21] By that time, it had been open for just over three months, in which "over 10,000 ozs. [of EBM] have been dealt with already, and supplies have been sent to leading Hospitals, and to all parts of the country."[22] Those who took part in the tour included Lady Baldwin, Lady Rhys Williams, the Viscountess Buckmaster, Dame Beatrix Hudson Lyall, Mrs Frances Carver, Dr Alan Moncrieff, Louis Rivett, Miss Edith Dare, Lady Howard de Walden, Dr Haden Guest, Mr and Mrs Sydney Walton, Francis Carver and Leonard Colebrook, who was head of the department of microbiology at Queen Charlotte's, conducting the research that led to the development and testing of Prontosil.

Queen Charlotte's was more closely involved than any other voluntary hospital with the Birthday Trust. Lady Rhys Williams was Honorary Treasurer of its Anaesthetic Fund between 1928 and 1939; Seymour Leslie was Appeal Secretary; and Louis Rivett, who had a consulting appointment at Queen Charlotte's, was one of the authors of the hospital's textbook, *Practice of Obstetrics*. When Lady Rhys Williams started her project to improve the maternity services in the Rhondda Valley, she persuaded the Queen Charlotte's committee of management to loan two district midwives for twelve months as Inspectors of Midwives. The fundraising style of Queen Charlotte's and the Trust were similar in the 1930s: the hospital organized a Persian Ball, with a visiting baby elephant that escaped briefly down a nearby mews, a Rio Ball, and a Le Touquet Ball; while the Trust had a Lace Ball, a British Porcelain Ball, and a Strauss Ball. And like the Birthday Trust, Queen Charlotte's was especially concerned to help poor mothers: in an interview in 1948, Miss Dare commented that, "The main work of Queen Charlotte's Hospital is for mothers, whose home circumstances are such that they must go to hospital for the rest and specialised care they need. I am proud to have been a 'poor person's matron'."[23]

WET NURSING

The collection of human milk for feeding to unrelated babies has a long history. According to Dr John de Louvois, a microbiologist who was responsible for the milk bank at Queen Charlotte's and Chelsea Hospital in the 1980s and early 1990s, "The ancient Egyptians believed that milk from mothers of male infants had curative properties due to the influence of the god Isis and because of this such milk was collected and fed to weak and sickly infants."[24] From the sixteenth century onwards, wet nursing – when a woman is hired to suckle another woman's child – became popular in Europe and was a major source of employment for poor mothers. In the days before the development of infant formula, it not only provided a means of saving babies whose mothers had died in childbirth or had insufficient milk, but also enabled mothers to be away from their baby for any length of time. Also, it was believed that breastfeeding spoilt a woman's figure and that sexual intercourse 'troubled' breast milk and should be avoided during the period of suckling. The use of wet nurses became common practice among the affluent classes: in eighteenth-century England infants frequently lived in the home of their wet nurse until they were old enough to walk and talk.

The development of infant formula in the second half of the nineteenth century was a major factor in the demise of wet nursing.[25] The first patent baby food was introduced in 1867 by Justus von Liebig, a German chemist.[26] Other chemists followed suit and by the early 1870s, the Nestlé Milk Food Company was distributing its product throughout Europe, Australia and the Americas.[27] These commercial baby foods enhanced the safety of bottle-feeding; previously, mothers had diluted and sweetened cow's milk. Poor mothers relied on diluted condensed milk from tins, which was devoid of vitamins A and D and of fats and led to a prevalence of rickets among children to whom it was fed; it also caused diarrhoeal illness because unfinished tins of the milk were quickly contaminated.[28] As the formula preparations became more popular, the number of advertisements in newspapers by wet nurses diminished.[29]

The increasing availability of infant formula was not the only reason for the disappearance of wet nursing. Donald Paterson and J. Forest Smith, paediatric physicians, stated in a text book on infant feeding that, "Wet nursing, where the infant gets the whole of its supply from the foster-mother, is not so popular in this country as it deserves to be, largely owing to a lack of *suitable foster-mothers with care in selection*."[30] This was consistent with current theories about the deterioration of the 'race'. The view that "too many children are born mentally and physically defective" by low wage-earners[31] was consistent with a common belief that poorer mothers were tainted by an intrinsic inferiority. Wet nurses, who were generally poor, would have been regarded by some as capable of transmitting their inferiority to the baby they were suckling. Wet nurses were one kind of domestic servant, a group of workers that was reduced by approximately a quarter following the First World War.

By the Second World War, wet nursing had become unfashionable in Britain. In the 1937 (sixth) and 1939 (seventh) editions of their text book, *Modern Methods of Feeding in Infancy and Childhood*, Paterson and Forest Smith had remarked that, "after a preliminary inquiry into the health of the foster-mother, and the obtaining of a negative Wassermann reaction, this practice [of wet nursing] may at times be the *only method of successfully rearing a weakly infant*."[32] This statement was removed from the eighth and ninth editions of this book, which were published in the 1940s, suggesting that by this time, wet nursing was no longer considered a reasonable option.

One response in the early 1900s to the disappearance of wet nursing was an experiment with infant milk depots, which were based on the Gouttes de Lait in France. These depots sought to provide a humanized milk that was closer to the formula of human breast milk and was sterilized or pasteurized. The project failed, because it was expensive to run and also because there was no effective technology available for killing bacteria without destroying the important constituents of the milk.[33]

Milk banking can be seen as a modern method of wet nursing, albeit "in a rather more disembodied form".[34] Queen Charlotte's had had a long association with wet nurses, so it was fitting that this hospital became the centre for the first milk bank in Britain. In earlier times, the hospital governors had "had the right to present patients; their ladies gave baby linen and sometimes employed discharged mothers as wet nurses."[35] From the mid-1800s until 1913, wet nurses were mentioned in the hospital's annual reports; also, a list was kept of women who had been approved as wet nurses, from which mothers could choose. The wet nurses provided by the hospital had an excellent reputation. In Charles Dickens's novel, *Dombey and Son,* which was first published in the middle of the nineteenth century, Miss Tox is able to find a "plump rosy-cheeked wholesome apple-faced young woman" as a wet nurse for little Paul Dombey (whose mother died immediately after his birth) through the assistance of Queen Charlotte's. Miss Tox mentions the hospital by name:

> I posted off myself to the Queen Charlotte's Royal Married Females [that is, Queen Charlotte's Hospital] . . . and put the question, Was there anybody there that they thought would suit? No, they said there was not. When they gave me that answer, I do assure you, my dear, I was almost driven to despair on your account. But it did so happen, that one of the Royal Married Females, hearing the inquiry, reminded the matron of another who had gone to her own home, and who, she said, would in all likelihood be most satisfactory. The moment I heard this, and had it corroborated by the matron – excellent references and unimpeachable character – I got the address, my dear, and posted off again.[36]

The Advantages of EBM

Wet nursing can only meet the needs of full-term babies, since the sucking and swallowing reflex, which is necessary for suckling, is not usually fully developed until between thirty-four and thirty-six weeks of gestation.[37] EBM has an immense advantage over wet nursing, because it can be fed to premature as well as full-term babies. Today, it is largely reserved for premature infants; 'term' babies are given it only in exceptional circumstances, such as those that develop following gut surgery. In the early years of the Bureau also, it was used to save the lives of premature babies. During the tour of inspection of the Bureau in July 1939, Dr Moncrieff and Mr Rivett each gave a short speech in which they stressed the point "that the scheme was to save life. Half of these could be saved if properly treated and supplied with human milk, especially Prematures."[38] The lives of many tiny infants were saved: "Only today," Miss Dare told the Annual General Meeting of the National Birthday Trust Fund in 1942, "we have a baby that weighted 3 lbs at birth perfectly healthy, beautifully formed, that is being fed on this milk. We have just finished supplying a tiny baby at Muswell Hill, this baby was followed for about two months daily after she left Hospital."[39]

In the early years, however, full-term and normal-sized babies were also fed EBM. Press coverage of the Bureau in 1939 showed photographs of nurses delivering milk to the homes of babies, which meant they had not been kept in hospital.[40] Since infant formula was now available, EBM was not strictly necessary for full-term babies. However, formulae had not yet been humanized to the degree achieved later, and the baby food companies were not accurate in their claims that formula was suitable for babies who were small and weak.[41] The Cow & Gate company went so far in one advertisement as strongly to suggest – without actually saying so – that the St Neot's Quads survived only because they were given Cow & Gate Milk Food:

> The case is almost a miracle . . .
>
> Never before – anywhere – have Quadruplets survived *when three of them were boys* [sic].
>
> An additional complication was that the babies were premature and were far less than normal birth weight – in fact Michael only weighted 2-lbs, 13-ozs.
>
> *Those in charge of this appallingly difficult case knew that the Quads' only hope of survival was to put them on Cow & Gate* [emphasis added].
>
> There could be no more convincing evidence that Cow & Gate is the most wonderful food in the world for all babies when natural feeding fails.[42]

But in fact, the quadruplets had been fed EBM, not Cow & Gate, in the first difficult months; over six weeks after the birth, the *St Neot's Advertiser* reported that their doctor was still "very anxious to secure offers of help in fetching [human] milk."[43] Even if they were fed infant formula later on, their survival in the critical early period was due to expressed breast milk.

Other candidates for EBM included orphans and those babies whose mothers had insufficient milk to feed their babies. This problem was often associated with poverty: one of the women who wrote a letter for *Maternity* (1915) said that having been "left six hours without a bite of food, the fire out and no light, the time January, and snow had lain on the ground two weeks . . . I lost my milk and ultimately lost my baby." Another woman stated, "Nearly all the young married women cannot give breast milk. . . . No, I think because they work so hard before, do not get enough rest, therefore have no milk. And, then, some will not begin with their own milk, because they know they have to go out to work." Some women were prevented from breastfeeding by physical difficulties. One of the mothers who contributed to *Maternity* said that with her fifth baby, she "had a very long illness through the doctor hurrying the birth, instead of giving nature a chance, and he was rough in handling me. Now, the result was a three months' illness, and my baby had to be brought up by bottle." Another woman said that when she looked back to "that first three years of my married life, I wonder how I lived through it. I was weak and ill, could not suckle my second baby." Yet another remembered having "a gathered [that is, septic or inflamed] breast. The doctor lanced it, and it ran for fourteen weeks after."[44]

The Operation of the Human Milk Bureau

The women who donated their breast milk to the Milk Bureau, many of whom had been patients at Queen Charlotte's, were from the poorer classes, like the wet nurses of previous times. From the very start, it was understood that they "would, of course, be paid for it". Payment was 2*d* for 1 oz of milk. "Not only does the provision of this milk save the lives of fragile babies," noted the Birthday Trust, "but the mothers who give it, themselves benefit. The extra money saves them going out to work, or provides them with extra nourishment, to the improvement of their own health and the progress of their babies."[45] Mothers could earn anything from 10*s* to £1 a week (£1 was paid for a total of 4 litres of milk),[46] and Lady Rhys Williams warned that "care would have to be taken to guard against mothers denying their own babies in order to make money."[47] Given the extreme poverty of many families and the incentive of earning each week a sum that is equivalent in value at the end of the century to £34, it is possible that some women sold more breast milk than was good for their health. Gillian Weaver, the current Coordinator of the Milk Bank at Queen Charlotte's (now part of the Hammersmith Hospitals NHS Trust), has observed that women whose diet is poor or borderline would find their nutritional status undermined by donating breast milk. Current advice from the Department of Health is that lactating women have additional food requirements, including 450–570 extra calories and 11 gm of protein; these are higher if a woman is fully breastfeeding her baby and also donating some EBM to a milk bank.[48]

A variety of tests were conducted in order to detect any possible dilution of the donated EBM with cow's milk or with tap water.[49] The suspicion that some women might try deviously to increase the volume of their milk, suggests a spirit of distrust between the donors and the hospital, which has entirely disappeared. Today, most mothers expressing their milk for the bank are doing this to feed their own baby, who cannot be directly fed for some medical reason. In those cases where women donate their milk for other mothers' babies, payment has been replaced by good will. "They don't get paid at all. I send them a thank you letter when they stop and that's it," states Gillian Weaver. "In fact," she adds, "often they're out of pocket if they offer to deliver the milk."[50]

In the Bureau's early years, the names of mothers who had more milk than they needed for their own babies were sent from the wards of Queen Charlotte's to the Bureau; nursing mothers were also recommended by the Medical Officers of the West London boroughs. Any disinterest on the part of the mother is likely to have evaporated in front of Miss Dare, who was "very persuasive".[51] Mothers were only selected, though, if they had a high standard of health and had carried their babies to full term. Some women could supply the clinics with as many as fifteen or sixteen pints of milk a week, especially in the early stages of breastfeeding.[52] The mother and her child were seen every day and records of the weight and progress of the child, as well as the amount of milk donated by the mother, were kept at the Bureau. If the child was not making proper progress, the milk was not accepted. Once a mother's milk had been tested, she was supplied with the necessary equipment of a simple water pump, towels, bottles and a container of dry ice in which the bottles of milk were kept for collection. These bottles were collected each morning from her home and a fresh sterilized bottle was left. Once brought to the Bureau, the milk was "tested for fat content, dirt and bacteria, and possible adulteration."[53]

The method of processing the milk was perceived as very modern and was given coverage in a full page, with illustrations, by the *Daily Herald* on 1 March 1939, the day of the Bureau's opening. The milk was treated at 65 degrees for one hour in order to render it safe, even though cows' milk at this time was heated for only thirty minutes at 62.5 degrees. At the end of the day, unused milk was frozen into small cakes, about the size of a half-crown. Sir Julien's nurse remembers that "they had to be collected very quickly, you know, refrigerated; it wasn't easy in those days like it is today to do this sort of thing." She adds, "they looked just like peppermint creams . . . I used to like peppermint creams until I saw these."[54] The Bureau was open all day and night and was ready to deliver the milk to any part of the British Isles at the shortest notice. Railways carried the milk at special rates.[55]

By June 1939, Sir Julien was able to report to a meeting of the National Birthday Trust Fund Executive Committee that the Bureau was rapidly becoming an institution "of national importance".[56] In the same month, in an interview with the *Daily Express*, Miss Dare estimated that in the first three months of the Bureau's existence, several hundreds of babies' lives had been saved.[57] The Trust decided in June 1939 to set up a special Sub-Committee for the Bureau in conjunction with Queen Charlotte's Hospital. Sir Julien agreed to serve, with Mr Rivett acting as representative of the Fund. Two doctors were appointed by Queen Charlotte's and Sir William Jowitt agreed to be the Chairman; the first meeting was held on the afternoon of 27 June 1939.[58] Sir Jowitt continued to chair the committee until the Bureau was taken over by the state in the early 1950s.

The Bureau closed briefly during the Blitz, chiefly because mothers were evacuated from the district. At a meeting of the Trust's Executive Committee on

These frozen tablets of expressed breast milk, weighing one-third of an ounce, have been described as looking like peppermint creams. (Reproduced courtesy of Queen Charlotte's and Chelsea Hospital, Hammersmith Hospitals NHS Trust)

17 October, there was general dismay at this closure. After all, argued Mr Rivett, the work of Queen Charlotte's had largely been resumed, even in its district work, and many of the London hospitals were also engaging in fuller activities.[59] By April 1940, Sir Julien was happy to report that the work of the Bureau had been resumed.[60]

The Bureau was highly valued in the years of war: the Minister of Health, Ernest Brown, was very interested to hear from Sir Julien in 1942 (over lunch in a private room at Claridge's) that milk banking had been shown in the USA greatly to reduce infant mortality.[61] Sir Julien impressed upon the Minister the need to undertake research into methods of preserving breast milk, so as to make it available on a wider scale.[62] The Minister brought the question of milk banking before the Advisory Committee on Mothers and Young Children, which included in its final report of 1943 an addendum by Arnold Walker on the matter of EBM. Walker argued that for a small number of infants, EBM was life-saving, especially for premature babies and for young infants following surgical operations (for example, for pyloric stenosis), or with diarrhoea or vomiting; he added, however, that he did not have any statistics to support this opinion.[63] After this, the CMO proposed to Mellanby that the MRC carry out an investigation into methods of storing EBM,[64] and a Conference on the Drying of Human Milk was held at the London School of Hygiene and Tropical

Medicine on 22 July 1943. Throughout all these discussions between scientists, though, no mention was made at any time of the role of Sir Julien Cahn and the Birthday Trust in the creation and the running of the milk bank that was so admired.

Despite this interest from the scientific community, the difficulty in wartime of obtaining equipment and the shortage of steel[65] meant that Queen Charlotte's continued to be the only hospital collecting and distributing human milk throughout the Second World War. The *Daily Mirror* reported on 30 April 1940 that "within three minutes of the broadcasting of an SOS and urgently calling for human milk for a sick baby [which was 2 lb 6 oz at birth] at Slough, Bucks, emergency hospital yesterday, a consignment was on its way by car from the bureau." In 1938, Donald Paterson had told Miss Dare that "we are instituting a scheme for freezing the breast milk and storing it at Great Ormond Street, but of course only on a small scale",[66] but in the end the hospital at Great Ormond Street decided instead to obtain supplies from Queen Charlotte's. In 1942, Miss Dare said that the Bureau was supplying about twenty-five hospitals, several of them London County Council Hospitals.[67] In the early 1940s, Miss Riddick suggested to Sir Julien a scheme whereby all the big provincial hospitals with districts would be encouraged to start a human milk bureau of their own, with Queen Charlotte's Bureau as a training centre.[68] Sir Julien was delighted with this plan,[69] but Mr Rivett pointed out the difficulty of the expense and also the risk of bombing, since suitable hospitals would be in the large cities; he proposed waiting for "happier times".[70]

JOINING THE NHS

Happier times finally arrived with the declaration of peace in 1945. The creation of the NHS shortly afterwards meant that it was the responsibility of the state to set up and run milk banks. Accordingly, the government indicated its wish to pay for the development of bureaux in the provinces. The Public Health Department of Cardiff told the Ministry of Health that it hoped to be the first centre outside London to set up a milk bank like "the one which has been such a success at Queen Charlotte's Hospital". It added, "intrigues are going on by other Medical Officers to try and get ahead of Cardiff in the establishment of one of these Human Milk Bureaux."[71] The Cardiff milk bank was opened in 1948; banks were also opened in Birmingham and Bristol in 1950, and in Leicester and Liverpool a little later.

Although there was no longer a role for the Trust in setting up milk banks, it continued for a while to run the Bureau at Queen Charlotte's, which shared its expertise with those who wished to learn about milk banking. The Trust's Annual Report for 1945–7 reported that various Local Authorities sent personnel to Queen Charlotte's Hospital for training by Miss Dare.[72] In 1951, 80,000 oz of milk passed through the milk bank, and milk was still being collected by midwives from mothers in their own homes at a payment of twopence per ounce.[73] At this time, the Bureau – which in 1945 had been "self-supporting for some time"[74] – had a debt of between £500–£1,000. This was eliminated when the charge to the consumer was raised from seven pence to nine pence per ounce, but the Trust's Executive Committee was "seriously perturbed to think that the National Birthday Trust Fund may be asked to contribute in the future to the finances of the Milk Bureau."[75] This seemed especially unreasonable when all the other milk banks in the country were funded and run by the state.

The Trust therefore transferred the responsibility of the Bureau to the NHS.[76] This transfer was consistent with the shedding by the Birthday Trust of other philanthropic endeavours, such as the Samaritan Fund, during the early postwar period. The health needs of infants were now the responsibility of the National Health Service. In 1952, the Trust indicated that it would willingly waive its claim to any assets, so long as it was not responsible for any further expenses. In June 1953, a new Deed was executed, as a result of which there was no further responsibility on the part of the Birthday Trust for the affairs of the Human Milk Bureau.[77]

THE FUTURE OF MILK BANKS

Milk banks went into a brief decline after 1950 and in the 1960s, many milk banks closed down: "With the increasing refinement of artificial feeds prepared from cows' milk, the appreciation of the value of human milk became temporarily under-rated."[78] In 1973, there were five large milk banks in Britain: at Queen Charlotte's Hospital in London, St David's Hospital in Cardiff, Sorrento Hospital in Birmingham, Southmead Hospital in Bristol, and the Royal Alexandra Hospital in Brighton.[79] Then, at the end of the 1970s, there was a renaissance of interest in the value of human milk and a Working Party on Human Milk Banks was set up in 1979 by the Committee on Medical Aspects of Food Policy. The terms of reference of this committee were "to advise about setting up Human Milk Banks and to make recommendations", and it produced a report in 1981 entitled *The Collection and Storage of Human Milk*.

Modern thinking has supported the idea that breast milk is the optimum food for infants, particularly in the first week after birth. Gillian Weaver explains that breast milk is best for premature infants, because "it's easier for the babies to tolerate breast milk, so they're more likely to get onto full feeds quicker with this, than if they start on formula. So breast milk is the ideal introduction to enteral feeds. And babies that have had gut surgery are often given breast milk as a reintroduction to enteral feeds."[80] There is clear evidence from controlled, prospective studies that human milk, even when it has been pasteurized, significantly reduces the incidence of infection in low birth weight infants at risk. A randomized study showed that low birth weight babies were six times more likely to develop necrotizing enterocolitis if they were not fed with breast milk.[81] Research findings pointing to the "beneficial effect of human milk on neuro-development" have also been produced,[82] but these are still inconclusive. According to the 1981 government report of the Working Party on Human Milk Banks, "research has emphasized the unique nutritional and protective qualities of both human colostrum and milk."[83]

A setback for milk banks was the spread of AIDS, since the HIV virus can be transmitted through breast milk. On 4 July 1989, the Department of Health issued guidelines to prevent the spread of the disease through milk banks and many banks were forced by the complexity of these requirements to close down. The National Childbirth Trust (NCT) reported that whereas in 1986, it knew of seventy active milk banks, in 1991 it knew of "only a handful which are still operating".[84] However, following a revival of interest in the special benefits of human milk for feeding sick and newborn infants, demands were made at a symposium on milk banking at the Sorrento Maternity Hospital in early 1993 for new national guidelines. These were produced in 1994 by an ad hoc Working Party[85] and have led to a doubling of milk banks between 1994 and 1996, from six to twelve. One of these is the milk bank at Queen Charlotte's. It is no longer housed in the splendid rooms provided by Sir Julien, but in a small prefabricated building. The only reminder of the early years is the name – Edith Dare – of an adjacent building.

CHAPTER EIGHT

War and the Welfare State

The Birthday Trust was largely inactive during the war.[1] "Yes, the N.B.T.F. still functions," wrote Miss Riddick, "but it is a less 'public' existence these days."[2] Few meetings were held and Sir Julien complained in 1943 that they were "very dull these days – no cakes, no tea and no scandal!"[3] The Midwives' Institute and the Queen's Institute moved briefly to the country in 1939–40 to avoid bombing raids, but the Birthday Trust kept the midwifery headquarters open throughout the war. On two occasions, time bombs had to be removed, but most damage from enemy action was limited to windows and ceilings. The private ledgers of the Trust were destroyed when the accountant's offices were struck in a fire raid on London in December 1939, so documents held by the Trust were sent for the duration of the war to Miskin Manor, Lady Rhys Williams's home in South Wales.

Miss Riddick had to organize the Fire Guard Rota and the conversion of two cellars under the pavement into air raid shelters. Everything required paperwork, especially obtaining rations: even the reduction of the soap allowance by one seventh generated a sheaf of correspondence.[4] The City of Westminster Food Office sent the news that, "Notwithstanding the fact that you are in possession of a form EA2/SA2 authorising you to obtain specified quantities of TEA/SUGAR, I would inform you that your weekly usage of the following foods as from 15/9/46 should not exceed . . . Tea . . . 2 ozs."[5] War brought extra expenses, like the darkening of windows and the boarding up of rooms. The interest from the Capital Fund soon proved inadequate to maintain the headquarters, so the Trust obtained permission from its solicitors to use some of the capital for this purpose.[6] Miss Riddick helped to cut expenses by working for half her usual salary.[7]

Daily life was grim. "We have had a very troublesome time in Croydon lately," wrote Miss Riddick, "with two land mines and several bombs. My own flat is rather a wreck and I had to spend one week with an arm in a sling."[8] Mrs Chudley was made so nervous by the bombing raids that in 1943, her doctor advised her to leave the city; Mr and Mrs Price then took over the running of the building. Many members of the Trust suffered personal tragedies during the war. Lady Rhys Williams suffered the loss in 1943 of her eldest son, Glyn, who was killed in battle in Tunisia. She herself made a substantial contribution to the war effort: having left the Women's Auxiliary Air Force (WAAF) because of bad bronchitis, she became Commandant of the Miskin Convalescent Hospital at her home, Miskin Manor.

During bombing raids, tin hats provided some protection to nurses and midwives during the Second World War. (Reproduced courtesy of the Queen's Nursing Institute)

Miss Riddick was not called up to do war work because her work for the Trust was regarded as essential. Midwifery was treated as a high priority by the government. Under the Emergency Medical Services, maternity homes were set up in the countryside, where they were less likely to be bombed. Many urban women were reluctant to leave their homes, however. A retired midwife recalls that in 1940, she was moved from South London to Lord Rothschild's country home at Tring, where carloads of expectant mothers were brought from London every week. Once they had had their babies, they were desperate to return home – "They used to say, 'We cannot stand this 'orrible 'ush. Somebody rattle a tin can or something!' Homing instinct. They couldn't stand the country."[9]

The Birthday Trust was determined to survive the difficulties of war. It rejected all requests for funds, explaining that, "The tendency at the moment is rather to conserve all funds as much as possible for use after the War."[10] When Lady Buckmaster pleaded with her fellow members of the Trust to help the women and children suffering in occupied Europe, she was told that "what funds we have are spent upon maternity work in this country".[11] This was an unusually parochial outlook at this time. Miss Edith Pye, President of the Midwives' Institute, was involved in helping children affected by the Spanish Civil War and was Honorary Secretary of the Famine Relief Committee, while Eleanor Rathbone took a leading role in efforts to rescue Jews from Hitler's Europe and to assist refugees.

END OF AN ERA

The Birthday Trust emerged intact from the Second World War and ready to start work again. However, it found itself in a new and less favourable situation, because it was no longer closely linked to the government of the day. The Labour Party swept to power in 1945, which brought the Trust tumbling down from the privileged position it had enjoyed between the wars. This was Labour's first clear majority in the Commons, enabling it firmly to shoulder aside the influence of wealth and privilege. The Prime Minister still spoke at dinners to support his wife's favourite charity, but the wife was Violet Attlee and the charity was the Save the Children Fund.[12] Many of the Labour Cabinet came from the ranks of the working class. Aneurin Bevan, Minister of Health, for example, was an ex-miner from the Tredegar region of South Wales, which had sent several 'deserving' women to the Trust's grand fundraising event at London's Guildhall in 1939. Now, just six years later, Bevan himself was in London, sent by the British electorate.

But in any case, the generation that had run the affairs of British society between the wars was no longer so vigorous – in 1946, Lady Londonderry turned sixty-seven, and Eleanor Rathbone died. Edith Summerskill, a Labour MP since 1938, was keenly aware of this shift: during a Commons debate in 1949, she retorted to an up and coming MP: "Do not teach your grandmother

Aneurin Bevan, Minister of Health, visits a maternity patient in South Wales, shortly after the start of the National Health Service on 5 July 1948. (Reproduced courtesy of Geoffrey Chamberlain)

how to suck eggs."[13] The closing of the era was clearly in evidence on the Birthday Trust. Baron Melchett had died in 1930, Viscount Snowden in 1937, Sir Alfred Pease in 1939, Sir Julien Cahn in 1944, Lady Baldwin and Margaret Balfour in 1945, and Lord Plender and Sir Comyns Berkeley in 1946. The medical experts who had played a key role in the 1930s work of the Trust had also died: John Shields Fairbairn in 1944, Thomas Watts Eden in 1946, and Louis Carnac Rivett in 1947. There were also a number of resignations from the committee by those who felt they no longer had sufficient energy for the work, like Lady Dawson, the Hon. Mrs Merry of Belladrum, Dame Beatrix Hudson Lyall and Lady Dalrymple-Champneys; Miss Dare retired as Matron of Queen Charlotte's in 1948. The Earl of Athlone left Britain in 1940 to take up the position of Governor-General of Canada. Some members did not actually leave the Trust but were less involved than they had been before the war: this was the case with Lady Cynthia Colville, for example, who stayed in the Trust until 1965.

The list of committee members after the war was still liberally sprinkled with titles, but these signs of nobility had become much less valuable. In 1959, when Lord Strathcona died, he was the first holder of the Strathcona and Mount Royal Barony to leave a legacy of less than a million pounds; he himself had inherited about five million pounds in 1914. After the Second World War, commented the novelist C.P. Snow, "the aristocrats, as they lost their power and turned into ornaments, shut themselves up."[14] In 1959, Lady Londonderry held her 80th birthday party at Londonderry House, which was attended by Harold Macmillan (the seventh prime minister to be a close friend), but this was a rare reminder of her lavish entertaining before the war. The Londonderrys had fallen on harder times: when a music concert was held at Londonderry House in 1955 to raise funds for the Trust and the Queen's Institute, a fee was charged for the use of the house. Coffee and light refreshments, an announcer and a "woman for the ladies cloakroom" cost extra.[15]

Not only was the Trust faced with removal from the centre of power after the war, but it also had to redefine its mission. The risk of maternal death, which had been the reason for its foundation, had fallen dramatically, so that in 1948 the rate was less than 1 for every 1,000 births, compared with over 4 in 1928, the year of the Birthday Fund's creation.[16] Furthermore, the state had now assumed responsibility for the welfare and health care of every citizen: the introduction of the NHS and the Family Allowance at last removed the need for charity (at least in theory).

It was imperative for the Trust to adjust to these new realities, if it was going to survive. One important step was the development of a new style of operation. It downplayed its ties with the Conservative Party (which became looser, in any case, after Lady Baldwin's death in 1945) and built new alliances with medical organizations. This wider base of support gave power to its role as 'outsider' and proved useful in its efforts to help shape maternity provision in the new NHS. It also reflected a shift in the nation as a whole: the power of the aristocracy was being rapidly usurped by the new professional elite.

The Trust channelled its energies and funds into research, which remained the focus of Trust work until the 1990s. Its research was no longer directed at poor mothers, but at all mothers. Also, the earlier narrow focus on maternity gradually expanded to a broader approach to reproduction that included babies. Mrs Baldwin's pre-war broadcast appeals from Chequers had talked of mothers and their material needs. But when a scientist in the Trust tried to raise funds over BBC airwaves in 1955, he spoke only of research and he referred to babies as well as mothers: the work of the Trust, he said, was to "undertake investigations and medical and statistical research – under the supervision of a medical committee – into problems affecting the health and welfare of expectant mothers and newly born children."[17]

In the early postwar period, the NBTF maintained the political identity that had underpinned its character between the wars. The former Conservative MP, Henry U. Willink, who had been Minister of Health in the Coalition government of 1943–5 and had published the 1944 White Paper on the NHS shortly after he became Minister in late 1943, told Miss Riddick, "Your Executive has realised *how fully in sympathy with your point of view the Conservative Party is.*"[18] The Trust's ties with the Conservative Party were probably responsible for the Labour government's decision not to invite any members of the Trust or the former Joint Council of Midwifery to join the Working Party on the Recruitment and Training of Midwives, which was set up in 1947 to enquire into the current shortage of midwives. This was a striking omission, since the JCM had produced a report in 1939 warning of a future shortage.

The Trust was not deterred from trying to influence policy, however, and in October 1947 set up an Evidence Sub-Committee to obtain evidence to supply to the enquiry. The committee consisted of Lady Rhys Williams, Miss G.B. Carter, Miss Josephine Barnes and Lady Dawson and was chaired by Charles Read, a consultant who was the first of several Trust members to become President of the RCOG.[19] The Trust's evidence had little impact. It was referred to only once, and only briefly, in the Working Party's report, which briskly informed the Trust (and also the RCOG) that they were not the proper organizations to conduct research into pain relief for childbirth. "Without belittling the valuable work of the Royal College and the National Birthday Trust," it observed, "we suggest that there is only one body in the country with the necessary experience in urgent operational applied research and sufficient resources to deal with the matter and that is the Medical Research Council."[20] In other words, it was the job of government, not the voluntary sector.

On 25 August 1953, a cocktail party was held to celebrate the Birthday Trust's twenty-fifth anniversary. A quiet occasion, with none of the lavish splendour of the interwar events, it effectively said farewell to that earlier period. Lord Strathcona paid tribute to Lady Baldwin and received much applause when he observed that, "Historians will one day record that greater services to the poor people in this country was done in this lifetime by Lady Baldwin." He

In memory of Lady Baldwin, Lord Strathcona unveils a photograph of her portrait at a cocktail party to celebrate the Birthday Trust's 25th anniversary, on 12 November 1953. (Reproduced courtesy of the Wellcome Institute Library, London)

Lady Rhys Williams in the early postwar period, when she became sole leader of the Birthday Trust. (Reproduced courtesy of Lady Susan Glyn)

then unveiled a photograph of Lady Baldwin's portrait by de Laszlo, which Sir Julien had given to her in 1937.[21] Following the deaths of Lady Baldwin and Sir Julien, there was a major change in the leadership of the Trust. Louis Nicholas became Chairman in 1944, but when he was forced to resign by ill health he was replaced in 1947 by Mr Espley, who was already a member of the Board of Management and the Finance Committee of Queen Charlotte's Hospital and was on the Joint Committee of Chelsea Women's Hospital and Queen Charlotte's. Lady Rhys Williams joined William Penman as a Deputy Chairman in 1950. She assumed more and more responsibility for the Trust's policy and work after the war and by the early 1950s she was regarded by all members as its sole leader.

A PRIVATE MEMBER'S BILL

The Trust became involved in the late 1940s in a Private Member's Bill for Analgesia in Childbirth, which aimed to make analgesia in labour a statutory right. The Bill was introduced to the House of Commons on 28 January 1949 by Peter Thorneycroft MP (who later became Chancellor of the Exchequer under Macmillan) and was seconded by the socialist, Mrs Manning. The Trust publicly supported the Bill and held a Press Tea to support the work.[22] The Bill produced a furore. At the Second Reading on 4 March,[23] Mr Thorneycroft said that although the Bill was supported by Conservatives, Liberals and Socialists, it was being treated as a party measure and that Bevan planned to kill it. In the ensuing discussion, Labour MPs accused Thorneycroft of party politics and said the Bill was unnecessary, since its contents were covered by the NHS; Conservative MPs said that the legislation for providing analgesia in childbirth was simply permissive, and ought to be made into a duty. Bevan was not sitting in the House during this discussion, but made a statement on the subject on 15 March,[24] insisting that the government was doing everything within its power to provide women with pain relief. When Thorneycroft took him to task on this, Bevan became angry and accused him of exploiting "human pain as a political stunt". One paper reported that the Bill "roused a number of storms in the House of Commons"[25] and the *Sketch* produced the following verse:

Getting Aneurin Bevan
Into Heaven
Won't be any easier
Even with analgesia.[26]

Several files at the Public Record Office are brimming with letters to Bevan, begging him to advance the passage of Thorneycroft's Bill, from individuals and such organizations as the Midland Federation of Housewives, the Cheshire Federation of Women's Institutes, Matrons of Nursery Schools, the Union of Catholic Mothers, and the Women's Section of Islington Borough Communist Party. A telegram from Streatham Hill in South London urged him, "Appeal your personal intervention save Analgesia Bill stop Pain more important than any policy."[27]

Bevan had good reason to assume that Thorneycroft was using the Bill to undermine the government, since he had attacked his health policy on a number of occasions.[28] Also, the presentation of a Private Member's Bill was in sharp contrast with the policy of Labour MPs, who had been "instructed to avoid private members' bills, to keep quiet and vote the government's legislation through".[29] But in any case, the Bill was certain to stir up hostility against the government from women, since it implicitly suggested that the Ministry of Health was not committed to the provision of analgesia for childbirth. The Labour MP, Dr Haden Guest, who was a member of the Birthday Trust, was suspicious of Thorneycroft's motives. He told the press that he supported the Bill in principle, but that it had become infected with political prejudice. The Bill would have been carried through the House without any trouble, he said, if it had been conducted in the way in which "a non-controversial measure ought to be conducted, on a level of professional understanding and common sense and with an honest desire to benefit people in this country without seeking any party advantage."[30] In any case, it would have been impossible for Bevan in the early years of the NHS to ensure that all women were offered analgesia.

Bevan may also have been suspicious of the analgesia campaign's close links with the Trust and, consequently, with the Conservative Party. This association was highlighted during the Commons debate, when frequent references were made to the pioneering work of Lady Baldwin. The very strength of the Trust in the 1930s, therefore, became a weakness and disadvantage in the postwar world of politics.

Now that the Bill had become "a political matter", said Miss Farrer, General Secretary of the National Federation of Women's Institutes, the large women's organizations would no longer press for it, since they had to maintain a strictly non-party policy. The Executive Committee of the Trust was worried about Mr Bevan's charges that attempts to press for the relief of pain in childbirth were a "political stunt",[31] because they feared that Labour MPs who had supported the Bill would withdraw their names out of party loyalty. But in fact, only two names were withdrawn and three more were added.

Dr Haden Guest and some other Labour MPs then proposed additional clauses to the NHS (Amendment) Bill, which would strengthen legislation covering pain relief in labour.[32] This was evidently prearranged by Bevan: a letter from him to Herbert Morrison refers to "tactics we might pursue in order to frustrate the Analgesia Bill". The best strategy, he thought, would be to arrange for "one of our own side" to put down an amendment to the National Health Service (Amendment) Bill as soon as it was published. This would remove any doubts that may have been created by Thorneycroft's propaganda, about the power of the Minister of Health to impose a duty on Local Authorities to provide analgesia.[33] At the second reading of this Bill, Thorneycroft told Bevan that he would be willing to withdraw his Private Member's Bill, so long as the new clause was accepted. The Minister declined the offer, on the grounds that the amendment had yet to be considered in committee.[34] However, he had already managed to defuse the power of the Private Bill and was seeking to assure the public that his Ministry was working hard to deliver pain relief for labour under the NHS,[35] and had already succeeded in increasing its availability. [36]

Thorneycroft's Bill finally died when it was defeated on its third reading in the House of Commons by 108 votes to 44, five months after its introduction.[37] The Bill was beneficial to the analgesia campaign, since it generated so much publicity in the press while it was passing through its various stages,[38] but it may have damaged Bevan's reputation in the eyes of some of the female electorate. One woman who described herself as a socialist warned Bevan of "the perfect chance it will give the Tories to get at millions of women if you do not pass the Bill. Absolutely millions of them who are too busy to take an interest in politics . . . will certainly not remain indifferent over a bill like this. It is bad enough that the thing has been put forward by a Tory. . . . We cannot afford not to pass the Bill, everything will count now."[39] Another Labour supporter warned that, "the indifference to the suffering of about half the electorate may seriously prejudice many voters against the Labour Party."[40] It is unlikely that Thorneycroft's Bill played much of a role in Labour's imminent loss of power, given the concatenation of events that led to the reduction in Labour's majority in 1950 and the end of Attlee's government in 1951. However, it did nothing to enhance its image.

FROM POOR WOMEN TO ALL WOMEN

By the end of the Second World War, there was massive, nationwide enthusiasm for the principles of the Beveridge Report of 1942, which recommended a high level of employment, family allowances, and a unified and universal system of social insurance that was underpinned by a national health service. "Support for Beveridge spread like forest fire," comments the historian Charles Webster, observing that "More than a quarter of a million copies of the full report were sold, and in many popular versions the 'Beveridge Plan' became known to all sections of the community, including the armed forces. Beveridge became the touchstone for a new social order . . ."[41] When the Labour Party was elected to implement the Beveridge proposals, many expected to see an end of Want, Disease, Ignorance, Squalor and Idleness, the five Giant Evils identified by Beveridge that divided the nation into rich and poor. Already, the war had forced women and men of different classes to mix together in a way that was unprecedented. Rationing helped to level the social classes further, by reducing differences between the expenditure of poor and prosperous families. Other changes, too, built bridges between the classes. The war produced a set of social services that responded to need, and milk and other nutrients were distributed by the state to expectant and nursing mothers and children. "No longer was it argued (as it often was before the war)," observed Titmuss, "that the condition of the people did not warrant such measures . . . It was the universal character of these welfare policies which ensured their acceptance and success. They were free of social discrimination and the indignities of the poor law."[42]

In keeping with these social developments, the Trust adopted a more democratic approach to its activities. At the beginning of the Second World War, the target group of the National Birthday Trust Fund was still women who were poor, just as it had been throughout the 1930s. But by the end of the war, the Trust referred in more general terms to the needs of "The Mothers of Britain".[43] In 1948, less than ten years after the Guildhall Reception that had made a clear distinction between rich and poor, it endorsed a resolution that there should be health care "for *all women*, which is equal to the best available to any".[44] In the same year, it took a major role in hosting a meeting on Safer Motherhood, which was directed at the public as a whole and not simply a handful of those who were rich and powerful. All tickets were free and the day's proceedings were broadcast on 9 June 1948 on 'Women's Hour' on the Light Programme (between items on 'First Aid' and 'What About Your Husband's Clothes?').

The Safer Motherhood event was also a watershed in the history of the Trust because it was the product of a collaboration with other organizations; these were the Married Women's Association, which was chaired by Lady Helen Nutting (who also belonged to the Trust) and which sought to improve the financial and legal status of the housewife, and the National Federation of Women's Institutes. Previously, the Trust had kept at a distance from other groups interested in women's health and welfare. Now that it no longer enjoyed the patronage of the ruling government, however, it needed to create other alliances. This wider base of support gave power to its new role as 'outsider' and strengthened its power to help shape maternity provision in the NHS.

In 1947, the Trust was pleased to hear that Miss Farrer of the NFWI would be willing to join the Executive Committee.[45] Also, Miss G.B. Carter took the view that, "It might be a good thing to get into direct touch with the PEP [Political and Economic Planning] Mothers and Children Group since they are obviously doing a lot of work in our province and overlapping would be a pity."[46] This interest in extending the Trust network did not stretch to the working classes, however: PEP, which described itself as "a voluntary association of people who are interested in the objective study of the economic and social problems which confront us . . . [and] includes people of all political parties and of none",[47] was an organization of highly educated intellectuals; and the NFWI had a largely middle-class leadership. At no time did the Trust invite on to any of its committees members of the Women's Cooperative Guild, all of whom were working class.

Political differences sometimes rippled to the surface of collaborations between the Birthday Trust and its chosen allies. Lady Rhys Williams was anxious to present its involvement with the Married Women's Association (MWA) and the NFWI as a firm partnership in the cause of Safer Motherhood, claiming, "we might well describe ourselves as a Combined Operations movement". None the less, she firmly disassociated the Trust from certain aspects of the Married Women's Association. During discussions about headed notepaper for the campaign, she instructed Miss Riddick to delay printing notepaper with the name of the Married Women's Association, "as there is a little trouble with the Assocn. over a communistic resolution, and Lady Helen and Lady W may resign; on the other hand they do not think the resolution will stand, as Dr Summerskill is not likely to pass it, being [that is, the resolution] against the Gvt. [sic]."[48] Nor did the choice of Dr Charles Hill as Question Master for the Safer Motherhood Brains Trust event (see page 175) reflect a neutral political position. On the one hand, he was an obvious choice because he was the popular 'Radio Doctor' on the BBC, dispensing homely advice.

But on the other hand, he was leading the BMA (of which he was Secretary) in its confrontation with Bevan, which at times became unpleasantly personal. Hill became a Conservative MP and Parliamentary Secretary in the Ministry of Food under Churchill's administration.

THE BIRTHDAY TRUST AND THE NHS

The Trust appears to have welcomed government acceptance of Beveridge's recommendation for a "comprehensive health service for everybody in this country", as set out in the 1944 White Paper.[49] The new health service, said the Trust leaflet *Happy Birthdays*, "provides a fresh opportunity" to give women the maternity care they need.[50] The most striking evidence of Trust support for a national health service is the eagerness of its members to claim credit for the idea. "It struck me last night," Lady Baldwin told Miss Riddick in June 1945, "while listening to W. Churchill's Broadcast and his propaganda for Maternity Welfare (Really what we of the N.B.T.F. have been preaching and propaganding for – [sic] years) that . . . *we were really the first in this work.*"[51] Three days before Lady Baldwin's death in 1948, Miss Riddick decided to insert the date of the Fund's foundation in the heading on its notepaper, in order to demonstrate that the Fund "had been the pioneer in maternal welfare work, and that many of the things we had advocated years ago had now become recognised essentials."[52] The belief that the basis for the NHS had been laid by the voluntary sector was common among voluntarists. "On their results," Dame Louise McIlroy informed *The Times*, "the new Act has been built."[53] This claim distorted the real picture. Local Authority mother and baby clinics, feeding programmes, even school dentistry and school medical examinations, had all introduced the idea of universal health measures, while the movement of the Left had campaigned vigorously for social reform. All these had worked together to shape an irresistible demand for a national health service for all.

The Trust's enthusiasm for a national health service did not at first extend to the kind of NHS that was created by Aneurin Bevan, the Labour Minister of Health. Willink had intended to maintain the voluntary sector and to base the hospital service upon the Local Authorities, which pleased the Trust because it had been closely associated with the voluntary hospital system between the wars. All its Cooperating Hospitals were voluntary, and it had an especially close relationship with Queen Charlotte's Hospital. Bevan, however, proceeded to nationalize the hospitals. He was highly critical of a system that appeared to him to discriminate against the poor. Many shared his view. In *The Citadel*, the novel by A.J. Cronin set in the period before the war, a doctor complains to his wife of the difficulties of obtaining a bed in a voluntary hospital for a poor patient: "They're not full up. They've plenty of beds . . . for their own men. If they don't know you they freeze you stiff . . . Isn't it hell . . . Here am I with this strangulated hernia and I can't get a bed."[54] Further support for the nationalization of voluntary hospitals came from consultants, who gained increased security, prestige and money from the 1948 settlement.

Lady Rhys Williams approved of Bevan's NHS once it had been in operation for a while. But in the 1940s, she recommended the kind of service proposed by Willink. In *Something to Look Forward To, Suggestions for A New Social Contract* (1942), she advocated a situation where the state would be responsible for the welfare of every individual, without the need for nationalization. "The idea that there is no hope of improvement of the present inadequate arrangements short of complete nationalisation," she insisted, "has been studiously pressed upon the public mind by those who desire a State-dominated world for its own sake, but such propaganda should not be accepted. . . ." The older, voluntary hospitals, she added, "have a greater tradition to sustain them, and reach, for the most part, a higher standard of medical and nursing care than the average Municipal Infirmary."[55]

The Trust was anxious about its own future under Bevan. At a meeting of the Executive Committee in 1946, Lady Rhys Williams said that although "it was *not desired to attack the [NHS] Bill itself*", there was much concern that "the loss of voluntary initiative would seriously handicap the future Health Services". A Resolution was passed, expressing concern that "grave harm will be done to the progress of medical science and the development of hospital services if the provisions of the NHS Bill are not supplemented by voluntary effort." A further Resolution was passed, which warned against the division of responsibility for maternity care between the various professional groups. The RCOG, which had already circulated to MPs a memo warning against the plans in the NHS Bill to share maternity care between different administrative bodies, was delighted with these Resolutions.[56] In fact, Labour wanted a unified administration, but this was not achieved because of the need to appease all the various interest groups.

Copies of the Trust Resolutions were circulated to all MPs and to interested groups. Voluntary hospitals and organizations were grateful to the Trust for taking a lead in their defence [57] and the College of Midwives reported that they, too, were doing "a good deal of propaganda on this subject".[58]

For some, it was difficult to accept the new health service; one such individual was Seymour Leslie, a member of the Trust who served on numerous committees in the voluntary hospital system. On behalf of the London Maternity Voluntary Services Joint Committee, which was sponsored by the Voluntary Hospitals Committee and the King's Fund, he complained to Miss Riddick that "the Minister is not yielding on any important points, and many of the Opposition efforts are disappointing too". He added that, "I have myself heard the Minister say that he would rather be cared for in a thousand bedded general unit, but we all know that the maternity department is usually the Cinderella in the large general units. 'Bigness for bigness' sake' seems to be the fetish with our rulers."[59] The Birthday Trust, however, chose not to complain about the NHS but to adapt. Having registered its objections to Bevan's plans for legislation, it did not resist their force. For example, the Executive Committee decided in the middle of 1949 that the representatives of the former 'Cooperating Hospitals' should no longer be referred to as such. Also "much doubt existed as to the correctness of their appointment", so they were given the opportunity to continue their association with the Trust as private individuals.[60]

The Trust sought to establish some kind of relationship with the Ministry of Health. Lady Rhys Williams, who had enjoyed such a productive relationship with Janet Campbell before the war, made overtures to Dr Dorothy Taylor, the Senior Medical Officer of the maternity welfare department at the Ministry of Health. Dr Taylor was perfectly friendly in response, but with none of the wholehearted commitment to the work of the Trust that was shown by Dame Janet Campbell in the 1930s.[61]

A MOTHERS' CHARTER

At a meeting in 1947 of the Evidence Sub-Committee that was gathering data to present to the Working Party on Midwives, discussion of the Ministry of Health's plan for the registration of maternity nurses led to the conclusion that "a Mothers' Charter should be drawn up, setting out the ideal maternity service from the mothers' point of view".[62] The Executive Committee was enthusiastic about the idea,[63] advocating "a revolution in the whole attitude towards motherhood: a Mothers' Charter."[64] Lady Rhys Williams duly produced a draft for the Charter, reporting on its contents to a meeting of the Evidence Sub-Committee. It listed the usual requirements demanded by the Trust, notably the provision of pain relief to every mother, and insisted that mothers should have 'the best service'.[65] This draft appears to have been the end of the story of the Mothers' Charter; no papers have been found which document further interest or action. In discussions of the Charter, there was no thought at any time of asking mothers for *their* point of view; rather, Lady Rhys Williams said the Trust was "in a position to offer evidence *on behalf of* the mother herself upon the requirements of an ideal maternity service . . ."[66] This plan for a Charter anticipates the flurry of so-called citizens' charters nearly half a century later, ranging from *The Patient's Charter* (Department of Health, 1991) to *The Charter on Maternity Services* (Department of Health, 1993) and *The Bus Charter* (London Transport, 1994).

The Married Women's Association, the Birthday Trust and the National Federation of Women's Institutes joined together in 1948 to form a Safer Motherhood Committee, to ensure that the needs of women were met by the new National Health Service. The committee was chaired by Lady Helen Nutting, Chairman of the Married Women's Association and also a member of the Birthday Trust Executive Committee. It arranged a public meeting in

London on 8 June 1948, to discuss the implications for women of the National Health Service Act. This was regarded as being "of paramount importance at this time",[67] since the NHS Act was going to be implemented less than one month later, on 5 July. It was called a 'Safer Motherhood' meeting, but had a different purpose from the 'Safer Motherhood' campaign of the 1930s, which had focused on the problem of maternal death. The organizers of the 1948 meeting insisted that it would not be held in any spirit of criticism of the proposed health service, but so that the government would "know what improvements the mothers want to see incorporated in the new service".[68] A Senior Medical Officer of the Ministry of Health was invited, so that the organizations represented on the platform could "act as a channel between the authorities and the mothers, and help to interpret the wishes of the latter."[69]

Lady Nutting wrote to interested people to explain that, "We have invited Women's Organisations to send questions as we are anxious to discover *from the mothers themselves* what they consider to be the most important and necessary requirements of a good service."[70] As in the case of the Mothers' Charter, however, mothers themselves were not in fact given an opportunity to offer their views. What they were offered was the chance to come to a meeting and put questions to a Brains Trust, modelled on the popular wireless programme, 'The Brains Trust', on which experts answered listeners' queries. The 'Brains' for this meeting were provided by Sir Eardley Holland, Miss Josephine Barnes, Lady Rhys Williams, Miss G.B. Carter and Dr Geoffrey S.W. Organe, and suitable questions from the public were read out and given an answer.

The Brains Trust experts agreed on most aspects of maternity care, and Eardley Holland's keynote speech, which argued that motherhood had to be safer not just in the narrow medical sense, but in the wider sense of its social and economic implications, was welcomed by his colleagues. On the subject of birth control, however, there was a difference of opinion. Sir Eardley and Miss Barnes advocated its practice, for the sake of mothers' health and to reduce illegal abortion. Lady Rhys Williams, however, insisted that it should not be given unless medically required. "It is necessary to make people want to have children," she argued, adding, "it is a very serious decision for the State to take to subsidise doctors to keep the birth rate down."[71]

A Resolution was passed at the meeting to record mothers' expectation that "the standard of the [National Health] Service shall be set at a level, for all women which is equal to the best available to any at the present time." It was stressed that this demand was not made in any spirit of opposition to the Ministry of Health.[72] A copy of the Resolution was sent to Bevan, in a letter calling for improvements in the safety, relief and comfort of women in labour. Signed by the Married Women's Association, the National Federation of Women's Institutes and the National Birthday Trust Fund, it stated that, "What we want for the Mothers of Britain by the Fathers of Britain, is that they should put their purse behind us."[73] Equating the 'Fathers of Britain' with the

SAFER MOTHERHOOD

Under the auspices of the
MARRIED WOMEN'S ASSOCIATION
NATIONAL BIRTHDAY TRUST FUND.
NATIONAL FEDERATION OF WOMEN'S INSTITUTES

at CAXTON HALL, WESTMINSTER
(St. James's Park Station)

on TUESDAY, JUNE 8th 1948, at 7 p.m.

Speaker:

Sir EARDLEY HOLLAND
M.D., F.R.C.P., F.R.C.S., F.R.C.O.G.

Question Master:

Dr. CHARLES HILL
M.D. (The Radio Doctor)

Brains Trust:

Sir EARDLEY HOLLAND
M.D., F.R.C.P., F.R.C.S., F.R.C.O.G.

Miss JOSEPHINE BARNES
D.M., M.R.C.P., F.R.C.S., M.R.C.O.G.

LADY RHYS-WILLIAMS
D.B.E.

Miss G. B. CARTER
B.Sc., (Econ.,) S.R.N., S.C.M.

Dr. GEOFFREY S. W. ORGANE
M.A., M.D., D.A., R.C.P. & S.

In The Chair:

LADY HELEN NUTTING
(Chairman, Married Women's Association)

SILVER
COLLECTION.

Tickets from:—
The Meeting Secretary,
Safer Motherhood Committee,
57, LOWER BELGRAVE STREET, S.W.I
SLOane 5076

W. J. BIRD & Co., Ltd. 7, Ludgate Broadway, E.C.4.

This Safer Motherhood meeting on 8 June 1948 was organized by the Birthday Trust, the Married Women's Association and the National Federation of Women's Institutes, to discuss the implications for women of the National Health Service Act. ([NBTF/G33/3] Reproduced courtesy of the Wellcome Institute Library, London)

government and the source of power was perfectly reasonable, since only one woman – Ellen Wilkinson – reached the Cabinet during this period.

A SAFER MOTHERHOOD SUB-COMMITTEE

After the Safer Motherhood meeting had been held, a special sub-committee was set up to pursue the issues that had been raised. The first meeting was held on 7 July 1948, two days after the inception of the NHS, and was attended by Lady Rhys Williams, who sat in the chair, Miss Josephine Barnes, Miss Carter, Frances Farrer, and Lady Helen Nutting. The outcome of this meeting was a decision to produce a leaflet for mothers, called *Safer Motherhood*.[74] As indicated by its eventual subtitle, '*Minimum Requirements of a Comprehensive Maternity Service*', the leaflet was a deliberate effort to influence the maternity component of the NHS. A draft leaflet was sent to Dr Taylor at the Ministry of Health, who found inaccuracies and said that some statements were too dictatorial.[75]

She was better pleased with the second draft, but asked for information to be added on the availability of services under the NHS; in particular, she wanted mothers to know that they could obtain a maternity outfit free of charge from their Local Health Authority, and that ambulances were available when necessary without charge.[76] The final version of the leaflet called for an increase in parentcraft lessons and antenatal care, domestic help where appropriate, better pain relief for labour, and support for the role of the midwife. It also suggested ways of improving the quality of a mother's pregnancy, by reducing waiting times to a minimum and making clinics bright and clean. It advocated afternoon rest periods, showing a mother her baby as soon as it was born, and not waking her up too early if she was in hospital.

No one knew quite what to do with the leaflets once they were ready. This problem was solved, though, when the Women's Group on Public Welfare said it would shoulder the responsibility. Miss Homer, the Group's Secretary, said that *Safer Motherhood* was "exactly what they wanted" and was anxious to circulate it as soon as possible to 109 Standing Conferences of Women's Organizations all over the country.[77] The Birthday Trust wanted the women's organizations to set up Safer Motherhood Committees all over the country, to monitor the growth of the new maternity service. Creating committees with "an encouraging if sometimes critical attitude towards the country's Health Service," said a letter accompanying the leaflet, would guarantee a high standard.[78] This plan for citizens to 'audit' the NHS was not developed any further, but over forty years later, the 1991 NHS reforms included a commitment to an audit of the health service, involving consumers as well as those working within the system. Evidently, the ideas that had produced the Birthday Trust plan never quite disappeared.

CHARITY BECOMES UNPOPULAR

Charitable relief had been much in evidence during the Depression. By the end of the war, however, the notion of 'charity' had become widely unpopular and Bevan claimed that "subvention by public funds and flag days is becoming increasingly repugnant to the conscience of the public".[79] The socialist J.B. Priestley's play, *The Inspector Calls* (1945), which demonstrated that charity was dangerous because it was dispensed on the basis of discretion, was a huge success in London's West End. There was a broad consensus of support for the idea of entitlement on the basis of need. When the National Health Service began in 1948, a leaflet explaining its operation promised that, "Everyone – rich or poor, man, woman or child – can use it or any part of it . . . *it is not a 'charity'.*"[80]

Since charity is largely dispensed by voluntary organizations, the

A government leaflet preparing families for the start of the National Health Service on 5 July 1948. (Reproduced courtesy of the Department of Health)

future of the voluntary sector looked grim. On the one hand, some government spokesmen pledged to protect it: "We must watch," warned Herbert Morrison, "for the State to take over more and more what formerly was done by voluntary action . . . Even where there would not be much financial saving, there are strong arguments for keeping the voluntary spirit alive."[81] Lord Pakenham insisted to the House of Lords that, "Democracy without voluntary exertion and idealism has lost its soul. All forms of democratic government were dependent on that same spirit, but the socialist form most of all."[82] But on the other hand, the increased role of the state in daily affairs was undermining the role of voluntary organizations. "It is all very sad, but I fear the worst after 1946," said Sir Frederick Menzies in dismay (even though, as former MOH for London, he had contributed actively to the demise of the voluntary sector).[83] The Charity Organization Society sensibly changed its name to the Family Welfare Association. Some organizations simply became redundant. The British Hospitals Association, for example, which had represented the interests of the voluntary hospitals for thirty years, was unable to continue its traditional function and was wound up in March 1949.

The Royal Maternity Charity, which had been founded in 1757, was a typically old-fashioned charitable organization. Its subscribers, explained the 1946 Annual Report, "have absolute discretion in selecting the nationality, creed and district of the patients to be helped, provided that they adhere to the fundamental rule of the Charity – 'Marriage and Necessity'."[84] With an eye to survival in these changed times, the Charity proposed a merger with the Trust; but after a period of negotiation, its committee pulled out of the plan. It turned out that Lady Rhys Williams had told the Charity Commissioners that the Trust would administer the other charity's funds, which had never been proposed;[85] she apologized profusely for this mistake.

Some voluntary organizations adapted successfully. The influential King's Fund, which had reserves of between five and six million pounds, underwent a radical transformation. It took the practical step, explains a historian of the Fund, of concentrating on patient care and the promotion of experimental projects.[86] It also took advantage of the fact that its constituency now included the former municipal hospitals, as well as those that were voluntary, by moving into issues of hospital planning and administration.[87] The Birthday Trust was equally determined to survive, through following the lines of modern scientific investigation.

TURNING TO BABIES

For more than a decade the Trust had concentrated on the needs of mothers. But now the fate of babies was seen as a priority, since for every thousand babies born in 1945, nearly 28 were stillbirths and over 45 died in the first four weeks of life[88]. This concern contributed to the shift away from mothers, to mothers and babies. In 1949, Professor Moncrieff advised the Executive Committee that, "it would be very necessary to *stress the baby side* . . . equally with that of the maternal aspects (even though it might be of lesser importance as far as the Trust itself was concerned)."[89]

The Trust also started to devote its energies to scientific research. The introduction of the National Health Service, observed the Trust's Annual Report for 1948, had not decreased the responsibilities of the Trust in the field of maternal welfare but rather, since the minimum requirements put forward for many years by the Trust were going to be provided, "has enlarged these responsibilities to the wider field of vital research into factors which still militate against safe motherhood and healthy childhood."[90] This shift to research required the recruitment of members with a scientific background. Previously, laypeople had dominated the organization and had initiated projects that were investigative in type, but not very 'scientific' in methodology. Genuine concern had been accepted as an adequate basis for venturing an opinion; and if that opinion was offered by someone who was rich and powerful, it was even more acceptable. Sir Julien Cahn, therefore, did not hesitate for a moment before recommending connecting the tap of the gas cylinder of a gas and air machine to a gramophone record saying, 'Bear down, dear, bear down'. He told Miss Riddick, "You might think of this when you have some time to develop the idea!"[91]

Miss Josephine Barnes was the first medical expert to join the Trust after the war; shortly after moving in 1946 into the London district of Belgravia, where Lady Rhys Williams lived, she was invited by her to join the General Committee. She had a previous Trust connection, because she had been Louis Rivett's House Officer at Queen Charlotte's. In 1947, it was decided actively to recruit more medical people to the Executive Committee, and Mr Rivett agreed to see what he could do.[92] He brought in Charles Read,[93] another consultant obstetrician, and two years later, Professor Moncrieff and Dr James Douglas joined the committee. In 1952, Elliot Philipp joined the Trust.

The shift to research also reflected the decline of the women's movement after the war (it did not revive until the 1960s).[94] After all, the Trust could have moved into issues like the campaign for equal pay, but the kind of single-minded feminists that had run the Trust between the wars were no longer on the committee (Lady Rhys Williams was not really one of these, because she was active in so many causes and campaigns). Lady Baldwin may have anticipated this when she urged in 1944, not long before her death, "that we invite some younger women and men to join our Executive Committee. We older ones are dropping out and it's good to have fresh blood to take our places."[95] A new generation of feminists to take over the Trust failed to materialize, however. This supports the argument of Martin Pugh, a historian of the British women's movement, that during the 1950s, "the failure of inter-war feminism to recruit a large body of young leaders became apparent."[96]

THE TECHNICAL ADVISORY SUB-COMMITTEE

In 1948, Lady Rhys Williams argued that the Trust needed a small group to provide it with technical expertise. She proposed that the sub-committee that had been set up to prepare evidence for the Working Party on Midwifery should be used for this purpose, but that it should be known in future as the 'Technical Advisory Sub-Committee'. The first meeting of this Technical Advisory Sub-Committee (TASC) was held in October 1948 and was attended by Lady Rhys Williams, as Chairman, Miss Josephine Barnes, Miss G.B. Carter and Mr Charles Read. "All detailed matters concerning the technical aspects of the work of the Trust," suggested Lady Rhys Williams, should "be put back on the Technical Sub-Committee, and not discussed at length at the Meetings of the Executive as at present." It would be better, she said, if the technical committee furnished concise reports and recommendations for the executive members. This was approved by all concerned.[97]

The Technical Advisory Sub-Committee became increasingly independent, selecting projects for research and advising on the methods and personnel required. In this respect, it was quite unlike the Research Committee that had supervised the nutrition experiments and the abortion enquiry between the wars. The Research Committee had had no powers of its own and was used simply for consultation; and when its members offered advice, they were often politely ignored. The Technical Advisory Sub-Committee also differed from the Joint Council of Midwifery, which had been concerned with the development of policy rather than the pursuit of research. A number of medical people had sat on the Council, but they were chosen because of their prestige and influence, not because of their scientific knowledge. The developing autonomy of the TASC occasionally led to conflict with members of the Executive Committee. In 1951, a memo by James Douglas intended for the eyes of fellow-members on the Technical Advisory Sub-Committee went to the Executive Committee by mistake. Penman, the Chairman, immediately planned ways of reducing the cost of the project described in the memo. This annoyed Dr Douglas, who felt that Penman was intruding into matters he knew nothing about.[98]

Guided by the TASC, the Trust funded various research endeavours in the early postwar period. In 1948, a three-year grant was made to Queen Charlotte's Hospital to enable Dr John Murray to carry out research into the Rhesus Factor and to re-open the Bernhard Baron Laboratories. In the same year, Dr Paul Polani, who became Professor of Child Health and Research Fellow at the Paediatric Research Unit at Guy's Hospital Medical School, carried out investigations with Dr Philip Evans into the causation of cerebral palsy. Also in 1948, a three-year fellowship was granted to Dr Cedric Carter at the Hospital for Sick Children, which formed the basis of a highly regarded study of Down's Syndrome. After this, funds were for the most part channelled into survey work (which is described in the subsequent chapters of this book). However, in 1959, a grant was given to D.J. MacRae, for the study of recording the action of the foetal heart, and another grant was given to Professor Ian Donald, which enabled him to carry out his early work on ultrasonics at Hammersmith Hospital. A further grant in 1961 enabled Dr John Wigglesworth, at University College Hospital to study the structure of the placenta and abnormalities related to toxaemia of pregnancy and placental insufficiency.[99]

The Trust also took upon itself the role of educating the public on the value of antenatal care. In 1945 it employed the latest technology – the Synchrophone Apparatus – to produce an illustrated lecture: this was played on gramophone records, with a 'frame' synchronized with the gramophone on which pictures appeared at appropriate times. The pictures showing pregnant women may have alarmed some of the lecture's audiences, since they are unexpectedly thin and flat-waisted and evidently well off. Few hospitals wanted to use the lecture more than once. They reported that their mothers had been "not very interested", preferring live talks by midwives, and that only the children had enjoyed the occasion.[100] The lecture was published in the form of a booklet called *The Expectant Mother*.

THE 'NEW MEN' OF SCIENCE

The Trust's move to become more 'scientific' and professional can be seen as part of a larger movement that was changing the lives of British people. Scientists had produced sulphonamides, penicillin and broad-spectrum antibiotics to cure puerperal fever, gangrene, pneumonia and tuberculosis, immunization against diseases such as whooping cough and polio, and life-saving techniques like blood transfusions. Technology in the home was also transforming people's lives. Non-iron fabrics, detergents, washing machines, fridges, and new gas and electric stoves and fires, which ended the burden of making coal fires, were the housewife's friend, while television brought welcome entertainment. Science had helped to win the Second World War and even the dropping of atomic bombs on Hiroshima and Nagasaki in August

The postwar confidence in science had its roots in the prewar period, as this advertisement for luggage 'planned on scientific principles' illustrates (Sketch 7 June 1939). (Reproduced courtesy of the Illustrated London News *Picture Library)*

1945 did not dent the optimism of the age, but underlined the role of science in every modern activity. Indeed, atomic power promised to bring ample warmth, power and comfort for next to nothing and with no dirt.

The Festival of Britain in 1951 celebrated not only the centenary of the Great Exhibition of 1851, but also "thrilling developments in modern scientific knowledge". It laid out the future of architecture, town planning and design, showing "a Britain full of hope and brightness".[101] The Paris Exhibition of 1937 had displayed colonial exhibits of 'native artefacts' and 'contented piccaninnies', and British life had been presented as a country house games room with Chamberlain in knickerbockers and fishing hat, surrounded by dogs. But in the London exhibition in 1951 and the smaller versions of the Festival all over Britain, there were no more colonies or country houses. One mother recalls that after her family's visit to the Festival, "My children had crystal structures (named) on their bed spreads, and the planets in their orbits on their curtains."[102] Hope for the future was symbolized by the Skylon, an extraordinary 300 ft 'vertical feature', marking the location of the Festival in the vicinity of what is now known as London's South Bank.[103] The Lord Mayor of London during the Festival of Britain year was Sir Denys Lowson, who later became Chairman of the Trust's Finance Committee.

A male doctor giving instructions to a pregnant woman. This illustration in The Expectant Mother, *an early postwar booklet by the Birthday Trust, presents a different image of maternity from the one dominating Trust literature in the 1930s, which stressed women's own expertise in pregnancy and labour. ([NBTF/G31/4] Reproduced courtesy of the Wellcome Institute Library, London)*

C.P. Snow described the scientists of the postwar age as 'The New Men', using this term as the title of a fictional account of the discovery of atomic fission and its consequences.[104] Snow's novel was a tale of 'pure' scientists, but his term was applicable to all the men and women of science. Obstetrics, for example, was a discipline of experts requiring data, statistics and research. Although most women still delivered their babies with the assistance of midwives, there was a growing view that the best care would be provided by highly trained obstetricians. The Trust's early postwar booklet, *The Expectant Mother*, showed an 'expert' giving advice to a mother: he is standing and looking down at her, while she looks up at him from a seated position. This was a different image of maternity care from that presented by the pre-war literature of the Trust, in which mothers had centred.

This presentation of men in a superior, more knowing, role, was consistent with the growing number of men who were Consultative Members of the TASC: by 1953, they outnumbered women by five (James Douglas, P.R. Evans, Professor Alan Moncrieff, John Murray, Charles D. Read) to one (Miss Lois Beaulah), though the few core members of the TASC were women. By 1960, there were ten men who were Consultative Members, and just one woman. On the larger committees, there were still many more women than men: in 1952, there were only four men out of sixteen members of the Executive Committee, and only seven out of forty-three of the General Committee. However, the role of the Executive and General Committees was increasingly limited to that of backing and supporting the scientists. Mrs Jenifer Gilbey, a lay member of the Trust, recalls that the "medical people did it all" and that the job of people like herself was to raise the money for their work.[105] This trend developed further over the next few decades, as the Trust became immersed in survey work.

CHAPTER NINE

Starting Survey Work: the 1946 Maternity Survey

In 1945, a Joint Committee of the Population Investigation Committee and the Royal College of Obstetricians and Gynaecologists was appointed to conduct a major investigation into the social and economic aspects of childbirth, called 'Maternity in Great Britain'. James Young, who had been a member of the JCM Research Committee, was Chairman of the Joint Committee, which is listed in table 9.1, and David Glass was Secretary. James Douglas[1], a medical doctor who was interested in social research, was appointed as the full-time director of the study in 1945 and Griselda Rowntree was taken on as his assistant in 1946, the year in which the study took place.

TABLE 9.1: JOINT COMMITTEE OF THE ROYAL COLLEGE OF OBSTETRICIANS AND GYNAECOLOGISTS AND THE POPULATION INVESTIGATION COMMITTEE FOR THE 1946 MATERNITY SURVEY

Chairman	James Young	RCOG and PIC
Secretary	D.V. Glass	PIC
	H.G.E. Arthure	RCOG
	Miss Josephine Barnes	RCOG
	G.F. Gibberd	RCOG
	Sir Eardley Holland	RCOG and PIC
	David Maxwell	RCOG
	Rufus C. Thomas	Co-opted
	C.P. Blacker	PIC
	I.G. Davies	PIC
	Miss C.L. Melly	PIC
	R.M. Titmuss	PIC
	Lady Rhys Williams	PIC
Director	J.W.B. Douglas	
Research Assistant	Miss Griselda Rowntree	

This was the first in a de facto series of national birth surveys in Britain: it was followed by the classic Perinatal Mortality Survey of 1958, the British Births survey of 1970, and then three surveys of special subjects in the 1980s–90s. The Birthday Trust took a leading role in all these surveys except the first, in which its role was accidental rather than planned, apart from a small grant for £200. The Trust's Miss Josephine Barnes and Lady Rhys Williams were both members of the Joint Committee, but as representatives of the RCOG and the PIC, respectively. Despite this slight involvement of the Trust, the 1946 survey is given this separate (albeit brief) chapter because of its importance as the first survey. It also generated a longitudinal study of the cohort of children that were born in the survey week; this follow-up was repeated with the 1958 and 1970 surveys. Table 9.2 lists all the birth surveys

Dame Josephine Barnes, who was on the Steering Committee for the 1946 survey and was Chairman of the Steering Committees for the 1958 and 1970 surveys. (Reproduced courtesy of Dame Josephine Barnes)

and follow-ups that were started by the maternity study of 1946, and figure 9.2 shows when data were collected for each of the three cohort studies.

A major reason for conducting the 1946 survey was concern at the apparent fall in the birth rate; it was set up, observed *The Times*, in order to enquire into the reasons for fewer births.[2] This is important for an understanding of the survey's focus: it asked about the social and economic, not the clinical, aspects of pregnancy and childbirth, because it wanted to know why parents were choosing not to have babies. In Britain, explained the survey report, "fertility has fallen very markedly since the 1870s. There are reasons for thinking that the medical and other costs associated with the birth of a baby may today be a serious deterrent to parenthood."[3] Dr Edith Summerskill said that the falling birth rate was the result of "a sit-down strike among mothers"[4] and Richard and Kathleen Titmuss observed that, "Millions of parents are revolting against parenthood".[5] Sir Leonard Hill, a 'Scientist, Father of Six, Wants Family Subsidies', reported the *Daily Mail*,[6] and the *Daily Mirror* said that Britain's peers wanted the government to 'Pay Wives to have more Babies' by introducing family allowances.[7] There were warnings of a decline in the 'White Population'[8]

TABLE 9.1: NATIONWIDE SURVEYS AND COHORT FOLLOW-UPS

	Name of Study	Birth Week	Extent	Number	Response Rate	Name of follow-up study
1946	Maternity in Great Britain (PIC and RCOG)	3–9 March	E, W & S	15,000 births	91%	MRC National Survey of Child Health and Development
1958	Perinatal Mortality Survey (NBTF)	3–9 March	E, W & S	17,000 births	98%	National Child Development Study
1970	British Births (NBTF and RCOG)	6–11 April	E, W, S, & NI (NI not in cohort)	17,000 births	95+%	British Cohort Study

SPECIAL SURVEYS

	Name of Birth Study	Births Surveyed	Extent	Number	Response Rate
1984	Place of Birth (NBTF)	1 August 1 Sep 1 Oct 1 Nov	E, W, S, and NI	512 units	99.1%
1990	Pain Relief in Labour (NBTF)	25 June– 2 July	E, W, S, and NI	10,000	66% (of midwives) 82% (of 2,500 followed-up mothers)
1994	Home Births (NBTF)	1 Jan– 31 Dec	E, W, S, and NI	7,136	not known at time of going to press

FIGURE 9.2: BRITISH LONGITUDINAL BIRTH COHORT STUDIES

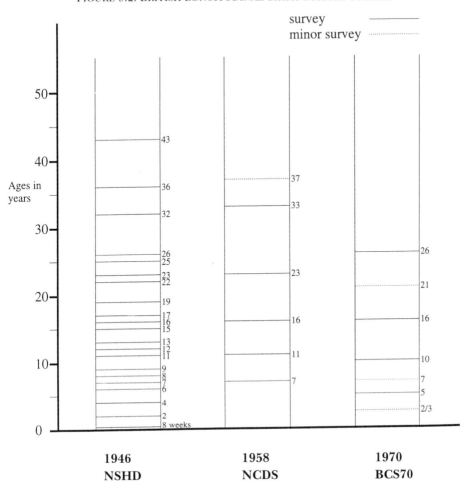

The three cohort studies: ages at survey sweeps.
Source: Adapted and updated from Ekinsmyth (1996) and Wadsworth, Peckham and Taylor (1984). Provided by Kevin Dodwell, NCDS.
Reproduced courtesy of the Social Statistics Research Unit, City University, London.

and the need for a rebirth of belief in 'Imperial greatness',[9] while the *Carlisle Journal* simply condemned 'Women Who Prefer Cars to Babies'.[10] A book published by Mass-Observation in 1942, *Britain and Her Birth-Rate*, starts its preface with an ominous warning of extinction: "Unless the trends of half a century are not only arrested but reversed immediately, the population of this country will diminish. Unless people decide to have larger families it will go on diminishing until *there is no one left*."[11]

At the end of the Second World War, the birth rate had become a major policy issue. In fact, though, Britain was on the brink of a baby boom, but nobody realized this at the time. A Royal Commission on Population produced a report in September 1945; the Commission had been appointed in 1944 and two former members of the Joint Council of Midwifery, Eardley Holland and Dame Louise McIlroy, served on its Biological and Medical Committee. The Commission's report referred to the "real" threat of a "gradual facing [sic] out of the British people" and warned of a dire effect on British social and economic life, migration to the Dominions, and Britain's position among the nations.[12] However, this report was out of date by the time it was published because of the rise in the birth rate, and it was not even debated in the House of Commons. Consequently, the issue does not feature in any important way in the final report of the maternity survey, which was published in 1948.

The survey had its roots in a pre-war enquiry into the public provision of maternity care, which had been initiated by Miss Winifred Burt (the same Miss Burt who had carried out statistical work for the JCM abortion study) and was then "amplified and completed" by Mr E. Grebenik and Miss D. Parry under the auspices of the Social Research Division of the London School of Economics.[13] At a meeting of the PIC in 1944, it was decided to pursue this investigation,[14] but in such a way as to uncover reasons for the fall in the birth rate and to help shape plans for the new health service.[15] Then, at the end of the war, the RCOG, which had recently published a report on *A National Maternity Service* (1944), agreed to collaborate on the project and appointed a number of representatives to join a Joint Committee. In order to publish the results while "the new Maternity Services were still in a fluid state", efforts were made to attract a publisher for the report as quickly as possible; to this end, it was decided not to ask for royalties.[16]

Surveys of this type are often regarded as innovations of the postwar period. There was so much going on in social and medical enquiry in the late 1930s, however, that the war was simply a hiatus in their development. Social surveys in York, London, Merseyside and elsewhere were conducted during the first third of the century, and a study in Newcastle was begun before the war, which was designed to identify and investigate the diseases of childhood in a representative sample of 1,000 families. The subsequent book, *A Thousand Families in Newcastle upon Tyne*, explains that, "We had gained experience of this kind of work in a survey of deaths in infancy in 1939[17] and we were busy with the extension of this inquiry in a study of morbidity when the war broke out. We postponed our work and resumed it in 1947."[18]

THE SURVEY WEEK

On the basis of all the births in Britain that took place in one week of March (3–9) 1946, 14,000 women were asked questions by health visitors about their pregnancy, labour, home life, and their circumstances before the baby was born. These took place in the mother's home, when the selected child was eight weeks old; by then, all the costs associated with preparation for the birth and with the birth itself were likely to be known. Douglas has since explained that the survey's design was largely determined by the challenge of obtaining a good sample with limited funds.[19] For example, the month of March was chosen so that students could be used to code the data (which was a tremendous job in the years before computers) in the summer vacation.

The extent of cooperation from health workers and mothers during the 1946 maternity survey was remarkable. Ninety-three per cent of the Local Authorities in England, Wales and Scotland agreed to take part, and 91 per cent (13,687) of mothers were successfully interviewed. The health workers were advised to instruct the mother that answering correctly "will enable us to make use of her experience *in planning better Maternity Services* [sic] which will benefit future mothers."[20] The readiness of mothers to help build a decent health service was part of the culture of the period: it was consistent with the public's enthusiastic approval of the Beveridge Report and of plans for the National Health Service, which was inaugurated just two years later in 1948.

A midwife weighs a baby following a home delivery shortly after the Second World War. Whereas 65 per cent of mothers gave birth at home in 1937, this figure dropped to 46 per cent in 1946, the year of the maternity survey. (Reproduced courtesy of the Queen's Nursing Institute)

The 1946 survey differed from the Birthday Trust work of the time, such as the Mothers' Charter and the Safer Motherhood project, because it not only claimed to ask mothers for their views, but actually did so. Only by heeding "the mother's comments and preferences", maintained the Joint Committee, could a satisfactory maternity service be established;[21] this meant that "the only people who can tell us what we want are the mothers themselves."[22] Consequently, mothers all over Britain were invited by health workers to give answers to a questionnaire about: their experience of the birth; work and income; other children; their care of the baby; antenatal care; confinement (such as place of delivery); when they got up after confinement; help in the house and care of the other children; extra nourishment during pregnancy; the home (such as number of rooms); maternity benefits; and the cost of pregnancy.

Initially, the committee took the view that health visitors should not call on "mothers of the Higher Income Groups".[23] This was consistent with the thinking that had led the Birthday Trust in the 1930s to direct nearly all its work at women who were poor. But in the spirit of universalism that underpinned the planned health service, it was soon decided that mothers of every class should be included, and that this comprehensiveness would be a key feature of the survey: "It was emphasised in the memorandum [sent to the authorities] that *mothers of all income groups* should be included in the survey."[24]

RESULTS OF THE SURVEY

The survey findings were published in *Maternity in Great Britain* in 1948; these are presented in summary form in table 9.3. The "main complaint" made by mothers in the enquiry was the lack of analgesia.[25] This complaint would not have arisen at all, if it had not been for Miss Riddick of the Birthday Trust. Reading an early draft of the questionnaire, drawn up by 19 March 1945, she noticed that it did not contain any reference to analgesia. She quickly penned (which shows her sense of urgency, since she usually used a typewriter for her correspondence) a note about this to Lady Rhys Williams: "Here are all the P.I.C. documents I have in the file. Re Questionnaire. Why not a question on analgesia? e.g. Did you have analgesic relief. If so – what kind and was it successful. If not – why not?" (she put an emphatic large cross next to the last two words).[26] No doubt Lady Rhys Williams promptly suggested a question on this important Birthday Trust issue.

Maternity in Great Britain offered a range of recommendations, including the provision of nursery accommodation, domestic help where appropriate, analgesia for every childbirth, a better standard of continuity during pregnancy, labour and the puerperium, better antenatal and postnatal care, a reduction in the costs of childbearing, and that birth control advice should be made readily available to all mothers.[27] These were all standard Birthday Trust demands, with the exception of increased contraception.

The 1946 survey broke new ground, because it was the first attempt to collect information from mothers on a national scale, producing a larger sample of the population than any preceding enquiry. Previously, this type of data had been largely collected on a local and ad hoc basis, by the Local Authorities. The 1946 sample was fully representative of mothers in all types of home and in all parts of the country. The data were welcomed by politicians and health planners, who needed information about individuals all over Britain in order successfully to provide the national and centralized health service that everybody was waiting for. This became a reality in 1948, the year that *Maternity in Great Britain* was published.

In the opinion of Dame Josephine Barnes, who has witnessed the evolution of the NHS from its start, from the point of view of an obstetrician working within it, "*Maternity in Great Britain* was a blue print for the maternity service we've had

TABLE 9.3: CHIEF FINDINGS OF THE 1946 MATERNITY SURVEY

1. *Antenatal supervision*
Many women did not put themselves under antenatal supervision until the last three months of pregnancy.

2. *Place of confinement*
The total proportion of institutional confinements in 1946 was 54 per cent. Some 5 per cent of those booked for home delivery were admitted as unbooked cases to hospital; among these the stillbirth and neonatal death rates were high. On average, women confined in an English hospital were not discharged until the thirteenth day after delivery.

3. *Relief of pain in childbirth*
Analgesia was given to 20 per cent of those mothers delivered at home (8 per cent of those attended by midwives, 48 per cent of those attended by doctors). Fifty-two per cent of those delivered in hospital were given relief. Rates were lowest in the metropolitan boroughs, where only 5 per cent of mothers confined at home, and 48 per cent of those confined in hospital, were given pain relief.

4. *Postnatal examinations*
Postnatal examinations were given to only one-third of mothers.

5. *Infant welfare centres*
Fifty-seven per cent of babies were taken to infant welfare centres before they were two months old.

6. *Costs of childbearing*
The most prosperous families spent nearly twice as much as the poorest group on first confinements. This difference increased with subsequent confinements.

7. *Unequal availability of services*
Inequalities were particularly noted in antenatal and postnatal supervision, the provision of maternity beds, and the giving of analgesia.

8. *Social inequalities*
In all aspects of maternity care, well-to-do mothers received better attention than those who were poor. Nine per cent of the average annual salary of professional and administrative workers was required for the average cost of pregnancy and delivery, compared with 16 per cent of the average annual salary of manual workers.

9. *Infant feeding*
By the end of the eighth week after delivery, 43 per cent of mothers were wholly bottle-feeding their babies. Babies were more often successfully breastfed in hospital than if they were born at home.

10. *Expectant mothers in gainful occupations*
Higher prematurity and stillbirth rates were found among those who worked during the last four months of pregnancy. Few mothers intended to return to work after the birth of their baby.

11. *Help in the house*
Less than 2 per cent of mothers were able to obtain the services of a home help during the last weeks of pregnancy and the lying-in period, though as many as 70 per cent would have liked one.

12. *Need for information*
Existing national statistics and local records were inadequate and sometimes misleading.

ever since."[28] Also, the results of the enquiry provided "yardstick data against which the changes brought about by the new system could be studied later."[29] The report stimulated further debate on the requirements of mothers in pregnancy and childbirth. During the Commons debate on Thorneycroft's Analgesia in Childbirth Bill (see pp. 167–70), references were made to the survey as an authoritative source by MPs on both sides of the House. Some readers of *Maternity in Great Britain* thought of new ideas in light of its findings: "If one might suggest," offered Dame Louise McIlroy in an enthusiastic review of the report, "the establishment of day nurseries at railway termini and in market towns would enable the mother to do her shopping and she would be relieved of all anxiety about her infant."[30]

A SAMPLE FOR LIFE

The survey had produced a sample of the population that was fully representative of children in Britain. Because of this, and because the Local Authorities had shown such a high level of support for the enquiry, the PIC decided to follow the sample for a further four or five years. According to James Douglas, the idea to do this occurred at more or less the same time to himself, David Glass and Richard Titmuss.[31] Douglas believed that a follow-up study of this type might answer questions about ill health that could not be answered in any other way, particularly questions related to social class.[32] This was an original plan: although there had been some follow-up research in the USA before the war, this was the first attempt at a national longitudinal study.

Owing to the limits of money and staff, it was decided to reduce the number of babies by about a half, to 5,362, ensuring that there were approximately equal numbers of each of the major social groups. The first follow-up studies of these children were carried out in 1948 and 1950 by a Joint Committee of the Institute of Child Health at the University of London, the Society of Medical Officers of Health and the PIC. At this stage information was collected from the mothers, though later the children themselves became the respondents. James Douglas and J.M. Blomfield used the data generated from these initial slices to write *Children Under Five*, which described the home environments in which young children were brought up in the early postwar period and which threw light on a number of problems concerning their health and growth during the pre-school period.[33] It dealt on a national scale with many of the subjects that had very recently been covered by local surveys, such as the 1,000 family survey in Newcastle upon Tyne,[34] a survey of morbidity in childhood that was conducted in Luton,[35] and the Oxford Child Health Survey of the development of children in volunteer families. These surveys had yielded a somewhat distorted picture, owing to local movements of the population and also the smaller size of the population sample.

Following up the 1946 children provided an ideal opportunity to study the results of the 1944 Education Act, which established for the first time the legal right of all children to secondary education. A study of the cohort children at school led to *The Home and the School* (1964), an account of their time at primary school, and then to *All Our Future. A Longitudinal Study of Secondary Education* (1968).[36] These studies, with their capacity for studying small groups in particular detail, were able to show which groups were failing to benefit from the education service. This "hidden selection" was not revealed by official statistics, since they could only provide isolated demographic facts that were not anchored to individual pupils.[37]

The survey has followed the 1946 babies all the way into mature adulthood, collecting data on their health and development, education, transition from school to work or higher education, work, marriage, parenting, and family life; some of the survey's key findings are presented in table 9.4. The design of the original birth study has had implications for the follow-up, since children born in the spring would begin to walk when there was no need for fires in the grate,

---

TABLE 9.4: SUMMARY OF FINDINGS FROM THE MRC NATIONAL SURVEY OF HEALTH AND DEVELOPMENT

The pre-school years
The study of the follow-up sample from the original maternity survey showed big class differences in survival, illness and growth. The importance of maternal care and health visitors' support for the health of children was shown, and was used to support contemporary arguments for the retention of public health community staff.

The school years
The study quantified the contemporary worry about the 'wastage of talent', and showed that many children of high measured ability did not pass the 11-plus examination. The study also showed the social class bias in the population going on to further and higher education, and in more recent times has shown the equally strong gender bias in that population, which was not discussed at the time. Educational attainment was shown to be greatly associated with the degree of parental concern for and interest in the child's progress.

Adulthood
The long reach of childhood is evident in adult health, income and family life. Childhood growth, development and socio-economic circumstances are strongly associated with physical health in middle life, and educational attainment is related to adult maintenance of health through eating, alcohol drinking, smoking and exercise habits. Educational attainment and socio-economic circumstances of the family of origin are also strongly associated with adult income and occupational attainment, as well as with age at marriage. Childhood family relations are one of the important sources of vulnerability to or protection against mental health problems in adult life.

Prepared by Michael Wadsworth, Director of the National Survey

---

which would reduce the number of accidents; also, the month of birth, by determining the year of school entry, has been shown to have considerable influence on a child's success at school. In the 1970s, it was observed that the choice of the survey week diminished the random nature of the sample, since babies are less vulnerable to infection in the spring than, say, in the winter. It could also distort associations, owing to the fact that shorter gestations commence pregnancy nearer to winter. In the early years of longitudinal surveys, however, none of these difficulties was realized.

The PIC continued to run the survey in the first few decades, largely supported by funding from foundations, especially the Nuffield and Ford Foundations and the Population Council, Inc. Smaller grants were also provided by the Birthday Trust, Great Ormond Street Hospital, and similar organizations. In 1962, the study was taken over by a Medical Research Council unit attached to the LSE; in the late 1990s the MRC is still running the survey, which is now known as the MRC National Survey of Health and Development. After James Douglas retired as director of the survey in 1979, it was based between 1979 and 1986 in the Department of Epidemiology and Community Medicine at the University of Bristol, under the direction of J.R.T. Colley. Then, in 1986, the direction of the study was taken over by Professor Michael Wadsworth at the Department of Epidemiology and Public Health at University College, University of London, who has written an account of the study, *The Imprint of Time. Childhood, History and Adult Life* (1991).[38] The National Survey stays in touch with cohort members by sending them a birthday card every year. The messages in the cards convey the gratitude of the survey team: "Of course,

---

We continue to be astonished at the long-term importance of childhood circumstances for adult health. Using information you have given us over the years we found that good home circumstances and health in the early years of childhood significantly reduced the risk of health problems in adult life. We found this in studies of illnesses like bronchitis, and in studies of lung function and blood pressure, as well as health in general. This does not, of course, mean that health in adult life cannot still be improved, for example by an appropriate level of exercise; one of our particular interests is the investigation of how far adult practice of a healthy lifestyle helps to maintain good health. But by showing the importance of childhood circumstances we have helped to change the climate of opinion about how health is generated, and therefore also the current ideas about how the good health of future populations may be most effectively developed. The trends are certainly in the right direction. Comparing the health of children at the time of your birth with that of children now it is evident that there has been a considerable improvement in all respects.

The message inside a birthday card sent by the MRC National Survey of Health and Development to members of the 1946 cohort. (Reproduced courtesy of the MRC National Survey of Health and Development)

none of our work could have taken place without your cooperation over the years."[39]

A mass of books and papers are still being produced on the basis of the generated data, on a remarkably wide range of subjects including 'The Prevalence of Bed-Wetting Among Children Aged 4–7 Years'. The kind of information provided by longitudinal studies like the National Survey could not have been produced in any other way, argues the sociologist Ann Oakley. "I don't think we knew that kind of thing, until these follow-up studies were done," she has commented. "They identify in a clear and powerful way the link between educational achievement and family background, and again the ways in which being born in a certain social class seems to be with you the rest of your life."[40] Further information of this sort was provided by the follow-ups of the 1958 and 1970 birth surveys, as chapters 10 and 11 will show.

CHAPTER TEN

The 1958 Perinatal Mortality Survey

At the end of the twentieth century, the National Birthday Trust Fund is best known for the Perinatal Mortality Survey it conducted in 1958. However, this survey began neither as a Birthday Trust study nor as an enquiry into perinatal death. It was the "brain child"[1] of Professor W.C.W. Nixon, Professor of Obstetrics and Gynaecology at University College Hospital (UCH) in London,[2] who was thinking about the possibility of a "field inquiry on the relative risks of hospital and home confinement". On 16 November 1954, he arranged a meeting to discuss this, to which he invited: Neville Butler, a paediatrician who also worked at UCH;[3] representatives of the Ministry of Health; James Douglas, who had directed the 1946 survey; J. Austin Heady of the MRC Social Medicine Research Unit, who was studying the social and biological factors in infant mortality and stillbirths, a joint study of the MRC with the General Register Office; and D.D. Reid of the Department of Medical Statistics and Epidemiology at the London School of Hygiene and Tropical Medicine. They concluded that such an enquiry would be a major undertaking and would have to be done on a large scale.[4]

The Birthday Trust became involved when Dr Dorothy Taylor at the Ministry of Health sent a report on this meeting to Lady Rhys Williams. "No doubt," she wrote, "you will now wish to consider whether the National Birthday Trust Fund would be prepared to set up such a technical group to study this complex problem."[5] Lady Rhys Williams, who would have known about or possibly met Dr Nixon, since he had been medical secretary of the special committee set up by the People's League of Health in 1935 to investigate the nutrition of pregnant mothers, was intrigued. In 1954, she convinced the Birthday Trust to give Nixon and Butler a small grant for a pilot study in Norwich, to discover whether there was any evidence that "mothers and babies are, in fact, safer in hospital than in their own homes". She arranged for them to meet James Douglas, the architect and director of the 1946 survey, who was enthusiastic about the project.

Douglas assumed that the original committee of the RCOG and of the Population Investigation Committee (which had become much less active following the postwar rise in the birth rate) would be reconstructed, but the Birthday Trust preferred to create its own. In April 1955 it created a "gigantic"[6]

TABLE 10.1: STEERING COMMITTEE FOR THE 1958 PERINATAL MORTALITY SURVEY

Chairman Miss Josephine Barnes

Sir Dugald Baird	J.W.B. Douglas
Lois Beulah	J.A. Heady
D.G. Bonham	F.M. Martin
J.P. Bound	Jean MacIntosh
G.B. Carter	W.C.W. Nixon
J. McClure Browne	Elliot E. Philipp
N.R. Butler	N.W. Please
A.E. Claireaux	Lady Rhys Williams

committee with seventeen members, who are listed in table 10.1, and fourteen nominated representatives of various related organizations. It was chaired by Miss Barnes, who had represented the RCOG on the 1946 committee; including Miss Barnes, nearly half the members of the committee were consultant obstetricians, and there were no midwives. The Ministry of Health, the Welsh Board of Health and the Department of Health for Scotland sent observers. In April 1956, Dr Hilda Roberts was appointed director of the survey, but she moved to Toronto later that year. The position was then given to Neville Butler, who nurtured the survey through every stage of its gestation. "Neville was a genius, there's only one way to put it. It wouldn't have existed without Neville; not with the excitement and the new ideas", claims one of the survey team, while another has remarked, "He had great insight. You come up with a problem and he'd be there, he'd often be there before anybody else. He could see a problem and he could come up with a solution."[7] His right-hand man was the obstetrician Dennis Bonham,[8] who was Professor Nixon's assistant at University College Hospital; in 1961, Nixon seconded him to work on the survey. Bonham has since recalled "the degree of missionary zeal and drive that was so much part of the survey" and the inspiration provided by Nixon.[9]

At the first meeting of the Steering Committee in April 1955, everyone agreed to Douglas's plan for a repeat of the 1946 survey, with questions added to discover the relative risks of home and hospital confinement.[10] However, this quickly developed into a broader and more general medical investigation into perinatal death. A key influence on this shift was Dr Alice Stewart, who worked at the Social Medicine Unit at the University of Oxford. In May 1956, Dr Stewart reported to Miss Riddick a long talk with Hilda Roberts, in which she and a colleague had "felt that any study of perinatal mortality, which was designed to show whether hospital or domiciliary service were best, was doomed to failure." But if the survey were to obtain facts about babies who died, she suggested, "and pairing this with facts about babies who had survived, it might

FIGURE 10.1: PERINATAL MORTALITY AND STILLBIRTH RATES – ENGLAND AND WALES (PER 1,000)

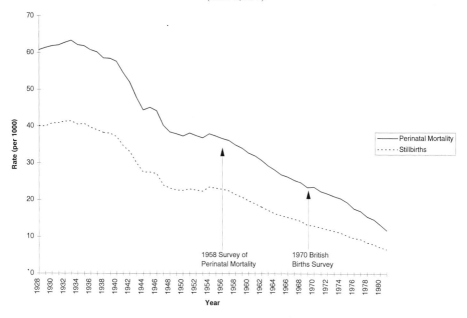

Source: A. Macfarlane and M. Mugford, *Birth Counts: Statistics of Pregnancy and Childbirth*, 2 vols (HMSO, 1984), pp. 10, 11

be possible to demonstrate the existence of special risks of death."[11] This possibility excited the survey team, since the rate of perinatal death was a cause for serious concern. As shown in figure 10.1, it had fallen sharply in the early 1940s, but then remained much the same: 38.5 for every 1,000 births in 1948, and 35 in 1958.[12] This was higher than in many other countries: in 1955, for example, the rate for every 1,000 births was 38.3 in England and Wales and 42.1 in Scotland, but 29.2 in the Netherlands, 27.8 in New Zealand, 25.9 in Norway, and 30.4 in the USA.[13]

HOME OR HOSPITAL

The question of where to give birth did not disappear, however.[14] If the survey results were in favour of hospital birth, thought Lady Rhys Williams, the RCOG would take the matter up in a big way, "as they are anxious to support 100 per cent hospitalisation".[15] Discussions on where to give birth were heavily informed by interest group politics. General practitioners opposed an increase in hospital delivery, because this would erode their own role in maternity care (they had tried to sabotage the 1936 Midwives Bill for the same reason). Consequently, the BMA representatives on the Steering

Committee "made a lot of noise and difficulty about the survey. They were looking out for the GPs . . ."[16] At a meeting in January 1963, Dr Leak of the BMA accused the RCOG of trying to ensure "that every woman should have her baby in hospital and they would use the survey as a slant on that."[17]

The Ministry of Health sought to maintain good relations with GPs. Lady Rhys Williams was dismayed in 1956 by a talk with Dr Taylor, from which it emerged that "The attitude of the Ministry would seem to be that things must be left very much as they are, and also that the G.P. must be left alone – in fact, all rather defeatist."[18] In 1961, Dr Butler told Lady Rhys Williams that a difference of opinion had arisen between the survey team and Ministry officials. "I have already been asked on the telephone," he complained, "to agree to the exclusion of one of the major reasons for the survey, namely, home and hospital deliveries."[19] Professor Nixon insisted that "home versus hospital" should not be left out, because it was the whole point of the study.[20]

In the end, though, the reports of the survey did not contain any specific study of the relative risks of home and hospital confinement. They are based on the assumption that hospital birth is safer, but this is not a specific finding of the research. This assumption is conveyed by statements like: "there is no doubt that the risk of perinatal death is lower in a well equipped and well staffed hospital than at home"; the high mortality ratio for forceps by consultant obstetricians "clearly reflects the difficulty of the case rather than the ability of the operator"; and the high stillbirth and neonatal mortality rate among caesarean sections are "naturally related to the severe complication necessitating section".[21] These statements and others like them may have been true, but were not actually proved. This would have been impossible, argues the epidemiologist Eva Alberman, who joined the survey team in 1963 and was brought on to the Birthday Trust a few years later.[22] "There are some questions," she believes, "that can't be answered from the sort of data that the Birthday Trust produced. I think we couldn't have answered about home births for mothers with very low risk, we just didn't have the information – of what time she went to hospital, what her home was like, and so forth."[23]

Before the war, the rate of death in childbirth was higher in some institutions than at home, because of the high rate of puerperal infection on the ward. This risk was greatly reduced by antibiotics, while the development of other medical techniques, like blood transfusions, further increased the margin of safety. Consequently, the issue of where to give birth had to be assessed anew. "I have looked up our Report of 1935," wrote Lady Rhys Williams in the late 1950s, "and find that . . . at the time, the Joint Council of Midwifery was not in favour of any great increase in the percentage of confinements taking place in hospital, owing to the increased risk involved." She added, "this decision would not necessarily apply at the present time as this Report was written before the sulphonamide drugs were generally available."[24]

FIGURE 10.2: BIRTHS IN INSTITUTIONS (%)

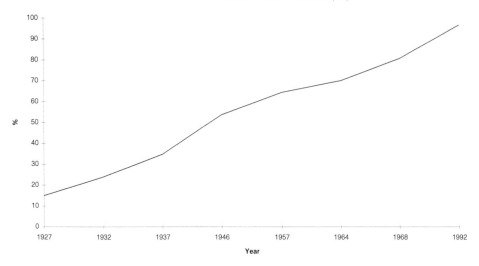

Source: Data provided in Rona Campbell and Alison Macfarlane, *Where to be Born?* 2nd edn (NPEU, 1994)

The numbers of women giving birth in an institution increased dramatically during the war, as shown in figure 10.2, because the Emergency Medical Services arranged for women in the cities to be taken to maternity homes in safer areas. "The local women were beginning to say, What about us?" recalls Sir George Godber,[25] who was then Deputy Chief Medical Officer at the Ministry of Health.[26] After the inception of the NHS in July 1948, the attraction of a hospital birth was enhanced. Not only was it free under the NHS, but it also spared a family the extra expenses of giving birth at home, like food, bedclothes, sanitary towels, extra washing, and adequate fuel.[27] Confinement in hospital also gave women the chance of a rest away from housework and the demands of their family. Miss Dare, the Matron at Queen Charlotte's, referred to "the complete rest women get there, especially mothers with heavy home responsibilities".[28]

In 1944, the RCOG had advocated that 70 per cent of confinements take place in hospital. In 1954, in *Report on the Obstetric Service under the National Health Service*, it recommended that all births should take place in an institution. It said that this would provide "the maximum safety for mother and child and, therefore, the ultimate aim should be to provide obstetric beds for all women who need or will accept institutional confinement"; a Reservation was added, giving Mr Arnold Walker's view that normal cases should be attended in their own homes. The report also recommended that GPs should not be permitted to give obstetric care unless they had received special training to do this.[29]

FAIR SHARES FOR MATERNITY IN THE NHS

The demand for beds outstripped supply. In order to secure a maternity bed, recalls one mother, she booked into a hospital while she was still trying to become pregnant.[30] Another mother who was living in lodgings with friends when she was three months pregnant, gratefully remembers the tremendous efforts made by her doctor to book her a hospital bed for her delivery.[31] The "notorious"[32] shortage was aggravated by the increase in the birth rate (of 30 per cent between 1956 and 1966) and also by the overall shortage of beds, which led hospital boards in the early 1950s "to divert beds now used for obstetric cases to other patients in greater need of hospital treatment . . ."[33] There was outrage at the closure of maternity beds. The Women's Cooperative Guild passed a Motion at their 1951 Annual Congress deploring "the lack of accommodation and facilities for maternity cases in our nationalized hospitals."[34] In early 1954, the Labour MP Barbara Castle asked the Minister of Health during Question Time in the House of Commons if he was aware that many women in her constituency of Blackburn were being "compelled to have their babies at home against their will owing to the shortage of the maternity beds?" She repeated this question two months later.[35] The Birthday Trust lodged a complaint with the Ministry of Health, objecting that "the interests of the mothers themselves are not given proper consideration."

The government's reaction was defensive: "Confinement which is expected to be normal," it insisted, "is as safe at home as in hospital."[36] It sought to prioritize needs in order to determine who should be allocated a bed: the second Confidential Enquiry into Maternal Deaths[37] advised "better selection of cases for hospital confinement based on the 'priority' classes".[38] To assist this selection, the Chief Medical Officer's report for 1955 identified the three most vulnerable groups, according to the mother's age and parity, and the Confidential Enquiry for 1958–60 also made detailed suggestions for selection. All these recommendations were based on the assumption that hospital care was safer; no attempt was made to discover the actual effects of the place of confinement or the relative risks of home and hospital delivery.[39]

Negotiations over beds and between doctors and consultants took place, of course, within the larger context of the NHS. Sir George Godber recalls "the tremendous change that took place in the 1950s. Planned development of specialist staff in hospitals was produced and the quality of specialist care and the amount of work done in hospitals was immensely improved."[40] This was followed by the Hospital Plan of 1962, which laid out a long-term capital programme for hospital rebuilding in order to provide "the most advanced diagnostic and treatment facilities for the entire population".[41] The cornerstone of the Hospital Plan was the idea of the district general hospital, with a maternity unit where full consultant cover would be on hand for all beds.

Unlike Lucy Baldwin, Lady Rhys Williams did not have any formal political power. She stood for election as a Liberal candidate in 1938 and 1945, but without success; after the war, she was a One Nation Tory in spirit, but did not belong to any political party. She had powerful connections, though. One Trust member recalls that at a meeting at London's Hyde Park Hotel, Cabinet Ministers and the Chairman of the Coal Board all came up to shake hands with her.[42] She made full use of her contacts. "If she wanted to argue for something to be done," recalls Sir George Godber, "she would promptly come and do it individually, rather than by formal approach. This worked, because if you start formal approaches, then people start formal defence. . . ."[43]

Her most influential friend after the war was Harold Macmillan, the Conservative MP who was Prime Minister between 1957 and 1963. "She is a great friend of mine. Although sometimes her ideas are not workable, sometimes they are quite brilliant," wrote Macmillan in 1956 to Miss Patricia Hornsby-Smith MP, who was Parliamentary Secretary to the Ministry of Health.[44] It was a family friendship: Macmillan's son Maurice (a Conservative MP who was consistently passed over by his father in the creation of the Cabinet) joined the Trust and in 1968, he became Chairman of the Appeal Committee set up to raise money for the Trust's 1970 survey.

The friendship between Macmillan and Lady Rhys Williams was built on mutual advantage. In 1956, while he was still Chancellor of the Exchequer, he sent Miss Hornsby-Smith a copy of a letter he had received from Lady Rhys Williams about a plan to unify the maternity services, with the comment, "I feel that she may be on to a good thing, both technically *and politically*."[45] Lady Rhys Williams sent plans not only to improve the maternity services, but also to simplify income tax; these ideas "are merely put up for you to look at," she explained, "because I think a radical change would *help your political reputation*."[46]

Lady Rhys Williams told a contact at the Treasury that her plans would undermine "the usual Labour Party propaganda to the effect that they alone care for the home and family." She explained that "mothers are already beginning to say that it is barbarous of the present Government to refuse them the right of being confined in hospital in every case, as they are in America, and Dr Summerskill is promising them that Labour will give them all a full fortnight in hospital for each baby. This would be fabulously expensive, needing new hospitals for over 200,000 cases a year, and cannot be done." She suggested as a solution to the problem putting the mother into hospital for her confinement, but sending her home within twenty-four hours to be nursed there. This scheme, she said, was "gloriously economical" and would release a great many beds for general use.[47]

She hoped Macmillan would use his influence to improve the maternity service. She wrote to James Young in July 1956, "I have seen Mr MacMillan [sic], to whom I made the suggestion that a Maternity Services Bill might be included in the present Government's last year programme. He is very interested in the idea . . . If the political 'tops' think well of such a bill, no doubt they will 'guide' the Committee to report in this way in time for the Bill to go through!" However, these proposals came to nothing. A Ministry of Health official told Macmillan that she had "very important objections" to them, such as the absence of any clear indication of the role of the GP.[48]

Lady Rhys Williams's friendship with Macmillan deteriorated in the 1960s. Already suspicious of his 'special relationship' with the USA, she felt betrayed by his support for Britain's application to join the Common Market, believing that this would diminish Britain's role in the world. For his part, Macmillan felt disappointed that, "Poor Roy Harrod and Juliet Rhys-Williams (dear, trusted, loyal friends) who used to be strong 'Europeans', have now changed round, and become violent opponents. This saddens me, for I am devoted to them both."[49] In 1963, the year of his retirement as Prime Minister, his annoyance developed into bitter criticism of "the economists – Harrod, Juliet Rhys Williams, Schwarz, Harold Wincott, Kaldor, and all the rest of this motley crew."[50] Roy Harrod, whose wife was a member of the Birthday Trust, was a Keynesian economist with whom Lady Rhys Williams had developed an alliance.

THE CRANBROOK REPORT

In April 1956, when the survey was still in embryo, the government set up a committee to review the maternity services. It was chaired by the Earl of Cranbrook, Chairman of the East Anglian Regional Hospital Board, so became known as the Cranbrook Committee.[51] This enquiry had been recommended by the Guillebaud Report, which had identified "a state of some confusion" in the maternity services.[52] In May 1956, the Birthday Trust was invited to provide written evidence to the Cranbrook Committee, along with fifty-nine other organizations and individuals. The Trust's written report focused on the problems caused by the division of responsibility in the maternity services, between hospitals, general practice and Local Health Authorities. There were echoes in the conclusion of the commitment to midwives that had informed the 1936 JCM Report: "the status of the midwife herself . . . should be raised, and every effort made . . . to attract the highest possible type to this important profession. We need to remember that it is not possible to dispense with the feminine attendant in midwifery."[53] The Trust gave oral evidence, too. On 11 October, Lady Rhys Williams, Professor James Young, Miss G.B. Carter and Miss Riddick presented themselves to Lord Cranbrook and his committee to elaborate on their report. The committee was not impressed and Lord Cranbrook remarked that they had "not gone far beyond saying that the maternity services were untidy administratively".[54] Seven days after this meeting, Lady Rhys Williams sent further details to Lord Cranbrook, explaining, "I think I gave poor answers to some of the questions". One reader of this letter, presumably a member of the government committee, added in pen, "I have written a clucking answer. I don't think this gets us any further or is worth having. It seems only to consist of vague generalities such as we heard a fortnight ago."[55] The Trust's proposals appear to have been less compelling than the suggestions made personally by Lady Rhys Williams to Macmillan, a point that was made by the Private Secretary for Health to the Private Secretary at the Treasury.[56]

Absent from the Trust's evidence to the Cranbrook Committee was any reference to the issue of place of birth, even though it was dominating Nixon's plans for the survey at this time. It was a key issue, though, in the evidence submitted to Cranbrook by the RCOG, which recommended 100 per cent hospital births in a statement that was based on the College's 1954 *Report*. The RCOG appears to have suspected a lack of support from the Trust and resented this. "I do not think the R.C.O.G. and the N.B.T. are at loggerheads over anything really," wrote Charles Read to Miss Riddick, trying to smooth things over, "and it would be a great help at unification if your report giving oral evidence could say that they in principle would uphold the RCOG Maternity Services Report of 1954."[57]

The eventual report produced by the Cranbrook Committee in 1959 contained fifty-nine separate conclusions, one of which was that the tripartite structure of the maternity service should be retained. The report devoted a whole chapter to 'The Place of Confinement: Home or Hospital?', presenting arguments for both; it recommended the maintenance of a good domiciliary service and hospital beds for 70 per cent of all deliveries, with normally a ten-day stay for the patient.[58] When the report was published in 1959, the rate of hospital births was 64.2 per cent. This meant that 70 per cent was a realistic target, which is likely to have been welcomed by the Ministry of Health. The Trust and many obstetricians were disappointed with the report, though, especially with its failure to recommend uniting the maternity services. Three years later, at a press conference to present the findings of the Perinatal Mortality Survey (PMS), Nixon argued that "The maternity services must be united; the Cranbrook Report must not be perpetuated." The Cranbrook Committee, he said, were "guilty men, and the next generation would point to them and say, 'You guilty men'. . . . Let us have a unified system of maternity care based on an obstetric consultant."[59]

STARTING WORK ON THE SURVEY

Much preliminary work, including several pilot questionnaires, went into the final questionnaire for the survey. Its scope was wide – it sought information on social and family background, details of past obstetric history, antenatal care and abnormalities during pregnancy, length and abnormalities of labour, analgesia and anaesthesia, and the sex, weight, progress, management and outcome of the infant.[60] The 'home or hospital' debate had dropped away as a main theme. Not only the content, but also the language, of the 1958 questionnaire were clinical in nature, unlike the questionnaire used in 1946.[61] In discussions of a draft questionnaire in early 1958, Dr Polani pointed out that while 'patient' was used in some questions, 'mother' was used in others; the committee then decided that 'patient' should be used throughout.[62] The 1946 survey, in contrast, used the word 'mother' throughout its questionnaire. Also, the questions are asked directly of the mother, who is addressed as 'you', whereas in the 1958 questionnaire, the mother is referred to indirectly, as 'she': questions are asked about 'the husband's' occupation, 'her father's' occupation and 'the patient's' household.

Austin Heady, who was a member of the Scientific Sub-Committee that was chiefly responsible for drafting the questionnaire, has described this work as "the most frustrating I have ever been involved in". Meetings went late into the night in order to produce recommendations for the questionnaire. But this work was frequently wasted, because "we would find at the next meeting that these had been changed without reference to us by people who were not members of our committee."[63]

At the beginning of 1957, the Ministry of Health offered to assist the Trust with the survey. This was the beginning of a cooperation over many years, covering the plans and preparation, the survey week itself, and the subsequent period of analysis. Sir George Godber remembers why he decided to offer Ministry support: "it's an actual advantage for an enquiry like this to be seen to be coming from some other source than the central department . . . so if it looks like moving, then you put your weight behind it."[64] His backing was similar to Dame Janet Campbell's support for the Trust in the 1930s, except that it was given officially. He told Lady Rhys Williams that he would hold consultations on the enquiry with the RCOG and the general medical services committee of the BMA, as well as senior administrative Medical Officers of the Regional Health Authorities.[65] He also persuaded Percy Stocks, formerly Chief Statistician to the General Register Office, to help with the survey analysis.

Relations between the Trust and the Ministry were strained at times. The fact that Dr Bransby was both a civil servant at the Ministry of Health and also Chairman of the survey's Scientific Sub-Committee generated some misunderstanding. "I was deeply shocked to hear from Miss Riddick this morning," complained Lady Rhys Williams to Mr J. Wrigley, the Ministry's chief statistician, "that a letter from me addressed to Dr Bransby in his capacity as chair of the scientific sub-committee of the Survey is regarded as a formal letter to the Ministry of Health."[66] In the summer of 1962, Percy Stocks announced that he would not do any more work on the survey, because the decision that twins should not be included was "more than I could digest". He explained, "I would not like to have to explain why they have been excluded from the mortality analysis."[67]

An invaluable contribution was provided by the Department of Obstetrics and Gynaecology at the University of Aberdeen, which was led by Professor Dugald

Baird,[68] and the MRC Obstetric Medicine Research Unit in Aberdeen, which were regarded as pioneers in showing the effect of the maternal physical and social background on perinatal mortality.[69] "Protected by this Aberdonian panoply," declared Nixon, "we felt as secure and inviolable as the foetus during the mid-trimester of pregnancy."[70] An early task of the Aberdeen group was to develop a classification of the causes of perinatal mortality for use in the survey.[71] These were devised in order to tell why, rather than how, a baby died. Using this method, the causes of perinatal death were divided into two broad groups: the 'environmental' group, due to the effect of unfavourable environmental influences on the mother; and the 'obstetrical' group, which were associated with complications of pregnancy and labour, many of which could be prevented by obstetric skill.[72]

The Aberdeen group took a leading role in conducting the survey in north-east Scotland and acted as advisors throughout the enquiry. They also wrote the last chapter of volume one and six chapters of volume two. Angus Thomson and Baird were anxious to have full control over their work. "The wires are getting crossed," complained Thomson to Butler in October 1958, "I therefore want to make it clear once more that the analysis of the mortality data is our concern alone."[73] Just before Christmas in 1958 he insisted, "we must be given complete responsibility for the whole task of analysing mortality rates . . . we have no axe to grind, except that the report on mortality should be scientifically as good as it can be made. Long experience suggests that this aim is best ensured by scientific freedom and full responsibility of reproduction being granted to one person: in this case Baird."[74]

THE SURVEY WEEK

March was initially proposed for the survey week in order to follow the model of the 1946 study, but Dr Mary Paterson of the Society of Medical Officers of Health suggested November instead, when the health and social services were usually fairly slack.[75] This was agreed, and the RCOG was duly informed that the survey would take place in November 1957.[76] By early summer, though, it was evident that they would not be ready in time.[77] Butler then proposed March 1958, pointing out that it would be easier for health visitors to have extra work in May than in January; also, the NHS year finishes at the end of March, so it would be possible to obtain help from people who had accumulated holiday time. A further advantage would be the opportunities of comparison with the 1946 survey, if the same months were used.[78]

These several postponements of the survey created problems for the Ministry of Health and General Register Office (GRO), which had been planning since 1956 to carry out a much smaller Perinatal Mortality Inquiry, looking at stillbirths and children dying under one week. Its chief purpose was to see whether information about the causes of stillbirth could be usefully recorded.

Although the two studies were "very different in scope and object", Sir George Godber was reluctant to have both running at the same time in case this confused the situation for the Birthday Trust.[79] The Perinatal Mortality Inquiry was eventually held between 1 July 1958 and 30 June 1959, after the PMS. It collected tables from thirteen Medical Officers of Health for Local Health Authorities. Dr Hirst and Dr Bransby were involved in both studies; one of their colleagues commented drily that they would have no difficulty dealing with the government records, after their experience of the notoriously detailed Birthday Trust questionnaire.[80]

In the Birthday Trust's chosen week in 1958, the weather was bitter – it was the coldest March for forty years. One survey mother remembers that her mother could not visit because the roads were so icy; she was also very uncomfortable, as her ward was barely heated by open gas fires.[81] The extreme cold may have been responsible for the larger than usual number of perinatal deaths,[82] since many of the working-class women giving birth at home would have had little bedroom heating (in Britain in the 1950s, it was rare for homes to have central heating).

Mothers who gave birth in the selected week were interviewed by midwives; their answers, as well as clinical information from all available records and other medical staff, were recorded on the questionnaires. Health workers were excited about the task, because Butler and Albert Claireaux, consultant morbid

Neville Butler, director of the 1958 Perinatal Mortality Survey, who has devoted his life to the health and welfare of babies.

anatomist at Queen Charlotte's Hospital, had gone on tours all over the country building up enthusiasm for the survey. In any case, there was a tremendous amount of good will among workers in the National Health Service at this time. "There was a culture in which nurses and midwives were very conscientious in collecting data," explains Eva Alberman. "Notes were well kept, and they regarded it as part of their duties to complete this sort of information."[83] Administrative help was given by every Regional Hospital Board and teaching hospital, as well as 195 out of 196 Local Health Authorities.

One mother who gave birth during the survey week has remembered the excitement of being told about the study, shortly after she had delivered her daughter. She regarded it as "quite an honour" and was eager to provide any information that would help other children; she was pleased, too, that her daughter was given the benefit of a rigorous set of medical tests that were not widely available at that time (her only disappointment was the lack of feedback about the survey findings).[84] Another mother does not recall anyone mentioning the survey while she was in hospital, though she was delivered by Josephine Barnes, the Chairman of the survey Steering Committee. She was told about the study some time later, when a midwife came to her home and invited her to take part. She and her husband were keenly interested, she says, but would have felt obliged to take part in any case.[85] "There was no such thing as an ethics committee or anything like that then," recalls Eva Alberman. "I don't know to what extent the mothers and midwives would have understood what 'consent' was. Because it was very much taken for granted that medical information could be used."[86]

THE PATHOLOGY ENQUIRY

An important part of the survey was the addition of pathological information, which was enhanced by adding all stillbirths and babies who died in the first week of life through the months of March, April and May. The idea for the pathology enquiry came from Dr White Franklin of the British Paediatric Association at a meeting of the Steering Committee in January 1956; he was deputizing for the Association's nominated representative. "If postmortem reports could be obtained and possibly even access to a section by a pathologist," he suggested, "it would be most helpful in finding the cause of death." Dr Butler agreed, but warned that there were few individuals interested in neonatal pathology who could give the cause of death with any certainty.[87] Soon after this discussion, Dugald Baird said that in his view, the pathology investigation would be a waste of time and would not produce any findings beyond those already established in Aberdeen.[88] None the less, the Steering Committee decided to go ahead.

A pathology sub-committee of leading paediatric pathologists was set up, chaired by Albert Claireaux. He and Butler decided to extend the investigation beyond the survey week to three months, in order to get sufficient figures to establish findings of statistical significance. A pilot investigation demonstrated that good results would be obtained by moving whole bodies to a regional centre, rather than organs or blocks. The Trust then asked about sixty pathologists with experience of obstetrics and the newly born to set up centres; this centralization was necessary because the standard of pathological work varied over the country. A very long questionnaire was produced (a "monster", recalled Claireaux with horror), asking for the main findings of the post-mortem and of an examination of body tissues through a microscope. The investigation went smoothly, even in the case of domiciliary deaths, which were difficult to collect. The bodies were transported in cardboard boxes, wooden boxes, parcels, and coffins, and some babies arrived in shoe boxes. In one area, it was found that the number of dead bodies was higher than that of registered deaths, and one body was found in a ditch.[89] Although Professor Baird had predicted problems with mothers having misgivings about bodies being taken away before burial,[90] this did not happen because of the huge public support for the survey. The pathologists performed an average of over fifty post-mortems each and found it unpleasant to work on so many macerated babies. "My lab looks a bit like a battlefield," reported Claireaux in 1962, "The blocks . . . are now at Queen Charlotte's . . . there are at least 1,000 cases waiting for me to have a look at."[91] In the event, an autopsy was carried out on 5,000 babies (85 per cent of those eligible).

It was very hard to specify the true cause of death, observed Claireaux. Asphyxia, for example, which is suffocation caused by a loss of oxygen in the blood, was often the immediate reason for death. It was actually caused by something else, however, such as placental failure, prolonged labour, difficulties with the cord, or a delay in the start of respiration. Furthermore, the cause of death was frequently multifactorial and "may go far back into pregnancy, or even earlier to involve the sociologist or geneticist."[92] Despite these difficulties, it was necessary to provide some kind of diagnosis, in order to produce a table that would give a picture of what was going on.

As far as the Ministry of Health was concerned, commented Dr Bransby, the pathology side was an essential part of the survey and "is unique in size and scope and in the information it will provide".[93] Dr Heady has since commented that, "This data set is/was really unique. There can have been nothing like it before or since. In this respect it is much more special than the results of the main study." In his opinion, these data have not yet been fully exploited.[94]

ANALYSING THE SURVEY DATA

By the end of 1958 there were some 25,000 completed questionnaires, with the mothers' names blacked out for reasons of confidentiality. "It's difficult to recall the excitement of the database, it was really very new," comments Eva

Alberman, adding, "The Birthday Trust broke new grounds in just developing the material that was there."[95] But behind this heady excitement was a tremendous amount of hard work. Once the mass of data had been collected, it had to be checked, coded, and transferred to punched cards; this was a formidable task in the years before computers. The Ministry provided a grant so that tabulations could be done by the Government Social Survey at the Central Office of Information. Coding was hampered by defects in punched cards, by impossible combinations of information on some cards,[96] and a "multiple births muddle".[97] When a mother was admitted to hospital two hours before labour commenced, this was sometimes coded as admission to hospital for causes other than pregnancy. Birth weight was coded in pounds and ounces, which were meant to correspond to groups of grams, but the conversion was not done by any recognized system.

Butler was soon exhausted. Like most of the scientists involved in the survey, he was not paid for this work but did it on top of his paid employment. Bonham has since recalled, "Neville was still involved in his clinical work and much of our time together was spent through the night. He used to travel with a car full of paper to our house at West Norwood after a clinical day at Swindon and we worked through until breakfast."[98] Bransby was worried that Butler "found the pace of life killing and had to have some respite . . . he has a very strong emotional tie-up with the survey, almost like a possessive mother."[99] His work as survey director became even more arduous when Bonham left Britain in December 1963 to take up the Chair of the School of Obstetrics and Gynaecology at the University of Auckland in New Zealand. "I never know where, or how far, we are getting with the survey analysis now that you have gone," Butler wrote to him, "so that an up to date précis always seems quite beyond my powers. Knowing me, you will appreciate this!"[100] Lady Rhys Williams urged Butler, "Please do try and get more sleep. If you continue to work at such a pace without more sleep and proper food, you will end by killing yourself – on the roads if not by illness."[101]

Mr Wrigley, the Ministry statistician, was also working on the survey data after work hours, but his contribution had to be anonymous, because he was a civil servant. He was so worn out by early 1963 that he decided to cut down on this extra work. He then gave it up altogether: in April, he told Lady Rhys Williams that he had resigned from the Ministry to take up a post in Rome.[102]

Analysis of the data became easier and also more sophisticated when computers were used. The shift to computers was expedited by Harvey Goldstein, a statistician who was brought in to work on the seven year follow-up study in the mid-1960s (which is discussed later in this chapter), but he was soon involved in the perinatal data set as well.[103] He introduced the method of analysis that is known as 'multivariate', because it allows several factors (which are known as 'variables') to be examined simultaneously. "You can throw in social class, maternal age, birth order, place of residence, a whole number of variables together like that," explains Goldstein, "and you can allow the effects of their association with each other, and then pick out what was really the important relationship with the effect that they caused."[104] The first computer used on the survey was an IBM. It was not the most powerful one, recalls Goldstein, but the most powerful one that worked for more than half an hour at a time. On one occasion,

> we'd booked the machines for the whole night. There were two of us, the other guy was a programmer. So we set off with about 10 boxes of punched cards and we got a taxi, and when we got in one of the card boxes dropped on the floor of the taxi and all the cards fell out, which was terrible because they had all been sorted. So we then had to sort them again. The we sat up all night till four or five in the morning trying to use these machines and on that occasion the machine stopped working, so we'd wasted a whole night.

Computers at that time took up a great deal of space, sometimes a whole large room. They were extremely valuable, so a security guard "sometimes locked us in the room to stop other people coming in, and he'd sit there and watch us, or read".[105]

The results of the survey were not actually published until 1963. "There never has been a delivery whose gestation period has been so long," Nixon observed wryly. "For the elephant," he added, "this is two years, but this survey, resembling perhaps the dinosaur, has had a gestation of five years. . . ."[106] In early 1959, Social Survey were already behind schedule. The Trust then gave some work to the Calculating Bureau of Birmingham, which discovered mistakes in the tabulations. In 1960, the work seemed to be grinding to a halt and was "very dark".[107] In autumn 1961, the Ministry of Health made arrangements for some work to be carried out at government expense by the English Electric Company Ltd, where new problems developed.

Pressure to start publishing the survey results was soon applied by the Joseph Rowntree Village Trust, which was the survey's major funding body. Mr Seebohm and Lewis E. Waddilove, representing the Village Trust, had offered £1,000 in 1956. At that time they regarded the survey as a repeat of the 1946 enquiry,[108] but were now concerned that the survey was outside their usual field of work. By November 1961, William Wallace, Chairman of the Village Trust, was complaining that the contribution had risen to £23,000.[109] Some bad feeling developed between the two trusts[110] and Sydney Walton (who had been instrumental in bringing the two parties together)[111] smoothed things over. He told Miss Riddick that he had had a "gracious" talk with Mr Wallace and that "All misunderstandings are cleared away." He then added with some delicacy, "May I make a suggestion for our splendid chairman [Lady Rhys Williams] to consider? If there is any communication to be made between the trust and the Trust, perhaps I could be used as the medium." In October 1962, the Rowntree Trust pleasantly but firmly refused to give any more money.[112]

FIGURE 10.3: NBTF EXPENDITURE 1964–6

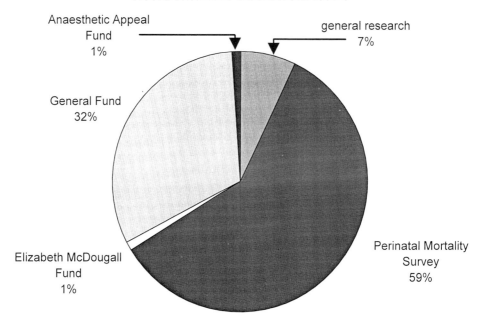

Anaesthetic Appeal Fund 1%

general research 7%

General Fund 32%

Elizabeth McDougall Fund 1%

Perinatal Mortality Survey 59%

Source: NBTF Annual Reports 1944–6
[SA/NBT/C19/11–13]

Lady Rhys Williams was in despair by 1962. "It is evident that a great deal of work will have to be corrected," she complained to Sir George Godber, who had become Chief Medical Officer in 1960, "and that the Ministry's timetable, on which all our plans are based, will not be carried out." She blamed the Ministry for this: "The difficulties have arisen chiefly," she said, "because the mechanical processes have been carried out by the Ministry at two different centres."[113] Sir George defended the Ministry on the grounds of "the invalidity of the original forms", which Lady Rhys Williams promptly refuted.[114] Meanwhile, she arranged for the Oxford Regional Hospital Board to do some of the analysis. Members of the Birthday Trust had offered private loans to pay for this, she explained to Sir George, in order to prevent a "complete failure"[115] and to meet "our commitments to the medical profession".[116] As shown in figure 10.3, the survey was already taking up well over half of the Trust's expenditure during this period of data analysis.

An editorial committee was set up, consisting of J.C. McClure Browne, Dennis Bonham, R.G. Law, Elliot Philipp, Percy Stocks and Neville Butler, and was chaired by Aleck Bourne (the same Aleck Bourne who in 1938 had openly terminated the pregnancy of a fourteen-year-old girl who had been raped).[117] As soon as a chapter was ready, it was put on a plane to Edinburgh for collection by the publishers, E. & S. Livingstone, who sent back the proofs for checking. The freight was provided free by the airline, since it was for a charitable purpose.

The first survey book, *Perinatal Mortality* (1963), is a straightforward account of the survey findings that examines singly the variables associated with perinatal mortality. The authors, Neville Butler and Dennis Bonham, paid tribute to the substantial contribution of the "Survey Team". The second book, *Perinatal Problems* (1969), is an in-depth study of high-risk pregnancies that was produced using multivariate analysis. It consists of sixteen chapters, edited by Neville Butler and Eva Alberman with the assistance of Lara Thomson and Jean M. Fedrick (who became Jean Golding on marriage).

The 1958 survey, which dealt with medical conditions and needed to use clinical terms, was a less accessible report than *Maternity in Great Britain*. However, the material in *Perinatal Mortality* is presented in as straightforward a way as possible, with the major tables on the right-hand pages, and commentary on these on the left-hand pages. The headings are easily comprehensible, but this was not achieved without a heroic struggle. Elliot Philipp was appalled when he saw the first drafts: "they were written in Butlerese and statisticalese," he recalls. "I said, what does this mean in English? Relationships were not called relationships, they were 'as a factor of' . . . and so on." Drawing on the experience of publishing some thirty books, he rewrote the headings on the tables:

> There were three of us sitting together, Dennis Bonham on one side of me, Neville Butler on the other side, and opposite us a typist. I'd say, "What does this mean?" And they would explain, when I said, "You really mean so and so". They said, "Oh yes". So then I said to the typist, "Type that out, table 21, so and so." We sat for two whole days.[118]

THE SURVEY FINDINGS

Since the key findings of the survey are presented in table 10.2, this chapter offers only a brief discussion of some of them. It was found that intrapartum anoxia was the most common cause of perinatal death at 22.9 per cent of the babies born in the survey week; 38.1 per cent of these babies weighed under 2,500 g. Fetal asphyxia was more common in parity 4, and 30 per cent above the

Mr Elliot Philipp, an obstetrician and gynaecologist, who joined the Birthday Trust shortly after the war and was a key member of the 1958 and 1970 survey teams. (Photograph by Guy Hills, reproduced courtesy of Elliot Philipp)

TABLE 10.2: KEY FINDINGS OF THE 1958 PERINATAL MORTALITY REPORT

MOTHERS' ATTRIBUTES INCREASING THE RISK OF PERINATAL DEATH

Biological:
1. Maternal height (lower height increased risk)
2. First or fifth or later born child
3. Maternal age (very young or over thirty-four)
4. Adverse obstetric history
5. Maternal hypertension in pregnancy

Social or behavioural:
1. Father in unskilled occupation or absent
   (their partners tended to be short and to have more babies at the extremes of reproductive ages)
2. Smoking in pregnancy

A mother who was at a disadvantage on all these counts had an average risk of perinatal loss over eight times that of a mother who had none of these risks.

BABIES AT HIGHEST RISK OF PERINATAL DEATH

1. Babies with congenital anomalies
2. Babies born considerably before their expected date
3. Babies of low birth weight (more often born to mothers at social disadvantage)

PATHOLOGICAL CAUSES

1. Lack of oxygen or trauma during labour was thought to account for one-third of the deaths
2. Death before labour and congenital malformations each accounted for another fifth
3. Immaturity, incompatibility between mother's and baby's blood group, and pneumonia together accounted for another 15 per cent

ADVERSE MEDICAL CARE FACTORS

1. The high emergency transfer rate to hospital of mothers of first babies booked for home delivery
2. More than half the mothers, particularly those at high risk, did not receive prenatal care until after the fourth month of pregnancy
3. About one-third had had no haemoglobin measurement in pregnancy
4. One in six did not have regular blood pressure measurements

Prepared by Eva Alberman, one of the two editors of *Perinatal Problems* (1969) average in social class 5. Most of the infants suffering from asphyxia, observes *Perinatal Mortality*, "were otherwise normal and born after 38 weeks gestation; clearly they constitute the group with the greatest potential for salvage."[119]

Of the survey births, 49.1 per cent took place in hospital; 36.1 per cent took place at home; 12.4 per cent took place in a General Practitioner Unit (GP Unit); and 2.4 per cent took place elsewhere (such as private nursing homes, taxis, the street, or an ambulance). Mortality rates were produced for each place of birth. For mothers booked and delivered in consultant staffed hospitals, the perinatal death rate was not much different from the overall mortality rate. For mothers booked and delivered at home, the perinatal death rate was half the national average. For mothers booked for home and later transferred to hospital, either late in pregnancy or during labour, the mortality rate was very high, over three times the national average. For mothers booked and delivered at GP Units, the mortality rate was fractionally higher than that at home. For mothers transferred from GP Unit bookings to a hospital delivery, the mortality rate was over three times the national average, just like the home-to-hospital transfers. For mothers who had not been booked anywhere, the rate of death was highest of all: five times the national average for those delivering in hospital, and very nearly the same for those delivering at home. The fact that so many more deaths occurred in hospital than at home and in GP Units, has been largely attributed to the booking of high-risk patients in hospital units and to the transfer of cases that went wrong at home and in GP Units.[120]

"The lessons brought out by the survey," observe Butler and Bonham in their preface to *Perinatal Mortality*, were "the need for better selection of women for hospital prenatal care and confinement."[121] For the obstetrical causes of perinatal death, wrote Baird, the improvement of medical treatment is likely to be "much more successful" than for the environmental causes. This was especially the case in the industrial areas of Britain, he said, where many mothers showed the effects on health and physique of inadequate living conditions and poverty; these would require a specially high standard of skill if deaths from mechanical causes were to be avoided.[122] It was therefore decided to use the survey data to find a way of identifying which women were at highest risk of having a stillbirth or neonatal death. A score was developed for each adverse effect: for example, since the risk of regular smoking after the fourth month of pregnancy was roughly comparable with that of being in social class 4 or 5,[123] or being under 62 inches in height, these were given a similar score. Once added up into a total, these scores could then be converted into an estimated mortality risk.[124] According to this system, the wife of a professional man having her second baby would achieve a mortality ratio of 55; whereas the wife of an unskilled worker having her fourth or subsequent baby would achieve a ratio of 198.[125] This identified the second woman as four times more in need of hospital and consultant care than the first.

This scoring system met one of the key recommendations of the Cranbrook

Report – that "A more careful selection of patients should be made for domiciliary confinements and for admission to hospital."[126] Its underlying principle was inherently democratic, since it offered a tool to the NHS to allocate scarce resources strictly on the basis of need. The system was generally welcomed and Sir George Godber reported in the mid-1960s that a summary had been sent out to chairmen of Maternity Liaison Committees. The value of these 'risk predictors' has been challenged, however. The medical statistician Alison Macfarlane has observed that the antenatal and labour prediction scores developed from the 1958 survey (and also the 1970 survey, which will be discussed in the next chapter of this book) have not been widely validated on other sets of data, so that their predictive ability is unknown. Also, studies in other areas that have attempted to use scores of this type to predict outcome have not had great success.[127]

Babies born to poor mothers, revealed the survey, suffered a higher rate of perinatal mortality than those born to mothers who were better-off. In social classes 1 and 2, the mortality rate was 6.7 per 1,000 lower than that for all classes, while in social classes 4 and 5, the rate was 3.9 per 1,000 above that for all classes. In social class 3, the perinatal death rate did not differ significantly from the average. Despite the postwar narrowing of class inequalities, therefore, "disparity still exists to a marked degree". This disparity was consistent with the regional distribution of perinatal death, which was shown by the survey to be lowest in the south and to increase gradually in a north-westerly direction. The higher rates of death in the north were shown to be due more to 'environmental' than to 'obstetrical' causes, related to the higher numbers of women in social classes 4 and 5 in that part of Britain. Better-off women, though, were more likely to give birth in hospital than those who were poor. *Perinatal Mortality* comments: "In the five standard social class groups the selection for hospital booking bears an inverse tendency to the overall mortality by class. The percentage selection for home delivery rises with lower social class so that the higher risk patients appear to be selected for home confinement."[128]

The PMS has been identified as one of a small number of studies in the 1950s to produce information about the prevalence of poverty in postwar Britain.[129] In 1955, the MRC Social Medicine Research Unit published a paper based on data going back to 1911, which showed that class differences in perinatal mortality were not narrowing.[130] This was usefully confirmed by the survey's findings, which challenged the comfortable assumption that poverty had been abolished by the welfare state and that social inequality belonged to the bygone era of the Depression. As Titmuss pointed out in 1958, behind the development of the social services known as the 'Welfare State', lay a kind of social inequality in which the better off, who had most power and occupational success, were still rewarded by much better services.[131]

'KITCHEN TABLE' DELIVERY

At a conference held in October 1962, Nixon, McClure Browne and Bonham claimed that the survey data showed it was safer for women to give birth in hospital than at home. Nixon, who was a passionate man, went further and said, "Surely it was known that the days of taking out an appendix on the kitchen table had gone, and yet delivery under similar conditions was perpetuated."[132] Horrified at hearing this because he knew it would infuriate GPs, Dr Butler pleaded with the journalists present not to draw the conclusion that the Trust wanted all women to have their babies in hospital. The press ignored him. "Lack of care kills 50 babies a week. Survey shows home is not best", was the sensational report in the *Guardian*. The *Daily Herald* referred to "shocks over babies born at home" and the *Daily Telegraph* said that "Specialists want crash plan on baby deaths. Deliveries 'in Kitchen Table conditions'."[133]

GPs were outraged. One letter to the *BMJ* complained that the figures had not been examined dispassionately, while another reminded readers that avoidable tragedies occurred in hospital as well as at home.[134] Butler sought to mollify the doctors. He explained to readers of the *BMJ* that these statements "were views expressed by individual doctors or organizations". He added, "The purpose of the press conference was to present facts accurately and not to present conclusions"; departures from this plan, he explained, had been largely the result of confusion generated by the rail strike.[135] The RCOG distanced itself as much as possible from the implied criticism of GPs.[136] Lady Rhys Williams vigorously backed Nixon. "A big survey I organised," she wrote to a friend a couple of weeks after the press conference, "has shown that over 100,000 mothers with 'high risk' conditions are still confined at home and the situation is growing rapidly worse."[137] Her position had changed radically since the Safer Motherhood meeting in 1948, when she had argued that, "For those who can afford to have a full time maternity nurse, I have absolutely no doubt at all that home is happier . . . The prejudice against having babies at home is entirely wrong."[138]

Nixon was much disliked by GPs after his attack on home delivery. Elliot Philipp recalls that, "they couldn't do anything to Nixon, he was all powerful because he was a genius, he had charisma, he was superb . . . so they got at him through Bonham, and they let it be known that Bonham, who was Nixon's assistant at UCH, was never going to get a consultant job."[139] Shortly after this, Bonham left Britain for New Zealand.

SHORTAGE OF HOSPITAL BEDS

After the disastrous press conference, the Birthday Trust hurriedly protested that it was interested only in data, not in opinions, and pointed out that "a factual book is being prepared for publication".[140] This was not entirely

TABLE 10.3: MATERNITY SERVICES EMERGENCY INFORMAL COMMITTEE

Professor Sir Dugald Baird	Dr John S. Happel
Miss Josephine Barnes	Dr J.A. Heady
Miss Lois Beaulah	Miss D. James
Professor D.G. Bonham	Miss M.K. Knight
Dr J.P. Bound	Dr W.N. Leak
Miss S. Briggs	Dr F.M. Martin
Professor J.C. McClure Browne	Dr Ann Mullins
Dr N.R. Butler	Professor W.C.W. Nixon
Dr W.C.V. Brothwood	Dr Mary Paterson
Professor N.B. Capon	Dr W.E. Smith
Dr A.E. Claireaux	Mr Elliot E. Philipp
Miss J.M. Darwin	Mr N.W. Please
Dr J.W.B. Douglas	Miss E. Renwick
Mr R.J. Fenney	Mr Arnold Walker
Professor D.V. Glass	Miss M. Wearn
Dr F. Gray	Juliet, Lady Rhys Williams
Mr John Hamilton	Miss A. Wood

accurate, however: it was also interested in the development of policy, based on the data that had been collected. At the same time that *Perinatal Mortality* was published, the Trust released the report of its Maternity Services Emergency Informal Committee (MSEIC), which had been created to propose emergency measures based on the survey findings. All the professional bodies associated with maternity were represented on the committee (listed in table 10.3), which was convened on 12 February 1963.

The report expressed concern at the shortage of hospital beds for maternity cases and of senior obstetrical staff and midwives. As a temporary measure, it advocated a policy of early discharge from hospital. So long as arrangements were made for the proper care of mother and baby on their return from hospital, it argued, the medical risks of this were less serious than those of not admitting her at all. This argument was influenced by the achievements of Dugald Baird in Aberdeen, where a low perinatal rate had been obtained "mainly because nearly 90 per cent of confinements in the city take place in a teaching hospital which also assumes responsibility for standards of care in local health authority clinics and in domiciliary midwifery."[141] The MSEIC suggested a reduction in the hospital stay from ten to eight days, but also referred approvingly to a scheme that had operated since 1956 in Bradford, where 40 per cent of cases were discharged on the second day after birth, so as to release beds for antenatal care and for cases of severe toxaemia; this was associated with a dramatic fall in the perinatal death rate.

Early discharge would not have been considered for a moment before the war, when it was regarded as imperative for a woman to stay in bed for fourteen days after delivery. One mother who gave birth in the 1930s recalls the midwife checking her feet for dust during the next two weeks, to see if she had been out of bed.[142] This fourteen-day rule was shown to be unnecessary during the war, when mothers had to get up to go to the shelters during air raids, recalls Elliot Philipp.[143]

It has been argued that early discharge increased the rate of hospital delivery, since the numbers of maternity beds in England and Wales increased by only 15 per cent between 1955 and 1968, while the total number of births increased by 18 per cent. The rise in the institutional delivery rate to 80.6 per cent in 1968, therefore, was achieved by a reduction in the average length of stay.[144] This is exactly what the Trust proposed in 1963. To this extent, the MSEIC report can be regarded as successful in achieving its objectives; however, it should not be regarded as an isolated influence, but as one that reflected current trends in thinking about maternity care.

The cover of this late 1960s Birthday Trust calendar shows a mother and baby after a hospital delivery. By 1968 the national figure for hospital delivery was over 80 per cent. ([NBTF/uncatalogued] Reproduced courtesy of the Wellcome Institute Library, London)

So topical became the issue of where to give birth after the 'Kitchen Table' fiasco, that it was the subject of a 'Panorama' programme on BBC television in May 1963. Miss Wood, General Secretary of the Royal College of Midwives, was one of the guests and told Richard Dimbleby, the programme host, that hospital delivery should reach 70 per cent (as proposed by the Cranbrook Report) and that home and hospital services should complement each other. Professor McClure Browne, who was also a guest on the programme, said that all births would be in hospital in twenty years anyway, and deplored the fact that eighty babies were lost every week from preventable asphyxia. "If every member of Parliament were an expectant mother," he argued, "we would see some action very, very quickly."[145]

Action *was* seen very quickly. By 1965, the Cranbrook Report's target of 70 per cent hospital delivery had been reached; and by 1968, the national figure (though concealing regional variations) was over 80 per cent. There were various reasons for this. One was the availability of beds following a decline in the birth rate, which had not been anticipated by the Hospital Plan of 1962; filling these empty beds was more cost-effective for the government than developing the domiciliary midwifery service. The demands of women's groups, such as the Association for the Improvement of the Maternity Services (AIMS), which had been set up in 1960 to campaign for more hospital beds, also had an impact. Another factor was the operation of interest group politics, in which obstetricians successfully undermined the role of GPs in obstetrics.

SMOKING IN PREGNANCY

An average reduction in birth weight of 170 g was observed in the babies of mothers who smoked after the fourth month of pregnancy; also, the perinatal mortality rate was raised significantly before, during and after delivery. This finding was achieved by multivariate analysis: "one was able to say, well it's not the social class of the mother, it's not the fact that it's her tenth baby or that she's 45 or 14 – the cause is smoking because that can have an effect on any mother no matter what."[146] It was also shown that the effects of smoking varied according to the mother's social class, with babies born into better-off families being less affected.

The idea that smoking might be dangerous for babies first occurred to Neville Butler about four months before the 1958 survey. "I read in *Reader's Digest*," he recalls, "that a nun, called Nun Simpson, had made the observation in a nursing home in California, that the babies weighed less where the mother smoked in pregnancy. And I thought, my God, why haven't I thought of it before? Because it would interfere with the oxygen."[147] The possibility of a relationship between smoking and pregnancy was occurring to several people at this time. It was first described by W.J. Simpson in 1957 and then by C.R. Lowe in 1959.[148] Concern about smoking grew in 1962, when the Royal College of

Physicians published *Smoking and Health*, which claimed that cigarette smoking was a cause of lung cancer. It was sold out within a week and Macmillan as Prime Minister took questions on it in the House of Commons. In August 1962, the *Medical Officer* reported that the US Public Health Service had published findings suggesting that premature births occur more frequently among mothers who smoke, than among those who do not.[149] In this process of discovery, the PMS played a key role. As the largest series of perinatal deaths yet analysed in relation to maternal smoking, it provided powerful confirmatory evidence of the dangers to the foetus of maternal smoking.

After an article containing the relevant analyses was published in the *BMJ* in 1972, Harvey Goldstein was asked to write up the results for *Concern*, the journal of the National Children's Bureau, and to give an estimate of the number of excess deaths due to smoking. *Concern* was circulated to the media, which led to 'Mums Cigs Killed 1,500 Babies' being splashed over the front page of the *Sun* on 8 September 1973. *Nature* responded by carrying a full page editorial arguing that Goldstein had drawn inferences about "causability" from "merely" statistical association; they added a phrase to the effect that pregnant mothers should be encouraged not to smoke, which undermined their own argument. A vigorous debate ensued in the letter section of *Nature* between Goldstein and those who contested his conclusions.[150] The association has subsequently been strengthened and it is now generally accepted that smoking is linked with low weight babies, along with factors like age and class.[151] Vigorous health education campaigns, especially by the Health Education Council, have sought to alert pregnant women to this risk and to encourage them to give up smoking. This relationship between mothers' smoking and the health of babies, believes Eva Alberman, was the single most important finding to emerge from the survey.[152]

The British perinatal mortality rate fell from 35 per 1,000 births in 1958 to 25 in 1967. Whether or not the PMS contributed to this fall, it is impossible to know, especially since the rate fell in a number of countries over this period. What is certain, though, is that the survey was in the vanguard of the campaign to reduce perinatal death; as a leader in the *Lancet* observed in 1969, its focus on the problem promoted wide discussion and a reappraisal of the maternity services.[153]

There were enthusiastic reviews of the survey books in the important medical journals of many countries of the world.[154] Maurice Macmillan congratulated the Trust, saying that the survey work had been praised and used by many other nations. It was not often nowadays, he added, that Britain could say she leads the world (Britain was losing the last vestiges of its Empire at this time: between 1960 and 1969, twenty-seven British colonies became independent), but "in this great humanitarian effort she has done so".[155] In 1971, an important report on perinatality produced by the Ministry of Health in France referred to the "données relativement exceptionnelles" of the survey.[156] In the year that

The Sun *made headline news on 8 September 1973 out of findings from the 1958 survey that associated maternal smoking with dangers to the foetus.*

Perinatal Mortality was published, the World Health Organization (WHO) set up an Expert Committee on Perinatal Mortality, which Bonham and Butler joined.

Several countries carried out their own perinatal studies in the 1960s and 1970s, copying the British model. Between 1970 and 1982, Neville Butler and Harvey Goldstein acted as advisors to the Cuban government, which carried out a perinatal mortality survey in 1973, looking at all births on the island in one week (4,400) and deaths over four months. During a visit to a Cuban town where they were going to advise on procedure for post-mortems, they were greeted by a poster saying, 'Viva la mortalidad perinatal'![157] Dr Butler recalls an attempt to initiate a national survey in the USA (where there had been a large Collaborative Study in the 1950s that was similar to the PMS, but was not nationwide). His presentation of the idea was greeted enthusiastically by representatives of all major health services and professional groups, until the question of litigation arose in relation to cases where something had gone wrong. Instantly, all discussions ceased.

FOLLOWING UP THE SURVEY CHILDREN

As in the case of the 1946 survey, there was no plan to conduct a follow-up of the PMS cohort until afterwards. The success of the first longitudinal study then generated interest in the 1958 children and the possibility of drawing comparisons between the two cohorts. "Speaking rather selfishly from the point of view of our own follow-up study," wrote David Glass to Miss Barnes in the summer of 1964, "we badly need a parallel inquiry which will be able to measure what, if any, changes have taken place in a number of important aspects of child development and education since we did our own study."[158] An opportunity for such a study arose out of a chance conversation at a Birthday Trust meeting between Neville Butler and Lady Plowden, a new member of the Trust, who was chairing a government committee looking into primary school education (the Plowden Enquiry). Butler told her about the potential of looking at the development and education of the 1958 children, which intrigued her. Subsequently, in 1964, the Department of Education and Science commissioned the newly launched National Children's Bureau (then called the National Bureau for Cooperation in Child Care) to collect information on all the 1958 children when they were seven; there were four sponsoring bodies, of which the Birthday Trust was one. This follow-up study of more than 14,000 children was directed by Neville Butler and the child psychologist, Dr Mia Kellmer-Pringle, Director of the National Children's Bureau; its first major publication appeared as an appendix to the Plowden Report.

This was the beginning of the National Child Development Study (NCDS), which has so far conducted five exercises to trace the members of the original study in order to monitor their physical, educational and social development. After the sweep of seven-year-olds in 1965, the next four took place in 1969 (at age 11), in 1974 (at age 16), in 1981 (at age 23), and in 1991 (at age 33). These have produced a wealth of data on health, class, education, housing, disability, employment, relationships with partners, and parenting; the key findings are summarized in table 10.4. Funds for the study have come mostly from public sources, although private trusts have funded some of the sub-studies. The Laura Ashley company gave money for a study of second-chance education, because

TABLE 10.4: SOME FINDINGS OF THE NATIONAL CHILD DEVELOPMENT STUDY (NCDS)

– At age seven height was shown to advance with increasing maternal height, social class and birth weight

– Children of mothers who smoked during pregnancy were shorter on average than children of mothers who did not smoke

– Average height was also shorter among children of younger mothers (i.e. under twenty-five years) than among children of older mothers

– Subjects in the 1958 birth cohort were shown to be taller on average than their parents and also taller than the 1946 cohort. The average height of women has not increased at the same rate as that of men; differences between social classes have shown only small fluctuations

– Overweight was nearly twice as common among seven-year-olds in the 1958 cohort than in the 1946 cohort, although the difference was less by adolescence

– Subjects with a chronic physical illness at any time during childhood had increased risk of psychosocial problems

– At age sixteen, 18 per cent had been prescribed glasses, but when these children were tested as part of the survey at that age, 27 per cent of these were found to have normal unaided visual acuity or only a minor defect

– Myopic children at eleven and sixteen achieved higher academic attainments than their normal sighted peers

– Children with severe speech difficulties at age seven had relatively poor school performance

– Both pneumonia and asthma or wheezy bronchitis up to age seven were associated with a significant excess in the prevalence of chronic cough at age twenty-three, after controlling for current smoking

– Chronic lower respiratory tract illness in adults is associated with poor home circumstances earlier in life

– Children at increased risk of handicaps not visible at birth could be identified from their perinatal circumstances (such as being a later-born child, or being delivered abnormally)

– Breastfeeding is associated with reduced risk of heart disease in adult life

– About 11 per cent of children were bed-wetting at age seven and approximately 5 per cent at age eleven

– Certain disadvantaged groups (in the poorest housing, low income and unfavourable family situations) appear to be at greater risk of poor behaviour

– Disadvantaged eleven-year-olds were shown to be more likely to have an accident followed by hospital admissions

– Teenage accidents, occurring at fifteen or sixteen years, were higher among those who had more conflict with their parents than in those who had less conflict

– At age eleven, children living in disadvantaged circumstances had more absence from school because of ill health compared with other children. Absences for more serious illnesses were more common among disadvantaged children

– Those who were disadvantaged were found to make less use of preventive health services

– Immunization is associated with reduced risks of childhood illness and adult health problems

– Risk of having an appendectomy was associated with a lack of household amenities

– Smoking was heavier among working-class than middle-class children

– A key predictor of children's educational achievement is interest shown by parents

– How schools are organized, including whether they are selective, has relatively little connection with educational attainment, but a change of Head can have marked effects

– Poor school attendance is associated with later marital breakdown, and with lower status occupations, less stable career patterns and more unemployment

– Children whose parents have basic literacy problems are likely to suffer from a diminished opportunity to acquire literacy and numeracy skills

– Poor economic conditions at birth disadvantage people in their subsequent employment and depress their adult incomes

– Children who experienced poor housing at seven, eleven or sixteen perform less well at school at sixteen

– Children who have been in care exhibit poor attainment and poor behaviour at school

– Children from lone parent families have lower school attainment, which is related to the material and socio-economic circumstances of such families

– Problems attributed to parental divorce or separation may have been present before the parental separation

– Women are economically dependent on men even in the early stages of partnership

Prepared by Peter Shepherd, member of the NCDS survey team

Bernard Ashley had left school at fourteen and wanted to help children faced with similar difficulties. The Leverhulme Trust funded a study of gifted children in 1969 and the Tobacco Research Council funded a smoking survey in 1978. The NCDS is now based at the Social Statistics Research Unit at City University in London and is directed by Professor John Bynner.

For the first three NCDS surveys, the cohort was augmented by adding immigrants born in the relevant week, who had been identified from school registers; it then became known as a national age cohort, rather than a birth cohort. No new immigrants were added after 1974, because of the difficulties of tracing them once the age group had left school. This led to a bias in the 1981 survey, since young people of Caribbean origin were under-represented by about one third, those from the Indian subcontinent by about one quarter and those from Ireland by about one tenth.[159] Assistance with the tracing of children has been provided by the Office of Population Census and Statistics (OPCS, which later became part of the Office of National Statistics) and the annual mailing of a birthday card has proved useful, as with the 1946 cohort study. A pre-paid reply slip is sent with the card, which asks questions about changes in address and the subject's life. The 1984 birthday card, for example, asked about the number of consumer goods in the household (such as a television, home computer and car), weight, experience of migraine, and date of birth of any children. The annual birthday card is the subject's single reliable link with the study. One member says that he has always enjoyed a sense of belonging to the cohort, ever since it made him feel special at school. When the card arrives, he explains, there is an "exclusivity about it, like belonging to a club. It's not the lodge business, of the secret wink and secrets. You're not actually 'a birthday card receiver' in any meaningful way, but it does mean that you belong."

The studies rely heavily on the willingness of cohort members like him. "After doing the 1981 questionnaire, I was worn out," he recalls, adding, "it took an awful lot of thought. And it was very intrusive, not in a bad way, but the questions asked about very private matters."[160] Once the child had been singled out for investigation, the mother's primary role in the study was forgotten; in one family, the child did not even know about the initial survey of 1958.[161] He has recalled the excitement of taking tests and then his disappointment at not being told his results: "I was a healthy relatively intelligent kid of seven who was quite competitive, normally competitive. The tests were fun, but I wanted to know my results." This cohort member has taken part in all five sweeps of the study, but been told virtually nothing about it. He was astonished to discover how many publications it had generated.[162] The absence of feedback has been a constant feature of the NCDS, with the exception of an *Observer* colour supplement – with a feature on the study – that was sent to cohort members. Wendy Moore, an NCDS member who has always taken an interest in the survey and is a journalist, has made a determined effort to find out about the survey findings and has written articles about them for the general public.[163]

Like the PMS, the NCDS has revealed a strong relationship between social class and quality of life: that children from disadvantaged backgrounds show reduced height and increased medical problems, as well as difficult behaviour and poor educational attainment. It has also shown that low birth weight is associated with socio-economic disadvantage in childhood and adolescence: that cohort members who weighed 6 lb or under at birth were more likely to experience socio-economic disadvantage.[164] It is in highlighting society's class divisions that the survey has probably been most influential, believes Wendy Moore. "From the start," she comments, "babies of working-class families were least likely to be born in hospital and most likely to be low weight. As children they were more likely to be short, suffer hearing loss, get winter coughs, become obese, do poorly at school, fall prey to serious illnesses, undergo psychological strains and end up in hospital after an accident. They made least use of preventive health measures."[165]

The size of the 1958 cohort, which belongs to the baby boom generation and is the largest sample of young people ever examined in this way in Britain, is one of the keys to its success. Only with such a very large sample, observed Dr Kellmer-Pringle, is it possible to have enough people in particular groups (for example, adopted children, gifted children, and those in care), so as to determine the outcome of a range of characteristics.[166] Incidence rates of fairly common conditions, such as congenital defects and speech problems, were easily calculated from a sample of this size. In addition, numerous sociological variables (such as social class, family size, and housing site) have been correlated with all sorts of medical, behavioural and educational measures. For example, smoking in pregnancy has been shown to have some influence on the physical and mental development of children,[167] and the data have also suggested that in very rare cases, the children of women who had influenza in pregnancy were at increased risk of developing leukaemia. Findings like these have major implications for the development of policy at the national level, and the NCDS has contributed substantially to the Plowden Report (1967) on primary education, to the Finer Report (1974) on one-parent families, to the Warnock Report (1978) on children with disabilities (which used NCDS data to show that the employment prospects for the disabled are severely and unnecessarily limited), and to the Court Report (1976) on child health services.

Now that the study is moving towards its fifth decade, it is proving useful to historians. David Crook, an historian of education, has commented on the "rich vein" of possibilities provided by the NCDS data for future collaborations between sociologists, historians and statisticians. He explains, "These data allow us to match the experiences of young people against studies of local, regional and national policy. Elsewhere in Europe, 'life histories' are an important theme for sociologists and historians, and the NCDS is a unique longitudinal study which may be interrogated by British scholars."[168] The surveys have uncovered not only changes over time, but also behaviour that stays the same. The most recent NCDS sweep revealed that although there was considerable support in the 1990s for the equal sharing of domestic work between men and women, little had actually changed and the routine household chores continued to fall largely on the shoulders of women.[169]

Comparing the lives of the 1946 and 1958 cohort groups is instructive. The second wave of children, for instance, were less likely to undergo tonsillectomy or circumcision than those born in 1946, but the later cohort were more likely to develop diabetes. A comparison with yet another cohort group became possible following the 1970 birth survey, which is the subject of the next chapter.

CHAPTER ELEVEN

British Births 1970 and Other Surveys

While the 1958 survey data were still being analysed, plans were started for a third births survey. Although there had been an overall fall in the perinatal death rate, from 35 for every 1,000 births in 1958 to 26.3 in 1966,[1] not everybody had benefited from this improvement. While the infant mortality rate among babies in social class 1 was on a par with the overall rate in Sweden, one of the lowest in Europe, the rate among babies born to poor families in inner city areas was "still equal to the average infant mortality rate over the whole country in the 1930s," reported the Trust in the 1970s.[2] This meant that problems facing poor mothers in the early years of the Trust had yet to be solved. A particular cause for concern was the proportion of babies born below 2,500 g. This low birth weight, which research was showing to be often avoidable and to be associated with intellectual impairment and other difficulties,[3] had stayed at 7 per cent since 1958 and was higher among poor families.

Although the nation had grown more prosperous, there was actually an increase in unemployment in the 1960s and in the numbers and proportion of the population in poverty, according to the sociologist Peter Townsend in *Poverty in the United Kingdom* (1979).[4] In this situation, a third births survey was invaluable, according to Frank Field, a social reformer and Labour MP who was an influential member of the Trust in the 1970s. As standards generally rise, he has explained, "it is important to have measurements for the poorest and those individuals who are most vulnerable."[5]

Some doubt was expressed, though, about the value of doing another national survey. James Douglas, the director of the 1946 survey and its follow-up, advocated a set of regional surveys instead, which would make the subsequent cohort easier to follow.[6] The Home Office showed little interest[7] and there was a risk that Medical Officers of Health would create obstacles to a third survey, since many doctors had been infuriated by the 'Kitchen Table' furore that followed the presentation of the 1958 data. Sir George Godber warned the Trust that opinion among the Medical Officers of Health was likely to be divided and urged them to find out about this before going ahead.[8] But perhaps the most serious difficulty for the Trust to overcome was the death of Lady Rhys Williams in 1964, which was swiftly followed by the death in 1966 of

William Nixon, the originator of the 1958 survey. It was as if the early postwar generation of the Trust had disappeared, just as Lady Baldwin's generation had passed away by the end of the Second World War. The time had come for a third generation to take over the Trust and to guide it through the last decades of the century.

In an effort to compensate for the loss of leadership created by the deaths of Lady Rhys Williams and Professor Nixon, the Trust created the post of a full-time director for the third survey and appointed the epidemiologist, Roma Chamberlain. She had worked in the Department of Health and had herself for a period run the Confidential Enquiries into Maternal Deaths. Since she had also acted as a ministry observer on the Perinatal Mortality Survey, she was ideally suited for the job. The obstetrician to the survey was a young man called Geoffrey Chamberlain, who was not related to Roma, despite their shared name. This led to occasional difficulties, because so many people assumed they

were married. "I once slept in a billiards room in Newcastle," recalls Geoffrey Chamberlain, "because the hotel was full and they had booked us into a double room because we were Dr Chamberlain and Dr Chamberlain."[9] Geoffrey Chamberlain was senior registrar at King's College Hospital to John Peel, the President of the RCOG, who recommended him to the Steering Committee in January 1968.[10]

With Roma Chamberlain as the full-time director, the management of the survey took on a more methodical style than had been the case with the 1958 study, which had been run by some brilliant but rather eccentric individuals. Roma Chamberlain insisted on having a full-time statistician, Brian Howlett,[11] and this core team of three was based at the Birthday Trust headquarters at Lower Belgrave Street. It was advised by a Steering Committee (see table 11.1) that was chaired by Josephine Barnes, who had represented the Population Investigation Committee on the first

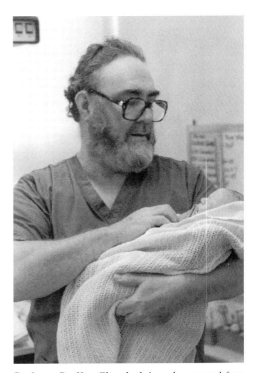

Professor Geoffrey Chamberlain, who emerged from the 1970 survey as a leading figure in the Birthday Trust. An obstetrician and gynaecologist, he is holding a baby he looked after through pregnancy and childbirth. (This photograph was taken in the labour ward by the baby's father and has been reproduced courtesy of Geoffrey Chamberlain)

TABLE 11.1: STEERING COMMITTEE FOR THE 1970 SURVEY	
Chairman	Roma Chamberlain
Josephine Barnes	Albert Claireaux
	A.M. Dickins
Members	James Douglas
Eva Alberman	J.A. Heady
Dugald Baird	Ann Mullins
J.C. McClure Browne	Elliot Philipp
Neville Butler	J.P.M. Tizard
Geoffrey Chamberlain	Cicely Williams

survey and then chaired the Steering Committee of the second. James Douglas, another veteran of the first two surveys, joined the Steering Committee for the third, and seven of the fifteen members on the committee had been involved in the previous survey. The supporting cast for the survey was huge. Miss Barnes advised having representatives from every organization with a related interest, in order to ensure their cooperation; this was especially important in the case of Medical Officers of Health, who would carry much of the responsibility for collecting the data.[12] These representatives joined the numerous groups that were set up: the Nominated Representatives, the Government Observers, the Initial Working Party, the four Working Parties on the Content of the Survey (Obstetric, Paediatric, Socio-economic, and Medical Care and Administration), and the Working Party on the Final Arrangements for the Survey. On the 1946 survey, no organizations had been represented at all, apart from the PIC and BCOG; in 1958, sixteen organizations (including government departments) had sent representatives; and in 1970, this figure reached twenty-three.

This third survey did not focus on death, as the 1958 survey had done, but on the care of babies who survived and on problems of morbidity; it emphasized this focus by calling it 'British Births'. Another difference was that right from the start, plans were made to build into the survey the basis for a subsequent longitudinal study: in the case of the 1946 and 1958 surveys, the follow-ups had been afterthoughts. Neville Butler was particularly anxious this time to study the period from one month to seven years, which had not been included in the 1958 study, in order to show the effect of events around birth on children's progress to seven years of age.

The Royal College of Obstetricians, which had jointly undertaken the 1946 survey with the PIC, took a key role in the third survey by offering professional backing and a guarantee of £10,000 for the salary of director.[13] Some members of the Trust had misgivings about this. During a discussion about survey notepaper, they expressed dismay at the proposed heading, 'A survey to be carried out by the National Birthday Trust Fund and the Royal College of

Obstetricians and Gynaecologists'; they were not convinced, they said, that the College's role would amount to an equal partnership.[14] A consensus was eventually reached on the phrase, '*Under the joint auspices* of the National Birthday Trust Fund and the Royal College of Obstetricians and Gynaecologists',[15] which appears on the covers of the two survey volumes. The survey had the wholehearted support of the President of the College, Sir John Peel, who believed it was "of the greatest importance".[16] His commitment may have been nourished by plans for the Trust to merge with the College, which were being developed at this time. They had petered out by 1973, but this did not diminish the College's association with the survey. The foreword to the first volume of the survey report, *British Births*, was written by Stanley Clayton, President of the College when it was published in 1975; and the foreword to the second volume was written by John Dewhurst, who was President when it was published in 1977.

THE PEEL REPORT

While plans were going ahead both for a third survey and also for the Trust to merge with the College, a committee was set up in 1967 by the Central Health Services Council to consider the future of the domiciliary midwifery service and the question of bed needs for maternity patients; chaired by John Peel, it was known as the Peel Committee. In 1970, it produced a report that has been described as "an important watershed in policy on the place of birth",[17] because it recommended that "*sufficient facilities should be provided to allow for 100% hospital delivery*. The greater safety of hospital confinement for mother and child justifies this objective."[18] The Peel Report has been widely regarded as the natural development of the 1959 Cranbrook Report, which had recommended a 70 per cent hospital delivery rate. In fact, though, these reports were not related: the Cranbrook Committee was set up by the Minister of Health and produced an official government report. The Peel Committee, on the other hand, as a Sub-Committee of the Standing Maternity and Midwifery Advisory Committee of the Central Health Services Council, was a relatively low status committee of the independent advisory machinery. The Peel Report was not, therefore, an expression of government policy, like the Cranbrook Report.[19]

The Peel Report relied heavily on the data generated by the Perinatal Mortality Survey. *Perinatal Mortality*, which is referred to as an authority at various points, is one of just fourteen independent (that is, not produced by the government or by professional associations) documents in the list of references. Of these fourteen, it is one of only two books; the rest are journal articles. Common to both the Peel Report and the report of the 1958 survey is the assumption of the greater safety of hospital confinement for mother and child, without actually establishing that this greater safety exists or even comparing the relative risks of home and hospital delivery. The relationship between the

Peel Committee and the Trust surveys was one of mutual influence: while his committee was still in progress, John Peel wrote in the foreword to *Perinatal Problems* that the 1958 survey had led "to re-thinking many obstetric procedures and to reorganising a good deal of obstetric practice";[20] then, in 1968, he offered the Trust the help of his committee in the design of the third survey.[21]

PREPARING FOR THE SURVEY

It was a major challenge to raise enough funds to carry out the study of British Births. A national survey was even more expensive now than it had been in the 1950s, and by the end of 1978, a total of £65,386 had been spent; between 1972 and 1976, more than half the Trust's expenditure was allocated to the survey (see figure 11.1). The Trust set up a special Appeals Committee, chaired by Maurice Macmillan, the Tory Opposition front bench spokesman on health, who described himself as "beggar-in-chief".[22] The main donors were the Variety Club of Great Britain, which gave £10,000, the Spastics Society, which gave £5,000, and the King's Fund, which gave £2,000. Some donations came from British companies that already had a relationship with the Trust, such as: British

FIGURE 11.1: NBTF EXPENDITURE 1972–6

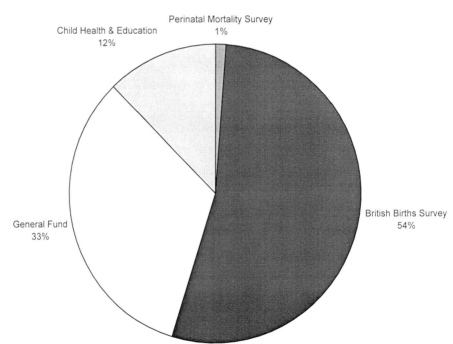

Source: NBTF Balance Sheets 1972–6
[SA/NBT/D1/3/12-13 & D1/4/1-3]

Oxygen Ltd, which led the market in the production of gas and air machines; the Glaxo Trust, which had been set up by the Glaxo company that had produced Minadex for the 1930s nutrition experiments; Pergamon Press, which was owned by Robert Maxwell, the husband of Elizabeth Maxwell, a member of the Birthday Trust; and the Sir Walter Gilbey Memorial Fund, which had been set up by the famous family of spirits merchants to which Walter Gilbey, the current Chairman of the Birthday Trust, belonged. Many individuals also gave contributions, like the Greek millionaire Aristotle Onassis. In 1966, to supplement its own fundraising efforts, the Trust employed Jeffrey Archer as Director-General, with the express task of raising funds for a third survey. When this proved unsuccessful, a professional fundraising company, Hooker Craigmyle, was then appointed to carry out an Appeal Campaign. This was launched by Princess Alexandra, who had become Patron of the Birthday Trust in 1966, at the Annual General Meeting of the Birthday Trust on 10 December 1968. However, funds were still insufficient and by September 1969, the two Chamberlains felt obliged to warn Miss Riddick, "We have considered whether we will be able to undertake the survey if more money is not forthcoming."[23] By the autumn of 1971, however, Sir Brandon had rescued the project, by persuading Sir Keith Joseph at the Department of Health and Social Security to give a two-year grant for 1972 and 1973, "so that the findings can be published without delay";[24] this amounted to £14,000 by the end of 1973. Additional funds for analysis slowly came in, including another £2,000 from the Royal College of Obstetricians and Gynaecologists in 1972.[25]

Numerous suggestions for the 1970 questionnaire were put forward, at meetings of up to fifty people in the Birthday Trust drawing room. The two Chamberlains hastily circulated a memo, warning that it would be impossible to include everything and pointing out that cohort studies ran into difficulties when more information was collected than it was possible to process.[26] Many questions were rejected: there was talk of collecting information on the mental health of the mother, but Peel took the view that this was "bristling with difficulties".[27] A question on the cost of pregnancy, which had not been investigated since the 1946 survey, was rejected on the grounds that this needed a special enquiry. It was also decided by the Steering Committee that questions about home births "should be omitted or treated with due caution".[28] This meant that the original aim of the 1958 survey, which was to study the relative risks of hospital and home confinement, did not feature at all in the 1970 survey.

The eventual questionnaire covered the care of mother and baby for the first week after delivery and there was also a section on the mother's social background, which the Working Party regarded as a key section of the enquiry.[29] This was the most comprehensive of the three survey questionnaires and took forty-five minutes to fill in. In 1966 Sir George Godber (grimly aware of the struggle involved in analysing the 1958 data) had warned against "a questionnaire so elaborate that it would defy statistical analysis",[30] but it was impossible to resist the pressure to include so many questions. When it was finally ready, recalls Geoffrey Chamberlain, "we did pre-pre-pre-pilot surveys, pre-pre pilots, pre-pilots, and pilots."[31]

The questionnaire had to be filled out by the midwife attending the mother. First she handed her a letter explaining what was involved and asking if she were willing to take part; if not, she was excluded from the survey. Throughout the questionnaire, the mother is referred to in the third person as 'the mother', just as in the 1946 survey. This made her more visible than in the 1958 survey, when she was simply 'the patient'. However, whereas the 1946 questions address the mother directly as 'you', the 1970 questions follow the 1958 model and refer to her indirectly, as 'she'/'her'. In the 1946 questionnaire, mothers' views had been actively sought. One question to the mother had asked whether "anything more could have been done to make your delivery or confinement more satisfactory. If so, give details", at which point the health worker conducting the interview is told to, "*Write in exactly what the mother says.*"[32] This concern to discover the views of mothers is not apparent in the 1958 and 1970 questionnaires. In volume 2 of *British Births*, in fact, the comment that, "The most important measure of analgesia is the degree of pain relief felt by the mother", is followed by the surprising statement that "*no attempt was made to collect data on this*". The survey was specifically designed to give an account of "the services we provided to mothers and babies before and after birth",[33] rather than the experience of these services by mothers.

THE SURVEY WEEK

It had been hoped to conduct the survey in 1968, but the inevitable delays made this impossible. In the event, the survey was held in 1970, in the week of 5–11 April.[34] This meant that there were exactly twelve years between the first and second surveys, and between the second and third, and that all three surveys took place at around the same time of year. The week was chosen partly on the advice of midwives, on the grounds that April is a slack period for annual leave and there is less winter sickness absence[35] (though it also meant that yet again, administrative difficulties were created by snow, sleet and rain). The 1970 survey did not collect data for three additional months of perinatal deaths, as the 1958 survey had done, because of its focus on life rather than death. It was the only one of the three surveys to include births in Northern Ireland: the Ministry of Health and Social Services in Northern Ireland had been planning to mount a perinatal survey of its own, but agreed to take part in the Trust study instead.

In the survey week, 17,196 babies were born to 17,005 mothers; one of these mothers had been born in the 1946 survey week.[36] There were 398 stillbirths and first week deaths and no maternal deaths (although one mother died the following week). As with the two previous surveys, the response was almost complete, at over 95 per cent. All NHS hospitals and GP Units took part except one hospital, which "has taken fright because of the size of the form".[37] Army and Royal Air Force hospitals also took part (but not the Royal Navy, which had no obstetric hospitals), as well as private maternity homes.

There was a postal strike in the middle of the survey, so nothing came into the office at Lower Belgrave Street for about two or three weeks. Then suddenly, sacks and sacks of big brown envelopes arrived. At one stage, there were four or five people sitting round the vast dining table, coding the forms as they came in. The coding was finished in about four months and was then put on to punch cards. About 120,000 punch cards were produced, with the potential for about 1,000 two-way and 15,000 three-way tables. It had been hoped that with modern data processing techniques using computers, a report would be out within six or nine months,[38] but this proved impossible because of the "enormous amount of data available".[39] Also, there were unexpected problems to be solved. For example, there was some confusion in answers regarding babies born between 12 and 1 o'clock. It was found that twice the expected number of babies were reported between 12 and 1 p.m., and only a quarter of those expected between 12 and 1 a.m. It was evident that midnight to 1 a.m. was widely regarded as p.m., so babies born between 12 and 1 o'clock had to be excluded from analysis.[40]

A scientific meeting to discuss the survey results was held at the RCOG on 9 June 1972. There was no 'Kitchen Table' fiasco this time. The findings were published in *British Births*, in two volumes (1975 and 1978). The first volume, subtitled *The First Week of Life*, was by Roma Chamberlain, Geoffrey Chamberlain, Brian Howlett and Albert Claireaux. It contains a chapter on the first minutes of a baby's life, which are key to a baby's survival: active methods of resuscitation are necessary for babies who fail to breathe spontaneously, in order to avoid brain damage. A new obstetrical concept introduced in this report was the expression of the number of babies who took longer than three minutes to establish respiration as a ratio of the total number of babies in the group analysed (the respiratory depression ratio or RDR), which was 54.3 for the first week deaths, compared with 4.3 for the survivors. This method of measurement has since been adopted as a clinical tool in many obstetric departments.

Volume 2 of *British Births*, subtitled *Obstetric Care*, was by Geoffrey Chamberlain, Elliot Philipp, Brian Howlett, and Keith Masters. While the production of volume 1 had been fairly straightforward, preparation for the second volume was riddled with difficulties. Roma Chamberlain had left the Trust to take up another job and Geoffrey Chamberlain needed to spend more time on his clinical work as a consultant, so the Trust had to find some other people to write the book. But every plan fell through. An emergency meeting was held and to everyone's relief, Geoffrey Chamberlain and Elliot Philipp stepped into the breach and offered to write the book themselves, at their own expense. Because they were working full-time as consultant obstetricians, they had to take unusual measures to get the job done. They took absence from their clinical work and went to stay at a quiet hotel, where they arranged for folding tables to be set up in their rooms. Chamberlain has recalled their intensive schedule:

> we worked from 8.30 in the morning, occasionally going into each other's rooms to borrow each other's calculators, and ask each other's opinions about things. We stopped at lunchtime, very firmly at 12.30 we'd have a light lunch of soup and bread. We would choose the claret for the evening then, so it could be decanted in the afternoon. We worked on in the afternoon until about 6.00 and then stop, we would cut off and go for a walk, have a bath, that was the rule. We'd have a glass of sherry, have dinner together pleasantly, then early bed at 9.30 or 10.00. I remember they were smashing dinners. Elliot and I used to talk and yarn over a decent claret but got on with our work in the day.

The statistician Brian Howlett and obstetrician Keith Masters visited them on several occasions to bring data and give assistance. By Friday, the data needed for the report had been analysed.[41]

In the survey week, 66.3 per cent of mothers of singleton babies gave birth in consultant beds in NHS hospitals, and 3.1 per cent in GP beds in NHS consultant hospitals. This meant that nearly 70 per cent of mothers delivered in hospital (as recommended by the Cranbrook Report of 1959), compared with just over 49 per cent in 1958. The number of mothers in GP Units was not much higher than in the previous survey: 15.4 per cent compared with 12.4. Only 12.4 per cent delivered at home, compared with 36.1 per cent in 1958.

The key findings of the survey are presented in table 11.2, so discussion here is brief. There had been an increase in smoking among pregnant women since 1958, and the babies of the mothers who smoked were smaller for their dates whatever their gestational age; if smoking women developed pre-eclampsia, their perinatal death rate was more than treble that of non-smokers with pre-eclampsia. Breastfeeding was found to be much less common in 1970 than in 1946, and two-thirds of the babies were totally weaned by the third day. The main factor associated with the decision to breastfeed was social class, with social classes 1 and 2 providing the highest proportion of breastfeeding mothers. However, the data were not capable of giving an explanation for this association.

The data revealed an increased use of oxytocics and episiotomy and an increased incidence of caesarean sections. Gas and oxygen had almost entirely replaced gas and air for pain relief, and there had been a considerable decline in the use of Trilene. The length of stay in hospital after delivery had been

TABLE 11.2: KEY FINDINGS OF THE 1970 BRITISH BIRTHS SURVEY

Mothers at highest risk of perinatal loss
1. Confirmation of the findings of the 1958 report regarding the biological and social relative risks of perinatal mortality, even though the absolute level of the rates had dropped since 1958
2. Matters for concern included the persistence of gradient of risk with social disadvantage, and the increase in maternal smoking during pregnancy

Changes in level and cause of perinatal death
1. The perinatal mortality rate had fallen to 23.7 from 33 per 1,000 total births
2. Main improvements seen were sharp drops in deaths due to pneumonia, massive pulmonary haemorrhage, blood group incompatibility, and those stillbirths due to lack of oxygen during labour
3. A new group of deaths emerging was that of the extremely immature babies weighing less than 1,000 g, who died shortly after delivery often without visible lesions, and accounted for 15 per cent of first week deaths
4. There was concern about the high rate of loss from respiratory disease in the remaining immature babies and the increasing importance of congenital anomalies, as other causes became less common
5. In contrast to the improved stillbirth rate there was still a high rate of death in the first week of life due to lack of oxygen

Medical care factors
1. The proportion of births at home had dropped from 36 per cent in 1958 to 12 per cent in 1970, although overall the percentage undertaken by midwives had remained at over 70 per cent
2. A far greater variety of methods of pain relief was available in 1970
3. Medical interventions, including induction of labour and instrumental delivery, had risen sharply between 1958 and 1970
4. The high proportion of babies admitted for special care was demonstrated
5. The high proportion of babies weaned by the third day of life was demonstrated
6. In 60 per cent of births there was a failure to use the type of thermometer which would ascertain a dangerously low temperature
7. There was often a failure to measure levels of blood sugar, bilirubin or calcium in babies with symptoms which indicated a need for such investigations

Prepared by Eva Alberman, member of the Steering Committee for the 1970 survey

reduced, and early discharge schemes were working in many hospitals. The induction rate in 1970 was 26 per cent. This was a trend that had swept Britain between 1960 and 1970 on the basis of the 1958 data, which showed that pregnancies lasting more than 42 weeks were associated with higher perinatal mortality rates than those that lasted 38 to 42 weeks. However, induced labours were shown to be three times as likely to end up with instrumental delivery than spontaneous labours. The induction rate started to come down in the 1970s, following the reports of research that questioned its value as a routine procedure in postmature pregnancy.[42]

Possibly the greatest impact of the 1970 survey was its contribution to the growing evidence on inequalities in health. It showed that the steep social class gradient in perinatal mortality rates that had been seen in 1958 persisted in 1970, ranging from 7.5 per 1,000 in the upper socio-economic group to 27.6 in the lowest. From the thirty-sixth week of pregnancy, furthermore, birth weight was heavier in the higher social classes. "There is nothing to contradict and everything to support the theory," observed the survey report in dismay, "that social class differences are widening rather than diminishing." Babies of unsupported mothers were shown to be particularly at risk. This was a group that had grown between 1958 and 1968 from 4.9 to 8.5 for every 100 live births, according to national statistics. The perinatal mortality rate of 36.4 per 1,000 for babies born to mothers in this category was almost twice that for births to married women, which was attributed by the Trust to social rather than medical reasons. Mothers in social class 5 and unsupported mothers, the report explained, had been suffering a more severe relative decline in the living standards of households with children, compared with most other groups of the population. It added that there had been both an increase in the number of people who were poor and a decline in family living standards, compared to the average. Yet another problem that chiefly affected the poor was the higher perinatal mortality rate for babies born to older and young mothers, since the majority of these were born to low income families.

No wonder, then, that the Birthday Trust concluded that the survey data offered "no room for complacency about our maternity services".[43] They could easily have glossed over or ignored this evidence of inequality, by attaching greater importance to the clinical findings, but instead made a policy decision to highlight the problem. Not only is it given even greater attention in the 1970 survey report than in the 1958 report, but it is also the primary focus of the last chapter of Volume 2, which lists the 'Conclusions . . . of the National Birthday Trust' and emphasizes the need for "Raising Standards to the Best". At this time, the Trust was heavily influenced by a new generation of social reformers who had recently joined and who worked for the Child Poverty Action Group (CPAG). This campaigning organization had been founded in 1965 at a meeting to discuss the extent of poverty in Britain; it has been said that poverty was 'rediscovered' at this meeting, which was held on 5 March at Toynbee Hall in London. The director of CPAG from 1969 was Frank Field, who became an influential member of the Trust in the 1970s. Field has regarded the work of the Birthday Trust as vital in the movement to reduce poverty, because it identified those who were most in need. In the chapter listing the Trust's conclusions about the 1970 survey, most of which he wrote himself, he stressed the need to raise the standards of all to the high levels achieved for social classes 1 and 2.

Two other members of CPAG who had by now joined the Birthday Trust were Margaret Wynn[44] and Virginia Bottomley. Mrs Bottomley, who later became Conservative Minister of State for Health (1989–92) and then Secretary of State for Health (1992–5), has explained that she was interested in the Trust because of its "focus on the circumstances facing the least advantaged".[45] Field, Wynn and Bottomley had all been brought on to the Birthday Trust Committee by Brandon Rhys Williams, a man of "blazing integrity"[46] who had inherited his mother's concern for the underprivileged members of society.

THE 1970 SURVEY AND THE SHORT REPORT

Although the 1970 survey report stressed that social and economic factors were a major influence on perinatal outcome, it focused on clinical measures as a way of "Raising Standards to the Best". Interestingly, the motto of *The Patient's Charter*, which was published by the Department of Health in 1991, while Virginia Bottomley was Secretary of State for Health, is 'Raising the Standard'. Whether or not this motto was developed as a result of the language used in *British Births*, it is evident that the phrase 'raising standards' was common in the language of discussions about the health services in the last quarter of the twentieth century. The survey report was particularly concerned that the most vulnerable mothers should receive adequate antenatal care. This view was based on the assumption that more antenatal care is beneficial, although this benefit is not actually established in the report. While there was plenty of evidence to show that good antenatal attendance is correlated with a low perinatal mortality rate, stated a review of *British Births* in the *BMJ*, there was little to prove that the two are causally related.[47] A key assumption of the survey report was the increased safety of hospital over home delivery, which had also been assumed throughout the 1958 report. And once again, this was not actually established. The higher perinatal mortality rate in consultant beds (27.8 for every 1,000 births, compared with 4.3 at home and 5.4 in GP Units) was simply accounted for by the fact that the births at greatest risk occur in hospitals.

Just as the 1970 Peel Report reflected the findings of the 1958 survey, so the 1980 Report of the House of Commons Social Services Committee on Perinatal and Neonatal Mortality (known as the Short Report, because the committee was chaired by Renée Short MP) was consistent with the findings of *British Births*. The enquiry was set up because perinatal mortality rates in England and Wales were falling more slowly than in many other developed countries, and because of the wide variations in the rates found in different socio-economic groups and geographical regions. The Short Report was influenced by the Trust in a number of ways (this is shown in figure 11.2, which describes the Trust's network of relationships during this period). First, Frank Field and Sir Brandon Rhys Williams were two of only ten

FIGURE 11.2: INSTITUTIONAL RELATIONSHIPS OF THE NBTF, 1970–80

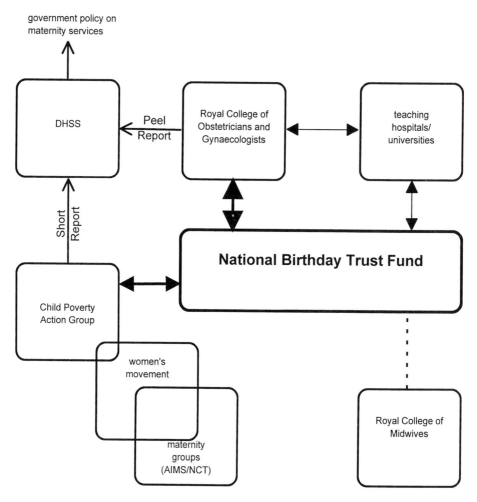

members on the Short Committee. Second, the Trust asked Elliot Philipp to speak on its behalf to the committee, and sent a memorandum from its Medical Committee; it also joined with other voluntary organizations, including CPAG and the Spastics Society, in the submission of a further memorandum. And third, the Trust's Eva Alberman was one of three specialist advisors helping the committee with its work.

The Short Report investigated the outcome of the maternity services and aimed "to secure more equality between mothers of different socio-economic classes". Like the Trust, therefore, it wished to 'raise standards to the best' for everybody; and like the Trust, it recommended an increase in antenatal care (though admitting to "our relative ignorance about the value of antenatal care") and a decrease in home births in order to achieve these objectives. It advised that an increasing number of mothers should be delivered in large units and that selection of patients should be improved for smaller consultant units and isolated GP Units. "Home delivery", it added, *"should be phased out further."*[48] A decade later, 98 per cent of women in the UK gave birth in NHS hospitals.

FROM THE WOMB TO THE TOMB

Soon after the 1970 survey, plans were made to follow up the cohort children. The first follow-ups of the 1970 survey, occurring at 22 months and 42 months, were carried out by Roma Chamberlain and were funded by the Medical Research Council. These were limited to a small group consisting of twins, 'small-for-dates' and postmature babies, and a 10 per cent sample of all babies born to married mothers. At 3½ years, the follow-ups were transferred to the University of Bristol and the study became known as the British Cohort Study (BCS70). It was led for two decades by Neville Butler, first at Lower Belgrave Street and the Department of Child Health at Bristol University with Jean Golding, and then at the International Centre for Child Studies (ICCS) in Bristol. When the 'children' reached their twenties, the direction of the study was taken over by Professor John Bynner at the Social Statistics Research Unit (SSRU) at City University in London. The SSRU at City University is the London base of ICCS and also the present home of the 1958 follow-up (NCDS). The Birthday Trust has provided some funding, along with government organizations like the Department of Education and Science, voluntary organizations like the Cancer Research Campaign, and companies such as Kellogg's Cereals. The key findings of the survey are listed in table 11.3.

The whole population of the 1970 cohort was contacted at five years of age. It was decided to trace all British children born in the survey week, including the 2 per cent of children whose births were not recorded and also those who had been born outside Britain. It was not difficult to reach the survey children through Family Practitioner Committees and Area Health Authorities, because their many names and addresses were accessible from the start, though confidentiality was maintained. The children born in Northern Ireland were excluded, because the civil disruption there made it "too sensitive an area to be included".[49] Nearly 80 per cent of the estimated population of 16,500 were traced at age five, and 92 per cent at age seven. A total of 13,135 children aged five were investigated, which led to *From Birth to Five. A Study of the Health and Behaviour of Britain's Five Year Olds*, which was edited by Neville Butler and Jean Golding. Topics in the book include maternal employment, the relationship between the child and her or his physical environment, 'soiling and wetting', temper tantrums, speech and hearing disorders, stomach aches, accidents, asthma and eczema, vision defects, use of the preventive health services, and immunizations.

Further follow-up studies were carried out at ten and sixteen years, when the total of children surveyed reached 14,900 and 11,632 respectively. A random

TABLE 11.3: FINDINGS FROM THE BRITISH COHORT STUDY 1970

Dangers of passive smoking	Passive smoking in the womb, in infancy or in early childhood was dangerous and increased the risk of SIDS (cot death) and of wheezy bronchitis. Increase in perinatal mortality, lowered birth weight and slower postnatal developments were risks of pregnancy smoking.
Birth weight and later blood pressure	The lower the birth weight the higher the blood pressure (diastolic) in mid-childhood.
Breastfeeding	Breastfeeding in itself has no independent preventive effect on risk of gastroenteritis or bronchitis. Breast-fed infants were slightly but significantly taller and brighter in childhood, the same as found in the 1946 and 1958 cohort studies.
Spectacles	Vision tests in mid-childhood showed that one in four children wearing glasses had normal vision, while even children with minor visual defects did as well at school without glasses.
Working mothers	Mothers in manual occupations had less risk of developing depressive illness.
Whooping cough	The dangers of whooping cough immunization were not confirmed and indeed those immunized against whooping cough performed better intellectually in mid-childhood than did the unimmunized. Infant whooping cough in the unimmunized carried a risk of mental impairment.
Feverish convulsions	Uncomplicated febrile convulsions occurred in one in twenty children under five but were only very rarely followed by epilepsy (3/1,000) and did not have any increased risk of mental, educational or physical impairment.
Literacy and numeracy problems	Nearly one in five 21-year-olds had literacy skills on testing which were below the level expec ted for GCSE. One in eight of 21-year-olds reported some reading, writing, spelling or number work difficulty. This represented no improvement compared to the 1958 cohort.

Good effect of pre-school education	Pre-school attendance for three months or more at LEA nursery/school or playgroup was associated independently with higher educational test results and behavioural scores at 10 years.
Dyslexia	One in forty of all ten-year-olds were found on specific testing to suffer from dyslexia. Many of these children had had difficulties at school, the true nature of which had not been recognized.
Diabetes	Certain conditions arising in childhood, notably childhood diabetes, wheezy bronchitis and eczema, appeared to have increased, compared with the 1958 cohort tested twelve years earlier.

Prepared by Neville Butler, former Director of BCS70

subsample of 10 per cent and 10 per cent controls were investigated for literacy levels and job experience at twenty-one years. Many cohort members were enthusiastic about taking part: "I think you are all doing a brilliant job," said one girl, adding, "I am glad someone is interested. Keep at it – I will!" Another commented that the survey "makes life interesting in a way. When someone asks you how you feel you've changed, you do stop and think."[50] However, there were also complaints, usually about the amount of work required to complete the questionnaires. One member complained, "Last year I completed my [questionnaires], and I don't mind telling you, I got pretty sick of them." Some of the cohort complained that they did not have the chance to meet other members. "Why can't we meet some of the 15,000 other people," asked one teenager, "because I myself only know one other girl who was born in the same week."[51] She was able to meet 4,000 of them in 1989, when Neville Butler threw an all-day party at Alton Towers Leisure Park to thank the nineteen-year-olds for taking part in the survey. He cut a giant four foot birthday cake for the 4,000 who came to the celebration, which must have been the biggest birthday party in the world.

A mass of data was collected: by the end of 1977, close to a quarter of a million computer cards had been punched and put on to magnetic tape. The findings have generated an extensive list of books and articles, with such varied titles as 'The role of breakfast cereals in the diets of sixteen- to seventeen-year-old teenagers in Britain' and 'Acute appendicitis and bathrooms in three samples of British children'.[52] At sixteen years, respondents kept a four-day Dietary Diary in which they recorded everything they ate and drank. This revealed that most teenagers ate a diet dominated by chips, fizzy drinks and sweets, and that on average they spent only eight minutes each day actually sitting down while eating, which was about half the average time of ten years before. Two-thirds of these sixteen-year-olds, who belonged to the first generation to be raised by parents who had grown up during the permissive 'flower power' years, wanted capital punishment restored and 70 per cent suggested more deterrents to crime, including flogging.[53]

The future of the 1970 cohort study is uncertain, however. This is due to the lack of secure funding, which meant that it was not possible to carry out the study planned for the cohort's mid-20s.

PLANS FOR A FOURTH SURVEY

In the early 1970s, Geoffrey Chamberlain and two leading obstetricians, Richard Beard and Stanley Clayton (who was President of the RCOG), decided that a research centre should be set up to enquire into perinatal mortality and to establish a permanent base to oversee national perinatal surveys. Despite support from a number of interested people, the idea foundered until 1976, when representatives of the RCOG and the British Paediatric Association broadened the scope of the plan and made a proposal for funding to the DHSS. In 1977, the DHSS approved the project and in 1978, the National Perinatal Epidemiology Unit (NPEU) was established in Oxford, directed by Iain Chalmers. A key component of its work plan was the formulation of plans for a fourth national perinatal survey in 1982 (so as to maintain the twelve-year interval that had now been established).

Jean Golding, who had assisted Neville Butler and Eva Alberman with the analysis of data for the second volume of the 1958 report, joined the NPEU with the main remit of investigating the possibilities of embarking on another national perinatal survey. As part of this process, experts in a wide variety of related disciplines were consulted, who expressed a number of doubts.[54] In 1979, Chalmers, as Director of the NPEU, submitted a report to the DHSS that advised against a fourth survey. It argued that although the three previous surveys had been "justifiably widely acclaimed", especially the 1958 study, they had provided few insights in the area of clinical practice:

> They have confirmed that the outcome of previous pregnancies is the best single predictor of the outcome of subsequent pregnancies. They have confirmed the steep social class gradient in perinatal loss, and the overwhelming importance of social and environmental variables in determining childhood morbidity. But, with the possible exception of smoking, they have contributed little to our understanding of the nature of these relationships.

In other words, said the report, survey data simply document important associations, but are not able to explain why they occurred or to identify the mechanisms that produced them. As a result, they are not capable of showing what kind of interventions might help those babies at risk of adverse outcomes.[55] On the basis of this report, the DHSS decided not to support a fourth survey.

Questions about the value of doing a national survey were quite different in the 1970s from 1946, when the first survey was done. At that time, two years before the start of the National Health Service, there had been a universal desire to create a 'New Jerusalem' that would improve life for everyone. Health workers taking part in the maternity survey were instructed to tell a mother that "she will enable us to make use of her experience *in planning better Maternity Services* which will *benefit future mothers*".[56] But by the time of the third survey, this spirit of building for the future had virtually disappeared. It had been replaced by the less exciting tasks of audit and measurement, and research was now a growing industry, producing a quantity of questionnaires to be filled in by overworked health workers in the NHS. By the 1990s, recalls Geoffrey Chamberlain, "on your desk there would always be three other people's questionnaires to fill in for something. You were filling in questionnaires until they were coming out of your ears."[57] Surveys were no longer the only source of comprehensive statistics; and in any case, as the NPEU pointed out, the statutory collection of perinatal data was about to be expanded by the Office of Population Censuses and Surveys.

Once the idea of a fourth national perinatal survey had been scrapped, the Birthday Trust examined new ways of working on behalf of mothers and babies. It no longer felt a responsibility for the perinatal period, since the NPEU had been specifically set up to carry out perinatal research and was investigating the relationship between social class variations and perinatal outcome, which had been so important to the 1970 survey. The Trust decided to continue its national survey work, but to limit it to single subjects that were related to the founding spirit of the 1930s. In the 1980s and 1990s, under the leadership of Geoffrey Chamberlain (Roma Chamberlain had died in 1978), it undertook three single-subject national surveys – on the place of birth, on pain relief, and on home births.

THREE SPECIAL SURVEYS

The first special survey was a Confidential Enquiry into Facilities Available at the Place of Birth, which took place in 1984, when 1 per cent of deliveries took place at home. It was a response to the Secretary of State for Health's statement that minimum standards of perinatal care could not be set until information had been gathered about available facilities.[58] This study was regarded as a direct successor to the previous surveys and followed the pattern of having a distinguished Steering Committee and a Working Party. It was directed by Chamberlain and by Philippa Gunn, a midwife, and run from the Birthday

Trust headquarters. It was funded by the Trust and a generous grant from the DHSS (this time, the RCOG "did not feel able" to join the Trust as co-sponsors).[59] The survey was not based on individuals, like the previous surveys, but on places. Two questionnaires were devised: one for hospitals and GP Units, and one for community-based deliveries. Questions were asked about staffing levels of midwives and doctors, and sample services like blood transfusion, resuscitation equipment and dedicated operating theatres. It was important to discover how the different 'on call' systems worked, since a baby suffering from asphyxiation or another urgent problem needs immediate expert attention. The survey covered four separate twenty-four-hour periods over 1984 – the first day of the months of August, September, October and November – in order to investigate a variety of working conditions. This was the last national survey before the reforms of the National Health Service in the 1990s.

The results of the survey were published in 1987 in *Birthplace. Report of the Confidential Enquiry into Facilities Available at the Place of Birth*, which was written by Geoffrey Chamberlain and Philippa Gunn. This reported a significant variation in the provision of equipment and services between units of similar size. It also revealed an important variation between the geographical regions; for example, there was a wide range of consultants on call at consultant units, from 58 in Wales for each 100 women in labour, to 18 in Oxford. There was an appendix on 'maternity unit profiles' that had been created by Miranda Mugford, an economist at the NPEU, which graphically portray how an individual unit relates to the overall distribution for items of staff and equipment. Using these profiles, any unit can compare its own facilities with the range for units of a similar size and type. *Birthplace* provides "much useful descriptive information about maternity services in the United Kingdom in the early 1980s", observes the statistician Alison Macfarlane, though she regrets that there had not been sufficient funds to link this information to stillbirths and infant deaths.[60]

The birthplace study was followed by a survey of pain relief in labour, which took place all over Britain in one week in June 1990 and is referred to in chapter 6. The survey team comprised Geoffrey Chamberlain, who directed the study, Ann Wraight, a midwife, who coordinated it, and Philip Steer, an obstetrician. The study was financed by the Birthday Trust with the aid of a grant from the Department of Health and was based at St George's Hospital, where Chamberlain was Professor of Obstetrics and Gynaecology, because the Birthday Trust headquarters at Lower Belgrave Street had been sold in 1989. Whereas previous investigations into this topic had been regional and hospital-based and addressed particular aspects, such as the long-term effects of epidural anaesthesia, this was the first time that the issue of pain relief had been the sole subject of a national study. It was also the first time that women's views had been sought as the basis of an enquiry into the subject; the organizers took the view that "most importantly, the woman's own appreciation of pain relief requires examining thoroughly to ensure that she is being offered the best agents."[61] This development was consistent with a growing trend of consulting the views of patients. Chamberlain has commented that when he started medicine in 1954, "we never used to ask patients, we just went ahead . . . If you got better it was due to the doctor, and if you did not, it was due to nature." This new acceptance that patients are whole human beings and need to have their rights protected, he added, "came in the 1980s, but then with a bit of a rush since the 1990s, and the Patient's Charter and such have improved this."[62]

It was decided to seek the views of everybody involved in childbirth: the mother herself, her partner in labour, and the health workers who surrounded her. An important part of the questionnaire was the space made available for mothers to answer with their own comments in an unstructured fashion, which produced unexpected and important information. For example, it led to the finding that women and their partners were unhappy about the level of pain relief for perineal suturing (after an episiotomy or a tear) and about the discomfort that followed it.

An assessment was made not just after the birth, but also several weeks after delivery, on the grounds that opinions about pain in childbirth change over time. One mother explained that when she first filled in the questionnaire, "the pain was fresh in my mind and if you had given me this questionnaire then I would have said the pain was horrific." Six weeks later, she added, she was not so sure: "as time goes on I am sure it will be the nicest experience I ever went through, with or without pain relief."[63] Ann Oakley was a member of the team and recommended using a postal questionnaire for the second stage. "If you want the truth," she has explained, "you have to ask the mothers directly and a postal questionnaire is the best way to do that, without the intimidation of a medical setting."[64] For the first stage, when mothers were preoccupied with their newborns, there was a 66 per cent response rate; for the second, it reached 82 per cent.

By the time of this survey, it was necessary to obtain permission from ethics committees before starting this kind of research. This meant that letters had to be sent off to 280 ethics committees all over the country, half of which replied with their approval within two weeks, and then a further quarter within two months. The last quarter were dilatory, approving in general but making very small objections. "There were all sorts of minute details, which I'm sure might be relevant for people who are blind, for example," recalls Chamberlain, "but when you're doing a national picture it's rather difficult."[65] These delays held up the data collection, which meant that quite a few women were lost from the survey. There were other practical problems, too. Ann Wraight had to pack and post hundreds of different sizes of parcels of questionnaires, since every hospital had a different number of births. When she took the first set to the Post Office,

I had to stand in line for ages, holding all the parcels. When I got to the

An example of the practical difficulties involved in research: a landrover loaded up with packages of questionnaires for the pain relief survey, ready for posting. (Reproduced courtesy of Ann Wraight)

counter, each one had to be weighed, franked and costed, and then paid for in cash. It was a nightmare. I had to get my husband to help, because armfuls of parcels had to be sent over the next two weeks – about 550 parcels altogether. I would load my car with the parcels at the end of the day, then spend the evening at home reinforcing them with string and tape. Then I loaded them into my husband's car, and the next day he would take them to the Post Office.[66]

The survey organizers relied heavily on midwives, "who carried out most of the real work". They asked the President of the Royal College of Midwives, Margaret Brain, to write the foreword to the final report, *Pain and its Relief in Childbirth* (1993). This was a significant change in practice, since the forewords to the previous survey reports had been written by obstetricians; indeed, the foreword to the second volume of the 1958 survey and to both volumes of the 1970 report had been written by presidents of the RCOG. The invitation to Miss Brain reflects a movement within the Trust, led by Chamberlain, to re-establish the close alliance with midwifery that had characterized the 1930s. This alliance had been strengthened when Ruth Ashton, the General Secretary of the RCM, joined the Trust in 1980. It was nourished by Iain Chalmers, who later became a Vice-President of the RCM, and who was a member of the Trust's Medical Committee in the 1980s. In the mid-1970s, he had supported Ann Bent, the Director of Education at the RCM, and other leading midwives including Miss Ashton, in efforts to construct and produce research-based refresher courses for midwives; the first course started in 1976.

After the pain relief survey, the Trust began an investigation into home births; this was the fourth national survey in which Geoffrey Chamberlain, who had become President of the RCOG in 1993, was involved. He, another obstetrician, Patricia Crowley, and Ann Wraight directed the study, which was entirely funded by the Birthday Trust. It sought to give a picture of home births in the 1990s: to discover the views of women about having babies at home, and also to compare the outcome for those who planned to do this, with that for those who planned to give birth in hospital. When it was conducted in 1994, almost 2 per cent of births (about 12,000 each year) were taking place in the home; approximately half of these were planned and booked. The data were being analysed and the report prepared when this history went to press.

THE MATERNITY MOVEMENT AND THE WINTERTON REPORT

From the mid-1970s, a consumer movement concerned with the maternity services was developing in the UK. It was spearheaded by AIMS, the National Childbirth Trust (NCT), and The Maternity Alliance. Organized by women and for women, it was concerned that the needs and wishes of pregnant women were not being met by the NHS. AIMS and the NCT were run by middle-class women who objected in particular to the virtual disappearance of home delivery, an issue that was tackled in books such as *Safer Childbirth?* (1990) and *Where to be born?* (1987).[67] They were also suspicious of the increased medical intervention in labour, such as the sharp rise in caesarean sections (in 1984, one woman in nine having a baby had a caesarean section, which was more than twice the number in 1972). Supporting policies to help poor women and babies was the chief aim of The Maternity Alliance, a spin-off from CPAG that was founded in 1980; it is an umbrella organization that is linked up to the trades unions and other interested organizations and provides information to all those parents who need it. These maternity groups were supported by feminists like Ann Oakley, who wrote *The Captured Womb* (1984), a critical history of the medical care of pregnant women; it gives an account of the medicalization of motherhood by male doctors and describes antenatal care as "an exemplar and a facilitator of the wider social control of women".[68] The novelist Zoë Fairbairns took this argument to a frightening extreme in her dystopian novel, *Benefits* (1979), which describes a Britain where the male government attempts full control of women's lives and reproduction by placing a contraceptive chemical in all the nation's water reservoirs – "The outward manifestations of women's menstrual cycles would remain unchanged, as would their ability to become pregnant after a short course of antidote tablets obtainable from government Women's Centres." The result is disastrous: babies all over the country are born with gross deformities and die within hours.[69]

In the early 1990s, a government committee (called the Winterton Committee after its chairman) was set up to re-examine the maternity services. Its particular focus was the management of normal pregnancy and birth and the quality of care, whereas the Short Committee had been concerned with the outcome of this care, particularly perinatal death. In the evidence that was presented to the Winterton Committee, a widespread view emerged that was deeply critical of the maternity services, especially of the massive shift to hospital delivery. Professor Sir David Hull of the British Association of Perinatal Medicine and the British Paediatric Association, for example, argued that "*it was a misunderstanding of the original statistics of the 1958 study that led to babies all being delivered in hospitals*. The data was there and was not scrutinised clearly enough. I think one has to look at it carefully but my view would be that babies can be safely delivered at home." Wendy Savage, an obstetrician, echoed this, claiming that the shift had "not been based on good scientific evidence". The reduction in perinatal death, she said, had been produced by a complex set of factors, including "Improvements in diet, housing, education and preventive health services, the ability to plan a family using contraception and abortion where necessary, and the consequent reduction in the proportion of older women and those of high parity." The Minister of Health, Virginia Bottomley, stated in her own evidence that "there was no reliable statistical evidence which established the superior safety of birth in consultant obstetric units as against home births and those in GP Units."[70]

The RCM, along with other midwifery groups, proposed the restoration of "a normal approach rather than a pathological approach to childbirth", paying greater attention to the needs and wishes of the mother. It advocated a move away from 100 per cent hospital delivery and an increase in home births, attended by midwives.[71] To support this argument, it drew on reports of recent research, in particular *Effective Care in Pregnancy and Childbirth* (1989),[72] which had been produced under the aegis of the NPEU. Key members of the team giving evidence were Margaret Brain, who wrote the foreword to *Pain and its Relief in Childbirth*, and Ruth Ashton. The College had made efforts from the mid-1970s to draw on new research to inform and to improve its practice, and to make the profession a research-based movement. A leading figure in this process was Julia Allison, Head of Midwifery Studies at the Norfolk College of Nursing and Midwifery. Concerned that midwifery practice and policy was governed by medical rather than midwifery research, she reviewed community midwives' records for 1948–72 on more than 35,000 home births in Nottingham; this retrospective study showed that babies of all weights survived at a greater rate if born at home.[73] The Birthday Trust has also contributed to making midwifery research-based, by funding a number of Research Fellowships for midwives in the late 1980s and 1990s.

The evidence given to the Winterton Committee by the President of the RCOG, Stanley C. Simmons, was quite different from that of the RCM. He warned against giving birth at home, on the grounds that such a delivery would be too far from the emergency facilities of a consultant unit. The Birthday Trust submitted a memorandum that took a middle position: it favoured a greater awareness of the needs of mothers, but opposed home delivery on the grounds that "antenatal and early labour diagnostic investigations do not have the precision to predict all cases that will go wrong". As a compromise, it recommended the use of a birth room in a hospital, to which a mother went for the few hours of her delivery, attended by her community midwife but within easy reach of obstetricians, paediatricians, anaesthetists and emergency equipment.[74]

The eventual Winterton Report concluded that improving the maternity services "requires an affirmation that the needs of mothers and babies are placed *at the centre*, from which it follows that the maternity services must be fashioned around them and not the other way round."[75] This was a triumph for midwifery groups and the maternity consumer movement. Ruth Ashton believes that it came about because the midwifery groups were now using research evidence to support their arguments. This was the very tool that had been used in the past by obstetricians, notably in the case of the Peel Report, which had relied so heavily on the 1958 survey data. But this time, the RCM was more than a match for the RCOG, which had not prepared as carefully as the midwives for the evidence session and did not draw on recent research data to support its argument. The session at which the RCOG and the RCM both gave evidence to the Winterton Committee was extraordinary, recalls Ashton, because the public area was packed with supporters of midwives and home delivery.[76] This demonstrated the shift that was occurring all over Britain at this time, at least among those (mostly middle-class) mothers who felt confident about their chances of having a safe pregnancy and childbirth.

Unfinished Business: the End of the Century

By the end of the 1980s, the Birthday Trust was no longer a vigorous organization: increased specialization on survey work may have produced ground-breaking results, but its very high cost had also planted the seeds of decline. To arrest this process, steps were taken to breathe new life into the Trust in 1989. First, 57 Lower Belgrave Street was sold for nearly £750,000, in order to release some badly needed funds. Second, the Honourable Susan

The Birthday Trust's final meeting at 57 Lower Belgrave Street in 1989. From left to right: Professor Eva Alberman, Miss Ruth Ashton, Professor Albert Claireaux, Professor Neville Butler, Dame Josephine Barnes, Professor Geoffrey Chamberlain, Mr Elliot Philipp, Mrs Margaret Wynn, the Hon. Mrs Helen Harmsworth, and Mrs Margaret Matthews. On the wall is a photograph of HRH Princess Alexandra, who became the Trust's Patron in 1966. (Reproduced courtesy of the National Birthday Trust Fund)

Baring, whose long history of work in human rights[1] made her an ideal figure to support the Trust's work in social obstetrics, was appointed as Chairman. And third, Christine Gowdridge, the Director of The Maternity Alliance, which was energetically pursuing its aim of helping mothers and babies who were poor, was brought into the Trust; this meant that two of the twelve members of the General Committee now belonged to the Alliance, since Margaret Wynn was a founder-member.

But these measures were unable to restore the Trust's earlier vitality. Despite the sale of the former midwifery headquarters, there was still not enough interest generated from the Trust's capital to fund a set of major research projects. Nor did it seem likely that a fourth generation of scientists would emerge to take the baton of leadership from Dame Josephine Barnes, Elliot Philipp and Geoffrey Chamberlain, who were reaching the point of retirement. Without the commitment and backing of a core group of professional scientists, it would be impossible for Susan Baring to take the Trust into the twenty-first century. The Trust had by now become so completely a research organization, that in order to survive it required the full participation of experts in its areas of research.

Slowly, the Trust wound down its affairs as an autonomous organization. It entered into negotiations to join forces with Birthright, the research arm of the

Diana, Princess of Wales, patron of Wellbeing, completes a jigsaw illustrating its new name and logo at a launch on 4 November 1993. The event also celebrated WellBeing's merger with the National Birthday Trust Fund. (Reproduced courtesy of WellBeing)

RCOG, which was founded in 1963 and funds medical and scientific research into women's health. This was agreed in 1991 and in a way, it was the final outcome of the Trust's unsuccessful negotiations in the mid-1960s to merge with the RCOG. On 4 November 1993, the Trust took part in a major event to celebrate the official merger of the two organizations, as well as the relaunch of Birthright under the new name of WellBeing (because many members of the public had mistakenly inferred from its name that Birthright was involved with the issue of abortion). Although in many ways a sad day for the Trust, this was a splendid event, honoured by the attendance of the Princess of Wales, who is WellBeing's patron. The Trust's Geoffrey Chamberlain provided a bridge between the two organizations, since in 1993 he had become President of the RCOG and WellBeing, as well as being a key member of the Birthday Trust. After this, WellBeing became the corporate Trustee of the Birthday Trust and provided the administrative offices and staff to run the Trust's affairs, which is represented by its own members on the WellBeing Council.

THE CUMBERLEGE REPORT

In the same year in which the Trust joined forces with WellBeing, the Department of Health issued *Changing Childbirth*, the report of the Expert Maternity Group that was chaired by Baroness Julia Cumberlege. This took the conclusions of the Winterton Report even further. It rejected the argument for 100 per cent hospital births, concluding that, "On the basis of what we have heard, this Committee must draw the conclusion that the policy of encouraging all women to give birth in hospitals cannot be justified on grounds of safety." Purchasers and providers in the NHS, it said, must ensure that home birth is a real option for the women who wish it. The shift to hospital birth, it added, had been based on presumptions based on unproven assertion. As part of its support for home delivery, it recommended an improvement in midwives' pay and conditions and an increased means whereby they might take on greater responsibility.[2]

The spirit of the Cumberlege Report recalls the Birthday Trust's vigorous struggle to improve the status of midwives in the 1930s and the Safer Motherhood campaign of 1948, which sought to ensure that women's needs were properly met by the new National Health Service. It is not surprising therefore that Virginia Bottomley has identified her experience of working in the Trust as an important influence on her support for the report, as Secretary of State for Health. "My time on the Birthday Trust," she has stated, "played a significant part in fashioning my thinking prior to my role in the Department of Health which in turn informed my support for the Cumberlege Report, *Changing Childbirth*." [3]

But a primary concern of the Birthday Trust, which has informed its work throughout the century, is absent from the report of the Cumberlege team. This is the impact on pregnancy and childbirth of poverty, which re-emerged as a problem in the 1960s. The "inescapable" conclusion of the 1980 Black Report, produced by the Working Group of Inequalities in Health, was that "occupational class differences are real sources of difference in the risk of infant mortality".[4] The problem of poverty has grown so rapidly over the decades that by the mid-1990s, nearly one in three babies was born into a family living on means-tested benefits.[5] Moreover, income inequality is increasing more sharply in the UK than in other Western countries,[6] and research following the 1970 survey has continued to show an unequal distribution in infant death and in the proportion of low birth weight babies.

Meanwhile, data on childbirth are inadequate. An important reason for not carrying out a fourth national birth survey was the expectation of improved official statistics, but these have not appeared, for two reasons. First, there has been a decline in the quality and completeness of data about the NHS and its activities; and second, agendas have changed, and new data collection systems have not yet been implemented at a national level in response to these new agendas. It is therefore difficult to monitor the impact of new policy, like that advocated by the Cumberlege Report, or to provide people at the local level with national data, as a base line for comparison with their own figures.[7]

THE FUTURE OF THE TRUST

The collection and publication of research data do not eliminate interest group politics or lead inevitably to the development of appropriate policy. However, they do provide concrete information, upon which negotiations and compromises can be based and against which policy can be evaluated. In the absence of reliable data, debate on the planning of maternity and perinatal care is likely to be vague and confused. Different interest groups – mothers, obstetricians, GPs, midwives, and politicians – base their arguments for preferred policies on personal experience, philosophical positions and clinical judgement. But with the use of survey data, there is a real chance that the needs of those who are poor and least powerful are not neglected and forgotten.

The unique contribution of the cohort surveys to the process of data collection was identified in the 1995 Department of Health report, *Variations in Health. What Can the Department of Health and the NHS Do?*[8] It may seem unfortunate, therefore, that the Trust has shrunk in its size and scope for survey work, especially now that the voluntary sector is flourishing again.[9] The charitable sector has been growing so rapidly that by the mid-1990s, there were 170,000 registered charities and on average thirty new charities registered with the Charities Commission every day.[10] The opposition to the notion of charity that emerged so powerfully after the Second World War has been replaced by massive support for charitable ventures that range from Band Aid to Red Nose Day. Many charities are plugging the increasing number of gaps in a disintegrating welfare state.

FIGURE 12.1 NBTF ASSETS AT END OF YEAR 1931–91, ADJUSTED FOR INFLATION

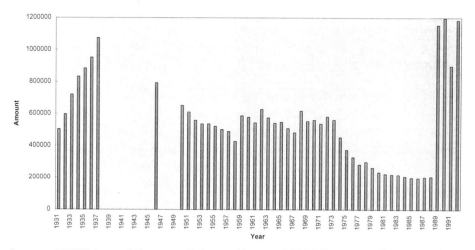

Source: NBTF Annual Reports, Balance Sheets, AGM Minutes. Inflation modifier: Central Statistical Office.
[SA/NBT/C17/1-C19/22, D1/3/10-D1/4/12, A1/1]

FIGURE 12.2 FINAL INSTITUTIONAL RELATIONSHIPS OF THE NBTF

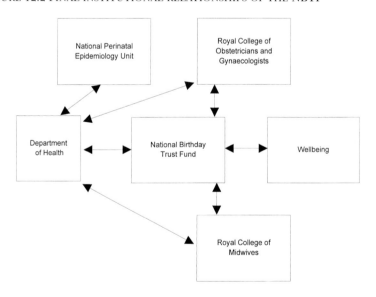

But the Birthday Trust still exists and still functions: although working in partnership with WellBeing, it has its own charity number, separate funds and bank account, and its own research projects. It is not in a position to fund a major national survey but it does have sufficient resources to continue its research in epidemiology and social obstetrics (see figure 12.1). Furthermore, it enjoys a unique network of contacts, as shown in figure 12.2, which had been slowly built up over the postwar period.

The Trust's focus complements the approach of the more clinically-oriented WellBeing, which funds medical research on infertility, menstrual and menopausal problems, incontinence and osteoporosis, and on methods to improve the screening diagnosis and treatment for gynaecological cancers and breast cancer. WellBeing's Director Rosie Barnes has welcomed the merger with the Birthday Trust precisely because of its concern with social issues: "it gives us a bit of flexibility to go more into the sociological areas which weren't within our remit as Birthright but can be now considered within a joint remit". Formerly a Social Democrat MP for Greenwich, she saw mothers bringing up children in very deprived areas, but without the means of improving the quality of their family's life. She is keenly aware, she says, of the need for decisions to be based on proper research and proper information, not on the opinions of a few lobbying groups who "always manage to get their views heard".[11] Her

Mothers and children on a London housing estate in the mid-1990s. (Reproduced courtesy of the Guardian*)*

influence on WellBeing is manifest in its publication, in conjunction with the RCOG, of *WellBeing of Women* (1995), a self-help manual on all aspects of women's health.

The Birthday Trust has continued to work on social issues relating to mothers and babies. It is conducting the Home Births Survey and helped to fund The Maternity Alliance to produce *Mother Courage* (1997), a book of letters written by mothers all over Britain who are struggling to bring up their children on a low income.[12] This book is a late twentieth-century sequel to *Maternity: Letters from Working Women*, which was published in 1915 by the Women's Cooperative Guild and which helped the Guild in its campaign for better conditions for mothers. The Maternity Alliance and the Trust believed that a contemporary version was needed, since the conditions faced by mothers coping with poverty at the end of the twentieth century are increasingly reminiscent of those suffered near the beginning.

The Cumberlege Report of 1993 was a victory for the articulate and well-off middle classes, who are at least risk of perinatal death and morbidity. But so long as social class differences persist, the story is not yet over. From its earliest years in the interwar period, the Birthday Trust campaigned to establish the equal right of poor and rich women to a safe childbirth and a decent start in life for their children. But at the end of the century, despite a huge overall improvement in maternal and perinatal outcome, this has by no means been achieved. The dreams of Lady Baldwin and Lady Rhys Williams have yet to be fulfilled: they will be the urgent work of the new twenty-first century.

Appendix A

The charity was set up "for the purpose of raising a capital fund (equal at least
to one shilling per head of the population of Great Britain), the income of
which fund is proposed to be accumulated (within legal limits) in and of the
capital fund or applied in or towards

(1) the cost of establishing or maintaining voluntary maternal hospitals and
training centres or classes for midwives or maternity nurses and generally
improving the professional ability and standing and emoluments of such
persons

(2) promoting friendly relations and co-operation between maternity and
similar services throughout the British Empire for mutual improvement and
advancement in constitution management and aims and for avoiding
overlapping in connection with appeals or otherwise or other waste and

(3) any other purposes connected with maternity and the welfare of
maternity patients and newly born children."

(Taken from NBTF Trust Deed, 2 April 1930 [NBTF/E1])

In the postwar period the activities of the Birthday Trust fell within the looser
criteria of object (3).

Appendix B

LISTS OF COMMITTEES

THE NATIONAL BIRTHDAY TRUST FUND 1928–93

Patron

HRH Princess Alexandra	From 1966

Presidents

Sir George Haynes	1966–81
Dame Josephine Barnes	1981–93

Chairmen

Ina, Lady George Cholmondeley	1928–30
Sir Julien Cahn	1930–44
Louis Nicholas	1945–6
A.J. Espley	1946–9
William Penman (Acting Chairman)	1949–54
Juliet, Lady Rhys Williams (Acting Chairman until 1957)	1954–64
J.D. Walters (Acting Chairman)	1964–5
Walter Gilbey	1966–71
Sir Brandon Rhys Williams	1971–88
Dame Josephine Barnes (Acting Chairman)	1988–9
Hon. Mrs Susan Baring	1989–93

Deputy Chairmen

William Penman	1944–58
Lady Rhys Williams	1950–4
J.D. Walters	1965

Vice-Chairmen

Ina, Lady George Cholmondeley	1931–4
Lord Strathcona	1931–57/8
Lady Baldwin of Bewdley	1932–45
Lady Rhys Williams	1934–50
Viscountess Dawson	1944–5

Honorary Treasurers

Marchioness of Londonderry	1929–35
Viscountess Buckmaster	1936–53
Mrs Frances Carver	1953–4
Hon. Thomas Sycamore	1957–8
Walter Nursaw	1964–89

Secretaries

Miss Ellaline Macey	1928–9
Miss Manningham-Buller	1929–33
Miss Meyer	1934–7
Miss Violet O'Reilly	1937–9
Miss D.V. Riddick (worked for JCM from 1934)	1939–72
Mrs M.C. Matthews	1973–93

NBTF Representatives on WellBeing Council from 1993

Hon. Mrs Susan Baring
Mrs Fiona Hodgson
Mrs Margaret Wynn

MEMBERS OF THE NATIONAL BIRTHDAY FUND 1929

Chairman and Founder

Ina, Lady George Cholmondeley

Honorary Treasurer

The Marchioness of Londonderry

Secretary

Miss Ellaline Macey

Committee

C.H. Andrews, Esq.
The Lady Annaly
Mrs Stanley Baldwin
Mrs P.A. Barran
Mrs Lloyd Baxendale
The Viscountess Bearsted
Commissioner Catherine Booth
Lady Bower
R.B. Cannings, Esq.
The Countess of Carlisle
The Marchioness of Cholmondeley

Honorary Treasurer
The Marchioness of Londonderry

Finance Committee
The Lord Ebbisham, Chairman
The Lord Annaly
The Lord George Cholmondeley
The Lord Plender
Sir W.H. Peat
Dr L. Haden Guest

Committee

*C.H. Andrews, Esq.
†The Lady Annaly
*Mrs P.A. Barran
†Mrs Lloyd Baxendale
The Viscountess Bearsted
The Countess of Bessborough
The Marchioness of Blandford
*Commissioner Catherine Booth
Lady Butterfield
*R.B. Cannings, Esq.
The Countess of Carlisle
The Lady Cynthia Colville
†The Lady Congleton
The Countess of Dalkeith
†Lady Dalrymple-Champneys
†The Lady Dawson of Penn
*Brigadier Edgar Dibden
†The Lady Ebbisham
The Countess of Ellesmere
†The Lady Greenwood
*Miss Alice Gregory
†The Hon. Lady Grigg
†The Lady Grizel Hamilton
†Miss Hartley

Lady Hodder-Williams
The Lady Howard de Walden
Dame Beatrix Hudson Lyall
*Lady Kimber
*S.B. Leigh-Taylor, Esq.
*W. Seymour Leslie, Esq.
The Viscountess Masserene and Ferrard
*Dr Annie McCall
The Lady Melchett
†The Hon. Mrs Merry of Belladrum
*Mrs Model
*H.A. Page, Esq.
†The Countess of Plymouth
Sir Frederick Richmond
†L.C. Rivett, Esq.
Mrs Rowe
Mrs Rowland
†The Lady St John of Bletso
Lady Stamp
The Viscountess Snowden
†Sydney Walton, Esq.
Miss C.L. Watney
†Lady Williams

*Hospital Representatives   †Executive Committee

MEMBERS OF THE NATIONAL BIRTHDAY TRUST FUND 1938

Trustees
The Rt. Hon. The Earl of Cromer
The Lord Wardington
The Lord Plender

Chairman
Sir Julien Cahn

Vice-Chairmen
The Lord Strathcona
The Countess Baldwin of Bewdley
Lady Williams

Honorary Treasurer
The Viscountess Buckmaster

Finance Committee
The Lord Ebbisham, Chairman
The Lord Annaly
The Lord George Cholmondeley
C.E. Fletcher, Esq.
Dr L. Haden Guest
Sir W. Henry Peat
The Lord Plender

Committee:

The Duchess of Abercorn
* Lady (William) Alexander
†C.H. Andrews, Esq.
†Mrs P.A. Barran
*Mrs Lloyd Baxendale
The Viscountess Bearsted
The Countess of Bessborough
*Mrs Beddington Behrens
*Sir Comyns Berkeley
†Commissioner Catherine Booth
The Duchess of Buccleuch
Lady Butterfield
†R.B. Cannings, Esq.
The Countess of Carlisle
*Mrs Francis Carver

The Lady Cynthia Colville
The Lady Congleton
*Lady Dalrymple-Champneys
*The Viscountess Dawson of Penn
†Colonel Edgar Dibden
*The Lady Ebbisham
The Countess of Ellesmere
The Viscountess Greenwood
†Miss Alice Gregory
* The Hon. Lady Grigg
*The Lady Grizel Hamilton
Miss Hartley
*Agatha, Lady Hindlip
Lady Hodder-Williams
The Lady Howard de Walden

*Dame Beatrix Hudson Lyall
* Miss Judith Jackson
Lady Kimber
†S.B. Leigh-Taylor, Esq.
†W. Seymour Leslie, Esq.
†Dr Annie McCall
*Mrs A.C. Macdiarmid
The Duchess of Marlborough
The Lady Melchett
* The Hon. Mrs Merry of Belladrum
†Mrs Model
†H.A. Page, Esq.
The Countess of Plymouth
*Mrs Cecil Raphael

Sir Frederick Richmond
*L.C. Rivett
Mrs H.B. Rowe
Mrs Rowland
*The Lady St John of Bletso
The Viscountess Snowden
Lady Stamp
Lady Vansittart
†Miss C.L. Watney
*Sydney Walton, Esq.

†Hospital Representatives
*Executive Committee

MEMBERS OF THE NATIONAL BIRTHDAY TRUST FUND 1946

Trustees
The Rt. Hon. The Earl of Cromer
The Lord Wardington
The Lord Ebbisham

Chairman
Louis Nicholas, Esq.

Deputy Chairman
W. Penman, Esq.

Vice-Chairmen
The Viscountess Dawson of Penn
The Lord Strathcona
Lady Rhys Williams

Honorary Treasurer
The Viscountess Buckmaster

Secretary
Miss D.V. Riddick

Finance Committee
The Lord Annaly
The Lord George Cholmondeley
The Lord Ebbisham, Chairman

C.E. Fletcher, Esq.
Dr L. Haden Guest

F.G. Mellor, Esq.
Sir W. Henry Peat

Committee

The Duchess of Abercorn
*Lady (William) Alexander
†C.H. Andrews, Esq.
†Mrs P.A. Barran
The Viscountess Bearsted
*Sir Comyns Berkeley
The Countess of Bessborough
The Duchess of Buccleuch
Lady Butterfield
The Countess of Carlisle
*Mrs Francis Carver
The Lady Cynthia Colville
The Lady Congleton
*The Lady Ebbisham
*A.J. Espley, Esq.
†Miss Alice Gregory
*The Hon. Lady Grigg
†Miss Katharine Guy
*The Lady Grizel Hamilton
†Colonel Fred Hammond
Miss Hartley
*Agatha, Lady Hindlip
Lady Hodder-Williams
The Lady Howard de Walden
Dame Beatrix Hudson Lyall

Miss Judith Jackson
*Mrs Karmel
Lady Kimber
†S.B. Leigh-Taylor, Esq.
†W. Seymour Leslie, Esq.
†Dr Annie McCall
*Lady Macdiarmid
The Duchess of Marlborough
The Lady Melchett
The Hon. Mrs Merry of Belladrum
†Mrs Model
The Countess of Plymouth
Mrs Cecil Raphael
Sir Frederick Richmond
*L.C. Rivett, Esq.
Mrs H.B. Rowe
Mrs Rowland
*The Lady St John of Bletso
The Viscountess Snowden
Lady Vansittart
*Sydney Walton, Esq.
†Miss C.L. Watney

†Hospital Representative
*Executive Committee

MEMBERS OF THE NATIONAL BIRTHDAY TRUST FUND 1955

Trustees
The Lord Ebbisham
Rt. Hon. The Earl of Halsbury
The Lord Lloyd of Dolobran

Acting Chairman
Lady Rhys Williams

Deputy Chairmen
William Penman
Lady Rhys Williams

Vice-Chairman
The Lord Strathcona

Honorary Treasurer
Mrs Francis Carver

Finance Committee
Sir George Aylwen
The Lord Annaly
The Lord George Cholmondeley
The Lord Ebbisham
The Lord Haden Guest
Sir Denys Lowson
William Penman

Committee

The Dowager Duchess of Abercorn
*The Lady Altrincham
*Miss Josephine Barnes
Mrs P. Austyn Barran
Mrs J. Biggs-Davison
Lieut-Colonel P.W. Bovan
The Viscountess Buckmaster
*Miss G.B. Carter
*Mrs Francis Carver
*S.P. Cherrington
The Lady Cynthia Colville
Edith, Lady Congleton
Lady Dalrymple-Champneys
*Lady Davson
The Viscountess Dawson of Penn
*The Lady Ebbisham
*The Dowager Lady Ebbisham
The Hon. Dame Frances Farrer
M. Finlay
Miss Katharine Guy
The Lady Grizel Hamilton

*Mrs Rod Harrod
Agatha, Lady Hindlip
Margherita, Lady Howard de Walden
Miss Judith Jackson
*Mrs David Karmel
Lady Macdiarmid
The Duchess of Marlborough
Mrs Donald Nicholas
Donald Nicholas
*Lady Helen Nutting
*Mrs E.C. Puttock
Mrs Cecil Raphael
*The Lady St John of Bletso
The Lady Tweedsmuir
The Lady Vansittart
*Sydney Walton
*Dr Brian Warren
Miss J. Wild

*Executive Committee

THE TECHNICAL ADVISORY COMMITTEE 1955

Miss Josephine Barnes
Miss G.B. Carter
Lady Davson
Lady Rhys Williams

Consultative Members of the Technical Advisory Committee 1955

Miss Lois Beaulah
Arthur C. Bell
J.W.B. Douglas
P.R. Evans
F.M. Martin
Professor Alan Moncrieff

John Murray
Professor W.C.W. Nixon
Paul E. Polani
Charles D. Read
Miss Hilda Roberts

MEMBERS OF THE NATIONAL BIRTHDAY TRUST FUND 1965

Trustees
The Lord Ebbisham
The Rt. Hon. The Earl of Halsbury
The Lord Lloyd of Dolobran

Acting Chairman
J.D. Walters

Honorary Treasurer
Mrs Francis Carver

Finance Committee
Sir Denys Lowson
The Lord Ebbisham
Walter A. Gilbey
William G. Nursaw (Hon. Financial Advisor to the Trust)

Committee

The Lady Altrincham
*Miss Josephine Barnes
*Mrs John Biggs-Davidson
Mrs Justin Brooke
Aleck Bourne
The Viscountess Buckmaster
S.P. Cherrington
Edith, Lady Congleton
Lady Dalrymple-Champneys
*Mrs Christopher Drew
*Christopher Drew
*The Lady Ebbisham
*Lady Glyn
*Mrs Walter Gilbey

*Walter A. Gilbey
Miss Katharine Guy
Lady Harrod
Margherita, Lady Howard de Walden
*Lady Hutchison
Councillor Percy Jones
Mrs David Karmel
Mrs Edith Lampitt
Lady Macdiarmid
Mrs E.L. Mallalieu
Mrs Donald Nicholas
Donald Nicholas
*William G. Nursaw
*Lady Helen Nutting

*Anthony Patten
William Penman
Elliot Philipp
*Mrs E.C. Puttock
Mrs Harold Quitman
Mrs Cecil Raphael
*Miss Hilda Roberts
*Miss Elspeth Rhys Williams
The Lady St John of Bletso
The Lady Tweedsmuir

The Lady Vansittart
William Wallace
*J.D. Walters
Dr Brian Warren
Neil E. Wates
Miss J. Wild

*Executive Committee

THE SCIENTIFIC ADVISORY COMMITTEE 1965

Miss Josephine Barnes
Lady Glyn
Elliot Philipp
Miss Hilda Roberts

Consultative Members of the Scientific Advisory Committee 1965

Sir Arthur Bell
C.O. Carter
J.W.B. Douglas
P.R. Evans
J.A. Heady

Professor J.C. McClure Browne
John Murray
Professor W.C.W. Nixon
Professor Paul E. Polani
Professor J.P.M. Tizard

THE NBTF GENERAL COMMITTEE 1971

Chairman
Sir Brandon Rhys Williams

Honorary Treasurer
Mrs Francis Carver

Honorary Financial Adviser
Mr William Nursaw

Committee
Lady Helen Nutting
Hon. Mrs Eric Harmsworth
Mrs David Karmel
Anthony Patten
*Dame Josephine Barnes

*Professor Neville Butler
*Mr Elliot Philipp
*Miss A.M. Dickins
*Dr Eva Alberman

*Medical member

The NBTF General Committee 1990

President
Dame Josephine Barnes

Chairman
Hon. Mrs Susan Baring

Committee

Professor Eva Alberman	Mrs Christine Gowdridge
Miss Ruth Ashton	Hon. Mrs Eric Harmsworth
Professor Neville Butler	Mrs Fiona Hodgson
Professor Geoffrey Chamberlain	Mr Elliot Philipp
Professor A.E. Claireaux	Mrs Margaret Wynn

Notes

CHAPTER ONE

1 Alison Macfarlane and Miranda Mugford, *Birth Counts. Statistics of Pregnancy and Childbirth* (HMSO, 1984), p. 271. This figure is based on the classification in use from 1911 onwards and does not include associated causes or deaths from abortion.

2 Message from the Queen, given in a report of a meeting on 28 February 1928 of the Maternal Mortality Committee [NBTF/uncatalogued box]. The message was read by Lady Cynthia Colville, Lady-in-Waiting to her Majesty, who joined the Birthday Fund shortly after it was founded.

3 'Maternity Services. National Birthday Fund Started', *The Times* (13 November 1928).

4 Minutes of NBTF General Committee, 29 January 1929 [NBTF/ B2/1(1)].

5 A shilling was worth 12*d* and there were twenty shillings to the pound. The shilling was replaced by a five pence coin after decimalization in 1970. A shilling in 1936 was comparable in value to £1.70 in 1994. This information was provided by the Central Statistical Office and allows for inflation.

6 Lady George (as she was usually known) was the second wife of Lord George Cholmondeley, younger brother to the fifth Marquess of Cholmondeley. Lord George served on the Trust's Finance Committee, continuing this work after their divorce. The family was further represented by the Marchioness of Cholmondeley, who was on the Executive Committee. In 1934 Lady George was awarded the OBE for her work for the Trust.

7 Edith, Marchioness of Londonderry was the founder and Director-General of the Women's Legion during the First World War and was the first woman to receive the military DBE. As chapter 2 of this book will show, she was a famous hostess and had a tremendous influence on political figures.

8 Mrs Baldwin became Lady Baldwin when her husband was created Earl in 1937; this change in title is reflected at the appropriate points in this history. She was well known for her interest in the welfare of women and young girls, which led to some merriment at a fundraising event when she told her audience, "I want every man in the audience to be responsible for at least one unmarried mother." (Interview with Mr Miles Huntington-Whitely, Lady Baldwin's grandson, by ASW, 8 May 1995.)

9 Correspondence between Macey and Chard, October and November 1928 [NBTF/F11/1]. Lady George and Lady Londonderry tried to recruit Mr Baldwin also, but he said that his position in the government made it impossible for him to join.

10 'Draft of Mrs Baldwin's Speech at the Mansion House', 11 December 1929 [NBTF/G1/1(2)].

11 Interview with Mr Miles Huntington-Whitely by ASW, 8 May 1995.

12 Lady Londonderry to *The Times* (April 1913).

13 Dawson to Riddick, 9 March 1946 [NBTF/F3/3]; Dawson to Manningham-Buller, 5 November 1931 [NBTF/F3/3]; Macey to Farnham, 10 October 1928 [NBTF/F11/1(5)].

14 Sir Julien inherited a fortune from his father's hire purchase furnishing empire and then won a share of one of the first prizes in the Stock Exchange Derby Sweep in 1929, just before joining the Fund. He was a member of the Magic Circle and a keen hunter. At his home Stanford Hall near Loughborough, which he acquired in 1928, he built a luxurious theatre and also a cricketers' wing, providing completely self-contained accommodation for visiting teams.

15 Interview with Mrs Molly Anderson by ASW, 10 April 1995.

16 'Miss Sketch's Diary', *Sketch* (5 April 1939).

17 Cahn to Manningham-Buller, 21 October 1931 [NBTF/F2/2/1(1)].

18 Lady Rhys Williams was the daughter of Elinor Glyn, an author of romantic novels and scriptwriter for Hollywood films, who was best known for the steamy passion of *Three Weeks*, which was banned at Eton, and *It*, which coined a new word ('it') for sex-appeal. *It* was published in 1926 and then made into a film in 1927, just one year before the creation of the Birthday Fund. Lady Rhys Williams, who also wrote novels, was active in the United Europe Movement, of which she became Chairman, and wrote several books on economics and taxation, including *An Economic Policy for Britain* (1963). Her husband had been a Liberal MP and a Minister in Lloyd George's government. The family owned land in the Rhondda Valley, receiving royalties on the coal. They lived just south of the coalfields, at Miskin Manor near Pontyclun, which gave Lady Rhys Williams the opportunity to see at first hand the suffering of miners' families during the Depression.

She was Lady Williams until 1938, when her husband Sir Rhys Williams assumed by deed poll the additional surname of Rhys, thus becoming Sir Rhys Rhys Williams; this made her Lady Rhys Williams. She became a DBE in 1937, as a tribute to her work for midwifery. These changes in her title are reflected at appropriate points in this history.

19 Unsigned letter to Jackson, 1 Jan. 1930 [NBTF/F3/2/1].

20 Bearsted to Cholmondeley, 11 July 1929 [NBTF/F5/1/1].

21 Interview with Jeffrey Archer by ASW, 31 March 1995.

22 He was Conservative Member for Kensington, South, between 1969 and 1974, then for Kensington from 1974 until his death in 1988, and was one of the first UK Members of the European Parliament. A 'One Nation' Tory, he was respected by both sides of the House, and was most active in the fields of social security and taxation and company law reform.

23 Known affectionately to his colleagues and friends as 'Bodger', Geoffrey Chamberlain was recommended

to the Trust in 1968 by Sir John Peel, President of the RCOG, to work on the 1970 perinatal survey. One of the UK's foremost gynaecologists, Professor Chamberlain has worked in the Royal Navy and was Head of the Department of Obstetrics and Gynaecology at St George's Hospital, London, until 1995. He served as President of the RCOG in 1993–4 and has produced many publications on his research on foetal development and the care of women in pregnancy and labour.

24 *Daily Express* (13 December 1928).

25 Minutes of NBTF Committee, April 1928 [NBTF/A1/1].

26 See Minutes of NBTF Finance Committee [NBTF/A/1].

27 Minutes of NBTF General Committee, 29 January 1929 [NBTF/B2/1(1)].

28 Minutes of NBTF Executive Committee, 6 February 1934 [NBTF/A1/2].

29 *Daily Sketch* (7 May 1929).

30 *Evening News* (11 December 1929).

31 Minutes of NBTF Executive Committee, 19 February 1931 [NBTF/A1/1]; Minutes of General Committee, 2 July 1928 [NBTF/A1/1].

32 Leaflet for the Kikuyu Alliance Women's Industrial Home, n.d. [NBTF/F/6/9].

33 Ross to NBTF, 9 October 1933 [NBTF/F/6/6].

34 NBTF to Bearsted, 22 September 1930 [NBTF/F5/1/1].

35 *Men Without Work, a Report made to the Pilgrim Trust* (Cambridge University Press, 1938), p. 139.

36 Margery Spring Rice, *Working-Class Wives* (1939; rpt. Virago, 1981), p. 198.

37 On behalf of the Minister of Health to the Marchioness of Salisbury, 20 January 1936 [PRO/MH55/653]; emphasis added.

38 Safer Motherhood leaflet (1939) [NBTF/G4/1].

39 NBTF to Rose, 5 May 1936 [NBTF/H4/1(2)].

40 'Suggestions Concerning the Future Policy of the N.B.T.F.', 5 December 1932 [NBTF/F2/5/1(1)].

41 In 1924, the year in which she was created a DBE, Dame Janet produced *Maternal Mortality*, which reported on an investigation into a sample of maternal

deaths and singled out the likely causes. Dame Janet also wrote *The Training of Midwives* (1923), *Obstetrics and Gynaecology Teaching* (1923), *The Protection of Motherhood* (1927), and *Infant Mortality* (1929), and collaborated with Isabella Cameron and Dilys Jones to produce *High Maternal Mortality in Certain Areas* (1932). Her work was influential in the Ministry of Health's decision to set up a Departmental Committee on Maternal Mortality and Morbidity in 1928, the year in which the Birthday Fund was founded. Dame Janet was a member of the committee, which was chaired by George Newman, the Chief Medical Officer. She was forced by the 'marriage bar' to leave the Ministry when she married the registrar of the General Medical Council in 1934.

42 Williams to Cholmondeley, 16 December 1929 [NBTF/F2/5/1(1)].

43 Williams to Manningham-Buller, 21 November 1932 [NBTF/F2/5/1(1)]; emphasis added.

44 'Suggestions Concerning . . .'

45 See Betty Cowell and David Wainwright, *Behind the Blue Door. The History of the Royal College of Midwives 1881–1981* (Baillière Tindall, 1981).

46 Sarah Perry, 'The History of District Nursing', a lecture prepared for use on behalf of the Queen's Nursing Institute (1996), p. 6.

47 See Monica E. Baly, *A History of the Queen's Nursing Institute* (Croom Helm, 1987).

48 Ministry of Health Minute, 8 August 1942 [PRO/MH55/1547].

49 Elizabeth Macadam, *The New Philanthropy* (George Allen & Unwin, 1934), p. 122. Macadam was the close companion of Eleanor Rathbone, whose work and influence will be referred to in the next chapter of this book.

50 After working for the JCM from 1934 until 1939, Miss Riddick became Secretary to the Birthday Trust. She played an increasingly important role in the Trust until her retirement in 1972, and was a key figure after Dame Juliet's death in 1964. She was awarded the MBE in 1958 for her many years of service to the Trust.

51 Information distributed by the NBTF to the press on the opening of the midwifery headquarters, n.d. [1933] [NBTF/E8/1].

52 A.M. Carr-Saunders and P.A. Wilson, *The Professions* (Clarendon Press, 1933).

53 Minutes of NBTF Finance Committee, 21 April 1936 [NBTF/B3/1].

54 Sir Julien was an extremely generous man. For example, he gave a large sum to the University of Wales to support agriculture and financed the Cahn Hill improvement scheme, to see what could be done to increase the fertility of 15,000,000 acres of rough hill grazing. In 1923, he provided a group of furnished almshouses for old people in the Nottingham area and in 1930, he gave Newstead Abbey, Byron's former home, to Nottingham.

55 Strathcona to Cholmondeley, January 1930 [NBTF/F3/1].

56 McDougall to Londonderry, 24 November 1936 [NBTF/D4/1].

57 This figure is based on information in 'Copy of Notes by Robert McDougall', 17 November 1936 [NBTF/D4/1].

58 NBTF to Bacher, 18 October 1928 [NBTF/F5/1/5].

59 Interview with Jeffrey Archer by ASW, 31 March 1995.

60 Cahn to Riddick, 12 October 1943 [NBTF/F2/2/2(1)].

61 See file [NBTF/F9/9/1] for letters giving examples of this.

62 Macey to Cholmondeley, 10 January 1929 [NBTF/F11/1(4)]. While most companies donated nothing or very little, the matchmakers Bryant & May were more generous. "You have only to evince considerable interest in their treatment of their workpeople," Lady George was told, "and ask to be shown the factory, and you can get anything." Macey to Cholmondeley, 19 January 1929 [NBTF/F11/1(4)].

63 Astor to Williams, 29 March 1933 [NBTF/U1/1].

64 Observation made in [1930][NBTF/G10].

65 Secretary of de Walden to NBTF, November 1929 [NBTF/G/9(1)].

66 *Brighton Standard* (21 October 1930).

67 Macey to Wren, 24 October 1936 [NBTF/F2/2/3].

68 Cinema advertisement [1929] [NBTF/G1/1].

69 Goodhart to Baldwin, 12 November [1936] [NBTF/H3/2/1].

70 These letters are in [NBTF/F3/2/2(1)].

71   *Nottingham Guardian* (10 February 1930).

72   *Express & Star* (February 1930).

73   Report by the Commissioner for the Special Areas (2 December 1935) [PRO/LAB 23/92].

74   Stewart to Baldwin, 3 January 1935 [PRO/LAB 23/92].

75   Stewart to Baldwin, 3 January 1935 [PRO/LAB 23/92].

76   Conference held at Ministry of Health, 14 January 1936 [PRO/LAB/23/92].

77   Haden Guest to Ebbisham, 27 July 1938 [NBTF/F5/3/1(b)].

78   Riddick to Preston at Glaxo Laboratories, 1 April 1947 [NBTF/B4/12].

79   Samples of cards [NBTF/N7/2].

80   NBTF Annual Report for 1968 [NBTF/C19/17].

81   Dame Josephine Barnes was made a DBE in 1974. She sat on the Committee on the Working of the Abortion Act (the Lane Committee) between 1971 and 1974, and on the Inquiry into Human Fertilisation and Embryology (the Warnock Committee) between 1982 and 1984. She was Vice-President of the RCOG between 1972 and 1975 and has also been President of the BMA, the Medical Women's Federation and the Women's National Cancer Control Campaign.

82   Mr Elliot Philipp has researched into all forms of pain relief in childbirth and rare blood diseases in pregnancy, and has pioneered key-hole surgery and micro-operations. He has been President of the Hunterian Society and of the Medical Society of London and serves on an Ethics Committee dealing with new fertilization techniques. He has published some 30 books and 300 articles and papers, and with Dame Josephine Barnes has produced several editions of *The Scientific Foundations of Obstetrics and Gynaecology*.

83   Fletcher Shaw to Blair-Bell, 23 January 1930 [RCOG/A1/6].

84   Professor William Blair-Bell, The History of the Origin and Rise of the British College of Obstetricians and Gynaecologists, vol. 2, p. 499 [RCOG/S33-2].

85   Interview with Geoffrey Chamberlain by ASW, 7 October 1994.

86   Interview with Neville Butler by ASW, 24 October 1994.

87   Interview with Harvey Goldstein by ASW, 7 October 1994.

88   Archer to Royle, 8 May 1967 [NBTF/N6/1/2(1)].

89   Archer to Carver, 5 September 1966 [NBTF/N6/7/8].

90   Michael Crick, *Jeffrey Archer. Stranger Than Fiction* (Hamish Hamilton, 1995), pp. 108–22.

91   Comment in letter, 5 May 1967 [NBTF/N6/1/3].

92   At the time he was Chairman of the Trust, Mr Walter Gilbey was Finance Director of International Distillers and Vintners, the international wine and spirits merchants which included W & A Gilbey Ltd. He moved in 1974 to the Isle of Man, where he has been a Member of the Manx Parliament since 1982. His wife Jennifer was also a member of the Trust.

93   Hutchison to Gilbey, n.d. [May 1969] [NBTF/E4/1/3].

94   Peel to Stephens, 17 June 1969 [RCOG/C8/6].

95   Peel to Riddick, 24 March 1969 [RCOG/C8/1].

96   Peel to Goodman, 10 September 1969 [RCOG/C8/2].

CHAPTER TWO

1   Notes made on 26 May 1993 by Mrs D.B., Derby, before interview with ASW.

2   Consequently, this book goes a small way towards the study of British aristocrats as "three-dimensional figures . . . members of the national elite of wealth, status and power", which David Cannadine calls for in *Aspects of Aristocracy* (Yale University Press, 1994), p. 244. Cannadine advocates examination of "the things that have always preoccupied aristocrats throughout history: getting and spending money, accumulating and wielding power, and revelling in prestige and authority" (p. 244). Cannadine's exclusion of women, with the exception of Vita Sackville-West, is inappropriate because many rich women wielded tremendous power, albeit often indirectly. For instance, Cannadine's statement that "Londonderry owed his job to

Macdonald's [sic] favouritism", ignores Lady Londonderry's role in generating this favouritism (p. 70).

3   Anne de Courcy, *Circe. The Life of Edith, Marchioness of Londonderry* (Sinclair Stevenson, 1992), p. 141.

4   *Circe*, p. 226.

5   Webb to Friends of Seaham, quoted in *Circe*, p. 218.

6   *Circe*, p. 229.

7   This information is given in William Buchan, *John Buchan: A Memoir* (Buchan & Enright, 1982), p. 192. I am grateful to George Chowdharay-Best for telling me about this book and its contents.

8   Chamberlain to Cholmondeley, 18 July 1928 [NBTF/F11/1(4)].

9   Circe [Londonderry] to Ti [Cholmondeley], 22 December [1929] [NBTF/F11/1(6)].

10   Quoted in H. Montgomery Hyde, *Baldwin. The Unexpected Prime Minister* (Hart Davis, 1973), p. 542. In his own book on Baldwin, Roy Jenkins has observed that Baldwin moved Londonderry from the Air Ministry to the Leadership of the House of Lords because "He was a heavy liability on a variety of grounds, and Baldwin was determined to be rid of him. He went with the worst of grace. . . . Once he was out he dropped some of the catering at Baldwin's request (there was no eve-of-the-session party in December 1935) and devoted himself to writing long letters of reproach to the Prime Minister." (1987; rpt. William Collins, 1988), p. 138.

11   Diary entry for 20 February 1936 in *Harold Nicolson, Diaries and Letters 1930–1939*, Nigel Nicolson (ed.) (Collins, 1966), p. 245; emphasis added.

12   As documented in Hector Bolitho, *Alfred Mond. First Lord Melchett* (Martin Secker, 1932) and Jean Goodman, *The Mond Legacy* (Weidenfeld & Nicolson, 1982).

13   Greenwood to Brown, 5 August 1942 [PRO/MH55/1547].

14   Sir Julien Cahn's Visitors' Book, held by the Cahn family, who very kindly gave ASW a photocopy [PP/JC].

15   Andrew Adonis, 'A better class of corruption', *Weekend Financial Times* (29/30 October 1994).

16   Bessborough to Manningham-Buller, [July 1930] [NBTF/F5/1/2].

17   Minutes of NBTF Executive Committee, 1 November 1938 [NBTF/U4/1].

18   Minutes of NBTF Executive Committee, 29 May 1934 [NBTF/A1/2].

19   Cutting sent by Baxendale to NBTF, 21 May 1930 [NBTF/F5/1/3].

20   Tennant, Tuckwell, Hughes, to Minister of Health, 24 July 1937 [PRO/MH55/679].

21   MH memo, 24 November 1934 [PRO/MH55/262].

22   Tennant to Manningham-Buller, 14 July 1931 [NBTF/CHECK].

23   Maternal Mortality Committee, *Maternal Mortality. A Report* (London, June 1932), p. 12.

24   MH minute, July 1937 [PRO/MH55/679].

25   MH memo, 8 September 1937 [PRO/MH55/679].

26   Tennant to Cholmondeley, 21 October 1928 [NBTF/F11/1(9)].

27   Tuckwell to Cholmondeley, 17 April 1928 [NBTF/F11/1(9)].

28   Chamberlain to Cholmondeley, 18 July 1928 [NBTF/F11/1].

29   Williams to Meyer, 4 July 1935 [NBTF/F2/5/2(3)].

30   Minutes of NBTF General Committee, 14 February 1929 [NBTF/A1/1].

31   Williams to Meyer, 14 November 1935 [NBTF/F2/5/2(3)].

32   Williams to *Daily Telegraph* (20 July, 1938) [PP/JRW].

33   D.V. Glass, *The Struggle for Population* (Oxford: Clarendon Press, 1936), p. 11. The social scientist David Glass was Research Secretary of the Population Investigation Committee from its beginning in 1936 to 1948, Vice Chairman from 1948 to 1959 and Chairman from then until his death in 1978. In 1946 he was appointed Reader in Demography at the LSE and in 1948 he was appointed Professor of Sociology at the LSE. He took an influential role in the survey work in which the Trust became involved after the war.

34   Interview with Mrs D.B., Derby, by ASW, 2 June 1993.

35   *Hansard*, 15 April 1935.

36   Draft of letter sent to *The Times* (30 March 1937), signed by Carr-Saunders, Horder, Huxley, Kuczynski, Blacker [EUG/D161].

37 PIC, *First Year's Work* (November 1937), p. 2 [LSE/PIC].

38 'Birth-Rate Plea by Lord Dawson, Quality Rather Than Quantity', *Daily Telegraph* (24 October 1936).

39 Williams to *Daily Telegraph* (20 July 1938).

40 *The New Philanthropy*, p. 208.

41 *The New Philanthropy*, p. 208.

42 Extract from note of interview with Dr Jones, signed Cunningham, 4 November 1920 [PRO/MH55/230].

43 Charles Webster, 'Saving children during the Depression', *Disasters* (September 1994), pp. 12–14.

44 Jane Lewis, *Women and Social Action in Victorian and Edwardian England* (Edward Elgar, 1991), p. 11.

45 Chamberlain's speech at NBF Inaugural Meeting [NBTF/C1].

46 The Hospital for Sick Children, Great Ormond Street; The London Hospital; the Marie Curie Hospital; and the National Children Adoption Association.

47 Minutes of NBTF Executive Committee, 17 October 1939 [NBTF/B2/6(1)].

48 Minutes of NBTF Executive Committee, 23 April 1940 [NBTF/B2/5(1)].

49 *Women and Social Action*, p. 302.

50 Buckmaster to O'Reilly, 14 June 1937 [NBTF/F4/2/1].

51 *Special Areas (Development and Improvement) Act* (HMSO, 1934), preface.

52 James Hanley, *Grey Children, A Study in Humbug and Misery* (Methuen, 1937), preface, pp. vii–viii.

53 Taken from *Hansard*, 20 November 1934, quoted in Alistair Horne, *Macmillan, 1894–1956*, vol. 1 of the official biography (Macmillan, 1988), p. 104.

54 Interview with Mrs R.H., Rhondda, by ASW, 3 August, 1991.

55 Interview with Mrs M., Phillipstown, New Tredegar by ASW, 1 August 1991.

56 Kathleen Dayus, *Where There's Life* (1985; rpt. Virago, 1989), p. 188.

57 Williams to Knollys, 19 June 1936 [NBTF/F2/5/2(4)].

58 Interview with Mrs W., Pontypridd, by ASW, 31 July 1991.

59 Notes made on 26 May 1993 by Mrs D.B., Derby, in preparation for interview with ASW.

60 These comments are taken from questionnaires filled out for the JCM abortion inquiry [NBTF/S9/17–19].

61 ASW is grateful to Sir Julien Cahn's family for showing her these photographs.

62 Committee against Malnutrition, *Unemployment and the Housewife*, report of public meeting 10 November 1936, p. 3.

63 Jackson to Manningham-Buller, 15 June 1932 [NBTF/F11/2].

64 *Sketch* (5 April 1939), p. 18.

65 Interview with Mrs G.J., Phillipstown, New Tredegar, by ASW, 1 August 1991.

66 Sister Superior, St John the Divine, to NBTF, 3 February 1939 [NBTF/G7/9/3].

67 Interview with Mrs G.J., Phillipstown, New Tredegar, by ASW, 1 August 1991.

68 Londonderry to prospective debutantes [NBTF/G7/9/2].

69 'Directions for Guard of Honour for Her Majesty the Queen' [1939] [NBTF/G7/9/1].

70 *Daily Mail* (30 March 1939).

71 NBTF to East Islington Mothers and Babies Clinic, February 1939 [NBTF/G7/9/3].

72 Riddick to J. Lyons and Co., 24 March 1939 [NBTF/G7/9/2].

73 Guildhall Reception. 'Instructions for Working Women' [1939] [NBTF/G7/9/3].

74 'Memo from Lady Williams with Regard to Advisory Leaflets', 1936 [NBTF/F2/5/2(4)].

75 B. Seebohm Rowntree, *The Human Needs of Labour*, new edn (Longman, Green and Co, 1937), pp. 9–10.

76 H. Montgomery Hyde, *Baldwin*, p. 270.

77 Quoted in W.J. Reader, *Imperial Chemical Industries. A History*, vol. 2 (Oxford University Press, 1975), p. 58.

78 BBC broadcast, 6 May 1926, quoted in G.M. Young, *Stanley Baldwin* (Rupert Hart-Davis, 1952), p. 117.

79 H. Montgomery Hyde, *Baldwin*, p. 271.

80 Pamela M. Graves, *Labour Women* (Cambridge University Press, 1994), pp. 163–4. Deirdre Beddoe has observed in *Back to Home and Duty* that local research is needed in order to find out more about the work of women in the Strike (Pandora Press, 1989), p. 146.

81 Notes made on 26 May 1993 by Mrs D.B., Derby, in preparation for interview with ASW.

82 Interview with Mrs R.W., Trealow, Rhondda, by ASW, 3 August 1991.
83 Reported in *Back to Home and Duty*, p. 146.
84 Storm Jameson, 'On Patriotism', *Civil Journey* (1935; rpt. Cassell, 1939), p. 256.
85 Bearsted to Cholmondeley, 11 July 1929 [NBTF/F5/1/1].
86 Quoted in H. Montgomery Hyde, *Baldwin*, p. 237.
87 Quoted in *Circe*, p. 300.
88 His novel, *We Live* (Lawrence & Wishart, 1939) tells of the industrial strife in South Wales from the time of the General Strike to the Spanish Civil War.
89 Quoted in *Imperial Chemical Industries*, vol. 2, p. 61.
90 David Cantor, 'The Aches of Industry. Philanthropy and Rheumatism in Inter-War Britain', in *Medicine and Charity Before the Welfare State*, Jonathan Barry and Colin Jones (eds.) (Routledge, 1991), p. 238.
91 Strathcona to Baldwin, 10 March 1936 [NBTF/F3/1]; emphasis added.
92 For a discussion of this and the workings of the Charity Organization Society in this period, see *Women and Social Action*.
93 Minutes of NBTF Executive Committee, 2 November 1937 [NBTF/B2/5(1)]; emphasis added.
94 Hebblethwaite to Williams, 19 December 1938 [NBTF/U4/3].
95 Pugh to Riddick, 21 August 1940 [NBTF/U4/1]; emphasis added.
96 Pugh to Meyer, 6 May 1937 [NBTF/U4/1]; emphasis added.
97 Pugh to Williams, 18 October 1938 [NBTF/U4/1]; emphasis added.
98 Williams to Pugh, 10 September 1936 [NBTF/F2/5/2(4)].
99 Pugh to Riddick, 31 August 1940 [NBTF/U4/1].
100 Pugh to Riddick, 15 January 1940 [NBTF/U4/1].
101 Lindsay Granshaw, 'The rise of the modern hospital in Britain', in *Medicine in Society*, Andrew Wear (ed.) (1992; rpt. Cambridge University Press, 1993), p. 214.
102 [NBTF/F6/1].
103 Gregory to Paget, 30 October 1934 [NBTF/F6/1(2)].
104 McCall to Williams, 30 June 1937 [NBTF/F6/1(4)].
105 *Circe*, p. 238.

106 Introduction by Tom Mann, to Wal Hannington, *Unemployed Struggles 1919–1936* (Lawrence & Wishart, 1936), p. xii.
107 Mary Chamberlain, *Growing up in Lambeth* (Virago, 1989), p. 97; emphasis added.
108 Women's Cooperative Guild Annual Report for 1930, p. 8 [WCG/BI].
109 Quoted in P. Brookes, *Women at Westminster* (Peter Davies, 1967), p. 34.
110 Vera Brittain, *Honourable Estate* (Victor Gollancz, 1936), p. 558.
111 *Circe*, p. 305.
112 *The Times* (1 April 1913).
113 Miss Eleanor Rathbone entered Parliament in 1929 as an Independent Member for the combined English universities and was re-elected at every following election until her death in 1946. She devoted her life to the cause of women's suffrage and social reform, and is remembered for her seminal book on family allowances, *The Disinherited Family*, published two years before the General Strike; she was in the House to witness family allowances pass into law in 1945. She was also concerned with the plight of refugees and displaced persons during the 1930s and the Second World War and was an outspoken opponent of Nazism.
114 See Martin Durham, 'Women in the British Union of Fascists, 1932–40', in Sybil Oldfield (ed.), *This Working-Day World. Women's Lives and Cultures(s) in Britain 1914–1945* (Taylor & Francis, 1994), pp. 101–10.
115 Eleanor Rathbone, *The Disinherited Family* (1924; rpt. Falling Wall Press, 1986), p. 345.
116 Lady Rhys Williams, Article for *British Weekly*. 'Family Allowances', 24 July 1939 [PP/JRW].
117 Juliet Rhys Williams, *Doctor Carmichael* (Herbert Jenkins, 1946), p. 21.
118 Mrs Baldwin's BBC Wireless Appeal, 24 February 1935 [NBTF/G7/5].
119 Virginia Woolf, *Three Guineas* (1938; rpt. The Hogarth Press, 1986), p. 79.
120 'Draft of Mrs Baldwin's Speech at the Mansion House', 11 December 1929 [NBTF/G1/2(2)].
121 Leaflet/Report of meeting of the Maternal Mortality Committee, 15 November 1932 (London), p. 8. The need for 'enlightened' mothers was seen as

a priority by the Ministry of Health. George Newman, Chief Medical Officer, referred to an "almost universal maternal awakening [sic] which really began to change the outlook of child health." *The Building of a Nation's Health* (Macmillan, 1939), p. 318.

122 Sir John Dewhurst, *Queen Charlotte's. The Story of a Hospital* (no publisher given, 1989), p. 155.

123 Baldwin to Hilton Young, 7 July 1933 [NBTF/F3/2/2(3)].

124 Hilton Young to Baldwin, n.d. [NBTF/F3/2/2(3)].

125 Minutes of NBTF Executive Committee, 23 February 1932 [NBTF/A1/2].

126 Minutes of NBTF Committee, 9 October 1932 [NBTF/A1/1].

127 *Labour Women*, p. 118.

128 Leslie to NBTF, 1929 [NBTF/C1].

129 'Notes for the Helping of Mothers and Children', n.d. [NBTF/F11/1(8)]. Whoever read these notes pencilled 'yes!' next to this one.

130 Jackson to Baxendale, 1936 [NBTF/F5/1/3].

131 Manningham-Buller to Cahn, 28 January 1932 [NBTF/F2/2/1(2)].

132 'His Master's Voice.' The Gramophone Company Ltd, to Meyer, 5 February 1936 [NBTF/F3/2/3(2)].

133 Quoted in *Circe*, p. 80.

134 GN to Secretary, 26 October 1932 [PRO/MH55/262].

135 Minutes of Annual Conference of the Conservative Party, 1929 [BOD/NUA2/1/45].

136 Martin Pugh, *Women and the Women's Movement in Britain 1914–1959* (Macmillan, 1992), p. 120.

137 Conservative Party, Campaign Guide, 1922, p. 981; quoted in *Women and the Women's Movement*, p. 129.

138 *Women and the Women's Movement*, p. 250.

139 November 1934 [PRO/MH 55/265].

140 MH memo 15 November 1934 and draft statement [1934] [PRO/MH 55/265].

CHAPTER THREE

1 Professor Blair-Bell, quoted in Ministry of Health, Final Report of the Departmental Committee on *Maternal Mortality and Morbidity* (1932), p. 146.

2 These and many similar comments appear in the letters in *Maternity. Letters from Working Women* (1915; rpt. Virago, 1978).

3 Tom Hanlin, *Once In Every Lifetime* (Big Ben Books, 1945), pp. 112–13.

4 'A Salaried Service of Midwives', *BMJ* (23 February 1935), p. 364.

5 *Nursing Notes* (October 1935), p. 137.

6 John Shields Fairbairn was a founder member and the second President of the BCOG. He taught midwives with the same enthusiasm as he did his medical students and became the second Chairman of the CMB. He conceived the idea of post-certificate training for midwives and was a pioneer in the establishment of antenatal work. His textbook *Gynaecology with Obstetrics* was ahead of its time and contains chapters on social welfare.

7 Thomas Watts Eden was a Fellow of the London Obstetrical Society and helped to found the BCOG in 1929. He became President of the Royal Society of Medicine in 1930. He played a conspicuous part in attempts to reduce maternal mortality and served on the Committee on the Causation of Puerperal Morbidity and Mortality from 1925 to 1928. He opposed the narrowness of specialization and insisted that obstetricians should keep in touch with normal midwifery by undertaking some private practice.

8 Louis Carnac Rivett was a founder member of the BCOG in 1929 and was elected a Fellow in 1936. One of the authors of the Queen Charlotte's Hospital *Practice of Obstetrics*, it has been said that he was one of the most spectacular and rapid gynaecological surgeons of all time. He was more involved than any other obstetric consultant in the work of the Birthday Trust in the 1930s.

9 Tuckwell to Williams, 6 December 1934 [NBTF/R8/1/1(5)].

10 Memorandum for consideration by the Midwifery Services Committee of the JCM, October 1934, by Juliet Williams [NBTF/R8/3/1].

11 *Report of the Joint Council of Midwifery on the Desirability of Establishing a Salaried Service of Midwives* (1935) [PP/ASW].

12 Janet Campbell, *Reports on the Physical Welfare of Mothers and Children. England*

and Wales. Vol. 2, Midwives and Midwifery (Carnegie Trust, Tinling & Co., 1917).

13   Dame Janet Campbell, *The Protection of Motherhood* (1927), p. 75.

14   Notes of Confidential Talk with Dame Janet Campbell [written by Lady Williams], 18 June 1934 [NBTF/R7/3/1].

15   Williams to Campbell, 31 May 1934 [NBTF/R7/3/2].

16   Williams to Eden, 24 May 1934 [NBTF/R7/3/2].

17   Dr William Oxley was a representative of the BMA on the JCM. A generalist attached to the East End Maternity Hospital, he was highly respected for his obstetric skills and although GPs were excluded as a rule from membership of the BCOG in 1929, he was invited to be a Foundation Member in 1929 and was elevated in 1931 to the Fellowship. At the BMA's annual meeting in 1929, he was able to report a maternal mortality in his own hospital of 0.64 per 1,000. Though critical of GPs' haste to use forceps, he stated that GPs were the "real obstetric specialists of the country". 'The Future of The Maternity Services', *Lancet*, 1 (1929), p. 209.

18   Maternal Mortality Committee, Report of Meeting held on October 27, 1930, pp. 11 and 18 [NBTF/uncatalogued box].

19   Memo on the JCM Report [PRO/MH55/652].

20   Summary of a National Maternity Scheme as outlined by Professor Blair-Bell in the Ingleby Lecture at the University of Birmingham, 4 June 1931. Reprinted in the *Lancet* (13 June 1931).

21   Quoted in Jane Lewis, *The Politics of Motherhood* (Croom Helm, 1980), p. 140.

22   *Birmingham Post* (21 July 1936).

23   *News Chronicle* (21 July 1936).

24   Women's Cooperative Guild Annual Report (May 1929), p. 20 [CWG/BI].

25   John S. Fairbairn, 'The Maternal Mortality in the Midwifery Service of the Queen Victoria's Jubilee Institute', *BMJ* (8 January 1927), p. 10.

26   Circular 1569, sent from Ministry of Health to Local Supervising Authorities, 18 September 1936 [PRO/MH55/700].

27   Williams to Campbell, 31 May 1934 [NBTF/R7/3/2].

28   Minutes of First Meeting of Midwifery Services Committee, 25 October 1934 [NBTF/R8/1/1(1)].

29   *Report of the JCM* (1935), Appendix C, p. 32.

30   Menzies to Manningham-Buller, 13 February 1934 [NBTF/U3/1].

31   Interview with Mrs M.M., Caerphilly, by ASW, 2 August 1991.

32   Walter Greenwood, *Love on the Dole* (1933; rpt. Penguin, 1969), p. 216; emphasis added.

33   Quoted in Midwives' Institute, 'The Midwife in Independent Practice Today' (1936), p. 13.

34   *Report of the JCM* (1935), pp. 10–11.

35   *Hansard* (30 April 1936) 311, 76, 1199.

36   Tom Harrison to *Time and Tide* (21 August 1937).

37   Interview with Mrs V.D.C. and Mrs S.D., London, by ASW, 27 March 1993.

38   Minutes of the Training and Distribution Sub-Committee of the Midwifery Services Committee, 26 February 1934 [NBTF/R1].

39   *The Nursing Times* to *Nursing Notes*, July 1935, p. 101.

40   *Reports on the Physical Welfare of Mothers and Children.*

41   Hannah Mitchell, *The Hard Way Up* (1968; rpt. Virago, 1984), p. 101.

42   'Address of Sir Kingsley Wood to the National Baby Week Council on 13 November 1935', *Nursing Notes* (January 1936).

43   'The Midwife in Independent Practice Today', p. 15.

44   'Maternal Mortality', *Nursing Notes* (June 1935), p. 84.

45   Irvine Loudon, *Death in Childbirth* (Clarendon Press, 1992), p. 218.

46   Interview with Mrs M.M., Caerphilly, by ASW, 2 August 1991.

47   Interview with Mrs G.T., Worcester, by ASW, 1 June 1993.

48   Quoted in *Death in Childbirth*, p. 217.

49   Ruddock West to Williams, 30 November 1935 [NBTF/R18].

50   *Men Without Work*, pp. 140–1. Data taken from Pilgrim Trust Unemployment Enquiry, Interim Paper by Dr Hans Singer, No. 14.

51   *Death in Childbirth*, pp. 244 and 246.

52   *Death in Childbirth*, p. 251.

53   Comment by Dame Josephine Barnes to ASW, 14 May 1996.

54   F.J. Browne, 'Maternity Services: The Part Played by Education of Medical Students', *BMJ* (22 August 1936), p. 384.

55   Interview with Mrs M.M., Caerphilly, by ASW, 2 August 1991.

56   *BMJ* (9 June 1934), pp. 1017–19.

57   Orde to Williams, 5 February 1935 and 31 January 1935 [NBTF/R8/4/3].

58   Carter to Williams, 11 September 1934 [NBTF/U3/2(1)]; emphasis added.

59   The *New Statesman* (8 December 1928).

60   Speeches at Inaugural Meeting of NBTF, 12 November 1928 [NBTF/C1].

61   Minutes of Midwifery Services Committee, 13 December 1934 [NBTF/R8/1/1(6)].

62   Memo from Sir Kingsley Wood to Maclachlan, 2 August 1935 [PRO/MH55/652].

63   See confidential note to Harry, Johnson, Gater, December 1935 [PRO/MH55/652]; and Minister to Harrison, 29 November 1935 [PRO/MH80].

64   Williams to Carter, 3 January 1935 [NBTF/U3/2(3)].

65   Dame Louise McIlroy, a consultant obstetrician and gynaecologist, joined the Scottish Women's Hospital for foreign service in 1914 and was awarded the Croix de Guerre in 1916. In 1921 she was appointed the first occupant of the University of London's Chair in Obstetrics and Gynaecology at the Royal Free Hospital. In 1929 she became a DBE and was elected a founder Fellow of the BCOG; she retired in 1934.

66   McIlroy to Meyer, 30 March 1936 [NBTF/R8/6/1].

67   Domiciliary versus Hospital Treatment, considered in Minutes of External Affairs Committee, 26 April 1935 [RCOG/T4/G3], pp. 11–12.

68   'A Salaried Service of Midwives', *Nursing Notes* (March 1935).

69   Memo to Sir Kingsley Wood, 9 January 1936 [PRO/MH55/653].

70   'To Our Readers', *Nursing Notes* (September 1935).

71   Sir Comyns Berkeley was a consultant obstetrician who was always interested in the training and teaching of midwives. He became a member of the CMB in 1930 and in 1936 succeeded Fairbairn as Chairman, an office he held until his death in 1946. He was involved in the founding of the BCOG and was its first Honorary Treasurer; however, he resigned following disagreements with Blair-Bell, the President. With Victor Bonney he published the classic *Textbook of Gynaecological Surgery*.

72   Comyns Berkeley to Maclachlan, 9 January 1936 [PRO/MH55/653].

73   Carter to Weale, 12 March 1935 [PRO/MH55/653].

74   Goodall to Williams, 28 June 1935 [NBTF/R8/5].

75   'Sir Kingsley Wood Replies to Questions', *Nursing Notes* (December 1936).

76   Sir Ewen Maclean, 'Maternity Services', *BMJ* (22 August 1936), p. 383.

77   Minutes of BCOG Council, 27 April 1935, Council Minute Book, pp. 145–6 [RCOG/A2M/2].

78   Eden to Williams, 29 April 1935 [NBTF/R19].

79   Williams to Fairbairn, 8 May 1935 [NBTF/16/1(7)].

80   BMA, 'Memorandum Regarding a National Maternity Service' (as approved by Council, 20 November 1935) [NBTF/R16/1].

81   Williams to Eden, 23 July 1935 [NBTF/R19].

82   Williams to Fairbairn, 8 May 1935 [NBTF/16/1(7).

83   Williams to Eden, 27 April 1935 [NBTF/R19].

84   Draft Agenda for meeting of JCM, 29 January 1936 [NBTF/R1].

85   Minutes of JCM, 5 May 1936 [NBTF/R1].

86   Minutes of JCM, 14 October 1936 [NBTF/R1].

87   Paget to Wood, n.d. [PRO/MH55/697].

88   Riddick to Greenwood, 4 July 1934 [NBTF/R16/1(8)].

89   Rhys Davies to Williams, 28 January 1936 [NBTF/R16/2].

90   *Hansard* (7 July 1936), 314, 118, 1079.

91   *Hansard* (30 April 1936), 311, 76, 1138.

92   'Better Britons', *Evening News* (1 May 1936).

93   *Behind the Blue Door*, p. 58.

94   Carter to Williams, 20 July 1936 [NBTF/R8/5].

95   *Nottingham Guardian* (1 May 1936).

96   For reactions to the draft of the Bill,

see correspondence in [PRO/MH55/697].

97 Minutes of meeting between Minister of Health and representatives of LCC, 16 January 1936 [PRO/MH55/652].

98 Salisbury to Kingsley Wood, 9 January 1936 [PRO/MH55/653].

99 Margaret Burnside to *Nursing Notes* (April 1935), p. 57.

100 'Rural Midwife' to *Nursing Notes* (April 1935), p. 58.

101 *Hansard* (7 July 1936), 314, 118, 1071.

102 *Hansard* (7 July 1936), 1109; emphasis added.

103 Report of Speeches at fundraising dinner at Guildhall, 8 May 1934, p. 22 [NBTF/G7/4(1)].

104 See *Women and the Women's Movement*, p. 159.

105 See figures on this in *Women and the Women's Movement*, pp. 57–8.

106 Women's Cooperative Guild Annual Report for 1937, p. 19 [CWG/BI].

107 Snowden to Inaugural Meeting, November 1928 [NBTF/C1].

108 Meeting held in Huddersfield, reported in 'Raising Status of Midwives', *Daily Telegraph* (9 January 1936).

109 Wood to Countess of Selborne, 5 May 1936 [PRO/MH55/697].

110 'A Salaried Service of Midwives'.

111 *Circular 1569*.

112 'Sir Kingsley Wood Replies to Questions', *Nursing Notes* (December 1935).

113 *Circular 1569*.

114 'Some Practical Points', *Nursing Notes* (December 1936).

115 MH Memo, n.d. [PRO/MH55/652].

116 See for example E.J. to Schuster [PRO/MH55/652].

117 'Address by Sir Kingsley Wood, Minister of Health, to Branch Representatives of the Midwives' Institute, 11 November 1936', *Nursing Notes* (December 1936), p. 150.

118 Interview with Mrs M.M., Caerphilly, by ASW, 2 August 1991.

119 *Circular 1569*.

120 *Daily Herald* (22 October 1936).

121 Frankenburg to Spencer, 23 May 1935 [PRO/MH55/697].

122 Report in *Nursing Notes* (December 1936).

123 Interview with Mrs M.M., Caerphilly, by ASW, 2 August 1991.

124 *Death in Childbirth*, p. 209.

125 Enid Bagnold, *The Squire* (William Heinemann, 1938) p. 171; emphasis added.

126 *Death in Childbirth*, pp. 254–62.

127 Baxendale to Meyer, 3 February 1936 [NBTF/F5/1/3].

128 MOH (W.R. Nash) Annual Report for the Urban District of Caerphilly (1937), p. 54 [NBTF/T19/1/5].

129 Interview with Mrs M.M., Caerphilly, by ASW, 2 August 1991.

130 Ann Oakley, *The Captured Womb* (1984; rpt. Blackwell, 1986), p. 107.

131 E. Sylvia Pankhurst, 'Will Marriage Become Compulsory in the Struggle for a New Race?', *Guide and Ideas for Competitors*, 21 November 1936.

132 Enid Fox, 'An Honourable Calling or a Despised Occupation?', *Social History of Medicine*, 6 (1993), p. 249.

133 Frank Honigsbaum, *The Division in British Medicine* (Kogan Page, 1979), p. 245.

134 Report of the Joint Council of Midwifery on the Desirability of Establishing a Register of Maternity Nurses (1939) [PP/ASW].

135 Cahn to Riddick, 30 June 1943 [NBTF/B2/14(2)].

136 J.D.C. to Dark, 13 May 1939 [PRO/MH55/662].

137 Rhys Williams to Elliot, 3 May 1939 [PRO/MH55/662].

138 For this reference and above, see memos in May and June 1939 in file [PRO/MH55/662].

139 Williams to *The Times* (24 August 1942) [NBTF/R21/2].

140 MH memo, 22 April 1940 [PRO/MH55/662].

141 MH memo, 22 April 1940 [PRO/MH55/662].

CHAPTER FOUR

1 MOH Annual Report for the Rhondda Urban District Council, 1933, p. 38; *Birth Counts*, p. 271.

2 A. Topping, 'Maternal Mortality and Public Opinion', *Public Health*, 49 (1936), pp 342–9.

3 Minutes of the Finance and Executive Committee of the BCOG, Friday 20 October 1933, p. 5 [RCOG/A3M-1/B37].

4   Fairbairn to Jenkins, 19 December 1933 [RCOG/B2/19].
5   Fletcher Shaw to Fairbairn, 16 November 1933 [RCOG/B2/19]; emphasis added.
6   Fairbairn to Cahn, 19 December 1933 [RCOG/B2/19].
7   Meeting of the Joint Committee of Queen's Institute and the NBTF, 2 March 1934 [PRO 30/63/359].
8   NBTF to Cahn, 1 March 1934 [NBTF/F2/2/2(1)].
9   For more on this, see the University of London Ph.D. by Enid Fox (1993), 'District Nursing and the Work of District Nursing Associations, 1900–1946', chapter 8. ASW is grateful to Dr Fox for sharing the results of her research and offering some useful leads.
10   Meeting of Joint Committee and the NBTF, 2 March 1934 [PRO/30/63/559].
11   MOH Report for the RUDC, 1934, pp. 13 and 34.
12   *Birth Counts*, p. 271.
13   Lady Williams, 'Malnutrition as a Cause of Maternal Mortality', *Public Health* (October 1936), p. 11.
14   The prices of these foodstuffs were: Ovaltine 1–8 oz: 1s 3d wholesale, 1s 10d retail; Marmite 1–4 oz: 7d wholesale, 1s 6d retail; Brandox 1–8 oz: 2s 4d wholesale, 3s 4d wholesale. [NBTF/F2/5/2(30).
15   Natyo was based on Rad-Jo-Malto, which was introduced to the Birthday Trust by Mrs Charlotte Smith, the wife of Rennie Smith MP. It was supposed to make "confinements easy. The preparation is a composition of herbs and other plant and mineral remedies and was discovered by a German some 25 years ago . . ."[NBTF/F10/2]. Demonstrating his faith in Natyo, Sir Julien wrote to the NBTF: "It looks as though our banking account in the near future will require some Natyo." (17 January 1935)[NBTF/F/2/2/2(2)].
16   MOH Report for the RUDC, 1935, pp. 38–46 [NBTF/T19/1/1] .
17   'Malnutrition as a Cause of Maternal Mortality', p. 11.
18   MOH Annual Report for the RUDC, 1935, p. 13.
19   John Boyd Orr and David Lubbock, *Feeding the People in War-Time* (Macmillan, 1940), pp. 32–3.
20   Interview with Mrs M., Phillipstown,

New Tredegar, by ASW, 1 August 1991.
21   Lady Williams, 'How They Live in the Distressed Areas', *Evening Standard* (21 July 1936), p. 7.
22   *Working-Class Wives*, p. 170.
23   *Men Without Work*, p. 140.
24   Richard M. Titmuss, *Poverty and Population. A Factual Study of Contemporary Social Waste* (Macmillan, 1938), pp. 247–9.
25   R.A. McCance, E.M. Widdowson, C.M. Verdon-Roe, 'A Study of English Diets by the Individual Method. III. Pregnant Women at Different Economic Levels', *The Journal of Hygiene*, 38 (1938), p. 611.
26   Charles Webster, 'The Health of the School Child During the Depression', in *The Fitness of the Nation – Physical and Health Education in the Nineteenth and Twentieth Centuries*, Proceedings of the 1982 Annual Conference of the History of Education Society of Great Britain, Nicholas Parry and David McNair (eds.) (History of Education Society, 1983), p. 71.
27   In 1934, it spent £16,829 16s 5d on its Milk Assistance Scheme. MOH *Annual Report for the RUDC*, 1934, p. 35.
28   W.A.R. to Minister of Labour, 1 November 1928 [PRO/LAB23/93].
29   Brooke to the Director, Conservative Research Department, 18 October 1935 [CRD/1/24/3].
30   Boyd Orr to Brooke, 17 October 1935 [CPA/CRD1/24/3].
31   Ball to Chamberlain, 1937 [CPA/CRD1/24/3].
32   Interview with Dr E.M. Widdowson by ASW, 9 August 1991.
33   Statement made at the plenary meeting of the League of Nations on 11 September 1935, by the Right Hon. S.M. Bruce of Australia. Quoted in *The Bulletin of the Committee Against Malnutrition*, No. 11 (November 1935), p. 62.
34   John Burnett, *Plenty and Want* (1966; rpt. Routledge, 1989), p. 271.
35   John Boyd Orr, *Food, Health and Income, Report on a Survey of Adequacy of Diet in Relation to Income* (Macmillan, 1937), p. 11.
36   MH memo, 17 June 1936 [PRO/MH55/697].
37   *Bulletin of the Committee Against Malnutrition*, No. 1 (March 1934), p. 2.
38   Mrs A.D. to NBTF, 26 June 1935;

NBTF to Mrs A.D., 4 July 1935 [NBTF/F8/3].

39 NBTF Executive Committee, 4 October 1935 [NBTF/A1/3].

40 Fletcher Shaw to Cahn, 29 May 1936 [NBTF/F2/2/2(1)]; Minutes of the BCOG Executive Committee, 20 March 1936, p. 22 [RCOG/T4/G8].

41 British College of Obstetricians and Gynaecologists, 'Report re adequate dietaries for pregnant women at certain income levels'[1936] [PRO/MH55/642].

42 UAB to NBTF, 18 June 1936 [NBTF/T1]; CAM to NBTF, 16 July 1936 [T1]; 'Comments on diets for pregnant women . . .' [PRO/55/642].

43 Ministry of Health – Dame Janet Campbell, Isabella D. Cameron and Dilys M. Jones, *High Maternal Mortality in Certain Areas. Reports on Public Health and Medical Subjects 68* (1932). Notes on this are contained in [NBTF/R8/7/1].

44 Children's Minimum Council, 'An Appeal for the Improvement of Child Nutrition', n.d. [CPA/CRD/1/60/7].

45 Committee Against Malnutrition, *Social Care of Motherhood* (Lawrence & Wishart, 1936), p. 5.

46 TUC General Council to Sir Hilton Young, 30 November 1934 [PRO/MH55/217].

47 Women's Cooperative Guild Annual Report for 1935, p. 8 [CWG/BI].

48 Memo, Commission for Special Areas, n.d.; Memo by Tribe, 3 December 1935 [PRO/LAB23/92].

49 Baldwin to Kingsley Wood, 27 November 1935 [PRO/LAB23/92].

50 Stewart to Baldwin, 3 January 1935 [PRO/LAB23/92].

51 Stewart to Ward, 16 June 1936 [PRO/LAB23/92].

52 Constance Braithwaite, *The Voluntary Citizen. An Enquiry into the Place of Philanthropy in the Community* (Methuen, 1938), p. 110.

53 NBTF to Picton, 7 April 1936 [NBTF/T1]; interview with Dr Widdowson by ASW, 9 August 1991.

54 Juliet Williams to the Editor of *Public Health* (November 1937).

55 She was helped to produce this paper by Percy Stocks, statistician at the Ministry of Health, and thanked him for this much later, when he was assisting with the analysis of the data generated by the 1958

Perinatal Mortality Survey. Rhys Williams to Stocks, 13 December 1960 [NBTF/M8/2/3].

56 Eden to Williams, 30 November 1936 [NBTF/R/19].

57 Machlachlan to Tribe, 23 November 1936 [PRO/LAB23/92].

58 In 1946, the Medical Research Council wanted to test a new drug called streptomycin, to see if it would cure tuberculosis in humans. But because supplies of the new drug were scarce, it decided to administer it to some people with tuberculosis and not to others, on the basis of selection according to a table of random numbers. This system produced a far more reliable control group than any used before and laid the basis for the development of the Randomized Controlled Trial (RCT). See Ann Oakley, 'Who's Afraid of the Randomized Controlled Trial? Some Dilemmas of the Scientific Method and "Good" Research Practice,' *Women and Health*, vol. 15(4), 1989, p. 26.

59 MOH (Dr A. Stuart Hebblethwaite) Annual Report for the County Borough of Sunderland, 1936, pp. 115–16 [NBTF/T19/2/2] .

60 Appeal from the Children's Minimum Council, n.d. [BL/CRD1/ 60/7].

61 MOH (James Grant) Annual Report for Gateshead, 1936, p. 48.

62 MOH Annual Report for Llantrisant and Llantwit Fardre Rural District Council, 1936, p. 9.

63 Langthorpe, Reckitt & Sons, to Williams, 11 March 1937 [NBTF/S2/2(1)].

64 Stewart to Ward, 16 June 1936 [PRO/23/92].

65 Minutes by ASM, n.d. [PRO/LAB23/92].

66 P.J. Atkins, 'White Poison? The Social Consequences of Milk Consumption 1850–1930', *Social History of Medicine*, vol. 5, No. 2 (August 1992) pp. 207–27, especially p. 224. Atkins describes the improvements in cleanliness of milk production after the First World War.

67 Memo from Brooke, 11 October 1935 [BL/CRD1/24/3].

68 Magee to Hamill, 22 June 1936 [PRO/MH55/642].

69 Williams to Browne, 9 December 1937 [NBTF/S7/2/1].

70   *High Maternal Mortality in Certain Areas.*

71   Medical Research Council, *The First 60 Years. History and Publications of the MRC Dunn Nutrition Unit, 1927–1987*, Alison A. Paul (ed.) (MRC Dunn Nutrition Unit, 1987), pp. 1–2. In 1896, Eijkman had identified B1, the vitamin essential for the prevention of a disease called beri-beri; and in the Thirties, Edward Mellanby identified the role of the fat soluble vitamin D in the development of rickets.

72   Oxley to Rhys Williams, 28 May 1938 [NBTF/R16/2].

73   See for example A.H.A. Wynn, M.A. Crawford, Wendy Doyle and S.W. Wynn, 'Nutrition of Women in Anticipation of Pregnancy', *Nutrition and Health* (1991), vol. 7, pp. 69–88, especially Figure 6, p. 83.

74   Celia Petty, 'Primary research and public health', in *Historical Perspectives on the Role of the MRC* (Oxford University Press, 1989), p. 104.

75   Williams to Elliston, 31 January 1938 [NBTF/T3(1)].

76   Reported by Pat Thane in 'Women in the British Labour Party and the Construction of State Welfare 1906–1939', in Seth Koven and Sonya Michel, *Mothers of a New World. Maternalist Politics and the Origins of Welfare States* (Routledge, 1993), p. 370.

77   See Geoffrey Chamberlain and A. Susan Williams, 'Antenatal Care in South Wales, 1934–1962', in *Social History of Medicine*, vol. 8, No. 3 (December 1995), pp. 480–8.

78   The Marmite Company, *Marmite: In Preventive and Curative Medicine*, n.d., p. 23 [NBTF/T10/1].

79   See correspondence in [NBTF/T3(1)].

80   'Extract from the Report of the Commissioner for the Special Areas in England and Wales for the year ended 30 Sept, 1937' [NBTF/R14/2/4].

81.   Eden to Williams, 2 March 1937 [NBTF/R19].

82   James Young became the first Professor of Obstetrics and Gynaecology at the British Postgraduate Medical School at Hammersmith Hospital. His *Textbook of Obstetrics and Gynaecology* ran to eleven editions. Very interested in the social side of obstetrics, he was Chairman of the Joint Committee of the RCOG and PIC for the 1946 *Maternity in Great Britain* survey (see chapter 9 of this book) and he helped in further survey work, such as the follow-up leading to *Children Under Five* (1958).

83   Dr Balfour had already conducted research into maternal nutrition while Chief Medical Officer to the Women's Medical Service in India; she had also taken charge in England of an investigation by the Children's Minimum Council into the supply of free and assisted milk to expectant and nursing mothers and children. Her involvement in the Trust nutrition work developed from a letter to Mrs Baldwin asking for information about the nutrition project, which led to Mrs Baldwin arranging for her to see Lady Williams. (14 May 1936; 15 May 1936 [NBTF/F3/2/4]).

84   Young to Williams, 29 July 1936 [NBTF/S2/1(1)].

85   Minute by ASM, 19 March 1937 [PRO/LAB23/93].

86   Interview with Dr Widdowson by ASW, 9 August 1991.

87   McCance to Mellanby, 28 April 1937 [NBTF/T2(2)].

88   'Report of the National Birthday Trust Fund Nutrition Scheme for Expectant Mothers (For the information of the Commissioner for Special Areas)' (September 1937) [NBTF/T1].

89   Margaret Balfour, 'Nutritional Therapy During Pregnancy', *The Proceedings of the Royal Society of Medicine* (June 1938) 31, p. 914.

90   These figures are taken from 'Malnutrition and Maternal Mortality', *Mother and Child* X, 6 (September 1939), p. 248.

91   This observation was of the distribution of foodstuffs in Gateshead. 'A Study of English Diets. III. Pregnant Women . . .', p. 616.

92   Nash to Williams, 4 November 1938 [NBTF/T8/2/3].

93   Rankin to Rhys Williams, 13 May 1938 [NBTF/T8/2/3].

94   Lady Williams, 2 March 1938 [NBTF/T8/1/1(1)].

95   Report by Dr Balfour on her tour of the North of England, July 1937 [NBTF/T15].

96   Taylor to NBTF, 5 November 1937 [NBTF/T8/1/3].

97   Lady Williams, 'Results of

Experimental Schemes for Reducing the Maternal Death Rate in the Special Areas of Glamorgan, Monmouthshire and Durham', *Public Health* (April 1937).

98 MOH *Annual Report for the County Borough of South Shields*, 1937, p. 113.

99 Stephens to NBTF, 3 March 1938 [NBTF/T8/1/2(1)].

100 Severn to NBTF, 24 September 1937 [NBTF/T8/1/2(1)].

101 Mrs P.H. of Sunderland to ASW, October 1991.

102 Information supplied by Margaret Wynn to ASW, February 1992.

103 Rennie to Williams, 17 February 1939 [NBTF/T10/3/1].

104 Campbell Lyons to Williams, 26 August 1937 [NBTF/T8/1/1(1)].

105 Nash to Williams, 21 May 1938 [NBTF/T13/3(2)].

106 Thomas to Riddick, 1 July 1938 [NBTF/T13/3(2)].

107 Unless, he said, expectant mothers were buying Marmite, but he did not see how this could be found out ('Report by Dr Margaret Balfour on the Tour of the South Wales Areas' (September 1937) [NBTF/T15]). Evidently this MOH was already convinced of the value of Marmite in the prevention of maternal death!

108 Jamieson to Riddick, 2 December 1938 [NBTF/T8/2/2(1)].

109 Williamson to Riddick, 24 October 1938 [NBTF/T8/2/2(2)].

110 Returns from Health Visitor, E. Richard, Cymmer, near Port Talbot, sent to NBTF on 25 April 1940 [NBTF/ T13/8].

111 Williams to Campbell Lyons, 1 September 1937 [NBTF/T8/1/1(1)].

112 NBTF to Thomas, 13 May 1939 [NBTF/T8/2/3].

113 Oddie to Williams, 8 February 1938 [NBTF/T13/3/(1)].

114 Good to Williams, 6 May 1938 [NBTF/T13/3(2)].

115 As in West Hartlepool – McKeggie to NBTF, 7 May 1938 [NBTF/T8/2/2(1)].

116 Islwyn Evans to NBTF, 26 May 1938 [NBTF/T8/2/2].

117 Juliet Rhys Williams to *Public Health* (July 1939).

118 Rhys Williams to Mellanby, 22 February 1939 (NBTF/T3).

119 Bradford Hill to Rhys Williams, 5 January 1939 [NBTF/T6/1].

120 McCance to Rhys Williams, 14 December 1938 [NBTF/T2(2)].

121 Telephone interview with Lady S.G. by ASW, 29 October 1991.

122 Islwyn Evans to NBTF, 26 May 1938 [NBTF/T8/2/2].

123 LAB Minute, 19 May 1938 [PRO/ LAB23/93].

124 Rhys Williams to Pye, 13 July 1939 [NBTF/T3(2)].

125 Rhys Williams to MOHs, draft, n.d. (but probably early June) [NBTF/T6/2].

126 Bradford Hill to Rhys Williams, 2 June 1939 (NBTF/T6/1).

127 Boyd Orr to Rhys Williams, 27 May 1938 [NBTF/T5/2].

128 This information is contained in Rhys Williams to McKinlay, 24 May 1939 [NBTF/T5/2].

129 McGregor to Rhys Williams, 24 May 1939 [NBTF/T5/2].

130 Boyd Orr to Rhys Williams, 27 May 1939 [NBTF/T5/2].

131 Johnstone to Rhys Williams, 25 May 1939 [NBTF/T6/2]; emphasis added.

132 Minute by Holloway, 15 March 1939; note added in different handwriting, 16 March 1939 [PRO/LAB23/93].

133 MRC Nutrition Committee, 'Report of the Nutrition Committee . . . on the administration of supplementary foods . . . by the Joint Council of Midwifery', 13 February 1939. The report is described and criticized in a Ministry of Health Minute to de Montmorency, 4 August 1939 [PRO/LAB23/94].

134 Rhys Williams to Mellanby, 22 February 1939 (NBTF/T3).

135 Mellanby to Rhys Williams, 30 March 1939 (NBTF/T3).

136 Rhys Williams to Haden Guest, 17 April 1939 [NBTF/T6/1].

137 Stewart to Rhys Williams, 24 May 1939 [NBTF/T3(2)].

138 Minute to Dalton, 9 September 1939; Minute from Dalton, 3 October 1939 [PRO/LAB23/94].

139 Minute by IDC, 5 August 1939 [PRO/ LAB23/94].

140 Rhys Williams to *Public Health*, July 1939.

141 Margaret I. Balfour, 'Supplementary Feeding in Pregnancy', *Lancet* (12 February 1944), pp. 208 ff.

142 Margaret I. Balfour, 'Supplementary Feeding in Pregnancy', first draft (1942), p. 11 [NBTF/T17/3/2].

143 McCance to Balfour, 17 July 1942 [NBTF/T17/3/2]; Dr Balfour's comments are written on a copy of this letter.
144 Rhys Williams to Balfour, 19 August 1942 [NBTF/T17/3/2].
145 Riddick to Balfour, 19 August 1942 [NBTF/T17/3/2].
146 Rhys Williams to Balfour, 28 October 1942 [NBTF/T17/3/2].
147 Margaret I. Balfour, 'Supplementary Feeding in Pregnancy', second draft (1942) [NBTF/T17/3/1].
148 J.H. Ebbs, F.F. Tisdall and W.A. Scott, 'The Influence of Prenatal Diet on the Mother and Child', *Journal of Nutrition*, 22 (1941), pp. 515–26.
149 'Nutrition of Expectant and Nursing Mothers', *Lancet* (4 July 1942), pp. 10–12.
150 Quoted in Horner, Editor of *BMJ*, to Balfour, 25 May 1943 [NBTF/T17/3/1].
151 Jackson of *Lancet* to Balfour, 26 May 1943 [NBTF/T17/3/1].
152 'Supplementary Feeding in Pregnancy'.
153 Interview with Dr Widdowson by ASW, 9 August 1991.
154 *Poverty and Population*, pp. 153–4; *The Bulletin of the Committee Against Malnutrition* (January 1938).
155 S. Mervyn Herbert, *Britain's Health* (Pelican, 1939), p. 135.
156 In 1989, for example, the historian John Burnett claimed that, "In 1934 experiments by Lady Williams in the depressed Rhondda Valley showed that no improvement in antenatal service reduced the high maternal mortality rate until food was distributed to expectant mothers – when this was done, it fell by 75 per cent." (*Plenty and Want*, p. 271). See also M. Mitchell, 'The Effects of Unemployment on the Social Conditions of Women and Children in the 1930s', *History Workshop*, 19 (spring 1985), pp. 105–27; and Keith Laybourn, *Britain on the Breadline* (Alan Sutton, 1990), p. 63.
157 *Hansard* (24 March 1938) 1373; emphasis added.

CHAPTER FIVE

1 This information is taken from questionnaires filled out in the late 1930s in the course of the JCM enquiry into abortion (discussed in this chapter). See the following files: [NBTF/S9/8; S9/15; S9/7].
2 East Midlands Working Women's Association, 'Memorandum to Inter-Departmental Committee' [1938] [PRO/MH71/23].
3 Interview with Mrs R. and the 'M girls', Pontypridd, by ASW, 31 July 1991.
4 The JCM abortion questionnaires from which this information is taken are in the following file: [NBTF/S9/11].
5 *Thompson's Weekly News* (2 December 1938). This is one of several cuttings in file [PRO/MH71/25].
6 This information is given in an MH list [n.d.] [PRO/MH71/18].
7 Ministry of Health, 'Statement of Evidence for submission to the Inter-Departmental Committee on abortion' (January 1938), p. 16 [PRO/MH71/18].
8 T.N. Parish, 'Report on a thousand cases of Abortion in St. Giles' Hospital, Camberwell', *Journal of Obstetrics and Gynaecology of the British Empire*, 42, 6 (December 1935), pp. 1107–20.
9 *Death in Childbirth*, p. 115.
10 Cunnington to Pyke, 8 March 1937 [ALRA/B3].
11 Statement by Mrs M. Williams of Leeds, quoted in 'Report of the Conference of the ALRA' (1936) [EUG/D1].
12 The JCM abortion questionnaires from which this information is taken are in the following file: [NBTF/S9/7].
13 Interview with Dr Mary Paterson by ASW, 12 August 1992.
14 *Death in Childbirth*, p. 115.
15 'Confidential Notes of evidence Given to Honorary Secretary of the Committee of Enquiry into Non-Therapeutic Abortion by Mrs X [sic]' (16 Feb. 1937) [NBTF/S1/6, in envelope formerly sealed, marked 'Strictly Confidential and Private'; a note inside indicates that this was sent in confidence to Mr Norman Birkett, Chairman of the Government Inter-Departmental Committee].
16 Helena Wright, 'Memorandum to the Inter-Departmental Committee', 1938 [PRO/HO326/29].
17 Robinson to Dawson, 1 October 1933 [PRO/MH71/20].
18 *Nursing Notes* (September 1937), p. 151.

19   Brown to Coleman, 20 October 1936 [NBTF/S3/1].

20   Williams to Burge, 22 September 1936 [NBTF/S2/1(2)].

21   Dr W.H.F. Oxley, 'Notes on the Abortion Enquiry' [n.d.] [NBTF/ S2/1(1)].

22   *Death in Childbirth*, pp. 250–1.

23   'Strictly Private. Notes on the Work of the Committee' [NBTF/S1/1/2].

24   'A Warning to Practising Midwives', *Nursing Notes* (December 1934), p. 1.

25   Women's Cooperative Guild *Annual Report, 1935* [WCG/BI].

26   Statement by Nurse Daniels in *Time and Tide* (19 December 1936).

27   Quoted in Janet Chance, 'The Case for the Reform of the Abortion Laws' (ALRA, [1930s]).

28   Barbara Evans, *Freedom to Choose. The Life and Times of Helena Wright* (Bodley Head, 1984), p. 142.

29   Meeting of the JCM Committee of Enquiry into Abortion, 6 November 1936 [NBTF/S1/2].

30   Meeting of the Legal Sub-Committee for the JCM Enquiry into Abortion, 9 March 1937 [NBTF/R3].

31   Williams to Burge, 22 September 1936 [NBTF/S2/1(2)].

32   Williams to Burge, 22 September 1936 [NBTF/S2/1(2)].

33   Eden to Williams, 28 October 1936 [NBTF/R19].

34   Eden to Williams, 3 October 1936 [NBTF/R19].

35   Williams to Roubikaine, 18 December 1936 [NBTF/S2/2].

36   Williams to Newnham, 1937 [NBTF/ S2/1(2)].

37   Meeting of Legal Sub-Committee for the JCM Enquiry into Abortion, 9 March 1937 [NBTF/R3].

38   Meeting of JCM Committee of Enquiry into Abortion, 15 April 1937 [NBTF/S1/4].

39   'B.M.A. on Abortion Law', *New Generation* (August 1936).

40   Eden to Williams, 28 October 1936 [NBTF/R19].

41   Lindsay to Athlone, 2 September 1936 [NBTF/R6/7]; MH memo, 14 May 1936 [PRO/MH55/627]; MH memo from MacNalty, 25 August 1936 [PRO/ MH55/627].

42   NCW to Minister, September 1936 [PRO/MH55/627].

43   Carter to MH, 13 October 1936; Machlachlan to Carter, 14 October 1936 [PRO/MH55/627].

44   Michael S. Teitelbaum and Jay M. Winter, *The Fear of Population Decline* (Academic Press, 1985), p. 42.

45   "In 1935 – the last year for which full figures were made available – there were registered in towns 573,593 births and 374,935 abortions (then still permissible by Soviet law). In the villages the proportion was higher. There were 242,979 births against 324,194 abortions. Moscow's figures were even worse, for the capital city of Soviet Russia recorded 70,000 births against 155,000 abortions." From 'Red Morality Drive', *News Review*, 25 November 1937.

46   *The Struggle for Population*, p. 30.

47   *The Struggle for Population*, p. 88.

48   Lady Rhys Williams, Article for *British Weekly*.'Family Allowances' (24 July 1939) [PP/JRW]; Williams to Briggs, *Daily Sketch* (1 May 1937).

49   HO Minutes, 19 December 1931 [PRO/HO144/21168].

50   *News of the World* (13 December 1931).

51   See for example Dr E.W.M. Phillips of Wales to Secretary of State, 11 March 1930 [PRO/HO144/21168].

52   Statement by Lindsay of Home Office, 15 December 1930 [PRO/ HO144/21168].

53   Interview with Dr Mary Paterson by ASW, 12 August 1992.

54   Robert Graves and Alan Hodge, *The Long Week-End, A Social History of Great Britain 1918–1939* (Faber & Faber, 1940), p. 105.

55   Margaret Owen, Fourth Annual Report of the Sheffield Women's Welfare Clinic, 1936–37, p. 6 [NBTF/S6/3(1)].

56   The questionnaires from which this information is taken are contained in the following files: [NBTF/S9/19; S9/8; S9/7].

57   Interview with Mrs R.H., Trealow, Rhondda, by ASW, 3 August 1991.

58   Women's Cooperative Guild *Annual Report, 1929*, p. 10 [CWG/BI].

59   Reported in *Freedom to Choose*, pp. 143–4.

60   Pyke to Williams, 3 December 1936 [NBTF/S2/2].

61   This has been demonstrated by two

historians: Jane Lewis in *Women in England, 1870–1950* (Wheatsheaf Books, 1986), pp. 17–18, and Barbara Brookes, *Abortion in England 1900–1967* (Croom Helm, 1988) p. i.

62 'Notes on the Abortion Enquiry'.

63 The questionnaires from which this information is taken are contained in the following files: [NBTF/S9/8; S9/15; S9/16(2)].

64 James Fenton, 'Notes on the proposed investigation into the prevalence of abortion amongst women of the working classes in Kensington' [NBTF/S1/6].

65 Eden to Williams, 15 September 1936 [NBTF/R19].

66 Gray to Williams, 15 December 1936 [NBTF/S6/1].

67 *Working-Class Wives*, pp. 22–3.

68 L. Carnac Rivett, 'The Report of the Abortion Committee of the Joint Council of Midwifery', *The Journal of the Royal Institute of the Public Health and Hygiene* (November 1941), vol. 4, No. 11, p. 265.

69 Johnstone to Balfour, 2 March 1938 [PRO/MH71/19].

70 Buchan to Williams, 13 February 1937 [NBTF/S6/3(1)].

71 Cunnington to Rhys Williams, 29 March 1938 [NBTF/S6/3 (1)].

72 For example, Williams to Williams, 5 February 1937 [NBTF/S6/3(2)]; also Smedley to Williams, 2 March 1937 [NBTF/S2/1(1)].

73 Statement by Machlachlan, 18 February 1937 [PRO/MH55/627].

74 Charles to Williams, 28 January 1937 [NBTF/S6/3].

75 Veitch Clark to Williams, 15 February 1937 [NBTF/S6/3].

76 Newsholme to Williams, 2 February 1937 [NBTF/S6/3].

77 Statement by Machlachlan, 18 February 1937 [PRO/MH55/627].

78 Young to Williams, 18 January 1937 [NBTF/S2/1(1)].

79 Note by MacNalty, 17 February 1937 [PRO/MH55/627].

80 PIC, 'Questionnaire on Fertility', 'Instructions and Notes' [PP/JRW].

81 Blacker to Williams, 8 April 1937 [PP/JRW].

82 'Abortion', statement by Machlachlan, 18 February 1937 [PRO/MH55/627].

83 Wood to Williams, 3 March 1937 [PRO/MH55/627].

84 Joint Council of Midwifery, *Interim Report of the Committee of Enquiry into Non-Therapeutic Abortion* (April 1937).

85 Williams to Buchan, 10 June 1937 [NBTF/S2/1(2)].

86 Goodall to Williams, 8 June 1937 [PRO/MH71/20].

87 Meeting of Extraordinary Meeting of Council, BCOG, 24 April 1937 [RCOG/A2 M/3].

88 Meeting of the Committee of Enquiry, 23 March 1937 [NBTF/S1/3].

89 MH memo, 8 February 1937 [PRO/MH55/681].

90 Berkeley to Williams, 14 November 1936 [NBTF/S2/1(1)].

91 Maclean to Wood, 30 April 1937 [PRO/MH71/19].

92 Meeting of the Committee of Enquiry, 5 October [NBTF/S1/5].

93 Wood to Williams, 3 March 1937 [PRO/MH55/627].

94 Hearder to NCW, 22 September 1936 [PRO/MH55/627].

95 Verbatim Report of Meeting of Abortion Enquiry, 5 October [NBTF/S1/5].

96 Ministry of Health and Home Office, *Report of the Inter-Departmental Committee on Abortion* (1939) (Birkett Report), p. iii.

97 Moshinsky to Pater, 4 October 1937 [PRO/MH71/19].

98 Oxley to Williams, 18 September 1937 [NBTF/S2/1(1)].

99 Berkeley to Williams, 15 February 1937 [NBTF/S2/1(1)].

100 Oxley to Williams, 22 November 1936 [NBTF/S2/1(1)].

101 Williams to Eden, 1 October 1937 [NBTF/R19].

102 Oxley to Williams, 25 September 1937 [NBTF/S2/1(1)].

103 Oxley to Williams, 22 September, 1937 [NBTF/S2/1(1)].

104 Verbatim Report of the Committee of Enquiry into Abortion, 5 October 1937 [NBTF/S1/5].

105 Williams to Young, 31 August 1937 [NBTF/S2/1(1)].

106 Kelly to Chrystal, 29 April 1937 [PRO/MH71/20].

107 Unsigned note, 16 November 1936 [ALRA/B3].

108 [PRO/MH71/18]. There is a copy of

the official form for this in the LSE archives [LSE Coll Misc/479/M1120].

109 Berkeley to Moshinsky, 26 August 1937 [PRO/MH71/20].

110 Meeting of Birkett Committee, 10 February 1939 [PRO/MH/71/29].

111 Evidence of BMA to Birkett Committee, 25 May 1938 [PRO/ HO326/31].

112 Evidence of BCOG to Birkett Committee, 15 December 1937 [PRO/ HO326/31].

113 Birkett Report, pp. 5, 11, 66–7, 93, 97–8, 128, 135.

114 'Note on Alterations to A.C. Paper No. 19D' by Dr Oxley, 26 October 1937 [PRO/HO326/29].

115 Interview with Mr Elliot Philipp by ASW, 6 July 1992.

116 Meeting of JCM Research Committee, 20 October 1937 [NBTF/R5].

117 Rhys Williams to Carter, 17 November 1938 [NBTF/R16/2].

118 Meeting of JCM Research Committee, 24 October 1937 [NBTF/R5].

119 Burt to Rhys Williams, 5 July 1938 [NBTF/S7/1/4].

120 Macgregor to Rhys Williams, 6 April 1938 [NBTF/S6/3(3)].

121 First meeting of the General Purposes Sub-Committee for the JCM Abortion Enquiry, 21 November 1936 [NBTF/R4].

122 Davidson to Young, 3 December 1936 [NBTF/S6/3(3)].

123 Rhys Williams to Burt, 4 August 1938 [NBTF/S7/1/4].

124 Burt to Rhys Williams, 25 October 1938 [NBTF/S7/1/4].

125 Burt to Riddick, 17 August 1938 [NBTF/S7/1/4].

126 Burt to Riddick, n.d. [NBTF/ S7/1/4].

127 The questionnaires from which this information is taken are contained in the following files: [NBTF/S9/17; S9/15; S9/16(1) and (2); S9/8; S9/11; S9/10].

128 JCM, 'Report of the Research Committee upon the Abortion Questionnaire Enquiry' (October 1938) [NBTF/R13/3].

129 McCance to Rhys Williams, 11 October 1938 [NBTF/T2(2)].

130 Rhys Williams to Carter, 28 November 1938 [NBTF/T2(2)].

131 Bradford Hill to Rhys Williams, 5 December 1938 [NBTF/T2(2)].

132 Rhys Williams to 'x' [form letter], 2 January 1939 [NBTF/S7/3].

133 L. Carnac Rivett, 'The Report of the Abortion Committee of the Joint Council of Midwifery', *The Journal of the Royal Institute of Public Health and Hygiene* (1941) vol. 4, No. 11, p. 268.

134 *The Disinherited Family*, p. 184.

CHAPTER SIX

1 Quoted in Nicky Leap and Billie Hunter, *The Midwife's Tale* (Scarlet Press, 1993), p. 168.

2 Report of LCC Central Public Health Committee (CPHC), 31 October 1933 [NBTF/H1/5].

3 Genesis 2:21.

4 Report of LCC CPHC, October 1933.

5 G. to Bevan, n.d. [1949] [PRO/ MH134/145].

6 *The Hard Way Up*, pp. 101–2.

7 Report of Dinner at Goldsmith's Hall, 8 May 1934 [NBTF/G7/4(1)].

8 Oatley to 'Lucy Baldwin's Birthday Trust Fund', 19 January 1938 [NBTF/ H3/2/1].

9 Report of LCC CPHC .

10 Rivett to Williams, 21 June 1930 [NBTF/F2/5/1(1)].

11 Manningham-Buller to Jackson, 13 March 1929 [NBTF/F3/2/1].

12 Ti [Cholmondeley] to Londonderry, 14 March 1929 [NBTF/F11/1(9)].

13 Cholmondeley to Londonderry, 18 March 1929 [NBTF/F11/1(9)]; J.M. Jackson to Miss Manningham-Buller, 14 March 1929 [NBTF/F3/2/1].

14 Transcript of Mrs Baldwin's Wireless Speech, given 28 April 1929, with pencil annotations showing 'As Spoken' [NBTF/ F3/2/1]; emphasis added.

15 Report of Dinner at Goldsmith's Hall; emphasis added.

16 Emphasis added; samples of stamps and flags are contained in file [NBTF/ G6/4].

17 Meeting of NBTF Finance Committee, 21 April 1936 [NBTF/A2/1].

18 Suggested draft for Middle Part of Letter to the NFWI [NBTF/H1/1].

19 Draft of Mrs Baldwin's speech at the Mansion House, 11 December 1929 [NBTF/G1/2(2)].

20 Judith Walzer Leavitt, 'Birthing and

Anaesthesia: The Debate over Twilight
Sleep', *Signs*, 6, 1 (autumn 1980), p. 154.
21   *Three Guineas*, p. 79.
22   Vera Brittain, *Honourable Estate*
(Victor Gollancz, 1936), p. 540; *Testament
of Experience* (Gollancz, 1957), p. 52.
23   Jacques Gélis, *History of Childbirth*
(Polity Press, 1991), p. 152.
24   Laetitia Fairfield, 'Anaesthesia in
Normal Labour' [c. 1933] [GLRO/
Ph/Gen/3/6]. I am grateful to Lara
Marks for drawing my attention to this
trial.
25   Report of LCC [NBTF/H1/5].
26   *Working-Class Wives*, p. 67.
27   'Anxious Daughter' to 'Mother',
4 February 1935 [NBTF/G7/5(1)].
28   These questionnaires are contained
in file [NBTF/S9/6/1].
29   Letters received as a result of the
press appeal, 1930 [NBTF/F3/2/2(1)].
30   From 'A Mother in Stockton-on-
Tees', 17 June 1931 [NBTF/F3/2/2(1)].
31   Hardy to the Minister of Health,
4 July 1938 [PRO/MH55/625].
32   Sparrow to Wood, 1 January 1936
[PRO/MH55/625].
33   H. Crichton-Miller, 'Preserving the
Race in Post-War Reconstruction', *BMJ*
(7 March 1942), p. 337.
34   *Britain and her Birth-Rate, A Report
prepared by Mass-Observation* (John Murray,
1945), pp. 113–14; emphasis added.
35   Bennett to Rhys Williams, 22 March
1945 [NBTF/H2/2(1)].
36   Cutting from *The Times* (1939) in
[NBTF/P15]; emphasis added.
37   Laetitia Fairfield, 'Pregnancy and
Feminism', *BMJ* (14 February 1914).
38   Oatley to NBTF, 19 January 1938
[NBTF/H3/2/1].
39   'Obstetric Analgesia', *BMJ* (22 April
1939).
40   Williams to Buckle, UCH, 21 October
1930 [NBTF/F2/5/1(1)].
41   Meeting of NBTF Committee,
11 November 1930 [NBTF/F6/1(5)].
42   Meeting of NBTF Committee,
27 January 1931 [NBTF/F6/1(5)].
43   Extract of minutes for NBTF
Committee, 28 November 1929, sent to
East End Maternity Hospital [NBTF/
F6/1(5)].
44   Meeting of NBTF Executive
Committee, 28 November 1929 [NBTF/
A1/2].

45   National Birthday Trust Fund,
Maternal Welfare (1936), p. 26.
46   Quoted by Virginia Woolf from a
letter sent by C.S. Wentworth Stanley to
The Times in 1937, in a footnote to *Three
Guineas*. Woolf adds that since chloroform
was first administered to Queen Victoria
on the birth of Prince Leopold in April
1853, normal cases on the wards had to
wait for seventy-six years and "the advocacy
of a Prime Minister's wife" to obtain this
relief (note 19, pp. 183–4).
47   Meeting of NBTF Finance Committee,
21 April 1936 [NBTF/A2/1].
48   Williams to Manningham-Buller,
18 March 1931 [NBTF/F2/5/1(1)].
49   L.C. Rivett, 'Chloroform capsules
during labour', *BMJ* (29 October 1933).
50   *Maternal Welfare*, p. 27.
51   Jackson to Williams, 1 April 1932
[NBTF/H1/1].
52   NBTF to LCC, 22 April 1931 [NBTF/
F7/4].
53   'Anaesthesia in Normal Labour'.
54   Report of LCC CPHC.
55   Fairfield to Williams, 30 June [1934]
[NBTF/F7/4].
56   This was reported in the *Lancet* and
the *BMJ* (June 1932).
57   Cahn to Sir, 28 July 1932 [NBTF/
H1/1].
58   Meeting of the NBTF Finance
Committee, 23 January 1934 [NBTF/
A2/1].
59   Meeting of NBTF Executive
Committee, 9 March 1932 [NBTF/A1/2].
60   First Meeting of the Medical
Committee of the NBTF, 13 October 1933
[NBTF/H1/1].
61   'Chloroform capsules during labour'.
62   Elgood to NBTF, 16 August 1933
[NBTF/H1/1].
63   Thierens to NBTF, 7 February 1934
[NBTF/H1/1(1)].
64   Completed forms from Springfield
Maternity Home, Greenwich and
Wolverhampton on the 'The Effectiveness
of the Capsules' are contained in file
[NBTF/H1/6(10)].
65   Elgood to NBTF, 16 August 1933
[NBTF/H1/1].
66   Elder to NBTF, 21 June 1933
[NBTF/H1/1].
67   Mentioned in reply by NBTF to
Matron, 4 November 1932 [NBTF/
H1/1].

68   Elder to NBTF, 27 June 1933 [NBTF/H1/1].

69   Quoted from an interview reported in *The Midwife's Tale*, p. 168.

70   Dooley to Sir, 14 June n.d. [1932] [NBTF/H1/6(1)].

71   Baldwin to Parker, 13 June 1934 [NBTF/H1/1].

72   Bird to Baldwin, 2 July 1934 [NBTF/H1/1].

73   Letters to NBTF [NBTF/H1/1].

74   Ennis to NBTF, n.d. [NBTF/H1/1].

75   Young in Onitsha, Nigeria, to NBTF, n.d [1933] [NBTF/H1/1].

76   Meeting of NBTF Medical Committee, 13 October 193[3] [NBTF/ H1/1].

77   Fletcher Shaw to Cahn, 19 December 1933 [NBTF/H4/1/1(1)].

78   *Maternal Welfare*, pp. 27–8.

79   Mellanby to MacNalty, 6 November 1936 [PRO/MH55/625].

80   BCOG, *Investigation into the use of analgesia suitable for administration by midwives* [1936] [NBTF/H4/1/1(1)].

81   Minutes of meeting of BCOG Analgesia Sub-Committee, 6 June 1934 [RCOG/T4/ J3].

82   Fletcher Shaw to Cahn, 28 May 1934 [NBTF/H4/1/1(1)].

83   Cahn to BCOG, n.d. [May/June 1934] [NBTF/H4/1/1(1)]; emphasis added.

84   For further details of this study see minutes of meetings of BCOG Analgesics Sub-Committee [RCOG/T4].

85   *Investigation into the Use of Analgesia.*

86   Pye to BCOG, 25 February 1936 [RCOG/B2/26].

87   Wren to O'Reilly, 9 February 1939 [NBTF/F2/2/2(1)].

88   For a discussion of this, see D.J. Wilkinson, 'Nitrous Oxide in the 1920s and 1930s', in *History of Anaesthesia Society Proceedings*, vol. 16 (Proceedings of the Joint Meeting with the Section of Anaesthetics, RSM, London, 10 December 1994), pp. 81–4.

89   Ellen P. O'Sullivan, 'Dr Robert James Minnitt 1889–1974: A Pioneer of Inhalational Analgesia', in *Journal of the Royal Society of Medicine*, 82 (April 1989), p. 221.

90   Elam to NBTF, 28 December 1933 [NBTF/F10/1/1].

91   Garry to NBTF, 19 April 1934 [NBTF/H2/1].

92   Williams to Rivett, 22 September 1934 [NBTF/F5/1/11].

93   Account of telephone call between Dr Minnitt and NBTF, 30 June 1934 [NBTF/H2/1].

94   Minnitt to Meyer, 8 May 1935 [NBTF/H2/1].

95   Interview with Mrs M.M., Caerphilly, by ASW, 2 August 1991.

96   'The Countrywoman Now Thinks for Herself', *News Chronicle* (2 June 1938).

97   Farrer Brown to BCOG, 7 June 1938 and 12 December 1938 [RCOG/B2/26].

98   Meeting of BCOG Analgesics Sub-Committee, 15 April 1942 [RCOG/T4/ J26]. Regarding pressure from the organizations mentioned, see correspondence in file [RCOG/B2/27].

99   Meeting of NBTF Finance Committee, 21 April 1936 [NBTF/A2/1].

100 Farrer to O'Reilly, 18 January 1938 [NBTF/F5/2].

101 Meeting of NBTF Analgesics Sub-Committee, 3 July 1939 [NBTF/ A1/15/1].

102 Chapman to O'Reilly, 15 February 1938 [NBTF/H3/1(1)].

103 King to Meyer, 16 November 1936 [NBTF/H2/1].

104 NBTF 'Report on Gas/Air Analgesia' (1948) [NBTF/H2/5].

105 'With regard to difficulties arising from C.M.B. Rule, quotations from Nursing Associations, collected by Lady Rhys Williams' [NBTF/H3/2/3(2)].

106 Extract from the Report of the BCOG into the use of Analgesics [NBTF/H3/1(1)].

107 Meeting of the NBTF Analgesics Sub-Committee, 29 March 1938 [NBTF/A1/15/1].

108 Meeting of NBTF Analgesics Sub-Committee, 3 July 1939 [NBTF/ A1/15/1].

109 Meeting of the NBTF Analgesics Sub-Committee, 25 July 1938 [NBTF/ A/15/1].

110 Meeting of NBTF Analgesics Sub-Committee, 1 December 1939 [NBTF/A1/15/1].

111 Greasley NA to NBTF, 7 July 1938 [NBTF/H3/3(2)].

112 Shearing to Baldwin, 3 February 1937 [NBTF/H3/2/1].

113 McVicker to Baldwin, 15 November 1938 [NBTF/H3/2/1].

114 Jones to Williams, 8 March 1937 [NBTF/H3/2/1].

115 West Hampstead DNA to NBTF,

27 May 1937 [NBTF/H3/3(1)].
116 Rhys Williams to Goodall,
7 November 1938 [NBTF/H3/2/1].
117 King to NBTF, 12 November 1934 [NBTF/F2/2/2(1)].
118 King to NBTF, 10 July 1935 [NBTF/H2/1].
119 King to NBTF, 25 September 1935 [NBTF/H2/1].
120 NBTF to King, 18 December 1935 [NBTF/H2/1].
121 Wren to Meyer, 10 April 1936 [NBTF/F2/2/2(3)].
122 King to Meyer, 16 April 1936 [NBTF/H2/1].
123 S. Shavaratman, Medical Super-intendent, DeSoysa Lying-In Home, Colombo, 'Report on use of Queen Charlotte's Gas/Air Apparatus', 14 April 1937 [NBTF/F2/2/3].
124 Wren to Meyer, 14 December 1936 [NBTF/F2/2/2(3)].
125 The BOC Group, *Around the Group in 100 Years* (1986), p. 24.
126 King to BCOG, 20 March 1937 [RCOG/B2/26].
127 BCOG to BOC, 19 April 1937 [RCOG/B2/26].
128 Chapman to NBTF, 3 May 1937 [NBTF/H3/1(1)].
129 The BOC Group, *Industrial Gases, The Invisible Fabric of the Modern World* (1984), p. 4 and preface.
130 Rivett to Secretary, BCOG, 17 September 1936 [RCOG/B2/26].
131 Mennell [to Fairbairn], 5 October 1936 [RCOG/B2/26].
132 King to Meyer, 12 March 1937 [NBTF/H3/1(4)].
133 Meeting of Analgesics Sub-Committee, 10 March 1937 [NBTF/A1/15/1].
134 Chapman to O'Reilly, 12 November 1937 [NBTF/H3/1(1)].
135 Meeting of NBTF Analgesics Sub-Committee, 3 July 1939 [NBTF/A1/15/1].
136 Meeting of NBTF Analgesics Sub-Committee, 29 March 1938 [NBTF/A1/15/1].
137 'Report on Gas/Air Analgesia'.
138 For example, the Liverpool Maternity Hospital: see letter to NBTF, 10 July 1937 [NBTF/H3/2/1].
139 London Hospital: see letter to NBTF, 15 March 1937 [NBTF/H3/2/1].
140 Leeds Maternity Hospital: see letter to NBTF, 12 July 1937 [NBTF/H3/2/1].
141 For example, St Thomas's Hospital: see letter to NBTF, 18 March 1937 [NBTF/H3/2/1].
142 Reported in minutes of NBTF Executive Committee, 6 April 1937 [NBTF/A1/3].
143 Northamptonshire NA: see letter to NBTF, 19 November 1937 [NBTF/H3/2/1].
144 Diana Palmer, 'Women, Health and Politics, 1919–1939: Professional and Lay Involvement in the Women's Health Campaign' (Ph.D. thesis, University of Warwick, 1986), p. 268.
145 'Medical Notes in Parliament', *BMJ* (5 August 1939).
146 Camp to NBTF, 10 August 1939 [NBTF/H3/1/1].
147 Department of Health for Scotland to Ministry of Health, 29 October 1937 [PRO/MH55/625].
148 *The Division in British Medicine*, pp. 158–9.
149 'The Midwife as Anaesthetist', *Lancet* (29 July 1939).
150 *The Division in British Medicine*, p. 159.
151 Joint Committee of the Royal College of Obstetricians and Gynaecologists and Population Investigation Committee, *Maternity in Great Britain* (Oxford University Press, 1948), p. 78.
152 *The Division in British Medicine*, p. 158, footnote b.
153 *The Squire*, pp. 100–2 and 145–6; emphasis added.
154 Interview with Dr Mary Paterson by ASW, 12 August 1992.
155 Interview of Mrs G.T., Worcester, by ASW, 1 June 1993.
156 Interview with Mrs R.H., Trealow, Rhondda, by ASW, 3 August 1991.
157 Interview with Mrs R., Pontypridd, 31 July 1991.
158 Meeting of NBTF Executive Committee, 24 October 1945 [NBTF/A1/5/1].
159 'Suggested Draft for Middle Part of Letter'.
160 Information given to Secretary of NBTF by Secretary of Midwives' Institute, Meeting of NBTF Analgesics Sub-Committee, 13 December 1939 [NBTF/A1/15/1].
161 *Maternity in Great Britain*, pp. 82–3.

162 'Report on Gas/Air Analgesia'.
163 'Anaesthetics for Mothers', p. 9.
164 *Maternity in Great Britain*, p. 86.
165 Women's Cooperative Guild Annual Report for 1946, p. 46; Annual Report for 1947, p. 49.
166 *Maternity in Great Britain*, p. 80.
167 *Britain and her Birth-Rate*, p. 113.
168 Letter to *The Lady* (21 May 1942).
169 Geoffrey Chamberlain, Ann Wraight and Philip Steer, *Pain and its Relief in Childbirth. Results of a National Survey Conducted by the National Birthday Trust* (Churchill Livingstone, 1993), p. 6.
170 Interview with Dame Josephine Barnes by ASW, 23 July 1992.
171 J. Barnes, 'Pethidine in Labour: Results in 500 Cases', *BMJ* (5 April 1947), p. 437.
172 See file [PRO/MH55/1602].
173 For an account of this see P.V. Cole, 'Entonox and Obstetric Analgesia', in *History of Anaesthesia Society Proceedings*.
174 See Elliot Philipp, 'Visit to Paris to study the Lamaze method of psycho-prophylactic approach to childbirth', 11 June 1959 [NBTF/B4/4].
175 *Pain and its Relief in Childbirth*, p. 6.
176 See chapters 5 and 6 of *Pain and its Relief in Childbirth*.

CHAPTER SEVEN

1 *Medical Officer* (19 August 1939), p. 73.
2 *Daily Express* (16 June 1939).
3 S.E. Balmer, B.A. Wharton, 'Human milk banking at Sorrento Maternity Hospital, Birmingham', *Archives of Disease in Childhood*, 67 (1992), p. 556.
4 American Academy of Pediatrics Committee on mothers' milk, 'Recommended standards for the operation of mothers' milk bureau', *Journal of Pediatric Medicine*, 23 (1943), pp. 112–28.
5 *St Neot's Advertiser* (6 December 1935).
6 Paterson to Dare, 12 July 1938 [NBTF/J1/1]; emphasis added.
7 Reverse side of photograph, kindly supplied by Georgina Going, Librarian of Queen Charlotte's and Chelsea Hospital, Hammersmith Hospitals NHS Trust; emphasis added.

8 Interview with Mrs M.M. by ASW, 28 November 1992.
9 Meeting of NBTF Executive Committee, 13 December 1938 [NBTF/J1/1].
10 Meeting of NBTF Executive Committee, 23 May 1939 [NBTF/J1/4].
11 *The History of Queen Charlotte's Hospital*, p. 200.
12 Statement for the press: 'Human Milk Bureau at Queen Charlotte's Hospital Block, Hammersmith' [July 1939] [NBTF J1/2].
13 *Birth Counts*, p. 10.
14 G.F. McCleary, *The Maternity and Child Welfare Movement* (P.S. King and Son, 1935), pp. 193 and 199.
15 Paterson to Dare, 12 July 1938 [NBTF/J1/1].
16 Lady Rhys Williams, 'A Baby', *Sunday Pictorial* (10 December 1939), p. 10.
17 Interview with Mrs M.M. by ASW, 28 November 1992.
18 Meeting of the NBTF Executive Committee, 23 April 1940 [NBTF/J1/4].
19 Interview with Mrs M.M. by ASW, 28 November 1992.
20 Professor Rosalinde Hurley's memories of the Queen Charlotte's Milk Bank, recalled in *Milk Banking News and Views* (September 1995), vol. 1 No. 2, p. 10.
21 Meeting of NBTF Executive Committee, 27 June 1939 [NBTF/J1/4].
22 Statement for the press [July 1939].
23 'Wonder Babies', *Sunday Pictorial* (20 June 1948).
24 John de Louvois, 'The Organisation of Human Milk Bank', n.d.; typewritten article [PP/HMB].
25 Diana Dick, *Yesterday's Babies. A History of Babycare* (Bodley Head, 1987), p. 36.
26 *Plenty and Want*, p. 164.
27 Rima D. Apple, *Mothers and Medicine. A Social History of Infant Feeding, 1890–1950* (The University of Wisconsin Press, 1987), p. 9.
28 *Plenty and Want*, p. 125.
29 *Yesterday's Babies*, p. 36.
30 Donald Paterson and J. Forest Smith, *Modern Methods of Feeding in Infancy and Childhood*, 7th edn (Constable and Co., Ltd, 1939), p. 27; emphasis added.
31 James Finlayson to Editor, *Daily Telegraph*, 14 July 1938 [PP/JRW].

32   *Modern Methods of Feeding in Infancy and Childhood*, 7th edn, p. 27; emphasis added.

33   For an account of these depots, see G.F. McCleary, *The Early History of the Infant Welfare Movement* (H.K. Lewis, 1933).

34   *Yesterday's Babies*, p. 36.

35   *Evening News* (1952), cutting in [NBTF/J1/1].

36   Charles Dickens, *Dombey and Son* (1848; rpt. Penguin, 1975), pp. 64–5.

37   Interview with Gillian Weaver by ASW, 21 January 1993.

38   *Nursing Notes* (August 1939), p. 137.

39   Annual General Meeting of NBTF, 23 June 1942 [NBTF/A1/4].

40   *Daily Herald* (1 March 1939).

41   For more on this in the USA, see *Mothers & Medicine*.

42   *St Neot's Advertiser, Hunts and Beds News* (21 February 1936).

43   *St Neot's Advertiser, Hunts and Beds News* (10 January 1936).

44   The letters from which these quotations are taken are collected in *Maternity*, pp. 24, 82, 122, 166 and 188.

45   Report for press [July 1939] [NBTF/J12].

46   'If you see a nurse on a motorcycle', *Daily Express* (16 June 1939).

47   Meeting of NBTF Executive Committee, 1 November 1938 [NBTF/J1/1].

48   Interview with Gillian Weaver by ASW, 30 September 1993. See Department of Health, *Dietary Reference Values for Food Energy and Nutrients for the United Kingdom: Report of the Panel on Dietary Reference Values of the Committee on Medical Aspects of Food Policy*, Report on Health and Social Subjects, 41 (1991).

49   'If you see a nurse on a motorcycle'.

50   Interview with Gillian Weaver by ASW, 21 January 1993.

51   Comment by Dame Josephine Barnes over the telephone to ASW, 22 January 1993.

52   Reverse side of photograph (see n. 7).

53   Statement for press [July 1939].

54   Interview with Mrs M.M. by ASW, 28 November 1992 .

55   'If you see a nurse on a motorcycle'.

56   Meeting of NBTF Executive Committee, 27 June 1939 [NBTF/J1/4] .

57   'If you see a nurse on a motorcycle'.

58   Meeting of NBTF Executive Committee, 27 June 1939 [NBTF/J1/4].

59   Meeting of NBTF Executive Committee, 17 October 1939 [NBTF/J1/4].

60   Meeting of NBTF Executive Committee, 23 April 1940 [NBTF/J1/4].

61   MH memo, 11 August 1942 [PRO/MH55/1547].

62   MH memo, 14 August 1943 [PRO/MH55/1547].

63   *Final Report of the Advisory Committee on Mothers and Young Children*, 3 April 1943 [PRO/MH55/1547].

64   Jamieson to Mellanby, 13 May 1943 [PRO/MH55/1547].

65   MH memos, 10 August 1944, 11 August 1944, 12 August 1944 [PRO/MH55/1547].

66   Paterson to Dare, 12 July 1938 [NBTF/J1/1].

67   Meeting of NBTF Executive Committee, 13 May 1942 [NBTF/J1/4].

68   Riddick to Cahn, 6 February 1942; NBTF/F2/2/2(1).

69   Cahn to Riddick, 12 February 1942 [F2/2/2(1)].

70   Riddick to Cahn, 21 February 1942 [NBTF/F2/2/2(1)].

71   Greenwood Wilson to Wade, 20 January 1945 [PRO/MH55/1547].

72   NBTF Annual Report 1945–1947, p. 5 [NBTF/C17/10].

73   MH memo, 22 July 1952 [PRO/MH55/1547].

74   NBTF to Dare, 24 May 1945 [NBTF/J1/1].

75   NBTF to Bell, draft, n.d. [NBTF/J1/4].

76   Riddick to Clayton, 15 February 1952 [NBTF/J1/4].

77   Walters to Riddick, 4 June 1953 [NBTF/J1/4].

78   *The Collection and Storage of Human Milk*, Report of a Working Party of Human Milk Banks, set up by the Committee on Medical Aspects of Food Policy (HMSO, 1981), p. iii.

79   'Human milk banking at Sorrento Maternity Hospital, Birmingham', p. 556.

80   Interview with Gillian Weaver by ASW, 30 September 1993.

81   A.F. Williams, 'Human milk and the preterm baby' *BMJ* 306 (19 June 1993).

82   A. Lucas, R. Morley, T.J. Cole,

G. Lister, C. Leeson-Payne, 'Breast milk and subsequent intelligence quotient in children born preterm', *Lancet*, 339 (1 February 1992), p. 261.
83 *The Collection and Storage of Human Milk*, p. iii.
84 'Human Milk Banking: The Way It Is', *New Generation* (December 1991), p. 22.
85 British Paediatric Association, *Guidelines for the Establishment and Operation of Human Milk Banks in the UK. The Report of an ad hoc Working Party following the Sorrento Symposium on Milk Banking, March 1993* (October 1994).

CHAPTER EIGHT

1 Riddick to ARP Office, 5 March 1940 [NBTF/E7/6/4(1)].
2 Riddick to Murley, 30 March 1942 [NBTF/F3/2/5].
3 Cahn to Riddick, 17 June 1943 [NBTF/F2/2/4(2)].
4 Riddick to City of Westminster Food Office, 30 April 1946 [NBTF/E7/6/5].
5 City of Westminster Food Office to NBTF, 17 September 1940 [NBTF/E7/6/5].
6 See copy of letter from Walters & Co., Solicitors, 19 January 1942, in Minutes of the Finance Committee, July 1942 [NBTF/C17/1].
7 Riddick to Cahn, 1 September 1939 [NBTF/B2/14(1)].
8 Riddick to Buckmaster, 10 October 1940 [NBTF/F4/2/1].
9 Reported by a midwife in *The Midwife's Tale*, p. 121.
10 Riddick to Buckmaster, 28 April 1941 [NBTF/F4/2/2].
11 Riddick to Buckmaster, 3 December 1943 [NBTF/F4/2/2].
12 See for example, Noel-Buxton and Violet H. Attlee to *The Times* (19 July 1948). Mrs Attlee was Chairman of the Dinner Committee of the SCF.
13 *Hansard* (4 March 1949), 717.
14 C.P. Snow, *Homecomings* (1956; rpt. Penguin, 1971), p. 227.
15 Londonderry House to Riddick, 18 January 1955 [NBTF/G28].
16 *Birth Counts*, pp. 271 and 276.
17 The appeal was made on Whit-Sunday, 20 May 1956; reported in NBTF Annual Report for 1955–6 [NBTF/ C19/2].

18 Willink to Riddick, 29 May 1946 [NBTF/K1/1]. This contrasts with other, more cautious replies, like that of Lady Megan Lloyd George: "I have carefully noted the Resolutions enclosed regarding the NHS Bill, and will bear your views in mind", Megan Lloyd George to NBTF, 4 June 1946 [NBTF/K1/1].
19 Meeting of Evidence Sub-Committee, 13 October 1947 [NBTF/K1/2].
20 Ministry of Health, Department of Health for Scotland, Ministry of Labour and National Service, *Report of the Working Party on Midwives* (HMSO, 1949), para. 108, p. 27 [GPA/13666].
21 de Laszlo also painted a portrait of Louis Rivett, which is currently hung at the RCOG, and Sir Julien Cahn.
22 Meeting of NBTF Executive Committee, 4 February 1948 [NBTF/ A1/5/1].
23 See *Hansard* (4 March 1949), 692–748.
24 See *Hansard* (15 March 1949), 1911–1922.
25 'Analgesia', *Greenock Telegraph* (5 August 1949).
26 'Citizenship by Alan', *Sketch* (14 September 1949).
27 See the letters in the following files: [PRO/MH/134/141, 144, 145].
28 Thorneycroft was also an active member of Design for Freedom, a campaigning group set up soon after the war that opposed regulation and advocated the principle of a united Europe. Lady Rhys Williams was also a member of this group and collaborated with Thorneycroft in some of its work. (Communication by ECB, London, to ASW, 18 August 1994).
29 *Women and the Women's Movement*, p. 308.
30 'No longer necessary', *Islington Gazette* (15 July 1949).
31 Meeting of NBTF Executive Committee, 16 March 1948 [NBTF/ A1/5/1].
32 See *Hansard* (1 July 1949), 1733–1747.
33 Bevan to Morrison, 11 May 1949. Morrison agreed "that you should arrange for an inspired amendment to be put down to the National Health Service (Amendment) Bill", Morrison to Bevan, 12 May 1949 [MH134/141].
34 Meeting of NBTF Executive

Committee, 29 June 1949 [NBTF/A1/5/1].

35 For example, Watson at the Ministry to Swindale, 7 April 1949; the substance of this letter was replicated many times. [PRO/MH134/145].

36 'Analgesia births more than doubled, progress under National Health Service', 221/12/49, No. 8 [PRO/134/141].

37 See *Hansard* (8 July 1949), 2545–2588.

38 Meeting of NBTF Executive Committee, 31 August 1949 [NBTF/A1/5/1].

39 Hall to Bevan, 11 March 1949 [PRO/MH134/144].

40 Lawrence to Bevan, 8 March 1949 [PRO/MH 134/145].

41 Charles Webster, 'Beveridge after 50 years', *BMJ*, 305 (17 October 1992), p. 901.

42 Richard M. Titmuss, *Problems of Social Policy* (HMSO and Longman, Green & Co., 1950), p. 514.

43 Safer Motherhood Committee to Bevan, 16 June 1948 [NBTF/G33/5(1)].

44 Quoted in Espley to various organizations, 5 November 1948 [NBTF/G33/1]; emphasis added.

45 Meeting of NBTF Executive Committee, 12 February 1947 [NBTF/A1/5/1].

46 Carter to Riddick, 9 September 1947 [NBTF/K1/2].

47 PEP, *Planning. Mothers in Jobs*, A Broadsheet, No. 254 (23 August 1946).

48 Note jotted down by Miss Riddick, n.d. [NBTF/G33/2].

49 Cmd 6502. *A National Health Service* (1944), p. 5.

50 *Happy Birthdays*, n.d. [1948] [NBTF/G4/3/1].

51 Baldwin to Riddick, 14 June 1945 [NBTF/F3/2/6]; emphasis added.

52 Riddick to Buckmaster, 22 June 1945 [NBTF/F4/2/3].

53 McIlroy to *The Times*, 26 June 1947.

54 A.J. Cronin, *The Citadel* (Book Club Associates, n.d.), p. 218.

55. Lady Juliet Rhys Williams, *Something to Look Forward To, Suggestions for A New Social Contract* (Western Mail and Echo, 1942), pp. 5 and 50.

56 Meeting of NBTF Executive Committee, 22 May 1946 [NBTF/K1/1]; emphasis added.

57 For example, the Salvation Army, the British Hospital Association to Miss Riddick, 6 June 1946; and the Mildmay Mission Hospital to Miss Riddick, 18 June 1946 [NBTF/K1/1].

58 Mitchell to Riddick, 15 June 1946 [NBTF/K1/1].

59 Leslie to Riddick, 31 May 1946 [NBTF/K1/1].

60 Meeting of NBTF Executive Committee, 29 June 1949 [NBTF/A1/5/1].

61 Reported by Lady Rhys Williams to Executive Committee, 11 June 1947 [NBTF/B2/15(1)].

62 Meeting of NBTF Evidence Sub-Committee, 22 October 1947 [NBTF/K1/2]; emphasis added.

63 Meeting of NBTF Executive Committee, 22 October 1947 [NBTF/A1/5/1].

64 'Notes Relating to the National Birthday Trust Fund', n.d. [NBTF/K1/3].

65 Meeting of NBTF Evidence Sub-Committee, 31 October 1947 [NBTF/K1/2].

66 'Notes Relating to the National Birthday Trust Fund'; emphasis added.

67 Nutting to relevant individuals, 19 May 1948 [NBTF/G33/1].

68 Press statement of the Safer Motherhood Committee, 1948 [NBTF/G33/1].

69 Transcript of speech by Lady Helen Nutting at meeting of Safer Motherhood Committee, 8 June 1948 [NBTF/G33/1].

70 Nutting to relevant individuals, 19 May 1948 [NBTF/G33/1]; emphasis added.

71 Transcript of Safer Motherhood meeting, 8 June 1948 [NBTF/G33/1].

72 Espley to Homer, 5 November 1948 [NBTF/G33/2].

73 Safer Motherhood Committee to Bevan, 16 June 1948 [NBTF/G33/5(1)].

74 Meeting of Safer Motherhood Sub-Committee, 7 July 1948 [NBTF/G33/5(1)].

75 Emergency meeting of Safer Motherhood Sub-Committee, 8 October 1948 [NBTF/G33/5(1)].

76 Taylor to Riddick, 18 October 1948 [NBTF/G33/5(1)].

77 Rhys Williams to relevant individuals, 14 September 1948 [NBTF/G33/5(1)].

78   Draft of covering letter to accompany leaflet, n.d. [NBTF/G33/5(1)].

79   Quoted and discussed in Charles Webster, *The Health Services Since the War* (HMSO, 1988), p. 79 and footnote 15, p. 414.

80   Cover of leaflet, *The New National Health Service* 1948; emphasis added [PP/AO]. ASW is grateful to Tendayi Bloom for alerting her to the relevance here of *The Inspector Calls*.

81   Morrison to Cripps, 15 January 1949 [PRO/T227/79].

82.   'Lord Pakenham's reply for the Government in House of Lords, 22 June 1949', *The Times* (23 June 1949).

83   Menzies to Riddick, 8 March 1946 [NBTF/G6/6 (1)].

84   1946 Annual Report of the Royal Maternity Charity [NBTF/B2/16(1)].

85   Tasker to Rhys Williams, 17 February 1948 [NBTF/B2/16(1)].

86   F.K. Prochaska, *Philanthropy and the Hospitals of London. The King's Fund, 1897–1990* (Clarendon Press, 1992), p. 163.

87   Geoffrey Rivett, *The Development of the London Hospital System 1823–1982* (King Edward's Hospital Fund for London, 1986), p. 278.

88   *Birth Counts*, p. 10.

89   Meeting of NBTF Executive Committee, 18 March 1949 [NBTF/A1/5/1]; emphasis added.

90   A scrap of the 1948 NBTF Annual Report [NBTF/C18/1].

91   Cahn to Riddick, 25 June 1943 [NBTF/B2/14(2)].

92   Meeting of NBTF Executive Committee, 12 February 1947 [NBTF/A1/5/1].

93   Meeting of the NBTF Executive Committee, 12 March 1947 [NBTF/A1/5/1].

94   For a discussion of this, see for example chapters 10 and 11 of *Women and the Women's Movement*.

95   Baldwin to Riddick, 2 October 1944 [NBTF/F3/2/6].

96   *Women and the Women's Movement*, p. 284.

97   Meeting of NBTF Technical Advisory Sub-Committee, 10 December 1948 [NBTF/B4/1(1)].

98   Notes on a conversation between Penman and Douglas, n.d. [NBTF/L2/1].

99   For detailed information about the Trust's early postwar research, see the documents in files [NBTF/J2–14].

100 Questionnaire returns on use of synchrophone lecture, 1945 [NBTF/G31/6/1].

101 Publicity leaflet about the Festival of Britain, 1951 [PRO/T227/77].

102 Mrs A. Wynn to ASW, July 1995.

103 Dan Cruickshank, 'The quest for Skylon', *Sunday Telegraph* (7 August 1994).

104 C.P. Snow, *The New Men* (Penguin, 1954).

105 Telephone interview with Mrs Jennifer Gilbey by ASW, 24 January 1995.

CHAPTER NINE

1   After qualification as a medical doctor, Dr Douglas researched on animal behaviour in Oxford and during the Second World War was involved in a study of air raid casualties. He was Director of the MRC National Survey of Health and Development from its beginning in 1946. He was Reader in Social Medicine at the University of Edinburgh and from 1962 was Director of the Medical Research Council Unit at the LSE.

2   'Maternity Survey. Inquiry into Reasons for Fewer Births', *The Times* (2 July 1947).

3   *Maternity in Great Britain*, p. 1.

4   Report of a meeting of the Married Women's Association, *Hampstead News* (15 June 1939).

5   R.M. Titmuss and K. Titmuss, *Parents Revolt: A Study of the Declining Birth-Rate in Acquisitive Societies* (Secker & Warburg, 1942), p. 11.

6   *Daily Mail* (26 June 1939).

7   *Daily Mirror* (22 June 1939).

8   For example, *Star* (11 July 1939) and *Jersey Evening Post* (11 July 1939).

9   *Daily Mail* (17 April 1942).

10   *Carlisle Journal* (30 June 1939).

11   *Britain and her Birth-Rate*, p. 7; emphasis added.

12   Statement by the Royal Commission on Population (September 1945), p. 5 [PRO/RC/495a].

13   *Maternity in Great Britain*, p. v. See E. Grebenik and D.J. Parry, 'The Maternity Services in England and Wales before the War', *Agenda* (May 1943).

14 'Problems of Maternity Child Welfare: History of Maternity Work', Meeting of PIC, 13 June 1944 [LSE/DPS/PIC/Minute Books of PIC].

15 *Maternity in Great Britain,* introduction, p. vi.

16 Meeting of Joint Committee, 1 April 1948 [LSE/DPS/PIC/Minute Books of Joint Committee].

17 See J.C. Spence and F.J.W. Miller, *Causes of Infantile Mortality in Newcastle upon Tyne,* 1939 (Newcastle Health Committee, 1941).

18 James Spence, W.S. Walton, F.J.W. Miller and S.D.M. Court, *A Thousand Families in Newcastle upon Tyne* (Oxford University Press, 1954), pp. 1–2.

19 Statement made by James Douglas in a video entitled, *Three Generations of Childhood,* filmed 29 March 1982, University of Bristol. This video was kindly lent to ASW by Professor Harvey Goldstein, who initiated and conducted it with Professor Michael Wadsworth.

20 *Maternity in Great Britain,* Appendix II, p. 223.

21 *Maternity in Great Britain,* p. 50.

22 *Maternity in Great Britain,* Appendix 1, 'Memorandum on the Procedure for Organising the Maternity Questionnaire Survey', pp. 219–20.

23 'Note on the Organisation of the Proposed Survey into Certain Aspects of Childbearing', 11 October 1945 [LSE/DPS/PIC/111/7/FU].

24 *Maternity in Great Britain,* p. 5; emphasis added.

25 *Maternity in Great Britain,* p. 86.

26 Riddick to Rhys Williams, n.d. [NBTF/L1/1].

27 *Maternity in Great Britain,* p. 91.

28 Interview with Dame Josephine Barnes by AO and ASW, 4 June 1991.

29 Introduction by D.V. Glass to J.W.B. Douglas, *The Home and the School* (MacGibbon & Kee, 1964), p. xi.

30 Dame A. Louise McIlroy, 'Maternity in Great Britain', *The World's Children* (February 1949), p. 46.

31 C.M. Langford, *The Population Investigation Committee. A Concise History to Mark its Fiftieth Anniversary* (PIC, 1988), p. 11.

32 Statement made by Douglas in video, *Three Generations of Childhood.*

33 J.W.B. Douglas and J.M. Blomfield, *Children Under Five* (George Allen & Unwin, 1958), p. 19.

34 These surveys were also followed up, leading to F.J.W. Miller et al, *Growing Up in Newcastle upon Tyne* (Oxford University Press, 1960), F.J.W. Miller, *The School Years in Newcastle upon Tyne 1952–62* (Oxford University Press, 1974), and numerous other publications.

35 R.N. Dykes, *Illness in Luton* (Leagrave Press, 1950).

36 For *The Home and the School,* see above; and J.W.B. Douglas, J.M. Ross and H.R. Simpson, *All Our Future* (Peter Davies, 1968).

37 *All Our Future,* p. xiii.

38 M.E.J. Wadsworth, *The Imprint of Time. Childhood, History, and Adult Life* (Clarendon Press, 1991).

39 Message inside a National Survey Birthday Card [NS].

40 Interview with Ann Oakley by ASW, 31 August 1995.

CHAPTER TEN

1 Foreword by John Peel, President of the RCOG, in Neville Butler and Eva Alberman, *Perinatal Problems. The Second Report of the 1958 Perinatal Mortality Survey* (Livingstone, 1969), p. vi.

2 William Nixon was elected Fellow of the BCOG in 1939 and succeeded Professor F.J. Browne as Professor of Obstetrics and Gynaecology in the University of London. His inquiring mind led him to initiate various researches, including the PMS. A member of the Expert Advisory Committee on Maternity Care for WHO, he was an adviser on this subject for many countries. He fought for the reform of the abortion laws and the importance of family planning in the curriculum. He was made a CBE in 1965.

3 Professor Neville Butler is Emeritus Professor of Child Health at the University of Bristol, and a Visiting Professor at the SSRU, City University, London. As Director of the Perinatal Mortality Survey, he was its driving force. Between 1965 and 1974 he was Co-Director of the National Child Development Study (1958 National Cohort), and between 1973 and 1985, he was Director of the Child Health and

Education Study (1970 National Cohort). He has published extensively on the cohort data, which he continues to analyse.

4   Reported in Taylor to Rhys Williams, 13 December 1954 [NBTF/M8/3/1(1)].

5   Taylor to Rhys Williams, 13 December 1954 [NBTF/M8/3/1(1)].

6   Interview with Albert Claireaux by ASW, 4 January 1995.

7   Interview with Harvey Goldstein by ASW, 7 October 1994.

8   Following his work on the 1958 survey, Professor Dennis Bonham went to New Zealand to be Head of the Postgraduate School of Obstetrics and Gynaecology at the University of Auckland. He was a key figure in the development of an integrated obstetric and perinatal service in New Zealand, which was associated with a reduction of perinatal deaths. He has been a member of the WHO Advisory Panel on Maternal and Child Health from 1965 and was awarded the OBE in 1973.

9   Dennis G. Bonham to ASW, 18 June 1995.

10   NBTF Annual Report for 1954–5, p. 7 [NBTF/C19/1].

11   Stewart to Riddick, 24 May 1956 [NBTF/M8/1/2].

12   *Birth Counts*, p. 10.

13   *Epidemiological and Vital Statistics Report*, World Health Organization, vol. 10, No. 11–12, 1957, and the *Demographic Yearbook 1961*, United Nations.

14   This has continued to animate vigorous debate into the late 1990s. For coverage of this debate, supported by key references, see Rona Campbell and Alison Macfarlane, *Where To Be Born? The Debate and the Evidence*, 2nd edn (National Perinatal Epidemiology Unit, 1994).

15   Rhys Williams to Macmillan, 16 July 1954 [PRO/MH94254/2/19].

16   Interview with Albert Claireaux by ASW, 4 January 1995.

17   Meeting of PMS Steering Committee, 16 January 1963 [NBTF/M1/9].

18   Reported by Riddick to Carter, 29 June 1956 [NBTF/K3/1].

19   Butler to Rhys Williams, 21 March 1961 [NBTF/M8/11/1].

20   Meeting of PMS Steering Committee, 16 May 1961 [NBTF/M1/7].

21   *Perinatal Mortality*, pp. 277, 174, 148.

22   Professor Eva Alberman joined the survey following a visit to Neville Butler to enquire whether the survey had produced any data on club feet, which she was researching at the time. She was Specialist Advisor to the House of Commons Social Services Committee, which produced the Short Report in 1980. Professor Emeritus of the University of London, she was a medical consultant to the Office of National Statistics (ONS).

23   Interview with Eva Alberman by ASW, 19 April 1994.

24   Draft letter, n.d. [NBTF/L1/1]; emphasis added.

25   While DCMO, Sir George was closely concerned with the establishment of the Confidential Enquiry into Maternal Deaths and the published triennial reports continuing through his period as Chief Medical Officer from 1960 to 1973. He was in close touch with Neville Butler over the launch of the 1958 survey and in a position to encourage the support given by Regional Hospital Boards and Local Health Authorities.

26   Interview with Sir George Godber by ASW, 4 November 1994.

27   Barnes to the Technical Advisory Sub-Committee, 26 April 1951 [NBTF/A1/5/2].

28   Interview with Edith Dare, 'Wonder Babies', *Sunday Pictorial* (20 June 1948).

29   RCOG, *Report on the Obstetric Service under the National Health Service* (July 1954), pp. 16, 17 [PP/ASW].

30   Communication by E.A. to ASW, 24 November 1994.

31   Telephone interview with Mrs J.M., Abingdon, by ASW, 7 June 1996.

32   *Perinatal Problems*, p. 21.

33   Grigson, Secretary of Regional Hospital Boards, Ministry of Health, to NBTF, 25 September 1953 [NBTF/F7/1/2].

34   Women's Cooperative Guild Annual Report for 1951, p. 32 [CWG/BI].

35   *Hansard* (21 January 1954); *Hansard* (4 March 1954).

36   MH Minute, 4 September 1954 [DHSS/94524/2/19]; quoted in *The Health Services Since the War*, p. 379.

37   The Reports on Confidential Enquiries into Maternal Deaths were started in 1952; 80 per cent of deaths were reported in this way from the start, a

figure that quickly reached 100 per cent. The reports of deaths were sent in and then analysed to see whether there had been any avoidable factors. Sir George Godber, who as CMO devised the Enquiries, together with Arnold Walker and Joe Wrigley, has described this as the first effective medical audit. Obstetric practice was changed in response to the information uncovered. In the case of haemorrhage, for example, previous policy had meant that an ambulance was called as immediate treatment. When it was discovered that this delay in treatment was very risky, a regional policy was developed of having it treated on the spot, often removing the placenta, before taking the mother to hospital. (Interview with Sir George Godber by ASW, 4 November 1994.)

38 Ministry of Health, *Report on Confidential Enquiries into Maternal Deaths in England and Wales 1955–57* (1960).
39 For a detailed discussion of this, see 'Mortality and the place of birth' in *Where to be born?*
40 Interview with Sir George Godber by ASW, 4 November 1994.
41 Virginia Berridge, Charles Webster and Gill Walt, 'Mobilisation for total welfare, 1948 to 1974' in *Caring for Health: History and Diversity* (Open University Press, 1993), p. 110.
42 Interview with Albert Claireaux by ASW, 4 January 1995.
43 Interview with Sir George Godber by ASW, 4 November 1994.
44 Macmillan to Hornsby-Smith, 16 July 1956 [PRO/T227/749]. I am very grateful to Charles Webster for telling me about this document.
45 Macmillan to Hornsby-Smith, 16 July 1956 [PRO/T227/749]; emphasis added.
46 Rhys Williams to Macmillan, 19 June 1956 [PRO/T227/749].
47 Rhys Williams to Powell, 5 July 1956 [PRO/T227/749]; emphasis added.
48 Hornsby-Smith to Macmillan, 13 December 1956 [PRO/T227/749].
49 Quoted in *Macmillan*, vol. II, p. 357.
50 Quoted in *Macmillan*, vol. II, p. 470.
51 Ministry of Health, Report of the Maternity Services Committee (Cranbrook Report, 1959), p. 1.
52 Cmd. 9663, *Report of the Committee of Enquiry into the Cost of the National Health*

Service [Guillebaud Report] (1956), para. 733, p. 263.
53 Evidence of the National Birthday Trust Fund for the Maternity Services Committee [PRO/MH137/269].
54 Second meeting of the Maternity Services Committee, 11 October 1956 [PRO/MH137/269].
55 Rhys Williams to Cranbrook, 18 October 1956 [PRO/MH137/269].
56 Permanent Secretary for Health to Permanent Secretary for Treasury, 19 November 1956 [PRO/T227/749].
57 Read to Riddick, 25 September 1956 [NBTF/K3/1(2)].
58 *Report of the Maternity Services Committee*, chapter 5.
59 Transcript of press conference on 24 October 1962 [NBTF/M11/2/1].
60 Introduction to Neville R. Butler and Dennis G. Bonham, *Perinatal Mortality. The First Report of the Perinatal Mortality Survey* (Livingstone, 1969), p. 1.
61 The 1958 questionnaire is given at the back of *Perinatal Mortality* and the 1946 questionnaire is at the back of *Maternity in Great Britain*.
62 Meeting of PMS Steering Committee, 15 January 1958 [NBTF/M1/5].
63 Austin Heady to ASW, 11 January 1996.
64 Interview with Sir George Godber by ASW, 4 November 1994.
65 Godber to Rhys Williams, 16 January 1957 [NBTF/M8/3/1(1)].
66 Rhys Williams to Wrigley, 11 November 1960 [NBTF/M8/3/2].
67 Stocks to Butler, 1 July 1962 [NBTF/M8/2/2].
68 As a result of Professor Baird's work, the perinatal death rate in Aberdeen was low relative to the rest of Britain. For 1953–62, the rate for primiparae in Aberdeen Maternity Hospital, where all primiparae in the city were confined, was 28 per 1,000, compared with the corresponding rate of 40 per 1,000 for the urban north zone of Britain, which includes Scotland as well as the north of England (*Perinatal Problems*, p. 252). Sir George Godber, who was CMO during this period, has commented that Baird "was the biggest figure in obstetrics this century. He built up a maternity service and a gynaecological service in NE Scotland that was probably the best in the

British Isles" (interview with Sir George Godber by ASW, 4 November 1994).

69 *Perinatal Mortality*, pp. ix–x.

70 Account given by Nixon in speech, transcript dated 23 November 1963 [NBTF/M12/3].

71 See Raymond Illsley and J.C. Kincaid, 'Social Correlations of Perinatal Mortality', Section K of *Perinatal Mortality*.

72 *Perinatal Problems*, pp. 281–2.

73 Thomson to Butler, 29 October 1958 [NBTF/M8/13(2)].

74 Thomson to Butler, 23 December 1958 [NBTF/M8/6].

75 Meeting of PMS Steering Committee, 16 January 1956 [NBTF/M8/3/2].

76 Council Minutes of the RCOG, 23 March 1957, p. 159 [RCOG/A2M/7].

77 Meeting of the PMS Steering Committee on 10 July 1957 [NBTF/M1/5].

78 Butler to Barnes, 23 May 1957 [NBTF/M8/11/1].

79 General Register Office memos, 30 July 1957, 6 September 1957 [PRO/RG26/254]. Also Godber to Taylor, 29 August 1957 [PRO/MH55/2419].

80 GRO memo, 24 June 1959 [PRO/RG26/254].

81 Interview with Mrs Toby Israel by ASW, 12 January 1995.

82 In the same way that the excess of sudden infant deaths of February 1986 was associated with the unusually cold weather of that month, as shown by M.J. Campbell, Laura Rodrigues, Alison J. Macfarlane and M.F.G. Murphy in 'Sudden infant deaths and cold weather', *Paediatric and Perinatal Epidemiology*, 93, 100 (1991), pp. 93–100.

83 Interview with Eva Alberman by ASW, 19 April 1994.

84 Telephone interview with Mrs J.M., Abingdon, 7 June 1996.

85 Interview with Mrs Toby Israel with ASW, 12 January 1995. Mrs Israel gave birth at Elizabeth Garrett Anderson Hospital in London, and had sought attendance by Miss Barnes because of her reputation as a woman obstetrician who had ideas ahead of her time.

86 Interview with Eva Alberman by ASW, 19 April 1994.

87 Meeting of PMS Steering Committee, 16 January 1956 [NBTF/M8/3/2].

88 Interview with Albert Claireaux by ASW, 4 January 1995.

89 Interview with Albert Claireaux by ASW, 4 January 1995.

90 Meeting of PMS Steering Committee, 15 January 1958 [NBTF/M1/5].

91 Meeting of PMS Steering Committee, 10 May 1962 [NBTF/M1/8].

92 Preface to *Perinatal Mortality*, p. ix.

93 Bransby to Rhys Williams, n.d. [13 March 1959] [NBTF/M8/3/1(1)].

94 Heady to ASW, 11 January 1996 [PP/ASW].

95 Interview with Eva Alberman by ASW, 19 April 1994.

96 Wrigley to Butler, 9 February 1962 [NBTF/M8/3/3].

97 Wrigley to Rhys Williams, 7 March 1962 [NBTF/M8/3/3].

98 Bonham to ASW, 18 June 1995 [PP/ASW].

99 Bransby to Rhys Williams, 4 August 1960 [NBTF/M8/3/1(1)].

100 Butler to Bonham, 28 January 1964 [NBTF/M8/11/2].

101 Rhys Williams to Butler, 4 May 1960 [NBTF/M8/6].

102 Wrigley to Rhys Williams, 28 February 1963 and 1 April 1963 [NBTF/M8/3/3].

103 Professor Harvey Goldstein is Professor of Statistical Methods at the Institute of Education. Prior to this, from 1971 to 1976, he was chief statistician at the National Children's Bureau. There are two main foci of his research interests: the first is the use of statistical modelling techniques in the construction and analysis of education tests; the second is the methodology of multilevel modelling.

104 Interview with Eva Alberman by ASW, 19 April 1994.

105 Interview with Harvey Goldstein by ASW, 7 October 1994.

106 Speech by Nixon, transcript dated 23 December 1963 [NBTF/M12/3].

107 Rhys Williams to Bransby, 11 November 1960 [NBTF/M8/3/2].

108 Waddilove to Riddick, 2 March 1956 [NBTF/M7/1/1(1)].

109 Waddilove to Rhys Williams, 2 March 1962 [NBTF/M1/8].

110 Waddilove to Riddick, 5 October 1961; Wallace to Rhys Williams, 14 November 1961 [NBTF/M7/1/1(1)].

111 Since William Wallace was the Chairman of the Rowntree Trust, Lady Rhys Williams wondered whether he might be willing to act also as the

Chairman of the NBTF: "he is exactly the man we want", she explained, adding that he had written *We Can Conquer Unemployment during the Depression* (Rhys Williams to Walton, 14 June 1956 [NBTF/ M7/1/1(1)]).

112 Walton to Riddick, 8 March 1962; Longman to Riddick, 26 October 1962 [NBTF/M7/1/2(2)].

113 Rhys Williams to Godber, 19 February 1962 [NBTF/M8/3/1(1)].

114 Godber to Rhys Williams, 2 February 1962; Rhys Williams to Godber, 27 February 1962 [NBTF/M8/3/1(1)].

115 Rhys Williams to Godber, 19 February 1962 [NBTF/M8/3/1(1)].

116 Riddick to Barnes, 9 March 1962 [NBTF/M1/8].

117 Meeting of PMS Steering Committee, 16 May 1961 [NBTF/M1/7].

118 Interview with Elliot Philipp by ASW, 14 June 1994.

119 *Perinatal Mortality*, p. 293.

120 See for example: Michael J. O'Dowd and Elliot E. Philipp, *The History of Obstetrics and Gynaecology* (Parthenon, 1994), p. 25; and *Where to be Born?*, p. 72 and the chapter 'Women transferred from home to hospital'.

121 Preface to *Perinatal Mortality*, p. xi.

122 *Perinatal Problems*, pp. 217 and 224.

123 Classification of social group was based on paternal occupation only and is as follows:

1. Professional or managerial.
2. Supervisory.
3. Skilled workers.
4. Semi-skilled workers.
5. Unskilled workers.

No husband – only mothers who have never been married.

Remainder – students, divorcees, widows, and those with insufficient information.

"'Husband's social class' is useful as a research tool," claims the second report, "not only because it accounts for the immediate way of life of a mother, but because it reflects her life history, the conditions of her upbringing, and her personal qualities" (*Perinatal Problems*, p. 18). However, this method of classification has been challenged by some feminist social scientists – see for example some chapters in E. Gamarnikow, D. Morgan, J. Purvis and

D. Taylorson (eds), *Gender, Class and Work* (Heinemann, 1983); and P. Abbott, 'Women's social class identification: does husband's occupation make a difference?' *Sociology* (1987) 21 (1), pp. 91–103.

124 See the tables on pp. 42–3 of *Perinatal Problems*.

125 *Perinatal Mortality*, p. 24.

126 Cranbrook Report, para. 327, p. 91.

127 Alison Macfarlane, 'No place like hospital?', *Nature*, 347 (25 October 1990), pp. 721–2.

128 *Perinatal Mortality*, pp. 52, 272, 282.

129 Harriett Wilson, 'How CPAG got "into politics". A personal memoir', in *Poverty* (December 1982), p. 30. The other studies she refers to are: Peter Marris's investigation of the circumstances of widows in East London (1958); Virginia Wimperis's study of unmarried mothers (1960); Dorothy Wedderburn's work on the economic circumstances of old people (1962); Margaret Wynn's book on fatherless families (1964); and Royston Lambert's work on malnutrition in Britain (1964).

130 J.A. Heady and J.N. Morris, 'Social and Biological Factors in Infant Mortality, Parts I–V', *Lancet* (1955) (I), pp. 343, 395, 445, 499, 554. This series continued with the following:

J.A. Heady and J.N. Morris, 'Social and Biological Factors in Infant Mortality, VI. Mothers who have their Babies in Hospitals and Nursing Homes', *British Journal of Preventive and Social Medicine* (1956) 10, pp. 97–106.

J.A. Heady and J.N. Morris, 'Social and Biological Factors in Infant Mortality, VII. Variation of Mortality with Mother's Age and Parity', in *Journal of Obstetrics and Gynaecology of the British Empire* (1959) 66, pp. 577–93.

S.L. Morrison, J.A. Heady, and J.N. Morris, 'Social and Biological Factors in Infant Mortality, VIII. Mortality in the Post-Neonatal Period', in *Archives of Disease in Childhood* (1959) 34, pp. 101–14.

See also the following book of tables: General Register Office, *Studies on Medical and Population Subjects No. 15 – Social and Biological Factors in Infant Mortality* by J.A. Heady and M.A. Heasman (HMSO, 1959).

131 Richard M. Titmuss, 'The Social Division of Welfare', in *Essays on 'The Welfare*

State' (1958; rpt. George Allen & Unwin, 1960), pp. 53–5.

132 Transcript of press conference on 24 October 1962 [NBTF/M11/2/1].

133 *Guardian* (26 October 1962); *Daily Herald* (26 October 1962); *Daily Telegraph* 26 October 1962.

134 Letters to *BMJ* (10 November 1962).

135 Butler and Bonham to *BMJ* (10 November 1962), p. 1255.

136 Lewis, Honorary Secretary RCOG to *BMJ* (22 December 1962), p. 1688.

137 Rhys Williams to Debenham, 11 November 1962 [PP/JRW].

138 Discussion during 'Brains Trust', Safer Motherhood meeting, 8 June 1948 [NBTF/G33/4].

139 Interview with Elliot Philipp by ASW, 14 June 1994.

140 Chairman, NBTF, to 'x' [form letter], 30 October 1962 [NBTF/M11/2/1].

141 *Perinatal Problems*, pp. 33–4.

142 Interview with Mrs R.H., Rhondda by ASW, 3 August 1991.

143 Interview with Elliot Philipp by ASW, 14 June 1994.

144 *Where to be born?*, p. 18.

145 Transcript of 'Panorama' programme 13 May 1963 [NBTF/M12/3].

146 Interview with Eva Alberman by ASW, 19 April 1994.

147 Interview with Neville Butler by ASW, 24 October 1994.

148 W.J. Simpson, 'A preliminary report on cigarette smoking and incidence of prematurity', *American Journal of Obstetrics and Gynaecology*, 73 (1957), p. 808; C.R. Lowe, *BMJ*, 2 (1959), p. 673.

149 'Smoking link with prematurity?', *Medical Officer* (3 August 1962).

150 The other scientists were Sharman and Lee. For the development of this debate see *Nature* in the following editions: 14 September 1973; 5 October 1973; 26 October 1973; 16 November 1973; 23 November 1973; 21/28 December 1973.

151 These other factors tend to be disregarded relative to smoking, in the health education of mothers. For a discussion of this, see Ann Oakley, 'Smoking in pregnancy: smokescreen or risk factor? Towards a materialist analysis', *Sociology of Health and Illness*, 11, 4 (1989), pp. 311–35.

152 Interview with Eva Alberman by ASW, 19 April 1994.

153 Leader in the *Lancet* (8 February 1969), p. 293.

154 Including *American Academy of Paediatrics* (Summer 1964); *American Journal of Obstetrics and Gynaecology* (November 1964); *Journal of the Irish Medical Association* (July 1964); *Fortshritte der Medizin* (May 1965); *Canadian Medical Association Journal* (28 March 1964); *Courrier, Centre International de l'Enfance* (28 April 1964); *New Zealand Medical Journal* (July 1964); *Rassegna Bibliographic della Stampa Obstetrico-Ginecologia* (November 1964); *South African Medical Journal* (June 1964); *Toxo-Ginecologia Practica* (January 1965); *Eugenics Review* (April 1964).

155 Mr Macmillan's speech to the AGM of the NBTF, 10 December 1968 [NBTF/C19/17].

156 P. 61 of the three volume report by Robert Boulin, *Pour une politique de la santé. Les grandes actions de santé I* (Ministère de la Santé Publique et de la Sécurité Sociale, 1971). 'La perinatalite' and 'les problemes de la naissance' are described as 'la priorité des priorités' (p. 18).

157 Communication by Butler to ASW, 26 January 1995.

158 Glass to Barnes, 4 August 1964 [NBTF/M8/8/1].

159 *NCDS User Support Group Working Paper 1 (Revised). The National Child Development Study (NCDS). An Introduction to the Origins of the Study and the Methods of Data Collection* (Social Statistics Research Unit, City University, n.d.), p. 15.

160 Interview with Simon Israel by ASW, 11 January 1995.

161 Interview with Mrs Toby Israel, 12 January 1995.

162 Interview with Simon Israel by ASW, 11 January 1995.

163 For example, Wendy Moore, 'Now we are Thirtysomething', *Health Service Journal* (5 March), p. 16.

164 M. Bartley, C. Power, D. Blane, G. Davey Smith, M. Shipley, 'Birth weight and later socio-economic disadvantage: evidence from the 1958 cohort study', *BMJ*, 309 (3 December 1994), pp. 1475–8.

165 'Now we are Thirtysomething'.

166 Comments made by Mia Kellmer

Pringle in video *Three Generations of Childhood*.

167 N.R. Butler and H. Goldstein, 'Smoking in pregnancy and subsequent child development', *BMJ* (8 December 1973), pp. 573–5.

168 David Crook to ASW, 20 March 1996. For Crook's use of the NCDS data, see Allan C. Kerchoff, Ken Fogelman, David Crook and David Reader, *Going Comprehensive in England and Wales: A Study of Uneven Change* (Woburn Press, 1997).

169 Elsa Ferri (ed.), *Life at 33* (National Children's Bureau, 1993), p. 32.

CHAPTER ELEVEN

1 *Birth Counts*, p. 10.

2 *British Births*, vol. 2 (Heinemann Medical Books Ltd, 1978), p. 262.

3 See S. Saigal et al, 'Comparative assessment of the health status of extremely low birth weight children at eight years of age: comparison with a reference group', *Journal of Pediatrics*, 125, 3 (September 1994), pp. 411–17; also N. Marlow, L. Roberts and R. Cooke, 'Outcome at 8 years for children with birth weights at 1250 g or less', *Archives of Disease in Childhood* 68, 3 (March 1993), p. 2890.

4 Peter Townsend, *Poverty in the United Kingdom* (1979; rpt. Penguin, 1983), p. 176. Most of the data in this book is based on a national survey conducted in 1968–9.

5 Personal communications by Frank Field to ASW, 26 September 1995 and 8 February 1995.

6 Meeting of BBS Steering Committee, autumn 1967 [NBTF/N1/1].

7 Meeting of BBS Steering Committee, 1 June 1966 [NBTF/N1/1].

8 Godber to Barnes, 19 August 1966 [NBTF/N1/4].

9 Interview with Geoffrey Chamberlain by ASW, 17 November 1994.

10 Meeting of BBS Steering Committee, 8 January 1968 [RCOG/C8/1].

11 Meeting of BBS Steering Committee, 25 September 1968 [RCOG/C8/1].

12 Meeting of BBS Steering Committee, 1 June 1966 [NBTF/N1/1].

13 Catterall to Riddick, 1 December 1967 [RCOG/C8/1].

14 Meeting of BBS Steering Committee, 2 October 1968 [NBTF/A1/9].

15 Meeting of BBS Steering Committee, 16 October 1968 [NBTF/A1/9]; emphasis added.

16 Peel to Evans, 19 December 1968 [RCOG/C8/2].

17 Rona Campbell and Alison Macfarlane, 'Recent Debate on the Place of Birth', in J. Garcia, R. Kilpatrick, M. Richards (eds), *The Politics of Maternity Care* (Oxford University Press, 1990), p. 218.

18 Department of Health and Social Security, *Domiciliary Midwifery and Maternity Bed Needs* (Peel Report) (1970), para. 277, p. 60; emphasis added.

19 ASW is grateful to Charles Webster for alerting her to this distinction.

20 Foreword, *Perinatal Problems*, p. v.

21 Meeting of BBS Steering Committee, 8 January 1968 [RCOG/C8/1].

22 Annual General Meeting of NBTF, 10 December 1968 [NBTF/C13/1].

23 Chamberlain and Chamberlain to Riddick, 17 September 1969 [NBTF/N5/5/1].

24 Cornish to Chamberlain, 9 September 1971 [RCOG/C8/1].

25 Clayton to Rhys Williams, 13 October 1972 [RCOG/C8/1].

26 Paper by Roma Chamberlain and Geoffrey Chamberlain [NBTF/N4/1/2].

27 Peel to Riddick, 6 February 1969 [RCOG/C8/1].

28 Meeting of BBS Steering Committee, 25 September 1968 [RCOG/C8/1].

29 Meeting of BBS Steering Committee, 25 September 1968 [RCOG/C8/1].

30 Reported at BBS Steering Committee, 27 July 1966 [NBTF/N1/1].

31 Interview with Geoffrey Chamberlain by ASW, 17 November 1994.

32 *Maternity in Great Britain*, pp. 86 and 229.

33 *British Births*, vol. 2, pp. 211 and 258; emphasis added.

34 Meeting of BBS Steering Committee, 8 January 1968 [NBTF/N2].

35 *Midwife and Health Visitor*, 6 (March 1970), p. 89.

36 Annual General Meeting of NBTF, 1970 [NBTF/C16/1].

37 Chamberlain to Catterall, 24 March 1970 [RCOG/A4/14/54a].

38 'Document for scientific advisory

committee', 1 December 1965 [NBTF/A1/8(1)].

39   Chamberlain to Jeffcoate, 18 October 1971 [RCOG/A4/14/30].

40   *British Births*, vol. 1, p. 114.

41   Interview with Geoffrey Chamberlain, by ASW, 17 November 1995.

42   See the following: I. Chalmers, J.E. Zlosnik, K.A. Johns, H. Campbell, 'Obstetric practice and outcome of pregnancy in Cardiff residents, 1965–1973', *BMJ*, 1 (1976), pp. 735–8; I. Chalmers, J.G. Lawson, A.C. Turnbull, 'Evaluation of different approaches to obstetric care I', *British Journal of Obstetrics and Gynaecology*, 83 (1976), pp. 921–9; I. Chalmers, J.G. Lawson, A.C. Turnbull, 'Evaluation of different approaches to obstetric care II', *British Journal of Obstetrics and Gynaecology*, 83 (1976), pp. 930–3; I. Chalmers, 'British debate on obstetric practice', *Paediatrics*, 58 (1976), pp. 308–12.

43   *British Births*, vol. 2, pp. 258, 259, 263.

44   Margaret Wynn was invited to join the Birthday Trust by Sir Brandon Rhys Williams following the publication of *Fatherless Families* (1964) and *Family Policy* (1970). See Frank Field, *Poverty and Politics* (Heinemann, 1982) on her influence. She was a founder member of The Maternity Alliance.

45   Interview with Virginia Bottomley by ASW, 18 September 1995.

46   Catherine Porteous, obituary in *Independent* (25 May 1988).

47   'Self-critical analysis', *BMJ* (17 February 1979), p. 473.

48   Social Services Committee, Session 1979–80, *Second Report. Perinatal and Neonatal Mortality*, vol. 1 (Short Report) (1980), pp. 52, 160, 161; emphasis added.

49   N.R. Butler and Jean Golding, *From Birth to Five* (Pergamon Press, 1986), p. 5.

50   'A future full of hope', *Sunday Mirror* (2 April 1989).

51   Letters to survey newsletter, *Youthscan Newsletter*, 2 (May 1987).

52   H.F. Crawley, 'The role of breakfast cereals . . .', in *Journal of Human Nutrition and Dietetics* (1993), 6, pp. 205–16; D.J.P. Barker et al, 'Acute appendicitis . . .',

British Medical Journal (1988) 296, pp. 956–8.

53   'Teenagers vote for hanging and stricter parents', *Daily Telegraph* (18 March 1988).

54   'An Introduction to the National Perinatal Epidemiology Unit and Annual Report for 1978', pp. 34–9 [NPEU].

55   I. Chalmers, 'Desirability and Feasibility of a 4th National Perinatal Survey', Report submitted to the DHSS (11 May 1979) [NPEU]. For the opinions of sociologists, see Ann Oakley, 'Comments on the Desirability and Proposed Study Design of a 4th National Perinatal Survey from a Social Science Perspective', also submitted to the DHSS [NPEU].

56   *Maternity in Great Britain*, p. 223; emphasis as in original.

57   Interview with Geoffrey Chamberlain by ASW, 17 November 1994.

58   Statement by Secretary of State, DHSS Health Circular (1980), HC(80)13, para. 3.

59   Meeting of NBTF Medical Committee, 17 March 1981 [PP/GC].

60   *Where to be Born?*, p. 93.

61   Request for funding for an inquiry into the relief of pain in labour, n.d. [1992] [PP/GC].

62   Interview with Geoffrey Chamberlain by ASW, 5 July 1995.

63   Quoted in *Pain and its Relief in Childbirth*, p. 14.

64   Interview with Ann Oakley by ASW, 5 July 1995.

65   Interview with Geoffrey Chamberlain by ASW, 5 July 1995.

66   Personal communication by Ann Wraight to ASW, 5 October 1995.

67   Marjorie Tew, *Safer Childbirth? A Critical History of Maternity Care* (Chapman and Hall, 1990); *Where to be Born?*

68   Ann Oakley, *The Captured Womb* (1984; rpt. Basil Blackwell, 1986), p. 2.

69   Zoë Fairbairns, *Benefits* (Virago, 1979), pp. 188 and 196.

70   Department of Health, *Health Committee Second Report, Maternity Services*, vol. 1 (Winterton Report) (1992), pp. x, xi; emphasis added.

71   Examination of witnesses (Miss Margaret Brain, Miss Ruth Ashton, Miss Beverley Bryans, Miss Anne Rider and Ms Lesley Page) by Health

Committee, 12 June 1991 [PRO/HC430II 1990–91], p. 130.

72   I. Chalmers, M. Enkin, M.J.N.C. Keirse (eds), *Effective Care in Pregnancy and Childbirth* (Oxford University Press, 1989).

73   Julia Allison, 'Midwives Step out of the Shadows. 1991 Sir William Power Memorial Lecture', *Midwives Chronicle and Nursing Notes*, 105, 1254 (July 1992), pp. 167–74.

74   Memorandum submitted by the National Birthday Trust (MS189), p. 853 [PRO/HC29III 1991–92].

75   Winterton Report, p. xciii; emphasis added.

76   Personal communication by Ruth Ashton to ASW, 23 October 1995.

CONCLUSION

1   The Hon. Susan Baring served as a Magistrate from 1965 to 1987 and has a long-term involvement in penal reform and probation; in 1983 she was awarded the OBE for her work in the probation service. She is currently Chairman of the British Institute of Human Rights, of the New Lease Trust (a Housing Association Trust for offenders and substance mis-users), the London Action Trust, which assists the work of the Inner London Probation Service, and the Advisory Council to the Centre of Medical Law and Ethics.

2   Department of Health, *Changing Childbirth* (1993), pp. 16 and 25.

3   Interview with Virginia Bottomley by ASW, 18 September 1995.

4   Peter Townsend and Nick Davidson (eds), *The Black Report* (1982); rpt. in *Inequalities in Health* (Penguin, 1992), p. 115.

5   Alison Macfarlane, 'Figures Bearing on Maternity Poverty', Appendix to *Mother Courage*; see n. 12.

6   See Tony Atkinson, *Incomes and the Welfare State* (Cambridge University Press, 1996).

7   See Alison Macfarlane, Miranda Mugford, Ann Johnson, Jo Garcia, *Counting the changes in childbirth: trends and gaps in national statistics* (NPEU, 1995); also Claire Middle and Alison Macfarlane, 'Recorded Delivery', *Health Service Journal* (31 August 1995), p. 27.

8   Department of Health, *Variations in Health: What Can the Department of Health and the NHS Do?* Cm. 1986 (1995), p. 15.

9   For a discussion of this see F.K. Prochaska, *The Voluntary Impulse. Philanthropy in Modern Britain* (Faber & Faber, 1988), p. 2.

10   Judy Hirst, 'Britain's Compassion Boom', in *Charity in the Nineties*, an extra section in the *Observer* (2 October 1994), p. 7.

11   Interview with Rosie Barnes by ASW, 11 September 1995.

12   Christine Gowdridge, A. Susan Williams and Margaret Wynn (eds), *Mother Courage. Letters from Mothers Living in Poverty at the End of the Century* (Penguin, 1997).

Bibliography

1. ARCHIVE SOURCES

Bodleian Library, Broad Street, Oxford OX1 3BG
Conservative Party Archives (CPA)
Conservative Research Department (CRD)
Conservative Central Office (CCO)
Miscellaneous (MISC)

Contemporary Medical Archives Centre (CMAC), Wellcome Institute for the History of Medicine, 183 Euston Road, London NW1 2BE
Abortion Law Reform Association (ALRA)
British Medical Association (BMA)
Grantley Dick-Read (GDR)
Eugenics Society (EUG)
National Birthday Trust Fund (NBTF)

Cooperative Women's Guild (CWG/WGG)
1) Bishopsgate Institute (BI), 230 Bishopsgate, London EC2M 4QH
2) Co-operative Union Library (CUL), Holyoake House, Hanover Street, Manchester M60 0AS

Glamorgan County Record Office
Rhondda Urban District Council (RUDC)

Greater London Record Office (GLRO), 40 Northampton Road, London EC1R 0HB
London County Council (LCC)

Home Births Survey, St George's Hospital Medical School, Cranmer Terrace, London SW17 0RE
Birthplace Survey (BS)
Pain Relief Survey (PRS)
Home Births Survey (HBS)

International Centre for Child Studies (ICCS), 86 Cumberland Road, Hotwells, Bristol BS1 6UG

London School of Economics (LSE), Houghton Street, Aldwych, London WC2A 2AE
Library: Miscellaneous (COLL MISC); David Glass papers (DG)
Department of Population Studies: Population Investigation Committee Papers (DPS/PIC)

Llwynypia Hospital, Llwynypia, Tonypandy, Rhondda CF40 2LX
Special Antenatal Clinics held at Carnegie Welfare Centre, Trealow

Mass Observation Archive, University of Sussex, Falmer, Brighton BN1 9RE

Milk Bank (HMB), Hammersmith Hospitals NHS Trust, Queen Charlotte's and Hammersmith Hospital, Goldhawk Road, London W6 0XG

MRC National Survey of Health and Development, University College London Medical School, Department of Epidemiology and Public Health, 1–19 Torrington Place, London WC1E 6BT

National Perinatal Epidemiology Unit (NPEU), Radcliffe Infirmary, Oxford OX2 6HE

Private Papers (PP)
  Sir Julien Cahn (JC)
  Geoffrey Chamberlain (GC)
  Ann Oakley (AO)
  Juliet Rhys Williams (JRW)
  Margaret Wynn (MW)
  Richard Titmuss (AO)
  A. Susan Williams (ASW)

Public Record Office (PRO), Ruskin Avenue, Kew, Richmond, Surrey TW9 4DU
  Ministry of Health (MH)
  Ministry of Labour (LAB)
  Home Office (HO)
  Treasury (T)
  Cabinet (CAB)
  General Register Officer (GRO)

Royal College of Midwives (RCM), 15 Mansfield Street, London W1M 0BE

Royal College of Obstetricians and Gynaecologists (BCOG/RCOG), 27 Sussex Place, Regent's Park, London NW1 4RG

Trades Union Congress Library (TUC), Congress House, Great Russell Street, London WC1B 3LS

2. NATIONAL BIRTHDAY TRUST FUND REPORTS AND PUBLICATIONS

Annual Reports and *Summarized Accounts*

Report of the Joint Council of Midwifery on the Desirability of Establishing a Salaried Service of Midwives, 1935

Maternal Welfare, 1936

Joint Council of Midwifery. Interim Report of the Committee of Enquiry into Non-Therapeutic Abortion, Part II. Appendices, April 1937

Report of the Joint Council of Midwifery on the Desirability of Establishing a Register of Maternity Nurses, 1939

The Expectant Mother, 1945; revised 1950

Happy Birthdays (leaflet), 1948; rpt. 1956

Safer Motherhood. Minimum Requirements of a Comprehensive Maternity Service, 1948

Report of the Maternity Services Emergency Informal Committee, October 1963

Butler, Neville R. and Bonham, Dennis G. *Perinatal Mortality. The First Report of the 1958 British Perinatal Mortality Survey*, Livingstone, 1963

—— and Alberman, Eva D. *Perinatal Problems. The Second Report of the 1958 British Perinatal Mortality Survey*, Livingstone, 1969

Barnes, Josephine. *Happier Birthdays. The Story of the National Birthday Trust*, Sixth Rhys Williams Memorial Lecture given at the RCOG on 16 June 1970, reprinted from the *Midwives' Chronicle*, December 1970

Chamberlain, Roma, Chamberlain, Geoffrey, Howlett, Brian and Claireaux, Albert. *British Births 1970. A survey under the joint auspices of the National Birthday Trust Fund and the Royal College of Obstetricians and Gynaecologists. Volume 1*, Heinemann, 1975

Chamberlain, Geoffrey, Philipp, Elliot, Howlett, Brian and Masters, Keith. *British Births 1970. A survey under the joint auspices of the National Birthday Trust Fund and the Royal College of Obstetricians and Gynaecologists. Volume 2*, Heinemann, 1978

Chamberlain, Geoffrey and Gunn, Philippa. *Birthplace. Report of the Confidential Enquiry into Facilities Available at the Place of Birth conducted by The National Birthday Trust*, John Wiley, 1987

Chamberlain, Geoffrey, Wraight, Ann and Steer, Philip. *Pain and its Relief in Childbirth. The Results of a National Survey Conducted by the National Birthday Trust*, Churchill Livingstone, 1993

3. GOVERNMENT ACTS, REPORTS AND PUBLICATIONS

Hansard

Commissioner for the Special Areas (England and Wales). *Annual Reports*

Ministry of Health/Department of Health. *Confidential Enquiry into Maternal Deaths. Annual Reports*

Department of Health. *Confidential Enquiry into Stillbirths and Deaths in Infancy. Annual Reports*

Ministry of Health, Consultative Council on Medical and Allied Services. *Interim Report on the Future Provision of Medical and Allied Services* (Dawson Report), Cmnd. 693, 1920

Ministry of Health. Campbell, Dame Janet. *The Training of Midwives. Reports on Public Health and Medical Subjects No. 21*, 1923

——. *Maternal Mortality. Reports on Public Health and Medical Subjects No. 25*, 1924

——. *The Protection of Motherhood. Reports on Public Health and Medical Subjects No. 48*, 1927

Local Government Act, 1929

Ministry of Health. *Interim Report of the Departmental Committee on Maternal Mortality and Morbidity*, 1930

——. *Final Report of the Departmental Committee on Maternal Mortality and Morbidity*, 1932

——. Campbell, Dame Janet, Cameron, Isabella D. and Jones, Dilys M. *High Maternal Mortality in Certain Areas. Reports on Public Health and Medical Subjects 68*, 1932

Special Areas (Development and Improvement) Act, 1934

Midwives Bill 1936 and *Midwives Act* 1936

Ministry of Health to Local Supervising Authorities. *Circular 1569*, 18 September 1936

Ministry of Health. *Report of an Investigation into Maternal Mortality*, Cmd. 5422, 1937

Ministry of Health and Home Office. *Report of the Inter-Departmental Committee on Abortion* (Birkett Report), 1939

Beveridge, W.H. *Social Insurance and Allied Services*, Cmd. 6404, 1942

Ministry of Health and Department of Health for Scotland. *A National Health Service*, Cmd. 6502, 1944

Royal Commission on Population. *Family Census. Instructions to Enumerators*, 1945

National Health Service Act, 1946

Ministry of Health. *Circular 118/47. National Health Service Act 1946*, 10 July 1947

Ministry of Health. *The New National Health Service* (leaflet), 1948

Ministry of Health, Department of Health for Scotland, Ministry of Labour and National Service. *Report of the Working Party on Midwives*, 1949

Festival of Britain (leaflet), 1951

Ministry of Health. *Report of the Committee of Enquiry into the Cost of the National Health Service* (Guillebaud Report), Cmd. 9663, 1956

Ministry of Health. *Report of the Maternity Services Committee* (Cranbrook Report), 1959

Ministry of Health. *A Hospital Plan for England and Wales*, Cmnd. 1604, 1962

Central Health Services Council. Standing Maternity and Midwifery Advisory Committee. *Domiciliary Midwifery and Maternity Bed Needs. Report of the Sub-Committee* (Peel Report), 1970

Department of Health and Social Security. *Prevention and Health. Reducing the Risk. Safer Pregnancy and Childbirth*, 1977

House of Commons, Session 1979–80. Social Services Committee. *Second Report. Perinatal and Neonatal Mortality, Volume 1* (Short Report), 1980

Department of Health and Social Security. *Inequalities in Health. Report of a Working Group* (Black Report), 1980

Department of Health, Committee on Medical Aspects of Food Policy. *The Collection and*

Storage of Human Milk. Report of a Working Party of Human Milk Banks, Report on Health and Social Subjects No 22, 1981

Social Services Committee, Session 1983–4. *Third Report. Perinatal and Neonatal Mortality Report: Follow-Up,* 1984

——. Session 1988–9. *First Report. Perinatal, Neonatal and Infant Mortality,* 1988

Department of Health. *HIV Infection, Breastfeeding and Human Milk Banking,* 1989

——. *Report of Expert Advisory Group on Folic Acid and Prevention of Neural Tube Defects,* 1991

——. *The Health of the Nation,* Cm. 1986, 1992

——. *Health Committee Second Report. Maternity Services. Volume 1* (Winterton Report), 1992

——. *Changing Childbirth* (Cumberlege Report), 1993

——. *The Health of the Nation. Variations in Health: What can the Department of Health and the NHS do?* Cm. 1986, 1995

4. OTHER REPORTS

British College of Obstetricians and Gynaecologists. *Report re Adequate Dietaries for Pregnant Women at Certain Income Levels,* 1936

——. *Investigation into the Use of Analgesics Suitable for Administration by Midwives,* 1936

Royal College of Obstetricians and Gynaecologists. *Report on a National Maternity Service,* May 1944

Joint Committee of the Royal College of Obstetricians and Gynaecologists and the Population Investigation Committee. *Maternity in Great Britain,* Oxford University Press, 1948

Royal College of Obstetricians and Gynaecologists. *Report on the Obstetric Service under the National Health Service,* July 1954

——. *Memorandum from the Royal College of Obstetricians and Gynaecologists,* 1956, submitted to the Maternity Services Committee of the Ministry of Health (the Cranbrook Committee) supplementing the College *Report on the Obstetric Service under the National Health Service,* 1954

——. Patel, Naren (ed.). *Maternal Mortality – The Way Forward. Some Implications of the Report on Confidential Enquiries into Maternal Deaths in the United Kingdom 1985–87,* January 1992

WellBeing, in conjunction with RCOG. *WellBeing of Women,* 1995

British Medical Association. *Memorandum Regarding a National Maternity Service,* 20 November 1935

——. *Report of the Committee on Medical Aspects of Abortion,* April 1936

British Paediatric Association. *Guidelines for the Establishment and Operation of Human Milk Banks in the UK. The Report of an Ad Hoc Working Party following the Sorrento Symposium on Milk Banking, March 1993*, October 1994

Children's Minimum Council. *An Appeal for the Improvement of Child Nutrition*, n.d. (mid-1930s)

Committee Against Malnutrition. *Unemployment and the Housewife*, Report of Public Meeting, 10 November 1936

——. *Bulletins*

County Nursing Associations. *Reports*

District Nursing Associations. *Reports*

Eugenics Society. *Annual Reports*

Kensington, Royal Borough of. *Report on Contraception and Abortion*, October 1937

Leeds Health for All. *Redressing the Balance: Health and Inequality in Leeds 1994*, 1996

London County Council, Central Public Health Committee. *Reports*

Maternal Mortality Committee. *Reports of Meetings*

Medical Officers of Health and School Medical Officers, especially for Rhondda Urban District, Sunderland, Gateshead, Llantrisant and Llantwit Fardre Rural District, County Borough of South Shields. *Annual Reports*

Medical Research Council. *Reports* of various committees

Midwives' Institute. 'The Midwife in Independent Practice Today', 1936

National Perinatal Epidemiology Unit. *An Introduction to the National Perinatal Epidemiology Unit and Annual Report for 1978*, 1978

——. *Annual Reports*

——. 'Desirability and Feasibility of a 4th National Perinatal Survey', 11 May 1979

NCDS (National Child Development Study), Social Statistics Research Unit, City University. *User Support Group Working Papers*

PEP (Political and Economic Planning). *Broadsheets*

Population Investigation Committee. *Annual Reports*

——. *Problems of Maternity Child Welfare: History of Maternity Work*, 13 June 1944

——. *A Record of Research and Publications 1936–1978*, 1978

Sheffield Women's Welfare Clinic. *Annual Reports*

Women's Cooperative Guild/Cooperative Women's Guild. *Annual Reports*

Bibliography

World Health Organization. *Epidemiological and Vital Statistics Reports*

UNICEF. *The State of the World's Children. Reports*

5. NEWSPAPERS, MAGAZINES AND NEWSLETTERS

Agenda
Birmingham Post
Brighton Standard
Carlisle Journal
Changing Childbirth Update. Quarterly
Newsletters of the Changing Childbirth
Implementation Team
Daily Express
Daily Herald
Daily Mail
Daily Sketch
Daily Telegraph
Evening News
Evening Standard
Everyman
Express & Star
Financial Times
Greenock Telegraph
Guardian
Hampstead News
Home & Country
Independent
Islington Gazette
Jersey Evening Post
The Lady
Liverpool Post
Maternity Action. The Bulletin of
The Maternity Alliance
Midwife and Health Visitor

Milk Banking News and Views
New Generation
New Health
New Statesman
News Chronicle
News of the World
News Review
Newsletter of the National Childbirth Trust
Nottingham Guardian
Observer
Picture Post
Sketch
Star
St Neot's Advertiser, Hunts and Beds News
Thompson's Weekly News
Sunday Express
Sunday Mirror
Sunday Pictorial
Sunday Telegraph
Sunday Times
Tatler
Thompson's Weekly News
Time and Tide
The Times
Vogue
WellBeing News. Branch Newsletters of
WellBeing
The World's Children
Youthscan Newsletter

6. PAPERS, PAMPHLETS AND JOURNAL ARTICLES

Abbott, P. 'Women's Social Class Identification: Does Husband's Occupation Make a Difference?', *Sociology*, 21, 1, 1987
'Address of Sir Kinglsey Wood to the National Baby Week Council on 13 November 1935', *Nursing Notes and Midwives' Chronicle*, January 1936
Allison, Julia. 'Midwives Step Out of the Shadows. 1991 Sir William Power Memorial Lecture', *Midwives Chronicle and Nursing Notes*, 105, July 1992
American Academy of Pediatrics Committee on Mothers' Milk. 'Recommended Standards for the Operation of Mothers' Milk Bureaus', *Journal of Pediatrics*, 23, 1943
Atkins, P.J. 'White Poison? The Social Consequences of Milk Consumption 1850–1930', *Social History of Medicine*, 5, 2, 1992
Baker, P.A. 'Illustrations from the Wellcome Institute Library. The National Birthday Trust Fund Records in the Contemporary Medical Archives Centre', *Medical History*, 33, 1989
Balfour, Margaret I. 'Nutritional Therapy During Pregnancy', *The Proceedings of the Royal Society of Medicine*, Vol XXXI, June 1938

——. 'Supplementary Feeding in Pregnancy: The National Birthday Trust Fund Experiment', *Proceedings of The Nutrition Society*, 2, 1 and 2, 1944

——. 'Supplementary Feeding in Pregnancy', *Lancet*, 12 February 1944

Balmer, S.E., and Wharton, B.A. 'Human Milk Banking at Sorrento Maternity Hospital, Birmingham', *Archives of Disease in Childhood*, 67, 1992

Barker, D.J.P. et al. 'Acute Appendicitis and Bathrooms in Three Samples of British Children', *BMJ*, 296, 1988

—— et al. 'Weight in Infancy and Death from Ischaemic Heart Disease', *Lancet*, 9 September 1989

—— (ed.). 'Fetal and Infant Origins of Adult Disease', *BMJ*, 1992

Barnes, J. 'Pethidine in Labour: Results in 500 Cases', *BMJ*, 5 April 1947

Bartley, M. et al. 'Birth Weight and Later Socio-economic Disadvantage: Evidence from the 1958 Cohort Study', *BMJ*, 309, 3 December 1994

Beinart, Jennifer. 'Obstetric Analgesia and the Control of Childbirth in Twentieth-Century Britain', in Garcia, J., Kilpatrick, R. and Richards, M. (eds), *The Politics of Maternity Care*, Oxford University Press, 1990

Berridge, Virginia, Webster, Charles and Walt, Gill. 'Mobilisation for Total Welfare, 1948 to 1974', in Webster, Charles (ed.), *Caring for Health: History and Diversity*, Open University Press, 1993

Browne, F.J. 'Maternity Services: The Part Played by Education of Medical Students', *BMJ*, 22 August 1936

Butler, N.R. 'The Problems of Low Birthweight and Early Delivery', *Journal of Obstetrics and Gynaecology of the British Commonwealth*, LXXII, 6, December 1965

—— and Goldstein, H. 'Smoking in Pregnancy and Subsequent Child Development', *BMJ*, 8 December 1973

Campbell, Dame Janet. 'Debate on Maternal Mortality', *Lancet*, ii, 1935

Campbell, M.J. et al. 'Sudden Infant Deaths and Cold Weather: Was the rise in infant mortality in 1986 in England and Wales due to the weather?', *Paediatric and Perinatal Epidemiology*, 93, 100, 1991

Cantor, David. 'The Aches of Industry. Philanthropy and Rheumatism in Inter-War Britain', in Barry, Jonathon and Jones, Colin (eds), *Medicine and Charity Before the Welfare State*, Routledge, 1991

Chalmers, I. et al. 'Obstetric Practice and Outcome of Pregnancy in Cardiff Residents 1965–1973', *BMJ*, 1, 1976

—— and Lawson, J.G., and Turnbull, A.C., 'Evaluation of Different Approaches to Obstetric Care I', *British Journal of Obstetrics and Gynaecology*, 83, 1976

——. 'Evaluation of Different Approaches to Obstetric Care II', *British Journal of Obstetrics and Gynaecology*, 83, 1976

——. 'British Debate on Obstetric Practice', *Paediatrics*, 58, 1976

Chamberlain, Geoffrey and Drife, James. 'Editorial', *Contemporary Reviews in Obstetrics and Gynaecology*, 7, 3, July 1995

—— and Williams, A. Susan. 'Antenatal Care in South Wales 1934–1962', *Social History of Medicine*, 8, 3, 1995

Cole, P.V. 'Entonox and Obstetric Analgesia', *History of Anaesthetic Society Proceedings*, vol. 16, 1994

Committee Against Malnutrition. *Social Care of Motherhood*, Lawrence & Wishart, 1936

'The Cranbrook Report', *Lancet*, 21 February 1959

Crawley, H.F. 'The Role of Breakfast Cereals in the Diets of 16–17 Year-Old Teenagers in Britain', *Journal of Human Nutrition and Dietetics*, 6, 1993

Crichton-Miller, H. 'Preserving the Race in Post-War Reconstruction', *BMJ*, 7 March 1942

De Louvois, J. 'Laboratory Monitoring of Banked Human Milk', *Med Lab Sci*, 39, 1982

Durham, Martin. 'Women in the British Union of Fascists, 1932–40' in Oldfield, Sybil (ed.), *This Working-Day World. Women's Lives and Culture(s) in Britain 1914–1945*, Taylor & Francis, 1994

Ebbs, J.H., Tisdall, F.F., and Scott, W.A. 'The Influence of Prenatal Diet on the Mother and Child', *Journal of Nutrition*, 22, 1941

Fairbairn, John S. 'The Maternal Mortality in the Midwifery Service of the Queen Victoria's Jubilee Institute', *BMJ*, 8 January 1927

Fairfield, Laetitia. 'Pregnancy and Feminism', *BMJ*, 14 February 1914

Finlayson, Geoffrey. 'A Moving Frontier: Voluntarism and the State in British Social Welfare 1911–1949', *Twentieth Century British History*, 1, 2, 1990

Foulis, M.A., and Barr, John B. 'Prontosil Album in Puerperal Sepsis', *BMJ*, 27 February 1937

Fox, Enid. 'Powers of Life and Death: Aspects of Maternal Welfare in England and Wales Between the Wars', *Medical History*, 35, 1991

——. 'An Honourable Calling or a Despised Occupation?' *Social History of Medicine*, Vol 6, No. 2, 1993

'General-Practitioner-Obstetrician Units', *Lancet*, 28 October 1961

Goldstein, Harvey. Letter to *American Journal of Obstetrics and Gynaecology*, 114, 4, 15 October 1972

Granshaw, Lindsay. 'The Rise of the Modern Hospital in Britain', in Wear, Andrew (ed.), *Medicine in Society*, Cambridge University Press, 1993

Harris, B. 'Government and Charity in the Distressed Mining Areas of England and Wales 1928–30', in Barry, J. and Jones, C. (eds), *Medicine and Charity before the Welfare State*, Routledge 1991

Heady, J.A. and Morris, J.N. 'Social and Biological Factors in Infant Mortality, Parts I–IV', *Lancet*, I, 1955

——. 'Social and Biological Factors in Infant Mortality, VI. Mothers Who Have Their Babies in Hospitals and Nursing Homes', *British Journal of Preventive and Social Medicine*, 10, 1956

——. 'Social and Biological Factors in Infant Mortality, VII. Variation of Mortality with Mother's Age and Parity', in *Journal of Obstetrics and Gynaecology of the British Empire*, 66, 1959

Hobsbawm, Eric. 'Looking Forward: History and the Future', paper delivered at the LSE, 8 October and printed in *New Left Review*, 125, February 1981

Kendall, Ian. *Mothers and Babies First? The National Insurance Maternity Grant in Historical and International Perspective*, The National Maternity Grant Campaign, November 1979

Langford, C.M. 'British Participation in the IUSSIP in its Early Years. A Report Prepared for the Working Group on the History of the IUSSIP', LSE, May 1984

——. *The Population Investigation Committee. A Concise History to Mark its Fiftieth Anniversary*, Population Investigation Committee, LSE, 1988

Lawson, Winifred. 'First Baby. Getting Ready for Confinement', *New Health*, June 1939

Leavitt, Judith Walzer. 'Birthing and Anaesthesia: The Debate over Twilight Sleep', *Signs*, 6, 1, Autumn 1980

Lewis, Jane. 'Mothers and Maternity Policies in the Twentieth Century', in Garcia, J., Kilpatrick, R. and Richards, M. (eds), *The Politics of Maternity Care*, Oxford University Press, 1990

Lucas, A. et al. 'Breast Milk and Subsequent Intelligence Quotient in Children Born Preterm', *Lancet*, 339, 1 Feb, 1992

Macfarlane, A. and McPherson, C.K. 'The Quality of Official Health Statistics', *The Journal of the Royal Statistical Society, Series A (General)*, 151, Part 2, 1988

——. 'No place like hospital?', *Nature*, 347, 25 October 1990

Maclean, Sir Ewen. 'Maternity Services', *BMJ*, 22 August 1936

'Malnutrition and Maternal Mortality', *Mother and Child*, X, 6, September 1939

Mann, S.L.O., Wadsworth, M.E.J. and Colley, J.R.T. 'Accumulation of Factors Influencing Respiratory Illness in Members of a National Birth Cohort and their Offspring', *Journal of Epidemiology and Community Health*, 46, 1992

Marlow, N., Roberts, L. and Cooke, R. 'Outcome at 8 Years for Children with Birth Weights of 1250g or Less', *Archives of Disease in Childhood*, 68, 3 Special No., March 1993

'Maternal Mortality', *Midwives' Chronicle and Nursing Notes*, June 1935

McCance, R.A., Widdowson, E.M., and Verdon-Roe, C.M. 'A Study of English Diets by the Individual Method. III. Pregnant Women at Different Economic Levels', *The Journal of Hygiene*, Vol XXXVIII, 1938

McCarrison, Sir Robert. 'Nutritional Needs in Pregnancy', *BMJ*, 7 August 1937

Mellanby, Edward. 'Nutrition and Child-Bearing [Summary of lecture]', *Nursing Notes and Midwives' Chronicle*, February 1934

Michel, Sonya and Koven, Seth. 'Womanly Duties: Maternalist Politics and the Origins of Welfare States in France, Germany, Great Britain, and the United States 1880–1920', *American Historical Review*, 95, 4, October 1990

Middle, Claire and Macfarlane, A. 'Recorded Delivery', *Health Service Journal*, 31 August 1995

'The Midwife as Anaesthetist', *Lancet*, 29 July 1939

'The Midwife Question', *Midwives' Chronicle and Nursing Notes*, XLVIII, 573, September 1935

Minnitt, R.J. 'Report to the Liverpool Medical Institute on the "Investigation of Gas and Air Analgesia in Midwifery"', 22 February 1934

Mitchell, Margaret. 'The Effects of Unemployment on the Social Conditions of Women and Children in the 1930s', *History Workshop*, 19, Spring 1985

Moore, Wendy. 'Now We Are Thirtysomething', *Health Service Journal*, 5 March 1992

Morrison, S.L., Heady, J.A., and Morris, J.N. 'Social and Biological Factors in Infant Mortality, VIII. Mortality in the Post-Neonatal Period', *Archives of Disease in Childhood*, 34, 1959

National Council for One Parent Families. *Born Poor*, National Maternity Grant Campaign, November 1979

'National Survey of Perinatal Mortality. First Results', *BMJ*, I, 6 May 1961

'NCDS User Support Group Working Paper 1 (Revised). The National Child Development Study (NCDS). An Introduction to the Origins of the Study and Methods of Data Collection', SSRU, City University, n.d.

Oakley, A. 'Who's Afraid of the Randomized Controlled Trial? Some Dilemmas of the Scientific Method and "Good" Research Practice', *Women and Health*, vol. 15, No. 4, 1989

———. 'Smoking in Pregnancy: Smokescreen or Risk Factor? Towards a Materialist Analysis', *Sociology of Health and Illness*, 11, 4, 1989

'Obstetric Analgesia', *BMJ*, 22 April 1939

O'Sullivan, Ellen P. 'Dr Robert James Minnitt 1889–1974: A Pioneer of Inhalational Analgesia', *Journal of the Royal Society of Medicine*, vol. 82, April 1989

Oxley, W.H.F. 'Prevention of Puerperal Sepsis in General Practice', *BMJ*, I, 1934

Pankhurst, Sylvia E. 'Will Marriage Become Compulsory in the Struggle for a New Race?' *Guide and Ideas for Competitors*, 21 November 1936

Parish, T.N. 'Report on a Thousand Cases of Abortion in St Giles' Hospital, Camberwell', *Journal of Obstetrics and Gynaecology, British Empire*, 42, 6, December 1935

People's League of Health. 'The Nutrition of Expectant and Nursing Mothers in Relation to Maternal and Infant Mortality and Morbidity', *Journal of Obstetrics and Gynaecology of the British Empire*, 53, 1946

Peretz, E. 'A Maternity Service for England and Wales', in Garcia, J., Kilpatrick, R. and Richards, M. (eds), *The Politics of Maternity Care*, Oxford University Press, 1990

'Perinatal Mortality Survey under the Auspices of the National Birthday Trust Fund. Report of Meeting 28 April 1961, Royal Society of Medicine', reprinted from *Proceedings of the Royal Society of Medicine*, 54, 12 December 1961

'Perinatal Mortality Survey', *BMJ*, ii, 1 December 1962

Perry, Sarah. 'The History of District Nursing', a lecture prepared for use on behalf of the Queen's Nursing Institute, 1996

Petty, Celia. 'Primary Research and Public Health', in Austoker, Joan and Bryder, Linda, *Historical Perspectives on the Role of the MRC*, Oxford University Press, 1989

Power, Chris. 'A Review of Child Health in the 1958 Birth Cohort: National Child Development Study', *Paediatric and Perinatal Epidemiology*, 6, 1992

'The Report on Abortion', *BMJ*, 10 June 1939

Rhys Williams, Juliet (see also Williams, Lady Juliet). Letter to *Public Health*, July 1939

Rivett, L. Carnac, 'The Report of the Abortion Committee of the Joint Council of Midwifery', *The Journal of the Royal Institute of the Public Health and Hygiene*, 4, 11, November 1941

Saigal, S. et al. 'Comparative Assessment of the Health Status of Extremely Low Birth Weight Children at Eight Years of Age: Comparison with a Reference Group', *Journal of Pediatrics*, 125, 3, September 1994

'A Salaried Service of Midwives', *Midwives' Chronicle and Nursing Notes*, March 1935

Schenk, Faith and Parkes, A.S. 'The Activities of the Eugenics Society', *Eugenics Review*, 60, 1968

Simpson, W.J. 'A Preliminary Report on Cigarette Smoking and Incidence of Prematurity', *American Journal of Obstetrics and Gynaecology*, 73, 1957

Singer, H.W. 'Unemployment and Health', Pilgrim Trust Unemployment Enquiry, October 1937

'Sir Kingsley Wood Replies to Questions', *Nursing Notes and Midwives' Chronicle*, December 1936

Smith, D.F. And Nicolson, M. 'The 1930s Nutrition Movement: Food, Poverty and Politics', in Kamminga, H. and Cunningham, A. (eds), *The Science and Culture of Nutrition 1840s–1940s*, Wellcome, Rodopi, 1994

Smith, Richard. 'Occupationless Health', *BMJ*, 291, 26 October 1985

'Smoking, Pregnancy and Publicity', *Nature*, 245, 14 September 1973

'Summary of Recommendations. Report of the JCM', *Midwives and Nursing Notes Chronicle*, March 1935

Thane, Pat, 'Women in the British Labour Party and the Construction of State Welfare 1906–1939', in Koven, Seth and Michel, Sonya (eds), *Mothers of a New World. Maternalist Politics and the Origins of Welfare States*, Routledge 1993

'Too Many Infant Deaths', *BMJ*, 7 December 1963

Topping, A. 'Maternal Mortality and Public Opinion', *Public Health*, 49, 1936

'A Warning to Practising Midwives', *Nursing Notes and Midwives' Chronicle*, December 1934

Webster, Charles. 'Healthy or Hungry Thirties?' *History Workshop Journal*, 13, 1982

——. 'The Health of the School Child During the Depression', in Parry, Nicholas and McNair, David (eds), *The Fitness of the Nation – Physical and Health Education in the Nineteenth and Twentieth Centuries*, History of Education Society, 1983

——. 'Health, Welfare and Unemployment During the Depression', *Past and Present*, 109, November 1985

——. 'Beveridge After 50 Years', *BMJ*, vol. 305, 17 October 1992

——. 'Saving Children During the Depression', *Disasters*, September 1994

Wilkinson, D.J. 'Nitrous Oxide in the 1920s and 1930s', in *History of Anaesthetic Society Proceedings*, vol. 16, 1994

Williams, A.F. 'Human Milk and the Preterm Baby', *BMJ*, vol. 306, 19 June 1993

Williams, A. Susan. 'Relief and Research: The Nutrition Work of the National Birthday Trust Fund 1935–39', in Smith, D. (ed.), *Nutrition in Britain in the 20th Century: Science: Scientists and Politics*, Routledge, 1996

Williams, Lady Juliet (see also Rhys Williams). 'The Joint Council of Midwifery', *Midwives* and *Nursing Notes' Chronicle*, XLVIII, 574, October 1935

——. 'Malnutrition as a Cause of Maternal Mortality', *Public Health*, October 1936

——. 'Results of Experimental Schemes for Reducing the Maternal Death Rate in the Special Areas of Glamorgan, Monmouthshire and Durham Carried Out by the National Birthday Trust Fund during 1934, 1935 and 1936', *Public Health*, April 1937

Wilson, Harriett. 'How CPAG got into politics', *Poverty*, December 1982

Winter, J.M. 'Infant Mortality, Maternal Mortality, and Public Health in Britain in the 1930s', *Journal of Economic History*, 8, 1979

Wynn, A.H.A. et al, 'Nutrition of Women in Anticipation of Pregnancy', *Nutrition and Health*, vol. 7, 1991

Wynn, Margaret and Wynn, Arthur. 'No Nation Can Rise Above the Level of its Women', Caroline Walker Trust, 1993

——. 'Has There Ever Been a Better Time to Have a Baby?' *Modern Midwife*, February 1995

Wynn, S.W. et al. 'The Association of Maternal Social Class with Maternal Diet and the Dimensions of Babies in a Population of London Women', *Nutrition and Health*, 9, 1994

Young, James, Hawthorne, C.O. and Nixon, W.C.W. 'Nutrition of Expectant and Nursing Mothers [Report of People's League of Health]'. *BMJ*, 18 July 1942

7. BOOKS

Abel-Smith, Brian. *The Hospitals 1800–1948*, Heinemann, 1964

Alberti, Johanna. *Beyond Suffrage. Feminists in War and Peace 1914–28*, Macmillan, 1989

Apple, Rima D. *Mothers and Medicine. A Social History of Infant Feeding 1890–1950*, The University of Wisconsin Press, 1987

Ashwell, Margaret (ed.). *McCance & Widdowson. A Scientific Partnership of 60 Years*, British Nutrition Foundation, 1993

Atkinson, Tony. *Incomes and the Welfare State*, Cambridge University Press, 1996

Austoker, Joan. *A History of the Imperial Cancer Research Fund 1902–1986*, Oxford University Press, 1988

—— and Bryder, Linda (eds). *Historical Perspectives on the Role of the MRC*, Oxford University Press, 1989

Bagnold, Enid. *The Squire*, William Heinemann, 1938

Balfour, M.I. and Drury, J.C. *Motherhood in the Special Areas of Durham and Tyneside*, Council of Action, 1935

Baly, Monica E. *A History of the Queen's Nursing Institute. 100 Years 1887–1987*, Croom Helm, 1987

Barry, Jonathan and Jones, Colin (eds). *Medicine and Charity Before the Welfare State*, Routledge, 1991

Bartrip, P.W.J. *Mirror of Medicine. A History of the BMJ*, British Medical Journal and Oxford University Press, 1990

Beddoe, Deidre. *Back to Home and Duty*, Pandora Press, 1989

Berkeley, Comyns, Fairbairn, J.S. and White, Clifford. *Midwifery by Ten Teachers*, 5th edn, Edward Arnold, 1935

Beveridge, William H. *The Pillars of Security*, George Allen & Unwin, 1943

Blair-Bell, William. 'The History of the Origin and Rise of the British College of Obstetricians and Gynaecologists', unpublished, RCOG/ S33–2

BOC Group, The. *Industrial Gases. The Invisible Fabric of the Modern World*, BOC, 1984

——. *Around the Group in 100 Years*, BOC, 1986

Bock, Gisela and Thane, Pat. *Maternity and Gender Policies. Women and the Rise of the European Welfare States 1880s–1950s*, 1991; rpt. Routledge, 1994

Bolitho, Hector. *Alfred Mond. First Lord Melchett*, Martin Secker, 1932

Boulin, Robert. *Pour une Politique de la Santé. Les Grandes Actions de Santé I*, Ministère de la Santé Publique et de la Sécurité Sociale, Paris, 1917

Braithwaite, Constance. *The Voluntary Citizen. An Enquiry into the Place of Philanthropy in the Community*, Methuen, 1938

Brierley, Walter. *Sandwichman*, Methuen, 1937

Brittain, Vera. *Honourable Estate*, Victor Gollancz, 1936

——. *Testament of Experience. An autobiographical account of the years 1925–50*, Gollancz, 1957

Brookes, Barbara. *Abortion in England 1900–1967*, Croom Helm, 1988

Brookes, P. *Women at Westminster*, Peter Davies, 1967

Browne, Alan (ed.). *Masters, Midwives and Ladies-in-Waiting. The Rotunda Hospital 1745–1995*, Dublin, A.A. Farmer, 1995

Buchan, William. *John Buchan: A Memoir*, Buchan & Enright, 1982
Burnett, John. *Plenty and Want*, 1966; rpt. 3rd edn, Routledge, 1989
——. *A Social History of Housing 1815–1985*, 1978; rpt. Routledge, 1986
Butler, N.R. and Golding, Jean. *From Birth to Five*, Pergamon Press, 1986
Campbell, Dame Janet. *Reports on the Physical Welfare of Mothers and Children. England and Wales. Vol 2, Midwives and Midwifery*, Carnegie Trust, Tinling & Co, 1917
Campbell, Rona and Macfarlane, Alison. *Where to be Born? The Debate and the Evidence*, National Perinatal Epidemiology Unit, 1994
Cannadine, David. *Aspects of Aristocracy*, Yale University Press, 1994
Carr-Saunders, A.M. And Wilson, P.A. *The Professions*, Clarendon Press, 1933
Chalmers, I., Enkin, M. and Keirse, M.J.N.C. (eds). *Effective Care in Pregnancy and Childbirth*, Oxford University Press, 1989
Chamberlain, Mary. *Growing up in Lambeth*, Virago, 1989
Chance, Janet. *The Case for the Reform of the Abortion Laws*, ALRA, n.d. (1930s)
Committee Against Malnutrition. *Social Care of Motherhood*, Lawrence & Wishart, 1936
Courcy de, Anne. *Circe. The Life of Edith, Marchioness of Londonderry*, Sinclair-Stevenson, 1992
Cowell, Betty and Wainwright, David. *Behind the Blue Door. The History of the Royal College of Midwives 1991–1981*, Baillière Tindall, 1981
Crick, Michael. *Jeffrey Archer. Stranger Than Fiction*, Hamish Hamilton, 1995
Cronin, A.J. *The Citadel*, Book Club Associates, 1983
Dally, Ann. *Women Under the Knife*, Hutchinson Radius, 1991
Darling, George. *The Politics of Food*, George Routledge, 1941
Davies, Margaret Llewelyn (ed.). *Maternity. Letters from Working Women*, 1915; rpt. Virago 1978
—— (ed.). *Life As We Have Known It, By Co-operative Working Women*, 1931; rpt. Virago, 1982
Dayus, Kathleen. *Where There's Life*, 1985; rpt. Virago, 1989
Dewhurst, Sir John. *Queen Charlotte's. The Story of a Hospital*, no publisher given, 1989
Dick, Diana. *Yesterday's Babies. A History of Babycare*, Bodley Head, 1987
Dickens, Charles. *Dombey and Son*, 1848; rpt. Penguin, 1975
Dick-Read, Grantley. *Natural Childbirth*, Heinemann, 1933
——. *Childbirth Without Fear*, Heinemann, 1942
Dingwall, Robert, Rafferty, Anne Marie and Webster, Charles. *An Introduction to the Social History of Nursing*, 1988; rpt. Routledge 1991
Donnison, Jean. *Midwives and Medical Men. A History of the Struggle for the Control of Childbirth*, 1987; rpt. Historical Publications, 1988
Douglas, J.W.B. and Blomfield, J.M. *Children Under Five*, George Allen & Unwin, 1958
——. *The Home and the School*, MacGibbon & Kee, 1964
—— and Ross, J.M. and Simpson, H.R. *All Our Future. A Longitudinal Study of Secondary Education*, Peter Davies, 1968
Dykes, R.N. *Illness in Luton*, Leagrave Press, 1950
Evans, Barbara. *Freedom to Choose. The Life and Times of Helena Wright*, Bodley Head, 1984
Fairbairns, Zoe. *Benefits*, Virago, 1979
Ferri, Elsa (ed.). *Life at 33*, National Children's Bureau, 1993
Field, Frank. *Poverty and Politics*, Heinemann, 1982
Fildes, Valerie, Marks, Lara and Marland, Hilary (eds). *Women and Children First. International Maternal and Infant Welfare 1870–1945*, Routledge, 1992
Fox, Enid. 'District Nursing and the Work of District Nursing Associations 1900–1946', unpublished University of London Ph.D., 1993
Gaffin, Jean and Thoms, David. *Caring & Sharing. The Centenary History of the Co-operative Women's Guild*, 1983; rpt. Holyoake Books, 1993
Gamarnikow, E. et al (eds). *Gender, Class and Work*, Heinemann, 1983
Garcia, Jo, Kilpatrick, Robert and Richards, Martin (eds). *The Politics of Maternity Care*, Clarendon Press, 1990
Gélis, Jacques. *History of Childbirth*, Polity Press, 1991

Glass, D.V. *The Struggle for Population*, Clarendon Press, 1936
Glyn, Anthony. *Elinor Glyn. A Biography*, Hutchinson, 1955
Goodman, Jean. *The Mond Legacy*, Weidenfeld and Nicolson, 1982
Gowdridge, Christine, Williams, A. Susan and Wynn, Margaret (eds). *Mother Courage. Letters from Mothers Living in Poverty at the End of the Century*, Penguin, 1997
Graves, Pamela M. *Labour Women*, Cambridge University Press, 1994
Graves, Robert and Hodge, Alan. *The Long Week-End. A Social History of Great Britain 1918–1939*, Faber and Faber, 1940
Greenwood, H. Powys. *Employment and the Distressed Areas*, George Routledge, 1936
Greenwood, Walter. *Love on the Dole*, 1933; rpt. Penguin, 1969
Grey-Turner, Elston and Sutherland, F.M. *History of the British Medical Association*, BMA, 1982
Hanley, James. *Grey Children. A Study in Humbug and Misery*, Methuen, 1937
Hanlin, Tom. *Once In Every Lifetime*, Big Ben Books, 1945
——. *Miracle at Cardenrigg*, Random House, 1949
Hannington, Wal. *Unemployed Struggles 1919–1936*, Lawrence & Wishart, 1936
Hardyment, Christina. *Dream Babies. Child Care from Locke to Spock*, Jonathan Cape, 1983
Herbert, S. Mervyn. *Britain's Health*, Pelican, 1939
Heren, Louis. *Growing Up Poor in London*, Hamish Hamilton, 1973
Heslop, Harold. *Last Cage Down*, 1935; rpt. Lawrence & Wishart, 1984
Honigsbaum, Frank. *The Division in British Medicine. A History of the Separation of General Practice from Hospital Care 1911–1968*, Kogan Page, 1979
Horne, Alistair. *Macmillan 1894–1956, Volume 1*, Macmillan, 1988
——. *Macmillan 1957–1986, Volume 2*, Macmillan, 1989
Hyde, Montgomery H. *Baldwin. The Unexpected Prime Minister*, Hart Davis, 1973
Jameson, Storm. *Civil Journey*, 1935; rpt. Cassell, 1939
Jenkins, Roy. *Baldwin*, Collins, 1987
Jones, Greta. *Social Hygiene in Twentieth Century Britain*, Croom Helm, 1986
Jones, Lewis. *We Live*, Lawrence & Wishart, 1939
Keown, John. *Abortion, Doctors and the Law*, Cambridge University Press, 1988
Kerchoff, Allan C. et al. *Going Comprehensive in England and Wales: A Study of Uneven Change*, Woburn Press, 1997
Kingsford, Peter. *The Hunger Marchers in Britain 1920–1940*, Lawrence and Wishart, 1982
Koven, Seth and Michel, Sonya (eds). *Mothers of a New World. Maternalist Politics and the Origins of Welfare States*, Routledge 1993
Laybourn, Keith. *Britain on the Breadline*, Alan Sutton, 1990
Leap, Nicky and Hunter, Billie. *The Midwife's Tale*, Scarlet Press, 1993
Lewis, Jane. *The Politics of Motherhood*, Croom Helm, 1980
——. *Women in England 1870–1950*, Wheatsheaf Books, 1986
—— (ed.). *Labour & Love. Women's Experience of Home and Family 1850–1940*, 1986; rpt. Blackwell, 1989
——. *Women and Social Action in Victorian and Edwardian England*, Edward Elgar, 1991
Light, Alison. *Forever England. Femininity, Literature and Conservatism Between the Wars*, Routledge, 1991
Loch, C.S. *Charity and Social Life*, Macmillan, 1910
Loudon, Irvine. *Death in Childbirth. An International Study of Maternal Care and Maternal Mortality 1800–1950*, Clarendon Press, 1992
Macadam, Elizabeth. *The New Philanthropy*, George Allen & Unwin, 1934
Macfarlane, Alison and Mugford, Miranda. *Birth Counts: Statistics of Pregnancy and Childbirth*, HMSO, 1984
Macfarlane, A. et al. *Counting the Changes in Childbirth: Trends and Gaps in National Statistics*, NPEU, 1995
Marmite Company. *Marmite: In Preventive and Curative Medicine*, n.d. (mid-1930s)
Marrack, J.R. *Food and Planning*, Victor Gollancz, 1942
Marsh, L.C., Fleming, A.G. and Blacker, C.F. *Health and Unemployment*, Oxford University Press, 1938

Mass-Observation, *Britain and her Birth-Rate,* John Murray, 1945

Mazumdar, Pauline M.H. *Eugenics, Human Genetics and Human Failings. The Eugenics Society, its Sources and its Critics in Britain,* Routledge, 1992

McLaren, Angus. *A History of Contraception,* 1990; rpt. Blackwell, 1994

McLeary, G.F. *The Early History of the Infant Welfare Movement,* H.K. Lewis, 1933

——. *The Maternity and Child Welfare Movement,* P.S. King & Son, 1935

Merry, Eleanor J. and Irven, Iris Dundas. *District Nursing. A Handbook for District Nurses and for All Concerned in the Administration of a District Nursing Service,* Baillière Tindall and Cox, 1948

M'Gonigle, G.C.M. and Kirby, J. *Poverty and Public Health,* London, 1936

Miller, F.J.W. et al. *Growing Up in Newcastle upon Tyne 1952–62,* Oxford University Press, 1960

——. *The School Years in Newcastle upon Tyne,* Oxford University Press, 1974

Mitchell, Hannah. *The Hard Way Up,* 1968; rpt. Virago, 1984

Moscucci, Ornella. *The Science of Woman. Gynaecology and Gender in England 1800–1929,* 1990; rpt. Cambridge University Press, 1993

Newman, Sir George. *The Building of a Nation's Health,* Macmillan, 1939

Nicolson, Nigel. *Harold Nicolson, Diaries and Letters 1930–1939,* Collins, 1966

Oakley, Ann. *The Captured Womb. A History of the Medical Care of Pregnant Women,* 1984; rpt. Blackwell, 1986

—— and Williams, A. Susan (eds). *The Politics of the Welfare State,* UCL Press, 1994

Oddy, Derek and Miller, Derek (eds). *The Making of the Modern British Diet,* Croom Helm, 1976

O'Dowd, Michael J. and Philipp, Elliot E. *The History of Obstetrics and Gynaecology,* Parthenon, 1994

Oldfield, Sybil (ed.). *This Working-Day World. Women's Lives and Culture(s) in Britain 1914–1945,* Taylor & Francis, 1994

Orr, John Boyd. *Food, Health and Income. Report on a Survey of Adequacy of Diet in Relation to Income,* Macmillan, 1937

—— and Lubbock, David. *Feeding the People in War-Time,* Macmillan, 1940

Palmer, Diana. 'Women, Health and Politics 1919–1939: Professional and Lay Involvement in the Women's Health Campaign', unpublished University of Warwick Ph.D. thesis, 1986

Paterson, Donald and Forest Smith, J. *Modern Methods of Feeding in Infancy and Childhood,* Constable, 1939

Paul, Alison A. (ed.). *The First 60 Years. History and Publications of the MRC Dunn Nutrition Unit 1927–1987,* MRC Dunn Nutrition Unit, 1987

Pember Reeves, Maud. *Round About A Pound A Week,* 1913; Virago, 1988

Perkin, Harold. *The Rise of Professional Society. England Since 1880,* Routledge, 1989

Petchesky, Rosalind Pollack. *Abortion and Woman's Choice,* 1984; rpt. Verso, 1986

Pilgrim Trust. *Men Without Work,* Cambridge University Press, 1938

Power, C., Manor, O. and Fox, J. *Class and Health. The Early Years,* Chapman & Hall, 1991

Prochaska, F.K. *Women and Philanthropy in 19th Century England,* Clarendon Press, 1980

——. *The Voluntary Impulse. Philanthropy in Modern Britain,* Faber & Faber, 1988

——. *Philanthropy and the Hospitals of London. The King's Fund 1897–1990,* Clarendon Press, 1992

Pugh, Martin. *Women and the Women's Movement in Britain 1914–1959,* Macmillan, 1992

Rathbone, Eleanor. *The Disinherited Family,* 1924; rpt. Falling Wall Press, 1986

Reader, W.J. *Imperial Chemical Industries. A History, Volume 2,* Oxford University Press, 1975

Reddick, Tom. *Never a Cross Bat,* Cape Town, n.d. (1979)

Rhys Williams, Lady Juliet. *Something To Look Forward To. A Suggestion for a New Social Contract,* Western Mail and Echo, 1942

——. *Doctor Carmichael,* Herbert Jenkins, 1946

Rivett, Geoffrey. *The Development of the London Hospital System 1823–1982*, King Edward's Hospital Fund for London, 1986

Roberts, Elizabeth. *A Woman's Place. An Oral History of Working-Class Women 1890–1940*, 1984; rpt. Blackwell, 1985

Rowntree, B. Seebohm. *The Human Needs of Labour*, new edn. Longman, Green and Co, 1937

Salmon, Jenny (ed.). *Dietary Reference Values*, HMSO, 1991

Singer, H.W. *Unemployment and the Unemployed*, P.S. King, 1940

Snow, C.P. *The New Men*, Penguin, 1954

——. *Homecomings*, 1956; rpt. Penguin, 1971

Snow, E.E. *Sir Julien Cahn's XI*, E.E. Snow, 1964

Spence, J.C. and Miller, F.J.W., *Causes of Infantile Mortality in Newcastle upon Tyne 1939*, Newcastle Health Committee, 1941

—— et al. *A Thousand Families in Newcastle upon Tyne*, Oxford University Press, 1954

Spring Rice, Margery. *Working-Class Wives*, 1939; rpt. Virago, 1989

Stocks, Mary. *Eleanor Rathbone*, Victor Gollancz, 1949

Teitelbaum, Michael S. and Winter, Jay M. *The Fear of Population Decline*, Academic Press, 1985

Tew, Marjorie. *Safer Childbirth? A Critical History of Maternity Care*, Chapman and Hall, 1990

Titmuss, Richard M. *Poverty and Population. A Factual Study of Contemporary Social Waste*, Macmillan, 1938

—— and Titmuss, K. *Parents Revolt: A Study of the Declining Birth-Rate in Acquisitive Societies*, Secker & Warburg, 1942

——. *Problems of Social Policy*, HMSO and Longman, Green & Co., 1950

——. *Essays on 'The Welfare State'*, 1958; rpt. George Allen & Unwin, 1960

Towler, Jean and Bramall, Joan. *Midwives in History and Society*, Croom Helm, 1986

Townsend, Peter. *Poverty in the United Kingdom*, 1979; rpt. Penguin, 1983

—— and Davidson, Nick (eds). *The Black Report*, 1982; rpt. in *Inequalities in Health*, Penguin, 1992

Trevelyan, John. *Voluntary Service and the State. A Study of the Needs of the Hospital Service*, Geo. Barber & Son, 1952

Vernon, Betty D. *Ellen Wilkinson 1891–1947*, Croom Helm, 1982

Wadsworth, M.E.J. *The Imprint of Time. Childhood, History and Adult Life*, Clarendon Press, 1991

Webster, Charles. *The Health Services Since the War, Volume 1. Problems of Health Care. The National Health Service Before 1957*, HMSO, 1988

—— (ed.). *Caring for Health: History and Diversity*, Open University Press, 1993

Woolf, Virginia. *Three Guineas*, 1938; rpt. The Hogarth Press, 1986

——. *Between the Acts*, 1941; rpt. Harcourt, Brace, Jovanovich, 1969

Wynn, Margaret. *Fatherless Families*, Michael Joseph, 1964

Young, G.M. *Stanley Baldwin*, Rupert Hart-Davis, 1952

Index

Page numbers in italics refer to illustrations (not to figures).